The R. J. Reynolds Tobacco Company

NANNIE M. TILLEY

The R. J. Reynolds Tobacco Company

The University of North Carolina Press

Chapel Hill and London

© 1985 The University of North Carolina Press

All rights reserved

Manufactured in the United States of America

Library of Congress Cataloging in Publication Data

Tilley, Nannie May, 1898-
The R. J. Reynolds Tobacco Company

Includes index.
1. R. J. Reynolds Industries—History. 2. Tobacco
industry—United States—History. I. Title.
HD9139.R4T55   1985   338.7'6797'0975   84-20811
ISBN 0-8078-1642-6

FRONTISPIECE
R. J. Reynolds photographed on his wedding trip in 1905

To John C. Whitaker

CONTENTS

ILLUSTRATIONS

R. J. Reynolds in 1905
frontispiece

between pages 372–73
Environment of R. J. Reynolds Tobacco Company, 1875–1891
Birthplace of R. J. Reynolds
Reynolds brothers
R. J.'s factory in 1884
R. J.'s price list, 1891
D. Rich, Walter Reynolds, and R. J.
R. J.'s white work force between 1893 and 1901
Check sent by R. J. to Josephus Daniels
Outing of R. J.'s salesmen, 1914
Clement Manly
Francis Burton Craige
John C. Whitaker
Meeting of department managers, 1948
Winston cigarettes' chief advertisement
Work in the truck and storage division
Whitaker Park plant
Albert Cuthrell
Office building completed in 1929
Chairmen of the Board
Joseph L. Graham
Dr. Samuel O. Jones

TABLES

Tables

P R E F A C E

Even before its absorbtion into R. J. Reynolds Industries, the R. J. Reynolds Tobacco Company, now nearing its 109th year, ranked in sales among the first sixty industrial corporations of the United States. Moreover, in the accumulation of net profits it was eighteenth in 1961, seventeenth in 1962, and eighteenth in 1963. Among the first sixty corporations listed by *Fortune* magazine, the company is one of only three with headquarters in the South. In addition, it is the largest corporation in this group with both administrative and executive headquarters in the southern United States.

In 1875 Richard Joshua Reynolds invested $7,500 in a new enterprise for the manufacture of flat-plug chewing tobacco. By 1963 the company that evolved from this small beginning produced all of the major types of tobacco products except cigars and snuff, listed its assets at $1,037,639,534, employed 14,932 men and women, sold products totaling $1,672,444,707, and paid $68,000,000 in dividends to 103,282 stockholders. In achieving this position the company was continually under the management of southerners—many of them natives of North Carolina.

Among the various employees and officers of the company who helped make this history possible, I am greatly indebted to the late John C. Whitaker. He became an employee of the company in 1913 and ended his career as chairman of the board in 1959. In 1950, he began to plan for a history of the company, and appointed Erwin W. Cook, Dell McKeithan, and W. S. Koenig to interview many of the oldest employees from Will Reynolds to the lowliest workman in Factory Number 8. Although Whitaker was unable to turn his full attention to the history until 1958, the material gathered by Cook, McKeithan, and Koenig proved to be invaluable.

My first information about such a history came in the fall of 1958 in a letter from William J. Conrad, Jr., then vice-president and secretary of the company, asking my advice on procedure. Understanding what lay behind this request, I began to consider the matter in the light of my long-time interest in the tobacco industry and my appreciation of the company's historic stand in support of the efforts of tobacco farmers to sell their leaf cooperatively. I flew to Winston-Salem and, with Charles B. Wade, Jr., made arrangements that, as the text of this volume will indicate, imposed no restrictions on me. At that time, however, I learned virtually nothing about the dearth of records pertaining to the company's history. My salary was set at $10,000 per year.

This study is an attempt to show how the R. J. Reynolds Tobacco Company developed into a leading tobacco manufacturer in the United States. It is, I believe, the first history of a major tobacco company based primarily on a direct interpretation of company records. Although it is a business history, I have endeavored to show what the company has meant to Winston-Salem and to North Carolina. Much of it is concerned with men, women, and politics as well as technical developments inside tobacco factories. Perhaps I have been overcautious in stressing Camel cigarettes and Bylaw XII as important factors in the development of the company, but I hope I have been equally careful to explain the role of labor, especially the part played by the CIO's "Operation Dixie" during the 1940s. Two factors have been kept in mind: the evolution of the company from an agrarian background and the consequent transformation of untrained employees into skilled laborers and highly trained technicians. Insofar as possible, in this most secretive of industries, I have tried to show the progress of the company in relation to that of other firms engaged in the manufacture of tobacco products.

In developing these themes I was constantly deterred by a scarcity of information. Prior to the establishment of the company's Records Center in 1954, there was a rigorous evaluation of all records in relation to what should be preserved for the operation of the company and what should be discarded. Many materials valuable to a historian were thus destroyed. Only those documents preserved in the secretary's department at first seemed intact. When I began with what was available in the Records Center, I soon found that the legal department had preserved its records in their entirety, but its officials were reluctant for me to use them. Eventually, however, I was able to examine what I desired, although hindered by the delay. The advertising department had also preserved all of its extensive records, which were very helpful. At times, however, I felt that the complete files of legal and advertising material in contrast to a paucity of records kept by other departments of the company would necessarily result in an unbalanced account of the development and growth of the company.

There were other difficulties in the research for this study. Although at no time did I wish to depend solely on company records, I did not anticipate so much reliance on newspaper statements and personal interviews. In the long and tedious research in newspapers and trade journals, Jane Robinson, by covering the files of *Tobacco*, relieved me of much drudgery; later, however, I examined various issues of that journal for materials related to, but not specifically concerned with, the company for background on the tobacco industry. A peculiar task of research fell to my lot, as a number of employees had secreted valuable files when the order for their surrender had come in 1954. It was weeks before I found three folders of special interviews with older employees conducted in 1950 by Erwin W. Cook, Dell McKeithan, and W. S. Koenig for the specific purpose of preparing a history of the company. The prime trouble lay in the fact that no person in the company had an overall knowledge of its records. Too, all officers and many employees were very busy. Under such circumstances it was impossible to move the records to a university library, an environment more conducive to scholarly research. Unlike in most large corporations, few doors in the Reynolds office building were ever closed except ocasionally for highly confidential conferences. As a result, this work was prepared in the midst of much physical activity and many pleasant but unscheduled visits from a variety of employees. On more than one occasion I despaired of completing the task on which I have spent almost exactly twice as much time as I originally deemed necessary.

With much of the data for this study coming from private records, I have considered a formal bibliography unnecessary, although some explanation should be given. The papers of Richard H. Wright (preserved in the Flowers Collection at Duke University Library in Durham) were the single most important original source outside company files. Local newspapers were very helpful. Weekly papers published in Winston and Salem during the last quarter of the nineteenth century include the *Winston Leader*, *People's Press*, *Western Sentinel*, and *Union Republican*. Thereafter, the files of the *Winston-Salem Journal* and the *Twin City Sentinel* proved invaluable. At different times in its history the *Twin City Sentinel* has appeared under so many different titles that I decided to use *Twin City Sentinel* as the citation in all appropriate instances. Of the trade journals consulted, *Tobacco* (published in New York City since 1886), the *Southern Tobacco Journal* (published in Winston-Salem since 1891), and the *Western Tobacco Journal* (published in Cincinnati since 1874) were most important. Of the numerous court records and government documents no single item was more helpful than the *Report of the Commissioner of Corporations on the Tobacco Industry* (3 vols., Washington, 1909–1915), although court records connected with the dissolution of the American Tobacco Company (1907–1911), the Kentucky Trial (1941–1946), and the New Jersey stockholders' suit (1940–1946) were also valuable. For the historical background of practices common in industrial management of the period, the study by Gordon S. Watkins and Paul A. Dodd (*The Management of Labor Relations*, New York and London, 1938) was of assistance.

Among the many who assisted me with the preparation of this manuscript, none was kinder or more helpful than the late Roy C. Haberkern, a company director from 1923 until 1955. He was a stern but helpful critic who constantly refused to venture information on any issues except those with which he was thoroughly familiar. Mrs. Haberkern, who seldom failed to recall personalities or pertinent dates, was likewise helpful. I learned much from both of them as I accepted their hospitality time after time. Recollections from William J. Conrad, Jr., were most useful, including many pertinent facts passed on to him by his uncle, D. Rich, who was an early director and R. J. Reynolds's right-hand man. He also helped me locate records and criticized almost every chapter, often catching errors as well as awkward phrasings. The late Bowman Gray, Jr., later chairman of the board of directors, read the typescript and made many useful suggestions and corrections, especially in Chapter 7. Charles B. Wade, Jr., then vice-president and company director, worked closely with me throughout my sojourn in Winston-Salem. He has both a historian's outlook and an expert's knowledge of North Carolina history and as such, I benefited greatly from our association. In many respects, however, I owe most to Louise A. Peterson, assistant secretary of the company. Her familiarity with the company records and her persistence in helping me locate them proved to be an invaluable asset.

I owe more than I can adequately phrase to John C. Whitaker, mentioned earlier in this preface, and to William T. Smither, retired director and long the manager of the advertising department. Though it is impossible here to acknowledge adequately the valued contributions of many others, I cannot omit mention of Clarence L. Johnson, Paul O. Pegram, Richard D. Moore, Edgar E. Bumgardner, Vernon Davis, Edgar H. Harwood, Samuel O. Jones, L. Heartt Bryant, Mebane E. Turner, Zachary T. Smith, Lee R. Salmons, Sidney J. Walters, James V. Dorse, Herbert R. Throckmorton, Erwin W. Cook, James C. MacLachlan, Jr., I. J. Miller, and Norman F. Matthews.

I was also aided to a remarkable degree by staff members of various libraries. At Duke University Library cooperation was complete, especially from Wilhelmine Lemon, Dr. Mattie Russell, and Dr. Benjamin E. Powell. At the public library of Winston-Salem, Paul S. Ballance and Jeannette Trotter gave me free range in all portions of the library. Anne Hendrix, Mae Kreeger Tillman, Margaret Julian, and others on the staff were of assistance. At Wake Forest University Minnie S. Kallam of the Z. Smith Reynolds Library was helpful. I am likewise obligated to staff members of the North Carolina State Department of Archives and History, the Virginia State Library, and the North Carolina State Library—especially to Lois Neal of the latter institution.

My former colleague, Professor Louis R. Harlan of the University of Maryland, favored me greatly by reading and correcting the manuscript. Melinda S. Belcher and Elizabeth F. Lewis typed the manuscript and its revisions. Mrs. Lewis, who was with me at the end, bore the chief burden and with her quick eye helped to eliminate many inconsistencies. My landlady in Winston-Salem, Sudie Byerly Stafford, aided me from her wide knowledge of local connnections and more than once steered me through cemeteries in search of accurate information.

Determining a starting point for such a history was simple indeed. Choosing an ending point necessarily was a function of the four-and-one-half-year period during which the volume was researched and written and events in the company at that time. The early 1960s represented yet another turning point in the company's history. Bowman Gray, Jr., became ill and was unable to function as chairman of the board with his usual vigor. His tenure marked the end of the Gray family's dominance in the management of the company. A slow decline in the sale of Camels was caused in part by the previous introduction of filter-tipped cigarettes, following the agitation over the cancer scare. Although a diversification committee had been established by the directors in 1957, little or nothing was accomplished in diversifying the products of the company until the 1960s, a movement inexorably leading to the current conglomerate, R. J. Reynolds Industries, Inc., of which the R. J. Reynolds Tobacco Company remains a leading, integral part.

This work, except for a few insertions, was completed in July 1964. Shortly afterward the manuscript was accepted by the University of North Carolina Press, initially edited, and returned for review by the R. J. Reynolds Tobacco Company and by me. The illness of Bowman Gray, Jr., and subsequent changes in the corporate structure and management were among some of the major reasons for delay in its ultimate publication. The more recent movement to publish this history can be attributed mainly to the energy of Nancy Susan Reynolds, the only surviving child of R. J. Reynolds. I am indebted to her and many others within and outside the family and company for their painstaking review and invaluable assistance in this undertaking. For encouragement and extensive help in proofreading I cannot thank my friend Louis Seabolt enough. Finally, responsibility for the inevitable errors in a work of this nature ultimately are mine; and all of the characterizations of persons and interpretations of events in this volume are solely my own—and are not intended to reflect the viewpoints of the present management of R. J. Reynolds Industries.

Commerce, Texas   N. M. T.
July 1984

PART ONE

Foundation, 1875–1899

CHAPTER 1

Background and Training
of R. J. Reynolds

The R. J. Reynolds Tobacco Company lives under the shadow of its founder from his bright-eyed portrait in the boardroom to his initials on posters in factory Number 8, warning lovers of the quid to restrain the functioning of their salivary glands. So great an influence has been exerted over the company by the vigorous and remarkable talents of its founder that his painting dominated the boardroom for forty-one years before any of his successors could summon the courage to hang the portraits of others on the same walls. In the expansion of the company his reputation has grown, taking "stature from the corporation" as it has grown in importance to overshadow the men who now manage it.[1] He was the expert who passed on formulas, planned buildings, influenced the location of railroads, set production figures, borrowed capital, and supervised the company's activities, all without the aid of engineering experts, survey makers, cost accountants, market analysts, personnel officers, public relations experts, or any other of the management specialists so commonly used in modern corporations.

Yet in many ways he did not resemble the typical nineteenth century industrial leader who relied chiefly on his own judgment. He readily accepted expert advice on such practical matters as advertising, traffic problems, new methods and machinery for manufacture, the erection of improved buildings, and even the feeble beginnings of a research department. Certainly he evidenced many characteristics of the modern corporate statesman and showed little or no interest in building up family dynastic power. Rather, he freely used his own funds to help many who wished to better themselves financially. It is, therefore, not an idle specu-

lation to assume that he would have accepted the aid of other specialists
in various areas had opportunities presented themselves. Just before his
death, he believed that his company as it then existed could make progress
for at least twenty years.[2] As it turned out, his prophecy held good for
almost forty years, or until his successors discarded his uniquely administered profit-sharing plan and developed new products for ensuring the
continued growth of the company. Scarcely any phase of his company's
career from his death in 1918 to the marketing of the Winston filter-
tipped cigarette in 1954 had not been carried into effect or anticipated by
Reynolds, the founder of the company that bears his name.

Richard Joshua Reynolds, unlike other successful manufacturers of tobacco in the postbellum South, achieved a leading position in three areas.
First, he rightly became known as the plug tobacco king, an acknowledg-
ment of his outstanding ability in the manufacture of chewing tobacco.
Second, while he was still in firm control of that position, his agile mind
busied itself with experimentation for a superior smoking tobacco. This
he accomplished in 1907, although he produced other brands before
combining different grades and ages of Burley leaf to produce his successful brand of Prince Albert. Third, when he was sixty-three, still vigorous
and aggressive, he made the first modern cigarette, a blend of flue-cured,
Burley, and Turkish tobaccos,[3] which revolutionized the cigarette industry.

Reynolds was in his prime as a manufacturer of a type of chewing
tobacco known as southern flat plug when his firm became affiliated with
the American Tobacco Company either by his design or by the force of
James Buchanan Duke (23 December 1856–10 October 1925). Certainly
Duke failed in his attempt to restrict Reynolds's operations to the manufacture of southern flat plug when the latter dared to produce and sell
smoking tobacco on a national scale. Reynolds, wide-awake and enthusiastic, emerged from the trust with his business intact and quite certainly
with wider vistas before his eyes. What was in the environment, training,
and education to produce such a successful individual as Richard Joshua
Reynolds, whose life spanned the years of the South when there was little
economic opportunity?

The Reynolds family settled early in Patrick County, Virginia, in the
area between the North and South Mayo rivers. Bordering the North
Carolina line on the south and the Blue Ridge Mountains on the west,
Patrick County is a mountainous area with an elevation ranging from 800
to 3,212 feet, the latter the summit of Richwood Knob, a peak of the Blue
Ridge. The easternmost area lies approximately forty-five miles west of
Danville, Virginia. The actual mountains of the county consist of a long
arm of the Blue Ridge in the west, Poor Mountain in the north, Bull and
Carter mountains, which lie northeast and southwest virtually dividing

the county into two areas, and Nobusiness Mountain, which occupies a broad area in southeastern Patrick County between the North and South Mayo rivers. Patrick's chief agricultural resource consists of a strip of relatively good tobacco land in the southern part of the county next to the North Carolina line. The county seat, first known as Patrick Court House but later renamed Taylorsville, has, since soon after the Civil War, been called Stuart in honor of its illustrious son, James Ewell Brown Stuart.[4]

By authentic legal record Abraham (often called Abram) Reynolds, the grandfather of Richard Joshua, purchased fifty acres of land "on . . . nobusiness fork of Mayo river" on 15 February 1814.[5] No doubt, however, the Reynolds family had lived in this same area much earlier. Walter R. Reynolds, writing to an interested individual shortly after the death of his brother, Richard Joshua, declared that his "ancestors as far back as great grandfather were born and lived in the southern part of Virginia. . . ." Although the family was often declared to be Scotch-Irish in origin, Walter Reynolds's strong impression was that it came from English stock. He conceded, however, that there was no absolute proof to back his impression.[6] To another the same writer stated that his grandfather, Abraham Reynolds, had several brothers who went west but that nothing had been heard of them since. Furthermore, Walter declared that his father, Hardin W. Reynolds, had only one brother and that he had died at the age of twenty-six.[7] These facts undoubtedly lend credence to R. J. Reynolds's frequent statement that Zachary Taylor Smith (19 February 1847–13 June 1938), R. J.'s first cousin on his mother's side, was his only close relative outside his own immediate family.[8]

The earliest of the family who can be definitely identified is Abraham Reynolds, who lived from 1 March 1781 to 3 May 1838. It was he who purchased land on the waters of Nobusiness fork of North Mayo River in 1814. In 1813 he had paid personal taxes.[9] By 1831 he owned 1,038 acres in the same general area, and in 1839 his estate included 1,080 acres and part ownership with Hardin W. Reynolds in an additional 376 acres on the waters of North Mayo River.[10] On 10 May 1809 Abraham Reynolds married Mary Harbour (7 March 1784–30 August 1853), the daughter of David Harbour.[11] They became the parents of two sons, Hardin William (20 April 1810–30 May 1882), the father of Richard Joshua Reynolds, and David Harbour (15 June 1811–20 September 1836), who died unmarried.

In addition to being a landholder of considerably more than the average acreage for his area, Abraham Reynolds engaged in other pursuits and became a man of means whose sons followed his example. Judging from a reference in 1865 to "Shucks in old Factory," Abraham operated some type of tobacco factory, which years later was used as a storage house. Similar reference in 1866 to "the old Store," then used as a tenant house, indicates that he also carried on mercantile operations. In addition, there is some proof that he may have engaged in amateur banking operations.[12] Not surprising, therefore, was his ability to advance substantial sums of money to his son David, who died only two years before his father's death, thus leaving Hardin W. Reynolds to inherit the property of both. In connection with a prolonged suit over David H. Reynolds's estate,[13] Joseph W. Varner declared in a deposition that Abraham Reynolds on one occasion handed his son David a thousand dollars or more, saying to him, "Do the best with this you can, my son." Testifying further, Varner stated that Abraham had but two children, that he could command money when he pleased, and "generally had money by him." These statements were based on twenty years of acquaintance with the Reynolds family. In view of the period and the nature of Abraham's activities, he was undoubtedly a very successful man.

The suit involving David Reynolds's estate also reveals much about his brief career that exemplifies the venturesome spirit and drive to succeed in business characteristic of many members of the family. According to the briefs and depositions connected with the settlement of his estate, David Reynolds, at the age of twenty-one in 1832, began peddling a stock of goods and made a considerable amount of money. On 26 December 1834 he formed a partnership with James M. Redd for speculating "in money, tobacco, and other things" at Ward's Gap in Patrick County. Some time in 1835 young Reynolds and Redd moved their business headquarters to Patrick Court House. There they continued to manufacture tobacco, which David peddled as far south as Georgia, often returning with loads of sugar, rice, coffee, molasses, and cotton domestics. They also sold apple brandy, French brandy, Madeira wine, and various staples. On one occasion David returned with three yards of petersham, a rough knotted woolen cloth used chiefly for men's overcoats, which he sold at five dollars per yard. Selling trips were also made to Danville, Richmond, and Lynchburg, all in Virginia. Such a trip to Georgia required ten weeks and no doubt great physical stamina. Varner further declared in his deposition that David Reynolds was very industrious, of good character, and prosperous in anything he undertook. Also in a deposition, Henry Aistrop stated that James M. Redd called David a "skinner" who made a handsomer profit on the goods he sold than did the other merchants of Patrick Court House.

David Reynolds had been on a selling trip to Georgia with 3,410 pounds of chewing tobacco shortly before his untimely death. According to the testimony of Abram Staples, David returned with twelve hundred dollars in cash in addition to several hundred dollars worth of groceries. This evidence definitely ties the uncle of R. J. Reynolds to the manufacture and sale of chewing tobacco in the 1830s. Furthermore, at the death of David Reynolds, according to the sworn word of Henry Aistrop, the firm of Reynolds and Redd had on hand 8,000 to 9,000 pounds of tobacco stems that had been accumulated from their manufacture of chewing tobacco. Abraham Reynolds died two years after the death of his son David, thus leaving Hardin W. Reynolds as the only heir to land and money far beyond the holdings of most inhabitants of Patrick County.

Quite possibly David Reynolds received his motivation to manufacture chewing tobacco from his father and his brother Hardin. As early as 1828, Hardin W. Reynolds saw greater possibilities in the manufacture and sale of tobacco than in total reliance on its cultivation. In that year his father sent him through the mountainous country rolling a watertight hogshead of tobacco for sale in Lynchburg—approximately a ten-day trip. Discouraged at the low price received, Hardin persuaded his father to let him make a crude press for manufacturing tobacco into twists, which he peddled into South Carolina. Certainly no record indicates any noteworthy prosperity on the part of the elder Reynolds until soon after 1828. At that time he and his sons apparently began growing more tobacco in addition to buying small lots from neighbors, all of which was crudely manufactured and peddled.[14] In view of the general conditions prevailing in Patrick County in 1835, it is entirely probable that Hardin W. Reynolds did indeed influence his father and brother to begin the manufacture of chewing tobacco in 1828. Joseph A. Martin, in describing Patrick County seven years later, wrote:

> The staple article of produce, on the south side of the Bull mountain is tobacco. . . . The principal portion of the slave population is on the south side of the county, which may in some measure account for the article of tobacco being more raised on that side than on the other. . . . The tobacco raised in the county is mostly manufactured and sold in the southern and western States. Immense quantities of this article are annually sent to the States of South Carolina, Georgia and Alabama, and sold at good prices for cash. Nearly every planter who raises tobacco to any extent is a manufacturer; but there are some who make a business of it, and purchase the article in the leaf from their neighbors, without prizing, at a very liberal price.[15]

The career of Hardin William Reynolds, so early interested in the manufacture of chewing tobacco, requires especial analysis as a factor in the life of his son Richard Joshua. In the first place, the records of Patrick County reveal that Hardin, as well as his father, was literate, no mean accomplishment for that area in the early nineteenth century.[16] He did not assume family responsibilities until he was thirty-two after inheriting the land and money amassed by his father and brother. No doubt by that time he also had accumulated considerable property by his own efforts. On 31

January 1843 he married Nancy Jane Cox (31 March 1825–7 March 1903) of the Quaker Gap community in northwestern Stokes County, North Carolina. She came from a family long settled in Stokes County, which lies immediately south of Patrick County.

According to family accounts, two or more Cox brothers came into the area near the time of the French and Indian War, and one of them, apparently Joshua Cox, the grandfather of Nancy Jane, fought in the war and in one engagement became the last man of his company to survive. Then captured by the Indians, he was, because of his great strength and magnificent physique (six feet six inches), adopted by the chief and his life was spared. After many months he escaped by swimming down the Susquehanna River until he reached a settlement. Later he came down the Appalachian Valley, eventually reaching Stokes County. Again from family accounts, it seems that before coming to America from London he had been a captain in the British Army. Joshua Cox also took a leading part in the Revolutionary War in his area and achieved local renown for having driven marauding Tories from his community.[17] Apparently he was also first to carry the highly prized good luck coin—a silver piece minted in Lima, Peru—which later came, generation by generation, to the next of kin with Joshua in his name until it reached Richard Joshua Reynolds. The coin supposedly imparted good luck to Reynolds and to all who rubbed it against their gold before departing for the Civil War and for World War I. At any rate R. J. Reynolds set great store by his inherited coin and no doubt kept in his mind a heroic picture of his great-grandfather, Joshua Cox, who, because of his brave exploits, his physical stature, and his bright red hair, long remained a legend in the Stokes-Patrick area.[18]

Not only did Nancy Jane Cox come from such determined ancestry but she was also a literate woman far more accurate and precise in her writing and spelling than her husband.[19] In fact, she wrote with ease and surprising grammatical correctness, though no one seems to know how she obtained her education.

At their marriage Hardin W. Reynolds and his wife settled on Rock Spring plantation near what is now Critz, Virginia, in a new brick house built on the land that Abraham Reynolds had purchased in 1814. Though Patrick County had little to offer any ambitious young man at best, Hardin made Rock Spring the center of a prosperous little empire based on farming and allied pursuits, the manufacture of chewing tobacco, and a mercantile business. Few opportunities for turning a profit escaped his eye and his energy was phenomenal. To this day his name remains in the area of Rock Spring as a symbol of thrift and industry.

Scant direct record of Hardin W. Reynolds's farming operations remains, although there are indications that he placed first emphasis on the accumulation of land. Long before his marriage he and Thomas Reynolds purchased 376 acres from Adrian Anglin through the executor, Greensville Penn. Thomas Reynolds disposed of his share to Abraham and Hardin W. Reynolds, the father apparently helping the son with the purchase.[20] At his death Hardin Reynolds had owned at least 8,000 acres of land in Patrick County and 3,000 acres in Stokes County, North Carolina, much of it acquired before 1865.[21] There is little indication that he ever parted with any substantial acreage. In fact, the last complete legal record left by Hardin is an agreement with a neighboring landowner that a third party should determine the correct boundary between their properties; in case either failed to accept the decision, he was to forfeit five hundred dollars.[22]

Such large landholdings, even in mountainous Patrick, demanded an extensive labor force, which, at first, consisted largely of slaves. By 1840 Hardin Reynolds owned nine slaves, by 1860 forty-nine, and by 1863 eighty-eight.[23] More important than mere numbers is the fact that thirty-three of them in 1860 were of working age—that is, older than twelve. Hardin's papers show that he frequently purchased single slaves always old enough to work.[24] Evidently during these years he conducted his farming operations from three centers; at least in 1855, for example, he registered the births of his slaves at Rock Spring, North Mayo, and Dan River.[25] His slaves, of course, were freed in 1865—by a segment of Major General George Stoneman's forces under the command of Colonel William J. Palmer, who reached Taylorsville on 7 April and remained in that area until 9 April 1865.[26]

For a short time after the emancipation of his slaves Hardin Reynolds evidently experienced some difficulty in handling freed slaves as laborers. The complaint of one of them elicited the following reprimand from Captain Asa Teal, an agent for freedmen stationed in Greensboro, North Carolina: "Sir a colored woman by the name of Ceby comes to this office and complains of You threating [*sic*] to Drive her from your plantation I suppose you are well aware wherein Freedmen have help raised [*sic*] a crop they are entitled to a Support You are hereby ordered to give this woman a home on your plantation or a support to do her till Christmas."[27] It is doubtful that Ceby's complaint caused Hardin any pronounced trouble because he had had experience with white tenants as early as 1855. On 15 September of that year he drew up a rent bond with Joel Tuggle, duly signed and witnessed, by which the latter rented "a place on the turnpike" pledging himself to erect a good fence around the place, to build a good tobacco house, and to pay Reynolds fifteen dollars in tobacco or other produce by 1 November 1856.[28] Hardin's papers after 1865 contain many such bonds, which generally detail the tenant's obligation to pay any indebtedness due him for supplies, to perform specific duties includ-

ing permanent improvements on the land, and to care for and use properly farm implements, tools, and livestock. By following this system of
farm tenantry Hardin was enabled to hold most of his property and required to pay increasing land taxes, which no doubt in a large measure
represented improvements made by the tenants. Scattered tax receipts
from 1866 to 1879 give a reliable record of his postbellum landholdings
in Patrick County and their increasing value (see Table 1-1).[29]

In his farming operations Hardin not only depended on shares of major
crops cultivated by his tenants, but also saw and exploited small opportunities characteristic of a rural economy. In 1859, for example, he collected
ten dollars from Lewis Pedigo for the services of a jack in the season of
two of the latter's mares. He also had the hides of various animals tanned
and on three occasions included the skins of kips—no doubt rabbit or
squirrel skins. The following agreement with Bainbridge Ferguson on 16
September 1867, in Hardin's own handwriting, reveals his drive to secure
every penny possible and the meager economic opportunities of his day
and locale, as well as his limited education: "This is to Sertify that I H. W.
Reynolds have a Greed to let B. Fogison have a Cow & Calf for which he
is to pay $1 per month for the milk of the Cowe for the winter months &
for the Faule and Somer months he is to pay $2 per month and he Bindes
him self to have the Cowe & Calf well Taken Good care off Giv the Calf
milk a Nuft to make it Growe and Do well and have the Cowe well atend
to." In 1879 Beasley Mabe and J. G. Lawson each obtained one barrel of
corn from Reynolds under their signed promises to repay the barrels of
corn "this fall." When Hardin died Joseph G. Penn owed him twenty-five
dollars for "one spotted bull" and by the date of settlement he also owed
the estate $4.50 for interest.[30]

Major products from Hardin's farm and from his tenants generally
included tobacco, livestock, grain, wool, potatoes, and flax. Census figures show that he grew 18,000 pounds of tobacco in 1849 but only 4,000
pounds in 1859, thus indicating, as his papers do, that he often accepted
tobacco alone for rent and that he purchased more each year for use in his
manufacturing.[31] The other farm products accepted from tenants were
often sold in his store as merchandise. Thus he frequently exacted two
profits—one directly from the production of his tenants and another by
means of manufacturing or selling what they produced.

Hardin's store, located near his dwelling, stood on the old Bristol-
Norfolk highway, which was for years a main thoroughfare across Virginia. The commodious building with its large cellar, no doubt for use in
handling leaf tobacco, was still sturdy and strong in 1960. In addition to
produce from his farms Reynolds sold ordinary commodities as well as
more sophisticated items. Of the countless sales of farm produce recorded
among his papers, few are more typical than the one made on 17 January

Table 1-1
Landholdings and Taxes of Hardin W. Reynolds in Patrick County, Virginia,
During 1866–1879

Year	Number of Tracts	Number of Acres	Amount of Taxes
1866	33	6,210	$ 86
1867	33	6,319	186
1868	33	6,419	222
1869	33	6,395	215
1871	33	6,395	277
1876	35	6,192	363
1879	35	6,300	367

Source: Papers of Hardin William Reynolds, in possession of Nancy S. Reynolds, Greenwich, Conn. The tax figures have been rounded off to the nearest dollar.

1843 by Julius Patterson, who purchased nine bushels of wheat, one and a half bushels of salt, one bushel of apples, two gallons of honey, ten barrels of corn, and one "sack bag." Reynolds also sold lead, cloth, plows, plow points, chewing tobacco, coffee, brandy, boots, wooden buckets, nails, sole leather, salt, herrings, sugar, molasses, candles, pistols, and axle trees. Among the more sophisticated articles he handled were coffee pots, collars, nutmeg graters, and paregoric, many of which were sold in quantity in the process of settling his estate. Though he also served as something of a banker for his area, Reynolds as a merchant could not easily deal with all his monetary problems. On 26 February 1874, for example, when paid with "One Five Hundred Dollar bill Series of 1869 No. 5527," he was, for lack of change, forced to give his customer his note for $250 to be paid thirty days later.[32]

A separate section of the inventory of Hardin W. Reynolds's estate includes the listing of 203 bonds or notes, ranging in size from $5.00 to $973.69, that were due the estate, thus indicating his role as a banker for the area. In general the notes had been made in 1881 and 1882, although two bore dates as far back as 1854. This number matches closely the 210 outstanding notes found among his papers with the oldest one dated 14 March 1837. The following list of larger promissory notes due Reynolds at his death by no means includes all in this category:

D. P. Allison	$ 90.14
John L. Anglin	855.59
A. J. Barbour	138.26

W. J. Craddock	202.04
William Critz	106.50
M. R. Dunkley	606.00
Ed Fulcher	87.92
A. M. Lybrook	750.00
R. G. Penn	116.29
R. J. Reynolds	1,674.00
A. D. Reynolds	2,500.00
Letty Reynolds	394.00
J. W. Taylor	61.79
John G. Lee, Peter A. Lee, and John R. Cobbs	2,500.00

He also ventured capital in far larger amounts. Near the beginning of the Civil War he invested the proceeds of his entire stock of manufactured tobacco in 213 bales of South Carolina cotton on the theory that it would deteriorate less rapidly than tobacco. Though this venture failed to materialize as he had planned, it did reveal sound financial foresight and the command of substantial capital.[33] Typical of Hardin's banking operations was a note of David W. Robertson for $74.48 made to Thomas M. Clark on 28 July 1859 and assigned by him to Reynolds on 22 October 1860. So far as his papers reveal, Reynolds seldom failed to collect his interest down to the last penny whether on notes or bills incurred at his store. Moreover, he frequently handed notes to the constable of Patrick County for collection.

In moulding the career of his son Richard Joshua, however, the operations of Hardin W. Reynolds as a manufacturer of chewing tobacco were more important than his agricultural pursuits, his mercantile operations, or his banking activities. Many references to the elder Reynolds as a tobacco manufacturer exist in statements of R. J. Reynolds and other members of the family, although they often do not agree as to sequence. There is no direct account of Hardin and the manufacture of tobacco as early as there is of his brother David. As noted above, however, it is more than likely that he began his manufacturing operations in 1828 and that he led his brother and his father into the same work. Tabulations from meager census returns indicate that his factory was a stable concern in 1850 (see Table 1-2).[34]

Among Hardin's papers there are no references to his manufacture of tobacco earlier than 1865—the date of a receipt from William C. Staples for branding tobacco. Three years later Reynolds paid excise taxes on 2,322½ pounds of tobacco manufactured in 1867, hired a Negro worker to prize tobacco, and paid a wagoner $39.53 for hauling 3,635 pounds of

Table 1-2

Available Operating Data for the Tobacco Factory of Hardin W. Reynolds,
1850, 1860, 1870

	1850	1860	1870
Capital invested	$1,500	$3,500	$9,000
Tobacco used	20,000 lbs.	25,000 lbs.	—
Value of tobacco used	$1,000	$2,500	—
Licorice used	—	250 lbs. at $75	—
Power	hand	—	hand
Machinery	—	—	Catt screw
Number of machines	—	—	10
Employees:			
male	8	7	10
female	—	7	5
children	—	—	7
Monthly cost of hands	$80	$70 males	—
		$42 females	—
Total wages paid in year	(slave)	(slave)	$400
Number of months in operation	—	—	5
Quantity of tobacco produced	15,000 lbs.	18,750 lbs.	—
Value of tobacco manufactured	$11,700	$3,000	—

Source: Based on figures given in original MS. Census Returns, Patrick County, Va., Industry, 1850, 1860, 1870 (microfilm, Virginia State Library).

manufactured tobacco to Charleston, then in what later became West Virginia. An indication of Hardin's failure to meet the new industrial age first came in 1878 when a Baltimore firm complained about receiving a bill for manufactured tobacco that had not arrived and could not be traced because there was no bill of lading. One year before his death Reynolds had difficulty with inventories and federal taxes. As the following letter to him from his son R. J. indicates, the latter was forced to aid his father. The letter probably reveals more about R. J. than the father, who by then had reached the virtual end of his career:[35]

I made the amended reports to balence your revenue account by there statement which they had made out without accepting the amended inventory of June 1st 1880 Walter [son of Hardin W.] only brought me the new Rev. book so I had no copy of 180 [1880] inventory and had to balence account according to there statement of inventory which made it rather bad showing and I got Harber [son of Hardin W.] to go to Danville and get the amended report that was sent when Walter was here and made new ones which makes your account balence and you are now OK with Gov. up to June 1st 1881 You ought to Keep coppy of all your inventories send you your book back by Mr. Noel Harber has placed to your Cr $1113 63/100 and give Check for your taxes enclose Tax receipt Much love to all Your son Dick

Though in the end age and change proved difficult for Hardin W. Reynolds, he was a successful and persistent manufacturer of tobacco. His success sent all five of his sons into the same business. His factory was a log building behind his dwelling in a field that even today is known as the "factory lot" despite the burning of the building about 1904.[36] According to the inventory of his estate, Reynolds owned such equipment for the manufacture of tobacco as box screws, iron levers, retainer pumps, shapes, and clamp bands.[37] He evidently operated his manufacturing business in a thoroughly systematic manner, if the possession of a "factory bell" is any indication. After 1865 Reynolds's sons and sons-in-law worked with him, usually as his partners. In 1867 Abram D., Reynolds's eldest son, became a partner in the business as manager of the factory and salesman of its products.[38] R. J. followed his older brother in the business at Rock Spring for a time as did Hardin Harbour, Reynolds's third son. Operations combining small tobacco factories, farming, and merchandising were not uncommon among the more enterprising in Reynolds's day and area.[39] His embryonic banking business, of course, rested on his success with other activities.

Hardin W. Reynolds, largely because of his economic status, was an outstanding figure in Patrick County and the surrounding area. Invariably addressed as "Captain Reynolds," he evidently held his title by virtue of service in the Patrick County militia.[40] Frequently he served in such capacities as commissioner for general elections and surveyor of roads; in 1846 he was inspector of the newly constructed county jail.[41] It has also long been held that in 1862 he furnished funds to obtain a sufficient supply of salt for the inhabitants of a large area of Patrick County for the remainder of the war. Actually in that year, when the Confederate government published a notice that all farmers needing salt might purchase a supply at Charleston (then in Virginia) at one dollar per bushel, Reynolds sent his oldest son with a four-horse team and a Negro driver to obtain salt. Other individuals from the area were largely unsuccessful in the same attempt, but young Abram D. Reynolds, taking along a load of manufactured tobacco to sell, succeeded in returning with 40,000 pounds of salt.[42]

Though severely limited in his ability to spell and write, Hardin Reynolds was evidently a faithful reader of newspapers, subscribing at one time or another to the *Southwestern Whig*, the *Union Republican*, the *Winston Sentinel*, and the *Hillsville Virginian*. He also subscribed to the *Richmond Christian Advocate* and contributed freely to Methodist causes. According to his son, he read these newspapers and kept informed on events covering a wide area.[43] As noted below, Reynolds sent his children to subscription schools, kept a governess at least for his youngest children, and entered all of them in the best colleges of the area. His prestige in the county, and no doubt that of his family, was enhanced by the possession of a carriage certainly as early as 1852 if not before.[44] His personal property in the year of his death included a "pleasure carriage" valued at two hundred dollars, books and pictures at three hundred dollars, and household furniture at three hundred dollars,[45] all no doubt nominal sums. His sturdy and roomy brick home faced Nobusiness Mountain and its plastered brick Doric and Ionic columned portico carried a distinction not often found in the area of Rock Spring. The outbuildings, still existing in 1964, reflect the conveniences of the day—a large kitchen separate from the main dwelling, a milk house, an ice house, and a granary. Most distinctive of all perhaps for such a mountainous region is the large level lawn, which by its springy turf still reveals the care once given it. Rock Spring became a post office with Reynolds, of course, the postmaster. He was not only a man of exceptional force but also of pride and common sense, concerned always that his children receive a good education. Soon after his death it was stated in a North Carolina newspaper that Captain Reynolds had "done more for Patrick County than any man who ever lived there."[46]

The great land suit of *Dr. William W. McCanless v. Hardin W. Reynolds*, which lasted from 1872 until 1884, served to make Reynolds's name well known in North Carolina at the very time his son R. J. was starting his business in Winston. It was the talk of the countryside from Stokes, Forsyth, and Davidson counties to Raleigh. It also illustrates the persistence of Hardin W. Reynolds. Brought by McCanless in Stokes County Superior Court in 1872, the suit revolved around the debts of Richard Cox to McCanless and to Hardin Reynolds, the brother-in-law of Cox. Cox deeded land to Reynolds, which, McCanless claimed, exceeded in value the prior agreements between Cox and Reynolds, thus preventing McCanless from being able to collect debts due him from Cox. Apparently the land in question was near the birthplace of Nancy Jane (Cox) Reynolds if not the birthplace itself. The case, tried in superior court in Stokes, Forsyth, and Davidson counties, went to the state supreme court four times with the Reynolds estate the final winner. This reckless expenditure of money for the best legal talent available excited many and moved the editor of the *Western Sentinel* to declare in 1878: "The suit is for a tract of land valued at some $1,500 to $2,000. The costs in the case now foot up near $3,000. Law is a luxury that must be paid for."[47]

Hardin W. Reynolds and his wife became the parents of sixteen children, eleven of whom were boys, though only seven of the group reached full maturity. In all, they were:[48]

Mary Joyce	10 January 1844–30 January 1888
Agnes Catherine	26 May 1845–18 June 1861
Abram David	13 August 1847–13 August 1925
Twin boys	20 April 1849–25 April 1849
Richard Joshua	20 July 1850–29 July 1918
Hardin Harbour	8 June 1854–21 June 1927
John Gilmore	13 March 1856–29 October 1862
Lucy Burrough	17 February 1858–18 July 1953
Nancy Bill	28 November 1859–31 October 1862
Ernest C.	14 January 1861–26 October 1862
William Neal	22 March 1863–10 September 1951
Twin boys	12 August 1865—born dead
Robert Walter	1 November 1866–6 March 1921
Nannie Kate	16 February 1870–16 August 1890

These children had advantages not available to many children growing up with them in Patrick County. Even the disaster that overtook three of them in 1862 originated from parental effort to protect them from the ravages of smallpox. Vaccination against the disease did not exist as a free public service during the 1860s. According to family accounts and birth records, John Gilmore (aged six), Nancy Bill (almost three), and Ernest C. (well over one year) died within five days of one another as the result of vaccinations against smallpox.[49] Supposedly Richard Joshua went to the Rock Spring, washed the vaccine from his arm, and thereby escaped danger.

Two other children died young. Agnes Catherine Reynolds, who lived to be sixteen, attended Salem Female Academy, a Moravian school in Salem, North Carolina, from 10 January to 1 June 1859, and in August of that year entered Danville Female College.[50] The youngest child lived to be twenty and was probably frail all her life. It was she who had a governess, Alice B. Crenshaw, at least from 1880 to 1882.[51]

The early education of five of the Reynolds children who reached maturity is documented to a degree by scattered tuition receipts among the papers of Hardin W. Reynolds.[52] It may well be that Nannie J. Walker, who received pay for tuition of the Reynolds children apparently in 1866 and who was present in the Reynolds home on 11 July 1866, served as a governess at Rock Spring. On that day she witnessed the signing of a receipt for Hardin W. Reynolds's payment to a household servant for the year 1865. There is evidence though that the early education of the Reynolds children began at the Shady Grove School—a subscription school near Rock Spring only a few feet from what is now Patrick Springs railroad station.[53] Fortunately their higher education may be traced with greater accuracy.

Of those who reached full maturity, Mary Joyce no doubt received her early schooling from her mother or from the local subscription school sponsored by her father. On 2 November 1857 she entered Salem Female Academy, located a few hundred yards from where her brother's factories would one day stand. Completing the two-year course, perhaps the best education then available for women in the South, she left the academy on 31 May 1859. Then with her sister, Agnes Catherine, she entered Danville Female College around 29 August 1859. At least Captain Hardin W. Reynolds held among his papers a receipt with that date for "seventy five dollars in advance for the board and tuition of his two daughters in D. F. College." Moreover Abram D. Reynolds declared in an interview in 1915 that his sisters attended Danville Female College (now Stratford Hall). According to another receipt, it is fairly certain that Mary Joyce attended Danville Female College a second year. Abram also declared in his 1915 interview that Mary Joyce "obtained distinction as a portrait painter."[54]

In 1867 Mary Joyce Reynolds married Andrew Murray Lybrook (18 January 1832–1 January 1899), a native of Giles County, Virginia. According to the catalogs of Emory and Henry College, Lybrook entered that institution in 1847 and received his B.A. degree in 1852. Soon thereafter he began to practice law in Patrick County and early fell under the influence of Hardin W. Reynolds. Lybrook, a bookish man, became a prominent citizen of Patrick County. He served as county judge, raised Company I of the 24th Virginia Regiment for the Confederacy, served as its captain, and represented his district in the Virginia state senate in the 1880s. In the senate he achieved statewide fame as a spokesman for the Readjuster movement.[55] As a partner with his father-in-law for some years, Lybrook was closely allied with the manufacture of tobacco, and two of his and Mary Joyce's children later became associated with the R. J. Reynolds Tobacco Company, one, George Richard, serving a number of years as secretary and treasurer.

Next among the children of Hardin W. Reynolds and Nancy Jane Cox to reach full maturity was Abram David Reynolds. Young "Abe" evidently received early instruction at the neighboring subscription school. When fourteen or fifteen his parents sent him to Edgewood Academy in Henry County for preparation to enter the Virginia Military Institute. Venturesome in spirit, brave, and intelligent, Abram David's chief interest in his one year's stay at the Virginia Military Institute lay in his desire to join the Confederate army. His parents insisted on at least a year's training in military tactics before permitting him to do so. Serving about one year in the Confederate forces, he emerged at the age of seventeen as a full-fledged major. About this time his father offered him five hundred dollars if he would complete his studies at Virginia Military Institute, but he preferred a business education. Later, for a brief time, Abram David attended Bryant & Stratton Business College in Baltimore.[56] One of his sons, Richard Samuel, worked for a time with the R. J. Reynolds Tobacco Company.

In the lineup of Hardin W. Reynolds's mature children Richard Joshua followed Abram David. In many ways these two seemed closer in spirit than any others in the family. Because R. J.'s education and earlier experiences are intertwined, and most important for this study, they will appear last in this account.

Fourth among the Reynolds children to survive childhood was Hardin Harbour. As various receipts among the papers of Hardin W. Reynolds reveal, he, too, attended a subscription school in Patrick County. In 1872 he entered the newly established Virginia Agricultural & Mechanical College, now known as Virginia Polytechnic Institute, and apparently completed the two-year course offered at that time.[57]

Lucy Burrough Reynolds, almost four years younger than Hardin Harbour, also attended subscription school in Patrick County. On 10 August 1871, however, she entered Salem Female Academy where she remained until May 1872. According to the records of Salem College and family accounts, she later attended Sullins College in Bristol, Virginia.[58] On 14 May 1878 Lucy Burrough married Robert Critz (18 September 1855–7 December 1924), who was a neighbor living near Rock Spring as well as a classmate of Hardin Harbour Reynolds at Virginia Agricultural & Mechanical College. Critz aided his father-in-law in his chewing tobacco operations at Rock Spring during the last years of the latter's life. He later became associated with Abram D. Reynolds in the manufacture of chewing tobacco in Bristol, Tennessee, perhaps as early as 1888. He remained in Bristol until April or May 1893, when he moved to Winston to become associated with R. J. Reynolds's rapidly expanding business. From that time until his death Critz served as the secretary and general amanuensis of the R. J. Reynolds Tobacco Company.[59] He was an excellent scribe, and the company's records contain copies of a countless number of his letters and much advertising copy in his handwriting.

The two youngest sons of Hardin W. Reynolds also attended the local subscription school and possibly received instruction from a governess in the Reynolds home. In 1882 both entered King College in Bristol, remaining there for several months. They then entered Trinity College in Randolph County, North Carolina—eventually to become Duke University. William Neal Reynolds's record there for 1882–83 and 1883–84 was good. Unlike R. J.'s handwriting his was that of a man somewhat accustomed to holding a pen and his use of the English language was fairly smooth and generally grammatical. There is no indication that his knowledge of figures approached that of R. J. Reynolds. On leaving Trinity he immediately joined the R. J. Reynolds Tobacco Company in Winston where he remained for the rest of his working life.[60]

Walter R. Reynolds, who changed the order of his given names, was educated much like his brother William, except that he made a better record at Trinity College and continued his education for two additional years at Randolph-Macon College in Ashland, Virginia. According to officials of that institution, Walter studied such subjects as philosophy and advanced mathematics. His letters, many of which still exist,[61] are remarkable for their clarity and conciseness. He was decidedly the best educated of the five sons of Hardin W. Reynolds and Nancy Jane Cox. Soon after leaving Randolph-Macon, Walter Reynolds, with his mother and sister, moved to Bristol, Tennessee, where he evidently worked with his oldest brother in the manufacture of chewing tobacco. Like his brother-in-law Robert Critz, Walter also joined R. J. Reynolds in Winston in 1893.[62]

Neither Hardin W. Reynolds's efforts to educate his children nor his success as a landowner and merchant equals for this account his importance as a tobacco manufacturer. It may well be that his greatest success lay in that area. All five of his sons pursued the same business. As noted above, the two youngest sons joined forces with R. J. Reynolds. After serving five years as manager of his father's factory and as salesman of the goods produced there, Abram David left Rock Spring in 1872 and immediately began to deal in leaf tobacco and to manufacture chewing tobacco in Bristol, Tennessee. He apparently was more than moderately successful. Clearly with his father's example in mind, he later purchased extensive tracts of land in the Bristol area and amassed a most comfortable but not extremely large fortune. Though he sold his manufacturing business in 1897, his other pursuits were based on profits from the tobacco industry.[63]

Hardin Harbour Reynolds likewise spent much of his mature life in the chewing tobacco business, though he was not too successful. Judging from various items among the papers of Hardin W. Reynolds, he made a partner of his son Harbour in 1876 at least in merchandising and in the manufacture of chewing tobacco. Apparently the son remained a partner until 1880. By 4 June of that year he had just arrived in Winston to work for R. J. Reynolds.[64] In 1885, however, Harbour Reynolds, as he was known to his intimates, began to manufacture chewing tobacco in Winston. Something of a wag, he achieved a degree of success with his Red Elephant chewing tobacco named for a well-known brand of whiskey and advertised as having one thousand spits to the chew![65] Largely because of the panic of 1893 and his naive belief that his customers would automatically pay their bills Harbour's tobacco venture in Winston failed.[66] Sometime between 1893 and 1897 he moved to Bristol to work with Abram David. According to the latter's recollections, Harbour remained with his firm for a short time after it was sold in 1897. The business was in turn sold to the American Tobacco Company in 1902. It thus appears that Harbour Reynolds left Bristol at least by that date. Soon afterward he established a chewing tobacco factory in South Boston, Virginia, and operated it successfully until a devastating fire destroyed much of the business of the town. Thereafter he retired to the Reynolds homestead at Rock Spring.[67]

It remains to outline the education and early experiences of Richard Joshua Reynolds, who derived a more grandiose fortune from the manufacture of tobacco than Harbour Reynolds ever imagined. Family stories recount that R. J. transported to his plant in Winston the only item saved from the fire that destroyed his father's old factory at Rock Spring—a licorice kettle. In his mind, however, he carried lessons far exceeding in value the price of a licorice kettle. He knew what he owed his father and, when describing his upbringing, seldom did he fail to pay tribute to Hardin W. Reynolds who taught him how to make a fortune.

In the first place, it is clear that R. J. Reynolds grew up in an atmosphere of comfort and well-being with exceptional opportunities for his day and area. He undoubtedly possessed a quick mind, although, according to his brother, an eye defect prevented him from visualizing words. Instead, he always saw separate letters, and not realizing his condition until relatively late in life, he never excelled in any subject except mathematics. In fact, declared Abram David in 1915, R. J., after entering Emory and Henry, "decided to abandon all other branches of study. It became necessary for him to originate all of his work in arithmetic, algebra, geometry, and trignometry [sic]."[68] Therefore, throughout his schooling, both in Patrick County and in college, he apparently paid far more attention to mathematics than to any other subject. Though handicapped by stammering as well as the eye defect, which generally passed for nearsightedness, his intelligence was apparent to all. One of the indications of his perceptive mind was told by an early teacher. During the Civil War years, on being asked what covered the mountains, his reply came instantaneously: "Rocks and deserters."[69] He could hardly have been more correct.

No receipts showing payment of R. J.'s tuition for early schooling exist among the papers of his father. He was, however, in school in 1860 according to the census enumeration made on 25 August of that year.[70] He must also have been in school somewhat later when he gave his pertinent description of the mountains of Patrick. Quite likely he was in the Shady Grove School, which some of the younger Reynolds children undoubtedly attended.

It is an assured fact that he attended Emory and Henry College for two years, probably at the instigation of A. M. Lybrook, his brother-in-law. In 1868–69 and 1869–70 he was enrolled there as a member of the "Select and Preparatory Class," living the first year in Fulton House and the second in Byars House.[71] It has never been claimed that Reynolds possessed any intrinsic interest or excellence in academic learning, although he wanted to excel in all branches of his studies when at Emory and Henry. According to Abram D. Reynolds, R. J. left college because he was able to make headway only in mathematics.[72] William Allen Blair (4 June 1859–2 March 1948), who knew Reynolds intimately, wrote that while he was attending school at home, he "'studied little and learned less.'"[73] Blair's inclusion of this phrase in quotation marks could indicate that it came from Reynolds himself, who generally downgraded his education and background perhaps in order to create a fellow feeling with his employees. Two other writers, certainly familiar with Reynolds's background, have frankly stated that he had "no particular taste for books" but that he possessed an unusual aptitude for mathematics.[74]

R. J. Reynolds therefore deserted his studies and began work in his father's factory at Rock Spring apparently late in 1870 or early in the following year. In his recollections Abram David described the move as follows:[75]

R. J. was at Emory and Henry College and as I returned from one of my Southern trips R. J. said he was going home with me and go to work My father was Very determined R. J. Should become a fourth partner [with Hardin W. Reynolds, A. M. Lybrook, and Abram D. Reynolds]— I took Dick out and Said do you want to Stay in Patrick 60 miles from a rail road all your life— If you do Come in as a ¼ partner or hire to me for two years and I will sell out to you and have Capt Lybrook to do the Same and you will be a half partner— He wanted to Know what Salery I would pay him I said the same I receive [$50 per month] he said thats a trade so we went to father and Dick said I dont Know any thing about this business and Abe had agreed to pay him 50$ a month and he thought he would learn

more on a Salery than he would as a partner— Our father Consented
and R. J. did good service for our firm for two years when Lybrook
and my self sold out to Dick and father—

Though R. J. in later years claimed a very early acquaintance with arduous
labor in his father's factory,[76] it is doubtful that in 1870 he could have
known much about all the details involved in manufacturing tobacco.
Late in life, R. J. also stated that he began his "career in growing and
manufacturing tobacco," and that he was promoted to the superinten-
dency of the factory at the age of eighteen.[77] Because he became eighteen
on 20 July 1868 and attended college from 1868 to 1870, he quite obviously had little or no time for serving as superintendent at that age.
Moreover, according to the usually reliable testimony of his brother
Abram, R. J. declared after his schooling at Emory and Henry: "I dont
Know any thing about this business." It is doubtful that R. J. in late 1870
or early 1871, when he began to work for Abram, could have known a
great deal about the purchase of leaf tobacco, licorice, and other supplies
for manufacturing, or about the sale of the manufactured product.

Work in tobacco factories in young Reynolds's early years differed quite
radically from the present. Factories generally were in operation about
four months a year, and the remaining months were devoted to the sale of
the manufactured product and to farming. When working for his brother
in 1871 and 1872, R. J.'s duties were connected with management of the
factory and sales expeditions, both of which had been allocated to Abram
in 1867.[78] In view of these facts, it is doubtful that R. J. made many of his
highly touted peddling trips until after he was eighteen.

One particular and frequently repeated story of R. J.'s early selling
expeditions must surely concern the period when he was working for
Abram. Traveling with a load of chewing tobacco into southwest Virginia,
Tennessee, and Kentucky, he found times hard, money scarce, and sales
virtually impossible to make. He decided to use the barter system, which
was then a frequent practice of tobacco salesmen. His tobacco disposed
of, R. J. started home with a load larger than at the outset of his trip and
with some agony of spirit as he reflected on his possible reception at Rock
Spring.

He arrived home late one night, with his wagon loaded to its
capacity with beeswax, tallow, ginseng, cowhides, sheep-pelts, bear
and wildcat skins, 'possum, mink and groundhog hides, rap [rag]
carpets, knit sox, yarn and homespun of various kinds, a few pieces of
valuable old furniture, with almost every other conceivable thing
which a country store took in exchange for the things the country
people had to have, stored away in that wagon, with three or four
horses and mules hitched on behind, and a solid gold-case watch in

his pocket, which was originally purchased by the owner for one hundred and twenty-five dollars, but accepted in payment for tobacco at thirty dollars.

One of his brothers, undoubtedly Abram, showed no pleasure at the idea of bartering $2,000 worth of manufactured chewing tobacco for such merchandise. Deciding to hold an auction sale and serve as his own auctioneer, R. J. sold all at a fair price except the watch, on which this brother bid $30. R. J. raised the bid to $90, obtained the watch, and used it for several years until he was able to sell it for $90. The profits from the sale amounted to 25 percent more than cash sales would have been, and R. J. soon started on another trip.[79] Though such stories may well grow in the telling, this one does fit into the general pattern of the time and the area.

Other of R. J.'s accounts of peddling chewing tobacco vary only in minor details. As the stories most often go, Hardin W. Reynolds, appreciating his son's determination and energy, decided to let him peddle manufactured tobacco on trial. With a small sum of money and enough food for a few days, R. J. drove over the Blue Ridge through Carroll, Wythe, and Smith counties. Finding no customers because the farmers he met were well supplied with homemade twist or blockade tobacco, he felt quite despondent. Evasion of the payment of federal taxes on manufactured tobacco generally prevailed for more than two decades after the Civil War, but R. J.'s tobacco was "tax paid" so that he could not meet the competition of blockade tobacco. A few more days of travel produced no sales. With both food and money exhausted, the young salesman picketed his team by the toll road on which he had been traveling, gathered up a supply of tobacco, and proceeded on foot over terrain not usually traveled by peddlers. Successful in selling enough to obtain food for himself and his team, he drove on to Morristown, Tennessee, where he sold the remainder of his tobacco.[80] This episode, of course, may well have happened, but it is something of a replica of Abram D. Reynolds's account of using somewhat similar tactics for securing forage in 1862 when on an expedition to get salt.[81] Nor is it possible to fix a date for R. J.'s trip to Morristown, although it very likely occurred while he was working for Abram.

It appears that R. J.'s next venture was a short period of study at the Bryant & Stratton Business College, in Baltimore, which was later merged with Strayer College. The records prior to 1904 were destroyed in the devastating Baltimore fire of that year. The fact that Reynolds later gave 1 July 1873 as the exact time of his entry into partnership with his father indicates that his stay at Bryant & Stratton came during the first half of 1873. Direct proof of Reynolds's schooling at the business college, however, must rest on his possession of a countinghouse edition of *Bryant &*

Stratton's Commercial Arithmetic, reprinted in 1871, which he kept almost to the end of his life. In it, in more legible handwriting than he was wont to use in later years, he wrote his name, "R. J. Reynolds Rock Spring Va." R. J.'s copy of the book, well worn but not abused, may be considered as evidence to support the frequent statement that he was something of an expert with figures. Part I of the arithmetic consists of a review of arithmetical functions whereas Part II gives basic explanations, illustrations, and problems pertaining to such items as profit and loss, insurance, bankruptcy, banks of exchange and discount, negotiable paper, partnership, errors on trials and balances, partnership settlements, and statistics, not to mention "Days of Grace and Time of Maturity." Also in Part II are rigorous problems involving mensuration of plane and solid figures, no doubt the basis of R. J.'s later aid to John Clark Whitaker (b. 7 August 1891), a 1912 graduate of the University of North Carolina. Whitaker stated that he had covered reams of paper in a futile attempt to determine the proper diameter for a paste can of given height in order to double its capacity. When Reynolds came by and asked Whitaker about his problem, he laughed and explained that he had a book that he had always found very helpful. Eventually, in 1917, forty-five years after Reynolds had used the book as a student, he gave Whitaker his countinghouse edition of *Bryant & Stratton's Commercial Arithmetic*. Furthermore, it was always R. J.'s firm intention to write a good, sound arithmetic textbook.[82]

More important, perhaps, than peddling or bartering chewing tobacco in rural areas was young Reynolds's experience in Baltimore. There he most likely attended school at his own expense. On Saturdays he solicited orders for chewing tobacco, thus becoming familiar with the nature of city trade and the methods of wholesale dealers.[83]

Returning from Baltimore, R. J. went into partnership with his father on 1 July 1873, under the firm name of H. W. Reynolds and Son, in the same factory he had known since childhood. This factory, sixty miles from a railroad,[84] was considerably removed from the center of the Old Bright Belt where flue-cured tobacco, a relatively new type, had emerged to assume leadership over the heavy type of leaf produced in the low valleys of Patrick County. Always aware of new trends in the tobacco world, Reynolds undoubtedly sought a bountiful supply of the increasingly popular flue-cured leaf as well as railroad facilities. As Reynolds phrased it in 1915, he "moved to Winston Salem for the benefit of railroad facilities, and on account of this town being located in the center of the belt in which the finest tobacco in the world is grown."[85] For the manufacture of tobacco his was a far wiser move than that of his brother Abram.

Richard Joshua Reynolds grew to be a man of unusual size with great energy, an independent will, and robust health. On his passport, issued in 1908, his height was given as six feet two inches.[86] He was apparently able to learn from his environment. One story told by R. J. in 1912 about his experience in peddling tobacco illustrates the point. Driving into a village of three stores, one large and two small, he called at the large store to find the proprietor busy. To save time he went to the small stores and sold some of his tobacco at both places. Returning to the large store, he boasted of his sales to the competing stores only to have the owner refuse to make a purchase. When asked why, the owner replied that he did not copy those little fellows but that they copied him. Smarting under his failure, Reynolds endeavored as he drove away to understand the store owner's reaction. He decided it was similar to his experience when sent to bring in the horses from grazing in the pasture; if he caught the lead horse, the others would follow, but no other horse had any influence over the group. R. J. theorized that men reacted in much the same fashion.

Another of his anecdotes may well illustrate Reynolds's quickness to assume control under most circumstances. As a youngster, when bullied by his older brother, R. J. often fought back. The father, to R. J.'s great annoyance, would then have them kiss and make up. On one such occasion R. J. bit his brother's lips until he screamed. He took his punishment, but after the next fight when ordered to kiss, he spoke through his clenched teeth, telling his brother to come on and give him a sweet kiss. Whereupon the brother refused to do so and thus received his thrashing. R. J. remained free of any further bullying.[87] Though of doubtful value as authentic historical evidence, the many anecdotes connected with the early life of R. J. Reynolds generally reflect a quick-thinking mind. His father's discipline and supervision, so evident in the above story, were matched, as far as stories go, by his mother's demands. Certainly R. J. showed great deference to her, especially during her years in Winston, where she eventually came to live some time after the death of her husband.

Because Reynolds became important to people in general only after he had achieved success, many of his interviewers wished to find the key to that success. Such questions often produced homilies in regard to his early days of labor. It is doubtful, however, that R. J. had quite as much interest in work for work's sake as was often intimated. Nevertheless he attributed his success to his father's training in the following words:[88]

> I was trained early in the value of work by my father, who was a successful planter and business man. He took a great deal of interest in training young men to work, and in this he gained a reputation for efficiency. Above all things else, he believed firmly in work. I have heard him say over and over again that all the talent, or ability, a man could possess, was worthless unless it was backed up by work.
>
> A short time before my father died, he requested me to train my two schoolboy brothers [William Neal and Walter Robert] to work

the same as he had trained me. One of these is sixteen years younger than myself and the other is twenty years younger.

Hardin W. Reynolds did indeed believe that his sons should work, chiefly, as Abram D. Reynolds declared in 1915, "to learn the business in [the Rock Spring factory]." In his recollections Abram referred to work necessary in the spring of 1865 when he wrote of his father: "He would say Evry now and then what will we do for bread— Negros all gone Corn planted no one to work it— I said father Dick and I can save your corn crop . . . Bro R. J. and my self saved the corn crop—I could plow all right R. J. did the choping and other hard work." In 1915, when he sought to rebut some of R. J.'s boasting of having risen from a lowly factory hand, the older brother declared: "No white man worked in his [Hardin W. Reynolds] factories except his sons, all of the labor on his plantations and in his factories being done by slaves." Clearly these statements mean that the sons of Hardin Reynolds worked at hard labor only in 1865 and that their work in the factory amounted to little more than learning the manufacturing process. Some of R. J.'s stories of severe manual labor in his early years actually refute themselves and show that his labor in some instances represented discipline imposed by his father. Testifying at the age of sixty-six, R. J. declared that he had fancied he liked manual labor better than schooling and persuaded his father to let him drop out of school temporarily. To this proposal his father reluctantly consented, taking care at the same time to give him the most difficult tasks available. First, at his own request, R. J. tried plowing with the understanding that he was to keep pace with one of his father's plow hands. After two days of drudgery, he reported to his father that he did not like plowing. Next, he was given the task of clearing land by cutting down trees and grubbing roots, the only terms being that he keep up with his father's laborers. A few days later, with blistered hands and an aching back, he announced to his father that he preferred school. It was from these experiences, R. J. claimed later, that he learned to remain with what he understood rather than to jump into work he did not understand.[89]

Here then was Richard Joshua Reynolds, who, sometime in the fall of 1874, sold his interest in the factory at Nobusiness Mountain as he prepared to move nearer the tobacco center of the South and modern transportation. He brought with him not only a willingness to work for a profit but also the experience of his father and grandfather in the manufacture and sale of chewing tobacco dating back to 1828 and his own dating from his earliest recollection. In some respects he had grown up in the Old South, but he was of the New South despite his firm recollection of taking horses into the woods for safekeeping when rumors spread in Patrick County that a segment of General George Stoneman's forces was approaching.[90] In addition, his brother Abram David had been a Confederate officer and his father, though not absolutely bankrupt, had been badly damaged by the Civil War. Nevertheless R. J. had enjoyed many opportunities denied to most young men in the South of his day. He had attended school and college, received a business education, and lived for a time in a city. He knew how to manufacture chewing tobacco. He knew how to sell manufactured tobacco. He knew how to handle taxes levied by the federal government. Equally important, if not more so, he was able to obtain a small amount of capital from his family. All in all, Reynolds had many advantages and he seized them with speed and energy.

His very success bred stories of early poverty and illiteracy. Those who did not succeed in making money built themselves a platform of superiority from which to view the millionaire. The workers in Reynolds's factories believed him to be virtually illiterate and thereby developed a fellow feeling for him. One retired worker, not in the least responsible for the rumors, referred to Reynolds as a man of no education. Upon being told that this could not possibly be true, the retired worker countered with what undoubtedly was true: "Well, they always said he had no education."[91] Reynolds certainly did not write with any smoothness, nor with any notable concern for grammatical rules; yet he was by no means illiterate. He readily recognized a well-written letter and often handed badly composed letters back to secretaries for revision. Frequently he ran contests among the secretaries in his company and offered prizes for the best-written letter. No doubt in the South of his day it was difficult to find secretaries with adequate training. The folklore about his illiteracy probably had its origin in the appearance of his signature, usually a hasty scratch that could be interpreted as the signature of a man who did not know how to spell his own name. It was also his custom not to dictate letters but to tell a secretary what to include—a practice no doubt a relief for a stammering and busy man. Much of the blame for the persistence of such stories, of course, may rest on R. J. himself whose reminiscences often stressed his supposed rise from early poverty. In reality, few successful men owed more to parental training and supervision than did R. J. Hardin W. Reynolds's insistence on a thorough education for his children no doubt reflected regret that his own education had been so inadequate.

These stories of R. J.'s illiteracy traveled about as rapidly as his brands of smoking and chewing tobacco. Repeated, the rumors seemingly became more truthful and soon were recorded facts. William Watts Ball, editor of the Charleston *News & Courier*, put in his diary shortly after R. J.'s death a ridiculous story once told him by Robert L. Gray, an editorial writer for the Columbia (South Carolina) *State*. This tale of virtual illiteracy on the part of Reynolds emphasized the latter's habit of not dictating letters. Obviously the story of his illiteracy had been ac-

cepted as truth by both men.[92] Wilbur J. Cash, in his brilliant interpreta-
tive work *The Mind of the South*, took even greater liberty with the facts
when he wrote the following words as the solid truth: "That Reynolds
had come to his destined fief, Winston, in true Dick Whittington style,
perched atop a tobacco wagon, and barefoot in his turn—that he had not
learned to read and write until he was already a rich man."[93] This would
have been a great affront to Hardin W. Reynolds, that proud and ambitious man, who was no doubt aware of the deficiencies in his son's education when he sent him to plow in his roughest field. But in 1874 young
Reynolds rode directly south into a community not too unlike the area of
his birth. There he remained supremely unmindful of gossip about his
background and education as he set about the business of developing his
fortune as well as that of others. Was he not the son of Captain Hardin W.
Reynolds of Rock Spring plantation?

CHAPTER 2

Laying the Foundation

Events connected with R. J. Reynolds's removal to Winston in Forsyth County, North Carolina, and his early years there as a manufacturer of chewing tobacco are seriously obscured by a paucity of documentary evidence. Nevertheless these early years may be partially reconstructed from records concerning his plant, the laborers, purchases of leaf, brands of chewing tobacco, sales, and capital. Reynolds's business progressed so rapidly during the first twelve years of its existence that its management demanded more than one man. During this period, R. J. constantly enlarged his plant, managed his sales through wholesale outlets, and obtained capital on a piecemeal basis largely from his family and wholesale tobacconists of Baltimore. Notwithstanding the multiple problems that confronted the young manufacturer as he went about organizing his new venture in business, he early became interested in and played an important role in the life of the community, particularly in its economic development.

Location of the New Factory

At the age of twenty-four R. J. Reynolds headed south from Nobusiness Mountain to an area that he evidently knew rather well. His association with tobacco must have brought him in contact with the Old Bright Belt and its superior leaf. In fact Patrick County, Virginia, is adjacent to Stokes County, North Carolina, and Henry County, Virginia, both in the Old Bright Belt. His choice of a new base of operations, sixty miles almost due south of Rock Spring, was Winston in the western area of the Old Bright Belt next to Salem, which had served as the seat of the Moravian church in the South since around the mid-eighteenth century. In this area, before 1870, comparatively little attention had been paid to producing the new type of tobacco, bright or flue-cured leaf, although as early as 1858 three experienced growers had introduced it into Forsyth County. Farmers in the vicinity of Winston eventually produced much bright leaf, usually of a heavy type more suitable for chewing than for smoking tobacco.[1] Major Thomas Jethro Brown (3 August 1833–17 July 1914) came from Caswell County to Winston in 1869, and, in an old livery stable, began operating an auction sales tobacco warehouse. Despite Brown's work in distributing seed to encourage the production of tobacco, not enough was grown to support a sales house. In 1872, however, Brown returned, and, in partnership with S. M. Hobson and Hamilton Scales (1821–7 September 1890) established a more pretentious and longer lasting sales house. Their auction sales house, the operators claimed, would ensure an adequate supply of tobacco for the manufacturing interests of Winston and afford "facilities for transportation which will enable speculators to compete with the Danville market in the matter of freights."[2] Though more interested in manufacturing than in speculating in leaf tobacco, Reynolds carried this letterhead on his stationery as late as 1883: "Dealer in Leaf–Manufacturer of Plug and Twist Tobaccos."[3]

Some say that young Reynolds rode from Nobusiness Mountain to Winston on horseback whereas others think he drove in a buggy or carriage; it makes little difference, because his mind was perhaps occupied with the advantages of a means of transportation more rapid than either. Stories from Walnut Cove in Stokes County, which had hopes for a railroad before Winston, hold that Reynolds, with a horse and buggy, spent a night at Piedmont Springs near the girlhood home of his mother as he moved toward Winston. Similar stories from the same area say that he stopped for a night in Danbury, the county seat of Stokes, and while there put his money in the care of the innkeeper. Still nearer Winston, at Walnut Cove, he reputedly spent the night with a large landholder, Dr. W. A. Lash, who owned all the land near the surveyed line for a railroad. Supposedly Reynolds wished to settle there, but Lash refused to sell him land for the projected factory. On the other hand, the story as broadcast over North Carolina is that Walnut Cove, once called Lash, was plotted on Lash's land, that Lash was an intimate friend of Reynolds and, upon finding that R. J. planned to start a tobacco factory, "did his best to persuade him to locate the plant in Walnut Cove," and that Reynolds "was very much interested in the suggestion and . . . promised to think it over."[4] Reynolds no doubt preferred the town with railroad connections already established. As early as the last weeks of 1870 or early in 1871 he had listened to his oldest brother talk about the disadvantages of being located sixty miles from a railroad. R. J. himself declared in 1915 that he located his plant in Winston "for the benefit of railroad facilities."[5]

Whatever the contradictory stories, R. J. Reynolds of "the county of Patrick and State of Virginia," on 19 October 1874 purchased on "Depot Street" in the town of Winston a hundred-foot lot that extended westward to Chestnut Street. Part of the R. J. Reynolds Tobacco Company's factory Number 256, as it stands today, occupies this lot, which Reynolds purchased for $388.50 from the "Congregation of the United Brethren of Salem and its Vicinity." In the light of the boom from the new railroad it is noteworthy that Reynolds paid more for his first purchase of land than the Forsyth County commissioners paid the Salem congregation in 1849 for the fifty-one-acre tract on which Winston was established.[6]

Nothing less that Depot Street would have satisfied young Reynolds. On 28 July 1873 the first regular train had arrived in the vicinity of Depot Street (now Patterson Avenue) from nearby Greensboro, North Carolina, over the Northwestern North Carolina Railroad, which was twenty-eight miles long. Edward Francis Belo (27 January 1811–2 October 1883), president of the railroad that began the transformation of Winston and Salem, was a member of the United Brethren, or the Moravians. In Greensboro, the Northwestern North Carolina Railroad connected with the Richmond and Danville system, later to become the Southern Railway. The editor of a Winston newspaper wrote in 1885:

> The completion of the North Western North Carolina railroad, extending from Winston-Salem to Greensboro, where it connects with the great Richmond & Danville system, ushered in a period of prosperity to Winston that nothing else could have produced, and the facilities that this railway have [*sic*] given our manufacturers and tobacco dealers have proved the very life-blood of the Twin-City [Winston-Salem]. This road is only 28 miles in length, so that we are in close connection with the great thoroughfares and great marts of the country. . . . It is currently understood that this road "pays better" than any other in the State, but how true this is we, of course, cannot say. We have two trains to and from Greensboro each day, and both freight and passenger traffic is heavy.

In the next breath the editor urged that another railroad be built from Winston and Salem northward via Martinsville to Lynchburg, Virginia.[7] When Reynolds arrived in Winston in 1874, however, all seemed satisfied with the single spur track to Greensboro, known as the Salem Branch Line. Conjectures to the contrary, it is extremely doubtful that anyone influenced R. J. Reynolds to settle by the railroad right-of-way in Winston. He had seen the trend of the times in Baltimore and he knew the

slow and difficult work of peddling chewing tobacco. In little more than
three months he fortified his position by purchasing another tract of land,
this time on the east side of the hundred-foot right-of-way of the Salem
Branch Line, the front or west side being parallel with the railroad track.
This purchase, surely the result of foresight, was apparently made on
special terms because the transaction for $261.75 was made early in 1875
but not legally recorded until 30 November 1880,[8] a delay quite foreign
to Reynolds's usual procedure.

What was Winston like when Reynolds showed so much faith in his
ability to succeed in this location? In the first place, it was the county seat
of Forsyth County established in 1849 next to Salem partly because it was
the center of the county and partly because Salem was an important
town—the center of industry and culture for the area. Actually for many
years Winston seemed of little importance to the Moravian center of
Salem. Throughout most of the 1870s Winston's population reputedly
stood at 400 to 500, although by 1878 it was supposed to have reached
2,500. Salem and Winston of 1877 have been described as "two quite
small neighboring towns" whose people were poor and depressed from
the trials of war and Reconstruction. The Moravian congregation had
lost its invested funds in the general disturbances of the Civil War. But in
1878 Winston contained fifteen independent tobacco factories.[9] Physically Winston consisted of frame buildings and unpaved streets "shoe-top
deep" with dust in summer and bottomless quagmires in winter. The
"twin cities" at the time of Reynolds's arrival undoubtedly constituted
something of a frontier region. In February 1877, for instance, John Eli
Gilmer (d. 31 March 1916), a leading merchant of Winston, shipped
$1,000 worth of furs.[10]

Another factor indicative of the undeveloped economy of the area during the 1870s and 1880s was the tremendous traffic in dried blackberries.
Far more important than the embryonic chewing tobacco venture of
Reynolds, the blackberry business helped give Salem a national reputation
and no doubt a feeling of superiority toward the struggling town of Winston. By 1877 the impact of the dried berry trade in Salem had reached
New York City: "The little town of Salem, N.C., containing only about
2,000 inhabitants, has shipped during three years over three million
pounds of dried blackberries, for which nearly half million [sic] dollars was
received."[11] Three years later a local editor cheered his readers with news
of blackberry drying and favorable indications for "an extensive trade in
this fruit."[12] The firms of Hinshaw and Bynum, Hinshaw and Medearis,
and Vaughn and Pepper engaged in a considerable business in dried blackberries until the late 1880s when the industry began to decline because
canned and evaporated fruits had come into use. According to the 1888
circular of Hinshaw and Medearis, dried blackberries were mostly con-

sumed by laboring people who, in such centers as St. Louis and Chicago, could not afford them if the price exceeded seven cents per pound. One Winston editor in 1907 and again in 1910 recalled with nostalgia the years when the dried blackberry "was a power . . . in the channels of trade and business."[13]

The New Factory

Signs other than those of the dried blackberry business confronted Reynolds in Winston as he prepared to build his factory. Three manufacturers were already producing tobacco by 1875; when the first factory was built, the machinery, equipment, and supplies were hauled in on Nissen wagons.[14] Hamilton Scales reputedly operated the first tobacco factory, beginning in 1872 in an old carriage shop and continuing until 1890 when he sold his plant to N. S. and T. J. Wilson. By 1875 Scales had built a new factory two and a half stories high, 60 by 34 feet, with a cooling room and a drying house.[15] Virtually all available accounts list Thomas Livingston Vaughn (19 January 1848–5 February 1932) as the second tobacco manufacturer to be located in Winston. A native of Stokes County, Vaughn apparently came to Winston in 1873 and was actually the first to erect a tobacco factory there—a brick building within a block of the courthouse.[16] He became an active and leading manufacturer among the many who settled in Winston. Other manufacturers came possibly in 1873 from nearby Davie County. Pleasant Henderson Hanes (16 October 1845–9 June 1925) and his brother, John Wesley Hanes (3 February 1850–23 September 1903), under the firm name of P. H. Hanes and Company, erected a little factory only 40 by 60 feet and "a story and a jump high."[17]

Next to appear was Reynolds, who built a factory 38 by 60 feet—a frame building; it was not the largest of the four then in Winston, although it did have two stories. Many sentimental accounts of this first building, "The Old Red Factory," have been given, especially in 1909 at the time of its abandonment to make way for an improved building.[18] In view of its numerous additions, it is doubtful that The Old Red Factory had any marked identity by 1909, although R. J. had not only obtained his start in this building, but, according to many verbal accounts, had also used the second story for his living quarters during his early years in Winston. Reynolds in 1915 described the early expansion of his factory as follows: "'We manufactured the first year 150,000 pounds, which was the capacity of the plant. From then on, about every other year, this factory was built on top, bottom and additions made to each end, until the business was increased to 1,000,000 pounds, having taken eighteen years to secure this volume.'"[19] Table 2-1, pieced together from newspaper items and pamphlets, all subject to the fallible memory and enthusiasm of R. J. Reynolds as well as to the human errors probable in the collection and printing of the information, nevertheless indicates expansion that doubtless soon obscured the original frame structure.

Newspaper accounts in the early years frequently touch on the growth of Reynolds's factory. In 1878 one local paper referred to the "considerable additions" that R. J. made to his plant in 1877 "in order to meet the growing demands of his trade" and to the fact that he found it necessary late in 1878 to enlarge further.[20] Following the completion of that work, the *Western Sentinel* editorialized: "R. J. Reynolds during the past winter has made large additions to his factory and will increase his work accordingly."[21] In December 1880 Reynolds decided to install a large "25-horse power" engine with the intention of "prizing," or pressing his chewing tobacco by steam, and on 21 April 1881 his significant new move received the following comment in the *Union Republican*, then the leading newspaper in Winston: "Mr. R. J. Reynolds has about completed an addition to his already large Tobacco Factory building and, has added an engine and attachments for running his machinery by steam in future. He will thus be enabled not only to do a much greater quantity of work in the regular tobacco season, but to operate the year round if desirable."[22] In this move, however, Reynolds had been anticipated by his chief competitor, P. H. Hanes and Company, which had added steam to its factory late in 1878 in order to "carry on operations during the winter months."[23] Again, in 1882, Reynolds, along with P. H. Hanes and Company and Bailey Brothers, made extensive additions to his building, causing a local editor to declare that "Mr. Reynolds enlarges every other year—this being the third addition if we mistake not."[24] Alert and active, Reynolds by 1883 had already so distinguished himself among Winston's twenty-three tobacco manufacturers that he was referred to in a local newspaper merely as "R. J. R.,"[25] the initials that were to become so well known in later years. Increased demand for leaf tobacco by manufacturers in Winston during the fall of 1882 induced T. J. Brown to issue a special circular from his auction sales house, calling attention to the greater number of sales made in order to satisfy the manufacturers. He specifically mentioned Bailey Brothers, the Winston Manufacturing Company, and "the large additions to Messrs. Hanes & Co. and R. J. Reynolds."[26] Clearly Reynolds was keeping pace with the best; it was during these years that he was never seen to walk. Instead he always ran.[27]

Table 2-1
Indications of the Growth of R. J. Reynolds's
Business During 1875–1887

Year	Factory Measurements	Hands	Capacity or Output (pounds)
1875	38 × 60 ft. frame structure 2 stories	30–40	150,000 (capacity and output)
1878	38 × 95 ft. brick and wood 3½ stories	75	250,000 (capacity)
1879	38 × 140 ft. brick and wood 3½ stories	175 (to be hired)	300,000 (capacity)
1880	38 × 128 ft. brick 3 stories	125	275,000 (output)
1885	90 × 215 ft. rear: 4 stories front: 3 stories steam fixtures and machinery	300 or more	1,000,000 (capacity)
1887	38 × 215 ft. plus brick addition 50 × 50 ft.	250–300 and partners added for 1888	500,000–750,000 (output)

Sources: For 1875: *Winston Leader*, 27 May 1879; *Western Sentinel*, 17 December 1885; *Manufacturers' Record*, 1 June 1916; *Winston-Salem Journal*, 25 April 1915. For 1878: *Guide Book of N. W. North Carolina Containing Historical Sketches of the Moravians in North Carolina* (Salem, N.C., 1878), p. 33. For 1879: *Winston Leader*, 27 May 1879. For 1880: J. D. Cameron, *A Sketch of Tobacco Interests in North Carolina* (Oxford, N.C., 1881), p. 19. For 1885: *Western Sentinel*, 17 December 1885. For 1887: D. P. Robbins, *Descriptive Sketch of Winston-Salem, Its Advantages and Surroundings, Kernersville, Etc.* (Winston, N.C., 1888), p. 35. In 1885, however, the dimensions of the original factory were given as 36 by 60 feet— *Western Sentinel*, 17 December 1885.

Labor

The nature of factory operations during this period demanded little more than a seasonal labor force. In accordance with the practices of the day, the early Winston manufacturers suspended operations during the winter months. Probably in part because of market techniques, it appears that the shift to manufacturing in the winter occurred somewhat slowly. In early May 1875 a local editor referred to the beginning of operations.[28] In May 1881, just as Reynolds completed installation of steam, another editor wrote that "Richmond factories are now at work with full force" and that the same was true of Winston manufacturers, "several of them with increased machinery." Another editor stated in October 1878 that "some two or three of them will continue work during the winter" but that the remainder had "about closed for the season."[29] This beginning of work in April or May and closing in October or November continued to be the general practice in Winston at least until 1886, when the editor of the *Union Republican* declared in December: "This year many of our more pretentious tobacco factories are still in operation, while others have been running day and night in order to close out the season's work."[30] Possibly 1886 did mark the beginning of somewhat continuous work by the "more pretentious," and Reynolds had obviously been in that class since the spring of 1881. At any rate, on 3 February 1887 R. J.'s early inauguration "of the rolling and twisting season" called for a special news item.[31] Yet, in 1886, when John Q. Adams, Sr., began to work in Reynolds's Old Red Factory, the absence of heat and lighting prevented work during winter months.[32] It is doubtful that the problem of continuous operation was fully settled before the advent of the Proctor Redrying Machine about 1898, but Reynolds was moving rapidly toward solving it.

For many years labor requirements necessarily fluctuated with seasonal conditions of manufacturing, a situation that induced one editor to write in 1877: "Suspension of the tobacco factories throw a good many colored employees out of work for the winter season."[33] It is therefore no wonder that the tobacco rollers in 1879 petitioned the manufacturers of Winston, declaring that they had suffered not only because of scarcity of work during the winter but also because of low wages received during the working season. As laborers they wished to become citizens, to have their grievances redressed, and to secure wages sufficient to permit an honest living.[34] No encouragement appeared in 1880. Tobacco manufacturers, astonished at the number of people seeking work in the spring of that year, reported that they were besieged with applications by letter and in person. "The supply of hands is greater than the demand," wrote a Winston editor.[35]

Records are available to permit a brief examination of labor in Reynolds's plant from 1 June 1879 to 31 May 1880. In that period the greatest number of hands employed "at any one time" was 110, of whom 55 were men over sixteen, 45 were women over fifteen, and 10 were children—all at an average daily wage of fifty cents. A skilled mechanic received one dollar per day. In an ordinary working day from May to November the laborer worked ten hours, but, if he worked at all from November to May, he remained on the job nine hours. At the time these figures were recorded, Reynolds had five employees regularly employed, one on three-quarter time, and six who were idle.[36] This view of his labor force fits the general picture of the period.

Of the five regular workers two were most likely Thomas Landon Farrow (31 July 1857–26 September 1911) and Henry Roan (7 December 1856–13 June 1925), though Roan, who worked regularly at night, was not then a full-time worker. Farrow began to work for Reynolds possibly in 1877 as a tobacco tagger, but by 1883 he headed the prize room, a position equivalent—at that time when Reynolds produced chewing tobacco only—to superintendent of manufacturing.[37] Sometime before 1882 Reynolds, hard pressed for help, persuaded Henry Roan, a telegraph operator, to do the bookkeeping as a regular employee at night. Later as the business expanded, Roan became R. J.'s regular bookkeeper, entering his full-time duties on 1 December 1882 at $1,200 per year. Two years later, on 15 November 1884, additional help came for the manufacturing area of the business when D. Rich (10 March 1862–21 October 1924), later to become treasurer and director, was hired to work in the rolling and casing division, a change that no doubt enabled Thomas L. Farrow to devote his full time to the prize room. Born in nearby Mocksville, Rich received little education and, at the age of thirteen, began to work as a stemmer in a Mocksville tobacco factory at ten cents per day. When he was eighteen, he came to Winston and worked four years for Bynum, Cotton and Jones, tobacco manufacturers. Joining Reynolds at twenty-two, ambitious and knowing only work, he returned to the factory at night, learned the bookkeeping system, and upon the death of the chief bookkeeper several years later succeeded to his position, thus beginning his climb in the company.[38] In such a way had the small business grown since 1875, when, according to the memory of his younger brother William, Reynolds had built his factory largely on credit and begun to manufacture chewing tobacco with a dozen Negro workers, doing the buying, supervising, selling, and bookkeeping himself.[39] William N. Reynolds knew the early circumstances of the business, for he joined the company in 1884 after having worked earlier with R. J. during vacation months. Not long afterward, R. J. assigned him the task of purchasing leaf.

According to the census data for 1879, the average yearly wage for a worker in tobacco factories in North Carolina was only $101.25.[40] In

March 1879, however, workers came into Winston to negotiate "with manufacturers for the approaching season's employment." In the 1880s, when railroad construction began to offer supplementary work for the winter months, their prospects tended to improve though at the expense of heavier drudgery.[41] Because the Winston-Salem area had relatively few Negroes, many of the laborers during these early years walked in from places as far distant as Patrick and Henry counties in Virginia. Many also came from Richmond and Danville "to find a season's employment in Winston's tobacco factories." Doubtless the testimony of Ed Penn in 1890, when identifying Willis Read, was typical: "I live in Winston, have been making my home for two years; I came here first in '82. I know Willis Reed; I know him when he came here in '88 in March or April; I got him a bench [to work as a lump maker for chewing tobacco] at R. J. Reynolds; his wife came the next week after he came."[42] When Reynolds's employees finished ten hours of work for six days a week, they walked to the store of Henry Dalton Poindexter (25 November 1849–23 November 1922), a leading merchant of Winston. There they were paid at a small window wired off from the rest of the store in such a way that they did not have a full view of the goods until their pay was in hand.[43]

In an era of great poverty, the Winston labor situation was similar to that of the entire South where an abundance of unskilled labor strove for wages of any description. Because of a proposed reduction in wages in 1887, about 2,000 workers in the Jersey City plant of the P. Lorillard Tobacco Company went on strike.[44] But strikes were not entirely foreign to the Winston-Salem area, where the Knights of Labor had established a lodge as early as 1886 and W. T. Pfohl of Winston had been appointed to work as a state organizer.[45] At any rate, a provocation similar to the one causing the P. Lorillard strike erupted into a general strike of the "rollers" in Winston in April 1889. These workers objected to an adjustment in wages adopted by all Winston tobacco manufacturers that reduced the rollers' pay of $3.00 and $2.00 per hundred pounds to $2.75 and $1.75, while increasing the wages of the "prize hands" from $1.00 to $1.25 per day. Crowds of Negroes milled around the streets and both strikers and manufacturers held meetings, the latter remaining firm in their stand. A local editor described the scene:[46]

A large number of the strikers assembled at the Negro Knights of Labor hall Tuesday night, and John Wade and others harrangued [sic] them until a late hour, advising a continuation of the strike. Although some of the more sensible Negroes advocated a resumption of work, they were outnumbered and outvoted, we understand, by the radical element present.

Although the wages of prize hands has just been increased . . . from $1 to $1.25 per day, an effort was made to draw them into the strike also. We could not learn definitely what the result of that attempt was. One prize-hand, who left before the meeting adjourned, told us he didn't care what action they took—he was going to work as soon as called on to do so.

He said that the tobacco season would not last all the year, and he didn't want to beg nor starve next winter, when he could, by working now, save up enough to support himself comfortably.

After the meeting adjourned a large number of strikers, headed by a bass drum (a very base one) and a fife marched about town, making the night hideous—a nuisance the repetition of which the city authorities should not permit.

Clearly the Negro workers were departing from their agrarian ways. The rollers nevertheless resumed work when some of the manufacturers sent to Danville and Reidsville for the schedule of wages paid there. When the schedule was read to the strikers, declared an editor, they realized that Winston manufacturers paid better wages than any other tobacco town in North Carolina or Virginia. But the "radical element" was not destined to subside so easily in years to come.

Other than references to rollers and prize hands there exist virtually no indications of the labor performed by workmen in the Reynolds plant during the early years. As in factories elsewhere, there must also have been leaf pickers, stemmers, licorice cooks, dippers, cappers, and shapers. The purchased leaf, of course, had to be made suitable for handling by means of steam in some cases, but more often in the early years, by atmospheric conditions. Leaf pickers then assorted the tobacco into wrapper and filler material for different brands of chewing tobacco. Usually stemmers next removed the midrib before the leaf was immersed by the dippers in the cooked mixture of sugar and licorice. Allowed to dry naturally, the leaf was then sprinkled with flavorings, which in Reynolds's case included brandy of various flavors. The stemmed and flavored leaf then went to the roller, sometimes called a lumper, who fashioned it into sizes suitable for twist or plug. The capper wrapped the lump with a leaf of superior color and texture known as a wrapper. Eventually the twist or plug went into the shapes ready for pressure that was generally applied by hand and main force in the prize room prior to the introduction of steam. There were other employees—some to stem the wrapping leaf, some to tag the finished product, and others to assist in packing the product for shipment. Crude scales were generally used to produce work as uniform as possible, the first effort at quality control.[47]

Purchase of Leaf

Based on the scant evidence available, it appears that buying, storing, and handling raw leaf proved to be troublesome for Reynolds, and, before the end of this formative period, he established an embryo leaf department. The supply, often uncertain as to quantity, quality, and type, frequently had to be sought in areas far from the new auction sales houses of Winston thus making transportation a problem. An excellent example is R. J.'s trip in 1882 to Saltville, some 150 miles northwest of Winston in the mountains of southwest Virginia. He drove some distance from Saltville to the farm of George W. Palmer to examine three barns of tobacco. Carefully inspecting the leaf on the lower tiers, Reynolds found it to be excellent. Upon being assured that the tobacco on the upper tiers was equally good, he bargained to purchase at twenty-four cents per pound the entire crop, which was shipped to Winston in two lots, one on 7 April and the other on 20 May. The shipment required eight or ten days. Meanwhile Reynolds had paid Palmer $2,569.13. Upon examination in Winston, part of the tobacco proved to be frostbitten and worthless. Reynolds sued Palmer in federal court during the April term of 1884. He obtained $1,278.48 from Palmer, although at considerable expense in legal fees and loss of the use of much-needed capital. His lawyers were the best the area afforded—Cyrus Barksdale Watson (14 January 1844–11 November 1916), James Turner Morehead (28 May 1838–11 April 1919), and John Henry Dillard (January 1819–6 May 1896).[48] This extraordinary case no doubt resulted from the extreme scarcity of good leaf in the crops of 1881 and 1883.[49] It also seems that Reynolds occasionally purchased leaf from other manufacturers, especially from small country manufacturers such as W. R. Doss of Copeland in Surry County, North Carolina.[50] Meanwhile, in 1883 and 1884 Reynolds also obtained leaf from dealers in Richmond, Danville, and other areas.[51] On 22 July 1884, when the manufacturing season was undoubtedly in full swing, the local editor considered one of Reynolds's leaf-buying expeditions to be important enough for comment.[52]

At length Reynolds joined a group of local men to erect a new auction sales house at a cost of $20,000—to be the largest and "most complete" of its kind in America. His purpose was to entice farmers to market more leaf in Winston. Evidently, however, he needed even more tobacco before this group of "the biggest moneyed men" in Winston and Salem could complete the building, because only four months later he purchased the Eagle Warehouse from Pfohl and Stockton for a price purported to be $7,000.[53]

Reynolds's large supplies of leaf presented a serious problem in the matter of storage. He was proud in 1885 to announce that for him it was not unusual to have as much as 600,000 pounds of leaf on hand at one time. This supply of leaf, of course, had to be stored until needed for manufacture. Anxiety over this matter caused him to rent the skating rink building in March 1882. With his storage facilities still inadequate, he proceeded in 1886 to erect a "roomy" storage building, four stories high and fireproof, on the Hannah Warehouse lot at Chestnut and Third streets, which he had purchased for $3,200.[54]

To make a difficult situation worse, Reynolds also experienced trouble from thieves who stole leaf tobacco from his buildings. Acting vigorously as always, he discovered the name of one thief which he published in a local newspaper together with a warning that those who came into posses-sion of any of the stolen leaf should return it to him and thereby avoid the trouble and cost of legal procedures that he was prepared to initiate. The last word of the episode came with the announcement that Reynolds had recovered one-half of the tobacco and "captured several of the thieves."[55]

Reynolds's work became so complicated that he soon placed his leaf business in the hands of his young brother, William Neal Reynolds. Will Reynolds, as he was generally known, apparently lacked much of R. J.'s exuberance and enthusiasm. He was, of course, almost thirteen years younger than R. J. Will spent the summers of 1880, 1881, and 1883 in Winston assisting his brother and the winter months attending school. It is clear that he joined R. J. on a permanent basis in Winston during the summer of 1884, and it is also clear that he first became head of the leaf department largely by accident. Will Reynolds frequently accompanied R. J. to auction sales houses to pick up the tobacco that the latter bought. One day as R. J. was talking with a group of men, Will bid on and purchased an allotment of tobacco. R. J. hurried to inspect Will's pur-chase, decided that it was an excellent bargain, and immediately gave his brother the task of purchasing leaf tobacco. According to Will Reynolds's memory in 1950, this occurred in 1885. Quite probably it happened somewhat later, although by 1888 Will Reynolds had temporarily become one of R. J.'s partners.[56]

Sales

In selling his products, it has been stated repeatedly that Reynolds did no country peddling from Winston. He probably considered such a method unprofitable long before the editor of *Tobacco* wrote in 1892 that the day had gone for any profit in peddling manufactured tobacco.[57] Reynolds's chief connections were with wholesale tobacco dealers in Baltimore. Will Reynolds stated very late in life that R. J. peddled the product made during his first year of manufacturing in Winston but that he soon went to

Baltimore and "made contracts with brokers" to furnish them plug under their own brand names.[58] There is, however, a definite indication that Reynolds used a peddler, one N. Dalton. From the record it seems that Reynolds let Dalton have manufactured tobacco on his own account to peddle at whatever profit he might make. Moreover Dalton's name has the word "peddler" written after it.[59] There are no company records of any type available prior to 1881, but Reynolds's ledger from 1881 to 1889 shows that he had accounts with forty-seven Baltimore firms as well as with firms in other areas of the South and in such places as Philadelphia, Cincinnati, and Pittsburgh. A newspaper account in 1885 seems therefore to be based largely on fact:[60]

> The market for the tobacco he [R. J. Reynolds] manufactures is exclusively among jobbers of the country, chiefly in Maryland, Pennsylvania, Ohio, Kentucky, Georgia, Alabama, Texas, Tennessee, and South Carolina. He has some customers to whom he sells as high as 175,000 lbs. per year and he has made single sales of 100,000 lbs. (in one sale of this magnitude the buyer took 90,000 lbs. of one grade). . . . Another fact we may make note of, and that is that, despite the very active competition that exists, Mr. Reynolds undoubtedly sells more tobacco in the city of Baltimore than any other two manufacturers in North Carolina.
>
> We question very much if there is another plug and twist tobacco factory in North Carolina, Virginia or any other State owned and operated by one man, that does so extensive a business as the one we here refer to—indeed we know of none in the whole country.

Another publication in 1888 carried essentially the same information: "Mr. Reynolds deals exclusively with jobbers and has no salesman on the road, the merit of goods being a sufficient advertisement for all the manufacture of the house."[61] There is even more emphatic proof of Reynolds's extensive trade in Baltimore during this period. As early as 1887 he used a printed form headed "Baltimore, _____ 188___" which contained an agreement for purchasing manufactured tobacco from R. J. Reynolds. In this agreement Reynolds allowed a rebate for each jobber buying one "hundred or more boxes on or before July 1st, 1887" provided each delivery contained lots of ten or more boxes. The jobber also agreed not to give more than a 2 percent discount for cash when selling Reynolds's products to retail dealers.[62]

Possibly Reynolds had salesmen on the road by 1886, because on 10 September of that year he obtained what was known as a drummer's license, which was required of all companies with salesmen on the road.[63] Yet, his knowledge of Baltimore and the help of his friends at Benjamin F.

Parlett and Company doubtless delayed any great expenditure for salesmen of that type. Benjamin Francis Parlett (9 July 1824–3 September
1884) established a wholesale tobacco business in Baltimore in 1843,
added a tobacco-manufacturing business at Danville, Virginia, in 1874,
and in 1881–82 owned a tobacco factory at Penn's Store in Patrick
County, Virginia. At the death of Parlett his sons took over the management of this chain operation, and the business flourished. When Benjamin
F. Parlett, Jr., retired, the business was continued for a time by his brother
John Fletcher Parlett (1 March 1853–14 October 1908), who finally
closed "the Danville factory and the Baltimore jobbing trade" and connected himself "with the R. J. Reynolds Tobacco Company, of Winston,
North Carolina, with which he was associated as a resident director and
manager of the Eastern territory."[64] In December 1887 the following
news item appeared in a Winston paper: "Mr. R. J. Reynolds, of this city,
will manufacture large quantities of plug tobacco for Messrs. B. F. Parlett
& Co., Baltimore."[65] It requires little imagination to see that Reynolds
was close to the Parletts long before John F. Parlett became a director of
his company, especially as Penn's Store in Patrick County is scarcely four
miles from Rock Spring. Close connections between other wholesale tobacco brokers of Baltimore and Winston manufacturers in 1887 also appear evident from the presence of John Wight, "celebrated broker" of
Baltimore, in Winston "again" to look after his "heavy trade" with local
tobacco interests.[66]

Despite Reynolds's connections with wholesale dealers, his ledger covering the years from 1884 to 1888 contains certain other intriguing items
insofar as sales are concerned:[67]

1884–86   J. W. Bitting "'Agt.'," Marlin, Texas, $438.61
1885   P. A. Ball, Baltimore, "traveling Expenses," $250
1885   T. H. Flood, "Traveling Expenses," $100
1885   S. H. Williams "'Agt.'," Washington, N.C., $88.19
1886   J. E. Morris, "Traveling Expenses," $950
1888   E. O. Douglas "(salesman)," $233.12

Unspecific as these entries may be, it is probable that they represent the
beginning of the sales force for dealing with wholesale tobacconists and
retailers. Reynolds undoubtedly occupied an advantageous position in
relation to the expenditures connected with sales. Certainly the situation
was not the same for all manufacturers of tobacco; in 1885, for example, a
person just in from the lower South reported "tobacco drummers as thick
. . . as bees in a clover field."[68]

Brand names, of course, represented chiefly a method for encouraging
sales. Actually the chewing tobacco manufactured by Reynolds in the early

years consisted of one brand insofar as the formula was concerned. According to Will Reynolds, it was shipped out in lots weighing fifty-six pounds to the box, and, at one time, R. J. made two brands differing only in size, one a seven-inch plug and the other twelve inches.[69] Such practice was doubtless general, and certainly difficulties in obtaining different types of leaf as well as a paucity of flavoring and sweetening agents would prevent any real diversity in brands. The brands represented largely the quality of the manufacturing process. In 1918, when demand for chewing tobacco was at its height, it would possibly have been difficult for a manufacturer to produce eighty-six distinctive brands. Yet, in 1886, Reynolds listed eighty-six different brand names. Will Reynolds declared that it was not until R. J. brought out Maid of Athens that he started to make his own brands but that Schnapps really made his reputation. The earliest record of Maid of Athens is 1886. Schnapps as a brand name appeared first in 1885, though spelled "Snaps," which Reynolds had intended to call it. The change in name was an accident. With some of this new brand ready for shipping, the labels arrived late, spelled "Schnapps," and Reynolds was furious. When a passerby remarked that Schnapps was one of the best drinks in Germany, he allowed the boxes marked "Schnapps" to go out and continued the German spelling.[70]

But some of his earlier brands may well have been his own property, and he listed them as his own before 1886—five of them as early as 1877. Only the brands shown in Table 2-2 seem to have been available for the years prior to 1886. With Schnapps and Maid of Athens on Reynolds's list for 1885 and 1886, it would seem that he began to shift to his own brands near the mid-1880s. Moreover, he knew the value of his initials, R. J. R., for he first registered them on 10 August 1886.[71]

This apparent shift to his own brands about 1885 renders a complete list in 1886 of more than ordinary significance (see Table 2-3); included is at least one on which he had already begun to center considerable interest, Maid of Athens. In the list provided in Table 2-3 there are obvious efforts to draw trade through appeals to such factors as flavors, state pride, familiar landmarks, national heroes, honest value, low cost, religious inclinations, pleasing chews, and Southern sectionalism. Some brands received the names of R. J.'s friends among the young ladies of his acquaintance, as well as that of his sister Lucy Reynolds. Noticeable also is the absence of Schnapps, listed in 1885 as Snaps. Most important of all was the use of his own name, which occurred six times.

In *Connorton's Tobacco Brand Directory of the United States for 1887*, Reynolds changed Dick Reynolds to Dick Reynolds's Best, Jake's Idea to Jake's Idea 4's, and Sam Jones' Vest Chew to Sam Jones Best Chew. He also added the following brands:[72]

Banana	Dixie's Delight	Live Indian (twist)
Capitol	Emma	Monumental
Daisy Girl	Golden Rain	Schnapps
Diamond	Jennie Winston	Watt Slaton
		Yellow Rose

In Reynolds's hustling plant, manufacture of these various brands involved duties other than those connected with prizing, flavoring, and leaf picking. Brandy was ordered from such firms as Goldsborough, Pitt, and Myers of Baltimore and labels from the Calvert Lithographing Company of Detroit, Louisville Lithographing Company, Krebs Lithographing Company of Cincinnati, or Burrow-Giles Lithographing Company of New York. Machinery, never identified by item, came from the H. M. Smith Machinery Company and the J. W. Cardwell Company, both of Richmond, Virginia. Along with four leading manufacturers of Winston and several others elsewhere, including Liggett and Myers Tobacco Company and P. Lorillard, Reynolds used Cardwell's well-advertised shapes early in 1887.[73] These were more monumental tasks than such casual

Table 2-2
Some Brands of Chewing Tobacco Made by R. J. Reynolds During 1877–1885

Year	Brands
1877	IXL, Old Reliable, Reynolds' Orange, Reynolds' Strawberry, World's Choice
1878	Before Any, Berry Foster, Black Crook, Bright Molly, College Select, Old North State, Old Reliable, Orange Twist, Strawberry Twist, World's Choice
1879	College Select, Old Hickory, Omaha State, Orange Twist, Reliable, Strawberry Twist, World's Choice
1880	Orinoko Pounds, Reynolds' Bright Twist, Strawberry Twist, World's Choice
1885	National, Orinoko, Snaps ("Schnapps"), Sure Pop, World's Choice (and "a host of others")

Sources: For 1877: *Western Sentinel*, 1 February 1877; for 1878: *Guide Book of N. W. North Carolina Containing Historical Sketches of the Moravians in North Carolina* (Salem, N.C., 1878), p. 33; for 1879, *Winston Leader*, 28 May 1879; for 1880, J. D. Cameron, *A Sketch of Tobacco Interests in North Carolina* (Oxford, N.C., 1881), p. 19; for 1885, *Western Sentinel*, 17 December 1885.

Table 2-3
All Brands of Chewing Tobacco Made by R. J. Reynolds, 1886

Ambrosia	Golden	Ready Cash
Arlington (twist)	Henry Clay	Red Brick
Autumn Peaches	Hickory	Reynolds' College
Beacon Light	Honey Dew	Select (twist)
Berry Foster	Hume's Favorite	Reynolds' 3-oz.
B.4 Any	Ida G	Strawberry (twist)
Big Jim	Jake's Idea	Richard's Extra
Black Crook	Jockey Club	R.J. Reynolds'
Bloomingdale	Keystone	A.A.A.A.
Boss	Legal Tender	R.J. Reynolds' Choice
Bridal Wreath	Little Mitie	Robert's Daisy
Bright Mollie	Lord Erskine	Rose Bud (twist)
Caromel [*sic*]	Lucy Reynolds	Sam Jones Vest Chew
Charter Oak	Lula Hurst	Sand Road
City Talk	Luxury	Seal (twist)
Cleopatra	Maid of Athens	Solace
Crescent	Mountain Eagle	Standard (twist)
Crown of Diamonds	My Pet	Sunny South
Dick Reynolds	National	Tar Heel
Dime Plug	Nickel Twist	Town Talk
Domino Twist	Old Cabin	Trumps
Dummitt Grove	Old Griff (twist)	Twin City Club
Eclipse	Old Hickory	Tyler's Center Shot
Eleanor Calhoun	Old North State	Uncle Dan's
Extra North Carolina	Old Reliable	Wade Hampton
Chew	Our President	World's Choice
Flanagan	Peerless	XXXX Henry County
F.X.J. Twist	Planter's Choice	Pounds
George Washington	Pride of the Forest	Zeb Vance
3-ply Twist	Purity	Zulu
Gold Cord	Randall	

Source: J. W. Connorton, ed., *Connorton's Tobacco Brand Directory of the United States for 1886 and 1887* (Chicago, 1886–93), pp. 9–79.

references indicate, although none of Reynolds's manufacturing supplies or equipment can actually be measured except his machinery and that only in dollars and cents. According to balance sheets from 1881 through 1887, the value of Reynolds's machinery alone in the last year was 51 percent greater than his entire original capital, generally said to be $7,500 (see Table 2-4). Meanwhile the value of his real estate holdings increased at a more rapid pace—from $10,726 in 1881 to $55,946 in 1887.

By 11 November 1875 the young manufacturer had come under the eye of Dun & Bradstreet, Inc., known then as Dun, Barlow & Company, which rated him as a tobacco manufacturer doing a good business and "altogether reliable." In his total net worth, estimated at $20,000 to $30,000 in June 1876, Reynolds held real estate valued at $3,000 to $4,000. The representative of Dun, Barlow & Company in May 1878 reported "Mr. Reynolds, now alone, to be worth $10,000 to $15,000, with good habits, a good business reputation, and good credit." His being "alone" meant that his silent partner had withdrawn, as will be shown later. By January 1879, his career and habits still "good, prompt, and reliable," he had raised his total worth to an estimated $18,000 to $20,000, $6,000 of which was in real estate with no encumbrances. At the end of 1879, however, the picture was not quite so rosy, although he was doing "a fair bus[iness] & making money." Rated as being worth $12,000 to $15,000, he remained of "good char[acter] & habits" and stood high in Winston.[74] Reynolds had evidently accomplished this standing on his own, because his silent partner had withdrawn and no legacy had yet been received from his father.

The actual value of Reynolds's real estate holdings, as shown in his balance sheets from 1881 to 1887 (see Table 2-5), indicates that the earlier estimate of Dun, Barlow & Company was a good one. The sudden jump in value from 1882 to 1883 may well reflect some of the inheritance received from his father, who would have approved of R. J.'s faith in real estate.

Table 2-4
Recorded Value of R. J. Reynolds's Machinery, 1881–1887

Year	Value
1881	$ 7,606
1882	7,358
1883	9,385
1884	9,890
1885	10,445
1886	11,446
1887	11,332

Source: Balance sheets of R. J. Reynolds, 1881–87.

Table 2-5
Recorded Value of R. J. Reynolds's Real Estate Holdings, 1881–1887

Year	Value
1881	$10,726
1882	13,543
1883	29,409
1884	34,334
1885	40,126
1886	50,224
1887	55,946

Source: Balance sheets of R. J. Reynolds, 1881–87.

Capital

Scarcity of capital no doubt placed Reynolds in the same category as others of Winston and Salem in 1889 who were ready "to welcome Northern capital" but unwilling to wait "for something to turn up."[75] From the scant clues available it seems that he engaged in considerable maneuvering to obtain capital during the early years of his business. Will Reynolds declared in 1950 that R. J. took half of the two years' profit from the Rock Spring factory—between $6,000 and $7,000—when he left for Winston. There he persuaded the Fogle Brothers, or possibly the Miller Brothers, to build his factory on credit.[76] R. J. Reynolds said in 1915 that he erected his first plant at a cost of $2,400 and began business with a capital of $7,500. One year later, however, he told a reporter that his factory, when equipped, cost $2,400, an expenditure that left him $5,100 for operating capital. The account usually accepted is that Reynolds arrived with $7,500, which sufficed for his lot, his factory, and his working capital during the first year.

At the same time, Reynolds stated in 1915 that he had a partner who evidently helped furnish his early capital. He bought the partner out two years later, which must have been early in 1877. In 1916 Reynolds said that the silent partner was A. M. Lybrook, his brother-in-law, but that the partnership existed only twelve months after which time he bought Lybrook's interest and paid him the principal plus 25 percent—apparently the profit for that period.[77] Fortunately, at least to a degree, there is evidence to settle this last discrepancy. In June 1876 Dun, Barlow & Company listed Reynolds's worth as $20,000 to $30,000, but in May 1878 it reported that he was "now alone" and worth only $10,000 to $15,000. It therefore appears that Reynolds bought Lybrook's interest at some point between June 1876 and May 1878. Yet in his ledger, Reynolds noted on 3 December 1877 that he owed Lybrook $1,826.24 and on 21 August 1879, $312.23, the former sum being marked "Transfd to Bills Payable" and apparently fully settled by 2 May 1881.[78] From a separate sheet laid in this ledger it is clear that the $1,826.24 represented interest due Lybrook and that Reynolds later borrowed from his sister, Mary Joyce Lybrook, who, according to family tradition, did lend her brother money after her father's death. It will also be recalled that R. J. owed his father $1,674 at the time of the latter's death in 1882. Actually Reynolds borrowed and repaid rather modest sums so constantly that he most likely could not recall the facts accurately. The only conclusion possible is that R. J. constantly needed capital, but at first failed to find any but comparatively small sums in his own family.

Will Reynolds recalled in 1950 that the bank in Winston, in reality perhaps the First National Bank of Salem, would allow his brother only $500 in credit during the first year of operations, but that he returned to Virginia and borrowed $1,500 from his father and an equivalent sum from a friend of his father. In this pinched situation he managed to survive the first year in Winston. He made some money that he deposited in the local bank and reported to the teller that he needed more credit. The teller sent a note to the president of the bank who asked to see Reynolds. Appearing much younger than he actually was, R. J. told the skeptical bank official that the money deposited had been made by his own efforts. He also told the president that he would take his account to Danville if he failed to secure more credit. Supposedly the president allowed the credit. In any event, Reynolds's ledger for 1881 to 1889 is filled with accounts connected with the Wachovia National Bank, which was founded in 1879.[79]

It may be readily accepted that R. J. borrowed from his family and from the local bank, but which friend of his father was able and willing to advance $1,500 in 1875 or 1876? Circumstantial evidence points to Benjamin F. Parlett, Sr. Parlett, who entered the tobacco business in 1843, was well known in Winston as early as 1882, when he spent "some days" there on business connected with the manufacture of tobacco. In December 1887, it will be recalled, Reynolds began to manufacture large quantities of chewing tobacco for "Messrs. B. F. Parlett & Co., Baltimore." Moreover, in 1881 Reynolds had an account with B. F. Parlett and Company of Danville totaling $1,122.10 and in 1884 another of $246.69 involving leaf tobacco. Parlett's factory in Danville had been established in 1877.[80] More important, however, is the fact that John F. Parlett, of the old B. F. Parlett and Company, on 6 February 1897 became a director of the R. J. Reynolds Tobacco Company under the North Carolina articles of incorporation. At that time, with capital badly needed, John F. Parlett was the only director outside the Reynolds family.[81] The Parlett family certainly occupied a key position for helping Reynolds obtain credit in Baltimore.

Reynolds often borrowed small sums from others. In the records available William S. Floyd, a tobacco dealer of Baltimore, ranks first. When the stockholders of the Winston High School sold a lot on Fourth Street to the highest bidder in 1882, R. J. Reynolds and William S. Floyd were the successful purchasers. This same Floyd, apparently connected with the Parletts, made at least fifteen different loans to Reynolds from 1881 to 1884. Often, however, the loans appear to have been made for very short periods and many of them undoubtedly represent the same money with frequent renewals. They ranged in size from $1,000 to $3,000. Significantly or not, some of Reynolds's loans from Floyd fell due at the Merchants National Bank of Baltimore with which Reynolds himself carried accounts only four years later. Two ledger pages—which, among existing records, list most of Reynolds's borrowings—show twenty loans from the Wachovia National Bank from 1881 to 1884, totaling $29,000 and ranging in size from $500 to $3,000. In one case a purchase amounting to $973.75 from J. D. Patton & Sons of Richmond, dealers in supplies for tobacco manufacturers, received credit for a sufficient length of time to be called a loan.[82] In view of his many small loans, with repeated renewals and repayments, and his increasing business, Reynolds undoubtedly suffered as much annoyance in obtaining capital as he did in securing leaf for his plant. It is obvious, too, that his need for capital could not be permanently solved by such methods.

Yet from 1875 to 1887 Reynolds had little need to worry about profit. Late in 1885, he considered business far better than in 1884 with collections "very satisfactory."[83] His balance sheets covering the years 1881–87 show that his net worth steadily increased (see Table 2-6). These figures do not reveal when he made his early decision to accumulate $100,000 and retire from the tobacco business because of its lack of promise. No doubt he came to be fired by statements such as the following, which appeared in a Patrick County newspaper in 1887: "Mr. R. J. Reynolds, of Winston, spent several days in this county last week. Mr. R. is said to be one of the wealthiest men in North Carolina."[84]

Other Activities of R. J. Reynolds

Reynolds's interest in other businesses, in real estate, in the development of the town, in local government, in public education, and in good horseflesh caused him to be well known to many. One illustration of his well-established position in the town appeared as early as 1881 when he

Table 2-6
Recorded Net Worth of R. J. Reynolds, 1881–1887

Year Ending 31 January	1882	$ 81,729
	1883	98,997
	1884	143,041
	1885	155,709
	1886	185,816
	1887	224,365
	1888	262,932

Source: Balance sheets of R. J. Reynolds, 1881–87.

suffered a severe case of typhoid fever. A local editor expressed concern over "one of our leading manufacturers" and pleasure at his recovery.[85]

Among his various interests he was probably most active in buying and developing property. In 1882 a house mover received compliments for moving one of Reynolds's tenement houses with the family "in occupancy" the same as if it were fixed "as immovable as the stars." His ledger shows an investment in 1884 of $6,910.50 in the Lafayette Mills of Company Shops, now Burlington, North Carolina; one of his financial backers, William S. Floyd of Baltimore, had a part in this investment. Early in 1887 he and John E. Gilmer began renovating the old Merchants' Hotel, which Reynolds had bought for $7,010 in 1886. A little later in the same year came news that he, "with a number of other gentlemen," was investing considerable capital in a booming real estate project at Mock's Mill in southeastern Virginia on the Norfolk and Western Railway. On R. J.'s balance sheet for 31 January 1888 appeared the sum of $6,800 representing the Gadsden (Alabama) investment in timberland, made with the intention of producing his own wooden caddies for use in shipping chewing tobacco. Apparently at this time he expected to compete with the Mengel Box Company because he felt it was overcharging him. Doubtless this action and Reynolds's later entry into the American Tobacco Company caused the Mengel company to establish a branch in Winston-Salem, where it still exists. In 1890 he was commended as a public benefactor for tearing down "the old Barringer Hotel, which has long marred Liberty Street"; his purpose, it was rumored, was to place "a handsome block of stores on this property."[86] Nor do these activities indicate the full extent of his interests in real estate. As revealed by the deed books of Forsyth County, he had purchased thirty-four tracts of land, chiefly in Winston, before the end of 1887.[87]

Reynolds also figured in real estate activities of a slightly different nature, possibly helping bring in capital to aid the growth of Winston. In 1880, he subscribed to thirty shares of stock in the Winston Water Company, although three weeks later at the time of the directors' meeting he had not paid; nor did he subscribe to an amount equal to the seventy-five shares taken by Bitting and Whitaker, another tobacco manufacturing firm in Winston.[88] He held deeds of trust on several pieces of real estate and industrial sites as security for loans made by members of the Parlett and Floyd families of Baltimore (see Table 2-7). These loans to people in Winston indicate that Reynolds played a role of some importance in securing capital for the development of interests other than his own. Not yet forty years old, he evidently centered on developing Winston into an industrial center—a somewhat amazing goal for a man of rural background in rural Winston where his chief rival in the manufacture of tobacco, P. H. Hanes, boasted of his two fine porkers, thirteen months old when butchered, weighing an average of 483 pounds each.[89]

Reynolds also showed considerable interest in local government, and, as early as 1879, entered the race for city commissioner. In a campaign involving thirteen candidates he ranked eighth in the number of votes secured. Five years later, however, he received virtually three times as many votes as in 1879 and was elected to the city commission on which he served as chairman of the sanitary and fire committees. His interest in good roads, already apparent in 1886, led to his appointment as supervisor of roads in Winston township, a post he held at least until 1890. In that year, however, candidates for the city commission ran on three tickets—Democratic, Citizens, and Colored Men—with three commissioners to be elected from each ward. Reynolds and others on the Democratic ticket met defeat at the hands of the Colored Men's ticket with the election of John B. Gwynn, John F. Hughes, and Rufus E. Clement. Of a different nature was the "Cleveland and Fowle Club," organized in 1888 by several hundred young Democrats, who, amid the roar of the band and the waving of red bandannas, elected Reynolds one of the twelve vice-presidents.[90]

R. J.'s interest in community affairs went further than mere local politics. In the late 1870s when Mayor Albert Burrow Gorrell (6 March 1840–9 December 1898) was presented with a petition asking that an election be called for voting a tax of twenty cents on the one-hundred-dollar property valuation and a sixty-cent poll tax to establish graded schools, the name R. J. Reynolds stood at the head of the list of thirty-nine Winston signers. Incidentally, the matter was discussed but a decision postponed.[91] Such vigorous pursuit of public education soon had its results, however. In 1880, a group of Negroes led by G. D. Wise, having subscribed $230.08 for building a graded school, continued their campaign which was evidently successful. Commenting in 1885 on the town

Table 2-7
Loans to Winston Builders by the Floyd
and Parlett Families, 1884–1890

Date	Lender	Amount	Borrower and Security
9 Jan. 1884	Nannie T. Floyd	$1,500	George W. Hinshaw—real estate
18 Feb. 1884	William S. Floyd	3,500	J. C. Nicholson and Jesse Pipkin—flour mill
16 Feb. 1885	William S. Floyd	3,000	Griffith & Jouffray—real estate
15 Aug. 1885	Mary E. Parlett	6,000	W. J. Cooper & Company—flour and grist mill
3 Feb. 1886	William S. Floyd	3,500	Jesse Pipkin & D. N. Dalton—flour and grist mill
8 Apr. 1886	William S. Floyd	3,000	H. A. Linebach—paper mill
31 Aug. 1886	Mary E. Parlett	6,000	C. P. Sides—Salem Flour Mill
26 Feb. 1887	Mrs. Anna T. Floyd	1,300	E. A. Oldham—real estate
28 Aug. 1887	William S. Floyd	3,200	Lewis H. Scranton—paper mill
3 Jan. 1888	Mrs. Anna T. Floyd	1,500	H. A. Watkins—real estate
3 Jan. 1888	John F. Parlett	4,500	P. A. Wilson—residence and hotel
14 Apr. 1888	William S. Floyd	3,500	D. P. Mast & R. B. Kerner—flour and grist mill
30 Jan. 1890	John F. Parlett	4,500	Martha A. Johnson—real estate

Sources: Forsyth County records (Office of Register of Deeds, Forsyth County Courthouse, Winston-Salem, N.C.), in order as follows: Deed Book, vols. 20 (pp. 65–67), 19 (pp. 283–85); Record of Mortgages, vols. 1 (pp. 30–32, 402–8), 2 (pp. 241, 243, 393–96), 3 (pp. 120–24, 596–99); Deed of Trust, vol. 4 (pp. 358–61, 582–84, 586–89); Mortgage Deed, vol. 5 (pp. 292–94); Record of Mortgage Deeds, vol. 7 (pp. 495–98).
Note: Griffith & Jouffray, borrowers on 16 February 1885, in that year erected a paper mill, with a daily capacity of one ton, to produce wrapping paper and newsprint—Edward Rondthaler, *The Memorabilia of Fifty Years, 1877–1927* (Raleigh, 1928), p. 48.

of Winston's notable work in public education, an author writing in the
New England Journal of Education declared: "Only four months from its
organization this school, with all the disadvantages of the mixed population of the new manufacturing community, is a model, and is thronged by
visitors from all parts of the country." The writer also commented on the
excellent beginning of the Negro school.[92]

Reynolds was active in other efforts to improve the community, one
being the establishment of the Forsyth Five-Cent Savings Bank. Designed
to encourage thrift among the tobacco workers in the Winston factories,
this bank resembled similar institutions in New England. At a meeting of
the directors in "the Twin-City Reform Club Room" in March 1888, R. J.
Reynolds was elected a member of the board and plans were made to open
the new bank for business on 1 June "in front of S. E. Allen's Hardware
Store, corner Main and Third Streets." By July 1889 a number of Negroes
had become depositors, and the treasurer, Edward Alexander Pfohl, reported resources totaling more than $16,000. Along with P. H. Hanes,
Reynolds served on a committee of the Forsyth County Immigration Society in 1885 to solicit funds for printing a pamphlet describing Forsyth
County, the object being to entice skilled labor to the Winston area.[93]

Aside from matters concerned with civic improvement, Reynolds evi-
dently played a somewhat dashing role in social activities. "Rollax," the
name bestowed on him by a local editor when describing the "Knights of
St. Patrick," who paraded the streets in 1884, no doubt gives the key to
R. J.'s nature. To the editor Irish names came easily for many of the
"Knights" wearing green ribbon, but the rollicking name of "Rollax" J.
Reynolds seemed especially appropriate for the young man described by
Polly Pepper as being six feet tall with "dark hair and eyes" and "a roseate
bloom on his cheeks. . . ." At any rate he attended a Mother Goose Dance
in the Farmers' Warehouse as one of King Cole's Fiddlers Three; the other
two were Benjamin Franklin Hanes and Frank Stockton.[94] He frequently
served in weddings as groomsman: with Kate Hanes at the wedding of
John W. Hanes and Anna Hodgin, with Mary Stanfield at the marriage of
Rod Cotton and Maggie Lea, and with Carrie Stockton at the marriage of
J. W. Morefield and Murphy Preddy.[95] As a member of the reception
committee, he frequently served at the social events of the year when the
Twin-City Club entertained the graduating class of the Salem Female
Academy or the visitors and ladies of the town. These facts lend credence
to Harbour Reynolds's observation soon after he came to Winston in
1880: "Dick is the biggest blood in Winston af[fo]rds more stile than any
one hear."[96]

Such parties may have furnished diversion for young Reynolds, but his
real recreational interests lay in fine horses and quail hunting. He kept
excellent hunting dogs and usually drove a double team for extra speed.[97]

He paid the taxes for several farmers in order to enjoy hunting privileges on their land.[98] As early as 1881, he owned "the fleetest span of close match[ed] mares in the South, if not in the U.S.," who according to one wag, "could go it double in two minutes and sixty seconds without the least fatigue."[99] His fleet of horses increased, and in 1887 he built on his factory lot a stable that amazed the countryside. Of brick, two stories high, it contained seven stalls, a carriage department, a feeding department, a nonfreezing hydrant, and a patented feeding arrangement. After additional description, a local editor vowed that its cost would not be less than $2,500—and would be "no doubt the most complete stable building in the State."[100] R. J.'s purchase of the expensive stallion Matador was perhaps the climax of his interest in good horseflesh.[101]

The day was fast approaching, however, when Reynolds would have less time for such pleasant pastimes as horse racing and lively parties. In fact, during the years prior to 1888 his interest centered to a great extent on the necessities for building an industrial community—public education, good city government, and development of real estate and local industry. Nevertheless, his general popularity and ability to mix with all, especially the more influential of the area, would serve him in good stead as he turned his interests to wider railroad connections, a superior type of chewing tobacco, a more modern plant, and the reorganization of his business. As he moved in these directions, it was the conviction of D. Rich that Reynolds could see further ahead than most people could see behind them.[102]

CHAPTER 3

Growth and Transition

The R. J. Reynolds Tobacco Company, a small-scale manufacturing unit in 1888, became, during the ensuing decade, an outstanding producer of southern flat-plug chewing tobacco, though by no means the only one. Numerous factors effected this transformation, one of the most important being the improvement of transportation facilities, which gave Winston connections with the Norfolk and Western Railway and freed it from domination by the Richmond and Danville railway system. R. J. Reynolds took an active part in furthering these developments, which led to the expansion not only of his company but also of tobacco manufacturing interests in Winston as a whole. With new sales opportunities available after the development of wider transportation facilities, Reynolds enlarged his plant, began advertising in a systematic manner, and established a sales department. The company also adopted improved machinery and made drastic revisions in its manufacturing processes so that its production increased virtually 400 percent from 1892 to 1898. Basic to these changes was the building of the Roanoke and Southern Railway.

Transportation

The Salem Branch Line gave Winston its first badly needed railway connections, although it also opened the way for the Richmond and Danville railway system (later the Southern Railway) to enter the town. Thereafter further efforts to expand transportation facilities for the town met opposition from the Richmond and Danville system. R. J. Reynolds played a leading role in this fight, which eventually resulted in the entry of the Norfolk and Western Railway into Winston. Shortly afterward, in an effort to place Winston on the main line of the Southern, Reynolds led a spirited but unsuccessful move to force the hand of John Pierpont Morgan (17 April 1837–31 March 1913), the organizer of the Southern Railway following the collapse of the Richmond and Danville.

The problem of transportation had been of concern to the Winston area as far back as antebellum days. In 1857 an unidentified North Carolinian urged Virginians of the Lynchburg area to build a railroad to Salem by way of Stokes County, "one of the finest tobacco growing sections of the State." The writer visualized a line from Charlotte, North Carolina, to Alexandria, Virginia. On 18 April 1857, business leaders of Lynchburg met to choose delegates for "the Winston (N.C.) Railroad convention to be held in June next, and to give some expression of the public sentiment relative to the proposed railway connections between this city and North Carolina." Nothing came of this, although the North Carolina legislature earlier had considered a charter for building such a line.[1]

Difficulties connected with the construction of the Salem Branch Line set the stage for a long struggle with the Richmond and Danville railway system—a struggle that ended many years after the brilliant efforts of R. J. Reynolds to place Winston and Salem on the main line of the Southern Railway and the many struggles of Joseph Lewis Graham (6 January 1869–3 November 1931) to obtain lower shipping rates for the company. It should be kept in mind that the collapse of the Richmond and Danville railway system during the panic of 1893 gave J. P. Morgan his opportunity to organize and develop the Southern Railway.[2] The Salem Branch Line of the Richmond and Danville system from Salem to Greensboro was the first modern transportation facility to enter the Winston-Salem area.

Chartered as the Northwestern North Carolina Railroad by the Reconstruction convention of North Carolina in 1868, the Salem Branch Line at its start was the result chiefly of the efforts of Edward F. Belo, Israel George Lash (18 August 1810–17 April 1879), Henry William Fries (5 March 1825–4 November 1902), and J. A. Vogel, of Salem, and Thomas J. Wilson, Joseph Walter Masten (3 March 1848–23 February 1927), and R. A. Wilson, of Winston, to whom the charter was issued. For the construction of the road Winston and Salem contributed $30,000, Forsyth County $100,000, and Greensboro $20,000, whereas the state of North Carolina appropriated $10,000 for each mile built.[3] Before the road received its irons, however, funds had been exhausted, and on 4 October 1872 the Richmond and Danville Railroad Company took over the unfinished road by means of a mortgage payable in ten to thirty years at the option of the company.[4] The Richmond and Danville then laid the rails. This was a remarkable accomplishment, but it nevertheless placed Winston and Salem manufacturers at the mercy of the powerful Richmond and Danville system—a rail line never distinguished for generosity and already despised by Winston tobacconists. In 1873, when referring to the Northwestern North Carolina Railroad, which by lease became a part of the Richmond and Danville system in 1871, William Asbury Whitaker (13 June 1844–6 December 1912) declared: "The North Carolina R. R. is the roughest handler in the world and would tear up the Devil if a chance at him could be had."[5] Reynolds, of course, had no part in the construction of the Salem Branch Line, but he undoubtedly came to feel the heavy grip of the Richmond and Danville, which at the outset of his Winston career controlled not only the Salem Branch Line but also the North Carolina Railroad from Goldsboro to Charlotte, North Carolina— a road built partly with state funds.

Meanwhile Winston received suggestions for other railroad connections with "open arms" because its citizens suffered "from discrimination of the Richmond and Danville line."[6] In 1879, the Baltimore and Ohio Railroad, which owned the Virginia Midland Railroad, projected a rail line from Danville via Winston and Salem southward; this line would have placed Winston on a main line with outlets independent of the Richmond and Danville. Winston voted $40,000 in bonds for the construction of that part of the Virginia Midland (or the North Carolina Midland) that would lie in Forsyth County, the agreement to be binding when completion of the road had been guaranteed. At that time, an agent of the Richmond and Danville, posing as a trustee of unknown capitalists, began a road from Danville toward Winston, parallel to the Midland, thus inhibiting the sale of Midland bonds. The Richmond and Danville then easily bought the Midland stock from the Baltimore and Ohio, which agreed to the sale on condition that the Richmond and Danville build the North Carolina portion of the road from Danville to Winston. Officials of the Baltimore and Ohio gave a Winston committee a copy of their agreement with the Richmond and Danville, and this the Winston representatives considered a guarantee that the line would be built. Winston commissioners then issued $10,000 of the bond that had been voted. They proved too trusting. During the following week all work on the Midland railroad stopped, and before an injunction could be obtained innocent purchasers of the bonds had lost $5,000. The Richmond and Danville asked why it should go to the expense of building a line from Danville to Winston and Salem when it already controlled the Twin Cities by way of a spur track from Greensboro.

Colonel Alexander Boyd Andrews (23 July 1841–17 April 1915), vice-president of the Richmond and Danville, eventually resumed work on portions of what would have been the Midland—an action undoubtedly motivated by Winston's contribution of $100,000 for a projected line to Roanoke, Virginia, which would connect with the main line of the Norfolk and Western Railway. Andrews then requested that the Winston commissioners issue the remaining bonds and place them with a trustee to be delivered to him upon completion of the Midland into Salem and Winston. But he offered no guarantee to build the road any farther than the boundary of Forsyth County. Bitter debate arose in Winston as to the wisdom of issuing the remaining bonds. Colonel Andrews could not, or would not, pledge to build the line to Mocksville for fear of losing funds from Davie County.[7] Eventually Winston and Salem succeeded in getting the successor of the Richmond and Danville to build a line to Mocksville and to extend the Salem Branch Line to Wilkesboro, but what the two towns wanted was an immediate and complete line to Charlotte on the main line of the Southern Railway leading to Atlanta. The road via Mocksville did not connect with Charlotte until 1899. Before that, however, Reynolds was to see one other opportunity to place his town on the main line of the Southern.

It was possibly at the outset of Winston's efforts to secure the Virginia Midland extension that R. J. Reynolds most actively interested himself in transportation problems. A story, long current in the Winston and Salem area, credits Reynolds with attempting to persuade the Richmond and Danville system to extend its line from Danville to Winston and Salem. He and several prominent men in the area had agreed to meet Captain Algernon Sidney Buford (2 January 1826–6 May 1911), president of the Richmond and Danville from 1865 to 1886, in Richmond. Finding only Captain Buford present for the meeting, Reynolds was so frustrated and angry that he immediately sold all of his Richmond and Danville stock, thereby making a clear profit of $30,000.[8] Though the story is doubtful in some respects, it reflects R. J.'s interest in rail connections for Winston and Salem and probably also his despair of ever receiving help from the Richmond and Danville.

When the opportunity arose for connections with the Norfolk and Western Railway, Reynolds plunged into work designed to hasten construction of the Roanoke and Southern. Nor was he alone in this effort. When Colonel John Crouch Moomaw (13 March 1837–16 August 1886), visiting points along the projected railroad in search of funds, reached Winston, he declared that the assembly that greeted him represented a capital of $2 million.[9] On 9 April 1886, the Winston Board of Trade held a "railroad meeting" and appointed delegates to attend a similar meeting in Roanoke on 20 April with instructions "to pledge Forsyth County to grade and cross-tie the road through said county—at a cost not to exceed $150,000." The delegates were George W. Hinshaw (22 April 1847–5 July 1918), John Cameron Buxton (30 September 1852–26 April 1917), Dr. William L. Brown (20 January 1831–16 March 1899), Thomas J. Brown, John E. Gilmer, and R. J. Reynolds, of Winston, and Henry W. Fries, Christian H. Fogle, Francis Henry Fries (1 February

1855–5 June 1931), and Henry Theodore Bahnson (6 March 1845–16 January 1917), of Salem. Reynolds and Dr. Brown were the only tobacco manufacturers of the group. Later meetings were well-attended.[10] Quickly, bills of incorporation were introduced into the legislatures of Virginia and North Carolina. At a consolidated meeting of the stockholders of the Roanoke and Southern on 18 June 1887, R. J. Reynolds became one of the directors.[11] The editor of the *People's Press* echoed the general enthusiasm at the prospect of an outlet "free of the Richmond and Danville syndicate" to points north, east, and west.[12]

By November 1887, affairs of the railroad were at a standstill because of the dissolution of the partnership of the Bullock Construction Company, the contractor for building a portion of the road. It was declared locally that "the moneyed men of Winston and Salem" would form a company to complete the work south of the Virginia state line. Soon, the Virginia and North Carolina Construction Company was organized. When the option of the Bullock company expired, the matter of construction fell to the executive committee of the Virginia and North Carolina Construction Company on which R. J. Reynolds served. Eighty-eight citizens petitioned for and obtained an election to determine whether Winston township should subscribe $100,000 in bonds for completing the North Carolina sector of the Roanoke and Southern line.[13] During this anxious period, the directors of the projected railroad from Winston, Martinsville, and Roanoke, including R. J. Reynolds, attended a successful meeting in Danville, after which the following announcement appeared:[14]

> The company has a charter to build a road from Roanoke *via* Martinsville to Winston, and has obtained 300 convicts from the state of Virginia. Some half million dollars have been subscribed to the road and the directors decided to begin work about the middle of April. About fifteen miles of the road between Martinsville and the North Carolina line are already located, and this will be built at once. Work will begin on the Winston end of the line about April 16th, and it is proposed to complete the line from Winston to Martinsville in twelve months. Work will begin on the Roanoke section a year hence. The Virginia and North Carolina Construction Company, chartered by the late session of the Legislature, will probably do the work. The company has nearly a half million dollars in the treasury to begin with, and we are assured by them that no fears are to be entertained regarding the building of the road. Capital together with men of brains are behind the work. Hurrah for the R. & S.

In this same strenuous period, Cyrus B. Watson, Junius Waitman Goslen (13 July 1840–16 August 1896), Francis H. Fries, and R. J. Reynolds attended a rally at Walnut Cove on 9 June 1888; each addressed the group in an attempt to persuade the people of Sauratown township, in Stokes County, to vote bonds for aiding in construction of the Roanoke and Southern. Goslen, editor of the *Union Republican*, declared that limited space forbade a synopsis of each speech in his paper:[15]

> . . . yet one of the most level headed reasons urged in favor of voting the subscription and one we feel should be put on record because of its general application to our Southern Section was made by R. J. Reynolds, Esq.,—by the way a most level headed man, too, is he. It was this: 20 years ago soon after the war, Northern capitalists invested largely in Western railroads. At the same time they advertised by flameing [*sic*] posters, write ups and in every effective way possible, throughout the South and North, attracting all emigrants and thousands of people from every section, so that for 15 years the whole tide of immigration flowed westward. The result was the upbuilding of im[mense?] cities with overflowing populations and a phenomenal growth of the whole section and an increase in railroad lines that not only brought immense worth to their owners but but [*sic*] placed their bonds at a premium.
>
> To-day the situation is changed. Northern capitalists are turning their attention Southward and are seeking investments here. If the same ratio in this direction is kept up for 30 years that has marked the last two, Mr. Reynolds argued that the bonds voted by the people of Sauratown township would be worth dollar for dollar and the investment regarded as a paying one.

Truly Reynolds's short speech indicated that his mind had dwelt with alertness and understanding on matters involving transportation and capital.

Nor was Reynolds alone in his enthusiasm. By 28 March 1889 the new station of the Roanoke and Southern in Winston had received its roof. Citizens went to the edge of town and boarded the train for a free round-trip ride to Walnut Cove. Soon P. H. Hanes and Company, possibly by way of a Labor Day celebration, gave its employees an excursion to Martinsville. The local editor felt that the progress on the road had been remarkable: "Home folks and home money," he declared, "are backing" the railroad.[16] Yet, he forgot his paeans to local enterprise when he recorded the fact that Colonel Francis H. Fries had closed a contract with the state penitentiary for at least two hundred convicts to work on a rugged portion of the road from Walnut Cove to the Virginia line.[17] No doubt many a local prize hand would have welcomed this labor as an opportunity to eke out his scanty income. A little later there was general indignation in Winston and Salem when Richmond and Danville forces, working by moonlight, laid a sidetrack that threatened to eliminate a portion of the right-of-way of the Roanoke and Southern. Only by swift action of the towns' commissioners was the dispute settled amicably.[18]

On 3 March 1892, only one month before regular passenger service was scheduled, came news that the line had been leased to the Norfolk and Western Railway for ninety-nine years. When asked for his opinion of this shift, R. J. Reynolds declared: "It will enhance the valuation of real estate in Forsyth County by at least four million dollars inside of ten years."[19] The entire community realized the significance of the new railroad. In his memorabilia for 1891, the Moravian bishop in Salem gave this enterprise great praise, declaring that the Roanoke and Southern Railway had not only "provided an important connection with the rest of the world" but had also "attracted other railroad enterprises, thus maintaining this place and advancing it as a business centre." He noted that the last rail on the 122-mile stretch had been laid "at Rocky Mount, Va., on Dec. 19th, 1891." The rail line, he marveled, had been built "in a time of great financial pressure at the cost of two millions of dollars." No longer would the people of the two towns fear "that a stand-still had been reached in their prosperity."[20]

A few years later, in 1897, R. J. Reynolds played a part in another struggle with the railroads, again more or less directly concerned with the old theme—the desire to establish Winston and Salem on the main line of the Southern Railway. It was during the administration of Governor Daniel Lindsay Russell. Russell (7 August 1845–14 May 1908), a Republican governor of a Democratic state, had been elected by a fusion of Republicans and Populists. (This was a stirring time politically and a day of hatred for railroads and monopoly in general.) It will be recalled that the North Carolina Railroad, curving from Goldsboro via Raleigh, Durham, Greensboro, and Salisbury to Charlotte, had been leased to the Richmond and Danville railway system. In 1871 arrangements for the thirty-three year lease, at an annual rental of $260,000, had been made under suspicious circumstances at a night meeting in what is now Burlington, North Carolina. Then in 1895 came the leasing of this same road to the Southern Railway, which had taken over the assets of the Richmond and Danville system as a result of the panic of 1893. The annual rental stood at $260,000 per year for the first six years and $286,000 for the remaining ninety-three years of the lease.[21] Governor Russell urged the legislature to repeal the lease to the Southern Railway. At that point a bill, generally believed to have been prepared by officials of the Southern under the shrewd leadership of J. P. Morgan, was introduced, calling for an investigation of the origin of the ninety-nine year lease. If the legislature became bogged down in the investigation, the bill to repeal the lease would be sidetracked and the hated lease would stand. In this bitter fight, filled with legislative maneuvers, Josephus Daniels (18 May 1862–15 January

1948), editor of the Raleigh *News and Observer*, fought for repeal of the lease, thus incurring the wrath of Colonel Alexander B. Andrews, who managed the lobbying for the Southern Railway. He withdrew Daniels's pass on the Southern—a courtesy generally accorded all newsmen by railroad lines.

At this point R. J. Reynolds entered the fight, which at that time overshadowed everything else that was happening in the state. He sent Daniels his personal check for one hundred dollars, dated 4 February 1897, with a letter of explanation. He hoped Daniels would use the check to defray his expenses when traveling on the Southern. Moreover, declared Reynolds, he believed that Daniels was fighting "in the interest of the people of North Carolina for three generations to come." Daniels published a facsimile of Reynolds's check with his letter on the front page of the *News and Observer*. In the same issue, in an editorial entitled "Mr. Reynolds and the Kind Offer," he declared that Reynolds was not afraid to fight J. P. Morgan and his rich corporation. Reynolds knew that the lease, if allowed to stand, would rob the taxpayers of $120,000 per year for the next century. Praising Reynolds as a wealthy man who stood with the people, Daniels expressed his gratitude for the check but declared he could not cash it. Rather, he would frame it so that it could remind all who saw it of the words of greatest price: "'a good name is rather to be chosen than great riches.'"[22] At a fully attended meeting of the Winston and Salem Chamber of Commerce on the same day a resolution was passed, with only three dissenting votes, recommending annulment of the lease. So intense was the feeling of the group that the names of the dissenters were published: Henry W. Fries, William A. Blair, and George W. Hinshaw.[23] When Daniels failed to cash Reynolds's check, R. J. subscribed for twenty copies of the *News and Observer* to be sent to his friends.[24]

Six days later, after the Seaboard Air Line Railway had offered $120,-000 more per year than the Southern was paying for its lease of the North Carolina Railroad, a counterproposal by Reynolds appeared in the *News and Observer*. With his associates, he offered to give the state $100,000 for an option on the lease at a rental of 8 percent, or an option of $25,000 at a rental of ten percent, which was equivalent to the offer of the Seaboard Air Line Railway. "What did this prove?" asked Daniels. Answering his own question, he asserted that it clearly established the fact that the North Carolina Railroad was worth more than the $400,000 per year offered by the Seaboard and that "the rich Winston tobacco manufacturer" believed the road to be worth at least $8,000,000.[25] Again Reynolds wrote, on 17 February, proposing to pay $5 per share for an option at $112 per share, though it was then quoted at $109, for 1,000 shares of stock of the North Carolina Railroad if the lease were annulled.[26]

Why was Reynolds so interested in controlling the North Carolina Railroad? He could thereby prevent the Southern from using that portion of the North Carolina railway from Greensboro to Charlotte, thus forcing the Southern to run its main line from Washington, to Danville, to Greensboro, to Winston and Salem via the Salem Branch Line, and on to Charlotte over the Mocksville road, which at that time was nearing completion. He would be on the main line from Washington to Atlanta. Even though unsuccessful, Reynolds had not hesitated to put up a financial fight against the wealthiest financier of the nation—referred to by Josephus Daniels as "Rothschild, Pierrepont Morgan & Co." Possibly no episode of R. J.'s career so clearly marks his willingness to challenge any hazard for the good of his business.

Expansion of Tobacco Manufacturing in Winston and Salem

Growth of the manufacture of tobacco in the Twin Cities did not await the laying of the last crosstie on the Roanoke and Southern, which "did more than anything else to fix the future of Winston and Salem."[27] In 1888 one writer described twenty-three tobacco factories chiefly in Winston. Possibly more zealous in their enumeration, officials of the Chamber of Commerce in 1890 counted thirty-three plug factories and three smoking-tobacco factories. Four years later at least thirty-eight firms made chewing or smoking tobacco or both. In 1896 Winston alone contained thirty-nine tobacco factories.[28]

Of far greater significance, however, was the output of Winston factories from 1887 to 1895, with the most marked advances coming after the Roanoke and Southern was assured (see Table 3-1).[29] No data seem to be available for determining R. J. Reynolds's share in this production prior to 1892, but, from that time until 1897, Reynolds virtually quadrupled his output. By 1897 he was making more than one-fourth of all chewing tobacco produced in Winston (see Table 3-2).[30]

Winston's boom began perhaps somewhat earlier than 1888. On 25 March of the previous year, the Winston Electric Light and Motive Power Company had been incorporated. According to one author: "The coming of the lights proved a seven days' wonder to the people of Winston and the surrounding country; the battery was near the jail, and at eight o'clock each evening when the current was turned on, there would be a crowd standing around to see the dazzling sight." The "dazzling sight" proved to be only a promise of better things to come; a violent thunderstorm in September caused all thirty-seven of the arc lights to burn out with one sudden flash.[31] The tobacco interests, strong in the belief in their destiny,

Table 3-1
Output of Winston Tobacco Factories, 1887–1895

Year	Pounds
1887	6,343,585
1888	7,252,250
1889	9,132,962
1890	9,686,980
1891	Not available
1892	10,926,085
1893	10,263,373
1894	11,231,751
1895	12,927,250

Sources: *Southern Tobacco Journal* in *Union Republican*, 12 January 1893; Nannie M. Tilley, *The Bright-Tobacco Industry, 1860–1929* (Chapel Hill, 1948), p. 589.

persuaded Henry E. Harman to move his *Southern Tobacco Journal* from Danville to Winston, where the first issue appeared on 16 January 1891.[32] On the side, R. J. Reynolds began experiments in the manufacture of fertilizer from tobacco stems and bone meal, expecting to organize a stock company, buy the mill in which the experiments were being made, and "go into the manufacturing of commercial fertilizers on a large scale."[33] In the same year, 1890, he and some of his fellow townsmen organized the West End Hotel and Land Company and the North Winston Loan and Improvement Company, in which "a northern syndicate" participated.[34] The brickmaking business also boomed in 1891,[35] and the editor of the *Southern Tobacco Journal* exulted: "Never before in the history of Winston has there been so much building in tobacco circles as this year. Several large factories have already been completed since the new year came in and in addition to these there are at present not less than nine large tobacco factories . . . under construction."[36]

Increasing duties and enlarging business interests induced Reynolds to form a copartnership, holding three-fourths of the business himself and assigning a one-eighth part each to William N. Reynolds and Henry Roan. Dated 2 January 1888, the partnership agreement of "R. J. Reynolds and Company" called for the general business of "manufacturing and selling plug and twist tobacco and transacting the business of Tobacco Manufacturing." Subject to mutual agreement of the partners, the contract was to be continued from year to year. R. J. Reynolds contributed $18,000 for his capital stock; each of the other partners contributed

Table 3-2

The Reynolds Company's Share of Winston Tobacco Production, 1892–1897

Year	Pounds Produced in Winston	Pounds Produced by Reynolds	Percent Produced by Reynolds
1892	10,926,085	1,085,929	9.94
1893	10,263,373	1,006,101	9.81
1894	11,231,751	1,215,328	9.98
1895	12,927,250	2,126,767	16.50
1896	13,033,406	2,846,039	21.83
1897	15,500,000	4,228,235	27.27

Source: Based on production data from comptroller's department, R. J. Reynolds Tobacco Company.
Note: The figures for 1892 and 1893 correspond exactly with those given by Reynolds in 1915—Winston-Salem Journal, 25 April 1915.

$3,000. Reynolds did not charge for his services, but his brother received the handsome sum of $750 per year and Henry Roan $1,000, both salaries to be charged to operating expenses. R. J. Reynolds also agreed to provide the firm the sum of $26,000 "as may be required from time to time when he has the money on hand" at 6 percent interest. In addition, he would furnish the factory building with all the necessary machinery and fixtures, the firm to pay him interest on these items at the rate of 10 percent beginning on 1 December 1889. On the cost of the storage house the firm agreed to pay interest at 10 percent beginning with the start of operations, except that no interest would be paid on that portion required by R. J. for storing "his own tobacco." The same terms applied to the "Hannah Ware House" building, utilized for reordering leaf tobacco, and to the new leaf-storage building of brick adjacent to the Hannah Warehouse. The firm was to bear the expenses of any necessary repairs on machinery and fixtures, which, however, were to be in good working order at the outset. R. J. Reynolds agreed to handle the draying at a cost of $240 per year, but it was clearly understood that the firm would pay the wages of the drayman. Also clearly stated was the acknowledgement that all "present tobacco brands" belonged to R. J. "individually." At the end of the agreement was a memorandum providing for continuation of the copartnership and blanks for signatures of the partners. These, however, were never signed.[37] Many years later Will Reynolds declared that R. J. felt that the junior partners fared too well under the agreement, each making $4,000 in addition to his salary. He also recalled that R. J. then changed the partnership to a stock company.[38]

The business then was incorporated under the laws of North Carolina on 11 February 1890. The Articles of Incorporation for the R. J. Reynolds Tobacco Company listed R. J. Reynolds with 1,700 shares and Henry Roan and W. N. Reynolds with 100 shares each. The capital stock thus stood at 1,900 shares, with a par value of $100 each; from time to time it might be increased to $1,000,000 by a two-thirds vote of the stock. The duration of the charter was set for ninety-nine years. Regular annual meetings came on the first Monday of January unless changed by a vote of the stockholders; the board of directors might include from three to seven members. Included were provisions that the stockholders were not individually responsible for debts of the company, that bylaws were to prescribe methods of filling vacancies among officers and directors, and that no additional shares were to be issued unless fully paid at par value.[39]

Accordingly, at the first meeting of the stockholders, 12 February 1890, the capital stock was set at $190,000, R. J. Reynolds elected president, William N. Reynolds vice-president, and Henry Roan secretary and treasurer, the three constituting the board of directors. General bylaws were also approved.[40] At this first meeting of the directors "in the office of the Co.," the yearly salary of the vice-president was fixed at $1,200 per year and that of the secretary and treasurer at $1,500. It was agreed to rent from R. J. Reynolds his Hannah Warehouse and his brick storage building, adjacent to the warehouse on Third Street, for $695 per year beginning 1 January 1890. It was also decided to pay R. J. Reynolds, from the same date, interest on the buildings, machinery, and money "which he had taken to his stock account." The last item of business at this first meeting was a decision to pay the president $240 per year for the use of his harness and two horses, although he was to feed them and keep them shod.[41] No other business appears in the minutes for 1890. These arrangements, with changes in personnel, salaries, and plant, continued until 4 April 1899, when a more drastic change occurred.

A great stir among Winston tobacconists before the actual completion of the Roanoke and Southern on 19 December 1891 evidenced itself in numerous ways. Early in January 1889, R. J. Reynolds made one of the largest shipments from one firm in one day in the history of Winston "as a tobacco city"—57,000 pounds—"billed to Washington and Baltimore."[42] Four months later a local editor wrote that the season was the busiest in the history of the town and that chewing tobacco was "hardly considered genuine without the Winston brand."[43] In May 1889, B. F. Hanes of the Model Tobacco Works began erecting a storeroom adjoining his factory; it was to be 40 by 81 feet, four stories high, and equipped with electric light facilities and a steam elevator. A mild announcement that he would build a larger factory came from P. H. Hanes in the fall of 1889; spring found him building the largest tobacco factory "ever erected in the Twin

Cities."[44] John W. Hanes, a member of P. H. Hanes and Company, summed up the situation in Winston as he saw it late in 1890:[45]

During the year we have added one large brick warehouse, seven mammoth tobacco factories, besides large additions to old factories by the score. . . .

We now boast with pride of the number and magnitude of our factories, and our output of chewing tobacco is larger than any city in Virginia or North Carolina. Our manufactured tobacco is regarded by jobbers everywhere as standard . . . and the name of Winston on a box of the same is a guarantee of its merit, and the fact that this is being taken advantage of by our competitors in other places is a matter of concern to which our manufacturers will have to give prompt attention.

The expansion continued into 1891, with large factories being built by W. W. Wood and Company and the Lucile Tobacco Works, owned by William A. Whitaker.[46] Finally, in 1892 it was announced that P. H. Hanes and Company had appointed Joseph Gans, prominent wholesale distributor in New York, as its representative in the eastern states. P. H. Hanes vowed that Winston needed a larger territory in which to sell because its production had become too great to be confined to a few southern states; for this he was lectured by the editor of *Tobacco* in New York and advised to go into the manufacture of smoking tobacco because disgruntled southern manufacturers could not compete with manufacturers who used Burley leaf in chewing tobacco.[47] In other words, the editor believed that southern flat plug could not compete with navy plug made of Burley leaf.

Other than building "a large and handsome" leaf-handling plant south of B. F. Hanes's factory in 1889,[48] what was Reynolds doing about expansion during this period? He gave up his original plan to retire with $100,000[49] and built factory Number 256, which stands today in the 256 group with "R.J.R. Tob. Co." across its front. In March 1891 he talked "of erecting THE tobacco factory of the South" and of having ordered "one million brick." At a meeting on 19 March 1891, the board of directors decided to buy R. J.'s lot on Chestnut Street, 100 by 259 feet, on which to build a tobacco factory according to plans to be drawn by C. R. Makepeace and Company of Providence, Rhode Island. Possibly Reynolds had this decision in mind in 1915 when he described his new factory as having a capacity ten times larger than his old one.[50] Astonishment greeted this announcement. The new building would stretch from Chestnut to Depot streets; it would stand six stories high, have a brownstone front, and resemble the plan of a northern silk mill; no stairs or elevators would occupy space on the inside; and, in short, there would be "no tobacco factory like it anywhere." It was to be so completely protected against fire as to be a first-class risk, saving half the current cost of insurance. Probably no factory in the South was more adequately equipped for fighting fire.

Ready for occupancy in the spring of 1892, the "mammoth" factory attracted the "attention of everybody" who passed along the street and received admiring salutes as "the largest plug factory in the State."[51] According to the drawing made of the factory for insurance purposes, it was well-planned, with stemming and drying on the sixth floor, rolling on the fifth, picking and sorting on the fourth, flavoring or sweetening and office space on the third, pressing on the second, and a shipping room on the first. Steam power, electric lights, and a Hahn watch clock added to its elegance and efficiency. The factory and leaf houses on each side were connected by tunnels and overhead tramways, thus adding to convenience and saving labor in the transfer of leaf tobacco to the factory. According to R. J. Reynolds, this modern factory had a working capacity of nine hundred hands and its smokestack had cost more than the whole of his first factory.[52]

The R. J. Reynolds Tobacco Company from its very beginning had guarded carefully against fire hazards and suffered little in this respect. True to its policy, which has continued until today, the company installed a complete sprinkler system in the new factory, two 6,000-gallon tanks above the highest line of sprinklers, a gravel-topped roof, and pumps capable of forcing water at 750 gallons per minute.[53] In 1895 Reynolds lost 130,000 pounds of leaf tobacco stored in the Jones-Cox factory, but the insurance, $11,000, covered all but a small portion of the cost.[54] Two years later, the explosion of a licorice pot scalded two employees, resulting in the death of William Hairston but in no property loss.[55] On 30 March 1897, about five o'clock in the morning, the tobacco-box varnish in a metal tank in the new factory was discovered to be on fire, and, "before it could be controlled, about twenty-one of the automatic sprinklers" extinguished the fire. The chief loss came from water, which damaged 70,135 pounds of manufactured tobacco.[56] Less than two years later when a small fire broke out in the drying department, the employees marched outside while the automatic sprinklers quickly extinguished the fire.[57] Installation of the automatic sprinklers and other meticulous efforts to prevent fire hazards were well worthwhile. P. H. Hanes and Company evidently took fewer precautions against fire hazards: from 1877 to 1893 they lost their main factory three times, the last fire destroying their new plant, the "second largest of the kind in the South." Ironically this devastating fire originated in Reynolds's old Hannah Warehouse but with small loss to Reynolds.[58] Even before the destruction of the Hanes plant, however, the

new Reynolds factory was capable of a greater production than any other
such factory in the Virginia-Carolina area.

Advertising and Sales

Simultaneously with the completion of his new factory and the Roanoke
and Southern Railway, Reynolds adopted an intensive system of advertising and began to develop a sales department. These changes, basic to the
spectacular growth of the R. J. Reynolds Tobacco Company from a small
plant to one of large-scale operations, mark 1892 as the pivotal year in its
history.

Perhaps no exact beginning date can be established for R. J.'s adoption
of changes in sales and advertising. An early price list, apparently the first
issued, became effective on 1 June 1891, shortly before the completion of
his new factory. The list carried six brands of chewing tobacco: R. J.
Reynolds' Level Best, R. J. Reynolds' Double Thick, R. J. R. Break
Pocket Piece, Zeb Vance, Belle of North Carolina, and Caromel. The
terms of sale permitted no rebates, no payment of freight, and no discount
except 2 percent for cash, but allowed the purchase of assorted lots of
five original packages, if of different brands. In 1892 tobacco jobbers
and wholesale distributors received Reynolds's announcement that "an
assorted price list" governing the sale of brands would become effective
on 10 June because agents of the company and the trade generally deemed
it advisable.[59] This actual price list for 1892 seems to be unavailable,
though price lists for all other years of the decade exist.

The first printed advertisement appeared in March 1892 in the *Iron Belt*
of Roanoke, Virginia, a publication unavailable and apparently unknown
today,[60] although it was probably a boosting periodical issued by the
Norfolk and Western Railway Company. The advertisement is actually an
appeal to wholesale dealers rather than to the consumer. According to the
custom of that day, the editor of the *Iron Belt* prepared an editorial, based
on the Reynolds advertisement but more clearly written. Both versions,
printed as handbills on paper of different colors and widely distributed as
further advertising, merit quotation:[61]

REYNOLDS VERSION

How the Bottom Rail gets on Top
and all be Benefitted by the Shuffle

Not by slight [*sic*] of hand, but in an open, fair handed way. Requires
years of hard work to accomplish it and benefit all who are instrumental in building it up. When they have this ability and are not

circumscribed as to territory, there is no limit as to what they can accomplish with the most popular chewing Tobaccos offered. We are reliably informed by the trade and chewers of Tobacco that R.J. Reynolds' Level Best, Double Thick 8-oz., and R.J.R. Pocket Piece, manufactured by R.J. Reynolds Tobacco Co., Winston, N. C., are the best goods on the market. They have recently equipped the largest and best Tobacco Factory in the South, and are now much better prepared than ever to make the shuffle.

EDITOR'S VERSION

READ

What the "Iron Belt" of Roanoke, Va., says
in an editorial under date of March, 1892,

in regard to

How the Bottom Rail gets on Top and
all be Benefitted by the Shuffle.

This is done by no slight [*sic*] of hand work, but in an open, fair handed, honorable way, which requires years of hard work and study to accomplish, and benefit all concerned. But few know how to run a business to the advantage of all who are directly and indirectly instrumental in building it up, and when they have this ability there is no limit to what they can accomplish provided their efforts have been in a line of business in which it is possible for them to meet competition without being circumscribed as to territory. We are reliably informed by the trade and chewers of tobacco that the brands, R.J. Reynolds' Level Best, Double Thick 8 oz., and R.J.R. Pocket Piece, manufactured by R.J. Reynolds Tobacco Co., of Winston, N. C., are the most popular chewing Tobaccos that are offered. As an evidence of the fact the rapid increased demand for these famous Brands has justified them in building and equipping the largest and best Tobacco Factory in the South, and they are now better prepared than ever to furnish goods that will leave a profit to the Jobber and Retailer and give satisfaction to the consumer.

Two years later, the R. J. Reynolds Tobacco Company began to advertise in a systematic manner. Testifying in 1915, Reynolds, whose memory was good but not infallible, declared that he began advertising in 1894 by spending $4,000 and in that year saw his business increase by more than 200,000 pounds. Thus encouraged, he spent $20,000 for advertising in

1895 and his business doubled.[62] Abundant evidence supports Reynolds's claims. The scrapbook for the 1890s, preserved in the advertising department, contains small envelopes labeled, "Sample of R.J.R. Double Thick 3 Break — On sale at 60 cts. per pound" and "Reynolds Suncured Tobacco is not so sweet as imitators." There are also pasteboard strips, 2 by 11 inches, with large letters showing "R.J. Reynolds 8 oz." and directions in small letters: "Please tack this card on upper edge of the box." On 23 October 1894 the company sent Cox and Corbin, of Macon, Georgia, 250 postcards carrying the following printed heading on the back: "Cox and Corbin, Wholesale Grocers, Agents for R.J. Reynolds Tobacco Co.'s Naturally Sweet Tobaccos," with space for a date, and the message "Expect me _____ and please save an order for me"—evidently for the use of its agent when preparing to call on jobbers. One leaflet, used possibly in 1895, begins with the statement "Tobacco Cure Institutes are being established all over the country for the cure of the Tobacco habit" and, after calling attention to many virtues of "R.J. Reynolds Double Thick, 8 oz.," ends with this sentence: "We advise those who use Tobacco, for the good of their health and teeth, to chew R.J. REYNOLDS 8 oz., as it is a well known fact that pure tobacco preserves the teeth." This leaflet is signed "Tobacco Institute."

Advertisements in the *Southern Tobacco Journal* and *Western Tobacco Journal* warned other tobacco manufacturers against infringing on Reynolds's trademarks. Posters called attention to the skeleton letters R. J. R. as the trademark of the company, warned imitators, and stated that, in areas where many consumers impressed the R. J. R. initials on their minds by using the words "Run John Run" or "Roll Jordan Roll," infringements were easily detected. The scrapbook also contains many locals from newspapers, generally in the South; often they consist of no more than "R.J.R. tobacco has come to stay. Try it." Credible or not, wording for wall and fence signs in the areas of Atlanta and Knoxville in January and February 1895 consisted of "R.J.R. 16 oz. sad man's cordial," "R.J.R. 16 oz. tobacco quiets the nerves," and "R.J.R. 16 oz. tobacco satisfies." Circulars containing testimonials from wholesale dealers, forms for advertising space agreements, premium lists for the redemption of tags, and a plain paper bag with the following printed in red letters: "R.J. Reynolds Tobacco Company's 'Naturally Sweet' R.J.R. Chewing Tobacco, Palatable, Without Drugs" all appeared during the 1890s.

Some advertisements seem to be more ingenious. One featured the "Schnapps Kicking Machine," whereby a chewer administered well-merited punishment on himself for having committed the folly of buying some brand of chewing tobacco other than Schnapps. These kicking machines, in use as early as 1897, remained popular for more than a decade. Schnapps "Kickers," of metal with a cord for hanging, should be placed "one to a store where Schnapps tobacco is on sale," Reynolds salesmen were advised on 23 March 1897. Only slightly less intriguing was the poster that gave the pedigree of R. J. Reynolds Double Thick in terms of the racetrack—surely the work of Reynolds himself. An advertising poster known as the Free Silver Circular encouraged chewers to bet on the stirring election of 1896 in the following manner:

FREE SILVER IN ITS TRUE SENSE!

In addition to the extreme low gold value that is expected by Tobacco Chewers for their hard earned money, WE WILL GIVE FREE SILVER MONEY under the conditions named, TO GET ADDITIONAL CHEWERS ON R.J.R. TOBACCO, which has the quality and price to hold them as permanent consumers.

YOU GET UNDER OUR R.J.R. TAG THE BOTTOM PRICE OF A DEPRESSED MARKET; also the quality that pleases nearly all classes of Tobacco lovers.

Our offer is as follows: If the United States should adopt Free Coinage of Silver during the administration of the President to be named by the Electors chosen on November 3rd, 1896, WE WILL GIVE R.J.R. TOBACCO CHEWERS 50 CTS. FOR EACH LOT OF 50 RED R.J.R. TAGS, delivered to us or our agents within 10 days from the date the Free Coinage is allowed.

We obligate ourselves to comply with the above.

R.J. REYNOLDS TOBACCO CO.
WINSTON, N.C.

If you inform your trade of our offer for R.J.R. Tags they will appreciate it, as it will enable them to save many Tags before our advertising matter can be posted.

At first the company wanted its salesmen to arrange for distribution of these circulars to residences, factories, workshops, and stores. Three days later, on 19 September 1896, all salesmen were instructed to confine distribution to businesses, houses, offices, workshops, and the streets. Again, on 6 October salesmen were urged to distribute the circulars "every where you go and have a good supply of them which we want given out by November 4th."[63]

Other forms of advertising appeared during the 1890s. Late in 1891 with his new factory nearing completion, Reynolds issued a calendar that captivated the editor of the *Union Republican*. In the following year the editor of the *Western Tobacco Journal* rhapsodized over the calendar for

1893 as "the most striking and handsome" seen that year and one "that will adorn the boudoir as well as the office"; it showed "a ravishingly beautiful olive skinned and dark tressed maiden."[64] Another advertisement, placed in 1893, made an appeal for trade on a national basis. In *Connorton's Tobacco Brand Directory of the United States for 1894* this advertisement appeared on the lower margin of every eighth page sixty-eight times: "Naturally Sweet, Mild and Palatable, Manufactured by R.J. Reynolds Tob. Co., Winston, N. C." Envelopes containing samples of the R. J. R. 16 oz. carried accounts of its excellence and the statement that the company, upon receipt of sixty cents, would deliver a trial plug to any address in the United States. In November 1893 a writer from Atlanta noted that R. J. Reynolds, who was "here last week," had a great trade there especially in Level Best and R. J. R.; moreover, they were the best advertised goods in the city.[65]

Evidently this status was heightened by the great acclaim received by Reynolds's products at the famous Atlanta Exposition of 1895. Dr. S. J. Blum and Nathaniel Vogler Peterson (16 May 1869–26 December 1938), of Salem, left Winston with a carload of materials to be placed in the exhibit hall in a space of 600 feet—the only exhibit from North Carolina. An editor from Winston declared that the exhibit occupied an attractive room "papered in imitation of plug tobacco, with an ornamental border of leaf tobacco, while the ceiling is a tasteful arrangement of granulated or smoking tobacco." The outside of the room bore "the well known trademark of the firm R.J.R. with doors in the lower part and windows in the upper part of the two Rs." When the Winston editor visited the exposition, Robert Edward Lasater (16 December 1867–15 July 1954) was in charge of the Reynolds stand. This assiduous attention to his duty at the age of twenty-eight may have been the beginning of Lasater's climb in the company, which led eventually to membership on the board of directors. The editor, a booster of Winston and Salem, continued his description of the exhibit:

> Tobacco cuts a small figure at the Exposition. We noticed only three exhibits of the manufactured product and the R.J. Reynolds Co.'s exhibit was the only one from the South, impressing us with the idea that many of our manufacturing concerns, as well as the Legislature, are lacking a proper spirit of enterprise and progress. It is to be regretted that there was not that concert of action among the Winston manufacturers of various lines that would have resulted in a grand and attractive advertisement for our city and section.

So impressed was the editor that he later ran a special account of the Reynolds display, describing the pyramid of tobacco boxes representing the various plugs made by the company, surmounted by a figure of " 'Liberty Enlightening the World' " well illuminated by varicolored lights.[66]

Reynolds and his employees used other methods to call attention to his brands. Other firms' advertisements in the *Southern Tobacco Journal* for 1893–94 generally remained the same from issue to issue, but Reynolds occasionally changed his copy. Beginning on 17 February 1894, and repeated several times, an empty space appeared carrying only the caption "This space is reserved for R. J. Reynolds Tobacco Co., Winston, N. C.,"[67] a technique used more masterfully later in the introduction of Camel cigarettes. As did other tobacco manufacturers, Reynolds frequently shipped in carload lots, the cars gaily decorated with huge banners bearing the names of the company and the brands being shipped. One notable shipment in 1894 included three carloads consigned to Haralson Brothers and Company of Atlanta. Another, by way of the Norfolk and Western Railway to Baltimore, carried the showy lettering of Le Roy Tise on its sides.[68] For a number of years such shipments frequently left the Reynolds company's back door on Depot Street. A most unusual choice of a spectacular position for an advertisement attracted wide attention in 1896 at the time of a lynching near Elkhorn, West Virginia. After the tragedy, C. P. Mahood, representing the company, tacked "R.J.R. tobacco signs" on the sapling to which the slain man had been chained.[69]

So went the Reynolds advertising well before the firm became a subsidiary of the American Tobacco Company, an event that some consider as the mainspring of R. J.'s penchant for advertising. In 1915, when describing his early use of advertising, Reynolds stated that he regularly reinvested "between two and three percent of his annual sales in advertising."[70] Apparently he impressed the importance of this belief on his company, as expenses for that purpose have been known to constitute approximately 81 percent of net earnings.

A modern factory and vigorous advertising suggest a vigorous sales department, but just how the Reynolds sales department actually developed during the 1890s seems largely forgotten. Salesmen were on the road as early as 1892 and possibly a few years before that. Rufus Tucker Stedman (12 January 1856–21 January 1931), long a sportsman and man-about-town, began traveling for Reynolds in 1892; yet it appears that he also worked in the main office during that same year.[71] Only fragmentary accounts of the personnel of the early sales organization may be given. According to official records, J. W. Young was the first salesman, hired on 6 June 1893. On 30 June, however, Martin Luther McKenzie (18 April 1863–15 April 1944), who worked the area around Montgomery, Alabama, had already resigned in order to be near his wife and young children. His possession of a leather sign case and a magnetic hammer furnished by the company as well as his good record as a salesman indicate that he had held the position for some time. William Emerson Brock (14 March 1872–5 August 1950), later a candy manufacturer and a United States senator, joined the company as a salesman on 1 January 1893 as did J. S. Jopling (d. 25 July 1915). Bowman Gray, Sr. (1 May 1874–7 July 1935), the Reynolds salesman par excellence, began with the company on 1 November 1895 at a salary of $5.75 per week.[72] Sometime before his death in February 1899, Arthur H. Smoot traveled for Reynolds, and L. W. Matthews began similar work in 1897.[73] Noteworthy, too, was the employment of "Miss Boogs" in the sales department at least as early as 1894. Miss Boogs copied letters and wording for advertisements in a flowing and even hand but evidently was not trusted with the type-writer—an instrument used in the company only by men until well after the turn of the century.[74] All in all, available records indicate that Rufus T. Stedman, employed in 1892, served as first head of the sales department, and that his department began operation in that pivotal year on a larger scale than previously.

Available information shows an early dependence on agents to supply the needs of jobbers and the evolution of a sales system with division managers and salesmen. Apparently it was first the duty of the sales de-partment to keep in contact with these agents and to furnish inducements for the jobbers who patronized them. Only a few agents may be named, such as Benjamin F. Parlett and Company of Baltimore and its heirs; Cox and Corbin, wholesale grocers of Macon, Georgia; and H. M. Kean of Philadelphia. It will be recalled that Reynolds had worked through the Parletts in the 1880s if not earlier. For a time prior to 1898, the Baltimore and Washington territory constituted a distinct division under the man-agement of John F. Parlett. Cox and Corbin evidently covered a large area, as Reynolds on 23 October 1894 mailed them 250 cards for use with jobbers. H. M. Kean served as broker or representative for the entire Philadelphia area. At the time of Kean's resignation, perhaps in 1898, the company wrote its Philadelphia jobbers asking them to mail all orders directly to Winston.

Of more importance is the blank form entitled "Agency Appointment made by the R. J. Reynolds Tobacco Co. of Winston, N. C." The Reyn-olds agents handled only brands shown on the company's price list. Pay-ment for each shipment was due in sixty days, but, if the agent paid cash within ten days after shipment, he received a 2 percent discount in addi-tion to his regular commission. Reynolds guaranteed to pay the agent's discount every ninety days unless he sold the goods at less than list price. That there was a printed form for use in appointing agents leads to the conclusion that the agent served an important role in sales, perhaps more in the early part of the decade than later.

Another type of contract used during the 1890s represented a method of sales destined to disappear after a time. Printed forms, entitled "Contract, Governing the Sale of Contract Brands of Tobacco Manufactured by the R.J. Reynolds Tobacco Company," covered special brands manufactured for a particular jobber, jobbers of a particular area, or agents turned jobbers. Cash Value, a two-ply twist made especially for the jobbers of Philadelphia, was no doubt a fair sample of a contract brand. Reynolds had many such brands. Often, as in the case of B. F. Parlett and Company, a brand listed by a wholesale dealer was also listed by Reynolds. In 1894, for example, the following listed as Reynolds brands were also listed in the name of B. F. Parlett and Company: Aggie Twist, Bantam Twist, California Twist, Little Idol Twist, Nerveless Light Pressed, Our Idea, Walter Raleigh Twist. During the same year Reynolds also made Rosenfeld's Natural and Rosenfeld's Rod for S. Rosenfeld of Baltimore.[75] This practice undoubtedly accounts for the great number of brands usually listed as Reynolds products. In the case of B. F. Parlett and Company and its successors, originally wholesale tobacconists and manufacturers, it is clear that Reynolds took over their manufacturing interests whereas the Parletts eventually became straight agents for Reynolds. Apparently this process marked the decline of commission merchants.

As the old order of catering to wholesale dealers with their own brands and salesmen and of using special agents began to weaken, R. J. instituted a modern sales department. As early as 1896 Reynolds salesmen began receiving barrages of instructions from the home office on such subjects as the proper use of advertisements, the need for sending in the following week's route list promptly, the proper way to fill in weekly reports, proper methods for treating dealers, the necessity for exerting greater energy, the desirable manner of working with jobbers' salesmen, the importance of adhering to the price list, the need to cease worrying dealers about brands already popular, the terms for writing orders, the significance of introducing new brands, and the importance of sending duplicate weekly and daily reports to the division manager. More than sixty years later emphasis would also be placed on daily and weekly reports, which by then had to be sent airmail, but, in fact, the differences between such letters of the 1890s and the 1960s were slight indeed. Samples labeled by Robert Critz or Rufus T. Stedman as letters "stirring up the salesmen" would later be called "pep letters," although the pattern was well established before 1900.

Other details in these early letters to salesmen resembled those of the 1960s. On 20 August 1896, salesmen were admonished to place goods "on the shelves of all the small dealers" and to sell to those retailers "that you can not reach through regular jobbers" through "some large retailer." Not only were salesmen urged, on 25 June 1896, to enclose "yellow duplicate orders each day with reports" but also to "mail every report the evening of the day it represents." In the matter of checking on the receipt of goods ordered by dealers, salesmen were asked in 1896 to find out "if other goods have been substituted by any jobber on orders you have sent him." If such substitution had been made, salesmen were asked to notify the home office promptly, giving the names of the jobber and the dealer. A welcome letter sent on 10 December 1896 permitted salesmen to begin their Christmas holidays on 21 December. Soon after the holidays, however, instructions urged them to size up the class of consumers whom the retailers supplied and to place their efforts on brands suitable for that trade, provided the retailer failed to have them. A new enticement reached the field in May 1897, when word came that shipments of two hundred pounds or more might be made to retail dealers "for account of jobbers" to points in any territory with freight prepaid. This seems closely related to the drop shipment plan used so long and so successfully by Reynolds. William N. Reynolds stated in 1951, perhaps erroneously, that drop shipments were used by his firm as early as 1886.[76] When the home office sent salesmen samples of R. J. R. 2's or Half Pounds, they were requested "to speak of this goods as twos or half pounds and not as 8 oz.; so that it will not be confused with R.J. Reynolds' 8 oz." Possibly inspired by sharp competition from the American Tobacco Company, the sales department in February 1898 emphasized the importance of a space on the daily report sheets for remarks; there the salesmen were to report anything beyond the regular order that might be of value or interest to the company.

These cautions and orders reached a high point in 1898. In April—almost exactly one year before the R. J. Reynolds Tobacco Company became a subsidiary of the American Tobacco Company—the following notice was sent to all salesmen:

> For a number of years it has been our policy not to confine the sale of our goods, but at the time these instructions were issued, we had not taken on additional jobbers in a few markets. We have now made open market in the whole field covered by us, and renew these instructions, except the sentence leaving it discretionary with our man under certain conditions to work with jobbers' salesmen, which we withdraw, and you are hereby instructed to work entirely independent of jobbers salesmen, and by carrying out these instructions give each jobber and his salesmen the full benefit of their efforts on our goods.

On 8 June salesmen were sent weekly report blanks with instructions to mail them "so as to reach us on or before Tuesday morning of each week," the deadline in effect for many years for the receipt of such reports. Duplicate copies were to be sent to the head of the division under whom the salesmen worked. While this is the first direct mention of division managers other than John F. Parlett, it is not made as if the division manager were a new position. On 12 August there came an urgent appeal for "a harmonious pulling together"—perhaps the Victorian rendition of the more recently adopted motto *teamwork*. This appeal to salesmen for teamwork did not prevent emphasis on the importance of a detailed weekly report on all salesmen by the division managers who were to evaluate their work. Was it fair or poor? Had the trade been worked closely, to the best advantage under the circumstances, leisurely, too hurriedly, very poorly, or how? Had the advertising been handled well, poorly, too little, or too poorly? These directions to division managers were concluded in an even sharper key: "State any item of his [the salesman's] expenses which you do not approve, and advise us of any amount we should deduct from his next remittance. Note carefully any towns which are not in satisfactory shape, keep a record of them, and be sure to see to it that they are given the necessary attention, and in this way bring up all the weak points in your division."[77]

Problems other than the supervision of salesmen confronted the growing sales department in the 1890s. To attract the trade west of the Mississippi River the company prepaid freight on all direct shipments of a hundred pounds or more to retail dealers of that area on the jobber's account. First made on 29 June 1898, this offer does not mention Texas, although the sample copy bears an inscription in the handwriting of Critz or Stedman: "To Texas jobbers offering to prepay freight on shipments of 100# direct to the retail trade W. of Miss. River." A notice of continuance of this offer on 9 February 1899 bears no reference of any kind to Texas. West of the Mississippi evidently covered a wide territory.

Of greater importance was the matter of rebates on listed brands. Apparently Reynolds used the rebate system to prevent price cutting by jobbers. As early as 1887 he had used a printed form with spaces to include the quantity bought, the brand, the price per pound, and the rebate per pound. On sales covered by this agreement, jobbers obligated themselves not to sell for less than a stated sum, which varied according to the amount purchased. All deliveries to the jobber were to be in lots of at least ten boxes. Reynolds, according to this agreement, would give no drawback "either by excess of 2% discount for cash, or by other means" unless the jobbers adhered strictly to the scheduled prices written into the agreement. If Reynolds charged any jobber with violating this agreement, he refused to pay the rebate until the jobber affirmed under oath that the charges were untrue. If Reynolds sustained such a charge against a jobber, the rebate would be forfeited and the jobber would settle at full prices. In order to make the violation of such an agreement doubly disagreeable to the jobber, Reynolds might indemnify himself from the full price collected from the offending jobber and parcel out the remainder to other parties with whom he held similar contracts. Space at the end of this agreement provided for the jobber's signature.

By 15 May 1893, the Reynolds price list for office use carried the following scale of prices and rebates on chewing tobacco brands:

	Cost Price per Pound	Rebate per Pound
R.J. Reynolds' Level Best	$1.00	$.20
R.J. Reynolds' Double Thick		
8 oz.	.65	.09
Triplets 3 Break 7½'s	.48	.08
R.J.R., 9 in. 4's	.43	.07
High Standard, 9 in. 4's	.43	.07
Belle of North Carolina,		
9 in. 5's	.34	.06
Maid of Athens, 9 in. 5's	.34	.06
Caromel, 7 in. 5's	.34	.06
Our Advertiser, 7 in. 5's	.34	.06

As early as 8 April 1895, the company issued a circular to jobbers listing the rebate per pound for sixteen brands of chewing tobacco. The prices on the regular price list were the same at the factory as the "box price" at which jobbers were allowed to sell. In view of that fact, Reynolds agreed to send with each invoice to jobbers a "Purchase Voucher" representing from five cents per pound on Belle of North Carolina to twenty cents per pound on R. J. Reynolds' Level Best, thereby including sixteen different brands. Each purchase voucher obtained by the jobbers covered a period of ninety days. The circular carried statements that these compensations were voluntary and that no purchase voucher would be honored unless signed by the jobber, which act would be "an affirmation that the terms printed on our price lists have been strictly lived up to during the life of each Voucher."

The purchase voucher remained in use, apparently without question except for a reduction of the ninety days to sixty, until the enactment of a severe antitrust law by the state of Georgia in 1896.[78] On 2 January 1897, the company "deemed it prudent" to withhold purchase vouchers in Georgia and by 8 January to issue a list of lower prices prepared especially for Georgia. The sample preserved in the scrapbook, on which this account is based, carries the following notation: "First system adopted after the passage of the Anti-Trust Law in Ga." Undated but apparently later, a credit memorandum by brands was issued for use in Georgia. The purchase or rebate voucher was abandoned on 31 March 1897 as the result of laws passed in several states. This was the "trust-busting" era with hatred for any practice savoring of monopoly and especial venom for the word "rebate," which had been made ugly by the railroads. After 31 March a system of voluntary compensations was adopted. The object and effect of these various schemes apparently remained the same—prevention of price cutting on the Reynolds brands by jobbers.

With the coming of the Spanish American War a problem of considerable proportions arose when federal taxes were raised in 1895 by 12 cents on the pound. As uncertainty about the tax continued to prevail, on 2 May salesmen were advised to go home for a vacation but to keep the sales department informed of their whereabouts. On 16 May the sales department notified jobbers that increasing leaf prices and the unsettled condition of the country forced the company not only to raise prices two cents per pound but also to accept orders subject to any forthcoming increase of the revenue tax. After the twelve-cent tax became effective, the company decided "to bear a part of the loss of the advance in tax," at least on Schnapps, and to fill orders on 6 in. 4's at 31 cents "delivered, on usual terms, with no trade discount or 'voluntary consideration.'" To close out a supply of R. J. R. 2's, manufactured with dark wrappers before the increase in taxes, it had to be sold at the same price but without any 10 percent consideration, discount on regular terms, or payment of freight. Our Advertiser smoking tobacco, and no doubt other brands, had to be sold before package sizes could be reduced to meet increased taxes.[79] Truly the expanding business before the end of 1898 had taught the company to synchronize its sales activities and its manufacturing with changes in public sentiment, in prices of raw materials, and in taxes.

Improvements in Manufacturing

Changes involving advertising and selling necessarily reflected changes in manufacturing methods. In this area, always difficult to fathom, Reynolds probably made his greatest strides. During the 1890s, he began to manufacture smoking tobacco, installed vastly improved machinery for making chewing tobacco, and revolutionized his formulas for chewing tobacco by introducing the use of saccharin. Advances made in this decade determined the continuation of the R. J. Reynolds Tobacco Company as a corporate entity through the tough competition of the 1890s, the affiliation with the American Tobacco Company, and the years after 1911, which saw the company advance to leadership among the successors to the old American Tobacco Company after its dissolution.

Reynolds's entry into the manufacture of smoking tobacco was a radical departure from the teachings of his father at Nobusiness Mountain. William N. Reynolds stated in 1944 that R. J. had begun manufacturing "a little granulated tobacco about 1890 or 1891, somewhere along there;

just in a very limited way."[80] This is doubtless correct, because early in 1891, just when plans for the new factory were taking shape, R. J. owned as personal property one stem grinder manufactured by H. M. Smith and Company and one granulator valued at forty dollars and probably acquired from an auction sale.[81] It may be safely concluded that in his spare time, whenever he found it, he was laying plans to eclipse Bull Durham and Duke's Mixture manufactured in Durham, North Carolina, although probably of more immediate importance was his desire to turn his scrap tobacco resulting from the manufacture of plug into a paying product. Of interest, too, is the fact that this tinkering with the stem grinder and granulator came twenty-eight years before Reynolds's sale of chewing tobacco products reached a peak but only sixteen years before he launched his spectacularly successful Prince Albert smoking brand. In *Connorton's Tobacco Brand Directory of the United States for 1895*, Reynolds listed his first known brand of smoking tobacco: 4A Naturally Sweet Cut Plug, derived no doubt from a plug brand called 4A Naturally Sweet. Because this directory was ready for distribution in December 1894, it is certain that 4A Naturally Sweet Cut Plug was in production at least by 1894.[82] This is the only available mention of such a smoking brand. It was not included in the first price list for smoking tobacco issued on 15 May 1895, which showed only Split Silk, Razor Back, and Our Advertiser (also named for a chewing brand of the same name). Split Silk was a long-cut type of smoking tobacco made by passing leaves through a shredding machine before flavoring; Razor Back was a cut plug manufactured from partially prepared plug tobacco; and Our Advertiser was a granulated type made of small, roughly cut pieces of tobacco and stems in a more or less pulverized state. Split Silk, listed at fifty-five cents per pound, ranked as Reynolds's choice brand of smoking tobacco; Razor Back, listed at thirty cents, stood next; and appropriately Our Advertiser, at twenty-one cents per pound, ranked last in quality.[83]

Reynolds was by no means the first manufacturer in Winston to make smoking tobacco. In the same year that Reynolds listed his 4A Naturally Sweet Cut Plug, other Winston manufacturers listed fifty-seven different brands, including ten brands listed by Taylor Brothers (William B. and Jacquelin Plummer),[84] a firm never forced into the American Tobacco Company. Before 1899 the Reynolds company distributed samples of Our Advertiser and enclosed cigarette papers and pipes in its regular packages. Split Silk, guaranteed as the best quality for pipe and cigarette, was submitted to the United States Army in 1897 for approval as tobacco to be purchased for soldiers, but Razor Back apparently received no special emphasis before 1899. It should be noted that the company also listed one other brand in *Connorton's Tobacco Brand Directory* before becoming affiliated with the American Tobacco Company—Occabot, which appeared at times on the Reynolds price lists.[85] Perhaps the inclusion of cigarette papers with Our Advertiser indicated that the growing cigarette business had not escaped the eagle eye of R. J. Reynolds.

During this same fruitful decade Reynolds adopted machinery of a revolutionary nature apparently well in advance of other manufacturers of southern flat-plug chewing tobacco. First and most important for the manufacture of chewing tobacco was the Adams Duplex Automatic Tobacco Press invented in 1889 and sold by the Adams Tobacco Press Company of Quincy, Illinois. Known generally as the Adams double-header machine, its chief advantage lay in the accurate weighing of each plug before it went into the machine for pressure. The machine had two chambers that worked alternately; while the tobacco for one plug was being weighed, another plug remained under pressure. No time was lost after the tobacco was pressed into shape for adding to or taking from the plug to make its weight correct. Its use produced a saving of two to three dollars per day on wrappers alone; the plug did not sponge up after being under pressure; and, according to its manufacturers, its capacity ranged from 2,000 to 2,500 pounds in ten hours.[86] As testimony of its excellence, the Adams double-header machine long remained the standard fixture in the chewing tobacco division of the R. J. Reynolds Tobacco Company, which in 1958 produced more chewing tobacco than in 1906.

With his usual acumen, Reynolds became the first manufacturer of southern flat-plug chewing tobacco to adopt the Adams machine. Possibly Henry E. Harman, of Winston, had seen this machine in operation in the Reynolds plant when he published a veritable panegyric on its performance in the *Southern Tobacco Journal* for 6 December 1897. At that time, Harman declared that the Adams machine had been used by Reynolds for several years. Furthermore, it was not adopted by Richmond manufacturers until 1899. On 28 February 1896, the Reynolds company informed its customers that it was "now fully equipped" with additional machinery to fill all orders for Schnapps. Undoubtedly this statement referred to the installation of more Adams machines. Demand for Schnapps, however, proved unusually heavy, and the wreck of one carload of machinery in transit—a catastrophe not immediately reported to Reynolds by the railroad—delayed full production for some time. Also of significance is the fact that the R. J. Reynolds Tobacco Company, on 27 March 1896, became an agent for selling the Adams press in Virginia and North Carolina at a commission of twenty-five dollars per machine with special terms for purchases of such machinery in the future.[87] In view of these various facts, it seems that Reynolds began to use the Adams machines by 1893 but did not fully equip his plant with them until 1897. Apparently the early adoption of the Adams press, together with improvements in his brand formulas, placed Reynolds in the forefront as a manufacturer of southern flat-plug chewing tobacco well before James B. Duke felt strong enough to attempt consolidation of the chewing tobacco industry.

Another outstanding machine transformed the handling of leaf tobacco, making the onerous task of redrying leaf much faster and more accurate. Reynolds became one of the first to install the Proctor Redrying Machine, which not only shortened the process of redrying but also offered economy in floor space, heat, and labor, not to mention reduction of fire hazards and consequently lower insurance rates. By 1898 the Proctor Redrying Machine, apparently ready for sale in 1895, had not been generally installed in factories and redrying plants. In that year, however, R. J.'s "Proctor truck system" seemed to be a familiar fixture in his plant.[88]

Other, less drastic changes came in the 1890s. A contract dated 12 December 1891 covered the purchase of an American Watchman's Time Detector, guaranteed for three years except for "Wear and tear on Battery and Wire," for ten stations.[89] This was obviously intended for use in the new plant ready in the spring of 1892. Reynolds's constant efforts to prevent destruction by fire no doubt led to this decision to install a mechanism for checking on his night watchman. His growing sales and improved facilities also eliminated the need to close down operations for any great length of time. In 1894 Reynolds stated with pride that he did not stop work for one day during the previous year's manufacturing season, which lasted from 1 March to 16 December 1893.[90]

Neither improved transportation facilities, intensive advertising, a modern sales force, nor more effective machinery can equal in importance the introduction of saccharin as a sweetening agent into the formulas of the Reynolds brands of southern flat plug. Unfortunately, because of brand secrecy and the passage of time, this highly important aspect of the business must be approached indirectly. Yet there is abundant proof that Reynolds stood among the first, if not the very first, to use saccharin to sweeten chewing tobacco.

The adoption of saccharin resulted from a conflict between chewing tobacco manufacturers who used Burley leaf and those who used eastern or bright leaf; during this period the former was produced west of the Appalachians and the latter in the Virginia-Carolina area. It was a very serious struggle between manufacturers of navy plug centered in St. Louis, Cincinnati, and Louisville, and those of flat plug in Virginia and North Carolina—especially in North Carolina. In fact, St. Louis remained the leader in the manufacture of chewing tobacco until surpassed by Winston-Salem in 1916.[91] The foundation for the eastward shift of the manufacture of chewing tobacco came much earlier. Burley leaf, somewhat spongy by nature, absorbed sweetening agents and flavorings more readily than the bright, or flue-cured, leaf and thus became pleasing to the palate of many chewers. The controversy, which raged in newspapers and trade journals especially during the 1880s and early 1890s, became so intense that manufacturers in the Virginia-Carolina area who dared to use Burley leaf did so as secretively as possible.

Saccharin, the discovery of Constantin Fahlberg, a German student studying at the Johns Hopkins University, was first noted in 1879 or 1880. The earliest available advertisement of saccharin in a U.S. tobacco trade journal appeared in 1894.[92] The editor of the *Western Tobacco Journal* referred in 1900 to the use of saccharin, or Heyden Sugar, its trade name, as a rapidly growing practice among tobacco manufacturers. His assessment of this practice indicates the difficulty of obtaining precise information on the subject: "Many manufacturers prefer (for their own benefit) to keep their experience with such articles to themselves, but those who will talk on the subject at all speak with enthusiasm of the good results they have obtained in several ways."[93] Less than two years earlier, however, he had analyzed the benefits to be derived from the use of saccharin in chewing tobacco. It greatly reduced the amount of sugar needed; it saved 1¼ to 2½ cents per pound on the cost of sugar; it eliminated the dangers of funk and mold customarily found in chewing tobacco heavily charged with sugar; it gave a lasting sweetness to the chew; and it acted as a preservative. The use of saccharin did not replace sugar; rather, it supplemented the use of sugar and licorice. North Carolina leaf would assimilate five pounds of sugar and ten pounds of licorice to one hundred pounds of tobacco without becoming gummy. That formula, however, did not produce a chew as sweet as the consumer wished. To obtain this, the manufacturer of flat plug merely added one or two ounces of saccharin to one thousand pounds of tobacco. The editor then cited an anonymous manufacturer in North Carolina who pronounced the use of saccharin in chewing tobacco one of the greatest aids to tobacco manufacturing that had ever been discovered. Each ounce of saccharin, the editor declared, contained sweetening power equivalent to thirty-three pounds of sugar. Because it was much less soluble than sugar, saccharin caused the maintenance of a sweet impression long after the other sweetening agents had been exhausted by the chewer. The advantages of saccharin coupled with the more durable quality of Virginia-Carolina leaf gave definite superiority to southern flat plug, and thus it is clear how Reynolds and no doubt other Winston manufacturers could advance bright leaf, which would absorb only about 15 percent of its weight in sweetening agents, over Burley, which readily absorbed 40 to 50 percent of its weight in sweetening materials.[94]

On the other hand, the version given in the Virginia-Carolina area by Henry E. Harman, writing in the *Southern Tobacco Journal* of Winston and Salem on 14 March 1898, held that saccharin had been introduced into the manufacture of smoking and chewing tobacco "some three years ago."

At that time, he declared, "the trade in the East was practically at a standstill" because western chewing tobacco with its enormous capacity for absorbing sweetening material seemed to be taking the lead. Harman wrote further: "The trade was demanding sweeter tobacco, but our manufacturers could not possibly meet the demand, for they were then putting on as much licorice and sugar as our non-absorptive leaf would take. Many were discouraged and it looked as if the Eastern flat goods trade had met its Waterloo." About this time, Harman stated, the New York chemical firm of Merck and Company secured control in the United States of saccharin, a product put up in Germany; it was more than five hundred times as sweet as sugar and was considered virtually harmless. Harman also stated that the *Southern Tobacco Journal* first called the attention of tobacco manufacturers to saccharin and that some began experimentation. The process proved slow and tobacco had to be aged in order to test results fully. Saccharin was found to be excellent and the most thorough experiments were made in Winston. Harman continued: "The second year only a limited number of manufacturers used Saccharin, but the suddenness with which their tobacco leaped into public favor soon convinced the others that their only hope lay in imitating their more enterprising competitors, and last year the great majority of flat goods manufacturers were using this wonderful sweetener."

With information probably secured from R. J. Reynolds, another writer unknowingly commented on the same point in the same year:[95]

> The R. J. Reynolds Tobacco Company started and operated, in 1875, the smallest tobacco factory in Winston, N. C. Their business increased in a small way until, in the year 1891, when they discovered how to manipulate Virginia and North Carolina tobacco, and to remove the difficulties that caused many chewers to prefer other classes of tobacco. They were convinced that they could produce chewing tobacco that would be the favorite of lovers of tobacco, and their knowledge would justify them in building and equipping a much more expensive plant than had been used in their class of tobaccos.
>
> They built an additional factory in 1891, which was five times larger than their business at that time warranted. . . . Their brands have proven such wonderful sellers that they have not only alarmed Virginia and North Carolina manufacturers, but Western manufacturers imitate the outward appearance of the R. J. Reynolds Tobacco Company's goods.

Had Reynolds really discovered how to manipulate tobacco in a new way and did this way include saccharin? Henry Harman said the use of saccharin required aging the tobacco. J. S. Oliver, in the *Open Door*, stated that, prior to Reynolds's first advertisement in 1892, it was customary to age the tobacco after it had been manufactured. This process, he declared, represented the best thought of the day. Oliver, who undoubtedly obtained his information from Reynolds along with a copy of the first advertisement of Reynolds's products, declared further:[96]

> The R. J. Reynolds Tobacco Co., after exhaustive experiments discovered that the tobacco must first be properly aged in the leaf, then manufactured into the finished product, if the highly desirable natural flavor, aroma, and strength were to be fully retained and greatly enhanced. . . .

> Only by inference could the R. J. Reynolds Tobacco Co. then tell the public just what they were able to do. Had they have [*sic*] taken the public fully and frankly into their confidence they would have invited other manufacturers to follow suit—to freely avail themselves of a reward which rightly belonged to them exclusively.

Oliver's account ties in with Harman's as well as with that taken from the *Charlotte Observer*. It is also well known that tobacco manufacturers always strive to maintain secrecy of their brands, and Reynolds was no exception.[97]

Furthermore, in the early 1890s Reynolds began talking about "naturally sweet" tobacco. In 1893 he declared that only a very small area of North Carolina, including Davidson, Surry, Davie, Forsyth, Stokes, and Rockingham counties, produced this "naturally sweet leaf," generally regarded as "a botanical freak." This "botanical freak," never before noted, was undoubtedly based on the use of saccharin in the manufacture of chewing tobacco. In Atlanta, in the same year, Reynolds displayed a plug of this *rare* leaf made as an experiment; this he intended to market under the brand name Naturally Sweet. At the same time, he diagnosed, in the manner of the sly fox, one difficulty of North Carolina manufacturers: ". . . they have all been, to some extent, striving to supply, by artificial process, the sweet tobacco demand, overlooking the fact entirely that this native sweet leaf, if properly cultivated, prized, and manufactured, will make the most delicious and lasting chew that can be made from tobacco."[98] The account of this interview ended with the statement that in all probability Reynolds would market a brand called Naturally Sweet, "as he has a large quantity of this leaf on hand." Actually no probability was involved because Reynolds had advertised his new brand Naturally Sweet as early as 14 October 1893 in a full-page advertisement in the *Southern Tobacco Journal*. In this advertisement he vowed that, since he began the manufacture of tobacco, he had confined his efforts entirely to the production of a naturally sweet chewing tobacco and had not used one dollar's worth of flavoring. Furthermore, he declared, he had registered his new brand Naturally Sweet.[99] On 19 September 1895, Reynolds's pasteboard signs included references to "Recent Experiments made by the expert manufacturers of R.J.R. Tobacco" that improved the chew and reduced the price 20 percent. On the same signs the same idea was also worded: "Natural growth improved on by experiments made by the expert manufacturers of RJR Tobacco."[100] Thus Reynolds condemned artificial sweetening while turning to the most artificial type then known. It should be noted that Constantin Fahlberg developed saccharin in Baltimore where Reynolds had close connections. There is no evidence available to show that any other manufacturer was first to use saccharin.

Thus, on more than a tentative basis, the conclusion may be drawn that Reynolds developed a new type of chewing tobacco based on the use of saccharin and a new method for aging leaf. The clinching proof lies in a contract that R. J. made to act as agent for the sale of Heyden Sugar, which was saccharin combined with bicarbonate of soda. By this contract of 16 January 1899, he was to use his influence "*as before*" to promote the sale of saccharin "in Virginia and North Carolina, excepting Danville, in connection with Mr. Watt Martin" (1860?–16 March 1920). By this arrangement R. J. was to obtain his requirements of saccharin at $7.50 per pound.[101] Martin, a close personal friend, lived in Winston and apparently with the aid of Reynolds began a profitable business in 1893 as a dealer in tobacco manufacturers' supplies.[102] Whether R. J. was actually first to use saccharin in his chewing tobacco or whether he was first to learn to age his tobacco properly, in the leaf instead of in the plug, matters little. Enough hints and records exist to show that something remarkable along this line emerged in 1891. However, Reynolds had to surmount a personnel crisis before meeting other problems.

Crisis in Organization, 1893

Plans for the new factory developed and production increased so rapidly after the company's incorporation by the state of North Carolina that Reynolds was soon forced to make changes in management, which at that time included him, his brother William, and Henry Roan. At the second stockholders' meeting, delayed from the first Monday of January until 19 March 1891 because of R. J.'s absence from town, the directors and officers were reelected. It was also decided to change bylaw number one so that annual meetings of the stockholders would fall on the first Monday of February rather than January.[103] At least the embryo corporation had learned that the business of the year could not be accounted for instanta-

neously. On the same day the directors, who were also the three stockholders, raised the vice-president's salary to $1,500 and that of Roan, the
secretary and treasurer, to $1,800. At this meeting apparently the ground
was laid for later disputes by the purchase of a lot on which to build the
new factory to be planned by C. R. Makepeace and Company.[104] No
further changes occurred until 15 August 1891, when the stockholders
decided that any of the three might endorse checks and drafts in the
company's name and receive and give receipts for all money due and
payable to the company. Moreover, all receipts and checks up to that time
handled by any of the three were ratified.[105] On the surface, it thus appears that nothing had occurred to destroy the harmony of the stockholders or directors.

Yet a sharp change in management occurred at the stockholders' meeting for 1 February 1892, simultaneously with the opening of the new
plant. Thomas L. Farrow, manager of the prizing department, who on 11
June 1891 had laid the first brick for the company's mammoth new factory, was added to the board of directors.[106] This was a sensible move.
Farrow had worked with Reynolds for sixteen years, longer than Will
Reynolds, D. Rich, or Henry Roan, and his qualifications were undoubtedly well known. Two meetings of the stockholders occurred on 7 March
1892. At the first one $95,000 from the 1891 earnings of $120,014 was
set aside to increase the capital stock to $285,000, a move that increased
R. J.'s holdings by 781 shares, Henry Roan's by 50 shares, and Will
Reynolds's by 119 shares. This left $25,014 as a dividend on the original
capital stock. When the same group met a few minutes later, Will Reynolds offered a resolution: "Inasmuch as the election of T. L. Farrow as a
member of the Board of Directors of this Company was held prior to his
having acquired any stock in this Company & whereas said election was
on that account void and of no effect, therefore be it resolved that the
stockholders proceed to the election of another director." Roan, after stating that Farrow had since become a stockholder, placed his name in nomi-
nation. Farrow was elected,[107] but this was by no means the last time such
an error would be made.

On 6 February 1893 Roan did not have the annual balance sheet quite
completed, and on 13 February a pending crisis involving Farrow and
Roan reached the minutes. It could in no way have been directly connected with the panic of that year, which did not affect the country until
June. On that day, Thomas L. Farrow and Henry Roan submitted identical letters of resignation from the board of directors, Farrow's dated 13
February and Roan's 11 February. Roan also wrote another letter resign-
ing formally as secretary and treasurer;[108] Will Reynolds assumed these
positions temporarily. What caused Farrow and Roan to resign, as accounts have been handed down, appears to have been a belief on Roan's

part that R. J. was a reckless plunger,[109] as perhaps he may have been. On 13 February 1893, however, Reynolds had good reason to believe that expansion of his business constituted a wise move. The Roanoke and Southern Railway had opened up possibilities of easily reaching a wider market in the mountains of Virginia, West Virginia, and nearby areas. He had been making drastic changes in his formulas that were just about to pay off. Farrow, although he may have been influenced to some degree by Roan, had apparently accumulated a rather tidy nest egg.[110] According to family tradition, the Dalton brothers, with whom Farrow went into business, argued with great persistence for him to join them, no doubt wishing to obtain the use of his money, his ability as a tobacco manufacturer, and an opportunity to spite R. J. Reynolds. It will be recalled that Reynolds's father Hardin W. had engaged in a land suit against Dr. William W. McCanless in the 1870s. Memories of the suit still persisted in the 1960s among descendants of the McCanless family. One of the Dalton brothers, Rufus I. Dalton (3 November 1855–18 February 1937), had married the daughter of McCanless in 1880.[111] At any rate, a description of the firm of Dalton, Farrow and Company in 1896 included a reference to Farrow that points to his valuable experience in the manufacture of tobacco as an important asset to the firm: "Mr. T. L. Farrow was for sixteen years with the R. J. Reynolds Tobacco Company, during which time he studied and mastered the business of manufacturing tobacco, in all its phases." Soon after he left Reynolds, Roan joined T. L. Vaughn and Company.[112]

R. J. solved his problems by persuading his youngest brother, Walter R. Reynolds, and his brother-in-law, Robert Critz, to take the respective positions of Farrow and Roan. Walter Reynolds, probably needed more immediately than Critz, was present on Farrow's last day at the Reynolds plant. Critz, however, did not appear at any stockholder's meeting until 29 May 1893; that day Will Reynolds resigned as temporary secretary and treasurer and Critz assumed his duties.[113] Insofar as the minutes reveal, Will Reynolds's chief duty as temporary secretary and treasurer was to sign the minutes of the stockholders' meeting on the last day of Roan's service, Roan having prepared them before leaving. On 24 February 1894, Critz became a director.[114] The company was now operated by R. J. Reynolds and his close relatives. Moreover, both Walter Reynolds and Robert Critz had experience in the manufacture of tobacco. Both had been trained at Rock Spring by Hardin W. Reynolds; in fact, it appears that Critz operated Hardin's old Rock Spring plant in 1889.[115] Then, from 1890 to 1893 Critz and Walter Reynolds operated a plug and twist factory in Bristol, Tennessee.[116] Thus, upon their arrival in Winston, the work of Hardin W. Reynolds in training his sons continued largely in the firm of R. J. Reynolds.

Table 3-3
Financial Profile of the Reynolds Company, 1890–1898

	Amount Owed	Stock Issued	Surplus	Gain	Stock Unissued	Assets & Liabilities
1890	$ 27,688	190,000	$ —	$ 50,747	$ 50,747	$ 268,434
1891	41,629	190,000	50,747	69,268	120,014	351,638
1892	43,373	285,000	—	56,159	56,159	384,532
1893	31,600	285,000	33,359	26,525	59,885	376,485
1894	37,561	300,000	36,552	58,364	94,916	432,477
1895	101,276	300,000	70,916	46,603	117,519	518,795
1896	115,450	300,000	99,519	92,084	191,603	607,053
1897	269,277	300,000	173,603	163,725	337,328	906,606
1898	269,978	300,000	276,706	159,234	435,940	1,005,919

Source: Consolidated balance sheets, R. J. Reynolds Tobacco Company.

Another serious blow struck the company before the end of 1893 in the death of W. D. Moore (1862?–27 July 1893), who had been chief book-keeper for three years.[117] Undoubtedly it was Moore's position to which D. Rich succeeded. These losses in three crucial positions within six months might well have halted a man less determined than R. J. Reynolds. To see the real outcome of the 1890s, however, it is best to examine his company's finances.

Table 3-3 represents a financial profile of the R. J. Reynolds Tobacco Company's business during the 1890s; it reflects increasing debt, the panic of 1893, the cost of factory Number 256 in the issuance of additional stock, and no doubt extreme competition from the American Tobacco Company.[118] Reynolds's continued expansion near the end of the decade meant chiefly an increasing debt for leaf tobacco. Panics pass and buildings may be paid for at the expense of personal funds. But, what of expansion dependent on additional debt for leaf tobacco and what of competition from the American Tobacco Company with its well nigh inexhaustible funds? In Table 3-4, the data for the production of chewing tobacco available after 1891 show a steadily growing output naturally with no hint of debt. Taken together Tables 3-3 and 3-4 indicate that the more Reynolds produced the larger grew the company's debt.

R. J. Reynolds's great need was capital for his constantly enlarging business. This he could not supply by means of energy and ingenuity, although the company had assumed a commanding position and had made considerable headway toward establishing a national market. Condi-

Table 3-4

The Reynolds Company's Total Production of Chewing Tobacco, 1892–1898

Year	Pounds
1892	1,085,292
1893	1,006,101
1894	1,215,767
1895	2,126,765
1896	2,846,039
1897	4,288,235
1898	5,331,312

Source: Production data, R. J. Reynolds Tobacco Company.

tions prevailing at that time in the U.S. tobacco industry were bound to affect the company. Where would Reynolds turn for the capital required for continued growth? Could he maintain the independence of his business? These questions point to the American Tobacco Company and its efforts to control and regulate the entire tobacco industry of the United States.

PART TWO

Under the Tobacco Combination, 1899–1911

CHAPTER 4

Affiliations, Acquisitions, and Consolidations

The years from 1899 to 1911 represent a unique period for the R. J. Reynolds Tobacco Company and indeed for all firms manufacturing chewing tobacco. Small manufacturers who had survived the financial vicissitudes of the 1880s and early 1890s were confronted with the American Tobacco Company's program to dominate the chewing tobacco industry. It was a time when manufacturers of chewing tobacco either failed or joined the Continental Tobacco Company, organized on 10 December 1898. From the beginning the American Tobacco Company exercised complete control over Continental, which in reality was a holding company. James Buchanan Duke served as president of both companies.[1] With his business steadily expanding and in dire need of additional capital, Reynolds apparently sought it from James B. Duke on a personal basis. As a result, in 1899 his company became a subsidiary of the Continental Tobacco Company and served as the agency for consolidating the flat-plug chewing tobacco industry of the Virginia-Carolina area. In that role, the R. J. Reynolds Tobacco Company acquired numerous tobacco factories located generally in the vicinities of Winston and Salem and Martinsville, Virginia. From the monotonous details connected with the acquisition of these factories, it is clear that many of them represented earlier consolidations. Operations of the R. J. Reynolds Tobacco Company during these years necessarily received supervision from the men who dominated American and Continental. Meanwhile Reynolds remained alert to all possibilities.

Affiliation with the American Tobacco Company

As R. J. Reynolds's business expanded during the 1890s so did his need for additional capital. He now required far more than the small sums that might be obtained from relatives or friends in the wholesale tobacco business. On 7 July 1898 he purchased a lot adjacent to Number 256 with the intention of constructing the following year a larger factory than the one he had built in 1891. The new factory was to be connected with Number 256 by iron bridges and tunnels.[2] But in addition to lack of capital, Reynolds's situation was complicated by the growing power of the American Tobacco Company and hatred of the public for that company, generally and no doubt properly considered as one of the most outright monopolistic businesses in the country. Despised by wholesale tobacconists who were forced to do business with it, hated by farmers who attributed low prices of leaf to it, and inveighed against by warehousemen and independent leaf dealers who saw in its operations a threat to their businesses, American had little popularity with the chewing public or with any notable sector of the general public.[3]

A brief analysis of the entry of the American Tobacco Company into the chewing tobacco business reveals the dilemma that confronted Reynolds. American had been formed in 1890 by Duke, who forced a consolidation of the leading cigarette manufacturing interests of the country through improvement of the Bonsack cigarette machine. Early in the following year American entered the chewing tobacco business by purchasing the National Tobacco Works of Louisville, Kentucky, thus acquiring the famous Battle Ax plug brand. In 1894 the company increased its sales "in a severe competitive fight in the plug-tobacco business" and the next year purchased the James G. Butler Tobacco Company of St. Louis. The American Tobacco Company continued to enlarge its grip on the navy plug business, which was based on the use of Burley leaf, and in the early fall of 1898 purchased the Brown Tobacco Company and the Drummond Tobacco Company, both of St. Louis. American now controlled a large segment of the chewing tobacco business. By price cutting and by refusing to sell cigarettes to wholesale dealers unless they also purchased its Battle Ax and other chewing tobacco brands, the American Tobacco Company reached a commanding position.[4] Profits on cigarettes compensated the company for losses on chewing tobacco. Independent manufacturers of chewing tobacco sought to hold back the tide but it was impossible. For a time during the 1890s R. J. Reynolds supported the *News and Observer* edited by Josephus Daniels and *Webster's Weekly* edited by John R. Webster in Reidsville, North Carolina, in their campaign to keep American from driving other tobacco manufacturers out of business in the state and, so they thought, to save the farmers from being subjected to a monopoly.[5] But their efforts proved futile against the Continental Tobacco Company, which acquired the firm of P. H. Mayo and Brother of Richmond, Virginia, a producer of flat plug.[6] Large-scale financiers aided in the formation of Continental, and other financiers who had been attempting to organize opposing independent manufacturers were brought into the company, so that its directors included such top-ranking figures from Wall Street as Oliver H. Payne, Herbert L. Terrell, Thomas F. Ryan, Grant B. Schley, William C. Whitney, Peter A. B. Widener, and Anthony N. Brady.[7] Continental, eventually to be merged with American, thus commanded immense capital at its formation and almost unlimited funds shortly thereafter.

Two points should be emphasized in regard to the formation of the Continental Tobacco Company: (1) through its many branches it entered the manufacture of flat plug, which was the particular product of Virginia and North Carolina, and (2) with the American Tobacco Company, it discontinued purchasing other companies outright and destroying their corporate identity. After this time both American and Continental followed the practice of holding a majority of the stock in companies that they acquired. This policy of dominating subsidiaries through control of a majority of the stock was based on two practical considerations: (1) control of a company through a majority holding, rather than by outright purchase, cost less, and (2) it permitted the subsidiary to retain its name and its officers with their loyalty, thus making for better relations and more profit.[8] By entering the combination as a subsidiary, the Reynolds firm lost neither its corporate identity nor a semblance of independence in the eyes of the public as it would have by being merged into the Continental Tobacco Company.

Without knowing with absolute certainty when or how Reynolds met this situation, it is safe to assume that it was not many days after 10 December 1898. James B. Duke's answer to this question may be correct:[9]

> After the Continental Tobacco Co. was formed he [R. J. Reynolds] came up with the idea of selling his business to them. I personally told Reynolds that the Continental Tobacco Co. had no organization to manufacture, or that knew how to manufacture his style of goods and that I would not favor buying it unless he should stay and run it, and that I did not think he was the kind of a man to run a business that he had no interest in—a rich man. I told him we would take two-thirds of it at the price he named because I thought it was a good investment and manufactured an entirely different class of goods

from what the Continental Tobacco Co. manufactured. They are sold in the Southern States and I did not consider they were in competition with the Continental Tobacco Co.'s plug because it is a different class of goods.

One thing is certain: Reynolds did not wish it known that he approached Duke. Later developments indicate that he desired to be viewed as an underdog who had been maltreated by the monopolistic American Tobacco Company. As one story goes, Reynolds conferred with James B. Duke, who said he would market his Battle Ax brand and destroy Reynolds. Thereupon R. J., whose price was $2 million, replied that it would cost Duke $2 million to do so.[10] In his later years William N. Reynolds stated that "a Mr. Cobb, vice president of the American Tobacco Company," hearing that Reynolds was trying to increase his capital stock, wrote R. J. to come to New York for a conference. On the other hand, a younger man, who served many years as Will Reynolds's secretary, later testified that R. J. went directly to Duke for additional capital.[11] Will Reynolds declared further that R. J. called on Cobb, undoubtedly John B. Cobb, vice-president of the American Tobacco Company, who asked how much stock R. J. wished to sell. When Reynolds stated his need for $300,000, Cobb suggested that he and James B. Duke take the stock. Supposedly they bought the stock, which the Reynolds brothers considered a personal matter. Stockholders in the American Tobacco Company then insisted that Cobb and Duke transfer their stock to the company.[12]

It is more likely that R. J. Reynolds approached Duke directly. In view of the situation in the tobacco industry at that time, it would have been unrealistic to do otherwise. Moreover, it was acknowledged many years later that, when Reynolds's business grew faster than his capital, he sold two-thirds of his stock to Duke and two of his associates in the belief that they were buying it for themselves and not for the Continental Tobacco Company, in whose name the stock was later issued.[13] R. J.'s often-quoted explanation to his friend Josephus Daniels of his entry into the tobacco trust lends weight to the conclusion that Reynolds sought out Duke in order to obtain capital:[14]

Toward the close of the session of the [N.C.] Legislature of 1899 a bill had been introduced authorizing the Reynolds Tobacco Company to increase its capital stock. Shortly after the session of the Legislature an announcement came from Winston-Salem which was a most astonishing one to those who thought that Reynolds was more than a match for Duke, that the capital stock of the R. J. Reynolds Company had been increased to five million dollars and the incorporators were R. J. Reynolds, W. N. Reynolds, J. B. Duke, George Gales, D. K. Faucette, and D. A. Keller. At the same time, it was announced that this company would be associated with the Continental Tobacco Company.

Not long after that I saw Dick Reynolds. We had long been very good friends and I expressed to him my great regret and disappointment that he had sold out to the Tobacco Trust. He said: "Don't you believe it. Sometimes you have to join hands with a fellow to keep him from ruining you and to get the under hold yourself." Then he narrated how the Dukes had gobbled up the Blackwells and the Hanes Company and said, "I don't intend to be swallowed. Buck Duke will find out he has met his equal, but I am fighting him now from the inside. You will never see the day when Dick Reynolds will eat out of Buck Duke's hands. If you will keep your eyes open, you will find that if any swallowing is done Dick Reynolds will do the swallowing. If Buck tries to swallow me he will have the belly-ache the balance of his life."

Meanwhile, in Reynolds's hometown rancor against the American Tobacco Company actually appeared before the company was first chartered in 1890. Rumors that the "trust" had been formed arose in the tobacco area of North Carolina and Virginia in mid-July 1889 and in the Winston-Salem area as early as June of that year.[15] Rumors regarding a combination of plug manufacturers continued to circulate in 1890 and again in 1892.[16] In February 1899 a local editor stated that a representative of the Continental Tobacco Company had been in town for a week or more attempting to add a number of Winston plug factories to that company. He called attention to the many unconfirmed rumors and one fact: the representative had approached a dozen or more Winston manufacturers. Whether or not any local manufacturers were entertaining Continental's proposals the editor did not know, but, he added: "Several of the larger concerns say very positively that they will not go into any combination, nor sell to the trust, and they mean what they say." The Continental agent, he then declared, was in Winston with his family, evidently prepared for a long stay if necessary.[17] Apparently Reynolds was giving no secrets away until the last minute, because he did not wish to incur unpopularity by announcing his association with the hated tobacco trust. A month later, however, the editor of the *Union Republican* tentatively identified the Continental agent as one Heath and repeated a general rumor that either two or six Winston tobacco manufacturing firms had given Heath options.[18] At last came news that the R. J. Reynolds Tobacco Company had closed its plant on 22 March 1899 for an inventory in order to increase its capital stock "under the provisions of the new charter," the object being "to erect a mammoth addition to the plant and to increase facilities in every way."[19] Yet the editor remained in the dark.

Actually the business, goodwill, and all property of the R. J. Reynolds Tobacco Company of North Carolina was transferred to the R. J. Reynolds Tobacco Company of New Jersey on 4 April 1899, as of 21 March;[20] hence arrangements for the inventory had probably been made prior to the closing on 22 March. The real meaning of these maneuvers did not reach the general public in Winston and Salem until 6 April when it was discovered that the charter came from the Mother of Trusts, as New Jersey was called, and not from the agrarian Tar Heel state. The editor's question at the end of the announcement revealed the general sentiment: "After the 'big fish' have swallowed all the 'little fellows' what then?"[21]

The Reynolds company's need of capital had been most urgent since early 1898 when the board of directors authorized the company to borrow as much as it needed up to $400,000. On 6 February 1899 an authorization for the same sum was approved by the directors. On that same day, R. J. reported that he had applied to "the present legislature" for an increase of the capital stock to $12 million—$4 million of preferred and $8 million of common—a move heartily approved by the stockholders.[22] It could be that Reynolds himself did not know early in 1899 that he would join the Continental Tobacco Company by 4 April. No doubt also he realized the significance of the general animosity toward the "Tobacco Trust."

New Capital and New Plans

What steps did Reynolds take now that his property and business had been chartered at the instance of the Continental Tobacco Company? First of all, the stock in the new company was authorized on the basis of a capital of $5,000,000 divided into 50,000 shares of a par value of $100 each. Of this original authorization, $2,100,000 was issued at the time of organization and owners of the R. J. Reynolds Tobacco Company of North Carolina received $1,721,300 with the balance of $378,700 subscribed and paid. Reynolds, members of his family, and John F. Parlett held 17,213 shares whereas the Continental Tobacco Company held 32,787 shares, representing almost two-thirds of the total unauthorized stock. The new company also was to pay the debts of the R. J. Reynolds Tobacco Company of North Carolina, unpaid on 21 March 1899, up to $333,739.[23]

Although Reynolds could no longer control his company, he could obtain capital, expand, and do the bidding of his board of directors composed of J. B. Cobb, George M. Gales, and D. A. Keller for one year each; William N. Reynolds and James B. Duke for two years each; and R. J.

Reynolds and C. K. Faucette for three years each. Within a matter of minutes after the transfer of the old company to the new, Gales, Keller, and Faucette resigned, and in their respective places Walter R. Reynolds, George W. Watts, and Benjamin N. Duke were chosen. The managers now were the Duke brothers and J. B. Cobb; the workers were the Reynolds brothers. R. J. Reynolds returned to Winston as president of the new company. B. N. Duke was first vice-president, W. N. Reynolds second vice-president, and George Richard Lybrook (21 November 1874–26 January 1902), nephew of the Reynolds brothers, secretary and treasurer.[24] Having completed organization in Newark, New Jersey, the group moved across the Hudson to 111 Fifth Avenue, where many a tobacco manufacturer had been forced to go. R. J.'s salary was fixed at $10,000, a sum no doubt astounding to him because his annual salary had been only $2,500. He believed in small salaries, hard work, and participation in company earnings. Will Reynolds, whose salary was set at $3,500, a raise of $1,000, was "to devote himself to the duties of buying leaf tobacco, and attending to the affairs of the Company as he formerly did." Appointed superintendent of the new company, Walter R. Reynolds again became "General superintendent of the Company's factories and manufacturing" at a salary of $2,500, an increase of $700 per year.[25]

On 11 April 1899 R. J. Reynolds took particular care to write his salesmen: ". . . this Company has not been sold to nor absorbed by any other company, is not and will not be known as a branch of any company. The business will be conducted under the management of the resident directors, Messrs. R. J., W. N. and W. R. Reynolds. Mr. R. J. Reynolds is president of the Company." With somewhat less accuracy, he went on to state that James B. Duke, of the American Tobacco Company, and others had taken stock in the R. J. Reynolds Tobacco Company. After listing the directors, he stated that no employees would be affected by the reorganization but that the company would "largely increase" its forces in every department, and that advantages gained by the reorganization should furnish an incentive to work with new zeal.[26] The same tone of independence pervaded the information given to the editor of the *Southern Tobacco Journal* before 13 April. The editor received correct facts relating to capitalization, directors, and officers, including the retirement of Robert Critz because of ill health. The remainder of the item accurately sums up R. J.'s intentions though perhaps with a tinge of braggadocio and some untrue statements:[27]

> While the Messrs. Duke and others of the American and the Continental are part owners of the new R. J. Reynolds' Tobacco Co., the Winston company will not be taken into either of the trusts nor be identified with them. It will be operated separately.

It has for some years been the largest manufacturer of flat goods in this country, its annual output having reached about 7,500,000 pounds. The facilities are to be increased, and it is expected that the production will be doubled, or over, before long. The contract for another factory building, of as great if not greater dimensions than the present one, is to be let as soon as plans can be drawn. Additional office forces and operatives, of course, will be employed, and the corps of salesman [sic] enlarged. The buyers on the leaf markets will be retained.

These are facts that have been obtained from authoritative sources.

R. J. Reynolds began to carry out these plans with great speed. Within one week of the appearance of the above summation, he had returned from a trip to New York to consult members of his company about plans for increasing production from 10 million to 15 million pounds. He also found that all aspects of the new building would be left entirely in his hands, and on 9 May 1899 he obtained plans from C. R. Makepeace and Company, which had designed Number 256 in 1891. On a lot at the southeast corner of Fourth and Church streets, which Reynolds purchased on 10 May, excavations began for Number 8 but trouble soon arose. A free running spring from the vicinity of the present Downtown Garage at Fifth and Main streets emptied water into the excavated area in a considerable rivulet. James Ballard Dyer (5 October 1869–19 August 1929), following Reynolds's orders, put 138 carloads of "Mt. Airy Rock" into the excavation before a solid foundation could be secured. Erected at a considerable distance from Number 256 for fear of fire, Number 8 for years was known as "the Flat-Top Building" in contrast to "the Old House," or Number 256.[28] The offices, which had once occupied a corner of the Old Red Factory and had moved in 1892 to the third floor of Number 256, facing Chestnut Street, now were moved to Number 8, where the arrangements, as befitted a New Jersey corporation, appeared much more pretentious. Instead of room for two offices, the space now occupied a considerable area extending all the way across the front, with the entrance on Church Street. In this area were R. J.'s office, a vault, the office of Will and Walter Reynolds, the mail and file department, possibly even then under the direction of Norman Blum, the secretary's office, a small office for Walter Reynolds's secretary, and a premium room larger than any other room except that of the sales department, presided over first by Rufus T. Stedman and later by Robert B. Horn. The new building had double the floor space of Number 256. As Number 8 neared completion, the Moravian bishop in Salem noted that the "new Reynolds factory which is rising is the largest building thus far erected in our city." Here the offices of the company remained until about the time of Reynolds's emergence into complete independence in 1911.[29]

Inside the two factories all was soon stir and bustle as supplies came in, machinery was installed, and production continued. An order of 66,000 pounds of glycerin indicated brisk activity. On 17 April 1899 Rufus T. Stedman purchased 200,000 waterproof cardboard signs for the smoking brand Our Advertiser to be ready for shipment on 10 May. Reynolds canceled his 1896 agency contract with the Adams Tobacco Press Company of Quincy, Illinois, and ordered for delivery on or before 15 December 1899 twenty Adams duplex presses, obtaining four of them free by virtue of his previous connections with the firm. On 10 November 1899 he bought twenty-four hydraulic shape presses with twelve-inch cylinders from Talbott and Sons of Richmond, Virginia. In the same year he arranged to get a Mayo-Hysore automatic machine "for drying, cooling and ordering tobacco of the capacity of 20,000 [pounds] per day of ten hours" to be "a duplicate of the machine built for the Continental Tobacco Company of Danville, Va., with the exception that steam pipes as is put in the machine for the American Tobacco Company at Kinston, N. C. and Timmonsville, S. C., each machine having a capacity of 20,000 [pounds] per day of ten hours." These machines cost more than $5,000 each. Again in 1899, the Kester Manufacturing Company of Winston and Salem agreed to furnish Reynolds two casing machines, one lump machine, eight combination box clamps, and six caddy clamps at a total cost of $3,011. Agreeing on 10 January 1900 to buy for $1,500 a softener from the Philadelphia Textile Machinery Company, Reynolds stipulated that cypress wood be used in its construction instead of pine. Two days later he ordered 40 million Schnapps tags, asking for 1 million per week and warning the manufacturer to be particularly careful in the shipment "as we are running prize schemes and are desirous that none of these tags become diverted from the usual channel." In New York early in 1900 he spoke with an agent of the manufacturers of General Electric Equipment Supplies about an "Intercommunicating" telephone system of six phones; shortly thereafter he installed the system.[30]

When Number 8 stood complete "with powerhouse and stack," it contained so many innovations that the leading U.S. tobacco publication featured it with photographs under the headline "Electricity in a Tobacco Factory." The writer referred to electrical equipment "recently" installed by the American Tobacco Company in its larger factories at St. Louis, Cincinnati, and Richmond but centered on "one of the most thoroughly modern and up-to-date tobacco factories in the world . . . that of the R. J. Reynolds branch of the American Tobacco Co., at Winston, N. C." The writer described the boilers and engines that generated power for operating tobacco dryers, forty duplex plug machines, machinery in the box factory, filler shakers, casing machines, wringing machines, tobacco steamers, and, among other things, a machine "used to drive a 42-inch fan for ventilating the factory." To a considerable extent similar machinery had been installed "for the same work in one of the other factories." With 315 "incandescent lamps" and motors "of the most approved patterns," the Reynolds factories were enabled "to produce an enormous output of manufactured tobacco under the most economic [sic] conditions." Finally, declared the writer, those who had recently visited and studied the methods followed by the leading tobacco factories in Europe "say that there is nothing either in England or on the Continent that can compare with the R. J. Reynolds plant in equipment."[31] Yet Reynolds had used few items not found in his "Old House" built in 1891. But with his new access to capital he had moved full into the twentieth century by beginning to rely on electric power instead of on his little twenty-five horsepower engine of the 1880s. It is doubtful, however, that these innovations alone could have produced a jump in production from 5,331,312 pounds of chewing tobacco in 1898 to 16,654,440 pounds in 1901. Nor is it likely that he could rely as heavily as before on the unskilled labor of the cotton choppers and blackberry pickers who still filled his factories.

Meanwhile James B. Duke did not so much as see Winston and Salem or one of Reynolds's factories until September 1903, when he came on his "special train" from Durham "to pay a social visit to Mr. R. J. Reynolds." At that time he did inspect the plant and approve R. J.'s plan to build another large storage house.[32] This visit in the grand manner, four years after he had acquired controlling stock in the company, illustrates the basic difference between Duke, the manipulator, and Reynolds, the doer. As general anger against the American Tobacco Company continued, it may be safely assumed that R. J. was learning from the ways of the manipulator.

Reynolds Takes Over the Flat Plug Industry

The R. J. Reynolds Tobacco Company, from its organization as a subsidiary of the Continental Tobacco Company on 4 April 1899, served as an agency to carry out the policy of consolidation in the manufacture of flat-plug chewing tobacco. In 1904 Continental was merged with the American Tobacco Company, and, with that formal move, the Reynolds company became a subsidiary of American in name as well as in fact.[33] This shift in organization made no real difference in policy or authority; the American Tobacco Company was the "Tobacco Combination," and it remained the task of the Reynolds company to consolidate the flat-plug industry of the Virginia-Carolina area. After a long and famous investigation the Commissioner of Corporations reported in 1909: "Through the R. J. Reynolds Tobacco Company the Tobacco Combination has been able to control the plug-tobacco business of the South with as great a measure of success as the Continental Tobacco Company met in its direct operations throughout the North and West."[34]

In following the various moves of the Reynolds company to carry out this policy, it is well to keep in mind that attempts were made to block these moves and that the money for buying out such firms as P. H. Hanes and Company came in part from Continental.[35] Whether this policy seemed distasteful to Reynolds and his resident directors is not known, but Will Reynolds stated many years later that the American Tobacco Company insisted that the Reynolds company purchase competitive firms in the Virginia-Carolina area. Some of these factories and their brands were of no value, he declared, and R. J. would not have bought them had he been allowed to follow his own judgment.[36] According to the Commissioner of Corporations, the three Winston-Salem companies purchased by Reynolds late in December 1900—P. H. Hanes and Company, B. F. Hanes and Company, and Brown Brothers and Company— together produced more than Reynolds in 1897. For 1900, the last year of independent operation by these three companies, Reynolds by far exceeded the other three companies, as the following figures indicate:[37]

Pounds	Producer
11,800,000	R. J. Reynolds Tobacco Company
8,000,000	Brown Brothers and Company
4,000,000	B. F. Hanes and Company
3,500,000	P. H. Hanes and Company

This remarkable advance by Reynolds in 1900 can only be attributed to his rapid addition of machinery in mid-1899 and the use of saccharin, not to the operation of Number 8, which did not begin production until July 1901. The conclusion naturally follows that the other three companies, comparatively strong in 1897, would soon have been reduced to unimportance in any event. It should be noted, however, that Reynolds acquired T. L. Vaughn and Company on 4 May 1900.

In following the policy of consolidation outlined by the Tobacco Combination, Reynolds first acquired the firm of T. L. Vaughn and Company, consisting of Vaughn, Madison Daughtry Stockton (10 April 1861–31 December 1944), and, ironically, Henry Roan, who had left Reynolds in 1893 because he felt him to be a dangerous plunger. There is some evidence that Vaughn may have approached Reynolds for this sale. In a letter dated 20 April 1900, which had been preceded by conversations, Vaughn proposed to sell the business at cost, although he first intended to list $10,000 as the bonus required for his brands. The typed figure of $10,000 has been crossed out and $1.00 substituted, whether by Vaughn or a representative of the Continental Tobacco Company it is not clear. The option was to expire on 5 May 1900. Two weeks later a local newspaper reported the sale with the information that Vaughn, because of ill health, had decided to retire from active business.[38]

Reynolds evidently sent Vaughn's letter of proposal to the Continental Tobacco Company without delay. Williamson Whitehead Fuller (28 August 1858–23 August 1934), counsel and director of Continental, replied on 26 April 1900, giving the R. J. Reynolds Tobacco Company detailed instructions for the transaction, followed by these two sentences to make the purchase legal and possibly secret in every respect: "*Do not have the paper registered.* Simply file it in your own safe." Evidently Fuller did not wish the sale to be publicized. He also suggested a partial payment of $50,000 or $60,000, a shift of the insurance on the Vaughn plant to the Reynolds firm, and necessary permits to be secured from the U.S. Department of Internal Revenue for the removal of the Vaughn machinery and tobacco. Fuller also clipped Vaughn's estimated cost figures from the sheet submitted by the latter and returned them to Reynolds marked carefully with instructions that the figures were "not to be made parts of the conveyance." In the contract of sale, dated 30 April 1900 and prepared, or at least revised, by Fuller, it was agreed that T. L. Vaughn and Company would write a circular letter to its trade explaining the sale and requesting patronage for the R. J. Reynolds Tobacco Company, would give Reynolds a list of its customers, and would allow until 1 June for the removal of machinery and other purchases. Other clauses in the contract of sale provided that the Vaughn company could sell its manufactured tobacco until midnight of 3 May, that Reynolds would pay all leases on buildings at the expiration date, that the insurance policies would be transferred to the Reynolds company, that Vaughn would furnish Reynolds a list of its salesmen with its contracts, that Reynolds would employ certain of Vaughn's employees, including William Vincent Garner (29 October 1862–31 August 1937), and that Vaughn would guarantee until January 1901 to keep in good condition the leaf tobacco acquired by Reynolds in the transaction. It was a tight contract followed by an inventory taken 9–11 May 1900. According to the inventory the value of the machinery and equipment amounted to $34,058, to which $10,000 was added in pencil presumably for goodwill. The Commissioner of Corporations reported the sale price as $90,506.[39]

By this purchase the R. J. Reynolds Tobacco Company received all of T. L. Vaughn and Company's trade names, trademarks, and brands, although according to the bill of sale the purchaser was chiefly interested in the name T. L. Vaughn and in sixteen of the one hundred different brands listed by Vaughn in 1899: T. L. Vaughn & Co.'s Natural Leaf, T. L. Vaughn & Co.'s Very Fine, Big Auger, Black Horse, Broad Ax, Elegant, Gold Wedge, King of North Carolina, Life Boat, Old Rover, Our Boy, Pot Rack, Red Apple, Red Snapper, Spot, and Stampede. On the bill of sale, the brands Jumbo and Opera had been inked out.[40] Red Apple or Apple served the Reynolds company as a best-seller for many years, and Black Horse has long continued in production. It may well be that one of the most valuable acquisitions in this purchase was the unfulfilled contract of William V. Garner, who served as superintendent of Number 8 for many years. Judging from the inventory and the final selling figure, T. L. Vaughn and Company received better than a fair price. The only hint of Vaughn's willingness to sell, however, came from a newspaper item that may have been a face-saving device. On the other hand, after the letter of proposal, the transaction moved along smoothly and rapidly. It is said that later, when in a fractious mood, Vaughn threatened to kill Reynolds, and for a time D. Rich and another employee stood guard over R. J.'s home at night.[41] The bitter antitrust feelings of the day made this sale an important event in the Winston-Salem area.

No such records exist for the acquisition of Brown Brothers and Company of Winston, although the general procedure bears a similarity to that of the Vaughn purchase. Originally known as Brown and Brother and composed of Dr. W. L. Brown (20 January 1831–16 May 1899) and Rufus D. Brown (1836–3 October 1893), the firm had begun operations in Mocksville before the Civil War. In 1877 the plant was moved to Winston. The death of Rufus D. Brown in 1893 and a disastrous fire in the same year seriously affected the business. But by leasing two factories and remodeling another plant, the firm produced 800,000 pounds of chewing and smoking tobacco and cigarettes in 1900. At that time it was considered the third largest tobacco manufacturing plant in Winston. The death of Dr. W. L. Brown in 1899 and the death of two sons-in-law, who were his partners, left only a son, who had withdrawn from the company to serve as secretary of the Southern Chemical Company.[42] It was not surprising, therefore, when a local newspaper announced that Brown Brothers and Company had been acquired by the R. J. Reynolds Tobacco Company and that the acquisition resembled that of T. L. Vaughn and Company because the owners wished to retire from business. Somewhat less gullible than the local editor, an editor in New York felt otherwise: "Two weeks ago TOBACCO stated that indications pointed strongly to the acquisition of two Winston, N. C., plug tobacco factories by the Continental Tobacco Co., or in its interest. This was following the acquisition of the Brown Bros.' factory there by the R. J. Reynolds Tobacco Co., of which Company's stock the Continental holds a controlling interest."[43]

On 30 November 1900 the directors of the R. J. Reynolds Tobacco

Company approved Brown Brothers and Company's proposal to sell its business to them, including all leaf tobacco, manufactured tobacco, trademarks, and goodwill, the last item valued at five dollars. Brown Brothers wished Reynolds to retain its salesmen and employees for the duration of their contracts, although this was not compulsory. The directors later approved a five-year lease of the leaf house and factory of Brown Brothers and Company and the payment of $67,615 for the business.[44] In 1894 the most popular brands made by Brown Brothers were Anchor, Brown's Mule, Cottage Home, Long Horn, Old Rip Van Winkle, Ruby, and Waverly. Of the ninety brands listed by Brown Brothers in 1899, Brown's Mule became one of the most profitable brands of chewing tobacco ever manufactured by the R. J. Reynolds Tobacco Company. Contemporary opinion held that the sales price did not constitute "any fancy figures";[45] this would seem to be true, although, in the absence of an inventory, such a conclusion perhaps should not be drawn. But the immense popularity of Brown's Mule for many years and its continuous production since 1894 demonstrate the bargain obtained by Reynolds. Brown's Mule is said to have been R. J. Reynolds's favorite chew. The story still goes among the older employees that once R. J., when on a train in West Virginia, spat out the window and accidentally hit a man in the face. As the man rushed into the car, Reynolds remained in his seat willing to make any kind of apology. But the man only wanted to know what brand R. J. used because he intended switching to it immediately.

The purchase of P. H. Hanes and Company by Reynolds involved none of the uncertain factors relating to the purchase of Brown Brothers and Company. A formal decision to buy the P. H. Hanes company came simultaneously with the decision to purchase Brown Brothers—on 30 November 1900, eight days after Hanes had submitted his proposal for sale.[46] After working in the tobacco factory of Dulin and Booe in Mocksville and for one year as a partner in that firm, Pleasant Henderson Hanes, with his brother John Wesley Hanes and Thomas J. Brown, moved to Winston and organized P. H. Hanes and Company. Later Brown retired from the partnership and two other Hanes brothers, Phillip (1 May 1852–1 March 1903) and Benjamin Franklin (1853?–24 August 1894), entered the firm. The company operated two plants, one in its own name and the other as B. F. Hanes and Company.[47] They were highly successful manufacturers, as their combined production of 7,500,000 pounds in 1900 indicates; in the words of the editor of *Tobacco*, they were "both large concerns, long established . . . enjoying a reputation far beyond . . . [their] surrounding locality."[48] It is probable that P. H. Hanes initiated the move for this sale or that he considered selling directly to the Continental Tobacco Company.[49] By rumor, still extant in Winston-Salem, P. H. Hanes went to Duke with that intention but found that Reynolds had preceded him.

P. H. Hanes, in his letter proposing to sell, offered to convey all of his company's brands, trademarks, symbols, goodwill, and the trade names of P. H. Hanes and B. F. Hanes to the Reynolds firm for $175,000. All real estate, machinery at a discount of 10 percent, furniture at a discount of 25 percent, casing and wrapping materials, tags, and so forth at cost, all leaf tobacco bought on markets other than Winston at cost when delivered in Winston, and all tobacco in process at two cents less per pound than when completely manufactured were offered at a total cost of $200,000 "in the stock of your Company out of the increase proposed to be made, at par, and the balance at cash." Hanes guaranteed payment of outstanding bills, the redemption of tags, and any outstanding lien. He gave Reynolds eight days to accept the offer with the hope that the matter would be "closed up" as expeditiously as possible. The inventory, which included 3,462,987 pounds of leaf tobacco and office furniture in Winston and Salem and in "the Baltimore office," amounted to $529,154. According to the bill of sale P. H. Hanes and Company received $471,951 in cash and 2,000 shares of capital stock in the R. J. Reynolds Tobacco Company. The Reynolds directors considered the true value of the Hanes plant to be $702,951.[50] In the bill of sale P. H. Hanes listed fifty-three different brands and indicated that Apple Jack, Early Bird, Greek Slave, Man's Pride, Missing Link, Natural Leaf, O. N. T., and Speckled Beauty were outstanding. He also listed two new brands not appearing on his list submitted to *Connorton's Tobacco Brand Directory of the United States for 1899*: Cutter and Maggie May. For the B. F. Hanes Company twenty-six important brands were listed including seven names not listed in the brand directory for 1899: Dick's Pet, Nectar Twist, Old Peach, Quaker City, R & D, Monumental City, and Special Drive. B. F. Hanes's best brands were B. F. Hanes' Best, Dick's Pet, Frog, Golden Chair, Natural Leaf, and Red Rabbit. Of all these brands Reynolds was perhaps happiest to get Early Bird, which had been a keen rival of Schnapps for many years.[51] Reynolds agreed to assume the contracts of twelve Hanes employees, among them E. G. Hester, Henry Arthur George (27 March 1872–4 December 1945), and Walter S. Lindsay, who served at different times as superintendent of Number 8 and Number 256 for the manufacture of chewing tobacco.[52]

An intriguing aspect of this transaction has to do with James Sloan (2 December 1871–29 October 1948), head bookkeeper for P. H. Hanes and Company. During the stir over the impending sale of the Hanes company in November 1899, Sloan resigned to accept a similar position with the American Tobacco Company in New York.[53] At a later date, however, he returned to Winston, joined the R. J. Reynolds Tobacco Company and eventually became a director, thus making it seem that Sloan went to New York to learn American's bookkeeping system. Perhaps Reynolds needed a more skillful bookkeeper for his rapidly accumulating businesses.

P. H. Hanes and Company was well paid for its business. Nevertheless, Reynolds profited from the purchase for many years, especially from the sale of Man's Pride and Greek Slave as well as from other Hanes brands. He also had obtained the chief rival of Schnapps. It is often stated in Winston-Salem that the basis of the Hanes family fortune lay in the 2,000 shares of capital stock in the R. J. Reynolds Tobacco Company obtained in 1899. Although there is no indisputable proof, it appears that John W. Hanes was slated to become first vice-president of the Reynolds company in charge of the factory and business formerly owned by P. H. Hanes and Company.[54] It is generally believed that Hanes refused the position because he wished to engage in some business more useful and uplifting to humankind than the manufacture of tobacco.[55] Despite the apparent satisfaction of the principals involved in the transaction, the purchase of the Hanes business by Reynolds caused much talk about the dangers of monopoly. A local editor wrote: "The R. J. R. Tobacco Co. will soon be 'Monarch of all it surveys' so far as the tobacco manufacturing industry in Winston is concerned. . . . When we state that the bulk of mail matter received for Winston goes to the R. J. R. Tobacco Co. the magnitude of business done by this firm is thus briefly told." Less than four months later he believed that "more people are employed by the R. J. R. Co. than by any other firm or corporation in the State."[56] The same editor also marveled at the pipes being run from the new Reynolds factory to the old one in order to transport power for operating machinery by hydraulic pressure. Moreover a pipe connection was made with the Hanes factory. This, he declared, meant the saving of an engine, fuel, and fireman—"a contest between labor and labor saving appliances."[57]

Reynolds's next acquisition came by a very different method. The firm of Pegram and Penn at Madison in nearby Rockingham County, operated as early as 1896 by Harry J. Penn and one Pegram, went into receivership in May 1902, with liabilities estimated at $40,000 and assets at about $20,000. Sold by the receiver at public auction on 1 June 1902, the plant fell to R. J. Reynolds, the highest bidder, for $550. Reynolds thereby obtained all of the firm's trade names, trademarks, goodwill, and brands, the most valuable of which were Magic, Nigger Baby, Our Favorite, Red Jacket, Sallie Jay, Seven Up, Tug of War, and Whole Chunk. Reynolds acted promptly in order to profit from this purchase by preparing a price list, which was ready by 10 July 1902, for Nigger Baby, Sallie Jay, Tug of War, and Whole Chunk "formerly manufactured by Pegram and Penn of Madison."[58] No worries about the growth of monopoly were expressed because of this acquisition.

No direct records are available for R. J.'s acquisition of the business of his brother, Abram D. Reynolds, in Bristol, Tennessee. In July 1897 it was widely reported that A. D. Reynolds, who had started from nothing and made a total profit of $525,000 in twenty years as a tobacco manufacturer, had sold his plant to a syndicate for $30,000. Supposedly the motivation for selling lay in his religious convictions against the sale of spirituous liquors. He had finally come to regard the tobacco business as incompatible with his convictions.[59] On 24 September 1897 the state of Tennessee granted a charter for the operation of the A. D. Reynolds Tobacco Company to John J. Hager, Anson King, Charles W. Bondurant, N. D. Bachman, Jr., and Hardin Harbour Reynolds, whose tobacco manufacturing business in Winston had failed as a result of the panic of 1893. On 17 January 1898, no doubt erroneously, the *Southern Tobacco Journal* reported that the transfer of Major A. D. Reynolds's tobacco business in Bristol to the R. J. Reynolds Tobacco Company had occurred on 1 January 1898. In Bristol, however, the charter of A. D.'s company was amended on 9 January 1899 "for the purpose of increasing the capitol [*sic*]" from $75,000 to $100,000. At that time the board of directors included five men to whom the charter had been granted. Among them were John H. Caldwell and Benjamin Lewis Dulaney (1857–4 March 1930), the latter a promoter of industry who engaged in the development of numerous businesses in the Bristol area. Again, on 8 May 1899, the same group (except that A. P. Pepper had replaced N. D. Bachman, Jr.) had the capital stock increased to $150,000.[60]

Nothing more appears until the A. D. Reynolds Tobacco Company of Bristol was purchased by the American Tobacco Company in 1902, when its annual output stood at 300,000 pounds.[61] Apparently Benjamin L. Dulaney served as president of the Bristol company in 1902 and continued to do so until the firm was liquidated in 1904. When testifying in the antitrust suit in 1907, Percival Smith Hill (5 April 1862–27 December 1925) identified Dulaney as "the gentleman with whom I negotiated the unfortunate transaction with the [A. D.] Reynolds Tobacco Company." On 15 August 1903 Hill wrote Dulaney urging him not to buy any leaf tobacco, intimating that the American Tobacco Company would take what it could off Dulaney's hands. Hill also asked Dulaney to take up with American's leaf department head the matter of selling some of the high-priced leaf that the Reynolds firm in Bristol had on hand. In conclusion, he wrote: "When you come to New York you seem to get away before the matter can be definitely determined upon." Hill told the prosecuting attorney that Dulaney bought tobacco when he didn't need it, and that "we" didn't want him to invest his money in tobacco "because he didn't seem to have much sense as to the way of buying it." Hill wrote on 21 August 1903 that May Queen smoking tobacco, the leading brand of the Bristol company, was practically dead in the Chicago area.[62] He did not recall when the American Tobacco Company purchased an interest in the Reynolds firm of Bristol, although he himself had carried on the necessary negotiations with Dulaney; nor did he recall any details connected with the acquisition. He stated, however, that May Queen smoking tobacco was still being sold in 1907, that the Reynolds company in Bristol still existed, that dividends were being paid on its stock, but that it was not an operating company. The factory, he declared, had been closed as a matter of economy and May Queen was being produced in another factory of the American Tobacco Company. When the prosecuting attorney produced a letter from the Reynolds company of Bristol, dated 4 July 1902 and addressed to Hill, the latter then recalled that American secretly acquired its interest in the factory about that time.

In further testimony Hill stated that the transaction had been a very trivial one, that Dulaney had had little to do with the management of the Bristol firm, and that he had had a number of interviews with Dulaney. Additional testimony by Hill revealed that another active brand of the firm was Bristol Club, that Dulaney wished Hill to have the Neudecker wholesale tobacco dealers in Baltimore stop giving the impression that the Reynolds firm "belongs to the Trust," that considerable friction developed between the American Tobacco Company and Dulaney's firm over the poor results of the latter, that Dulaney wished on 11 August 1903 to borrow money from American in order to purchase 500,000 pounds of leaf tobacco, that Dulaney carried on all his dealings with the American Tobacco Company through Hill, that Dulaney had great faith that his new brand, Union Lad, would sell in Cincinnati but that some losses would be incurred at first, that Dulaney wanted American to subsidize his firm's actual net losses incurred in such a campaign, and that on 3 September 1903 Dulaney strongly objected to American's excessive charges in buying leaf for his firm. Hill also said that Dulaney wrote him a lengthy letter on 21 September 1903 filled with complaints against Hill and the American Tobacco Company. In it Dulaney answered Hill's complaint of not being able to see him in New York by stating that in the previous week he had called at Hill's office for three consecutive days, waiting in vain one entire morning to see him. Dulaney declared that Hill had promised to furnish his firm leaf at cost and carriage and to remove all opposition of the American salesmen to the Bristol brands, but, instead, Hill had perpetrated such frauds as furnishing his company with $500 worth of second-hand machinery for $2,500. In conclusion Dulaney wrote: "Now, Mr. Hill, let us deal frankly with each other; and if it is your intention to put our company out of business let us do so amicably and save every dollar possible to the stockholders."[63] Hill, of course, contended that the Bristol firm was incompetent. He may have been correct, but stories of such tactics by American, rampant during these years, accounted for R. J.

Reynolds's tendency to put on a show of having been forced into the American Tobacco Company.

Hill's account generally agrees with the time factors revealed by the Commissioner of Corporations: that American acquired the Reynolds company of Bristol through the purchase of 58 percent of its capital stock for $140,000 in 1902 but that the company was discontinued on 30 June 1904.[64] Hill's further testimony explained the liquidation of the Bristol firm but revealed nothing concerning R. J.'s acquisition of his brother's old business. Because the Bristol firm could not make any money, Hill declared, he and Dulaney, who represented the minority stockholders, agreed to sell the assets, to pay off the stockholders, and, as far as the value of the brands was concerned, to turn the brands over to the American Tobacco Company for manufacturing, paying the stockholders a royalty. This arrangement, Hill declared on 2 August 1907, prevailed at that time.[65] It must follow, therefore, that the flat plug brands of A. D. Reynolds's old business went to the R. J. Reynolds Tobacco Company and the smoking tobacco to American. At any rate R. J.'s firm manufactured some of the brands listed by the A. D. Reynolds Tobacco Company in 1899. Yet the Commissioner of Corporations reported that the R. J. Reynolds Tobacco Company acquired the Reynolds Tobacco Company of Bristol in 1902. However the American Tobacco Company handled the matter with its Winston subsidiary, R. J. Reynolds obtained at least seventy-six brands for his ever-growing list.

Unlike Reynolds's previous direct acquisitions, the purchase of Liipfert, Scales and Company of Winston was made in secrecy. Secrecy in many of American's acquisitions undertaken during 1902–4 was followed by years of concealment of true ownership.[66] As a matter of fact, however, Liipfert, Scales and Company itself represented acquisitions of several companies of the Winston-Salem area. It was descended from Hamlen, Liipfert and Company, a partnership including Chesley Hamlen, Frank Julius Liipfert (25 July 1866–2 April 1927), and Melvin S. Hamlen. Liipfert, Scales consisted of Frank J. Liipfert, James Kirkpatrick Norfleet (10 March 1870–2 November 1930), Robert Comer Norfleet (14 September 1872–3 July 1941), and James S. Scales (19 June 1840–22 January 1916). Significant also is the fact that Hamlen, Liipfert and Company began work with the factory and machinery that they had obtained from the receivership sale of Bynum and Crutchfield, an older tobacco manufacturing firm of Winston.[67] Of their many brands, some were created by the company, some by its predecessor companies, some by W. T. Gray and Company prior to 1892, some by Bynum, Cotton and Company prior to 1895, some by Lockett, Vaughn and Company prior to 1900, some by Casey and Wright prior to 1900, and others by the company of Thomas Albert Crews (18 April 1860–24 December 1940) of Walkertown, near

Winston.[68] It should be noted also that James S. Scales had manufactured tobacco in the 1870s under the tutelage of Randall Duke Hay (2 December 1827–23 October 1885), then in nearby Madison.[69] It is evident that numerous tobacco manufacturing companies had failed long before R. J. Reynolds began consolidating the flat-plug industry under the aegis of the American Tobacco Company.

In response to a proposal from the R. J. Reynolds Tobacco Company for the purchase of a two-thirds interest in its business, Liipfert, Scales and Company gave the following conditions on 24 June 1903: Liipfert, Scales was to be reorganized with a capital of $300,000; the Reynolds company would pay $200,000 for 2,000 shares of stock and Liipfert, Scales $60,000 for 1,000 shares; the Reynolds company would pay in cash or stock $20,000 for brands and goodwill and $26,000 for real estate and machinery; the new company, which was to be chartered under the same name if possible, would take over at cost such items as leaf tobacco, supplies, labels, tags, all ledger accounts considered good at the time of inventory, and the old firm's liabilities. The new firm would retain Frank J. Liipfert, Robert C. Norfleet, and James K. Norfleet in their respective departments at an annual salary of $5,000 each, and continue all existing contracts with employees of the old company. This proposal evidently got a cold reception, because two days later the Reynolds company received a modified plan by which Liipfert, Scales and Company offered its brands and goodwill with no price attached, accepted the annual salaries of $3,333 for Liipfert and the Norfleets, and raised the value of real estate and machinery by $300.[70] An agreement dated 18 August 1903 followed, guaranteeing that the cost of real estate and machinery would not exceed $27,300, that a full schedule of all debts and an inventory would be submitted to the Reynolds company, that Reynolds would be permitted to inspect the books and records of Liipfert, Scales, and that, as soon as possible after the inventory, the partners would form a new corporation under the laws of North Carolina with a capitalization of $300,000. The partners were to subscribe for 1,000 shares and the R. J. Reynolds Tobacco Company for 2,000 shares all to be paid in cash. Then came the "secrecy" clause: ". . . since it is proposed that the connection of the Reynolds Company with the said new corporation shall not be publicly known, the said subscription by the Reynolds Company may be by its nominees instead of by it directly and the certificates of stock may issue to its nominees, to be by them endorsed in blank and delivered to the Reynolds Company instead of said certificate issuing directly to said Reynolds Company." Another clause provided that immediately after the formation of the new corporation, the Reynolds company would sell to it the P. H. Hanes Company's new factory on Church Street for $40,000 in cash.[71]

Next in the file chronologically, and appropriately so, comes a letter marked "personal" to R. J. Reynolds, president of the R. J. Reynolds Tobacco Company, from Junius Parker (24 September 1867–11 June 1944), assistant counsel to the Continental Tobacco Company, stating that he had made his office copy of the contract or agreement with Liipfert, Scales and Company and that he was returning the original because "your Company, and not any of our Companies here, is the proper party to hold the original."[72] Soon the local newspaper, dutifully but none the wiser, carried statements that the Liipfert-Scales Company, its new name, had been granted a charter with an authorized capital of $300,000 and that the new company had purchased the six-story brick factory formerly occupied by P. H. Hanes and Company at a cost of $25,000 to $30,000.[73]

Possibly as a part of its plan to become affiliated with the Reynolds company, the Liipfert-Scales Company served as the means for acquiring yet another firm. On 31 March 1904 Thomas A. Crews and James W. Crews, tobacco manufacturers in Walkertown under the firm name of T. A. Crews, agreed to sell all their manufactured tobacco, brands, tags, goodwill, formulas, trademarks, and secret processes to Liipfert-Scales for $1,000.[74]

The Liipfert-Scales Company prospered under the new arrangements, which continued to be a secret from the public. The Commissioner of Corporations reported that the stock of the company was increased to $400,000 in July 1906, and to $500,000 in 1907. He estimated that the value of its goodwill was $100,000 and that the percent of earnings on the total assets amounted to 6.5 in 1905, 12.3 in 1907, and 15.1 in 1908. His report also indicated that loans to the company, principally from the R. J. Reynolds Tobacco Company, amounted to almost $200,000 in 1905 and 1906, to $45,000 in 1907, and to more than $300,000 in 1908. He reported that control of Liipfert-Scales "was kept secret for several years." Actually this policy of secrecy was ordered from 111 Fifth Avenue by the Continental Tobacco Company. On 19 April 1904, two months before the formal proposal of the R. J. Reynolds Tobacco Company to purchase the Liipfert-Scales Company, the following directive came from 111 Fifth Avenue to George W. Coan, secretary of the Reynolds company: "Your Board should also ratify the L. S. deal, and if your entire Board is not conversant with this latter transaction you might arrange to have those members who are conversant with the deal attend the meeting. You of course realize that we must not exploit these matters too much before the public." When questioned about this item, Coan stated that authorities at Reynolds sometimes referred to Liipfert-Scales by name and sometimes as "Number 14."[75] It should be kept in mind that while Reynolds controlled two-thirds of the Liipfert-Scales Company, the Continental Tobacco Company controlled two-thirds of the R. J. Reynolds Tobacco Company. But by these deals and counterdeals Reynolds had garnered at least thirty-five additional brands of chewing tobacco made by Liipfert-Scales and nineteen brands of T. A. Crews as listed in the 1903 brand directory.[76] After the decree dissolving the Tobacco Combination, the Reynolds company purchased the one-third interest in the Liipfert-Scales Company held at that time by James S. Scales, Robert C. and James K. Norfleet, P. O. Leak, and Frank J. Liipfert and merged the subsidiary into its own operations without further secrecy.[77]

Consolidation of the southern flat-plug industry was incomplete, however, until manufacturers in the area of Martinsville, Virginia, could be merged with the R. J. Reynolds Tobacco Company. At the same time as it purchased a controlling interest in the Liipfert-Scales Company, the Reynolds company obtained a controlling interest in D. H. Spencer and Sons (Incorporated) of Martinsville. This firm was a combination planned in 1903 by Reynolds for merging D. H. Spencer and Sons (controlled by D. W. Spencer), Spencer Brothers (controlled by J. D. Spencer of Danville and J. M. Spencer of Martinsville), and B. F. Gravely and Sons (controlled by H. C. Gravely). The few stockholders came generally from the Gravely and Spencer families, long connected with the production of well-known brands of chewing tobacco in Henry County, Virginia.[78]

The first move involved D. H. Spencer and Sons, Spencer Brothers, and R. J. Reynolds Tobacco Company, which agreed in December 1903 to form a corporation under the laws of Virginia with an authorized capital of $500,000—$300,000 of common stock and $200,000 of 6 percent noncumulative preferred stock. As soon after the formation of the new company as possible D. W. Spencer was to sell his business, brands, and formulas to D. H. Spencer and Sons (Incorporated) and was not to engage in the manufacture of tobacco for fifteen years. J. D. and J. M. Spencer likewise were to convey all their business to the new corporation. On 4 March 1904 H. C. Gravely agreed to convey all of his business to the new corporation.[79] On 23 July 1906 D. H. Spencer and Sons (Incorporated) presumably decided to turn over its formulas, recipes, treatments, patent rights, copyrights, trademarks, and brand symbols to the R. J. Reynolds Tobacco Company for one dollar. A part of the agreement called for an inventory in order to arrive at a price for the factory and its equipment. To handle the details of this transaction Reynolds received the expert advice of Ambrose Hammet Burroughs (8 May 1859–19 June 1929), then assistant counsel to the American Tobacco Company.[80] What Reynolds paid for control of the stock in D. H. Spencer and Sons (Incorporated) was never known to the Commissioner of Corporations. The fact that R. J. had control remained secret for a number of years.

There was discord involved in the purchase of D. H. Spencer and Sons (Incorporated). On 12 March 1907 J. H. Spencer, president of the firm, wrote to the R. J. Reynolds Tobacco Company that his company refused to execute the paper presented to him on that day by Walter R. Reynolds until it was changed. His explanation is highly suggestive:[81]

> Our objection to the paragraph stricken out is that it makes us say that we offered to go out of business as an inducement to get you to buy the concern of D. H. Spencer and Sons, Inc. This is not in accordance with the facts in the case, and you can readily see that we can not sign a paper containing any such clause.

> Our objection to the other clause stricken out is that it purports to say on its face that we were receiving valuable consideration for good will, brands, etc. and for going out of business. This also, as you know, is not in accordance with facts.

> We are perfectly willing to execute the contract as amended by us, or any other contract that will carry out our agreement of July 23, 1906, but will go no further.

The Commissioner of Corporations nevertheless reported that D. H. Spencer and Sons (Incorporated) was closed in 1906 and its brands were produced thereafter in the Reynolds plant in Winston. Whatever human feelings were aroused, the papers on the purchase of the firm by the Reynolds company contain an inventory, dated 26 February 1907, attached to a rough draft of a sales agreement on which $314,255.49 is written as the price Reynolds paid in cash. On the back of a certificate for 1,500 shares of preferred stock in D. H. Spencer and Sons (Incorporated) issued to the R. J. Reynolds Tobacco Company on 16 November 1906, there is in handwriting: "Paid $75,000.00 on the within stock. March 25-1907—same being a 50% dividend in liquidation thereof." In connection with this quotation it is perhaps pertinent to note that R. J. Reynolds, when reporting to his directors on 2 September 1904, stated that D. H. Spencer and Sons (Incorporated) had increased its preferred stock to $300,000 and its common stock to $500,000. He also said that he had subscribed $50,000 for preferred stock, with which he had received as a bonus $100,000 of the common stock of D. H. Spencer and Sons (Incorporated), the $50,000 to be carried on the books at par and the common at one-half par.[82]

Secrecy also dominated the operations of D. H. Spencer and Sons (Incorporated) after it became a subsidiary of the R. J. Reynolds Tobacco Company. It, too, was referred to by a number. An official of the Continental Tobacco Company, on 18 January 1904, advised George W. Coan that the bookkeeper, who was to install American's system of bookkeeping in the plant of D. H. Spencer and Sons (Incorporated) under the auspices of the Reynolds company, be given an anonymous name. Under the circumstances the Continental official felt that secrecy was advisable. On

6 April 1904 Caleb Conley Dula (8 February 1864–26 December 1930), a director of the American and Continental tobacco companies, stated that one of his associates had received a letter, with a note enclosed, from D. H. Spencer and Sons (Incorporated) requesting Continental to discount the note and place the proceeds to its credit in the Second National Bank. Dula's explanation of the way this simple transaction was handled indicates that it was American and Continental who insisted on secrecy, not Reynolds:[83]

> Mr. [Herbert D.] Kingsbury took this matter up with Mr. R. J. Reynolds to-day and it was decided that it would not be policy [*sic*] for us to take up this note and that the R. J. Reynolds Tobacco Company had better loan this money to Spencer and Sons, we to loan the money to the R. J. Reynolds Tobacco Company. Agreeable to the above, we have issued check payable to the R. J. Reynolds Tobacco Company which Mr. Reynolds has endorsed and the amount of $50,000 has been deposited to the credit of D. H. Spencer & Sons, in the Second National Bank. I hand you herewith note of Spencer & Sons, Inc., and you will please, therefore, have your demand note drawn for $50,000, dated April 6th, and send to Continental Tobacco Company. Note bears interest at 5% per annum. In making your entries the name of D. H. Spencer & Sons need not appear in your Bills Receivable account, simply six months note, dated April 6th, payable at Second National Bank, New York.

Despite the letter J. H. Spencer wrote to the Reynolds company on 12 March 1907, Dula testified as follows on 4 December 1907: "The Spencers have been personal friends of mine of long standing in Virginia, and they were anxious to sell their business and become connected in some way with some larger interest, and they took the matter up with me just as a personal matter—I don't remember just what I did if I did anything about it—I might have arranged a meeting with Reynolds, or something of that kind, but I don't know that I did that even." Beyond that, Dula said, he only knew about the negotiations because he had enough confidence in Reynolds "to know he would hold his own."[84]

According to the report of the Commissioner of Corporations, Reynolds's last important acquisition while in the Tobacco Combination came through using D. H. Spencer and Sons (Incorporated) "to carry on a destructive competitive warfare against the Rucker and Witten brands." The commissioner further declared that Rucker and Witten, finding it "impossible to maintain itself against this competition . . . sold its entire business to the R. J. Reynolds Tobacco Company in 1905."[85] The Rucker and Witten Tobacco Company of Martinsville, Virginia, was itself the product of a combination of other firms. A resumé of its component firms throws considerable light on the conditions prevailing in the chewing tobacco industry during the years of Reynolds's consolidation of the flat-plug business. To begin, in 1872 the Sparger Brothers Company, consisting of James H. Sparger (10 September 1849–28 April 1922) and Benjamin Franklin Sparger (29 September 1853–29 September 1946), established a factory for the manufacture of chewing tobacco near Mount Airy, North Carolina. Later moving into Mount Airy itself, about forty miles northwest of Winston, the Sparger Brothers' business appeared to flourish for a time. In 1896 the plant supposedly had an annual capacity of 2,500,000 pounds, but by 1900 it was bankrupt. Thereupon it was merged with Hadley and Smith, also of Mount Airy.[86] Hadley and Smith, composed of James Alfred Hadley (9 May 1853–22 October 1916) and Alfred E. Smith (22 February 1862–30 November 1929), began to manufacture chewing tobacco in 1890 and by 1896 had three salesmen on the road selling its products from Baltimore to Texas. In 1900, however, it was consolidated with Rucker and Witten and four years later moved to Martinsville.[87] Early in 1905 the Rucker and Witten Tobacco Company acquired the business of W. T. Hancock of Richmond, Virginia, a firm that had existed about thirty years.[88] With its three acquisitions, Rucker and Witten probably considered itself strong enough to meet the competition of the Tobacco Combination or at least to sell out to it on favorable terms. Whether or not it became weakened by machinations of the American Tobacco Company through D. H. Spencer and Sons (Incorporated) is a moot question. The Spencer company met the same fate.

The Rucker and Witten Tobacco Company, with Pannill Rucker as president, Ancil D. Witten, James A. Hadley, and B. A. Rives as vice-presidents, and C. B. Keesee as secretary and treasurer, was thus a fairly new firm in 1905. On 28 July 1905 Pannill Rucker called on Caleb C. Dula, vice-president of the American Tobacco Company, a second time with a proposal to sell his company's assets "on a fair basis" to the R. J. Reynolds Tobacco Company provided he and his father-in-law received a guarantee that they might purchase $100,000 worth of stock in the Reynolds company at par. His original request had been for twice as much. Dula finally told Rucker that he would recommend $25,000 worth at par. Promptly reporting this information to R. J. Reynolds, Dula prophesied that Rucker, if he had not already done so, would call on Reynolds within a few days.[89] After Reynolds had bargained to purchase the Rucker and Witten Tobacco Company, he described its condition: "They have been working 75 salesmen, and their prices range from two to four cents per pound less than we get for similar tobaccos. Their heavy losses began about six months ago, and we believe their average loss per pound for the last six months is not less than 8 cents per pound, and as their losses were not very heavy up to twelve months ago, they might have something left after paying their indebtedness."[90]

On 8 August 1905 representatives of Rucker and Witten made a preliminary agreement to sell their entire business to the Reynolds firm. Accounts receivable and money on hand or on deposit were excepted. Members of the firm, including the officers and W. T. Hancock, agreed to have an inventory prepared by 31 August 1905. They also promised not to engage in the manufacture of tobacco for fifteen years either alone or jointly "with any other person" as "a shareholder, director, manager representative, agent or servant or otherwise." Nothing, however, prevented members of the firm from buying or selling stock in the R. J. Reynolds Tobacco Company, the American Tobacco Company, or any other firm at that time controlled by Reynolds or American. Likewise, members of the Rucker and Witten firm might enter the service of any such company. These last clauses also permitted Reynolds to employ W. T. Hancock and Pannill Rucker to buy $25,000 worth of Reynolds stock.[91] On 15 August 1905 the twenty-two stockholders of the Rucker and Witten Tobacco Company voted to accept $5,000 plus a fair evaluation of their assets, the value to be determined by two persons, one selected by the seller and one by the buyer. In case of disagreement these two were to choose a third person whose decision would be final.[92] There were to be no disputes over agreements and inventories as with the Spencer purchase. Counsel Burroughs and Vice-President Dula, from their Fifth Avenue offices, prepared contracts and in general supervised this purchase more closely than any other made by Reynolds while it was a subsidiary of the American Tobacco Company. The final act of the transaction occurred on 19 December 1905, when Rucker and Witten received $512,899 for their brands, goodwill, and tangible assets. According to the inventory, this meant that the sellers received $46,622 for their intangible assets—brand names and goodwill.[93]

Public reaction to the absorption of the Rucker and Witten Tobacco Company by the "Trust" produced a letter of refutation from Pannill Rucker, probably at the instigation of the R. J. Reynolds Tobacco Company. Rucker asserted that the Reynolds company was "a distinct concern in itself, and not a branch of the American Tobacco Co. or any other business." He declared that it would be an injustice to the Reynolds management to term it a branch of any business. In commenting on this letter, the editor of *Tobacco* declared that it was sent broadcast through the daily newspapers and that it indicated "the existence of a sentiment against concerns controlled by the trust which is coming to be gradually recognized, even by those who are financially interested in such concerns." In a technical sense, the editor continued, it was probably true that Reynolds maintained "the semblance of a company organization apart from the trust." He noted sarcastically that President Rucker had forgotten that when the Continental Tobacco Company absorbed the Reynolds company an announcement had come from "trust headquarters, at 111 5th Avenue, that the Continental Tobacco Co. would take over the plug tobacco business of the Reynolds Co., while the brands of smoking tobacco would be turned over to the American Tobacco Co."[94]

This last statement was undoubtedly true. On 10 June 1901 the resident directors of the R. J. Reynolds Tobacco Company, on the motion of Walter R. Reynolds, voted to sell to the American Tobacco Company all the business property, brands, goodwill, and materials pertaining to all smoking tobacco that the company had purchased from T. L. Vaughn and Company, Brown Brothers and Company, P. H. Hanes and Company, and B. F. Hanes and Company. The motion also set the price at $28,984 and authorized the president and secretary to transfer this property to American.[95] There is no available record that any other smoking brands obtained by Reynolds in the process of consolidation were transferred to American. Certainly as early as 1906 R. J. Reynolds had embarked on a more independent course. He showed by later actions that he was acutely aware of the sentiment against the American Tobacco Company and aware that the federal government had begun investigations. No other proof need be produced than his introduction of a new brand of smoking tobacco in 1907. This was the famous Prince Albert—to be treated in Chapter 6.

Another bit of evidence fits into the grand and methodical scheme of the American Tobacco Company. The Continental Tobacco Company on 2 September 1902 received title to nine brands of chewing tobacco from its affiliate, the Neudecker Tobacco Company, a wholesale firm of Baltimore, although it was agreed that the Neudecker firm would be the sole user of these brands as long as its aggregate purchases amounted to at least 5,000 pounds annually. Shortly thereafter Continental transferred its rights in this contract to the R. J. Reynolds Tobacco Company, which became virtual owner of the nine Neudecker brands: Big N, Big Plug, Big Schooner, Big Steamer, City Stock, John's 7, Neudecker's Own, Royal Blue, and Sword.[96] This arrangement, of course, was not new to the Reynolds company, which had long manufactured brands specifically for wholesale dealers, including Neudecker. By this transaction all of Neudecker's work was committed to Reynolds. It is clear that the effort of the Tobacco Combination to allocate plug brands to Continental and smoking brands to American was not haphazard.

There are hints but no proof that Reynolds obtained two other chewing tobacco firms. One was reputed to be the business of M. L. or M. A. Walker of Winston.[97] In 1907 R. J. wrote Caleb C. Dula to find out whether it would be feasible for him to purchase the firm of W. P. Pickett and Company in High Point, North Carolina, a short distance from Winston. Dula agreed to the purchase but there is no available evidence that Reynolds carried out the plan.[98]

Supervision by the Tobacco Combination

Indisputable evidence exists to prove that management of the R. J. Reynolds Tobacco Company cooperated on the surface with the men who owned two-thirds of the stock of the company, although R. J. Reynolds constantly protested his independence of the Tobacco Combination. In reality, Reynolds sometimes cooperated only after pressure had been exerted. The business acumen that had led him into the combination did not desert him from 1899 to 1911. He saw the necessity of cooperation in 1900 when he wrote Caleb C. Dula in a somewhat flippant manner:[99]

> I write to say that after getting the factories that we have bargained for, it appears to me that we should adopt the C. T. Co's method of handling the trade and conform to their policies as closely as the conditions will allow.

> We have a price list ready to go to the press soon after the transfer of the factories bought, and, "The above price list is subject to no rebate or discount, other than two per cent for cash." We intend to give five per cent to those who assist us in securing additional business and will earn the money.

> You will please let me know the "song and dance" you require before making such offers and when payable.

Reynolds's exact quotation from the price list refers, of course, to a change in his operations in order to comply with the practice of the American and Continental companies, although he states his determination to follow his own plan when deemed advantageous. R. J.'s determination to give a 5 percent discount at times and his sarcastic use of "song and dance" in connection with Dula's requirements reveal his attitude as one of unhurried compliance.

This particular "song and dance" in reference to sales was not the only facet of Reynolds's business to fall under the surveillance of 111 Fifth Avenue. Also involved were the requirements that R. J. visit New York frequently for conferences, the use of scrap tobacco in the manufacture of smoking tobacco, the reluctance of the Continental Tobacco Company to allow Reynolds to manufacture smoking tobacco, reports to Duke and his associates on leaf purchases and the sales of finished goods, and other matters of a similar nature. Sometimes Reynolds reversed the procedure and obtained services from the more widely-organized Tobacco Combination, thus undoubtedly enlarging his own operations and learning many lessons from his enforced association with these men of great capital.

R. J. Reynolds undoubtedly made many visits to 111 Fifth Avenue at special requests. Percival S. Hill testified in 1907 that, though he saw Reynolds on his frequent visits to New York City, he, Hill, had held no conferences with him about his business. Likewise, Caleb C. Dula, in the same year and in a similar capacity, stated that he had not conferred with Reynolds when the latter occasionally visited New York. Early in 1908, George W. Coan testified that Reynolds went to New York as often as five or six times a year, but that on his return he never gave him to understand that he had conferred with any officials of the American Tobacco Company unless he happened to refer in a general way to having been at the office of that company. These cagey answers, of course, accorded strictly with the letter of the law. As a matter of fact, on 6 December 1900 Dula wrote not only for Reynolds to come to New York but also for him to bring with him two or three of his "head men," whom he expected to use "in augmenting in the field such of our methods, if any . . . [he] should decide to adopt." Dula also wrote Reynolds on 26 June 1901 that James B. Duke had received R. J.'s letter but thought it advisable for him to come to New York as soon as he could leave Winston "not later than about July 1st." Four years later, on 13 September 1905, Dula referred to his business plans for "the next time Mr. Reynolds is here."[100] From these conferences and letters it is quite obvious that Reynolds and his resident directors received constant supervision from the Tobacco Combination.

Perhaps no specific question caused greater friction between the R. J. Reynolds Tobacco Company and the Tobacco Combination than the matter of scrap tobacco, which was closely allied to the manufacture of smoking tobacco. It was clearly the combination's intention to allocate the production of all chewing tobacco to the Continental Tobacco Company and the production of cigarettes and smoking tobacco to the American Tobacco Company. In fact, American, after it had merged with Continental, manufactured about 1,500 brands of cigarettes and smoking tobacco, in addition to owning a great many inactive brands.[101] Reynolds no doubt earlier had utilized his scrap tobacco—a significant by-product from the manufacture of plug—for the production of smoking tobacco. Evidently in 1899 he wished to produce smoking tobacco on an even larger scale. It is doubtful that any analysis of this situation could be more revealing than the following letter written by R. J. Reynolds on 11 March 1901 to John B. Cobb, first vice-president of the American Tobacco Company and director of the Continental Tobacco Company:[102]

On my return here I conferred with Hanes and the home officers of the R. J. R. T. Co., and our arrangement was satisfactory to them and, if to your Company, we will record the following on our books:

Bargained to the American Tobacco Company our scrap tobacco in stock and hereafter accumulated from the crops of '99 and 1900, delivered in hogsheads on cars here at a discount of 20% on the average cost of each crop, as shown on our Leaf Department books. We are to have the privilege of using a part of the above scrap to supply whatever trade we can get on Our Advertiser granulated smoking tobacco, without advertising the brand.

We also agree to allow you 30% discount on 1901 crop, a recorded average on it as shown by our leaf department books; you also to have the privilege of taking other crops at the same price. All scrap to be received when the stock on hand amounts to one car load. Terms net cash. Both companies reserve the right to annul this agreement any time after two years by giving six months notice to that effect.

In consideration of you taking our scrap at the above prices, we agree, during the life of this agreement not to advertise any brand of granulated smoking tobacco, or make any concession on our plug tobacco to secure business on granulated smoking tobacco.

To avoid any other controversy in regard to the scrap and smoking business we accept your offer of 30% discount on future crops, and if satisfactory this matter will not likely ever come up again.

We will also pass a separate resolution, confirming the sale of the smoking business of T. L. Vaughn & Co., Brown Bros. Co., P. H. Hanes & Co. and B. F. Hanes at cost to us.

Other facts indicate that Reynolds never intended to relinquish the manufacture of smoking tobacco. It is significant that his price list for 31 January and 20 February 1901 carried the following brands of smoking tobacco: Canvas Back, King of North Carolina, Our Advertiser, Red Apple, Razor Back, and Split Silk—all except the last two granulated. Thereafter in 1901, and until 28 July 1902, the price lists showed at least two of the following brands of smoking tobacco: Our Advertiser, Razor Back, and Split Silk. Beginning on 28 July 1902, however, the price lists carried only Our Advertiser until 15 November 1905, after which the following smoking brands appeared: Cotton Bale, Cream of North Carolina, Hot Sausage, and Old North Carolina Mixture.[103] Evidently as indications of an antitrust suit by the U.S. government against the American Tobacco Company grew, Reynolds became emboldened to manufacture smoking tobacco on a larger scale.

Despite the fact that the Reynolds price lists carried Our Advertiser as the only smoking tobacco in 1904, James B. Duke must have had some suspicions. On 12 September 1904 Charles N. Strotz, manager of the department of manufacturing for the American Tobacco Company, wrote Reynolds that he had been instructed by Duke to obtain the following with reference to Our Advertiser: one five-pound carton "with cigarette paper or anything else you pack with it" to show how Our Advertiser goes to the trade; samples of leaf, scrap, and stems used in its manufacture; and the cost and proportion of each of these samples.[104] All this was sent to Duke. Reynolds listed four different brands for the greater part of 1905, but not Our Advertiser, which did not reappear until 27 November 1905. Then, in 1907, he listed two new brands, Refined on 22 March and Prince Albert on 18 December. On 2 December 1907 Percival S. Hill testified that there was not and never had been anything but open competition between his company and the Reynolds company in the marketing of smoking brands. He did state, however, that his company had corresponded with the Reynolds company when "their salesmen in putting up their signs of smoking tobacco covered up some of the American Tobacco Company's signs." Such conduct, Hill declared, was not decent.[105] In view of these circumstances, much of the testimony given early in 1908 by George W. Coan, of the R. J. Reynolds Tobacco Company, seems no more than a surface reflection of the terms supposed to exist between the two companies. His replies to leading questions from Junius Parker, counsel for the American Tobacco Company, indicate that the Reynolds company at the time it became a subsidiary of the Tobacco Combination had insufficient business in smoking tobacco to use all of its scrap, that Reynolds's smoking business had greatly increased since 1900, and that new brands had been developed and marketed.[106] Coan, of course, told the literal truth without going beneath the surface. Although the government was seeking to destroy the great power of the Tobacco Combination, the American Tobacco Company still held two-thirds of Reynolds's stock.

The testimony of William N. Reynolds in later years indicates that the dispute between his company and American over smoking tobacco reached even greater intensity when the Reynolds company brought out Prince Albert:[107]

They [the American Tobacco Company] never did [stop us], but they tried to block us every way they could when we started making Prince Albert Tobacco. They claimed the brand. They threatened to sue us if we didn't stop making Prince Albert. They tried to keep the trade from buying it from us, from taking on Prince Albert, and that was when my brother [R. J. Reynolds] and I got hold of some friends that had money to help us, and we decided we would go up there [to

New York City] and either buy them out or sell it to them. . . . They declined to buy or sell, either. . . . We didn't have any trouble with them after that.

Probably more exasperating to the management of the R. J. Reynolds Tobacco Company than the bickering over smoking tobacco was the matter of sending detailed weekly, monthly, and semiannual reports to the American Tobacco Company concerning such items as leaf purchases and sales of manufactured products. So far as available records indicate, Duke first called for weekly statements on leaf purchases by Reynolds early in 1903. When relaying Duke's wishes to Reynolds, William H. Schroeder, auditor of the Continental Tobacco Company, sent specific blanks for use in reporting purchases and the cost of Virginia wrappers, southern leaf, Burley, and dark western leaf. Schroeder's letter contained two very pertinent paragraphs:[108]

> In order that the statement that goes to Mr. Duke should not contain any figures that might be duplicated by reason of leaf having been transferred from one company to another, it will be in order for you to eliminate from your figures any leaf purchased by you from this company, the American Tobacco Company, and any of our other companies. However, leaf that is being bought for you by our Richmond Leaf Department should be shown on your statement, as it will not be included on ours; furthermore leaf that is being bought by you for account of our Danville Leaf Department should not be shown with your purchases, as it will be included in ours.

> We should like to have you commence making this statement at once, and send same for the week ending February 14th, if possible.

Neither Thomas B. Yuille, manager of American's leaf department, nor George W. Coan could remember when these weekly reports were discontinued. Questions by the government's examining attorney, James Clark McReynolds (3 February 1862–24 August 1946), intimated that it was shortly after the beginning of preparations for the antitrust suit against American, although Yuille claimed that he had ordered the weekly reports on leaf purchases stopped because they were of no value. It appears, however, that monthly reports on leaf purchases were continued at least into 1907, and at one time prior to 1907 daily reports had been required.[109]

The Reynolds company also submitted reports on manufactured products—the cost of manufacturing each brand, the amount of each brand sold, and the net result for each sale. These were daily and weekly reports on which Duke's auditor kept a sharp eye. When Reynolds failed to send a report because of the duration of one of his selling schemes, Schroeder immediately reminded him, and, as late as 11 January 1907, John B.

Jeffress, Jr., the assistant auditor, sharply called the attention of the Reynolds company to errors in the totals given for shipments of chewing and smoking tobacco. At one time in 1903 these reports included not only shipments by brands but also the different markets to which each brand was shipped. Early in 1907 Percival S. Hill professed to know little about these reports on manufactured tobacco, although he acknowledged that he regularly saw the Reynolds monthly financial statements.[110]

There were other means by which the Tobacco Combination looked into the management of the R. J. Reynolds Tobacco Company from 1899 until 1911—doubtless more than the scanty records available indicate. One of the most blatant involved the names and salaries of employees. In May 1907 the following came from the auditor at 111 Fifth Avenue:[111]

> I beg to acknowledge receipt of your valued favor of the 3rd inst., enclosing statement of the names and salaries paid to employees at No. 14 [Liipfert-Scales Company], and thank you very much for your prompt attention. While I believe that you have kept me posted as to the changes in the salaries at the R. J. Reynolds Tobacco Company, still I think a revised statement as of May 1st, would be a check on the records that we have. We never have had a statement of the salesmen of the R. J. Reynolds Tobacco Co. and I think it would be a good scheme to let us have this as of May 1st, giving the names, salaries paid to them and their territory.

When questioned about "a Mr. Lutz," whom the Duke interests wished to remain under an assumed name while he was in Martinsville, Virginia, George W. Coan stated that Lutz, an employee of the American Tobacco Company, had come to Martinsville "to install the same system of bookkeeping with D. H. Spencer and Sons as we were using."[112] The American Tobacco Company and the Continental Tobacco Company thus saw to it that their method of bookkeeping was used by Reynolds and then by D. H. Spencer and Sons (Incorporated) as soon as it was purchased by Reynolds. Auditors from 111 Fifth Avenue also frequently came to Winston in order to check on the bookkeeping of the Reynolds company.[113] Possibly R. J. and his resident directors needed assistance on some matters, such as the declaration in 1900 of a scrip dividend to mature in five years when capital was needed for the purchase of new businesses and property. It might have come as something of a surprise to the company's legal staff of 1960 to read R. J.'s letter of 11 December 1900 to Junius Parker, stating that the resolution for a scrip dividend "as drawn by you" had been adopted at a regular meeting of the board of directors on 6 December.[114]

R. J. Reynolds managed well the fiction that his was an independent company. No doubt he was behind the revival of George W. Coan's memory in 1908 when Coan testified concerning the resignations of George W. Watts, Benjamin N. Duke, James B. Duke, and Caleb C. Dula as directors of the R. J. Reynolds Tobacco Company. When asked why these men resigned, Coan at first could give no reasons. But, on the following day, he asked if he might go back to that point. Thereupon he declared somewhat indirectly that R. J. Reynolds had long been anxious for some of his faithful employees to be more closely identified with the company and that these resignations gave him that opportunity. Coan also remembered that prior to these changes it had often been difficult to obtain a quorum for directors' meetings.[115] The author actually came in contact with one former chairman of the board who, although he had joined the company in 1913, still believed the old Reynolds fiction that the company had never been affiliated with the American Tobacco Company.

It could scarcely have been accidental that though he directed a subsidiary company Reynolds managed to get his own working directors and a solid foothold in the smoking tobacco business. The day of the dissolution of the Tobacco Combination saw Reynolds with two foundation stones for moving ahead. In the first place the R. J. Reynolds Tobacco Company had been aided by the American Tobacco Company in securing "fully 90 per cent of the total flat-plug tobacco manufactured by the Combination."[116] In addition, Reynolds had refused to abdicate as a manufacturer of smoking tobacco. He undoubtedly retained more than a semblance of independence. After going through American's extensive records, the Commissioner of Corporations wrote correctly: "The R. J. Reynolds Tobacco Co. has insisted that while the Combination had technical control through ownership of a majority of the stock, nevertheless, its management was practically independent of the Combination. There seems to have been in fact a considerable degree of independence in the management of this company."[117]

CHAPTER 5

Management and Labor under the Tobacco Combination

While his company remained a subsidiary of the American Tobacco Company, R. J. Reynolds evidently knew that he must drive hard or some other subsidiary would lead the flat-plug industry. In this effort, Reynolds surrounded himself with able men, organized new departments, built factories, increased production, strengthened his sales department, increased his labor force, and vigorously launched several new smoking brands aimed directly at competition with Duke's Mixture and Bull Durham, both owned by American. Reynolds also learned many lessons from American; after the decree of 1911 dissolving the old American Tobacco Company (and thus the Tobacco Combination), his firm emerged as leader of the flat-plug industry and as a potential leader in the manufacture of smoking tobacco. Throughout this period he consistently maintained to the public that his was an independent business in which the American Tobacco Company was merely a stockholder. At the same time, labor and management seemed closer than in subsequent years.

While connected with the Tobacco Combination, R. J. Reynolds jealously guarded the independence of his organization and also managed to profit from his enforced association with the business of James B. Duke. During these years the R. J. Reynolds Tobacco Company obtained assistance in planning buildings, in the purchase of leaf, and in the sale of its products. Reynolds cooperated with Duke's organization at times when forced to and at other times when it was to his advantage. These efforts resulted in a greatly increased business and a necessarily enlarged office force, which moved into a new building in 1911. Despite the great rejoicing at freedom from the Tobacco Combination a few weeks later, the R. J. Reynolds Tobacco Company had become greatly expanded and improved from 1899 to 1911.

Expansion and Change in Management

Reynolds reorganized his management and held it intact until after 1911, enlarged his sales department, laid down the beginnings of a research department, began a legal department, employed a traffic manager, enlarged the payroll department, and ventured into more advertising.

On 4 April 1899, at Newark, New Jersey, the three Reynolds brothers of Winston, Benjamin N. Duke and George W. Watts of Durham, almost one hundred miles east of Winston, and John B. Cobb and James B. Duke of New York City all became directors of the R. J. Reynolds Tobacco Company of New Jersey. Without the highways, fast motors, and executive planes of today, this situation at times left the working directors in a difficult position when in need of a quorum. One of the early official acts of the president of the new company lay in requesting Clement Manly (12 March 1853–26 November 1928), R. J.'s first regular legal adviser, to write Benjamin N. Duke requesting his and Watts's presence for a directors' meeting preferably on 20 June. Urgency in this case came from the need for formal approval of an action, already made by the Continental Tobacco Company, shifting the principal office of the R. J. Reynolds Tobacco Company from Newark to Jersey City, New Jersey. At this meeting Reynolds also desired to discuss some contracts with Duke and Watts.[1] The next available communication between Reynolds and his Durham directors showed that he desired to profit from any knowledge accumulated by the American Tobacco Company. A builder commissioned by Reynolds to plan a new leaf house wrote B. N. Duke, at the behest of R. J. and William N. Reynolds, for permission to examine "the system of ventilation" that American had installed in a leaf house in Durham.[2] Reynolds could afford to be a rubber stamp for a time if in the process he might assimilate any new methods or ideas that the Tobacco Combination had developed or obtained from the various companies that it had engulfed. As Reynolds expressed it later, he did not intend to be swallowed by "Buck" (James B.) Duke.[3]

At no time when it suited his convenience did Reynolds seem hesitant to use the widespread facilities of the Tobacco Combination. Prior to 1906, before the Reynolds company had expanded its buying organization, the American Tobacco Company purchased leaf for Reynolds on the markets at Durham, Oxford, and Wilson in North Carolina and at Chase

City in Virginia. During the same period the American Snuff Company, also strongly allied to if not a subsidiary of the Tobacco Combination, purchased leaf for Reynolds. Likewise, buyers for the Continental Tobacco Company accommodated Reynolds, in 1904, 1905, and possibly earlier, by acquiring Green River lugs and Burley leaf from the market at Louisville, Kentucky. Reynolds's use of Burley at that early date was confined to the manufacture of a few navy brands acquired from the firms absorbed after 1899. R. J., of course, paid for these services; nevertheless they were favors that he freely accepted.[4] These purchases no doubt gave Will Reynolds some inkling of what would be required of him in obtaining Burley leaf for Prince Albert.

In the sale of manufactured goods the Reynolds company also profited from its alliance with the Tobacco Combination. Actually, by 1907 the exclusive Metropolitan Tobacco Company handled some of Reynolds products in New York City. Metropolitan represented a combination of about fifteen New York jobbers to which the American Tobacco Company gave exclusive control of the wholesale distribution of its goods in Greater New York. Not exactly a subsidiary of the Tobacco Combination, the Metropolitan Tobacco Company was nevertheless closely bound to it by a generous commission Metropolitan received for handling the combination's goods. Subsidiary companies of Metropolitan also controlled part of the sales in New Jersey. In 1907, however, Adolph D. Bendheim, its president, did not think that his firm received any extra discount from Reynolds.[5]

In 1901 the Reynolds company wrote Caleb C. Dula that it had "the trade now so we can handle the jobbers on the second period in the same way your Company does." When the jobbers "kick on the load we will write them similar letters to those furnished us by your Company," the letter continued. Although there is no proof, this sounds suspiciously like the quota system coupled with drop shipments. In 1902 Dula wrote Reynolds requesting some concession in time to discount the bills of L. E. Valloft of the Southern Tobacco Company of New Orleans, because by "his arrangements with us he, of course, is bound to give your goods the preference over all other similar kinds, and I think his account will show a steady increase in output of your goods." Furthermore, after the sales board met at 111 Fifth Avenue, it sometimes, if not regularly, informed Reynolds of jobbers who should be dropped for unreliability in the payment of bills.[6] All in all, it appears that R. J. Reynolds received considerable aid from the Tobacco Combination and that his company was in no way reluctant to receive this support. It was a matter of getting ahead, although R. J. took pains to leave the impression that he was tied to the villainous Tobacco Combination under duress.

When the company began operating under the combination its officers were R. J. Reynolds, president, W. N. Reynolds, second vice-president, and George Richard Lybrook, secretary and treasurer—all elected on 4 April 1899. Benjamin N. Duke's position as first vice-president was largely honorary.

The first change in officers came early in 1902 at the death of the young secretary and treasurer, a nephew of the Reynolds brothers.[7] The office fell to George W. Coan (28 October 1867–23 November 1939), originally from Ridgeway, Virginia, about eight miles south of Martinsville. How Coan came to the company is shrouded in some mystery. A graduate of Eastman's Business College in Poughkeepsie, New York, Coan began in the business world as a bookkeeper, serving in that capacity for six years. He then was one of the organizers of a bank in Martinsville before becoming owner of the W. A. Brown Tobacco Company, also of Martinsville. According to what apparently is an official biography, Coan sold his business to the R. J. Reynolds Tobacco Company in 1899 and moved to Winston as R. J. Reynolds's private secretary. Yet, according to his own testimony given in 1908, he had manufactured tobacco prior to July 1899 but had sold his business to his brother-in-law, who had since continued to manufacture tobacco. At the time of his death, the local newspaper reported that Coan had sold out to the R. J. Reynolds Tobacco Company in August 1899 and then moved his family to Winston.[8] There are no available records showing that Coan ever sold his tobacco business to Reynolds. It does not appear that Coan held stock in the company until 1903, when he was listed as the owner of 200 shares.[9]

A reorganization of considerable import in the management of the Reynolds company occurred after the Continental Tobacco Company merged with the American Tobacco Company on 19 October 1904. This merger—prompted by the case of the Northern Securities Company, a holding company as was Continental—gave American ownership of 33,323 shares of Reynolds stock, a controlling interest, of course. Previously it had not quite controlled a majority of Continental's stock.[10] R. J. Reynolds claimed that he somehow forced this new reorganization of his company, but it is more likely that he requested it without being successful until after 19 October 1904. Judging merely from the terse items in the minutes, no thought was given to such a reorganization at the stockholders' meeting in April 1904, when James B. Duke was reelected to the board of directors for a three-year period, nor in April 1905, when Benjamin N. Duke was reelected for a similar term. At any rate, at some point between 4 April and 16 August 1905, Benjamin N. Duke resigned as first vice-president. In the same interim Benjamin N. Duke, James B. Duke, Caleb C. Dula, and George W. Watts resigned as directors, and William N. Reynolds became first vice-president and George W. Coan, Robert B. Horn, and C. A. Hopman became directors.[11] Hopman, of Jersey City, was a statutory director, but the others were country-bred, working directors who lived in the Winston-Salem area. This reorganization left the R. J. Reynolds Tobacco Company with the following working directors:

R. J. Reynolds, president and chief executive
W. N. Reynolds, vice-president in charge of leaf buying
W. R. Reynolds, superintendent of manufacturing
George W. Coan, secretary and treasurer
D. Rich, head bookkeeper and director of hiring employees
R. B. Horn, sales manager

Presumably Reynolds had learned all that was necessary from the Tobacco Combination; his duty now was to earn sufficient dividends to please his stockholders—particularly his chief stockholder. With but one change, this board of directors remained the same until some time after the dissolution of the old American Tobacco Company in 1911. It was largely with this board that Reynolds accomplished much of the modernizing that was done after 1899.

The sales department naturally expanded during this period. When testifying early in 1908, Coan declared that in 1899 the greatest part of the Reynolds business was in Baltimore, whereas before then he believed that the company had no more than a handful of salesmen, two or three in each of the following states: West Virginia, Georgia, South Carolina, Alabama, and Tennessee. It is difficult to determine much about the sales department immediately after Reynolds entered the Tobacco Combination except that Rufus T. Stedman continued for a time as head of the department. On 17 December 1900, R. J. wrote Caleb C. Dula of the Continental Tobacco Company that Stedman was "the most loyal man that we have ever employed" and that he would "drive whatever policy we decide is best for the business." Reynolds also stated that George F. Dwire, a promising young man who was "Hanes' nephew," would serve as Stedman's assistant. In the same letter Reynolds revealed that Stedman would accompany his division managers to New York in order to obtain selling instructions from Dula.[12] Apparently Fred Watson became Stedman's assistant sales manager in 1902, but Reynolds brought in another man from the road who pushed Stedman out—a matter that angered Watson.[13] The man brought in from the road was evidently Robert Byron Horn (8 January 1870–20 September 1918). A native of East Bend in Yadkin County, North Carolina, a graduate of George Peabody College, and long principal of the Yadkin Valley Institute at nearby Boonville, Horn came to Winston in June 1902. He was hired as a Reynolds salesman on 23 July. After advancing to a weekly salary of $28.85 by 16 May 1903, he entered the main office of the Reynolds company on 1 July 1903. Though he became a director in 1905, Horn apparently was not steady and made questionable financial proposals. As legend goes, Reynolds discharged him in 1907. At any rate the company files contain his letter of resignation dated 8 January 1907.[14]

Horn was succeeded by Joseph D. Noell (1866–22 November 1912), a native of Danville, Virginia, who had been with the Reynolds sales force since 1 January 1898. When called to the home office in March 1907, Noell, a division manager with headquarters in Richmond, Virginia, supervised a sales area extending from Norfolk, Virginia, to Cincinnati. According to William Thomas Smither, who served as Noell's office boy in Richmond and accompanied him to Winston, Noell was a huge man physically and an excellent writer. One of the first things he did was to compose a letter to the division managers, then about twenty-five in number, explaining how he was the focal point between the salesmen and division managers on one hand and the Reynolds management on the other. R. J. Reynolds considered the letter so excellent that he had copies made for possible later use. By 1908, according to George W. Coan, about 170 salesmen solicited trade for the Reynolds company in the southern states from Maryland to Florida, and in Texas, Oklahoma, Arkansas, Ohio, Pennsylvania, New Jersey, Delaware, and New York. In 1913, very soon after Noell's death, at least twenty-four new division managers began work, in addition to those employed previously.[15]

During at least a part of the period from 1899 to 1911, the sales department included two managers, although one apparently handled the advertising. In July 1902, George F. Dwire, when commended for having originated a pasteboard disc to be attached to wagon wheels for advertising Schnapps, was described as being from the "company's advertising department."[16] Two years later, if not earlier, Richard Samuel Reynolds (15 August 1881–29 July 1955), one of R. J.'s nephews who had joined the company in 1903, served as "one" of the sales managers. That Richard Reynolds worked in the advertising section of the sales department is indicated by the fact that he, with Vann McNair, was scheduled in 1910 to publish a house organ entitled "Cross-tie Philosophy." "Cross-tie Philosophy" was planned to contain "shop-talk, news of the firm's traveling men, and business talks of various kinds." This projected house organ, apparently never published, may have been planned by N. W. Ayer and Son, a pioneer advertising agency retained by Reynolds as early as 1910.[17]

Advertising also included the work of a number of men who posted signs, generally around stores, crossing division lines in their duties. During 1906–9 division managers, among whom were Percy Reynolds Masten (7 August 1867–22 March 1924), F. P. Johns, Charles Ardea Kent (2 March 1868–9 August 1927), Bowman Gray, Sr., N. L. Mahan, A. Hume March, and H. L. Terrie, together had as many as fourteen men putting up posters from Baltimore to Dallas, Texas.[18] These facts do little more than indicate the growth of the sales department from 1899 to 1911. If it may be assumed that the department grew in proportion to production for these years, its expansion was fivefold.

Also indicative of the company's growth, as well as its alliance with the Tobacco Combination, was the establishment of a Winston branch of the Mengel Box Company in 1903. Originally an independent concern in St. Louis, the Mengel Box Company, manufacturers of wooden boxes for packing chewing tobacco, had been rechartered on 13 July 1899 at the instigation of the Continental Tobacco Company. Mengel soon controlled two similar companies and had factories in St. Louis and Louisville, Kentucky, before establishing a branch in Winston that was designed to supply tobacco-packing boxes for the factories in the Atlantic Coast states. In choosing a location between the Norfolk and Western and the Southern Railway, the Mengel officials placed their plant convenient to the Reynolds factories.[19]

Another sign of maturity came with the establishment of an incipient research department under William Owen McCorkle (25 August 1867–2 August 1943). Though he apparently had little or no formal training, McCorkle was first referred to as the flavorer or the chemist. His chief equipment, long preserved in the research department, consisted of a Bunsen burner and an old cup with "U.S. Navy" on it. McCorkle served as keeper of Reynolds's brand book and, after 1907, as "Custodian of the Denatured Rum Storeroom" in factory Number 8. Pete J. Crim, head of the casing department in factory Number 256, was custodian of rum in Number 256, but it was McCorkle's duty to keep all records and make the proper reports to the United States Department of Internal Revenue. Evidently Reynolds depended on McCorkle to help devise the flavoring for Prince Albert smoking tobacco.[20] Though McCorkle may have become somewhat eccentric in his later years, often boasting that R. J. could not fire him because he knew all the brand secrets, there is evidence that he had worked out the beginning of Reynolds's codes for brand formulas by 1910 when R. J. wrote his brother Walter to increase the amount of G3 in Red Bird chewing tobacco. G3 consisted of crushed stems and may have been concocted first by Reynolds, although it was also later used by the American Tobacco Company. It is quite possible, too, that McCorkle took charge of the information on flavoring sent Walter Reynolds by E. T. Jester of the American Tobacco Company.[21]

In this same period, although evidently well after 1899, Reynolds began a legal department. With ready access to the lawyers of the American Tobacco Company and his own able consulting lawyer, Clement Manly, Reynolds perhaps had no vital need for such a department in the early years. The learned, Chesterfieldian, and able Manly was senior member of Manly and Hendren, a legal firm long close to the R. J. Reynolds Tobacco

Company. In eastern North Carolina prior to 1890, Manly had been associated with Furnifold M. Simmons, later a U.S. senator and long a political power in the state. Shortly after arriving in Winston, Manly became an intimate friend of R. J. Reynolds and served as legal counsel not only for Reynolds but also for the Wachovia Bank & Trust Company and the Southern Railway.[22] In view of Manly's connections with a strong bank, a powerful political leader, and the Southern Railway, his value to the Reynolds company may be conjectured but unfortunately not specified in detail. Apparently both R. J. Reynolds and Manly saw the need for additional legal assistance shortly before the decree dissolving the old American Tobacco Company, and, as if anticipating coming events, the R. J. Reynolds Tobacco Company in 1908 sought to employ Aubrey Lee Brooks (19 May 1872–10 January 1958), a prominent attorney of Greensboro and senior member of the firm, which in that same year admitted Samuel Clay Williams to its membership. Failing to secure the services of Brooks, Reynolds in 1911 employed as his first full-time lawyer, Francis Burton Craige (23 December 1875–11 January 1945), a successful attorney from nearby Salisbury. Craige's office was in the R. J. Reynolds office building, but, according to a local newspaper, his work did not conflict with that of Manly and Hendren, who had served for a number of years as general counsel for the Reynolds company.[23]

Expansion of business and of railroad facilities before 1911 produced a need for expert knowledge of shipping facilities as well as for full-time legal advice. The American Tobacco Company took the initiative in improving the handling of Reynolds freight. On 2 October 1900 Charles S. Keene, traffic manager for American, wrote the R. J. Reynolds Tobacco Company:

> Will you please write this Department giving an outline as to the territory you are at present shipping your manufactured tobacco. Also give us data concerning supplies and leaf received, showing the quantities in which you receive them and the points shipped from.

> We desire this information in order that we may get in closer touch with your business, and probably we will be able to help you in the way of routing rates, etc., etc. A prompt reply is solicited.

In the light of testimony by George W. Coan, it is clear that before 1906 the Reynolds company corresponded with Keene in regard to traffic problems. Coan stated early in 1908 that his firm no longer sought such information from Keene because the Reynolds firm had employed a traffic manager of its own more than a year and a half earlier.[24]

The man hired in 1906 for the traffic work, Joseph L. Graham, was one of the ablest men whom Reynolds drew around him from 1899 to 1911.

Born in Augusta, Georgia, Graham's education in the public schools, in a commercial college, and in the reading of law gave assurance of an excellent background for handling traffic. His entire experience had been concerned with industrial traffic, first with the Central of Georgia Railroad and then with the Ocean Steamship Company of Savannah. According to local newspapers, he was held in high esteem by the Interstate Commerce Commission and the North Carolina Corporation Commission: "One of his first big successes came in the Winston-Salem coal case, in which he was instrumental in having removed the serious handicaps of discriminatory freight rates. This was followed by many other successful efforts, of both a city and statewide effect. His participation in the southeastern rate investigation brought wide attention." Six years before joining Reynolds, he had served as president of the National Freight Claims Association.[25] Much of his work in the Winston-Salem area came to fruition after 1911. He became a director of the company on 2 April 1912, just as the R. J. Reynolds Tobacco Company stood free of the American Tobacco Company. Though Graham handled traffic problems from 1906 until his retirement, it is interesting that he did not become traffic manager in name until 1914. Records do not reveal the cause of Graham's election to the directorate before his actual appointment as traffic manager. He had the reputation of being a man of fastidious nature, superior education, and good taste—perhaps outstanding in the Reynolds organization of his day. These were the characteristics that impelled D. Rich to seek Graham's criticism when he wanted a letter worded with complete precision.[26] Again Reynolds had demonstrated his ability to judge men and to prepare for the "day of freedom," as he termed the date that marked the dissolution of the old American Tobacco Company.

How else did growth manifest itself during the Babylonian captivity? The establishment of a payroll department represents one such move, although no available information on its actual beginning, possibly under Walter Brown, the only known employee of that department until Charles M. Griffith (31 January 1885–10 November 1956) entered it on 1 April 1907. Griffith, no doubt well prepared for the tedious details of counting out the cash, came from the closing premium department, where he had counted tags since 1 January 1905. Just how Brown alone had handled the payroll for the 3,066 employees in the office and factories reported by Griffith for 1905 seems lost. It was surely not child's play. During that period, however, payment of the employees of the two factories came every two weeks—Number 8 and Number 256 on alternate weeks.[27]

After Griffith joined the payroll department, the first crisis was the bankers' panic of 1907. The situation in Winston and Salem was serious for five weeks, where there was no cash on hand to meet payrolls. On Saturday night, 23 November 1907, various manufacturers of the towns, and no doubt merchants and bankers as well, met at the Wachovia National Bank and decided to use certificates of deposit, or individual checks of deposit, for meeting payrolls. These certificates were the same as cash, declared the *Union Republican*, and no one should be so foolish as to take less than their face value because they were backed by the bankers and businessmen of the towns and accepted by the merchants. Full information came to the factories on 27 November in the form of a 9-by-6-inch poster carrying the following with reference to "Deposit Bank Checks," a name R. J. Reynolds preferred to "scrip":

> Our Next Pay Roll, Saturday, November 30, 1907, will be paid one-half in our Deposit Bank Checks, and one-half in cash. Until further advised by us, all Pay Rolls after above date will be paid by our Deposit Bank Checks. Amounts less than One Dollar will be paid in money.

> The Deposit Checks will be made in convenient denominations, of $1.00, $2.00 and $5.00, and will be received on deposit by any of the Winston-Salem banks; also good at face value with members of the Retail Merchants' Association.

Fortunately this crisis soon subsided and the use of scrip was abandoned at the beginning of the new year. The editor of the *Union Republican* acknowledged his pleasure at this turn of events and declared that scrip had been a power in maintaining business stability during the crisis.[28]

But with the beginning of weekly payrolls on 19 September 1907, two additional employees came into the department, no doubt in part because of the 25 percent increase in the production of plug tobacco that year. The department continued to grow until it contained thirty-five people during World War II. During the early years, employees in this department often worked overtime especially before the plant closed for holidays or when the circus came to town. Long before the days of armored cars and printed checks, members of the payroll department, carrying guns and watching for robbers, accompanied wagons of money to be paid the employees. For many years payment followed this pattern, with wages paid in bills in multiples of fives and in silver for the odd dollars and change. On one occasion, a sack of 1,000 one-dollar coins was dropped and burst on the street in front of the Wachovia National Bank without loss. Even under such conditions no member of the payroll department was ever bonded until 1929 and then only because other companies provided similar protection as a guarantee to the stockholders.[29] Expansion of the payroll department came largely after August 1905 and occasioned no known repercussions from 111 Fifth Avenue; though this expansion represented a move closely tied to the production of smoking tobacco, payroll was a service department and perhaps of no interest to the American Tobacco Company.

This, however, was not the case with the Amsterdam Supply Company, which was organized in 1903 to serve as a purchasing agent for the American Tobacco Company and its affiliated corporations. Of the 2,350 shares, American held 1,092 and the Reynolds company 96 shares. Other facts indicate that the Reynolds company did not come to terms with the Amsterdam Supply Company until 1906, a rather late date. In the Reynolds files a penciled note headed "Motion GWC W RR" contains a resolution that the company make a contract with the Amsterdam Supply Company in accordance with a proposal, made to the company on 20 February 1906, that the president be authorized to take stock in the Amsterdam Supply Company, and that the treasurer be directed to make a list of the company's total purchases for the year 1906. This motion was passed on 23 February 1906. George W. Coan testified early in 1908 that Reynolds bought such items as pens, ink, and writing paper from the Amsterdam Supply Company. But, he added, "Anything that we buy, we buy where we get the best prices. We buy through the Amsterdam Supply Company when we can save anything by buying through them." Morton W. Reed, president of the Amsterdam Supply Company, stated one month earlier that his company gave each corporation orders to buy elsewhere if the prices were better. Reed also stated that he sold at a commission of one percent.[30] Reynolds's late entry into the plans of the Amsterdam Supply Company and Coan's first impulsive statement concerning the trifling purchases of Reynolds from that company are quite suggestive.

So far as records indicate, Reynolds showed no reluctance to enter the cooperative insurance plan adopted by the American Tobacco Company for the protection of its controlled companies. It was probably advantageous to do so because the plan was motivated by the increasing rates charged by insurance companies—particularly in the South prior to 1907. Reynolds also owned stock in the Factory Insurance Bureau, or the Factory Inspection Bureau, as it was also called. American officials checked the reports of their inspectors, and, when their recommendations had not been followed, requested explanations.[31]

Apparently unrestricted in any way by the American Tobacco Company, the R. J. Reynolds Tobacco Company began constructing an office building in 1910. Erected on the lot known as "the Masten Corner," this first office building, which faced Main Street at Fifth, is known today as Number 38 and has long been utilized by the electric shop. With plug business expanding and Prince Albert sales climbing at the rate of 4 million pounds per year, more space was needed for bookkeeping and other clerical work so that manufacturing might expand in Number 8, the building that had seemed so adequate in 1900. On 11 July 1911, only four months and five days before pronouncement of the final judicial decree dissolving the old American Tobacco Company, the office force moved into the new building.[32] In timing, this move seemed in part a preparation for the day of freedom. Office equipment and procedure also appeared to be in the process of change as the moving day approached, although department heads in the factories had no offices and used boxes instead of chairs. Filing cases in 1909 generally consisted of licorice boxes accumulated from the manufacture of plug.

With the exception of "Miss Boogs," the amanuensis of the 1890s, Victoria Hudson, who came from Charlotte, North Carolina, equipped with stenographic skills, appears to have been one of the earliest women employees in the office. It is more than probable, however, that Fallie Elizabeth Hilton (b. 9 October 1880), later Mrs. John C. Walker, was the first woman employed in the office. Closely following her came Annie Leonard, Lelia Idol Trivett, and Lizzie Kimball. At this time all invoices were prepared with pen and ink; copies entered in pencil in a "tissue book" constituted the only record of invoices kept by the company. In 1911, however, typewriters were adopted for preparing invoices and entering orders. Other than a few pages evidently prepared in New York, the minutes remained in handwritten form until 1917. At the instigation of George W. Coan, a complete filing system for general correspondence, a cash-credit filing system for the purchasing department, and a voucher system for the sales department were installed in 1909 with upright, golden oak cabinets, index cards, and folders. This was known as the "Y and E" system—a startling advance over the licorice-box system. In 1905 one Burroughs adding machine, the only one then owned by the company, stood in the secretary's department where it could be used by bookkeepers only at odd times.[33] According to Frank George, who began to work in the billing department in October 1906, just before the opening of the new office building the departments and their heads were somewhat as follows:

ledger	D. Rich (also treasurer)
bill of lading	C. F. Cromer
cost	?
payroll	Walter Brown
leaf	Robert S. Galloway
mail and file	Norman Blum
damaged goods	?
secretary	George W. Coan
premium	George F. Dwire
sales	Robert B. Horn

| purchasing | Walter R. Reynolds (later assisted by his secretary, Roy C. Haberkern) |
| billing | E. P. Miller |

James Sloan, the auditor, exercised general supervision over the payroll, bill of lading, and cost departments, and Robert B. Horn had the same authority over the premium and sales departments.

The premium department, booming at this time because of heavy sales of chewing tobacco, contained forty-four people who, like others in the office, worked from 7:30 A.M. until 6:00 P.M. every day in the week except Saturday when closing time came at 5:00 P.M. During this era of the quid, small metal tags stuck onto the manufactured tobacco bore the brand names. As an encouragement to trade, the company gave premiums in exchange for specified numbers of tags, the trading stamps of their day. In 1902, for example, a brisk chewer might obtain a dinner set for 2,000 tags, an English steel razor for 75, a ladies' mackintosh for 1,000, a calendar clock for 600, a Mason and Hamlin organ for 14,500, or almost any article from a buggy to a bed for the requisite number of tags. Schnapps and Brown's Mule were most popular; from a chewing and poverty-stricken South their tags rolled into Winston by regular, registered, and express mail. H. Floyd Hauser, who began to work in the office in 1899, declared later that the matter of counting tags proved simple compared with the task of interpreting the letters that came with the tags—often so undecipherable that a man might receive a baby carriage when he wanted a shotgun. Messengers were kept busy bringing tags from the post office, but the great annoyance in the redemption of tags lay in thievery. Such tempting premiums were offered that one of the Reynolds night watch-men and a guard in charge of a street crossing of the Southern Railway connived at making a rich haul of tags in 1901, but they were arrested and sent to jail. Somewhere along the way a thief might also steal tags from a package and substitute a similar weight in rocks. On one occasion a Pin-kerton detective investigated a theft of this nature for Reynolds. Disposal of used tags proved to be such a problem that in 1904 the directors ordered the erection of a foundry on the north side of Fourth Street for the destruction of tags returned under their "offers of redemption"; it appears that the old wells used for the disposal of tags were being tapped by thieves. Perhaps the advertising value of tags had been largely ex-hausted in 1906 when a notice ran in approximately six hundred news-papers that the R. J. Reynolds Tobacco Company would discontinue its premium department on 1 January 1907. This produced such a last-minute rush of tags that the backlog could not be cleared away until the following April.[34]

Except for the redemption of tags, R. J. Reynolds's advertising methods from 1899 to 1911 remained much the same as during the 1890s. There were newspaper advertisements, handbills, stickers, posters, window displays, large signs on carload shipments, and the usual pasteboard signs at public spots. In 1907 he again displayed his goods at a widely advertised exposition, as he had done earlier in Atlanta, this time at the Jamestown Tercentenary Exposition. During these years advertising expenses reached a peak in 1905. It is possible that this high point was a result of the launching of Reynolds or Apple Sun Cured, a plug designed to compete with a similar brand known as Grape. Grape was manufactured in Richmond, Virginia, by the R. A. Patterson Tobacco Company, which was taken into the Tobacco Combination and held secretly from the time of its purchase on 4 August 1903 until 29 April 1905. Reynolds knew in 1903 of its purchase; he had Grape analyzed and emerged with Apple Sun Cured, which he evidently pushed heavily in 1905.[35]

Reynolds also maintained a sample department, directed for much of this period by Harvey E. Enochs. Here were the samples of plug and smoking tobacco to be handed out by salesmen or mailed out in reply to Reynolds's offers. All told, the company advertised rather heavily while in the Tobacco Combination, and, judging from the expenses for gratis goods shown in Table 5-1, many samples were distributed.[36]

In determining the growth of organization and consequent division of labor in the company, the team and storage department, later truck and storage, deserves mention. The years 1899–1911 were the last in which there was complete reliance on horse-drawn vehicles, as the use of motor trucks began in 1913 with the first purchase of a chain-driven Garford truck. H. Floyd Hauser, first employed by the company on 11 December 1899, became head of the team and storage department about 1905 when the stables stood at the lower end of Number 256. This was a seven-day job, beginning at five A.M., because the company's five or six teams were fed and watered whether working or not. Leaf tobacco had to be transported from the auction sales house, often until eight o'clock at night, and ultimately from there to the manufacturing plant. With an ordinary dray two hogsheads of tobacco could be hauled at one time; at length, however, Samuel J. Nissen, a manufacturer of wagons, built an improved dray that permitted a load of three hogsheads. With all their drays, the team and storage department could haul only about 150 hogsheads per day. This meant late hours and difficult work during the leaf-marketing period when countless lots of tobacco had to be hauled from the auction sales house and about fifty hogsheads moved from storage to the manufacturing plant each day.

Loading and unloading these heavy hogsheads caused difficulties and injuries. Using skids and ropes, workmen stood atop the wagons and

Table 5-1
Expenses for Advertising and Gratis Goods of the Reynolds Company,
1900–1911

Year	Advertising	Gratis Goods	Total
1900	—	$ 16,168	$ 291,964
1901	—	15,529	430,074
1902	—	—	614,443
1903	—	—	765,603
1904	$582,169	130,311	—
1905	—	186,276	1,142,879
1906	—	—	—
1907	—	—	591,398
1908	227,233	98,734	—
1909	123,418	148,029	271,447
1910	215,301	111,302	326,603
1911	402,563	—	—

Source: Am. Tob. Co. et al. v. U.S., Record on Appeal, docket no. 9137–9139 (6th Cir., 1944), exhibits, 6:1096–1275, 3253–54. The figures have been rounded off to the nearest dollar.

raised or lowered the hogshead largely by brute force. It was not unusual for a man's legs to be completely crushed by a runaway hogshead of tobacco. Improvement in this area of the team and storage department came very slowly. In fact, hogsheads were moved on and off trucks in 1940 much as they were in 1904.[37] Ultimately, loading platforms on a level with the trucks helped considerably not to mention the use of fork-lift trucks in other aspects of loading. Tobacco leaf was stored in houses built for that purpose, in old factories that Reynolds had bought, and often in an auction sales house that had been rented after the sales season. Usually Burley leaf was stored in the auction sales houses, as the market-ing period for that type of leaf began approximately with the close of the Winston-Salem market.

The actual transporting of leaf did not compare in difficulty with its storage. Much damaged leaf came from one early storage building that lacked sufficient ventilation. When hot weather and a sweat caused mold, R. J. sent carpenters to cut windows in the upper walls of the building, thus correcting that particular situation. When constructing new storage buildings, the carpenters left ventilating openings at the tops and bottoms of the buildings. With rain or snow the tobacco in the hogsheads against the walls often molded and many times there was a total loss as the mold spread in the tightly packed tobacco. Often, too, when snow blew in, it was swept off by workmen only to fall on the next layer of hogsheads and cause additional trouble. In fair weather or foul, especially the latter, Hauser generally made his inspection trips from one storage point to another on horseback.

Labor and the Work Environment

With increasing production, the labor force of 2,932 in 1905 grew to 4,201 by 1910.[38] Untrained and generally illiterate, laborers of this period fortunately found an abundance of handwork, including such tasks as moving boxes of leaf tobacco, stemming the leaf, and sweeping floors. To the foremen, who did the hiring, fell the duty of teaching these laborers to perform these simple jobs. Apparently during the earlier years of the business, areas generally contiguous to Winston and Salem furnished an adequate supply of labor. As the business expanded, however, many laborers came from South Carolina. Children of all ages were employed in the factories, although in 1903 the North Carolina legislature endorsed a weak statute against the employment of workers under twelve years old. The gradual introduction of machinery such as the Adams double acting plug machine promised to end the indiscriminate hiring of children under twelve. Despite the low wages paid during these years, there appears to have been little or no complaint on the part of the workers, whose pay was probably as adequate as that of most laborers in the area. No doubt also, the Negroes who left tenant farms in upper South Carolina fared about as well in the factories of the R. J. Reynolds Tobacco Company as they had on cotton farms, because they were able to have gardens and livestock in the rural confines of the Winston-Salem area of that day.

Labor during the years from 1899 to 1911 remained largely handwork, although labor-saving machinery such as the Adams double acting plug machine was rapidly coming into use. In this era of chewing tobacco many of the laborers were Negroes.

When Ed Blakely began to work in a leaf house in November 1900, scarcity of labor was so pronounced that foremen often sent him to find hands in the town. During this period Charles Hunt, a reliable and judicious Negro, was sent to South Carolina for additional laborers. There, apparently in the area south and southeast of Charlotte, Hunt rounded up tenant farm families to whom five dollars per week seemed like salvation. On his first trip he is said to have gathered together a trainload of people who came to Winston in boxcars. They lined up on Fifth Street to be examined by foremen who hired them in groups without reference to pay or the nature of the work to be done. Foremen continued to do the hiring until 1919, when the employment office became the hiring agency for the company. Many of these South Carolinians proved to be excellent laborers and, happy in their new-found prosperity, sent home for their relatives and neighbors to join them. Police officers from South Carolina actually came for one man, who had contracted to make a crop before coming to Winston. Hunt made several additional trips. Charlie Wells came from near Newberry, South Carolina, in 1908 and remained with the Reynolds company until retiring in 1961. His first job was loading freight cars by means of a two-wheeled truck, which involved much lifting of heavy loads; today it involves no greater effort than pushing a button. Incidentally, Wells's pay of one dollar per day sometimes amounted to not more than three dollars per week because he worked only when needed. The South Carolina Negroes at one time could be distinguished from others by their references to "barrels" of tobacco and to "Reynolds Tobacco Mill," nomenclature brought from an area where the term "cotton mills" was the only indication of industry.[39]

It was the duty of the foremen to give these untried workers some semblance of training—no doubt often an exasperating duty that may in some measure account for the haughty attitude assumed by many foremen. Though much of the work did not require a high degree of skill, the factories contained some dangerous machinery, belts, and elevators, one of which in 1903 nipped off the toe of Robert Jones as he stood too near the door. Such injuries as the laceration of the hand of a young white man, Luther Lee Loggins (d. 30 July 1963), came frequently from the Adams press, or the lump machine, as it was generally known. Untoward accidents also occurred such as the painful injuries received in 1903 by Andrew Hunt, who was driving the R. J. R. tobacco box dray when his team became frightened by a fire engine on Fifth Street.[40] There was also the matter of thievery, which made foremen generally suspicious. The jailing of two people for stealing forty pounds "of lump" from the company in 1900 could, however, in no way excuse Louis F. Owen for cursing Charlie Wells and cruelly docking his meager wages because he took out a bundle of waste wood to use for kindling his fire at home.[41]

A description of the type of work required by the manufacturing process may clarify the need for so much unskilled labor during the period dominated by the production of chewing tobacco. Many of the jobs received names that are now obscure; some, however, remain in use. Actually the work of the more modern leaf-processing department and the manufacture of chewing tobacco occurred in the same factory, and the division between the two processes did not seem as sharp then as they were by the 1960s when the leaf-processing department was responsible for redrying, stemming, casing, and blending. According to the fading memories of many older workers, there were such general laborers as doormen, janitors, mechanics, and sweepers hired to sweep the floor while learning the business, job hands who were called on for any duty, truck rollers who pushed heavy loads of tobacco across the floor on trucks, or "mules" as they were generally called, car unloaders, coal shovelers, and plumber's helpers generally required to check on sprinklers.

In the preparation of the tobacco leaf for manufacture, there were hogshead openers, untiers who removed the tie leaf from the butt ends of bundles of leaf, pickers who removed trashy leaves and foreign matter and separated the remaining leaves into wrappers (excellent leaves for wrapping each plug) and fillers (leaves for filling the inside of the plug), and classers who graded the leaves chosen for wrappers into groups according to color, body, and type. The untying line usually ran the length of the picking and classing room. Here it should be noted that hogsheads had been opened in the sweat house by the reordering crew. If the manufacturing department was in a great hurry, the tobacco often received no steaming but went through the reordering machine, which dried and reordered the leaf to make it pliable and easier to handle. In this process, workers often used axes to cut molded leaves from the sides of the hogsheads for discard. Weighers weighed the leaf into drafts or lots of about forty pounds and draft boys then hurried across the floor giving each picker about five drafts, which constituted a normal day's work for a woman picker. Draft boys kept pretty busy lifting boxes of leaf from the mules. During this first phase of the work, stemmers handled each leaf of the filler and removed the woody midrib, leaving the filler leaf, which with flavoring composed the inside of the plug. Wrappers went to wrapper packers, who literally packed these superior leaves into neat flat packs ready for the wrapper receiver, who distributed them in the machine room to wrapper stemmers for removal of the midrib. Thereupon the stemmed wrappers went to the cappers to use for encasing the lump, or partially made plug. Often, too, when it was too dark for pickers and classers to work efficiently, they went to an upper floor to hang newly purchased bundles of leaf on sticks before they went into the Proctor Redrying Machine.

In the meantime, the stemmed filler traveled a different route to the casing and drying room, where it was cased. It was then shaken into a loose mass, hand-forked onto the blending bed, and sprinkled with flavoring. The blending bed was little more than a large area of the floor surrounded with boxes of tobacco ready to be pitched on the floor to receive flavoring. The filler, pliable, went to the machine room, later known as the lump-making department. In addition to the machines for making lump there were twisters who seized packs of filler, encased them in a wrapper, and twisted the lot into a twist which then received pressure. Some chewers preferred twist to plug perhaps as a relic from simpler days.

Plug was made in the machine room. Lump makers, or "machine boys," as they were called after adoption of the Adams press, took a lump of filler that had been weighed and dropped it into the machine where it received pressure, while the machine boy placed a second lump in the other chamber of the machine. Machine boys occasionally lost a hand when miscalculating the action of the press. Cappers then received wrapper leaves in halves from the wrapper stemmer and covered the lump with the wrapper. Usually taken into the prize room by hand, the wrapped lumps were put into steel shapes—often with divisions of 3 by 6 inches—by shape hands who lifted the heavy sinkers, or slabs of iron keyed to the divisions of the shapes, onto the shapes. Hydraulic pressure was then applied until the plug was thoroughly pressed. "Look-over boys" stacked these pressed plugs into their arms and let them fall one by one, like a pack of cards, watching for streaked, dark, or torn wrappers. In many cases the faulty plugs were returned to the shapes for additional pressure to force the excess casing from the filler and thus leave the wrapper leaf unstreaked. Pot mill hands, also in the prize room, placed the plugs into pot mills for making indentations to show where the retailer might cut the plug and where the taggers were to place the brand tags. The time in the pot mill was adjusted to the degree of darkness desired for the wrapper. Gummers packed the finished plugs into boxes, or gums, to be carried to the sweat house under the direction of Walter Reynolds, where they sometimes remained for sixty days. By the 1960s this time period had been greatly reduced and in some cases eliminated. In the sample room during the early years, the plug-wrapping department of the 1960s, labelers applied labels to the boxes; stampers affixed the revenue stamps; and the chew, the most popular form of manufactured tobacco until about 1918, stood ready for shipment. Often the stamper was a young Negro boy who somehow managed enough saliva to keep working for several hours at a time.

This piecemeal view of the tasks involved in the manufacture of chewing tobacco from 1899 to 1911 can do little more than suggest the great amount of handwork necessary. It also illuminates the statement frequently heard in Winston-Salem during the 1960s: if the Reynolds company's present volume of production required laborers on the same scale as in the years described, the city would be as large as Chicago.

Based on the recollections of many, this account is no more than a rough description. It does not include the work of such people as Harry Spencer, a Negro who came to Reynolds from Brown Brothers and Company perhaps in 1899. Walter Reynolds wrote W. L. Brown for information on a mixture for black twist that Brown had formerly manufactured. Brown replied, giving Reynolds the specific proportions of olive oil, rum, and glycerin. But, he added: "Harry Spencer (Colored, I think he now works for you) was our twist and pot mill hand for re-pulling twist for 8 or 10 years I think. If you would put him on the job he knows all about how much to have the boys apply & how to do it."[42] Nor does the description of the processes contain any of the lore about the consideration that R. J. Reynolds accorded the laborers. One example of this concerns Henry George, head of the press room in factory Number 256, who kept a great deal of live steam pouring into the room in order to keep the tobacco in good working condition. One day as R. J. passed through the room, he objected to its sickening heat and ordered the steam reduced. On a similar occasion in the prize room of Number 256 he saw the shape hands working with perspiration pouring from their bodies. Immediately he gave orders for a ten-minute cooling-off period before closing time. That directive was still followed in the 1960s.[43]

All in all, the management, from R. J. to many of his foremen, regarded laborers in a paternalistic fashion. Under such circumstances, workers would appeal directly to Reynolds in attempts to better themselves. Nor did he always refuse such appeals. When R. J. entered a factory, it was not unusual for a group of laborers to ask for a raise. Although he frequently put them off by saying that he paid all he could afford, he sometimes increased their wages on the spot.

The large number of floor sweepers usually found in the factories were hired at Reynolds's insistence for the purpose of training more men. Though R. J. gave such orders, he did not necessarily follow his own policy. Doakes Scales, an old Negro who operated the boiler in Number 256, allowed no one to come near his mechanical pet. His death in 1906 left the company seriously handicapped because no one had been trained to take over the job. R. J.'s chief mechanic solved the problem by inducing John Petree, boiler tender at Fries Cotton Mill, to join Reynolds and learn to pamper Scales's boiler. In a short time Petree became chief engineer for Number 256. Later in life Petree declared that his tools were of the simplest kind: a monkey wrench, a screw driver, a hammer, a hand ratchet, a cold chisel, and a calking iron—tools that by 1950 had long since given way to electric drills, air drills, electric welders, and air hammers. Reynolds also showed great deference to his laborers on other occasions. When he decided to make a new plug brand or to change a flavoring formula, he did not send test plugs to his directors, who were all good chewers, but looked among the laborers for expert chewers whom he invited to his office. There they would sit, chew, spit, and consider. If the group decided to change the formula, it was done and the conference was repeated. R. J. indulged in no foolishness with the laborers but appeared dignified and businesslike.[44]

Foremen, on the other hand, did not have Reynolds's ability to charm, flatter, or impress the laborers. They, of course, had difficult jobs in handling undisciplined laborers, who fought and cursed on the slightest provocation, but many of these early foremen also used fighting and cursing as a means to increase production. One of the greatest offenders in this respect was a foreman by the name of McKinsey in a stemming room. Usually accompanied by an informal bodyguard, McKinsey entered fights freely and as long as he had the advantage his bodyguard stood back; otherwise, the bodyguard knocked out McKinsey's opponent. A disturbance of a slightly different nature arose in Number 256 when an intoxicated subforeman heard the superintendent of the building, R. E. Lasater, approaching his floor. Crawling into a drier, the subforeman left his feet exposed, thus forcing Lasater to pull him out. Arless Hauser, a foreman in Number 8's lump-making room, stated later that the habit of fighting among employees remained widespread in 1911. He succeeded in restraining the habit in his department by calling the police who took the offenders away; the resulting fines proved to be excellent deterrents. Some foremen preferred to handle fighting, cursing, spitting on the floor, and other such offenses by docking wages. This method was used by a foreman named Nichols, who posted signs on the walls and even on the ceilings to call attention to his one-dollar fines for a great variety of offenses.

Boys aged twelve or younger often began to work at the Reynolds company with the permission—but possibly more often at the instigation—of their parents. Fathers of these boys regularly came to the factories on Saturdays to collect the wages earned by their sons. Occasionally when a boy ran away from his work, his father would catch him, punish him, and return him to the factory. If such desertions became too prevalent, the foremen cooperated with the parents by locking the doors to prevent escape. At that time it was routine to use corporal punishment to control children and, when foremen in the factories whipped a boy for loafing or destroying property, the parents rarely objected. In the stemming department especially small children accompanied their mothers to work, many of them occupying nooks and corners in the factories or attempting to help with the work—often according to the whim of the foreman.[45]

It was a rough and riotous time with as many as sixteen saloons in Winston during the early years of this period, but reforms were on the way. Children would soon be removed from the factories by state action. The time was also rapidly approaching when foremen would have the power of employment taken from them and company officials would turn their thoughts to the many personnel problems. The following 1909 letter from William V. Garner, superintendent of Number 8, and Walter R. Reynolds, director and manager of the department of manufacturing, to the foremen contains many suggestive warnings. It also indicates that neither Garner nor Reynolds perhaps understood how to meet the situation:[46]

> Beginning June 1st, we wish to tabulate and keep for future reference, occurrences in your department, both favorable and unfavorable to your management. At the end of any given period we will be in position to judge as to your fitness for present responsibilities and worthiness for promotion.
>
> Extensive additions are planned, which will from time to time make new openings which it would be our pleasure to fill from your ranks.
>
> Were you called at any time, for one man completely schooled to take a position of like nature to your own, and you failed to furnish such, this would reflect upon you and would be a serious bar to your advancement. Therefore, begin at once to devote your every spare moment to drilling and developing your assistants; exact of them the same watchfulness of their help as you exercise over them, or in plainer words, "teach them how to teach their help." Point them to such as you know to be expert workers, have them study these first, and points thus gained they will eagerly communicate to others of less experience.
>
> Have them note and report to you, ones that show intelligence and skill in their work, likewise those, to the contrary and in due time check up their reports and such as cannot be brought up to the standard, help to weed out. In this way, those well recommended from posts requiring but little skill, can be given opportunity to learn skilled work; their old places being given to new, or green help. Insist upon neat and cleanly house, tools and machinery; cuspidors that are daily cleansed at places needed, giving no excuse for spitting on floors, fining those caught doing so; gradually educate all help to wearing clothes free from rags. If persistently ragged, have a shearing occasionally, and your help will soon become ashamed of this, and will leave such clothes at home, and will adopt cheap but substantial overalls, which are washable.
>
> Provide safe appliances and tools for your workers, and in the event you judge any machinery or elevator in your department is not properly safeguarded, you should immediately report same to this office.
>
> We will note carefully when inspecting your departments, how well you have construed and exercised these suggestions, and hope that we will not find two or more foreman [sic] grouped in idle gossip, as we regret to say, we have seen in the past; but that their duties will be

so interestingly outlined by you, that it will be their pleasure to devote all of the working hours in furtherance of plans, the successful issue of which will result in their, your and our advancement.

No doubt the extensive additions referred to by Garner and Walter Reynolds were chiefly the four additions to Number 256, each as large as the fine new factory built by Reynolds in 1891. The number of laborers undoubtedly increased from 1899 to 1911 in proportion to the increase in the size of the plant, which was rapid indeed. During its years as a subsidiary of the Tobacco Combination the R. J. Reynolds Tobacco Company built a total of fourteen major structures, only four of which appear to have been leaf houses. They appear in Table 5-2 as used and numbered in 1958. Not included in Table 5-2 are a number of buildings, such as those purchased from P. H. Hanes and Company, sweat houses, other leaf storage sheds in Winston and one at Critz, Virginia, and new and enlarged stables at the intersection of Vine and Depot streets for the team and storage division.[47] Generally the more pretentious of these buildings were designed by J. E. Sirrine and Company, of Greenville, South Carolina, a firm with considerable experience in designing cotton factories. Building contracts often went to E. C. Bowman and Company, also for many years a contractor and builder in the Winston-Salem area. Then E. C. Bowman and Company moved to Lexington, Kentucky, later obtaining the services of Reynolds's early superintendent of construction, F. P. Solomon, who left early in 1913.[48] It was in Number 256, probably in the fifth section, that the company in 1909 installed its first Hamilton-Corliss generator, which some said would supply the power needs for years to come—a prophecy only slightly overstated because it was not discarded completely until 1959. Weighing more than ninety-four tons, it was a wonder in its day.[49]

The concern of Walter Reynolds and William Garner for the appearance, training, and behavior of their rapidly expanding corps of foremen and employees was not the only indication of activity along that line. In May 1902 the wages of some four hundred employees were increased by 10 percent; in 1906 the work period was reduced from eleven to ten hours per day with no cut in wages. To that bit of encouraging news, the editor of the *Union Republican* added a statement characteristic of the general tenor of the times: "And some will argue that corporations have no souls." On the other hand, C. T. Dixon recalled that in 1903 a person starting work at $4.50 to $5.00 per week might not receive an increase in wages until everyone in the room received an increase, thus making it possible for some to work as long as fifteen years without a raise. Despite the raise for four hundred employees in 1902, the average weekly wage of cash payroll and leaf department employees and subforemen in 1905

Table 5-2

Major Structures Built by the Reynolds Company During 1900–1911
(as Numbered and Used in 1958)

Year	Structure	Use
1900	Number 1 at 8	Packing, lighters, smoking office
1900	Number 43	Stemming and blending
1901	Number 3	Leaf house in Danville, Va.
1902	Number 1 at 1	Leaf house
1903	Number 5 at 8	Plug manufacture and strip preparation
1904	Number 25	Leaf equipment storage
1907	Number 4	Construction shop
1907	South Boston, Va.	Leaf house and office
1909	Number 2 at 256	Smoking, storage, and strip preparation
1909	Number 5 at 256	Pipe shop storage
1910	Number 3 at 256	Cigarette storage
1910	Number 6 at 256	Pipe shop
1910	Number 4	Leaf house in Danville, Va.
1911	Number 38	Electric and cooper shop (main office until 1929)

Source: Description of Company Properties, secretary's department, R. J. Reynolds Tobacco Company.

amounted to only $3.87 per week, whereas in 1910 it reached $4.87.[50] Though such small increases represented only nominal improvement, the income of Reynolds employees doubtless stood as high as that of the average farm tenant.

Effects of the panic of 1907 and poverty in the agricultural area surrounding Winston and Salem go far to explain the general acceptance of the prevailing wage. During these years, however, there was in the area a growing interest in the Socialist party. So great was the general regard for the tenets of socialism that "a large sized audience" heard Eugene V. Debs give a lecture in the auditorium on 28 March 1911, although an admission fee was charged;[51] nor was this the end of such ideas in Winston and Salem. But there is little in the way of actual evidence to show any effort at organization among the employees from 1899 to 1911. In 1898 three hundred workers in Brown and Williamson's factory protested a reduction in wages but remained out only a short time until their requests were met.[52] Henry Fisher, motivated by fear of the Tobacco Combination, succeeded in organizing the white and Negro workers of Brown Brothers and Company and P. H. Hanes and Company when they were on the eve of absorption by Reynolds. This union, which had a large membership in the North and Middle West pledged to use products from independent factories, did no more in Winston and Salem than organize the laborers of these two firms so soon to cease operations.[53] The policies of the Tobacco Combination thus erased Fisher's efforts to organize the workers. On 5 October 1900 about fifty Reynolds machine hands receiving sixty cents per day struck for $4.50 per week and thereby threw a number of wrapper stemmers out of work. Reynolds, stating that these boys were green, inexperienced workers who were being paid all they were worth, offered them one dollar per day if they would produce eight hundred pounds of lump in that time; some returned but others sought new jobs. Another strike in 1902 must have been more important, although few details appeared in the local newspaper; the company offered some concessions and the strikers returned to work. A very reasonable request came from Reynolds employees in 1908 when they petitioned for a shutdown on Saturdays—a move heartily approved by the local editor because the weather was excessively hot and business generally slow.[54]

During 1899–1911 it appears that the chief trouble among laborers resulted from injuries on the job—surely no surprise in factories filled with children, unskilled laborers, and increasing numbers of machines. In 1901 it was announced in a local newspaper that the company would employ no more children under the age of twelve, a policy endorsed "by the last general assembly."[55] This announcement probably embodied a policy rather than actual practice. Evidence indicates that similar problems connected with labor were demanding increasing attention. Dempsie Archie, a twelve-year-old Negro boy, had three fingers crushed on 23 February 1906, but, rejoiced the *Union Republican*, the "company furnishes free treatment to injured employees at Slater Hospital and Dempsie is in good hands."[56] This change in policy, made possibly in 1905 or 1906, came as the result of a recommendation to R. J. Reynolds by Clement Manly. Evidently suits such as that of *Rolin v. R. J. Reynolds Tobacco Company* induced Manly to recommend free hospital treatment for employees injured in any of the company's factories. In *Rolin v. R. J. Reynolds* involving the loss of the plaintiff's hand, the defendant won in the December term of the Forsyth County Superior Court in 1905. This was the first case to reach the state supreme court under the state child labor law enacted in 1903. The plaintiff's testimony is of value in illustrating conditions that prevailed in the plug factories of the company. Obviously the machine in question was the Adams duplex press:

I commenced work for the defendant about a year ago, May, 1904. I went in there one Monday morning. Mr. Nichols, boss man in the room, spoke to me and asked me if I wanted to weigh fillers. I told him yes. He took me over and put me to weighing; then he put me to cutting lumps on a table. They were making 3-inch work. I worked at that place three days in one fortnight, and in the second fortnight six days. After cutting lumps I then was a sweeper on the floor, I cleaned up about machines and around on the floor. The evening at 4 o'clock we got out of the factory. The weigh-boy went down the house to wash his hands. The man that run the machine went down the house to clean up another machine. I was cleaning up the one I worked at. The weigh-boy ran up and threw a piece of cut tobacco in the machine. I reached my hand in there to take it out. He pulled the lever and run the machine caught my hand and tore it off. I don't know the fellow who took me out of the machine. Mr. Nichols took me up in the house above, and said Did you not tell me you were 12 years old? I said, No. I was 11 years old in June, 1903. When cutting off lumps I was 12 inches away from the machine. No one explained to me the dangerous character of the machine, nor told me anything about it. I was born 4 June, 1892. I would not have been hurt if the boy had not pulled the lever. The machine was set, and you had to pull the lever that made it work and set it. At the time I was hurt I worked by the side of John Dillon all that day. Table and truck between me and the machine. The lever is in front of the machine. I did not get a lump and try to press it in the machine. He, Dillon, had pressed a lump that day for me. It was not after quitting time when I was hurt. If it was, all hands had not gotten out of the factory. No one told me to clean up the machine. I saw others cleaning up the machine and I did so. No one ever asked me to clean up the machine or do anything about it. It was a part of my duty to clean up around the machine. Will Hairston is the name of the boy that pulled the lever of machine on me. He is working down there in the factory now. There was a belt attached to the machine running at the time. No one told me to clean up around the machine. Other boys were at work cleaning up.

Willie Rolin obtained no compensation for the loss of his hand because the judge believed that the enacting law had been repealed or that the first section had been omitted from the revised code.[57] Yet the decision to send injured employees for immediate treatment represented some progress toward a more humane consideration of labor.

CHAPTER 6

A National Product and Financial Stability

The R. J. Reynolds Tobacco Company of New Jersey began operations in 1899 apparently in complete agreement with the plans of the Tobacco Combination, whereby the Reynolds company, except for a few slow-selling brands of smoking tobacco, was limited to the production of flat-plug chewing tobacco. As the years went by and R. J. Reynolds became more concerned with the increasing popularity of smoking tobacco compared with chewing tobacco, he determined to begin the manufacture and sale of smoking tobacco—if possible, on a national scale. Not wishing to be left merely as the producer of flat plug, Reynolds developed five new brands of smoking tobacco, at least one aimed at a national market. Success with Prince Albert smoking tobacco may well be regarded as a turning point in the company's history. This had been accomplished by 16 November 1911, when the old American Tobacco Company received its final notice of dissolution from a U.S. circuit court. This should not be interpreted to mean that the R. J. Reynolds Tobacco Company failed to profit from its years in the Tobacco Combination; it had profited both because of and in spite of the American Tobacco Company.

Prince Albert: A National Product

Reynolds's entry into the smoking tobacco business apparently took on new life in 1904, which saw his production virtually doubled over that of the previous year. The increase in the consumption of chewing tobacco, he declared in 1909, had by no means kept pace with the output of

Table 6-1
Annual Per Capita Consumption of Chewing and Smoking Tobacco in the
United States, 1900–1911

	Pounds of Tobacco	
Year	Chewing	Smoking
1900	2.39	1.31
1901	2.38	1.44
1902	2.28	1.51
1903	2.29	1.58
1904	2.22	1.80
1905	2.09	1.92
1906	2.16	2.01
1907	2.16	2.10
1908	2.06	2.07
1909	2.15	2.17
1910	2.17	2.30
1911	1.98	2.23

Source: Neil H. Borden, *The Economic Effects of Advertising* (Chicago, 1947), p. 216.

smoking tobacco.[1] Statistics indicate that Reynolds held a correct view of the situation (see Table 6-1). When his production of smoking tobacco surpassed one million pounds in 1907, before Prince Albert, it seemed clear that Reynolds was achieving more than merely saving the scrap tobacco, a by-product of plug manufacture. This development was clearly the most significant made by R. J. Reynolds while his company functioned as a subsidiary of the American Tobacco Company. It was during this period that the fast-selling Prince Albert began to seem like a national favorite. The idea that provoked Reynolds's decision to emphasize the manufacture of smoking tobacco while his firm was still dominated by the American Tobacco Company appears most distinctly in the 1917 supplemental petition of the company in regard to excess profits taxes. Of this decision Harry H. Shelton, counsel for the Reynolds company, wrote with partial accuracy: "He [R. J. Reynolds] kept alive the competition that did exist in the tobacco industry. In 1908 and 1909, while the suit for the dissolution of the 'Tobacco Trust' was still pending, the Reynolds Company began to enlarge and develop the smoking tobacco branch of its business. This proved to be a remarkable success."[2] Almost twenty-five years later P. Frank Hanes, general counsel, director, and later a vice-president, declared that Reynolds had planned Prince Albert "as a national seller."[3] Standing by itself this statement is perhaps incorrect, because Reynolds actually developed five distinct and new smoking tobacco brands from 1906 until 1910: Refined, Prince Albert, B. F. Gravely & Sons Special, George Washington, and Stud—in that order. Prince Albert did not hit its stride until 1910, or Reynolds would probably have launched yet another brand in the hope that one of them would capture the national taste among smokers.

The earliest available reference to Refined is 2 March 1906, when the R. J. Reynolds Tobacco Company registered it with the *Connorton Tobacco Brand Directory*,[4] although it did not appear on the price list until 22 March 1907. Refined was thus almost two years older than Prince Albert, which first appeared on 18 December 1907.

Scattering his shot in all directions on the smoking tobacco field, Reynolds developed another brand, a cut plug for smoking or chewing. Evidently he based this brand, George Washington, on his old brand of chewing tobacco called George Washington 3-ply Twist in 1887 and simply George Washington Twist in 1903.[5] Reynolds shipped his first package of George Washington cut plug on 8 May 1909, and, either because of encouraging sales or because he wished to guarantee his title to it, he soon desired to use the bust of George Washington on the new brand. This symbol he knew to be the property of the American Tobacco Company. When in New York in April 1910, he called twice in one day on an assistant counsel of American about assigning the bust of George Washington to the R. J. Reynolds Tobacco Company for "a tobacco trademark." Possibly ignorant of R. J.'s intentions, the counselor investigated the matter and wrote him on 27 April 1910, enclosing an assignment of "the design of the bust of George Washington" with the goodwill pertaining to that trademark, all made entirely legal by the signature of Caleb C. Dula.[6] The term "smoking tobacco" appears nowhere in the correspondence, and it is doubtful that Dula knew exactly why Reynolds desired the bust of George Washington. Advertised as the greatest American cut plug, ready for the pipe, George Washington became a steady but not a sensational seller. By 1912, however, the brand did so well that a machine builder was commissioned to construct an automatic packer for the George Washington 3½-ounce package. In operation by August 1913, the packer wrapped the tobacco in foil for insertion into cloth bags.[7] George Washington eventually appeared in a cylindrical tin humidor and was still on the market in 1964, still with its same patriotic bust on a blue background sprinkled with stars as an additional symbol of patriotism.

Stud, a trademark originally used by Allen Washington Turner of Macon, Georgia, as early as 1884, was registered by him on 19 August 1890. On 7 December 1909, however, through the wholesale firm of A. J. Long

Cigar and Grocery Company, Turner transferred the title of Stud to the R. J. Reynolds Tobacco Company.[8] No doubt R. J.'s love of horseflesh as well as the virility inherent in the name influenced him to make this particular purchase. Refined had been designed to compete with Bull Durham, then selling more than 12 million pounds annually for the American Tobacco Company; Stud was evidently to strike at Duke's Mixture, at the time selling 17 or 18 million pounds for the same company. Granulated bright tobacco like Duke's Mixture, Stud first appeared on Reynolds's price list on 3 January 1910, with special attention called to it.[9]

Reynolds's attempts to compete with the American Tobacco Company for the smoking tobacco trade seemed foolhardy, but in 1910 Prince Albert began to move fast, its production reaching 2,015,809 pounds. As a subsidiary in the Tobacco Combination, the R. J. Reynolds Tobacco Company was supposed to concentrate on the production of flat-plug chewing tobacco, Reynolds having delivered to American the various brands of smoking tobacco obtained through the purchase of three Winston plants in 1899 and 1900. Partial figures for Reynolds's total production of smoking tobacco from 1897 through 1911 (see Table 6-2) perhaps indicate that he soon determined to ignore the plans of the company that held two-thirds of his stock.[10] Four years after the dissolution of the old American Tobacco Company, production of Prince Albert reached 24,-602,800 pounds and continued from that point until it reached its peak of more than 56,000,000 pounds in one year.

Prince Albert evidently grew in part out of the failure of Refined, in which Reynolds had placed great faith. In fact, this new brand of granulated bright leaf, so easily manufactured from leaf on hand, received a gold medal for its excellence at the Jamestown Tercentenary Exposition of 1907.[11] Its early reception promised success until substantial quantities molded while in the hands of dealers and had to be repossessed at a loss by the company. Too much water had been put in the casing. In a company that has stressed omission of unpleasant references to its employees, past or present, it is still relatively easy to find that W. T. Hancock, Jr., who had charge of making Refined, was immediately discharged.[12] The Reynolds company however, did not desert its new brand. Refined, in cloth bags wrapped in weatherproof and transparent glassine paper, was tried again. A letter to the sales force in 1911 urged that its excellence be emphasized: "You can do so now with full assurance that all past mistakes have been corrected and that *Refined* to-day is of a good quality and is being manufactured by as good a process as any 1-oz. granulated smoking tobacco on the market."[13] Refined remained on the price lists and, according to Ernest Wyatt Fulton, formerly superintendent of the smoking division, was not discontinued until 15 November 1944.[14] It evidently yielded a small

Table 6-2
The Reynolds Company's Total Production of Smoking Tobacco, 1897–1911

Year	Pounds
1897	209,600
1898	Not available
1899	Not available
1900	88,894
1901	287,943
1902	238,960
1903	397,472
1904	658,365
1905	880,341
1906	859,481
1907	1,242,168
1908	1,799,824
1909	2,862,099
1910	5,424,780
1911	10,749,131

Sources: The figure for 1897 is from *Report of the Commissioner of Corporations on the Tobacco Industry*, 3 vols. (Washington, D.C., 1909–15), 1:104, 387, which gives the 1906 production figure as 875,000 pounds. The remaining figures are from Recapitulation of Shipments by Year—cost records, comptroller's department, R. J. Reynolds Tobacco Company.

profit during that long period, but the mistake of one man ruined the reputation of Refined early in its career.

According to William N. Reynolds, as his brothers R. J. and Walter had dinner with him one night, they fell to discussing the unfortunate situation of Refined. It was R. J.'s idea to develop another brand based on bright leaf. Walter Reynolds, who had constantly urged the use of Burley, finally accused R. J. of trying to push water uphill in order to help the farmers of the Virginia-Carolina area. At length, R. J. agreed with Walter. Soon Will Reynolds began his first purchases of Burley leaf in Kentucky— a matter certainly not to be entrusted to the buyers of the American Tobacco Company because smoking tobacco was involved. Without experience in buying from a Burley cooperative pool, Will Reynolds eventually but with difficulty obtained the help of Theodore Hamilton Kirk, of Louisville, Kentucky, who later joined the company and became a director. Much of the difficulty in purchasing Burley during the early years of Prince Albert, according to Will Reynolds, came from the American Tobacco Company. At one point in his negotiations with officials of the

Burley pool, Reynolds was told that under the circumstances he would have to obtain his Burley from American.[15]

So the Burley brand of smoking tobacco was born, but how and why was it christened Prince Albert? The first available mention of the name appears on 20 June 1907 in a letter of R. J. Reynolds to the Woodward and Tiernan Printing Company of St. Louis, requesting that one of their "best artists" prepare a sketch "for the front side of the label for our brand 'Prince Albert.'" Reynolds enclosed a rough sketch except for a center oval space in which he wished "the picture of King Edward in a Prince Albert coat" to appear. The picture should be "of such length as to show the entire Prince Albert coat to advantage." After giving detailed directions for the background and size of letters, Reynolds referred to an enclosed photograph, which he had evidently secured from Underwood and Underwood of New York, and about which he was concerned because of its failure to show the full length of the coat. But, he added, "your artist, we suppose . . . can fit the King out in the latest frock."[16] Soon, however, Reynolds solved the question of the coat. When reading the Richmond *Times-Dispatch* for 14 July 1907, his quick eye noted an illustration captioned "Mark Twain's Interview With The King and Queen At Windsor Garden Party." There stood the king resplendent in a Prince Albert coat— a style that he had originated in earlier years. Reynolds tore off a large portion of page four of the sports section and wrote promptly—on 17 July—to the *Times-Dispatch* for advice as to whom he should address to obtain "the drawing from which this plate was made." Back came the reply dated 20 July and promptly Reynolds wrote to the North American Syndicate in Philadelphia for a copy of the drawing. Informed by the manager of the syndicate that he might purchase "an albumen print from this copy for two dollars," Reynolds on 25 July sent the money requesting that the print be forwarded to Woodward and Tiernan.

The remaining problems concerned the work of Woodward and Tiernan, to whom Reynolds wrote on 20 July:

> . . . we have decided to change the wording in this label to read as follows: Prince Albert. Crimp Cut. Now King. Long Burning Pipe and Cigarette Tobacco.
>
> Instead of arranging the words "Prince Albert" around the top of the oval, as on the former sketch, let same go straight across the label in a nice, clean, neat lettering of a slender stroke, letting the spaces between the letters be of the same width as used in forming the outline or stroke in letters. The word "Crimp" to appear at the top of the oval on the left, and the word "Cut" at the top of the oval on the right. Of course these two words should not appear in as large and as prominent letters as the words "Prince Albert." The words "Now

King" are to appear at the bottom of the oval straight across. The line reading "Long burning pipe and cigarette tobacco" to be displayed in neat, easily read letters, in the best possible arrangement in two or three lines as you find the space will measure to the best advantage. We enclose a little rough sketch, which will perhaps more clearly define our ideas to you, and we hope you will put one of your best and most careful artists to work on this revised sketch immediately, and let us have same at earliest time possible.

Frank C. Banks, chief of Woodward and Tiernan's art department, replied on 2 August, sending the revised sketch in which he had taken no liberties with the king's position, although he was "built from the ground up." This position of the king, when surrounded "with a group of ladies and talking with the famous Mark Twain looked very nice," declared Banks. When the surroundings were eliminated, however, the king looked "a little bit peculiar." By that time R. J. Reynolds was enjoying a vacation at Bretton Woods, New Hampshire, but his fellow workers, among whom were Joseph D. Noell, Walter Reynolds, and George W. Coan, wrote R. J. on 7 August that they had authorized Woodward and Tiernan to make certain minor changes and would send him the latest revised sketch for approval. In conclusion, they showed that R. J. Reynolds was the final and sole arbiter of the label for Prince Albert: "Also, when you have the wording ready that goes on the back of the box, send it to us, and we will use our best efforts to get it arranged in a sketch that will meet your approval."

Such infinite care in providing a label for a tobacco product is some indication of R. J.'s determination to produce a brand that would catch the eye and taste of the smoking public.[17] His next national seller would soon require the same painstaking care.

Experimentation with the production of Prince Albert naturally began on a small scale. Sam Mitchell reputedly built the first drying machine—no larger than an office desk—for use in developing the brand. Reynolds experimented for some time before obtaining a mixture to his satisfaction. William O. McCorkle changed the flavoring and sweetening agents until R. J. was satisfied with the formula. Cased in Number 8 and cut in Number 256, the first sample emerged in the presence of C. T. Dixon, William V. Garner, McCorkle, and R. J. Reynolds. It consisted of Burley leaf of different grades and ages, but no rum.[18]

For some reason, however, Reynolds claimed in an advertisement of 11 September 1911 that the Prince Albert formula had been the work of an eminent German scientist who dearly loved his pipe and experimented with smoking tobacco as a side line. Also according to this advertisement, the company had acquired the formula, set experts to perfecting it, and spent "a bunch of money" in doing so. A patent on this marvelous process had been granted on 30 July 1907, and two years later the company was prepared "to manufacture Prince Albert on a vast scale."[19] This claim might be dismissed as mere advertising, but amazingly Reynolds had provided a basis for it. Or was it a ruse to avoid pressure from his largest stockholder? The so-called patented process was first filed in 1897 by Dr. Emil Alexander de Schweinitz, a native of Salem who was educated at the universities of Virginia and North Carolina and in German universities.[20] Of no actual connection with the formula for Prince Albert, this process amounted to little more than a method for sterilizing the leaf in an infusion of licorice, although it also involved the use of bacteria from a superior grade of leaf before fermentation. It was not patented in de Schweinitz's lifetime, but on 19 October 1906 the executor of his estate and a patent lawyer in Washington sold a one-half interest in the process to R. J. Reynolds. With an affidavit from Reynolds as to the efficacy of the process, a reconsideration was submitted to the patent office, where similar claims had interfered with the granting of the patent. Samples of leaf with and without treatment by the de Schweinitz process were submitted anew. By 19 March 1907, patent office examiners allowed the granting of the patent and nothing remained except to pay a fee of twenty dollars. Four days later Clement Manly wrote the patent attorneys in Washington: "Mr. Reynolds does not wish to take out the patent on the allowed application of de Schweinitz, Ser. 622,034, filed Feb. 4, 1897, for Treating Tobacco, at this time, and desires to know how long the matter can stand as at present." The law provided that the final government fee be paid within six months of the date of allowance—on or before 19 September 1907.[21] The letters patent were mailed from Washington on 30 July 1907.[22]

Why did Reynolds deliberately postpone obtaining the patent from 19 March to 30 July? In view of his troubles over the manufacture of smoking tobacco, it seems likely that he was waiting for the threatened antitrust suit against the American Tobacco Company by the U.S. government. This suit was formally started on 19 July 1907.[23] It is evident that the date—30 July 1907—carried on the Prince Albert tin would or could prove a safeguard to Reynolds in preventing any adverse action by the American Tobacco Company, then in distress for attempting to control the entire tobacco industry. As matters stood, according to the testimony of William Reynolds, American could only make threats. This maneuver also gave Reynolds the opportunity to place a high-sounding statement on his red tins: "Prince Albert tobacco is prepared for smokers under the process discovered in making experiments to produce the most delightful and wholesome tobacco for cigarettes and pipe smokers. PROCESS PATENTED July 30, 1907"—a pronouncement that remained on Prince Albert tins until 25 July 1960. By that time the reason for such wording had long since been forgotten, if indeed anyone besides R. J. Reynolds had ever known it. Several attempts at wording have been left in the file pertaining to the de Schweinitz patent; one ends: "The proof of the success of this great discovery is in the smoking of our brand 'Refined'—most harmless tobacco for smokers." On the price list for 20 July 1907 appears the completed attempt, much like the blurb used for Prince Albert: "Proof of the Great Discovery is in the smoking of Refined. The process, which makes 'Refined' granulated the most harmless tobacco for cigarette smokers, was discovered by eminent scientists and tobacco experts, after many years of study and experiment to produce the most delightful and harmless tobacco for cigarettes and pipe smokers. Patent applied for." Reynolds used virtually the same advertisement for Prince Albert except that a patent could be claimed.

To reveal Reynolds's full intentions in his drive to establish a national brand of smoking tobacco it is well to examine another flue-cured brand —B. F. Gravely & Sons Special. This brand, priced at the level of Prince Albert, first appeared on the descriptive price list for 20 April 1908. The plug brand Gravely's Special was the property of F. A. Davis and Sons of Baltimore, although it had been manufactured for them by B. F. Gravely and Sons until the Reynolds company acquired its brands.[24] Working through Bowman Gray early in 1908, Reynolds obtained permission of F. A. Davis and Sons to use the term "Gravely's Special" for a brand of high-grade smoking tobacco. The *Reynolds Illustrated Price List*, issued with the descriptive price list of 3 January 1910, also revealed R. J.'s thinking as he sought to establish a popular smoking brand. One side of the picture of the can carried "B. F. Gravely & Sons Special" with "Pipe Tobacco" at the top and "Crimp Cut" at the bottom. In the center an oriental-appearing figure smokes a pipe and holds a sheet of paper carrying the following totally inaccurate statement insofar as this smoking brand was concerned: "Established by B. F. Gravely & Sons Leatherwood." Thus Reynolds sought to leave the impression that these two old and respected names in the chewing tobacco industry—Gravely and Leatherwood—were involved in the development of his new brand of crimp cut, flue-cured smoking tobacco—a type of leaf in which R. J. had great faith. Furthermore, the concluding statement on the page devoted to the new brand carries the following (including the italics): "B. F. Gravely & Sons brands have a *national reputation* as the highest grade tobaccos in the world, and have always commanded the highest prices."[25] This advertisement not only indicates Reynolds's shrewd ways but also his determination to place a smoking brand in the category with Duke's Mixture and Bull Durham and make a national seller of it. He had set several traps with that intention in mind. Had Reynolds, in his serious entry into the production of smoking tobacco, not used all means at his command, buttressed by determination, sly maneuvering, and steady effort, his business at the end of the antitrust suit would have been merely a slowly declining flat-plug business with little hope for the future.

The production, packing, wrapping, stamping, and labeling of smoking tobacco on a large scale undoubtedly taxed the Reynolds·plug organization and forced it into new paths on very short notice. With production of Prince Albert jumping from less than 250,000 pounds in 1908 to more than 14,000,000 pounds in 1912, action in many areas became necessary. On 11 February 1910 the company employed its first advertising agency, N. W. Ayer and Son of Philadelphia. Six months later Reynolds salesmen arrived in San Francisco to "make an effort to establish their brand of smoking tobacco with the California trade."[26] Of such developments comparatively little has been left in the records of the company.

Apparently, though, Split Silk, Refined, and even Prince Albert were first made in the Old Red Factory next to Number 256.[27] According to the memory of Thomas F. Bryant, Reynolds workers packed the first Prince Albert into cloth bags for sale at five cents each. When packing in tin cans was added, the company purchased them already manufactured from the A. E. Heekin Can Company of Cincinnati. Later, Bryant says, it was decided to purchase the lithographed tin from Heekin, cut it to correct size, and manufacture the can as a part of the factory process involved in the production of smoking tobacco.[28] Evidence gives proof for Bryant's assertion. On 12 June 1909 the tin box was in use in Reynolds's factory. Six days later, the A. E. Heekin Can Company contracted to furnish Reynolds with a sufficient supply of lithographed tin to make a minimum of 5 million completed Prince Albert cans in one year.[29] The *Southern Tobacco Journal* commented in 1911 that Prince Albert was a twentieth-century wonder that had grown to worldwide proportions, its success due to judicious advertising and wise and aggressive salesmanship. Facilities in June 1911 did not permit space to meet the ever-increasing demand for both plug and smoking tobacco.[30]

Prince Albert had made its early reputation in cloth bags packed by pouring the tobacco through a funnel into the bag and stepping on a lever that sent a wooden plunger down to pack the tobacco.[31] This method of packing was probably done with the Lawrence Smoking Tobacco Packer, as the sales of Prince Albert rose. As early as 14 January 1909 Walter R. Reynolds wrote to an agent for tobacco machinery, Richard H. Wright of Durham, North Carolina, that his company was considering the installation of a Wright Automatic Foil Package Machine and wished to know its cost and estimated capacity. Incidentally, Reynolds wished to produce a one-ounce paper packet of smoking tobacco like the Union·Leader brand. Wright called on Reynolds in Winston three days later to give full particulars on the automatic packing machine. The machine, however, was not

Wright's but one developed and manufactured by Rose Brothers of Gains-borough, England. By 1 February Reynolds had ordered an automatic packer with a rotary feed.[32] The machine cost $4,050, net, a price that caused R. J. Reynolds concern; he was worried that it might not meet the approval of the Committee of Manufacture and Construction at 111 Fifth Avenue.[33] The machine, shipped from England on 3 April, arrived in Winston on 10 May 1909.

Meanwhile Walter Reynolds had been active in finding out the exact size of the machine in order to make room for it and in obtaining the type of foil to use on the packages of Prince Albert.[34] Despite his desire to begin using the automatic packing machine as early as possible, the "other machinery," adjuncts to the packer, had not arrived by 10 May. Yet, by 13 May 1909 Reynolds was asking Wright for information about "the automatic labeling machine to be used in connection with your packer." This machine, however, was not ready for the market; "radical changes" had been made necessary because of the accumulation of paste. Walter Reynolds also sought to learn from Wright the exact width of cotton duck belting used to convey the packed tobacco from the packing machine to the stamping table.[35]

The summary on 12 June 1909, written by Louis Fischer, the mechanic who installed the one-ounce foil automatic packer, reveals other problems that had to be solved as the sales of Prince Albert continued to mount—problems involving waste, labor, wrapping, packing, and hand machines versus additional automatic machinery, especially an automatic packer for tins of Prince Albert:[36]

> I had a long talk with Mr. W. R. Reynolds this afternoon in reference to another Tobacco packing machine, which is to wrape [wrap] the tobacco in glacing [glassine] paper and then has to be put into a tin box either by hand or automatically. I tested the glacing paper in the present machine and am positive, that it will make the packet good enough to be put in the tin box. Reynolds dont care to have a fancy packet, just so that the wrapper holds long enough to be put in the tin box without opening up, besides the packet or rather the tobacco can be pressed much more than on a regular machine. . . . In reference to puting [putting] the packets into tin boxes I suggest making cheap hand fixtures to push them in by hand, say have four girls sitting on the side of a carayer [carrier] table to do that operation, or we may adopt a second small mould wheel with about half the number of pockets and apply steel springs, which project on the side of the small wheel, about the same shape as in Mr. Bracy's Cup Machine where the cups are sliped [slipped] in a mouth piece and the pack pushed in then the tin boxes could be put on these Steel springs by

hand and let the present plunger push the packets out of the large Mould Wheel into the small one and another plunger to push the packets in the tin box, the boxes then could drop on a conveyor belt to be carried away, two girls then could insert the little card [coupon] and close the boxes. If we adopt this idea, we could safe [save] the labor of two girls. At present Reynolds have three machines [obviously hand packers] with eight operators on each and only turn out 8000 boxes on each machine in ten hours, this means 24 operators to turn out 24,000 boxes and an awful lot of waste besides. I figure that we can turn out 25,000 boxes on Wright's Packer [the Rose machine] with 9 operators and if we arrange the machine to put the packets in the tin boxes automatically than [then] I believe, that we can make or rather fill 25,000 tin cans with 7 operators. These advantages I made clear to Mr. Reynold [sic] & Br. and would like Mr. Wright to make a proposition to them in reference to price etc. The machine which I just finished works very satisfactory and Mr. Reynolds will forward a check to Mr. Wright during next week. Please find enclosed letter from R. J. Reynolds Tobacco Co. expressing their satisfaction with the machine.

Walter Reynolds wrote Wright on 2 July 1909 that the company did not then care for a packer for the tin cans because there were plans on which he wished to work before taking up the matter any further.[37]

Judged almost solely on the basis of correspondence in Wright's papers, the question of an automatic packer for the two-ounce tin cans was not solved to Reynolds's satisfaction until 10 April 1912. Meanwhile empty cans had to be sent to England, suitable paper found, tests run, broken parts mended, the machine rebuilt once in Baltimore, and a multitude of other chores attended to, not the least of which was to ward off Wright's insistence on selling his machine before it was adequately tested. At length, on 6 July 1910 Walter Reynolds consented to install "a new style [Rose] machine for packing tobacco in tin cans" in order to give it a "thorough trial."[38] The trial lasted slightly more than one and a half years. Meanwhile, Reynolds's regular supplier, presumably the Amsterdam Supply Company, had not been able to find any glassine paper of the proper weight, and Rose Brothers in England could send only "a few sheets" for testing.[39] On the last day of March 1911, the machine had been installed, and, according to Wright, his mechanic had succeeded in getting packets of tobacco into the tins and Reynolds should place his order for it as soon as he had used it enough to be satisfied.[40] Wright was far too sanguine. Robert E. Lasater suggested several changes, whereupon Wright wrote Rose Brothers that "the brass tops on the present push out were ripped off in the first half hour" and replaced with steel, that the driving pulley was too narrow, and that compression was insufficient to pack "this springy tobacco deep enough" into the cans.[41] As a result, Walter Reynolds sent Rose Brothers six pounds of Prince Albert tobacco with instructions to restore it to its original pliability after its long journey to England and continued his search for suitable wrapping paper.[42] Despite complaints from customers about the thick paper around the tobacco that Reynolds had packed in a few tins, Wright nevertheless insisted on the use of thick paper for the machine. He felt that the complaints possibly came from friends of operators in the hand-packing department.[43]

Wright continued altering the machine for packing Prince Albert in tins until it was torn down and many parts rebuilt. Mechanics from the Briggs and Shaffner plant in Winston and the Detrick and Harvey plant in Baltimore, a branch of the Bethlehem Steel Company, assisted while Reynolds's men watched critically.[44] Reynolds's chief assistants were undoubtedly as anxious to have the machine made acceptable as were Wright and his men. Increasing orders by July 1911 forced Reynolds to install ten new foot presses for packing tins of Prince Albert.[45] At last, on 9 August 1911, Walter Reynolds informed Wright that the last paper selected by his mechanic, Fischer, had proved satisfactory in Lasater's opinion. It was a fifty-pound paper, 24 by 36 inches, the obtaining of which had caused the Amsterdam Supply Company unusual trouble. Even so, the machine could not operate for at least another sixty days because the manufacturer of this paper did not have it in rolls.[46] R. J. Reynolds did not completely share his brother's approval of the paper, although in a letter to Wright on 10 August he acknowledged that the machine performed well and that he found no fault with the paper other than its weight. The company had ordered another supply of the paper and would continue to make trial shipments of tins lined with the paper. He would use the fifty-pound weight if it proved practical, but he expected to continue the search for a thinner paper. He also stated that he did not wish to discuss with Wright the question of additional machines "for use in the near future" because "we would not consider the purchase of any machines until after we have received practical results from the experiments now being made."[47]

Experimentation, tearing down, and rebuilding of the automatic tin packer continued. In January 1912, Reynolds intimated that he might buy as many as ten machines for packing Prince Albert tins if they proved satisfactory.[48] With success so near at hand, Fischer packed more than 2,800 pounds on 7 February 1912, but in doing so "the Top Pressor Cam roller . . . wore almost" three-sixteenths of an inch and had to "be replaced with a hardened steel roller and pin." This was not a serious handicap at the moment because the supply of suitable paper had again been exhausted.[49] Wright claimed two weeks later, when a fresh supply of paper arrived, that the machine gave a better performance, although there was still some jamming caused apparently by the use of glassine paper. Walter Reynolds requested and received permission to try out the machine in the absence of Wright's mechanic.[50] Early March found Wright still hopeful, although Fischer continued laboring to get the tubes on the conveyor chain before giving the machine another, and final, test.[51] Trying again to make a sale, Wright wrote to R. J. Reynolds on 6 April 1912:

> . . . the more I think of it the greater the injustice you are doing yourself in delaying placing your order for some Prince Albert machines for your two ounce tins. I think it is due you that you go up to your works and see this machine in operation, for I never saw a machine do better work than this machine did while I watched it for an hour yesterday morning. I saw absolutely no fault or objection, or cause of complaint of the way this machine works now, and when your force has had a few days more experience two boys will be ample to put the tins on the tubes, doing away with the third boy who is now opening up the lids of the tins, as the two boys who put them on can easily open them. I notice in taking up a tin they lift the lid any way, and it would be just as easy to open it up as it is to lift it after it has been opened by a third boy. This cuts down the force at that end to two boys. Then four weighers complete the number necessary to operate the machine up to the point where the coupons are put in. This, of course, is no part of the machine's work. So that with six operators you can easily get the rate of fifty tins per minute, or 30,000 [3,750 pounds] per day of ten hours. Now you can figure what these six boys cost you, four to weigh and two to put on the tins, who produce 30,000 tins per day by hand. . . . The difference of course, will be the net saving, and I think you will find it considerably in excess of $25.00 per day net saving, which would be at the rate of $650.00 per month per machine.

Wright, of course, was especially fearful at this time that Reynolds might wait and buy a machine being developed by Rufus Lenoir Patterson, who then lived in Winston and was a founder of the Automatic Packing and Labeling Company, later to become the American Machine and Foundry Company but a subsidiary of the American Tobacco Company by 1902.[52]

At last Reynolds was satisfied with the tubes and Wright agreed on 10 April 1912 to install in the Reynolds plant ten of his tobacco packing machines, duplicates of the one that had been subject to so much experimentation. Reynolds refused the rotary feed and the checking device designed to fix personal responsibility for errors in packing. At a cost of $4,000 each, all of the tobacco-packing machines were to be tested, including the five to be built by Rose Brothers and the five by Wright. The contract stipulated that the first machine made in England should be delivered within three months and the first made in the United States within five months. Wright also agreed to give the R. J. Reynolds Tobacco Company an option for two years on ten additional machines of like construction. In addition, he allowed the company a discount of five hundred dollars for "valuable aid and assistance" in developing the machine.[53] On 30 April R. J. Reynolds wrote Wright, "We are in a great hurry for the Prince Albert machines purchased from you and hope you will leave nothing undone to make quick delivery." As an indication of American dependence on western Europe, a situation still prevailing to some extent, when the top plunger tension arm of this packing machine broke on 10 May 1912, a temporary repair was possible but it was necessary to get a new one from Rose Brothers in Gainsborough, England.[54]

On the eve of the company's freedom from the American Tobacco Company, development of the automatic packing machine for Prince Albert tins stood as the one fortunate turn of the wheel for the R. J. Reynolds Tobacco Company; nor, in view of the protracted "aid and assistance" furnished by the company, can this accomplishment be called pure luck. Not only Robert E. Lasater, but also Tom Parrish, superintendent of the smoking department, had watched Fischer and made suggestions as he went about his work.[55] Likewise Charles McChristian, Reynolds's head mechanic in the smoking department, showed considerable interest in Fischer's work.[56] There is evidence that the experiments conducted in the Reynolds plant benefited Liggett and Myers in the packaging of their Velvet smoking brand. Just as the experimentation was about complete, Clinton W. Toms wrote to Wright about a packing machine and wax paper for inserting Velvet into tins similar to those used for Prince Albert. It is probable that, through Wright, Lasater actually and unknowingly tested the paper that Liggett and Myers used for its Velvet brand.[57]

A big money-maker, accounting for almost half as many pounds as all of Reynolds's plug brands in 1912, Prince Albert appeared in packages other than cloth bags and two-ounce pocket tins. On 7 December 1910 came the first shipment in one-half pound, cylindrical, hermetically sealed tins, and on 1 April 1911 a one-pound can of the same style appeared.[58] Just as the Prince Albert pocket tin was imitated by Liggett and Myers's Velvet, so Reynolds's two humidors, as the one-half- and one-pound cylindrical and hermetically sealed cans came to be called, inspired imitation. In February 1912, A. E. Heekin wrote the Reynolds company that his firm was "being asked by people in the tobacco business to quote them prices on humidors 8 ounce and 16 ounce, such as we are manufacturing for you." Considering his firm as a virtual branch of the R. J. Reynolds Tobacco Company, Heekin did not wish to do this and suggested that Reynolds attempt to secure a copyright on the design of this package. One of the would-be imitators in 1914 was evidently the American Tobacco Company with its "new Tuxedo 40¢ humidor."[59] Also, it was rumored in August 1914 that the P. Lorillard Tobacco Company was preparing to market a package of smoking tobacco quite similar to the Reynolds humidor packages.[60] George A. Ackermann, a former employee of the A. E. Heekin Can Company, obtained a design patent for the humidors, which he assigned to the Reynolds company on 12 March 1913, to be held for fourteen years.[61]

The tin-box shop, or more properly the metal can division, was established in 1909. It was a dangerous place in which to work, and for many years there were men in the smoking tobacco division minus thumbs and fingers from long work in that shop. A. C. Hege and his brother Ben reputedly played a prominent role in the tin-box shop, Ben being the subject of many jokes, much teasing, and more than ordinary danger because of his long, black beard.[62] A rough outline of the dangerous handwork of that day offers a sharp contrast to the completely automatic production of cans today, the last hazard having been overcome in 1954 by means of magnetic and suction devices that neatly pick up the tin, one sheet at a time, and feed it into the slitting machine. As Thomas F. Bryant remembered it in 1950, in the early years the lithographed tin was first cut to correct size, hauled by hand on a carrier to a worker who notched the tin in preparation for attaching a hinge to close the top, hauled from there to a man who inserted the wire for the hinge, and again moved by hand to the bodymaker who pressed each piece of tin over a shape to mold the body of the can. At this point the bodymaker pushed a foot pedal, thereby uniting the vertical edges of the can. He made only about thirty cans an hour, but with set wages there was no incentive to increase the pace. The bodies of the cans were then hauled in barrels to the worker, who attached bottoms that had been made by the A. E. Heekin Can Company with dies purchased by Reynolds at a cost of $250 each. There were no experienced diemakers in the company at that time and those brought from Baltimore refused to stay. Apparently the old Brown Brothers plant, now Number 8-5, served as the first tin-box shop.[63]

Hand packing came next, and according to W. E. Snyder, who served as a master mechanic in the Prince Albert section of Number 256-9 from 1918 to 1958, that called for one woman employee to put the paper on a shape (the inverse of the can), another to put the Prince Albert can over the paper-covered shape, still another to weigh and pour the tobacco into the now paper-lined tin box, a strong man to pack the tobacco in the can, another woman employee to fold the ends of the paper over the tobacco, another to drop in a coupon, another to close the package and place it in a tray, and a final woman employee to affix the revenue stamp.[64] The date of Reynolds's freedom from control by the American Tobacco Company did not mark the end of hand packaging, although the first automatic packer

had been introduced in 1909. Meanwhile the gradual mastering of automatic packing continued far beyond 1911, many details being worked out
by Hans Fritz Richter, master mechanic and general superintendent of the
tin-box shop from 1912 until his death.

Despite all the hand packing, shifting to automatic packing, buying of
cloth bags, and making of tin boxes, the R. J. Reynolds Tobacco Company could not keep up with the demand for Prince Albert, although
factory space was ample. The following circular to jobbers, dated 24 April
1911, indicates the difficulty: "The manufacturer who builds the machinery for assembling the tin boxes, has simply been unable to furnish us the
machinery fast enough to keep up with the unprecedented increase in the
sale of this brand [Prince Albert]. We have been working a night force
regularly in this department for some time. We have also provided facilities for the manufacture of a larger number of our own tools and machines."[65] Yet, they ran behind on shipping Prince Albert, although nothing had been left undone.

Possibly this situation had prompted an earlier drop shipment offer
whereby one carton of twenty-four 5-cent bags of Prince Albert was offered with an order of not less than two gross of any two or more other
brands of Reynolds smoking tobacco, with the proviso that only one
carton of Prince Albert would be permitted to a retail dealer with any
shipment regardless of size. What could have been better at the time than
to have B. F. Gravely & Sons Special, George Washington, Our Advertiser, Razor Back, Split Silk, or Stud ride to smoking fame on the strength
of Prince Albert? All of these were available in the drop shipment described above. Reynolds had caught the national fancy with one brand.
This the Commissioner of Corporations acknowledged when he wrote of
the sales of smoking tobacco by the companies that succeeded the American Tobacco Company: "The sales of all four of the successor companies
in 1912 and 1913 show substantially different relations. . . . The decreases
were not due so much to the falling off in the sales of . . . three companies
as to the remarkable development of the smoking-tobacco business of the
R. J. Reynolds Tobacco Co., particularly in the sales of one brand."[66]

What effect did the high-pressure advertising of N. W. Ayer and Son
have in this turn of smokers to Prince Albert? One authority has stated
that, to be effective, advertising must be based on an acceptable product.[67] In the case of Prince Albert this conclusion seems accurate inasmuch as Reynolds singled out only Prince Albert of his several brands of
smoking tobacco to be advertised nationally. Surely he chose the brand
that had demonstrated greatest public acceptance. The Prince Albert national advertising campaign began in 1910. On 16 April the *Saturday
Evening Post, Collier's Weekly*, and the *Literary Digest* carried advertisements of Prince Albert specifically directed to jobbers and retailers. At the

same time wholesale grocers, tobacco dealers, and druggists received a poster that was a facsimile of the advertisement appearing in the *Saturday Evening Post*. On it was a coupon to be sent with eight cents for a can of Prince Albert. The poster also mentioned the opportunity for a jobber to make "a living profit" by "a special deal" offering thirty-six 10-cent cans for $2.79—providing a jobber with a handsome margin of profit. In May 1910, the news of the pipe tobacco that "can't bite your tongue" went to readers of various monthly magazines such as *Review of Reviews* and *Munsey's*. During the same general period, at intervals of ten days to two weeks, an unknown young lady, who wrote a very feminine hand, sent cards to jobbers. "Gladys B.," the lady in question, invariably wrote from a different city showing different men enjoying "A Smoke without a Sting" or one that "Hits the High Spot." Always the lady sat on a can of Prince Albert or on the sand watching a similar can emerge over the horizon. "Here's the Joy Smoke," she wrote, and jobbers supposedly wondered why "Gladys B." should write to them from Atlantic City while on her vacation.

The campaign continued. Appearing in practically all nationally circulated magazines were urgent messages such as "Stop Broiling Your Tongue" and in tobacco journals the offer of one-fourth of a gross of Prince Albert ten-cent cans for $2.79. By August 1910, dealers read in their trade journals that customers would not be satisfied with a substitute because "we control the process that takes the tongue-blistering bite *out* of the tobacco—so there can't be even a near substitute." Posters showing some of these advertisements went to retail dealers throughout the United States, calling attention to the "Joy Smoke" that could be smoked "red hot" or "just easy like." The copy, in easy, everyday language, emphasized the "Joy Smoke" in all types of magazines from the *Army and Navy Register* to the *Pacific Monthly*, often in full-page advertisements until early December 1911, when stress began to fall on the glass humidor of Prince Albert as a Christmas present for pipe or cigarette smokers.[68] A few days after the Reynolds company acquired independence came the climax, as the local editor saw it, in advertising Prince Albert. On an electric signboard high above the skyscrapers in New York near the famous Flat-Iron building night after night appeared a mammoth electric display. The lights that blinked on and off revealed a tall man, the words "Prince Albert," and finally a "great glow" at the man's feet as the following emerged: "The Nation's Joy Smoke, R. J. Reynolds Tobacco Company, Winston-Salem, N. C."[69]

The company thus entered its years of independence with a new money-maker selling on a national scale—not simply a great number of chewing brands used chiefly in the South. The sales force had not been greatly augmented because of the addition of one new outstanding product, but Reynolds had only begun. The year after the dissolution decree found him busy with plans to make cigarettes. So intent was he on this problem in late 1912 that Richard H. Wright advised his mechanic to steal out of Winston on the sly for the Christmas holidays to inspect machinery then being built in Baltimore: "You can tell Reynolds that you are called away to get a man out of trouble and that you will return as soon as you can to get the cigarette making machine up and started, but that you will have that finished well in advance of the time he will get in other machines ready to start up the manufacture of cigarettes, and that you will try to get back from this trip in time to install some P. A. 2 oz. machines which will probably have arrived by that time."[70] Thus, long before the R. J. Reynolds Tobacco Company had mastered the wholesale production of smoking tobacco, it was ready to try its luck on a new product.

Financial Results of Affiliation with the American Tobacco Company

The handling of financial matters of the R. J. Reynolds Tobacco Company during its years of affiliation with the Tobacco Combination involved at least two factors that may be discussed only from fragmentary records: (1) borrowed capital, and (2) the foundation of a profit-sharing plan. In contrast to its earlier years the company spent a tidy sum from 1899 through 1911. The annual reports, given only in the minutes, are not conspicuous for their clarity. They do indicate that money was coming into the business from some source, which we know to have been the Continental Tobacco Company in part, and that the value of goodwill was used to balance the books. Because no rational consolidated balance sheet may be compiled, it seems advisable to present the company's assets in Table 6-3, prepared largely from the reports given in the minutes listing only the items consistently measured.[71]

The Commissioner of Corporations in 1911 had access to more complete figures than the author. In his report, released in that year, he included a table showing the assets and earnings of the company from 1900 through 1908 (see Table 6-4). The increase in earnings was phenomenal. It should be noted that the profits of the company in 1897 amounted to $163,725 and in 1898 to $159,234, but in 1900, the first full year of operation under the Tobacco Combination, the profit was only $43,871. Nevertheless, the output of the company increased greatly in 1901 and enormously so in 1902—to about five and a half times that of 1898. The sharp increase in earnings in 1901 resulted in a large measure from the decrease in taxes that had been levied to support the Spanish-American

Table 6-3
Recorded Assets of the Reynolds Company, 1899–1911

Year	Real Estate, Machinery, & Fixtures	Leaf, Manufactured Stock, & Operating Supplies	Goodwill, Patents, & Trademarks[a]		Capital Stock
			Reynolds Reports	Commissioner of Corporations Report	
1899	$ 300,363	$1,062,969	$1,000,000	$1,175,010	$2,100,000
1900	679,806	1,927,476	1,175,015	1,175,010	3,600,000
1901	721,812	2,740,783	1,172,708	1,175,010	3,600,000
1902	780,771	3,659,655	1,072,893	1,175,195	5,000,000
1903	851,541	2,530,958	1,072,943	1,175,195	5,000,000
1904	830,902	3,555,898	922,943	1,175,195	5,000,000
1905	1,025,376	4,135,428	927,943	1,180,195	5,000,000
1906	1,043,863	4,384,450	928,443	1,180,695	7,525,000
1907	1,143,926	3,791,672	1,146,831	1,399,083	7,525,000
1908	1,165,616	4,674,191	1,146,831	1,399,083	7,525,000
1909	1,298,726	4,875,247	1,146,856	Not available	7,525,000
1910	1,500,118	6,133,369	1,146,923	Not available	7,525,000
1911	1,996,595	6,730,989	1,147,123	Not available	7,525,000

Sources: Minutes of the Board of Directors, R. J. Reynolds Tobacco Company, secretary's department: vol. I, pp. 62 (1899), 97 (1900), 133 (1901), 169 (1902), 195–96 (1903), 233 (1904), 286 (1905), 309–10 (1906), 341–42 (1907); vol II, pp. 21 (1908), 60 (1909), 106 (1910), 158–59 (1911); and Report of the Commissioner of Corporations on the Tobacco Industry, 3 vols. (Washington, D.C., 1909–15), 2:191 (goodwill). The figures have been rounded off to the nearest dollar.

aIt should be noted that the Commissioner of Corporations, reporting goodwill *alone*, consistently exceeds the Reynolds figures, and that they seldom agree.

Table 6-4
Investment and Earnings in Direct Business
of the Reynolds Company, 1900–1908

		Earnings		
Year	Total Assets	Amount	Percent of Total Assets	Percent of Tangible Assets
1900	$4,474,161	$ 43,871	1.0	1.3
1901	4,815,452	544,033	11.3	14.9
1902	5,685,574	879,150	15.5	19.5
1903	5,948,751	977,810	16.4	20.5
1904	6,767,064	1,094,274	16.2	19.6
1905	8,173,896	1,095,988	13.4	15.7
1906	7,440,262	575,474	7.7	9.2
1907	7,551,381	1,174,169	15.5	19.1
1908	8,502,310	1,653,036	19.4	23.3

Source: Report of the Commissioner of Corporations on the Tobacco Industry, 3 vols. (Washington, D.C., 1909–15), 2:192–93. The figures have been rounded off to the nearest dollar.

War. The sharp decrease in profits in 1906 may be attributed to increased advertising expenses. It is clear that the Reynolds company benefited greatly during the years of association with the American Tobacco Company. The Commissioner of Corporations declared that the rate of earnings, both on total and tangible assets, was less than the rate for American and Continental. He believed the reasons for this to be that Reynolds worked in a more competitive field than either of the other companies and that its products sold at a lower average price than the chewing tobacco of the parent companies. It is nevertheless true that profits from three of Reynolds's brands—Brown's Mule, Schnapps, and Apple Sun Cured—amounted to 70 percent of the entire profit of the Tobacco Combination on flat plug in 1910.[72]

Funds for this remarkable expansion, so far as available records reveal, came from capital stock, surplus earnings, borrowing in the form of scrip dividends, bank loans, and at least one loan from the Continental Tobacco Company. At the outset, $2,100,000 of the original authorization of $5,000,000 for common capital stock was issued, with $1,721,300 given in exchange for the business of the R. J. Reynolds Tobacco Company of North Carolina. The balance, $378,700, was used to obtain working capital. Another issue of $200,000, authorized on 31 December 1900, was part of the purchase price of the business and property of P. H. Hanes and Company. This acquisition, of course, represented expansion. All other issues were for the purpose of procuring additional capital for expansion and for handling an increasing volume of business. Other issues of stock before dissolution of the American Tobacco Combination were for $1,300,000, authorized on 31 December 1900, and $1,400,000, authorized on 12 July 1902. On 15 February 1906 stockholders voted to increase the authorized capital stock to $10,000,000, and shortly thereafter $2,500,000 of that increase was issued in common stock. Also at that time the directors approved the issuance of $25,000 in stock to a "named individual," undoubtedly Pannill Rucker, for which he paid in cash. No other stock issues occurred until after dissolution of the Tobacco Combination became effective.[73] Nothing like an adequate sum for its remarkable expansion came from the company's capital stock.

Available details of Reynolds's borrowings from the Continental Tobacco Company are limited to one 90-day loan of $100,000 on 6 November 1902.[74] Yet, according to the *Report of the Commissioner of Corporations on the Tobacco Industry*, that was evidently a minute sum compared with what must have been borrowed from that source:[75]

> The tangible assets of the company at the time of the purchase in 1899 amounted to $924,990, and the good will entered on the books to balance the capitalization of $2,100,000 amounted to $1,175,010. From the time of acquisition in 1899 to the end of 1900 the investment of the company increased greatly, due in part to the acquisition of the business of P. H. Hanes and B. F. Hanes, made possible by money borrowed from the Continental Tobacco Company and from the sale of its capital stock. At the end of 1900 the tangible assets amounted to $3,299,151. From this figure they increased continuously until at the end of 1905 they were nearly $7,000,000. In 1906 and 1907 they were somewhat less, but in 1908 they exceeded $7,100,000.

It will be recalled that in 1899 and 1900 the very heavy expenses of the Reynolds company embraced not only the purchase of other plants but also the building and equipping of Number 8, considered at the time to be the most complete plant of its type in existence.

In addition to the capital from stock issues and surplus earnings, the company at least employed borrowed funds as follows from 1901 to 1908:

1901	$ 875,000
1902	650,000

1903	1,090,000
1904	2,025,000
1905	3,425,000
1906	Not available
1907	Not available
1908	600,000

After 1905, according to the Commissioner of Corporations, loans decreased greatly but there was "considerable addition to the investment from surplus earnings."[76] The minutes of the company, however, reveal no loans for 1901 nor for several other years. Nevertheless, the information available may indicate that, as the years passed and the business increased, funds generally came from farther north (see Table 6-5). There were frequent authorizations for the borrowing of considerable sums but no indication of their sources. Some of these loans were fixed on demand, more at ninety days, some at four months and six months, and an occasional one for one year. The interest charges, when indicated, ranged from 4½ to 6 percent.[77] These notes, of course, received approval from the directors—a far cry indeed from the mid-sixties when the treasurer could borrow up to $100 million without consulting even one director.

From 6 December 1900 to 18 December 1905, Reynolds used for varying lengths of time a total of $3,120,179 issued as scrip dividends.[78] According to the statement of the Commissioner of Corporations, working capital was usually reserved before the declaration of dividends; the amount of working capital, however, was never given, but, judging from extra dividends frequently declared, it must have been considerable. Finally on 7 July 1910, with Prince Albert booming and Camels probably in mind, the directors decided to discontinue the extra dividends for that quarter because of the increased requirements of the company, which necessitated "the borrowing of considerable money."[79]

The common capital stock of $7,525,000, divided into 75,250 shares of par value $100, was issued in three major allotments—in 1899, 1900, and 1906. Until 1906 it was held rather closely by R. J. Reynolds and his relatives, John F. Parlett, the Hanes family, and the American Tobacco Combination. In 1901 the true and complete list of stockholders entitled to one vote consisted of twenty-six holders (see Table 6-6).[80] R. J. Reynolds's close relatives on the list were his two brothers, his sister Lucy and her husband, and a nephew, G. R. Lybrook. Holdings of the Continental Tobacco Company may be grouped with the few shares held by John B. Cobb, James B. Duke, Benjamin N. Duke, and George W. Watts. Most of the other stockholders were employees of the company. Thus R. J.'s plan for his employees to own stock in the company and participate in its earnings had begun to be something of a reality at this time. Among

Table 6-5
Borrowings of the Reynolds Company, 1902–1911

Year	Source	Amount
1902	Continental Tobacco Company	$ 100,000
	R. J. Reynolds (personal funds)	90,000
	Merchants' National Bank of Baltimore	75,000
	National Park Bank of New York	75,000
	Wachovia National Bank, Winston	40,000
	People's National Bank, Winston	30,000
1903	No statement of sources and amounts	
1904	National Park Bank of New York	250,000
1905–7	No statement of sources and amounts	
1908	Philadelphia National Bank	300,000
1909	Philadelphia National Bank	350,000
1910	National Park Bank of New York	650,000
	American Tobacco Company, New York	500,000
	Philadelphia National Bank	500,000
	Merchants' National Bank of Baltimore	50,000
1911	National Park Bank of New York	1,000,000
	Philadelphia National Bank	450,000
	Fourth Street Bank of Philadelphia	200,000
	National Shawmut Bank, Boston	100,000

Source: Minutes of the Board of Directors, R. J. Reynolds Tobacco Company, vols. I, passim, and II, p. 116, passim, secretary's department.

employee-stockholders were William E. Brock (division manager at Chattanooga), George F. Dwire (in charge of advertising), W. T. Eaton (leaf buyer), Bowman Gray (division manager in Baltimore for the Northeast), Carl W. Harris (later head of the sales department), Eugene G. Hester (at one time a division manager in Florida), Clement Manly (counsel), L. A. Myers (division manager at Macon, Georgia), and D. Rich, who became treasurer just prior to the dissolution of the American Tobacco Combination.

The year 1906 marked a definite change. The Continental Tobacco Company had been merged with the American Tobacco Company in 1904. American then assumed Continental's holdings in the R. J. Reyn-

Table 6-6
Stockholders of the Reynolds Company, 1901

Stockholder	Location	Number of Shares
W. A. Blair	Winston	5
W. E. Brock	Winston	50
J. B. Cobb	111 Fifth Ave., N.Y.	3
Continental Tobacco Co.	111 Fifth Ave., N.Y.	23,990
Lucy B. Critz	Winston	217
Robert Critz	Winston	150
D. F. Crowell	Winston	10
B. N. Duke	Durham, N.C.	2
J. B. Duke	111 Fifth Ave., N.Y.	3
G. F. Dwire	Winston	50
W. T. Eaton	Winston	20
Bowman Gray	Baltimore, Md.	115
J. W. Hanes	Winston	1,000
P. H. Hanes	Winston	1,000
Carl W. Harris	Winston	10
Eugene G. Hester	Winston	50
G. R. Lybrook	Winston	200
Clement Manly	Winston	90
L. A. Myers	Winston	10
John F. Parlett	Baltimore, Md.	350
R. J. Reynolds	Winston	7,168
W. N. Reynolds	Winston	1,072
W. R. Reynolds	Winston	333
D. Rich	Winston	50
M. A. Walker	Winston	50
George W. Watts	Durham, N.C.	2

Source: Minutes of the Board of Directors, R. J. Reynolds Tobacco Company, vol. I, pp. 93–94, secretary's department.

olds Tobacco Company. In 1906 the directors of the Reynolds company issued 25,000 additional shares of stock, and several stockholders could not or did not take their allotments. As a result, the new list of stockholders, made before the end of the period for subscribing to the new issue, included new names, among them two firms of stockbrokers— Moore and Schley, and Hallgarten and Company—which together held 5,442 shares. The American Tobacco Combination now held 49,990 shares. No other significant change in the number and type of stock-holders occurred until the final dissolution decree of 16 November 1911. But in Table 6-7, the list of new stockholders for April 1906 shows a somewhat wider distribution of ownership and a greater number of Reynolds employees than listed for 1901.[81]

While it cannot be categorically stated that Reynolds initiated this attempt, the presence of his signature on four of the seven lists of signatures of stockholders attached to a consent and waiver, dated 23 February 1906, indicates that he stood in the forefront of the move to secure stock for his employees. This also marks the date of the authorization to issue new stock in 1906. Twenty-six stockholders, including the Reynolds group, the Haneses, at least twelve stock-holding employees, and Caleb C. Dula, acting for the American Tobacco Company, signed a consent and waiver notice to relinquish for a period of two years all rights to subscribe to an aggregate of 1,000 shares of capital stock at par, none of which was to be sold for less than par—$100. According to the third stipulation of this consent and waiver, all of the $100,000 of this stock "shall issue to members of the organization and individuals who, in the judgment of the directors, are useful to the organization." The purpose of this consent and waiver was "that the organization be strengthened, and we and all other stockholders benefitted [sic] by thus interesting in the corporation and its future, men useful to the corporation."[82]

Other facts indicate that Reynolds entered wholeheartedly into this profit-sharing plan in 1906. P. H. Hanes authorized Reynolds to allot to employees of the R. J. Reynolds Tobacco Company 550 shares of his rights in the new stock issue of 16 March 1906, provided the employees deposited with Reynolds for Hanes $50 for each of the 550 shares so allotted. This authorization, to be fulfilled on or before 12 March, was witnessed by R. J. Reynolds on 8 March 1906.[83] Hanes claimed that the 550 shares was all that he would sell; yet he offered additional rights in New York. Caleb C. Dula made this fact known to Reynolds, who immediately arranged to buy all the stock that Dula could get from Hanes.[84] Why Hanes should have preferred to sell his stock in New York when Reynolds wanted it for his employees is something of a mystery. In March 1906, Reynolds wrote Charles A. Kent in Memphis, L. A. Myers in Macon, and W. E. Brock in Chattanooga, offering to get stock for them.[85] In R. J.'s correspondence with Bowman Gray and Joseph D. Noell it is very clear that both had purchased Reynolds stock through the American Tobacco Company. The statement to Noell on 20 March 1906 reads: "We will hold this 25 shares, together with the 50 shares, that the American Tobacco Co. held, all as collateral security for the enclosed note." To Gray Reynolds wrote on the same day: "The enclosed settlement covers your notes, which we have taken up from the American Tobacco Co. and the

Table 6-7
New Stockholders of the Reynolds Company, April 1906

Stockholder/Employee	Location	Number of Shares
W. B. Birchfield	Marion, Va.	50
George W. Coan	Winston	346
Marion G. Follin	Winston	30
R. S. Galloway	Winston	30
Charles A. Kent	Memphis, Tenn.	50
Robert E. Lasater	Winston	95
Percy R. Masten	Winston	95
Joseph D. Noell	Richmond, Va.	75
R. W. Ogburn	Montgomery, Ala.	30
George W. Patterson	Winston	38
Cyrus W. Scott	Houston, Tex.	50
James Sloan	Winston	70
W. Z. Stultz	Charlotte, N.C.	30

Source: Minutes of the Board of Directors, R. J. Reynolds Tobacco Company, vol. I, pp. 278–79, secretary's department.

same are herewith enclosed, together with their statement." As this correspondence indicates, it was R. J.'s custom to accept an employee's note, buy stock for the employee, and allow dividends from the stock to pay off the note. Bowman Gray replied to such a letter from Reynolds: "It is understood that you are to apply the profits which are distributed, as payments on the note."[86] Undoubtedly Reynolds served his chief employees on the same basis. Robert B. Horn, who held three shares on 23 February 1906, held 248 shares on 3 April.[87] Where did Reynolds learn the value of thus drawing the energies and loyalties of his employees into such close identity with the company? The answer might be *from the American Tobacco Company* were it not for the difference in the nature of the profit-sharing schemes adopted by Reynolds and American in 1912.

In December 1905 Reynolds began to plan for the new stock issue in 1906. It was not only a new stock issue but also authorization of additional stock up to a total of $10 million. Reynolds wrote Ambrose H. Burroughs, counsel for the American Tobacco Company, for information on correct procedure. Burroughs sent Reynolds a form for a special directors' meeting in Winston and another for notifying stockholders twenty days in advance of a meeting. Upon receiving the instructions, Reynolds wrote that "we thoroughly understand them."[88] On 15 February 1906,

Burroughs wrote George W. Coan that the stockholders had met and voted on that day to authorize the increase in capital stock. At the same time he sent Coan the minutes of that meeting for transcription on his minute book, a blank form for an affidavit that notices of the meeting had been mailed (a matter that had been omitted), and a certificate of increase that Reynolds had signed and Coan was to sign and return with the filing fee.[89]

But a few more pointers from tobacco headquarters were needed. On the following day R. J. Reynolds talked with Junius Parker at 111 Fifth Avenue about the routine for handling a special meeting of the company's directors on 23 February. On 17 February Parker sent Reynolds detailed instructions marked in proper order for consideration. Paper A, relating to the declaration of dividends, should be passed first by the Reynolds directors; Parker also noted that "the dividend should cover approximately your surplus." Immediately following mention of "your surplus," Parker added a sentence both elementary and mystifying—elementary in defining that a declared dividend is a "fixed debt from the corporation to the stockholders" and mystifying in another part of this sentence that "checks should be sent out after you have received cash from the stock subscription." Apparently Reynolds was in serious need of capital. Paper B concerned the handling of the new stock not taken by stockholders at the time of issuance. "Strictly speaking," wrote Parker, "all stockholders who take stock are entitled to ratably subscribe for the proportion of those who do not take stock." Paper C was a letter to be written by the secretary of the Reynolds company to all stockholders "giving them an opportunity to take their proportionate part of the issue." Paper D bore on the matter of issuing stock to Pannill Rucker and "the other stock needed to members of the organization by virtue of the consent of all the present stockholders." Parker commented further on this point: "This would save particular stockholders who are willing to do it, such as you and the American Tobacco Co. from incurring a loss by providing to Mr. Rucker and the other employes [sic] a larger amount of stock than their proportion, and it seems to me that all of your stockholders would realize the fairness and wisdom of signing such paper." Parker then urged Reynolds not to issue stock to Rucker or to anyone else until all stockholders had signified their consent by signing paper D. Reynolds also received instructions on paper E, which was a resolution providing for the issuance of new stock.[90]

Perhaps this letter indicates Reynolds's need for advice. It might also mean that, contrary to the desires of his largest stockholder, R. J. had used the surplus for expansion. It undoubtedly means that he knew little about the authorization of new stock. One thing is certain: Reynolds favored a profit-sharing plan. Perhaps these lessons were the last needed by the R. J. Reynolds Tobacco Company as it emerged from the control of the American Tobacco Combination on 16 November 1911—a date that might better be given as 1 January 1912. The company, still operating under the leadership of its founder, stood on the threshold of a new career. Yet the president and founder, though ready with new plans, was now over sixty years old.

PART THREE

Expansion of the Company, 1912–1940

CHAPTER 7

Independence and New Directions

"I have written the book; others need only to follow it when I am gone," declared R. J. Reynolds some years before his death, when asked how the business could be maintained without him.[1] In this chapter the remaining years of Reynolds's leadership, 1912 to 1924, will be considered as a unit; leadership in subsequent years fell into the hands of men chosen or groomed by him. It seems best to consider first the position of the company in 1912, then its plan for employee participation in profits, the listing of its stock on the New York Stock Exchange, and last, its entry into the manufacture of cigarettes.

Position of the Company in 1912

On 2 June 1911, shortly after the final appeal in the antitrust suit was decided in such a manner as to prohibit further legal quibbling by the American Tobacco Company, the R. J. Reynolds Tobacco Company mailed its salesmen circular S-13-C. The salesmen were told that there was nothing in the latest decision to prevent the company from continuing its business "as a separate and distinct concern under the management of the splendid organization which [had] established the business and brands." The salesmen were also informed that, to meet the growing demand for its product, the company had let a contract for the construction of a five-story factory designed to have more space than any building then owned by the organization. More, a new office building would be ready for occupancy on 1 July 1911.[2]

On 15 November 1911, one day before final approval of the plan to dissolve the American Tobacco Combination, another circular went out to the Reynolds salesmen. No contemporary evidence seems to illustrate quite so well the agitation then prevailing in tobacco circles:[3]

> Regarding the plan for dissolution of The American Tobacco Company, recently approved by the United States Circuit Court, you will likely be asked many questions as to the effect of this decision upon the R. J. Reynolds Tobacco Company; and for your information, this is to say that R. J. Reynolds Tobacco Company's business will go along the same as heretofore, under the management and control of its officers and directors at Winston-Salem, N. C. So far as we are concerned, the decision of the Court simply requires that The American Tobacco Company shall part with the stock held by it in the R. J. Reynolds Tobacco Company, and, therefore, that part of our stock formerly owned by The American Tobacco Company will hereafter be owned by many and various individuals throughout the country.
>
> Newspaper reports have produced the impression in some quarters that in the dissolution and division of the business and properties of The American Tobacco Company, a part of same would be allotted to the R. J. Reynolds Tobacco Company. This is an entire mistake. The R. J. Reynolds Tobacco Company retains its own properties and business, and no part of The American Tobacco Company's business will be in any way allotted to, or conveyed to us.
>
> Shortly after the Government's suit was instituted against The American Tobacco Company, some four and a half years ago, experts were sent out from Washington to make a thorough investigation of our Company. The reports made by these experts in regard to our Company were entirely favorable and very gratifying to us; therefore, our Company has never been exercised as to the outcome of the much talked of litigation; indeed, we took no active part on it; never employed counsel, and so far as the final decision in its effect upon R. J. Reynolds Tobacco Company is concerned, it is no more than we confidently looked for, and it is needless to say, the outcome is entirely satisfactory to us.

But six days after the final dissolution decree, Reynolds salesmen received a letter headed, "News of Freedom." According to this communication, the decree was in "keeping with the spirit of '76." The American Tobacco Company would be forced to give up its stock in the Reynolds company and no longer directly or indirectly hold any interest whatsoever in the ownership or management of the R. J. Reynolds Tobacco Company. In addition, the salesmen were exhorted to let the trade know the truth: again the trade was to be informed that the company had always been a separate and distinct concern owning its own property and directing its own affairs. At no time had American dictated the policy of the R. J. Reynolds Tobacco Company.[4] There appears to be some lack of logical connection between the latter statements and the opening welcome of freedom. R. J. Reynolds had managed his years of captivity with remarkable acumen. He had escaped any changes of organization, loss of brands, loss of tangible property, or rechartering problems. He had gained financial stability, built up a large plant, learned the ways of financial maneuvering, and used the last four years of his connection with the Tobacco Combination to enter areas forbidden by the American Tobacco Company.

Nevertheless, at the end of 1911 his firm stood far below the leading tobacco manufacturers in sales. Percentages of production of chewing tobacco, smoking tobacco, and cigarettes for the larger firms connected with the Tobacco Combination at the end of 1911 are shown in Table 7-1. Reynolds stood at the foot of the list in every category except chewing tobacco and next to last in that area.[5] But in 1912 and 1913 its sales in the first two categories rose significantly (see Table 7-2), largely because of Reynolds's earlier daring venture into the production of new brands of smoking tobacco. Moreover, in 1913 the company made some progress, albeit small, in the sale of cigarettes.[6] In no comparison of the "Big Four" in 1912 could the R. J. Reynolds Tobacco Company appear imposing. In assets and value of sales for 1912, the company was only one-third as large as P. Lorillard and less than one-fourth the size of Liggett and Myers; Reynolds held only one-twelfth the assets and made one-fifth the sales of the American Tobacco Company.[7] To unbalance the situation even further, at the time of dissolution the navy plug business went to Liggett and Myers, P. Lorillard, and American; Reynolds, of course, held the small quantity he had secured from Brown Brothers and Company. The dissolution left the American Tobacco Company and Liggett and Myers, as well as Reynolds, with flat plug. At no point did Reynolds hold a lead or even a superior position.[8] The claim by Reynolds officials many years later in another antitrust suit is true: that the company through aggressive policies "lifted itself up from a position of relative unimportance in the industry to one of leadership, largely at the expense of its alleged co-conspirators."[9]

First Profit-Sharing Plan

Obviously after 1911 the R. J. Reynolds Tobacco Company would be strictly on its own financially. For that reason the capitalization of the

Table 7-1
*Percent of Tobacco Produced by Successor Companies
of the Tobacco Combination, 1911*

	Percent in Volume	Percent in Value
Chewing Tobacco		
American	25.32	22.98
Liggett and Myers	33.83	37.84
Reynolds	18.07	15.49
P. Lorillard	3.73	4.64
Smoking Tobacco		
American	33.08	40.53
Liggett and Myers	20.05	16.47
P. Lorillard	22.82	18.88
Reynolds	2.66	2.73
Cigarettes		
American	37.11	33.15
Liggett and Myers	27.82	21.03
P. Lorillard	15.27	26.02
Reynolds	00.00	00.00

Source: R. J. R. Tob. Co. et al. v. U.S., *Brief for Appellants*, docket no. 9139 (6th Cir., 1944), p. 74.

company and of its rivals is of interest. The so-called "Big Four" of later years began business in 1912 with capital stock as follows:[10]

American	$92,701,800
Liggett and Myers	36,800,200
P. Lorillard	26,463,200
Reynolds	10,000,000

Actually, the Reynolds company did not bring its capitalization to $10 million until 23 August 1912, when it issued its remaining authorized stock of 24,750 shares.[11] Incidentally, American reduced its capital stock by amending its charter instead of dissolving the corporation as did P. Lorillard.[12]

Certain other changes regarding its stock marked the independence of the R. J. Reynolds Tobacco Company. The Equitable Trust Company of New York became the stock transfer agent and the Central Trust Com-

Table 7-2
*Percent of Tobacco Sold by Successor Companies
of the Tobacco Combination, 1912 and 1913*

	Percent of Total Quantity Sold	
	1912	1913
Chewing Tobacco		
American	23.7	21.9
Liggett and Myers	46.0	47.4
Reynolds	24.4	24.8
P. Lorillard	5.9	5.9
Smoking Tobacco		
American	39.8	38.4
Liggett and Myers	21.8	23.0
P. Lorillard	26.6	24.6
Reynolds	11.8	14.0
Cigarettes		
American	40.1	38.5
Liggett and Myers	40.5	37.2
P. Lorillard	19.4	24.1
Reynolds	00.0	00.2

Source: Report of the Commissioner of Corporations on the Tobacco Industry, 3 vols. (Washington, D.C., 1909–15), 3:12.

pany, also of New York, became the registrar of stock. An official resolution terminating all connections with the American Tobacco Company went to the United States Circuit Court for the Southern District of New York. A new director in the person of Henry A. Oetjen, of Jersey City, replaced C. A. Hopman as statutory director. The list of stockholders became somewhat lengthy as the 49,998 shares held by American fell into the hands of such individuals as Thomas F. Ryan, Irénée S. duPont, Oliver H. Payne, P. A. B. Widener, Nelson W. Aldrich, James B. Duke, Anthony N. Brady, and Gertrude V. Whitney, and such stockbrokers as Hallgarten and Company, Moore and Schley, and the Northern Finance Company. To these individuals and stockbrokers, as well as numerous others—including officers of American, Liggett and Myers, and P. Lorillard, as constituted in 1912—went two-thirds of Reynolds stock, for the dissolution decree awarded Reynolds stock to the holders of common stock in the old American Tobacco Company.[13]

On the surface, at least, immediately after the dissolution the management of the Reynolds company felt no particular trust in certain of its large stockholders, known as "the New York crowd," because they had controlled and dominated the old American Tobacco Company. Be that as it may, the Reynolds management at once planned to get its stock into the hands of North Carolinians. What might be called an informal profit-sharing scheme was adopted to promote cooperation between employer and employee, to decrease waste, and to place company stock in friendly hands. On 4 January 1912, the directors authorized the president and treasurer to lend the employees from the company's surplus funds, on 6 percent demand notes, the sum of $145 on each share of stock thus hypothecated, "this value being less than the book value of the stock."[14]

This was but the first step. R. J. Reynolds learned that the New York majority stockholders had agreed to bonus plans for the officers of Liggett and Myers, P. Lorillard, and American by which they would receive a percentage of the earnings of their respective companies in excess of the sum earned by their properties in 1910. Apparently R. J. and his brother William N. Reynolds then approached "the New York crowd" and won their approval as stockholders to a bylaw of a different type. This was Bylaw XII, aimed at encouraging Reynolds employees to buy stock then held by the same "New York crowd" as well as stock then about to be issued.[15] Evidence from the opinionated and blunt George Washington Hill, Sr., long close to James B. Duke, corroborates this view. When asked if Duke had suggested such bylaws to the executives of the successor companies of the old American Tobacco Company, Hill replied: "He (Duke) told me that he was going to put the same by-law into effect in all companies, practically; I mean, I understand there were some changes that I didn't know about at the time. He didn't discuss the details, of course, with me." In addition, Hill said that he believed Bylaw XII in principle to be in the charters of all the successor tobacco companies. Testifying further, he added: "I have always known that the Reynolds Tobacco Company had a bylaw of some sort. It has always been my understanding that that particular bylaw was technically different from the other companies'. It has always been my understanding that Mr. R. J. Reynolds was the originator of that bylaw." Hill had also known that the Reynolds bylaw required actual ownership of the company's stock and that such ownership was available to all Reynolds employees.[16]

The bonus bylaw of the Reynolds company was quite different from those of its competitors. It can only be assumed that R. J. received support for his particular type of bylaw either because Duke knew that none of his henchmen would be present in Reynolds management or because he felt no great enthusiasm for the future of a company capitalized at such a low figure with only one national selling product. If this surmise is true, it follows that Duke did not yet understand Richard Joshua Reynolds. The exact date of the adoption of Bylaw XII by the stockholders of the American Tobacco Company is unavailable to the author, but most likely it was the first such bylaw adopted by any of the successor companies. Each year a sum that exceeded the net profits earned during 1910 by the business that belonged to American was to be ascertained. The treasurer was then authorized to pay 10 percent of such excess to the president and vice-presidents of the company, the president to receive one-fourth and each vice-president one-fifth of the remainder. With this bylaw continuing in effect until 1949 without amendment and with company profits generally increasing, it may be readily seen that this arrangement was a happy one for the top officers.[17]

The stockholders of Liggett and Myers Tobacco Company adopted a similar bylaw on 11 March 1912, except that it contained a section providing for pro rata distribution of such profits in case of changes in the offices of president or vice-presidents and for reversion of such profits to the general account in case of a vacancy. The question of what constituted profits was sharply defined in this bylaw, which was amended in 1929—certainly a more propitious time for a downward revision than 1949.[18] On 12 March 1912, the stockholders of the P. Lorillard Tobacco Company adopted a bylaw similar in every respect to that of Liggett and Myers. On the following day, however, P. Lorillard's board of directors adopted Bylaw XIII, providing that five percent of the net profits exceeding the net profits of 1910 be set aside for distribution by the directors to any other employees of the company whom they deemed worthy of such reward. Both bylaws were revised in 1921 to include more people.[19] The wording of the bonus bylaws of Liggett and Myers and P. Lorillard and their similarity to the American bylaw indicate one mind behind all three.

The stockholders of the R. J. Reynolds Tobacco Company adopted Bylaw XII, the profit-sharing bylaw, on 23 August 1912:[20]

All of the Company's Officers and Employees who have owned its stock and been in its Employ for not less than twelve months may be allowed, in the discretion and at the option of the Board of Directors, beginning with the year 1912, to participate in proportion to the stock thus owned, in the Company's Annual profits which are in excess of the percentage of profits earned during the year 1910, to wit: 22.19%, not exceeding, however, 10% of these profits, in excess of 22.19% of its entire outstanding issue of common stock, taking into account pro rata, any increase or decrease thereof made during the year.

Reynolds thus set a fairly definite ceiling on the sum to be used for participation in company profits. Moreover, not only officers but also employees might share in profits if they owned company stock. One block to what might be called democratic participation of employees in the company's profits lay in the phrase "in the discretion and at the option of the Board of Directors."

Allocation of stock for purchase by officers and employees does appear to have been handled on a democratic basis, the author having discovered only one instance in which a director held more than his allotted share by using the name of an underling. This, of course, cannot be substantiated, largely because of the reluctance of former officials to discuss the matter. This stock was common stock, the only type then issued. Known informally for many years as "A" stock in order to differentiate it from other classes of common stock issued later, it attracted Reynolds employees from men in overalls to the president. In some cases it was owned by workers who did not understand many two-syllabled words. Frequently they inquired about "anticipation" stock—indeed a most apt malapropism.[21] In practice the stock of a deceased person or of one leaving the company's employ could be sold or given to anyone. As was usually the case, it went to another employee, thus making it possible for a person of little value to the company to profit exorbitantly and in some cases to draw on participation rights sums far in excess of salary. The same held for directors. On the other hand, many employees, needing all their wages for living expenses, could not aspire to ownership of A stock.

For the period in which it began to function, however, the Reynolds plan was unique in the tobacco industry, an incentive to many more than the presidents and vice-presidents. Its ownership bred a community of interest. In one case, many years after the plan began, a young office girl went to a stockbroker in the Reynolds building to investigate the purchase of A stock. When given the facts, she said nothing but later called John C. Whitaker, a director, told him the details involved, and asked his advice. Thereupon she purchased the stock.[22] The story often told of a Winston-Salem youngster who had received a horde of Christmas presents may well be true in spirit. After examining his array of toys, he began weeping and said that he had set his heart on some Reynolds "A" which he did not get.[23] In the 1940s Samuel Clay Williams, chairman of the board, declared that A stock was not a bonus and that almost 80 percent of it was owned by North Carolinians.[24] This, of course, became true because of the policy of the directors in disposing of the stock that in 1910 earned 22.19 percent of its capital. When the new issue of $2,475,000 in common stock was voted on 23 August 1912, it too became participating stock if held by an employee.

R. J. Reynolds believed that the participation stock would serve as a check against speculation and as an inducement for valued officers and employees to become permanently interested in the company. On 8 August 1912, when Reynolds made this observation, prior to the functioning of Bylaw XII by a few days, 48 employees and officers owned stock in the company.[25] Table 7-3, covering the years of full operation of Bylaw XII, checked against similar figures in other sources as completely as possible, reveals the success of this plan for directors and other employees.[26]

Other matters connected with the participation stock indicate the effort to remove control of the company from "the New York crowd" by establishing a broader base of ownership. Regarding the issue of $2,475,000 in capital stock approved on 23 August 1912, George W. Coan, apparently writing to employees on the sales force, informed them of Attorney General George W. Wickersham's interpretation of the court's decree in the dissolution suit. Because Wickersham held that certain individuals who had been officers and directors of the American Tobacco Company before 1912 did not have the right to subscribe to the new issue of Reynolds stock, the Reynolds management assumed that these rights in the new issue would be offered for sale on the market. Coan then added:[27]

Some of the Company's employees have given their orders to purchase the stock, and as those who may wish to become Stockholders can likely get the stock on a more favorable basis by joining in together and buying under one name (instead of going into the market and bidding against each other), we will be glad to nominate a purchaser here for the stock that any of the employees of the Company may desire to buy, with the understanding that said nominee is to use his best judgment as to price, and with the further understanding that if he has orders to buy more stock than he is able to get at a fair price, the full amount so purchased will be pro-rated in proportion to the number of shares each employee orders.

According to the present price of the stock and the rights in the new issue, the new stock will likely sell at around $235.00 to $250.00 per share. If you desire to become a Stockholder in the Company as herein outlined, please advise us, sending a cash deposit of $25.00 per share on the number of shares you wish to purchase, with the understanding that you will pay a balance of $75.00 per share in cash when the stock is purchased, making a total cash payment of $100.00 per share, and the Company will take your demand note for the remaining cost of your purchase, with the stock so purchased as collateral, charging you interest at the rate of 6 per cent per annum, or possibly 5 per cent, according to conditions. All dividends and distributions on account of the stock will be applied as credit on notes thus carried and employees will be expected to otherwise curtail

Table 7-3
Effects of Bylaw XII on Stock Participation, 1912–1948
(in Shares of Stock)

Year	Directors	All Other Employees	Total Participating Shares	Retirement & Investment Fund	Non-participating Shares	Total Shares
1912	18,476	664	19,140	—	80,860	100,000
1913	33,186	5,507	38,693	—	61,307	100,000
1914	33,929	5,507	39,436	—	60,564	100,000
1915	33,219	6,261	39,480	—	60,520	100,000
1916	34,985	7,716	42,701	—	57,299	100,000
1917	36,656	7,616	44,272	—	55,728	100,000
1918	12,606	8,009	20,615	—	79,385	100,000
1919	13,057	8,287	21,344	—	78,656	100,000
1920	63,296	36,900	100,196	—	299,804	400,000
1921	74,615	55,740	120,355	—	279,645	400,000
1922	98,498	75,641	174,139	—	225,861	400,000
1923	110,239	89,075	199,314	—	200,686	400,000
1924	117,489	87,962	205,451	—	194,549	400,000
1925	118,067	88,180	206,247	—	193,753	400,000
1926	137,715	112,044	249,759	—	150,241	400,000
1927	139,415	113,938	253,353	—	146,647	400,000
1928	184,504	155,511	340,015	—	59,985	400,000
1929	460,623	358,329	818,952	—	181,084	1,000,000
1930	460,647	350,406	811,059	—	188,947	1,000,000
1931	460,447	340,108	800,555	—	199,445	1,000,000
1932	451,408	324,706	776,114	—	223,886	1,000,000
1933	338,408	316,370	654,778	200,000	145,222	1,000,000
1934	327,641	324,062	651,703	200,000	148,297	1,000,000
1935	280,450	379,707	660,157	200,000	139,843	1,000,000
1936	280,450	374,854	655,304	200,000	144,696	1,000,000
1937	263,450	391,064	654,514	200,000	145,486	1,000,000
1938	262,533	396,240	658,773	200,000	141,227	1,000,000
1939	255,550	405,142	660,692	200,000	139,308	1,000,000
1940	238,480	413,174	651,655	200,000	148,345	1,000,000
1941	233,980	424,863	658,843	200,000	141,157	1,000,000
1942	171,488	414,328	585,816	200,000	214,184	1,000,000
1943	167,240	413,823	581,063	200,000	218,937	1,000,000
1944	161,660	418,355	580,015	200,000	219,985	1,000,000
1945	177,990	402,433	580,323	200,000	219,677	1,000,000
1946	145,605	397,662	543,267	200,000	256,733	1,000,000
1947	116,125	390,040	506,165	200,000	293,835	1,000,000
1948	111,485	397,121	508,606	200,000	291,394	1,000,000

Source: Exhibits Introduced, *R. J. R. Tob. Co. v. U.S.*, docket no. 254–54 (U.S. Court of Claims)—legal department, R. J. Reynolds Tobacco Company. Except for 1923, the number of shares held by directors agrees with the number given in exhibits presented in *Bookman v. R. J. R. Tob. Co. et al.*, docket no. 129–544 (Chancery of N.J., 1946)—legal department, box 806C, Records Center, R. J. Reynolds Tobacco Company.

same from time to time, as long as the Company carries them. Of course, in the event no purchase of stock is made, the $25.00 per share deposit you may make with us will be returned.

It appears evident that the August 1912 stock issue was on Reynolds's mind in January of that year when the directors authorized the lending of surplus funds to employees for the purchase of company stock. Additional support for this conclusion may be drawn from the list of stockholders who received a letter and resolution regarding subscription rights in the new stock issue. Among them were at least eighteen who at one time or another had served as directors of the old American Tobacco Company:[28]

George Arents (dir.)	W. H. McAlister (dir.)
A. N. Brady (dir.)	T. J. Maloney (dir.)
Paul Brown (dir.)	Northern Finance Company
A. H. Burroughs	O. H. Payne (dir.)
J. B. Cobb (dir.)	Thomas F. Ryan (dir.)
W. B. Dickerman	R. K. Smith (dir.)
B. N. Duke (dir.)	Charles N. Strotz (dir.)
J. B. Duke (dir.)	George W. Watts (dir.)
C. C. Dula (dir.)	C. A. Whelan
Robert B. Dula (dir.)	G. J. Whelan
George W. Elkins	H. P. Whitney
William Elkins Estate	Payne Whitney
Howard M. Hanna (dir.)	J. E. Widener
George A. Helme (dir.)	P. A. B. Widener (dir.)

Additional light on the financing of participation stock for Reynolds employees is shed in a paragraph of a letter written by R. J. Reynolds from a Philadelphia hospital on 6 June 1918, about seven weeks before his death. To begin with Reynolds asked Harry H. Shelton, counsel for the company, to leave a day earlier on a projected trip to Washington in order to bring his will to Philadelphia for the addition of a codicil: "At the time my will was made my Company stock was worth $500 to $600 per share and as it is now down in price I want to add a codicil so that my estate will continue to carry the stock for my employees, which I am now carrying and under the same agreement." Accordingly, on 10 June 1918 the codicil, dictated and signed by R. J. Reynolds, was witnessed by D. Rich, George W. Orr, and Harry H. Shelton. Reynolds attached the codicil by "way of assisting or encouraging some of the employees of R. J. Reynolds Tobacco Company, I have, from time to time loaned ... money with which to purchase stock of said Company." He referred specifically to loans for taking up subscription rights in another class of stock but specified that the other class be exchanged for common or participating stock.

He ordered his executor to continue to carry these notes with the same collateral as originally drawn. In another section he made similar stipulations in regard to additional collateral that he had obligated himself to deposit in certain banks carrying loans to some officers of the company for the purchase of its stock should the banks demand such collateral.[29]

As indicated by his reference to a different class of stock, Reynolds had another and more adroit plan for placing voting or participating A stock in the hands of his employees. This move may be classified as the most original of his career—unless it is surpassed by his production of the first modern cigarette—because it permitted him to place control of his company in the hands of people of North Carolina, then one of the most poverty-stricken areas of the South. Despite all efforts to secure a majority control of his stock, in 1917 "outsiders" still controlled more than 55 percent. In that year the directors, in need of additional capital, considered putting out a new issue of stock. Instead of looking northward for a corporation lawyer, Reynolds went to nearby Greensboro and hired Samuel Clay Williams. Williams had studied corporate law at the University of Virginia and had nine years of successful practice behind him when he joined the R. J. Reynolds Tobacco Company on 1 July 1917 as assistant counsel.[30] Williams's first definite assignment was to prepare a plan and a charter amendment under which a new class of stock would be offered to the existing stockholders. With the special aid of R. J. Reynolds, Williams drew up the plan and the charter amendment for a new stock issue, not only for increased capital but also for use in trading A stock from "outsiders." Incidentally, the directors wished to request authorization for a 7% Preferred Stock of 200,000 shares amounting to $20 million. They also requested authorization for 100,000 shares of Class B Common Stock, the new issue so much desired. The changes, when adopted, would raise the total authorized capitalization to $40 million. Presented to the directors on 4 October, the entire plan was approved by the stockholders on 1 November 1917.[31]

On 7 February 1918, it was decided to issue 50,000 shares of the newly authorized Class B Common Stock to be offered first at par, $100, to all holders of common or A stock in the proportion of one share for every two shares of A stock held.[32] The idea had been to create a new stock comparable in every way to A stock except in voting and participation rights. Class B Common Stock had no voting rights and no participation rights, but it had the same book value, the same ordinary dividend rights, the same rights on liquidation, and the same rights on new stock issues as did A stock. Holders of A stock retained exclusive rights under Bylaw XII to participating dividends as well as regular dividends.[33] Reynolds remembered the purpose of this new stock in his last illness and placed in the codicil of his will a provision that the Class B Common Stock rights (for the purchase of which he had lent certain employees money) should be converted into common or A stock.[34] Because no "outsider" could participate other than by receiving regular dividends, why not exchange A stock for Class B Common Stock? Both paid handsome regular dividends; moreover, common or A stock commanded a higher price than Class B Common Stock.

With the release of R. J. Reynolds's large holdings of participation shares of A stock at his death in 1918, the holdings of the directors were reduced by approximately two-thirds and the plan for placing more A stock in the hands of employees required additional implementation. A scheme for such a shift reached the minute book, possibly after William N. Reynolds had visited with "the New York crowd." On 1 May 1920 the directors approved a plan to amend the charter. Both A stock and Class B Common Stock were changed in par value to $25 and a new class of common stock known appropriately as New Class B Common, par value of $25, was to be issued and 1,600,000 shares set aside for a 200 percent stock dividend to be paid to holders of A stock and Class B Common Stock. With the payment of this handsome stock dividend on 16 August 1920, the capital stock of the company stood as follows:[35]

	Par Value Per Share
$10,000,000 of common or A stock	$ 25
$50,000,000 of New Class B Common Stock	$ 25
$20,000,000 of 7% Preferred Stock	$100

Needless to say, the shift of A stock to "the Winston-Salem crowd" increased rapidly, and by 1924 its members held a majority of the A stock that carried all the voting power. Thereafter, at least until 1948, Reynolds employees controlled the company, although "outsiders" continued to hold substantial amounts of A stock. The blackberry pickers of early years had now begun to arrive. So determined were they to obtain "anticipation" stock that, according to local legend, they used their salaries to buy it instead of promptly paying their regular bills. Then, paying their bills only once a year, they came forth with gleaming new cars or other signs of prosperity. In a more serious vein it may be claimed that the R. J. Reynolds Tobacco Company, through its Bylaw XII, managed to regain control of its business and to create a considerable wealth, much of which remained in the South—all this at a time when northern investments in southern industry generally meant that profits flowed back to the North.[36]

Many are the stories that have been told about the wonders of A stock and the wealth that accrued to employees who held it. Some of them are true, but the title of a magazine article, "The Town of a Hundred Millionaires,"[37] stretches the matter beyond credibility. There were many crises, as, for example, when Carl Wainwright Harris, head of the sales and advertising departments, died in December 1937 holding 15,000 shares. According to the bylaw as amended in 1915, yearly profits from A stock went to the employee holding it on the last day of the calendar year. The problem at Harris's death was to find an employee or employees who could manage the immediate purchase of 15,000 shares.[38] Frequently, too, new employees in modest positions held grandiose ideas of riches to be obtained by holding great blocks of A stock. The plans of a man hired for a seasonal job of five months in the Danville leaf plant are typical:[39]

> Mr. B. K. Jones will likely not be with us after this season, as his salary is not large enough to justify him remaining with us as a season man. He was under the impression when he accepted a position with us as season man, he would be able to get a larger block of stock than was allotted him. You will recall he asked for 200 and was allotted 50. We pay him $300 per month for the season which is about five months.
>
> I have not encouraged him since then that he would be able to get much more stock in allotments.

Jones, obviously with some capital, expected to obtain a block of stock far out of proportion to his services and thus to live easily from regular dividends and profits on the participation stock obtained by working five months during a calendar year.

More serious was the predicament of Vernon Davis, a salesman who, by virtue of a loan, held seventy-five shares in 1942, when net earnings had been reduced because of increased taxes. At the time virtually all stocks had declined. Davis's broker called for additional collateral or a payment of approximately $650. Unable to furnish either, Davis asked his new division manager for advice only to find him in the same position and inclined to follow a Fabian policy. Meanwhile Davis's broker wrote that the holder of the note would consider a minimum payment of $200 and a directive to the company to send all dividend and participation checks to the note holder until the margin on the loan was restored. On the pretense of being out of town, Davis ignored the broker's letter and proceeded with his own plan by mailing a check to his broker for $20 as a down payment instead of $200 and wiring the company to divert his participation payments to the holder of the note.[40] In this way he retained control of his A stock, largely by bluffing the holder of his note.

On the New York Stock Exchange

Participation or common stock was not the only type of Reynolds stock authorized before 1924. Reference has been made to Class B Common Stock and New Class B Common Stock, and to the issuance of preferred stock on 14 October 1914. On 30 October 1914, the directors notified the stockholders that they intended to list preferred and common stocks on the New York Stock Exchange.[41] This preferred stock had been authorized 2 March 1922 but not then listed on the New York Stock Exchange. But, judging from what occurred during later successful efforts and according to the memory of William C. Smith, long in charge of the stock transfer department, the first effort to list the stock on the New York Stock Exchange failed because of inadequate distribution of the stock.[42]

While the details of the declaration of a 200 percent stock dividend were being settled, S. Clay Williams went over the entire situation with representatives of the New York Stock Exchange under the declaration of intention to list company stocks as soon as plans could be completed. This move demonstrated the end that the directors had in view. In 1922, when charges for listing stock were increased, Williams unsuccessfully used this earlier but rather vague connection with the stock exchange in an effort to lower listing charges from $26,000 to $8,000.[43]

Finally, however, the company succeeded in listing its stock on the New York Stock Exchange on 16 March 1922, although James A. Gray, a vice-president and in general charge of financial matters, seemed reluctant to divulge some of the information necessary for the application. John W. Hanes, Jr., then associated with a brokerage firm in New York, assured Gray that the information "will not be anything that your competitors do not give out, nor will it be anything which could in any way be detrimental to your business."[44] Gray relented and Williams began to work on the application immediately—24 January 1922.[45]

The application, filed in the office of the stock-list committee on 7 March 1922, was criticized for being too lengthy. Thereupon, noted Williams, who was well-known for his verbosity, one of the secretaries attempted to reduce it but ended with an even longer application. Gray and Williams were staggered when they learned that because of a changed rule their filing fee would be $26,000 rather than $8,000; they protested vigorously but paid. When questioned about avoiding the publication of quarterly statements, Williams successfully explained the Reynolds position, although he failed to give any details. When the amounts of taxes paid the federal government for 1917 to 1921 inclusive were requested, a regular requirement after the levying of the excess profits tax, he stated: "We refused flatly to make any such showing and told the Secretary that we would tear up our application and give up the plan of listing before we would show these amounts." A letter of explanation later, according to Williams, caused the stock-list committee to consider the Reynolds position well taken; yet the committee felt some qualms about tax rebates from the federal government. On being told that the rebates might be handled in any way except by showing that they were earned during the year received, Williams replied: "We can handle this very easily as an adjustment of surplus applicable to former years." One member of the committee insisted that the inclusion of directors in participation profits should be clearer than what was implied by the phrase "officers and employees." This was accomplished by inserting a footnote to Bylaw XII. Criticized for not listing all the company's brands, the Reynolds representative explained that Reynolds did not wish to appear to advertise. The company was commended for its modesty and permitted to insert the names of its principal brands. Incidentally, it is doubtful that anyone could have compiled a complete list of such brands. The omission of mention of Class B Common Stock, none of which was outstanding, was covered by an explanatory paragraph.

In handling the application Williams and Gray learned that approval by action of the stock-list committee had to be reviewed by the board of governors of the New York Stock Exchange before any stock could be traded. Learning that the next regular meeting of the board of governors fell on 22 March 1922 but that a fee of $500 would produce a special meeting within twenty-four hours, Williams described his and Gray's action tersely: "To allay rumor we paid." They experienced difficulty in obtaining "R.J.R." as their abbreviation on the exchange because "R.J.N." was used by the Reading Railroad. But they stood manfully for their valuable initials and received permission to use them on the following day. The only real trouble concerned the distribution of common and New Class B Common Stock. It was easy to satisfy the committee regarding the latter but not so with common or A stock. Williams wrote: "It was not so easy to convince him [Chairman Robert Gibson of the stock-list committee] that the distribution on Common was such as to guarantee that stock a satisfactory record on the Exchange. At one time there was very substantial doubt as to our being able to get the Common Stock listed." When the stock-list committee ordered 1,500 printed copies of the Reynolds application for distribution to members of the exchange, Williams and Gray ordered 500 to be delivered in Winston-Salem. With the resolution of a few other minor items, the plan for listing stock on the New York Stock Exchange had become an accomplished fact.[46] This important step placed the company somewhat on a par with other companies of the tobacco industry. It virtually coincided with the end of the Reynolds brothers' leadership, which was passed to Bowman Gray, Sr., only two years later.

In some measure the matters objected to by the stock-list committee later caused annoyance for the company—notably the question of interim reports and the handling of the participation plan. It should be emphasized that R. J. Reynolds, though he died in 1918, had carefully planned the moves that led to the listing of the company stock on the New York Stock Exchange in 1922. It should be noted also that only New Class B Common Stock and 7% Preferred were listed in 1922; common or A stock was not sufficiently well distributed for listing until 1927.

The Camel Revolution

R. J. Reynolds was not unaware of the importance of cigarettes as far back as 1898; in that year he offered with each three-ounce bag of Our Advertiser smoking tobacco a "Cigarette Book," the common name for a packet of cigarette papers for customers' use in rolling their own.[47] It has been claimed that Bowman Gray, Sr., came from Baltimore to Winston-Salem in 1909 for the specific purpose of discussing with Reynolds the feasibility of manufacturing cigarettes. Sometime prior to 1912, while still in Baltimore, Gray frequently urged the company to begin the manufacture of cigarettes, which he saw as the coming tobacco product.[48] The year 1909, when Prince Albert was beginning its rapid growth, could not have been a propitious time for such a venture. More than likely Reynolds began to manufacture cigarettes because of their increasing popularity, although he may well have been stirred by the success of Prince Albert and the mere joy of "throwing down the gauntlet to the American Tobacco Company" by becoming its competitor in all leading types of manufactured tobacco.[49] William N. Reynolds, whose stories often tended to denigrate his brother, declared in 1950 that R. J. believed the common canard that cigarette paper was harmful—a belief then about as strong as the prevailing dislike for the American Tobacco Company. In North Carolina the general opinion of cigarettes reflected not only ideas relating to health but also politics, religion, and economics, all of which may be summed up to mean antitrust sentiment. At length, R. J. reputedly permitted Walter R. Reynolds to have cigarette paper analyzed by three chemists, one in New York, one in Pittsburgh, and another in Chicago. According to Will Reynolds, when reports of the harmless nature of the paper came in, R. J. began to manufacture cigarettes.[50] Reynolds's earlier inclusion of cigarette papers with bags of smoking tobacco creates some doubt about the truth of this story.

The earliest available factual record of R. J.'s desire to manufacture cigarettes is dated 4 March 1912. At this point Walter Reynolds, then on a trip to New York City, wrote Rufus L. Patterson in regard to secondhand

Russian cigarette machines. Patterson replied immediately that most of them had been scrapped, although the American Tobacco Company and John Bollman Company of San Francisco still had some in operation. American, according to Patterson, could spare one of the secondhand machines. In reference to Reynolds's statement that his firm had not fully determined the best machine to adopt, Patterson indirectly recommended the Standard Cigarette Machine built by his company (American Machine and Foundry Company). He informed Reynolds that he was building one hundred of these machines for various tobacco companies. On his return to Winston-Salem, Walter Reynolds wrote Patterson early in April: "We are still undecided, as to whether we will go into the cigarette business at the present time and will, therefore, not place an order for the machine as yet."[51] This probably reflected a decision not to buy a secondhand machine rather than reluctance to enter the cigarette business as soon as possible. Meanwhile rumors in Winston-Salem that Reynolds would begin producing cigarettes appeared in print. The editor of the *Southern Tobacco Journal* declared that the Reynolds company had a good brand that it expected to do well.[52]

By November 1912 there was no more hesitancy. On 9 November Reynolds interviewed tobacco machinery agent Richard H. Wright about a machine for packing cigarettes in foil "and an auxiliary machine known as the cup filling machine for inserting the packets [of cigarettes] after [they were] wrapped in foil into cups." Described as a machine that would make from sixty to seventy-five cups per minute, it was priced at $2,000. In cigarette terminology, the "cup" is merely the outside wrapper or pouch of a cigarette package that has been properly folded and glued to hold. Wright needed to know the exact size of the cigarette before he could start building either the packer or the cup-making machine. In his follow-up letter Wright felt called upon to explain that three separate machines were necessary: a cup-making machine, another for placing and wrapping the cigarettes in a foil mounted on tissue paper, and a cup-filling machine for inserting the wrapped packets of cigarettes into the cup.[53] Six days later the local tobacco journal dutifully reported additional hints that Reynolds would manufacture cigarettes.[54]

At last Clement Manly announced, on 6 February 1913 at a meeting of the Winston Board of Trade, that the R. J. Reynolds Tobacco Company planned to manufacture cigarettes. He told of the purchase of machinery, although his main purpose lay in requesting that the Board of Trade adopt a resolution opposing the Clark bill, then pending in the North Carolina legislature, which would prohibit the manufacture and sale of cigarettes in the state. This the Board of Trade hastened to do after hearing that the passage of such a bill would mean a grievous loss to Winston-Salem "in that Mr. Reynolds would be compelled to move his cigarette factory to

Richmond or to some other point outside the State." A few days later the Winston Tobacco Association adopted a similar resolution.[55] So great was general interest that the sales department, on 12 February 1913, told its men in the field to disregard rumors in the daily press because "it will be a long time before we shall be in position to offer cigarettes to the trade in your territory."[56] The new venture continued to hold great interest for local people, but on 8 April the word was that it would be June or July before Reynolds could start producing cigarettes in the old Liipfert-Scales building, which had been built and occupied for a time by P. H. Hanes and Company (now Number 43). The delay, Reynolds declared, was caused by the manufacturers of cigarette machinery, who were unable to fill orders.[57] July came but the inquisitive *Southern Tobacco Journal* editor could not learn the names of the cigarettes to be made.[58]

Various puzzling questions confronted the Reynolds firm as it prepared to enter this more sophisticated branch of the tobacco industry. During these many trials, the model generally followed was the Fatima, a Turkish blended cigarette. Originally developed by Cameron and Cameron Company of Richmond and later purchased by Liggett and Myers, Fatima was the first cigarette packed in the present style cup package.[59] In December 1912 the superintendent of manufacture did not know what size paper to purchase for making cigarettes. He considered the correct width to be about $1^{15}/_{16}$ inches but did not understand how to use millimeters in measuring cigarettes until advised by the engineer of a machine builder; nor did he receive any definite clarification from that source. By January 1913, however, he could, as his letter indicates, convert millimeters into inches: "We have checked over our figures as to the width of this paper and find that we were in error in stating 31 mm equal to 1 15/16″. We also believe that you are in error in stating that 31 mm equal to 1 1/16″. One millimeter, we find, equals .03937″, 31 mm. 1.22047″, or 1 7/32″ plus. This, we find to be approximately the width paper used on the 'FATIMA' cigarette."[60]

Cigarette manufacturing was a strange new area for these users and manufacturers of plug tobacco—requiring the hiring of experienced men, the purchase of new machinery, more careful attention to patent rights, more meticulous study of packaging, and numerous other details including trademarks and labels. Other cigarette makers in general could not be expected to relish the entry of a vigorous new manufacturer. R. J. Reynolds supposedly sought to place a Winston-Salem mechanic in a cigarette factory in order to learn the details of manufacture, but the man in question refused to accept the assignment.[61] Eventually, however, Reynolds located at least three men with the necessary experience: Richard Lee Dunstan, John Emmitt Stone, and Henry Lee Lorraine, Jr.

Richard Lee Dunstan joined the Reynolds firm on 1 May 1913. Dunstan's first work in a tobacco factory had been with Allen and Ginter as tally boy in the production of hand-rolled cigarettes. Absorbed by the American Tobacco Company in 1890 and allotted to Liggett and Myers in 1911, Allen and Ginter had been an early producer of cigarettes, although prior to 1890 it had not been too successful in adopting machinery for their production. Sometime in the 1890s American sent young Dunstan to Philadelphia, where he worked for seven years as superintendent of a branch factory manufacturing small cigars. From there he was transferred to Danville, Virginia, to superintend another small cigar branch. In 1912, he was moved to Richmond to work in a smoking tobacco branch. In 1913 he resigned and on 1 May began to work in Reynolds's cigarette department. As superintendent of the cigarette division, Dunstan, an exceedingly energetic man, devoted the remainder of his working years, until 1 January 1948, to the manufacture of cigarettes for the R. J. Reynolds Tobacco Company. On 5 February 1913, three months before Dunstan's arrival, R. J. Reynolds had signed a contract with the American Machine and Foundry Company for the purchase of five Standard Cigarette Machines to be delivered in the latter part of April.[62] Dunstan was thus employed at the right moment.

Though plans had been formulated when he arrived, Dunstan, who carried in his pocket rough sketches for the layout of cigarette machinery, found many rough spots to iron out before the first cigarette was produced. Ironing out rough spots in cigarette production remained his task until retirement. Dunstan's aid to Walter R. Reynolds, who was floundering in his new task, proved to be of great significance in the development of the Camel cigarette. For almost thirty-five years he served as the key man in producing Camels, and, as a mark of his great value to the company, he was not retired until he reached the age of seventy-seven, just before the production of filter-tipped cigarettes. Perhaps there is no better way to evaluate his services to the company than to quote his letter of 27 May 1936 to Roy C. Haberkern, then a director and chief purchasing agent:[63]

> In reference to our 'phone conversation of yesterday, requesting information on Cigarette Machines.
>
> We wish to advise that we have 425 cigarette machines. Some of these machines were purchased in 1913—all machines were purchased at a speed of 450 per minute. These machines are in most excellent repair. We have made a great many improvements on these machines. We have worked over the feeder hopper and made a dustless feeder. We have also enlarged the paste cans so as to be able to run nine hours with one filling of paste—each machine has two paste cans. We have also put on a revolving sealer. The revolving sealer

permits the cleaning of the sealer while the machine is in operation. We have also changed the cut-off and are now using what is known as the Muller cut-off which permits us to run these machines from 800 to 830 cigarettes per minute. We are also using what is known as the hand catcher instead of the automatic catcher.

These 425 machines are equipped with 111 United Feeders and 314 Comas Feeders. We would be pleased to furnish you with any further information you may desire.

The writer would advise that should you be able to sell any of these machines to our competitors, that we not allow them to purchase just two or three machines, as they will only be learning just what improvements we have put on same.

Dunstan had been associated with John Emmitt Stone at Liggett and Myers; when he realized his need for additional expert aid in starting the new cigarette machines, he returned to Richmond and persuaded Stone to join Reynolds. It so happened that Stone had just returned from New York, where he had helped establish a cigarette factory that Liggett and Myers later decided not to operate. He was therefore in good practice for the work awaiting him at Reynolds when he arrived on 14 July 1913.[64] Stone, a mechanic, became chief operator of cigarette-making machines and continued to work in that general capacity but with enlarged duties. He was present when the first cigarette emerged from a machine in the old Liipfert-Scales building on 17 July 1913.

Henry Lee Lorraine, Jr., joined the company on 19 January 1914, probably also recruited by Dunstan. He had worked as an assistant foreman in the Allen and Ginter branch first for the American Tobacco Company and then for Liggett and Myers from 1906 to 1913, and for Swift and Company for one month before being located and hired by Reynolds. An expert mechanic, Lorraine became well known for his hobby of being able to repair any clock brought to him. He served in the cigarette department for approximately thirty-nine years.[65]

This trio, Dunstan, Stone, and Lorraine, apparently with no regrets at leaving Allen and Ginter, were the most important Reynolds employees in the production of cigarettes, and trainers of a countless number of foremen. Both before and after hiring them, Reynolds worked at the task of obtaining equipment and supplies. To bolster his slim knowledge of machines for cutting cigarette tobacco, he again wrote to Richard H. Wright for information. In his reply Wright referred to the Pease cutter, which "used to be very popular," the Adt cutter, which was "very excellent," and the Robert Legg cutter, "a very popular cutting machine for long cut as well as cigarettes." But Reynolds was not to be taken in by such a superficial report. In some way he learned of Eduard Quester's cutter, a heavy German machine capable of slicing through massive quantities of tobacco. As early as April 1913, Reynolds sought Wright's help in purchasing one of these foreign-made machines because the cutters he had were "for long cut tobacco." Eventually Wright located a new Quester machine already in New York and persuaded Clinton W. Toms of Liggett and Myers to sell the cutter to Reynolds. On 2 July, Walter Reynolds and his helpers worked to assemble the Quester cutter, which on a full day's run could shred about 7,000 pounds of leaf tobacco.[66]

No less annoying was the question of the best cup-making machine to adopt. Before purchasing an English cup-making machine, the Reynolds officials had doubted that it would serve their purpose, although Wright offered them a five-year monopoly on the use of the machine. When held directly to the point by Burton Craige, Wright stated that he had not allowed a patent to be issued on the machine in the United States. Thereupon Craige, on 27 November 1912, wrote Wright that a U.S. patent would be necessary before Reynolds officials would consider purchasing it. Again, five days later, Craige explained the necessity for a patent on the cup-making machine. At last Wright acknowledged that it was not possible to obtain a patent on the cup itself as that style had been used in England a great many years. At the same time Wright declared that he had earlier explained this fact to R. J. Reynolds, Will Reynolds, and other officers of the company at a meeting in Winston-Salem. He pointed to the great speed and small waste characteristic of his machine, but, after investigation and testing, Reynolds officials purchased only one such cup-making machine, although much time was spent in making the decision.[67] At length Reynolds changed to the Ludington cup machine; by August 1914 he had ordered "a large number" for delivery at an early date.[68]

The size and style of packages for the cigarettes was the subject of much deliberation. Should they be sold in packets of eight, ten, or twenty, and should they be sold in cups, hinged boxes, or slide boxes? Failure to come to an early, firm decision on these questions kept the matter of purchasing machinery undecided for some time. On 19 December 1912, Walter Reynolds ordered one foil-packing machine for packages of eight cigarettes and another for twenty, only to cancel the order by a long-distance telephone call on the following day.[69] Four weeks later Reynolds reinstated his order for a foil packer and cup filler for an eight-cigarette packet.[70] All the delay did not arise from the company's indecision. On 16 January 1913 the Ludington Cigarette Machine Company of Waterbury, Connecticut, in preparing to build a machine for Reynolds, sent sample packages but without allowance for the use of foil wrapping.[71] After the style for the two sizes of packages—eights and twenties—had apparently been settled again, Reynolds officials met on the afternoon of 5 Februaary 1913 and decided to change the style of wrapping both eights and twenties to one similar to that followed by Liggett and Myers with the Fatima—a radical change evidently made in order to utilize "a cheaper equipment for wrapping." Three days later Walter Reynolds clarified this move:[72]

> We have learned through inside sources that a machine has been made for packing "FATIMA" cigarettes which uses identically the same wrapper and cup as the hand packer. We believe the source of our information is correct; however, it would be well to check this up if there is any way in which you can do it. In all probability, Mr. Toms [of Liggett and Myers] can give you this information, provided, of course, he does not know for whom you want it.

Finally on 15 February 1913 Walter Reynolds requested Wright to stop work on both packing machines "until we can come to some definite decision as to size of packages." Two days later, he declared that his firm had decided to drop the idea of making a package for eight cigarettes.[73] This time the officials had decided to use a ten-cigarette package in a draw box similar to the one used for Piedmont cigarettes made by the American Tobacco Company. This involved another problem. R. J. Reynolds insisted on a device "for cutting and scoring the shell from a continuous roll of enamelled card board" instead of having the lithographer do this. According to the machine builder, the lithographer could do a clearer and cleaner job on such work.[74] By 11 July, however, Reynolds decided to change "the ten cigarette package in order to pack them in the same size box as is now used for the Sovereign" cigarette, also made by American. Four days later, however, Walter Reynolds believed that his company had been wrong in that decision and countermanded the order. Requesting his machine builder to await the result of experiments to determine exactly what his company wanted, Reynolds hoped to give a final decision on 16 July. Largely because the Reynolds sales force deemed it necessary, the company decided three days later to use a box similar to that in which Sovereign cigarettes were packed.[75]

Choosing a cigarette-making machine was complicated by another problem, and as Walter Reynolds's letter indicates this problem also involved another:[76]

> The machine we talked with you about is known as the "Standard" cigarette machine, and we understand that three or four hundred of these have been built within the past two years and are giving eminent satisfaction.

> We will not be able to get the automatic feed with these, however; as this is controlled by the American Tobacco Company for some

months as yet. We will be glad to have your advice as to what hand feed you consider the best satisfactory. In getting the STANDARD MACHINES it is understood that the builders are to fit their machine with any hand feed we select.

Though Reynolds spoke of a hand feed, his firm intended to use the automatic feed if possible. On 13 February, Walter Reynolds stated that the American Tobacco Company had refused to allow his company the use of the automatic feed. Nevertheless he wrote the Bonsack Cigarette Machine Company for further details. Just before 13 July, however, when in New York, Burton Craige found that the patent on the Bonsack feed had expired; thus for the time being, the Reynolds firm would not be forced to use the hand feed.[77]

A decision on the size of packages apparently was made in late July 1913. The ten-packet size would be put out in a sliding box the same length as the Piedmont and the twenty-packet in a cup or pouch like the Fatima. Reynolds officials kept in mind, however, the possibility of packing some of the same brand of cigarettes by tens as well as twenties.[78] By mid-September a delay in the construction of the twenty packer instead of the ten offered no problem to the company because the ten packer was needed "to help out with orders." The machine for the twenties, however, arrived in Winston-Salem on 27 September 1913, shortly before the first Camels were placed in trade.[79] Clearly the Reyno cigarette came into production first, packed in a sliding box of tens, while the Camels packed in cups of twenties, as they are today, came on the scene somewhat later. This order was probably also true for the Red Kamel tens and the Osman twenties. The Red Kamel was packed in a hinged box of ten cigarettes—the cigarettes being oval in shape.[80]

Entering the cigarette business involved more problems than securing machinery and deciding on the sizes of packages. Experimentation on formulas had to be done and suitable brand names chosen. R. J. Reynolds, never a man to risk all on one shot, decided to produce three different types of cigarettes in order to test the taste of the smoking public and thus arrive at a brand that would be accepted. No doubt he followed the same general plan that had caused his success with Prince Albert. Cigarettes, when introduced in the United States, had been Turkish, but, by the time of dissolution of the American Tobacco Combination, six types of cigarettes were being produced: (1) first-class Turkish cigarettes, (2) straight Turkish, (3) pseudo-Turkish packaged and adorned to resemble Turkish cigarettes, (4) Turkish blend or a blend of Turkish and bright (flue-cured leaf), (5) straight Virginia, made of bright leaf produced in Virginia or the Carolinas, and (6) miscellaneous consisting of mouth-piece cigarettes and uncased straight Burley cigarettes with a small amount of Turkish leaf. None of these variations were very strongly favored by the public at this time.[81] Of the variations, however, the Turkish blend had become somewhat popular as an adaptation of the Turkish cigarette, and among the Turkish blend cigarettes Reynolds chose as his target the fast-selling Fatima. He did not copy its formula but produced a Turkish and domestic blend; on his very earliest packages he described the formula simply as "Blended Cigarettes." Probably his recent success with Prince Albert had impressed on him the virtues of Burley leaf for use in smoking tobacco, and from his earliest years he had been indoctrinated with a belief in bright leaf. These two types of leaf constituted his domestic blend until 1916 when Maryland tobacco was added because of its exceptional burning qualities. Turkish leaf was used for its taste and aroma, and no doubt also for its inevitable association with cigarettes. In the tobacco trade an old saying persists that Turkish leaf used with domestic leaf is comparable to the use of salt and pepper in food. It may be, too, that the association in the public mind of Turkish leaf with cigarettes influenced Reynolds to use it in his blend. According to James Walter Glenn, experimentation with the Camel blend was carried on strictly by him, by James B. Dyer, and by R. J. and W. N. Reynolds.[82]

Perhaps no one has described the impact of this revolutionary new cigarette, the first truly American cigarette, better than the American Tobacco Company's George Washington Hill in his frank answer given when asked what important event in the cigarette business occurred in 1913. Seldom does one tobacco manufacturer speak so frankly and in such complimentary terms of a rival, but it should be kept in mind that Hill's statement came in 1944 during a suit that charged the major tobacco companies with oligopolistic practices:[83]

> Reynolds introduced Camels. I recall the first newspaper campaign was a teaser. I thought it was a joke; I thought they were wasting their money. "The Camels are coming," was their caption. It was not any joke. In town after town, when they introduced Camels, other cigarette brands were swept to one side. As I told you, the Fatima brand was the one great outstanding brand, and it capitalized on the Turkish taste in those days, the trend towards Turkish cigarettes, and, as I described, they had on the Fatima package "Turkish Cigarettes" large, and the word "blend" small. They [Liggett and Myers] were not particularly fond of the word "blend"; they wanted to show "Turkish."

> Camel went them one better. It showed on its package "Turkish and Domestic Blend," and the domestic part our people analyzed as largely burley. This brand was put on and swept other brands to one side. I worked the road in those days, and it was very discouraging.

Territory after territory swung over into the Camel column. Our brands could not stand up against it. Our salesmen were down because everybody was talking about this new taste in cigarettes. The public wanted the new taste. The public commented on the new taste, and that is what we in the Sales Department got — "Well, yes, you make good cigarettes, but they don't taste like Camels," and that was what we were up against.

And Camels introduced price competition, too, because Camels were put up to sell at 10 cents a pack — in the oval package of 20s, against the Fatima, the Zubelda, the Omar brand of the American, the Zubelda of Lorillard, the Fatima of Liggett & Myers, Turkish blends at 15 cents, and Camel was 10 cents.

Well, I went back home after my road work and I went to Mr. P. S. Hill, and I told him that if things went on like they were, we would not be in the cigarette business very long, so, "Well," he said, "What are we going to do?" . . .

So, my father and I talked it over a great deal, and finally I said to him, "Well, we will have to go to Charley Penn." Charley Penn was our vice president in charge of manufacturing plug tobacco and up until that time had had nothing to do with the manufacture of cigarettes at all. "Charley Penn knows how to handle burley tobacco and dip it. We will have to try and have Charley Penn blend us a cigarette that is better than Camels." So we experimented and we got Mr. Penn into the picture. . . .

Meanwhile, my father told me to get up a name, and I went through the old brands of the American Tobacco Company and I found a brand that was put out in smoking tobacco called Lucky Strike, and I thought that was a good name, but I did not like the package, because the package was kind of Elizabethan—had a lot of curlicues and scrolls on it, so I got an artist to work on the package, simplified it, and made the nice circle without any curlicues, and wrote the first things we put on the package and got the package all right, at least, I thought it was all right.

In the meanwhile, Penn had experimented in connection with blends, and he had a blend which our people thought was really [a] good burley blend, made under the processing that we had previously only used in connection with plug and smoking tobaccos, but never in connection with cigarettes. This tobacco had to be wrung out on a wringer. It was dipped into this mixture and wrung out on a wringer, and our first machines were used at the Mayo branch in

Richmond, Virginia, and we shipped this burley tobacco wrung out on a wringer up to the 22nd Street factory [in New York City]. . . .

Now, we had to put out Lucky Strike. The competition of Camel forced us to put out Lucky Strike. . . .

But, Fatimas was a 15-cent pack; Turkish blend cigarettes 15 cents a pack. Camels had capitalized on the Turkish atmosphere by the minarets and mosques on the Camel package.

I won't tell you what they said about Camels, the mosques and the minarets, but Camels came out at 5 cents less; at 5 cents less, and, Mr. Reynolds put on the back of his Camels, and it is there to this day, "Do not look for premiums or coupons as the cost of the tobaccos blended in Camel Cigarettes prohibits the use of them." . . .

I have forgotten what Camels were doing, but they were doing plenty. And, Liggett & Myers had come in. Now I don't know what the other fellows' blends are, but my report is from my men that the Chesterfield cigarette definitely changed its blend. It was a Virginia [flue-cured] cigarette originally. At any rate, they made a cigarette which has had a great popular appeal. They came into the picture.

Lorillard was still sticking by the old things, and if my recollection serves me, I don't think Lorillard got into the burley type of cigarette until Old Gold came out in 1926.

So the Camel became the agent for producing the modern cigarette industry. It should be noted that George Washington Hill credited Reynolds not only with a revolutionary brand, but also with a revolutionary change in prices and advertising as well as with the elimination of premiums. By late December 1913, the editor of *Tobacco* declared that the Camel had "already been accepted as a standard brand wherever it has been offered to the public." He noted that the blend of "Turkish and domestic tobaccos had received instant recognition as well as much sincere praise."[84] Walter Reynolds wrote on 14 December 1914 that the "rush for Camels is now on, and we are running all the packers to full capacity. It looks as though we will have to run over time this month, to supply the demand."[85] The first carton of Camels had been established in interstate commerce about fourteen months earlier, on 3 October 1913, by a sale to Charles E. Hughes and Company of Danville, Virginia, by Rice Gwynn.[86]

The other cigarette brands introduced by Reynolds in 1913—Reyno, Osman, and Red Kamel—offered no originality in formulas. The Reyno, a straight Virginia cigarette, contained flue-cured leaf from Virginia and the Carolinas. The top of its sliding box was ornamented with the seal and mottoes of Virginia and North Carolina.[87] The Osman was a Turkish blend and the Red Kamel was perhaps a straight Turkish cigarette.

None of the four Reynolds brands introduced in 1913 was named idly. Tobacco manufacturers tend to place great faith in the name of a product, but in the case of the Reynolds brands, from plug to filter tip, the telling point has been the formula. As the stories go, R. J. Reynolds desired short, simple names easily pronounced and symbolized by a picture. But Reynolds lived in an age and a section where literacy was not high. Though his chewing brands ran the gamut from Razor Back to Cleopatra, he could easily vary the names to influence different segments of his market. With Prince Albert he had aimed at a national product but stressed a simple name and a familiar picture. So it was with his cigarettes. The name Reyno is self-explanatory—the adaptation of a Virginia-Carolina name for a Virginia-Carolina tobacco. This was ineffective, but perhaps not because of R. J.'s failure to hold clearly to his principles of simplicity and graphic representation. With the name Osman, doubtless Reynolds, an avid reader of newspapers and a man with a remarkable memory, made the choice. The cigarette was named for General Osman (1837–1900), the Turkish field marshal who held off the Russians 143 days at the siege of Plevna. On his return from imprisonment in Russia, Osman became war minister for Turkey and held that post until about 1885. The Turkish flavor of the name is obvious. An undated excerpt from a letter, pasted on the photograph of General Osman preserved in the company museum, indicates that it was more difficult to secure this photograph than it had been to obtain one of Prince Albert.

In naming the Camel Reynolds again followed his ideas of simplicity and pictorial representation. Various stories about the naming exist. Because Fatima, the target aimed at, was a Turkish blend carrying the picture of an oriental dancing girl, it was decided to have the new brand savor of the Near East. Among the strong competing names were Kismet and Nabob, though many others were considered. So much favor was given to the word "Kamel" that at one point A. Hoen and Company, lithographers of Richmond, were ordered to use it in the preparation of a label. Finally "Camel" won the day and on 24 September 1913 the lithographers submitted an acceptable label, although this camel was a sad, shaggy animal with two-pronged hoofs, an awkward stance, short pointed ears, and a drooping neck. The background of temples, minarets, oasis, and pyramids was much as it is today except for sharpness of outline. Underneath the camel appeared the words "Blended Cigarettes," which were replaced by "Turkish & Domestic Blend Cigarettes." The directors did not especially care for Hoen's first depiction of a camel. Could this one-humped dromedary pass as a camel? Burton Craige consulted his *Encyclopaedia Britannica* and found that a dromedary was a camel but a camel was not a dromedary.

This settled the question and the directors felt justified in using the one-humped dromedary and calling it a camel. It was also decided to use the camel because of its yellowish color and to have the same color dominate the package, much on the principle that inspired the use of yellow on taxicabs as the color most likely to attract attention. Little was left to chance. At this time the famous inscription concerning coupons stood as follows: "The cost of the Tobacco blended in Camel cigarettes prohibits the use of inserts and coupons." This wording had been arrived at by a slow process. Many versions were submitted to, and by, the directors over a period of several weeks. With a young secretary, Roy C. Haberkern, Reynolds rode in his carriage to his farm in the hills of East Winston giving serious thought to the wording to be used and dictating many phrasings of the statement. Young Haberkern made copies of these various suggestions, which were presented to the directors the following morning.[88]

In preparing the Camel for its dizzy climb the label had to be improved and the name legitimized. Matters needing improvement included the dromedary's figure, an unfortunate cloud effect on the oriental sky, the phrase on the back panel, and the shadows cast by the pyramids. Scarcely had the directors accepted the first label before they decided to change the wording on the back panel to read: "Don't look for Inserts or Coupons, as the cost of the Tobaccos blended in CAMEL cigarettes prohibits the use of them." It is often stated that the skilled hand of Katharine Smith Reynolds (17 November 1880–23 May 1924), wife of R. J. Reynolds who had excellent training in languages at what became the Woman's College of the University of North Carolina (now the University of North Carolina at Greensboro), made further changes in this revision. On 31 October 1913, A. Hoen and Company was sent instructions to change "Inserts" to "Premiums," and so with minor changes in capitalization the warning has since remained, although it has now lost its significance.[89]

As to the appearances of the camel itself, prior to the showing of Barnum and Bailey's circus in Winston-Salem on Monday, 29 September 1913, Roy C. Haberkern asked R. J. Reynolds about photographing both a camel and a dromedary as a guide for improving the label. Reynolds consented, and on Monday morning, with the offices and factories closed for the circus, as was customary, young Haberkern contacted the superintendent of the menagerie. In an unpleasant humor on that rainy morning the superintendent refused in extremely profane language. Thereupon Haberkern referred to Reynolds's practice of closing offices and factories for the circus, intimating that this practice might be discontinued. The superintendent, named Patterson, softened and stated that he must have a letter from the company stating that the name Barnum and Bailey would not appear in Reynolds's advertising. Haberkern raced to the office building, climbed through a window, wrote the letter, and signed R. J.'s name to it. Upon its receipt Patterson conceded. At two-thirty Haberkern returned to the circus grounds with a local photographer named "Ferrell." Patterson brought out a dromedary and a camel. The dromedary, unwilling to pose without stretching his neck sidewise to watch the photographer, received a slap on the nose from Patterson. At once the animal raised his tail, threw back his ears, and closed his eyes as the photographer snapped the picture. The camel proved more tractable about posing, but on the following day the directors chose the picture of the insulted dromedary over the two-humped camel. The company, on 31 October 1913, sent a copy of the picture of "Old Joe," as the dromedary was known by the circus help, to A. Hoen and Company asking that it be reproduced for the Camel label without the background, halter, and man in charge. Satisfied with the result, the Reynolds company on 18 December 1913 ordered one million labels from A. Hoen and Company.[90]

Perhaps more involved is the story of the name "Camel." As early as April 1913, Burton Craige began inquiries to learn whether the names "Osman," "Camel," "Aga," "Oracle," "Rembrandt," and "Danube" were used by the tobacco industry, expressing special interest in the status of the first three.[91] A firm of New York attorneys wrote the company on 3 July 1913 that a Camel brand had been sold to Salvatore Ragona of New York City by the receivers of the Imported Tobacco Manufacturing Company.[92] In an effort to secure a clear title to the camel name, Burton Craige went to New York in July to see Ragona but found that he had purchased the name "Red Kamel," not "Camel." For three hundred dollars Ragona assigned his rights to Red Kamel, its goodwill, the die, and 5,000 manufactured cigarettes to the R. J. Reynolds Tobacco Company.[93] Reynolds's New York lawyer, formerly with the American Tobacco Company, now considered the titles to Reyno, Osman, and Camel to be clean.[94] On that basis, by 11 November Reynolds was about ready to make Red Kamels, and six days later was preparing to launch them in interstate commerce in order to obtain a valid trademark. But early in December Thomas B. Gilbert, a division manager for the company, found Red Kamels on sale in the Jewish districts of Philadelphia—not Reynolds's Red Kamel, but a Red Kamel made by J. Friedberg, of the Turco-Russian Cigarette Company of Philadelphia, who had purchased the brand from Salvatore Ragona of New York.[95] On 12 December 1913, Burton Craige declared that Reynolds was marketing Camels and had "sold a limited quantity of Red Kamel cigarettes."[96] But at the same time Red Kamels, made by another company, were also being sold in Ohio. Ragona protested that he had not sold die or anything else relating to the Red Kamel to Friedberg other than a job lot of mixed boxes that included some for the Red Kamel.[97] The matter became so important to the company that R. J. Reynolds himself called on Ragona, but evidently only to feel out the ground.[98] When he went to see J. Friedberg, Burton Craige found that the Turco-Russian Cigarette Company owned the Red Kamel on assignment from Salvatore Ragona. Reynolds wired Craige to buy Friedberg's title, his entire stock of 200,000 manufactured Red Kamels, 15,000 boxes, and 5,000 cartons—the cigarettes to be stored in the Philadelphia office of Thomas Gilbert and the remaining items to be sent to Winston-Salem. The cost was $3,000.[99] Reynolds thus purchased the Red Kamel twice and manufactured it until May 1936, obviously to protect the Camel brand.[100]

At the same time Reynolds apparently allowed the Red Kamel to supersede the Osman, which was of essentially the same type. Expanding on the virtue of these brands in 1914, Percy Reynolds Masten (7 August 1867– 22 March 1924) declared that the introduction of Camels should help the sales of Reynos and Red Kamels. "These three cigarettes are entirely different," he wrote.[101] Priced at eight dollars per thousand, the Red Kamel retailed at ten for ten cents and, like the Camel, carried no premiums. Bowman Gray, Sr., wrote F. C. Moore, division manager in Duluth, Minnesota, that Red Kamels were "making as remarkable success in the ten for ten line as CAMELS have in the 20 for 10 line." Furthermore, he had "personal knowledge of a great many people who have smoked Pall Mall and other 25¢ cigarettes for years, who are now regular smokers of Red Kamels."[102] Meanwhile a Red Kamel lighter was introduced as a means for advertising. Quite different from Reynolds's well-known lighters of the 1950s, the Red Kamel lighter was of cast metal, 8½ inches long and 7¾ inches high. So complicated was the operation of these lighters, involving the use of benzene or gasoline and a sparking metal, that they were apparently entrusted only to division managers to be placed in the best hotels, pool halls, and tobacco stores. All this befitted an elegant cigarette with a cork tip.[103] Yet no selling devices seemed effective with Reynos, Osmans, or Red Kamels, whose combined production from 1913 to 1924 is shown in Table 7-4.

The Osman, soon replaced by the Red Kamel, had a short life—from October 1913 until February 1915.[104] It was different with the Reyno, first manufactured on 17 July 1913. Reputedly, R. J. Reynolds paid much attention to the Reyno, perhaps because of his long-standing belief in the virtues of flue-cured or bright leaf. Packed ten to the box and retailed for five cents, Reynos first appeared on the price list for 1 September 1913 and did not disappear until about 1946. A "pep" letter from Percy R. Masten to Artemus D. Porcher, a division manager at Columbia, South Carolina, on 4 October 1919 insisted that Reynos were selling "more satisfactorily than any new 5¢ brand of cigarettes ever handled." Masten urged Porcher to sell all the Reynos "we can make for the present without

Table 7-4
Combined Production of Reyno, Osman,
and Red Kamel Cigarettes, 1913–1924

Year	Number of Cigarettes
1913	33,663,000
1914	117,598,000
1915	170,217,000
1916	272,905,000
1917	328,982,000
1918	298,469,000
1919	209,205,000
1920	162,087,000
1921	80,679,000
1922	37,519,000
1923	15,941,000
1924	6,451,000

Source: Recapitulation of Cigarettes Shipped Each Year—cost records, comptroller's department, R. J. Reynolds Tobacco Company.

giving them away."[105] A general letter to division managers on 27 October held that the Reyno was making a great record—"a more wonderful one, for the time the cigarette has been on the market, than any other brand of smoking or chewing tobacco this company has ever put out, not excepting the National Joy Smoke."[106] Obviously this was largely whistling in the dark. During these years the sales department required division managers to reply to all "pep" letters to ensure that they had been understood. The reply of John W. Alspaugh, division manager in the Winston-Salem area, is still remembered with relish: "I understand that you think that they want Reynos to sell well." For the rest of the year salesmen were urged to include Reynos in drop shipments, to display Reyno window posters, and to give samples freely.[107]

In addition to a coupon valued at one cent, a 20 percent rebate to customers, special offers were made in 1914 involving the Reyno Indian Head Art Picture and two "beautiful rugs" known as the Indian and Forest Stream series.[108] Finally in a letter on 15 September the company urged its salesmen to put up posters and "Push Reynos to the limit." With the outbreak of World War I came advertisements of a different nature with an offer of Reyno Scene Maps and a new Aerial Fleet war poster.[109] In a letter to its representatives on 9 November 1914, the sales department insisted that the one-cent introductory coupon was only a temporary

Table 7-5
Shipments of Camel Cigarettes, 1913–1924

Year	Number of Cigarettes
1913	1,145,000
1914	425,473,000
1915	2,255,310,000
1916	6,522,793,000
1917	11,923,640,000
1918	14,485,991,000
1919	20,822,994,000
1920	18,564,931,000
1921	18,333,338,000
1922	21,430,126,000
1923	30,069,015,000
1924	31,424,218,000

Source: Recapitulation of Camel Cigarettes Shipped Each Year—cost records, comptroller's department, R. J. Reynolds Tobacco Company. With slight variation, these figures are similar to those in Robert E. Lasater's Production Book for Factory 256, 1907–47—R. J. Reynolds Tobacco Company museum.

proposal for inducing smokers to become Reyno users. So the drive continued for some time. The Reyno, however, achieved no great popularity and in 1929 or 1930 it was dropped from the price lists,[110] although its production continued for some time—34,100 in 1945, 15,000 in 1946, and 1,000 in 1947.[111]

The impact of Camels on the market may be shown to better advantage. In a day when cigarette smoking was of small consequence compared with chewing tobacco, or to a lesser degree compared with smoking tobacco, the production of Camels from 1913 to 1924 stood as shown in Table 7-5. For the second time in five years R. J. Reynolds had hit the bull's eye in public taste.

It was the considered opinion of Samuel Clay Williams that the Camel formula had more to do with its success than any other factor, although he felt that the volume and policy of the advertising had also been of great importance. Advertising of tobacco products before the advent of the Camel, declared Williams, had generally been scattered without making any impact for any given brand. He felt that the originality of R. J.'s advertising policy lay in the fact that he spent heavily on one brand, giving it the most intensive and extensive advertising possible on billboards, in magazines, and in newspapers.[112] That Reynolds was following the pattern used with Prince Albert seems clear from the account of Julian L. Watkins. Watkins, once a member of the firm of N. W. Ayer and Son, obtained his information from William M. Armistead, an Ayer executive who handled the Reynolds account for many years. Reynolds offered Ayer $250,000 to introduce the Camel brand—a handsome sum indeed for 1913. Until then cigarettes held sectional appeal, with Piedmonts being popular in the South Atlantic states, Fatimas in the East and Middle Atlantic area, Home Runs and Picayunes in New Orleans, and a mouth-piece cigarette in San Francisco. According to Watkins, Reynolds had studied the various sectional brands of cigarettes before becoming convinced that the Camel brand could overcome all others.[113] An account in the *United States Tobacco Journal* for 5 December 1914 stated that the R. J. Reynolds Tobacco Company began marketing the Camel "precisely" as it had gone about "making a national — well-nigh — a world-wide success of 'Prince Albert,' the smoking tobacco which is said to have put three pipes where one was smoked before."[114]

N. W. Ayer and Son, feeling that possibly Reynolds employees had flattered him about the excellence of the new brand, advised that Camels be tested on the market. Ayer recommended that the cigarettes be distributed to 125 of the best retail stores in Cleveland with the understanding that a carton would be left on the counter and that figures would be furnished on repeat orders. Orders were repeated without advertising, and the same plan was tried in each of the 87 Reynolds sales divisions in the country. Ayer then began the first advertisement, a teaser display with the single caption "Camels," which gave no indication of the product involved or the meaning of the caption. The second advertisement, still showing one spirited camel, carried the words "The Camels are Coming!" and the third the words, "Tomorrow there'll be more CAMELS in this town than in all Asia and Africa combined." The fourth advertisement carried the same camel and the sentence "CAMEL Cigarettes Are Here!" together with a description of the cigarette, its price, its high-grade tobaccos, and its expert blending. Camels began moving in nearly all areas except New York City, which had been left until last. The Metropolitan Tobacco Company, in effective control of sales in that city, told Reynolds that if he kept his salesmen out of the city, Camels would be distributed in about 17,000 stores in one week, as soon as Metropolitan felt certain the product would sell. Reynolds, who probably had no other recourse, agreed, and sales opened late in New York. Camels grew from fourth to first place in five years, securing about 40 percent of the entire cigarette business.[115]

The New York debut came during the first week of December 1914. By 5 December, about ten out of every eleven stores normally handling tobacco goods carried Camels. As the saying went, Camels *humped* themselves and took their message, by advertising not only in magazines and newspapers but on billboards as well, to all parts of the country. Most distinctive was the two-page advertisement carried in the *Saturday Evening Post* for 12 December 1914, which marked the first time cigarettes were ever advertised in that paragon of virtue and circulation. No greater honor could have come to Camels than the acknowledgement by competitive manufacturers that Camels were doing very well on the New York market during their first week in Gotham.[116] The tremendous increase in expenditures for advertising, from $798,423 in 1913 to $2,163,888 in 1915, indicates the truth of the analyses by Watkins and the *United States Tobacco Journal*.

Advertising of the Camel during its early years rested in part on the theme that no premiums were given because of the cost of the tobaccos in the blend. Therefore, most advertisements, as in the last of the introductory teaser series, mentioned the expert blend and its reasonable price:

High grade tobacco and expert blending give *you* a cigarette that *will not* bite the tongue and leaves no cigaretty after taste (you know what that means!) in the mouth.

Every time you buy another brand you're simply wasting money and pleasure.

On sale all along the line—20 for 10¢.

By means of the caption "Camels now a Standard Seller," dealers learned early in 1915 that the Camel had arrived. N. W. Ayer and Son, in *Printer's Ink* for 18 February 1915, also reminded dealers that "The Blend's the Thing." Advertisements in trade journals and in the *Saturday Evening Post* later in 1915 insisted that "Camels Have Won in a National Way."[117] Confidential details occasionally appeared in pictures showing how the revenue stamp was placed over the end of the package to seal it and to preserve the quality of the blended tobacco. Advertising naturally decreased during World War I; in 1917 and 1918 none was recorded in the scrapbooks of the advertising department. The same themes were picked in 1920 and 1921: "Why Man — We Made This Cigarette for You," "Compare Camels with any Cigarette at any Price," "I've tried them all but give me a Camel," or, "It took Years and Years to develop Camel Quality." "Quality not Premiums" met the eye from the pages of newspapers and magazines ranging from the Jewish *Forward* to the *Wall Street Journal* and to most other publications with any circulation worth mentioning.[118]

Three enduring themes were evolved during this period: (1) the idea of selling cigarettes by the carton, (2) turning the edge of criticism to profit by the use of huge handbills offering rewards, and (3) the slogan "I'd Walk a Mile for a Camel." Who conceived the idea of selling Camels by the carton, a new move in the industry, is apparently lost. So far as available evidence is concerned, the first advertisement containing this theme appeared in the *Saturday Evening Post* for 31 July 1915. The campaign continued, and soon selling by the carton became more general with all cigarette manufacturers. This scheme appealed particularly to dealers.

So-called malicious slanders against the successful Camel were to be expected in the highly competitive tobacco trade. As George Washington Hill testified, other manufacturers were forced to change their formulas and lose money while doing so. Such malicious lies were used against the Camel, according to company officials in their righteous indignation, that they could not conceive of any "set of men resorting to such unprincipled methods." In the spring of 1917 the company released a series of posters, some as large as 14 by 17 inches, with black and red letters on a yellow background. One was entitled "The Stench of a Contemptible Slanderer is Repulsive Even to the Nostrils of a Buzzard." Others were headed "$10,000 Reward."[119] In an effort to find the source of some of these rumors, in 1916 and 1917 the company employed the Pinkerton Detective Agency at a total cost of $1,114.10. A penciled note to Bowman Gray from William M. Armistead on the bill dated 31 December 1916 runs in part: " . . . so far as I can judge this is correct—money thrown away, but the satisfaction of trying, I suppose is worth the price."[120]

It is difficult to ascertain the exact nature of the rumors. The inventor of a tobacco stemming machine, Frederick I. Billings, who had spent considerable time in Reynolds's factories, wrote Walter R. Reynolds on 28 May 1917 from Baltimore, stating that he had seen two of Reynolds's counterblasts against the rumors in a local newspaper and that soon afterward one of his friends had mentioned one of the advertisements. The friend had declared that he had been smoking Camels "but was going to quit doing so, as a Tobacco man had told him that they contained salt-petre which he considered very injurious." Billings, of course, had informed his friend that it was not true.[121] Dealers and jobbers were generally exempted from blame in spreading the injurious slanders. No specific falsehoods are listed in Reynolds's posters, but the method may be gleaned from an excerpt from the broadside published in April 1917:

> In at least one city where passengers are permitted to enter both the front and rear doors of street cars, during the crowded hours one of the slanderers would board the car at the front end, and within a few blocks one of his same kind would get on the rear end. They would work their way back through the crowd until they got in talking distance near the center of the car, then salute each other as old

friends and proceed, in a loud voice to maliciously slander CAMEL cigarettes. After making their little speech they would catch an incoming car and carry on the same performance.

Roy C. Haberkern recalled that the American Tobacco Company was suspected of spreading rumors that employees in the Reynolds cigarette department had such diseases as leprosy or syphilis. He also recalled that R. J. had the Winston-Salem *Journal and Sentinel* print thousands of posters offering rewards for the identity of slanderers of the Camel. It was an easy matter to give the posters nationwide circulation working through the eighty-seven division managers and their numerous salesmen. The posters usually began with an offer of a $500 reward to each of the first twenty persons who furnished satisfactory proof of the identity of the slanderers "together with the names of the persons, firms or corporations paying them to circulate a lie to injure the sale of Camel cigarettes." Always they called attention to the excellence of the Camel cigarette, its tremendous sales, its low price, or its Turkish and domestic blend. It was the opinion of Roy Haberkern that these posters not only refuted the rumors but also served to advertise the Camel.[122] According to one authority, ". . . the cigarette advertising to this time and all the attacks were as nothing compared to the advertising war for market domination by a single brand which was soon to come. It really began with the introduction in 1914 of Camels."[123]

Although not so exciting as the campaign against the "vile slanderers" of the Camel, the development and use of the slogan "I'd Walk a Mile for a Camel" has probably been more important in advertising. In 1919, when advertising was resumed after World War I, the major effort for a time centered on billboard advertising managed by Martin Francis Reddington, who handled Reynolds's outdoor advertising from 1912 until 1927. In the latter part of 1920 Reddington brought a number of large-sized posters into the office of Bowman Gray, Sr., for examination. Among them was the famous design "I'd Walk a Mile for a Camel," which had been inspired by a chance remark on a golf course. The players, discovering that they were out of cigarettes, sent a caddy for a fresh supply. While waiting, one of the golfers remarked, "I'd walk a mile for a Camel." Reddington, one of the group, immediately saw the advertising value of this remark and later worked it into a poster, using a New Haven fireman as a model. Used on billboards throughout the country, first apparently in January 1921, the slogan appeared in newspaper and magazine advertisements in May and June 1921 and has since been kept alive.[124]

Advertising slogans do not become well known without the expenditure of large sums. Table 7-6 shows that Reynolds's advertising costs rose

Table 7-6
Expenses for Advertising and Gratis Goods
of the Reynolds Company, 1912–1924

Year	Advertising	Gratis Goods	Total
1912	$ 435,370	$ 141,153	$ 576,523
1913	681,570	116,853	798,423
1914	1,251,413	237,111	1,488,524
1915	1,901,330	262,558	2,163,888
1916	1,947,919	285,270	2,233,190
1917	708,184	210,954	919,138
1918	408,997	154,963	563,960
1919	5,356,491	694,848	6,051,339
1920	6,188,478	512,381	6,700,859
1921	8,042,208	702,518	8,744,726
1922	4,927,169	884,419	5,811,588
1923	5,342,466	966,141	6,308,607
1924	6,444,926	1,670,353	8,115,278

Source: Am. Tob. Co. et al. v. U.S., Record on Appeal, docket no. 9137–9139 (6th Cir., 1944), exhibits, 6:3253–54. The figures have been rounded off to the nearest dollar.

almost steadily from 1912 to 1924, except for two years during World War I. At no time before the advent of the Camel did the company's advertising costs reach such heights. The cost of samples, as indicated by gratis goods, also increased rapidly.

The Reynolds company's new and modern cigarette, perhaps partly because of advertising, paved the way for increased use of Burley. Actually had Burley leaf not been brought into the manufacture of cigarettes, its production might easily have declined almost in direct proportion to the decline in popularity of chewing tobacco. Greater demand for flue-cured leaf undoubtedly accompanied the rise of the cigarette because of the sheer volume of production. Of more importance for the production of Burley, however, was the shift in emphasis to a grade known as "flyings," which had formerly been sold as trash tobacco at a very low price. Thin in body and without much elasticity or any noticeable amount of oil, "flyings" grow on the lowest part of the plant. These pale, porous leaves became most sought after by makers of the new type of cigarette originated by Reynolds.[125] Reputedly Reynolds held a monopoly on such Burley leaf for some time after 1912. Like the cigarette industry as a whole, the producers of Burley leaf had their ideas of value literally turned downside up by the Camel.

During all the stir and work connected with beginning the manufacture of cigarettes, the R. J. Reynolds Tobacco Company on 15 June 1914 registered as a manufacturer of cigars,[126] but apparently Reynolds dropped his ideas of entering the cigar business because of being swamped by work connected with the runaway Camel.

CHAPTER 8

Effects of Expansion on Leaf Handling and Labor

The period of expansion from 1912 to 1924 was marked by rapidly changing conditions, within and outside the company, affecting in major ways the leaf operations of the company, the work force, and the work place. This chapter chronicles these conditions, the entry of local politics and the union on the labor scene, and management's response.

None of the changes after 1912 affected so many people as those involving leaf buying, leaf storage, and leaf processing. The lines separating these areas are by no means clear, partly perhaps because of the seasonal nature of much of the work. Consider, for example, the case of Thomas Winfield Blackwell. During his long career with Reynolds from 1900 until his death in 1943, Blackwell purchased leaf or supervised its purchase, worked in manufacturing, and, as plant manager, was concerned with the stemming and storage of leaf tobacco.[1] Leaf processing, whether performed in a factory or in a leaf plant, involved the employment of much unskilled labor for the tedious work of hanging bundles of leaf on sticks for the redryer, removing the sticks from the hot dryer, and stripping the leaf from the stems. These processes, though not destined for any revolutionary improvement from 1912 to 1924, did undergo considerable change with chief emphasis on a search for machinery to handle the stemming problem.

Changes in Leaf Buying Practices

When R. J. Reynolds first came to Winston, the farmers marketed their leaf throughout the calendar year. By 1916, however, the crop was largely marketed from October through February, and by 1924 this contraction of the marketing season in the East had become sharper.[2] As cultivation of tobacco spread, loose-leaf auction sales followed a routine schedule, with sales first in Georgia, next in South Carolina, then in eastern North Carolina, thence to mid-North Carolina, and eventually to the Old Belt of Piedmont North Carolina and Virginia. Tied to these changes were the sales of Burley leaf in Kentucky and neighboring areas so that Burley sales immediately followed the sales of flue-cured leaf, ending usually in January or February. The same company buyers served all these areas. The overlapping of sales in the Georgia-Carolina-Virginia area with those of the Burley area was still somewhat marked in 1912.

Until shortly after 1924 there were also frequent attempts by farmers to sell their leaf cooperatively—attempts that the Reynolds officials appeared to support. R. J. Reynolds early prided himself on his friendly relations with the farmers, evidently, and perhaps rightly, believing that he helped create opportunities for them.[3] Farmers of the South and West endeavored to fight the agricultural depression of the 1880s and 1890s by organizing themselves into groups for cooperative buying and selling under the name of the Farmers' Alliance. This movement, vigorous in the Virginia-Carolina area, affected Forsyth County. Planning to operate an auction sales tobacco warehouse in Winston, delegates of the alliance in October 1890 approached the president of the Winston Board of Trade who appointed a committee to extend courtesies and aid to the delegates. On the committee were R. J. Reynolds, Thomas L. Vaughn, W. W. Wood, Pleasant H. Hanes, John W. Alspaugh, George W. Hinshaw, R. B. Crawford, and Dr. Henry T. Bahnson—the first four being tobacco manufacturers. Hanes reported on 5 December not only that his committee had met with the delegates of the Farmers' Alliance, but also "that the Alliance had made arrangements to make use of the warehouse belonging to Mr. R. J. Reynolds after the first of next March, and also that the Alliance intended to purchase a lot and erect a warehouse next summer."[4] Thus it was Hanes who helped accommodate the farmers, not Wood or Vaughn. Again in 1912, when the Farmers' Union attempted the same thing, in many cases building storage houses and redrying plants, the Reynolds company purchased the entire holdings of 800,000 pounds of leaf of the Stokes County Farmers' Union Warehouse Company at Walnut Cove.[5] In the same year Reynolds purchased for $40,000 the Burley farmers' storage warehouse in Lexington, Kentucky, for conversion into a redrying plant.[6]

The last great effort of tobacco growers to recover from the tolls taken from their crops by speculators and warehousemen, the Burley Tobacco Growers' Cooperative Association[7] and the Tri-State Tobacco Growers' Cooperative Association[8] of the early 1920s, was supported wholeheartedly by the R. J. Reynolds Tobacco Company and by the Liggett and

Table 8-1
Sales of Burley Tobacco Growers' Cooperative Association
to Tobacco Companies, 1921–1924

Tobacco Company	Pounds of Tobacco
Reynolds	230,378,890
Liggett and Myers	175,875,586
P. Lorillard	11,681,248
American	9,125,884
Imperial	0
Export Leaf	0
All others	49,320,110

Source: Reavis Cox, *Competition in the American Tobacco Industry, 1911–1932* (New York, 1933), p. 173.

Myers Tobacco Company, but by no other tobacco manufacturers save in a nominal fashion (see Tables 8-1 and 8-2). Based on size of company and profits Reynolds as the largest purchaser from the farmers' cooperatives was in the top rank, although Liggett and Myers supported the farmers almost as well proportionately. On the other hand, the American Tobacco Company, close behind Reynolds in profits, made only a faint gesture toward patronizing the cooperatives.[9] These conclusions, however, are drawn without knowledge of the total leaf holdings of each company and may be open to question.

The official policy of the R. J. Reynolds Tobacco Company indicates complete support for the cooperative movement. The company made its first purchase from the Tri-State Tobacco Growers' Cooperative Association—1,073,150 pounds—in May or June 1922.[10] On 10 February 1926, when many felt the association to be doomed, the board of directors of the Tri-State association announced the receipt of the largest check ever sent them—one for $2,039,941.07 from the Reynolds company.[11] In addition, William N. Reynolds, in order to bolster confidence in the association, wrote the leaf manager in April 1924 that his company had "bought large quantities from your Association during the last two years" and that his company's relations with the association had been "entirely pleasant and satisfactory."[12]

The large amounts of tobacco purchased from these cooperative associations indicate that the leaf department had grown considerably since R. J. Reynolds made his way into southwest Virginia to buy the single

Table 8-2
Sales of Tri-State Tobacco Growers' Cooperative Association
to Tobacco Companies, 1922–1924

Tobacco Company	Pounds of Tobacco
Liggett and Myers	93,709,359
Reynolds	77,254,270
Export Leaf	31,024,400
American	5,186,650
Imperial	485,953
P. Lorillard	0
All others	125,678,365

Source: Nannie M. Tilley, *The Bright-Tobacco Industry, 1860–1929* (Chapel Hill, 1948), p. 462.

crop of George W. Palmer. It expanded rapidly after the advent of Prince Albert and Camels.

Will Reynolds's first assistant in buying leaf tobacco was William T. Eaton, a pinhooker hired perhaps in the late 1890s when auction sales warehouses adopted the practice of double sales. As a pinhooker, as leaf dealers with small capital were called, Eaton had haggled with Will Reynolds for $1,000 per year because he planned to accumulate enough money to retire at the end of twenty years. Overhearing the argument, R. J. Reynolds called his brother into his office and told him to pay Eaton what he asked because the man had long-range plans—a goal unheard of from a pinhooker.[13] Another significant change came in 1907, when Will Reynolds went to Kentucky to purchase Burley leaf for Prince Albert and met Theodore H. Kirk, who became superintendent of leaf buying in 1912. It appears, however, that Kirk gave most of his attention to the purchase of Burley leaf, which he knew so well.[14] This left the task of purchasing flue-cured leaf to Eaton, who evidently was succeeded by Thomas W. Blackwell. These three men—William Reynolds, Eaton, and Kirk—laid the foundation for the leaf-buying department.

Changes in Leaf Storage Practices

Storage and handling of newly purchased leaf have always been problematic for the tobacco industry. The Reynolds storage facilities before 1900 remained in Winston-Salem generally near Number 256, but the turn of the century saw not only the beginning of additional facilities in Winston-Salem but also the development of storage facilities in Danville, Virginia, where a redrying plant was also built.[15] So rapidly were storage houses erected in Winston-Salem that the editor of the *Southern Tobacco Journal* wrote on 15 December 1902 of one leaf house built "this year" and the immediate letting of a contract for another. In rapid succession came the erection of a leaf house at Critz, Virginia, in 1901, a storage house and a redrying plant at the corner of Church and Fifth streets in 1903, an additional storage building in Danville in 1903, the purchase of two lots in South Boston, Virginia, in 1904, another storage house at Fifth and Vine streets as well as one on the east side of Church Street between Fifth and Sixth streets in the same year, and one in Richmond, Virginia.[16] In April 1904, the company contracted with the Southern Railway to construct on the Reynolds property three industrial sidetracks for the "mutual convenience" of both.[17] Apparently in June 1906 E. C. Bowman and Company contracted to build a large leaf-tobacco storage house at the corner of Chestnut and Fifth streets.[18] In the following year came the erection of a sweat house on the southwest corner of Chestnut and Fifth streets and the rebuilding of the reordering and storage plant in South Boston, Virginia, valued at $150,000, which had been destroyed by fire.[19] (The sweat house served as a place for steaming hogsheads of dried leaf to soften it before it was transferred to the stemming room.)

Though Reynolds had leased what were known as "the Vaughn factories" on Tenth Street in Richmond before 1904, it appears that these were purchased in 1910, remodeled, and enlarged for use as a rehandling plant.[20] No doubt this was done in order to care for the extensive purchases of sun-cured leaf for the chewing brand Apple Sun Cured. Almost simultaneously two new storage sheds arose in Winston-Salem.[21] In 1911 the company, contracting its holdings in Martinsville, planned storage shed Number 37 on East Fourth Street and boilerhouse Number 5 on Depot Street.[22] Thus storage facilities and redrying plants had greatly increased by the time Prince Albert began to flourish.

The purchase and storage of leaf tobacco rapidly became vastly more complicated not only because of expense, space, and aging requirements but also because of the different types in use by 1913. Caring for flue-cured, sun-cured, Burley, and Turkish leaf demanded more complex facilities. Fire hazards and the need for additional space were never-ending problems. Because of the aging process, any increase planned in manufacturing meant a proportionate trebling of storage facilities. Additional facilities by 1912 required the installation of telephone service to a storage house in the northern part of town. A new storage plant in 1913 and a "mammoth sweathouse building" in 1914 were added in Winston-Salem.[23] Many other buildings were constructed from 1912 to 1924 including the Kelly and Ashland storages off Indiana Avenue in 1913, the Ziglar sheds (between Twenty-fifth, Twenty-seventh, and Liberty streets and the Norfolk and Western tracks) in 1919, and the Tiretown storage houses (later a part of Whitaker Park) started in 1921. In 1922 spur tracks from the Southern Railway line to the Tiretown sheds became necessary.[24] A new sweat house became so well-known for its excellence and ingenuity of construction that in 1916 a Liggett and Myers official requested permission for his builders to inspect it.[25] A group of storage houses erected on East Fourth Street in 1915 evidently represented a change in policy looking to the concentration of leaf tobacco in Winston-Salem "if possible, instead of storing it on the other markets and shipping it to the city when needed."[26]

In 1917, by one account, leaf storage and processing facilities included twelve redrying plants and thirty-seven storage warehouses outside Winston-Salem.[27] The Reynolds purchases on the Danville market in 1919 were more than double those of the American Tobacco Company, almost double those of Liggett and Myers, and not far below those of the largest purchaser—the Export Leaf Tobacco Company.[28] The beginning of an extension to the Danville redrying plant in 1918 gives further indication that purchases there were expanding.[29]

Expansion in the Burley area followed the same pattern. In Lexington, Kentucky, the editor of the *Leader* commented in 1913 on the property of the Reynolds company in warehouses, storage houses, and redrying plants, to which extensive additions, including a power plant, were then being planned.[30] A new plant in Louisville promised employment for 1,000 people in 1920.[31] Another important step occurred in 1920 when the company moved into the relatively new tobacco area of eastern North Carolina by establishing a redrying plant at Wilson.[32] At this time, however, Reynolds apparently had no rehandling plants in the new tobacco belt of South Carolina. Based on the only completely reliable data available for this period, the company in 1922 owned ten rehandling and redrying plants—one in each of the following towns: Wilson and Winston-Salem in North Carolina; Danville, South Boston, Martinsville, and Richmond in Virginia; and Lexington, Louisville, Maysville, and Springfield in Kentucky.[33] Purchases of green and redried leaf from 1912 to 1924, as shown in Table 8-3, may perhaps make somewhat clearer the increasing volume of the leaf department in both buying and processing.[34] End-of-calendar-year inventories for four years during this period (the only data available) may reveal something of the carry-over problems with inventories:[35]

Year	Pounds
1916	93,744,655
1917	96,082,399
1923	215,141,670
1924	157,490,921

Sooner or later all of this tobacco reached Winston-Salem and remained with the leaf-processing department until needed. The difficult tasks of buying, transporting, and redrying leaf tobacco, keeping the various types separate and identified by grades and years as well as a multitude of other duties demanded constant attention. These were the tasks that occupied James B. Dyer so completely that he refused to become a director in 1912. "R. J., I ain't got time," he said when pressed to serve. Dyer held to this decision until threatened with discharge unless he attended directors' meetings.[36] On 13 April 1914 he became superintendent of the leaf department in Winston-Salem.[37]

During these years, chiefly under Dyer's supervision, the team and storage division began its metamorphosis into the truck and storage division. The shift from horse-drawn drays to trucks, starting in 1913, led to the abandonment of the new stable, about 72 by 200 feet, built in 1908 at the intersection of Vine and Depot streets.[38] No doubt the use of motor vehicles had not been completely accepted in 1916 when R. J. Reynolds added seven Percherons, five mares, and two colts to his stock at Reynolda farm.[39] The first order for a truck was given on 27 June 1913—a standard Model K Four Ton Garford Chassis with solid rubber tires—at a 20 percent discount from the list price of $3,850. This purchase was not settled until Paul Nissen Montague, a local salesman for Garford trucks and organizer of the first Ford agency in Winston-Salem, demonstrated the truck to management including R. J. Reynolds. To their amazement Montague with his new machine transported one-half of the hogsheads handled during an entire day when all the teams were on duty. Moreover, this chain-driven vehicle hauled six hogsheads at one load on the very day when R. J. Reynolds, firmly attached to fine horses, belittled the idea of substituting a machine for a horse.[40] Reynolds, however, was a practical man ready to be convinced of more advantageous methods. At this time the company owned thirty draft horses and seventeen to twenty drays equipped with roller bearings.

On this occasion and for some time afterward there were prophets of doom among those who handled the teams. Sitting high in their drays, supported by special orders from R. J. himself about the proper treatment of their teams, these drivers had the freedom of the town—from auction sales house to storage sheds to factories—in a little kingdom of their own. They showed extreme jealousy toward Arthur Casey, who was hired to

Table 8-3
Total Purchases of Green and Redried Leaf by the Reynolds Company,
1912–1924 (1 July to 30 June)

Year	Pounds
1912	62,303,689
1913	67,650,820
1914	66,895,754
1915	73,927,533
1916	78,068,202
1917	125,058,284
1918	126,125,259
1919	137,696,716
1920	169,775,668
1921	153,335,649
1922	145,503,005
1923	260,571,302
1924	126,433,066

Source: Purchases and Prices of Leaf *as Made*, box 1579C, Records Center, R. J. Reynolds Tobacco Company.

drive the first Garford truck; John Brendle, who drove Packard truck No. 1; Wade P. Casey, brother of Arthur and driver of Packard No. 2; and others who rapidly followed them, including Fred York, Jim Ford, and Ward Weaver. At first these trucks were stored at night in a rented building on Fourth Street across from warehouse Number 68. With more than a dozen trucks in this department by 1920, Dyer hired James Paxton Davis—a veteran of World War I who had been in charge of an army motor pool—to supervise purchases, maintenance, and operation of the truck fleet. When the rapidly expanding fleet outgrew its rented quarters, the garage was moved to the basement of Number 65 on Chestnut Street, where gasoline tanks and hand-operated pumps were installed. This arrangement sufficed for only a short time. In 1923 the company erected a new garage on Linden Street between Fourth and Fifth streets which became the headquarters for the truck and storage division.

Later, of course, the truck and storage division was tremendously expanded. The Garfords, Packards, Paiges, and Seldens gave way to other makes. During the marketing season, trucks transferred tobacco from auction sales warehouses in many states to redrying plants and thence to storage warehouses. This division was also responsible for transporting supervisors of the buying force from market to market. Its year-round duties included maintaining storage warehouses, supplying processing plants with tobacco, hauling strips from plant to plant, transporting hogshead materials to the cooperage shops, furnishing trucks and drivers to the shipping department for transporting finished products to loading points, among a multitude of other tasks. A general dispatch truck also stood ready to haul laundry, rags, machine parts, and miscellaneous items.[41]

By 1913 the storage and care of Turkish leaf had become another job of the leaf department. For about ten years the company bought Turkish leaf from the Standard Commercial Tobacco Company. Ery Euripides Kehaya and Savo Kehaya from Greece were president and vice-president of this company, evidently a foreign firm transferred to, or formed in, the United States. Three other vice-presidents were J. Valensi, R. S. Amado, and George O. Jones. The treasurer, William Asbury Whitaker, however, originally came from Winston-Salem. And in 1919 a newly elected vice-president, J. Turner Farrish, had local connections, having once lived in Winston-Salem. Whitaker, son and namesake of a pioneer tobacco manufacturer of Winston-Salem, was the brother-in-law of Ery E. Kehaya and the brother of John C. Whitaker, an employee of the Reynolds company since 1913 who was destined to hold its highest offices. This importing company, consisting of men from Turkey, Greece, and Winston-Salem, was thus closely allied to the Reynolds company. In 1917 and 1918 Reynolds had purchased more than 3 million pounds of Turkish leaf per year from Standard. In June 1919, Walter R. Reynolds expected shortly to draw up a contract with Standard for the delivery of a minimum of 3 million pounds from each of the crops of 1919, 1920, and 1921. Relations with the Standard Commercial Tobacco Company remained entirely cordial in September 1921, when Bowman Gray, Sr., sent William Joseph Conrad, Jr., to Europe to assist representatives of Standard in buying up all Prince Albert smoking tobacco that had been sold by the American government to the French government during World War I.[42]

The contract for Turkish leaf for the crops of 1919, 1920, and 1921 had been duly made, but "certain controversies" arose, presumably "on account of [the] Smyrna fire." By 1924 William A. Whitaker no longer served as treasurer of the Standard Commercial Tobacco Company.[43] Whatever the reason, in 1922 the R. J. Reynolds Tobacco Company organized its own subsidiary, headed by James W. Glenn of the leaf department, for the purchase of Turkish leaf. Known as the Glenn Tobacco Company, this subsidiary, in cooperation with the Alston Tobacco Company, not only purchased Turkish-type tobaccos for Reynolds on a set commission but also did the same for the P. Lorillard Tobacco Company. Turkish-type leaf is produced in the Near East, parts of Russia, Italy,

Korea, China, Japan, and other areas of the world. It was the duty of the Glenn Tobacco Company to buy Turkish leaf in Macedonia, Thrace, and Bulgaria; the Alston Tobacco Company handled the same task in Turkey, Smyrna, the islands of Greece, and Italy. Reynolds and P. Lorillard paid the subsidiary all expenses for tobacco bought on their orders, plus one-half cent per pound, in proportion to the amount each company ordered.[44] Rumors persisted that the subsidiary was formed because of unethical practices of the Standard Commercial Tobacco Company, though possibly it was because of the sharply competitive market for Turkish leaf that developed in the wake of the rise of Camels. Certainly, after 1913 much more Turkish leaf was needed.

To the many who have assumed that the amount of Turkish tobacco in Camel cigarettes was negligible, the mosques and minarets on the label adding more Turkish flavor than the leaf itself, it may be of interest to examine the data on the purchases of imported Turkish leaf from 1912 to 1924, as shown in Table 8-4.[45] The total cost of this tobacco by years ranged from $60,722 in 1913–14 to $23,303,086 in 1923–24. In examining these data it is well to recall that the Camel cigarette did not become a fast-seller until December 1914. By 1914, therefore, the leaf department instead of buying single local crops was making large purchases in several states and across the sea in the Old World.

Taxation on stored leaf became an issue in 1921 when the state of North Carolina adopted a law requiring the reevaluation of property. This was to be a bone of contention for years to come. Tobacco manufacturers felt that taxation on the same leaf stored for three years somehow meant triple taxation. In an effort to reduce the assessed valuation on their stored leaf, Liggett and Myers and the American Tobacco Company brought their cases before State Revenue Commissioner A. D. Watts.[46] On 16 May 1921, the State Board of Equalization reduced by $12,750,000 the assessed value of leaf stored in Durham County by Liggett and Myers and the American Tobacco Company. Allen J. Maxwell, a member of the State Tax Commission before the creation of the North Carolina Department of Revenue and in 1921 the Commissioner of Corporations, held this reduction to be an impeachment of the action of the State Tax Commission in making the assessment. The Reynolds company's position in this controversy appears in the following analysis:

Upon investigation it was found that the largest company in the state, having more stock (of leaf) on hand than both of these Durham companies, had voluntarily adopted as the basis for making its return the basis known as "book value," made up of the original cost plus carrying charges added from time to time as the tobacco was redried, processed and aged. In the opinion of the company and

Table 8-4
Purchases of Imported Leaf by the Reynolds Company, 1912–1924
(1 July to 30 June)

Years	Pounds
1912–13	176,079
1913–14	112,681
1914–15	1,160,885
1915–16	1,972,112
1916–17	4,274,584
1917–18	4,835,130
1918–19	3,762,657
1919–20	15,245,174
1920–21	6,150,620
1921–22	11,879,128
1922–23	15,370,954
1923–24	23,230,365
1924–25	9,069,387

Source: Purchases and Prices of Leaf as Made, box 1579C, Records Center, R. J. Reynolds Tobacco Company.

other companies that basis was considered conservative value for such stocks of tobacco on January first, 1920.

Naturally much of this leaf stock had been bought when the average market value stood much higher than it would for many years after 1919.[47] State Revenue Commissioner Watts defended the decreased assessment of Liggett and Myers and the American Tobacco Company based on testimony from prominent citizens of Durham. Maxwell replied to Watts, who then expected Josephus Daniels to continue the attack.[48] Possibly at this time the R. J. Reynolds Tobacco Company was preoccupied with a bigger issue in its efforts to obtain the same scale of remuneration for tobacco sold to the United States Navy during World War I as sold to the Army. Or, possibly R. J. Reynolds had set this pattern when the income tax was levied during Cleveland's administration; at that time he had meticulously prepared his report amid general clamor for the law's abrogation. In 1913, moreover, he told a newspaper reporter that the new income tax law was a good one designed to tax the man who had the money.[49]

Changes in Leaf Processing

The taxation of stored tobacco was a matter for top management, but stemming the leaf, an expensive item, was the everyday concern of James B. Dyer and Henry Straughn Stokes, many foremen, and countless laborers. Stokes, employed by the company in 1902 immediately after his graduation from Hampden-Sydney College, had the reputation of being the first college graduate hired by Reynolds. Although essentially a leaf man, he became assistant general manager of manufacturing on 5 July 1917 and a director in 1937.[50] His career thus illustrates the converging lines of leaf processing and manufacturing. Among other duties, Stokes had general supervision of those who stemmed the leaf. According to Jesse Shumate Davis of the blending division, hand stemming to some extent continued into the 1950s. The difficulties of the task with inexperienced hands, he asserted, were such that he could not dwell on them without lapsing into strong language.[51] Laborers were transient and undisciplined, and the task seemed ill-adapted to solution by machinery. This menial and monotonous work, which belonged neither in the leaf department nor in the manufacturing department, received constant attention from management. Burton Craige's statement in 1914, when analyzing the work of a more-or-less satisfactory stemming machine, indirectly placed this responsibility in the leaf-processing department. "The Manufacturing Department complained of the unusual amount of stems left in the strips and refused to use them," declared Craige. Furthermore, he stated, stemming with this machine resulted in 2 percent more scrap than did hand stemming, and, in view of "the cost of these tobaccos, this is quite an item with my client."[52] The stem, which of necessity was purchased in the leaf from the farmer, at that time represented about one-third of the cost of the leaf. This meant pure waste for the manufacturer, although some of the stems of bright leaf were used especially in the manufacture of smoking tobacco.[53] In 1912, when the average cost of bright leaf stood at something more than 15 cents per pound, Reynolds sold stems to the Virginia-Carolina Chemical Company at the rate of $5 per ton; in 1924 the company may have fared slightly better by selling stems to the Tobacco By-Products and Chemical Corporation for $11 per ton when the average price of leaf was 21.6 cents per pound.[54]

It was more difficult to stem Burley leaf with machinery than to stem bright leaf.[55] R. J. Reynolds attacked this problem with his usual vigor by trying to develop a satisfactory stemming machine. When the Reynolds company emerged from the old American Tobacco Company, there were a number of stemming machines to choose from. A summary by Richard H. Wright probably represented the true status of the problem in 1913:

"There are so many stemmers upon the market now that a patented stemmer does not appeal to one and is not very attractive unless it is very simple, comparatively inexpensive to build, does a larger quantity and better quality of work than those already on the market, and at a much lower price."[56] In addition, many of these stemming machines were earlier controlled by the American Tobacco Company through the Standard Tobacco Stemmer Company, a holding company capitalized at $1,730,000 but carried on the books at a nominal sum. Moreover, it had no plant before 1912.[57] With the bankruptcy of the Underwood Stemming Machine Company and the acquisition of its assets by the Standard Tobacco Stemmer Company, that company and the Tobacco Stemming Machine Company of Baltimore (successor to the Continental Tobacco Machine Company) remained as the major firms attempting to develop a satisfactory stemming machine. Before 1912, however, Reynolds had purchased a five-sixths interest in the invention of Peter P. Shouse, and in 1909 with Shouse and the Briggs-Shaffner Machine Company undertook its development.[58] In 1912 a man named Day secured a trial order from Reynolds to test a tobacco stemmer.[59]

In the next year the company showed unusual interest in a stemmer developed by James P. Scovill of Ohio, and R. J. Reynolds, who handled the matter himself, allowed the machine to be tested in one of his factories.[60] Apparently having met defeat in all these, Reynolds turned to the Tobacco Stemming Machine Company and had a test machine, the invention of Frederick I. Billings, installed early in 1913. Somewhat pleased with the model, the company placed ten of these machines in its plants in December 1913, the price to be fixed by a twenty-six day test. The cost of operating the machines amounted to $2.13 per hundred pounds of stems removed, against the cost of hand stemming at $2.50 per hundred pounds. On this basis one Billings machine would save $276.83 in one year. This machine did not reduce markedly the number of laborers, because the ten machines required fifty-nine laborers (three floor sweepers, three searchers to put strips in hogsheads, one stem searcher, where stems were delivered by carrier to the basket, one man to move tobacco to the machines, twenty laborers to untie bundles, ten feeders, one oiler, and twenty drop-leaf stemmers). Despite the meticulous manner in which the test was run, some friction arose over the results.[61]

In the exchange of correspondence about this test, the attorney for the Tobacco Stemming Machine Company referred to the fact that R. J. Reynolds and others of the company had noted that more strips remained on the stems than in the case of hand stemming. But the Reynolds people, he said, had not considered this an important matter as all the Reynolds stems were "thrashed."[62] Just what thrashing stems involved in 1914 is especially intriguing in view of the present-day tippers and thrashers used on the lines of the strip preparation department. An attachment for the Billings machine, known as the butter and cutter device, held particular interest for Reynolds early in 1914.[63] By November the Tobacco Stemming Machine Company was building thirty additional machines for Reynolds, and in October 1920 the company placed an order for eighty Billings machines.[64]

Meanwhile, on 8 May 1915 the R. J. Reynolds Tobacco Company, in the name of the United Cigarette Machine Company, purchased 64,654 shares of common and 918 shares of preferred stock in the Tobacco Stemming Machine Company, with an option on additional shares deposited in escrow with Reynolds. An arrangement with the Tobacco Stemming Machine Company covered the handling (under Reynolds supervision) of pending litigation brought by the Standard Tobacco Stemmer Company. On 13 October 1915, the United Cigarette Machine Company purchased from Reynolds a one-half interest in the stock and option of the Tobacco Stemming Machine Company for $5,000. In the litigation regarding a patent being used in the Reynolds factory, the Tobacco Stemming Machine Company won. These maneuvers in the name of the United Cigarette Machine Company show that the R. J. Reynolds Tobacco Company could steal a march on a successor of the American Tobacco Company in the style of that organization. This was probably not too difficult, for Reynolds used the services of Ambrose H. Burroughs, once counsel for the old American company. After winning the suit, the United Cigarette Machine Company and the R. J. Reynolds Tobacco Company, one and the same, exercised their option to buy 53 percent of the voting stock of the Tobacco Stemming Machine Company. Thereafter, at meetings of stockholders and directors, new officers were elected, a small working fund was created, and supplements occasionally were added to the working fund. It is interesting that Mumford DeJournett Bailey, Jr., the inventor of a tobacco-stemming machine in 1907 and also in the same year vice-president of the Southern Stemming and Manufacturing Company of Washington, D.C., along with M. D. Bailey, Sr., and William A. Blair—all from Winston-Salem—together held 205 shares of common stock in the Tobacco Stemming Machine Company.[65] Thus the R. J. Reynolds Tobacco Company came to control the company that handled the Billings machine, as well as other stemming machines like the Richter Tobacco Stemming Machine, which Reynolds helped build and improve.[66] The next improved stemming machine used by Reynolds—the Pasley machine, first tested in 1929—was built in the Reynolds plant under a contract with Thomas E. Pasley and George W. Agee, a contract permitting the company to manufacture this stemmer under shop rights.[67]

Hand stemming, mechanical stemming, and strip preparation units were in simultaneous operation as late as 1953, but the turning point

Table 8-5

Chronology of Leaf Processing Changes by the Reynolds Company During 1875–1935

Year	Event	Location
1875	Hand stemmery established	Old Red Factory
1892	Hand stemmery established	256
1901	Office of Leaf Processing established	8 Picking Room
1901	Hand stemmery established	8
1901	Redrying plant established	1
1901	Sweat house established	23
1901	Leaf-picking rooms established	8 and 256
1901	Inventory records maintained	256-2
1913	Sweat house established	10
1913(?)	Hand stemmery established	43
1915	Hand stemmery enlarged	43
1916	39 Billings stemmers added	43 (top floor)
1916–17	Richter stemmers added	256-2
1917	Richter stemmers added	256-2 (smoking)
1917	Large hand stemmery established	65 (4th and 5th floors)
1918	Richter stemmers moved	65 (top floor)
1919	Leaf-processing office moved	38
1920	Richter stemmers discarded and hand stemmery established	65 (top floor)
1920	23 Billings stemmers moved from 43 (top floor)	43 (5th floor)
1920	16 Billings stemmers moved from 43 (top floor)	65 (5th floor)
1923	Hand stemmery under smoking and stemming divisions (then SMD) established	64
1923	Two floors and sweat house used for storage	64
1924	21 Billings stemmers added to SMD	43 (5th floor)
1924	50 Billings stemmers added	65
1924	42 Billings stemmers added to SMD	Maysville Stemmery
1924	43 Billings stemmers added in new stemmery	60 (South)
1924	Hand stemmers transferred from 43, 8, 64, 256	Old Bailey Building
1925	42 Billings stemmers added	65 (South)
1925	Sweat house completed for stemmeries at 60 and 64	30
1928	43 Billings stemmers moved from 43	60 (North)
1930	New hand stemmery established (300 hands)	38

Table 8-5 (continued)

Year	Event	Location
1934	Maysville stemmery closed and 43 Billings stemmers moved and 2 added	60 (North)
1935	Experimental SPD unit established	43 (top floor)
1935	12 Pasley stemmers added	256-2
1935	Hand stemmery discontinued	43

Source: Lee R. Salmons, "History and Development of the Leaf Stemming and Blending Process at the R. J. Reynolds Tobacco Company"—in possession of Mr. Salmons, leaf-processing department, R. J. Reynolds Tobacco Company, as of 1963.
Note: The information is a partial summary, considered reasonably accurate, and is provided for illustrative purposes.

appears to have been reached in 1935 when the first experimental strip preparation department (SPD) unit was installed on the top floor of Number 43. (SPD was preceded by the stemming machine department, or SMD.) A chronology of management's struggle to develop more efficient procedures in leaf processing is provided in Table 8-5.[68]

It appears from the data in Table 8-5 that the company began installing its Billings stemmers after the tests in 1913 and 1914 and continued to rely on them until 1935. At no time, however, did the Billings machine operate without the aid of handworkers to stem the "drops." The Richter machine, apparently never equal to the Billings in efficiency, was discarded after Richter's widow sued for royalty payments on the machine invented by her husband while he was an employee of the company. Under contracts signed 11 September 1911 and 8 November 1912, any of Richter's inventions applicable to the tobacco industry while he was in the company's employ was to be used by the company. Any profits derived from the sale of such inventions by Richter and the company were to be divided between them. Though the company settled the disagreement with Richter's widow by paying her $5,000, it apparently did not use the stemmer again. Because the company acquired only thirty-six Pasley machines and did so only shortly before installation of the SPD lines, it appears that the Billings stemming machine was the only one of importance in the operations of the leaf-processing department. Despite the installation of a large hand stemmery as late as 1930, the direct labor cost of hand stemming in 1935 ran between $3.75 and $4.25 per hundred pounds of finished strips in contrast to $2.75 and $3.00 for the same amount on the Billings machine. Hourly production at Number 65 in 1935 amounted to 180 pounds per machine but to only 125 pounds at Number 60. According to a recapitulation by Lee R. Salmons in 1935, 1,565 employees were engaged in hand stemming and 2,750 served in the machine stemming division.[69] Continuation of stemming by hand when machine stemming had proved more economical may be attributed to three factors in descending order of importance: (1) the difficulty of stemming Georgia-grown leaf by machine because of its condition when marketed (loose rather than in neat bundles), (2) the practice of selecting certain choice leaves for chewing tobacco during the stemming process, and (3) consideration for the hand stemmers.

Labor and Politics

Wages and hours and their connection with local politics, and the appearance on the scene in 1919 of the Tobacco Workers International Union of the American Federation of Labor (TWIU-AFL), are so inextricably woven together during these years that no one of them can be discussed alone. Surviving records do not indicate any basic changes in labor conditions from the early years of the Reynolds company until after 1912. Over the next decade, however, there were many changes, caused possibly by the ferment of World War I, the deaths of R. J. Reynolds, Walter R. Reynolds, and D. Rich, and the passage of the child labor laws—all in a period of tremendous growth based on the popularity of Prince Albert, Camels, and such chewing brands as Days Work and Apple Sun Cured. The changes involved working conditions, wartime wages, efforts of management to solve personnel problems, inflated prices of consumer goods, and a brief attempt to move manufacturing to other areas.

These factors must also be considered against a background of southern arrogance toward labor, especially toward the many Negro laborers. "Nigger, take off your hat when you come in this office," was the standard greeting of D. Rich to any Negro who might fumble with his ragged hat. This astounded Roy C. Haberkern, a native of Indiana.[70] Rich's attitude was shared by many southern whites of that period, whether on the farm or in the factory—a far cry indeed from the day in 1961 when the chairman of the board told foremen point-blank that both races would work and eat together at the Whitaker Park plant.

There is no way to estimate the decline in morale that undoubtedly followed the death of R. J. Reynolds. It was the implicit belief of the laborers that "Mr. R. J." could prevent layoffs or anything else that might affect them adversely. Noah Eugene Hartley declared that once, when a slack sales period hit the company, more than 1 million pounds of finished chewing tobacco stood in the shipping room. William V. Garner asked Reynolds whether hands should be laid off and work stopped for a time. Reynolds advised him to continue production and boarded a train a few days later evidently to see salesmen. Whatever he did, declared Hartley, it was effective and in a few days the surplus disappeared.[71] This feeling of being protected prevailed in the company during the life of its founder.

As noted earlier, a strong interest in socialism had prevailed in Winston-Salem since 1911, when people of the town had filled a hall to hear Eugene V. Debs. The local Socialist party was led by Jacquelin Plummer Taylor, a tobacco manufacturer with Taylor Brothers. A benevolent man, he tried to advance the interests of the working class, and in so doing became an enthusiastic Socialist. He was charitably described by a local newspaper at the time of his death, not as an extremist or radical, but as an advocate of a "conscientious and workable Socialism."[72] Taylor's success in urging reform through the Socialist party was surprising in view of prevailing attitudes among southern leaders.

In 1916 Socialist party candidates in Forsyth County campaigned whole-heartedly at such points as Waughtown, the county courthouse, Pfafftown, Vogler's Store, Brookstown, and Lewisville. Furthermore, George Ross, "a Socialist speaker of national reputation," was scheduled to spend a week in Forsyth County.[73] In December of the same year a large group assembled at the city high school to hear Rose Pastor Stokes lecture on "What Socialists want and why they want it." A little later John Spargo, introduced by Mayor Oscar B. Eaton, made a strong impression. Mrs. Kate O'Hare, associate editor of the *National Rip-Saw* and a Socialist speaker of international reputation, addressed an audience that "taxed the capacity of the room." A local editor wrote: "This is Mrs. O'Hare's third speech in this city and her ability as a speaker, together with her wit and sarcasm, won her many friends here."[74]

During the period wages paid by the Reynolds company became an issue in a political campaign, causing a disturbance that may have been a factor in the 10 percent raise that came in 1916—the first beyond the old wage rate of five dollars. Alfred Eugene Holton, a Republican of Winston-Salem, ran for the North Carolina Senate against James Alexander Gray, brother of Bowman Gray, Sr., vice-president of the Wachovia Bank and Trust Company and soon to become a vice-president of the R. J. Reynolds Tobacco Company. A member of the state legislature in 1881 and 1883 and chairman of the state Republican Executive Committee from 1892 to 1900, Holton had been duly rewarded with the position of United States District Attorney by President McKinley—a post that he held until 1914. At a propitious time in 1916,[75] also the year of a presidential campaign, Holton made a statement about the low wages in Winston-Salem. When Andrew Fuller Sams introduced the Democratic candidate for governor at a political rally in Winston-Salem on the night of 30 September, he took that opportunity to dispute Holton's charges, noting that the average daily wage in the town was $1.635. Sams also declared that $1.42 was the true wage paid by "the manufacturing concern which employs the largest amount of labor," based on wages paid men, women, and children "exclusive of all foremen, office men, stenographers, and traveling salesmen." This, of course, represented the average wage paid by the R. J. Reynolds Tobacco Company. Sams declared that Holton's dissatisfaction had arisen from his having been removed from the "pie counter." Immediately a local newspaper lined up with the company by asking: "With these facts before him, will Mr. Holton retract or will he throw honor to the winds and persist in his efforts to win votes by false pretense?"

Holton responded in a paid advertisement in the *Winston-Salem Journal*—covering most of a page—attacking the local Democratic organization, which, he contended, controlled the municipal government, all public utilities, the stockholders of the *Winston-Salem Journal*, the R. J. Reynolds Tobacco Company, and the Wachovia Bank and Trust Company.[76] He described William N. Reynolds and Clement Manly as stockholders of the *Winston-Salem Journal*, R. J. Reynolds as political manager of the Reynolds company and brother-in-law of the Democratic candidate for the state legislature, and Manly as counsel for the Reynolds company, the Wachovia Bank and Trust Company, and the Southern Power Company. Furthermore, stated Holton, R. J. Reynolds had earlier charged the Southern Power Company with the extortion of 1,000 percent profit on electric light bills. Holton then declared that the local Democratic organization, though it maintained that wages were not a subject for legislation, nevertheless had advocated and secured a city ordinance placing a prohibitory tax of five hundred dollars on labor agents "for the purpose of preventing laborers from leaving the city, and to keep down their wages. If they can pass laws against laboring people, why can they not pass laws for them?" asked Holton. He accused the Board of Trade of having as its main purpose the prevention of the entry into Winston-Salem of other manufacturing interests, especially the Liggett and Myers Tobacco Company, thereby keeping laborers' wages and farmers' prices for leaf tobacco at a low level. He claimed that one of Winston-Salem's leading manufacturers had gone to Washington with his attorney and secured a ruling from the Wilson administration that the establishment of a certain manufacturing firm in the city would be in violation of the Sherman Antitrust Act. In return for this ruling, he charged, citing the *Winston-Salem Journal*, the same company had contributed $10,000 for Wilson's reelection. Holton then stated that, as published in the *Winston-Salem Journal* on 7 April 1916, Winston-Salem paid the lowest average daily wage of five centers in North Carolina.[77]

These charges produced bitter denials from R. J. Reynolds, R. Jarvis Smothers, Will Reynolds, and Clement Manly. R. J. replied first on 19 October in the *Winston-Salem Journal*: Holton's statement, "grossly at variance with the facts," reflected on the business integrity of himself and his associates. The charge that he had gone to Washington to prevent another manufacturing concern from entering Winston-Salem was ludicrous; it undoubtedly was. Perhaps with more than necessary unction R. J. then met another of Holton's implied charges: "As to the intimations that some of the factories of the R. J. Reynolds Tobacco Company have been closing down several days each week, this is also absolutely untrue. During the Wilson administration, we have been busy every day, while some of the factories have run nights to supply the demand for our products. The only time that our factories have closed was on holidays, and then only for the pleasure of our employees." He also declared that the $10,000 contributed to the Wilson-Marshall campaign had been given by him personally and that no other person or company would pay any part of it.

Holton's reply, perhaps a little weak, came promptly. He declared that his information about the trip to Washington had been corroborated by a statement from a leading officer of the R. J. Reynolds Tobacco Company. Holton declared that this official, having heard of his intention to attack the company on the subjects of taxation and wages, had called on him and stated that the company was paying taxes, the employees were content, he did not want Holton "to stir up the laborers," and the company had had a hard struggle with Liggett and Myers. Holton then fell back on the old antitrust accusation that Reynolds, by virtue of having been in the American Tobacco Company for years, had destroyed some thirty independent tobacco manufacturers, thus bringing down the price of leaf tobacco to farmers and depressing the wages of laborers. Had this not happened, he charged, no one could estimate the extent of wages with so many companies competing. In conclusion, he declared that Reynolds had paid the $10,000 to the Wilson administration with his own check because he knew that a corporate contribution was a criminal offense.[78]

R. Jarvis Smothers responded immediately, ridiculing Holton's reasoning. The hand of R. J. Reynolds seems evident in preparing Smothers's statement. Smothers wrote in the *Winston-Salem Journal* that if thirty or more tobacco factories had continued to operate in the town, labor would have competed for jobs and the firm able to work longest and pay least would have been the most successful. Few factories would have had the capital to buy expensive machinery and furnish work for the entire year; wage earners would have walked the streets about four months each year as they did when thirty-odd factories operated in Winston-Salem. Firms operating in this way could never have created a nationwide demand for Winston-Salem goods, and, all in all, Mr. Holton was ignorant of the principles of industrial evolution.[79] A more objective observer might have acknowledged that laborers neither had lived a luxurious life when thirty-odd factories operated in the area, nor had their situation greatly improved in 1916.

Clement Manly and Will Reynolds replied in the same issue of the *Winston-Salem Journal*. Manly simply listed the accusations that applied to him and branded them falsehoods. Will Reynolds assumed that he was the high official of the company to whom Holton had referred. Before the campaign began, Reynolds declared, he had heard that Holton intended to attack the Reynolds company "in an effort to dissatisfy its employees." Thereupon he had approached Holton to give him the facts, telling him that his company paid wages equal to any in the tobacco industry regardless of location. He also admitted telling Holton about the payment of taxes on stock in another state. But, he declared, Holton was not telling the truth if referring to Will Reynolds as corroborating the allegation that the Reynolds company had prevented any manufacturer from locating in Winston-Salem. In conclusion, he declared that Holton did not deserve election to any office and that it was "but natural that such a man . . . should attempt to deal blows below the belt."

Holton's answer in a paid political advertisement a few days before the election recalled that both R. J. and William N. Reynolds had been adjudged guilty as collaborators in the American Tobacco Company and claimed that R. J. Reynolds had discriminated against the state by not incorporating his company in North Carolina.[80] Although this dispute may have caused disaffection among the Reynolds employees, it had no marked influence on who was elected. James A. Gray won the state senate seat by a vote of 4,259 to 3,379. The local Republican newspaper commented that Holton had been "the leading factor on the Republican side" and that among other things he had awakened a sentiment for "workmen's compensation."[81]

The entire squabble with Holton might well have passed as politics typical of a presidential election year but for one fact. On 21 July 1916, the board of aldermen of Winston-Salem had adopted an ordinance regarding labor agents that most likely indicated fire beneath the smoke. The ordinance specifically placed a license fee of five hundred dollars on any firm engaged in procuring labor to be used in another state or territory or on any individual who solicited labor to be used in another state. A less severe form of this regulation had been passed by the North Carolina legislature in 1908, evidently in order to control farm tenants. The Winston-Salem ordinance, issued under the authority of the state act of 1908, however, was directed at industrial labor. On 23 May 1919, while representatives of the TWIU-AFL sought to organize the Reynolds employees, the ordinance was revised to place a similar fee of five hundred dollars not only on labor agents but on every firm or corporation that attempted to secure laborers for "employment *outside the City of Winston-Salem*."[82]

Attitudes of and toward Labor

On 6 September 1917, the directors of the Reynolds company decided to borrow within the next sixty days $10 million for a variety of reasons, chiefly to meet the increased costs of supplies and labor because of the military draft and the federal child labor law.[83] More significantly, six months later the directors, after a discussion not detailed in the minutes, deemed it advisable to form a labor committee consisting of Walter R. Reynolds, Lasater, and Dyer,[84] men who managed manufacturing and leaf processing. Winston-Salem, though not a large industrial center, could not escape the industrial strife that became nationwide in 1919 with wages as the predominant cause.[85]

A few available illustrations serve as a background for the many changes from 1912 to 1924. A strange situation prevailed among the laborers, perhaps because of the closeness to the blackberry patch and other aspects of agrarian independence. Laborers were plentiful but they frequently quit, stayed out for a time, were laid off, or fired. A loud order from a foreman, "get your bucket and your money and go home," served as the standard form of discharge. Often, however, such orders were disciplinary and the worker was free to return the following day. On many occasions messengers went out on the order of foremen to search for needed workers, as was the case when John Needham was asked to find ten or fifteen classers. The door-knocking efforts of Needham and his companion produced only one classer who consented to report to the factory.[86] According to Edgar E. Bumgardner, a long-time employee of the company, even after 1912 the average employee did not regard his job as permanent. Workers from rural areas, remaining on the job until able to buy a new suit, often returned to Yadkin or Wilkes counties, relatively backward areas, to show off their newly purchased finery. During blackberry or hog-killing seasons, young women would leave their work for more delectable food and the joys of outdoor life.[87] Labor turnover from 1920 through 1924, the earliest years for which such data are available, was as follows:[88]

Year	Percent
1920	167.60
1921	87.20
1922	99.62
1923	163.07
1924	118.50

Another reason for the rapid turnover of labor lay in the enticement of many Negro workers to the North, especially to the Pittsburgh area, during the early 1920s. Often becoming dissatisfied there, they would return to Winston-Salem but find it difficult to secure their former jobs. Later on, after observing this happen to friends and relatives, laborers tended to stay on the job and the turnover never again reached such high proportions as in 1920, 1923, and 1924.[89]

The great power of the foremen prior to 1919, and often their unscrupulous use of it, no doubt made difficult situations for laborers. There was no employment office until 1919. Yet foremen had their troubles and not all of them were autocrats. Perhaps the experiences related in 1950 by Cora Robertson Brewer reveal the difficulties of both foreman and worker in the factory. Cora, who had a third-grade education, moved to Winston about 1897 with her mother and sister from the town of Buffalo in Patrick County, Virginia, where, according to Cora, they never had anything and didn't know anything. At a very early age Cora became a worker on the untying line before learning to pick and class leaf. When she took her eleven-year-old son to John C. Whitaker for a job, he arranged for her to leave her place as a classer in Number 8 to work in Number 4 near her son. Her first task there consisted of reworking damaged packages of Camels made by the night shift. Finding the work so slow and tedious that she could earn very little on a piecework basis, she decided to return to Number 8. Instead, she was persuaded to remain where she was and try working as an inspector on a cigarette machine. The packages came at her so rapidly that she overlooked some imperfect ones only to have the two stamp girls, one on each side of the line, throw them back at her. Enduring the situation as long as possible, she eventually decided to quit but allowed her foreman to persuade her to stay as a stamper. She found this trying, especially when working on packages made by a green "cupper," who was so slow that earnings on the piecework basis were meager indeed. By the time she became more adept at stamping, her foreman was transferred to Number 256 and her new foreman did not like her. In 1919 the helpful foreman, then in Number 256, advised Cora to come to his factory but by that time the company had adopted a rule that no employee could quit at any time and go to another foreman for a job. For a time she obtained work with the Mengel Box Company before returning as a stamper to Number 256 under her favorite foreman. Again he was transferred, this time to Number 97, and a foreman prejudiced against her took his place. He gave her untrained cuppers, seven in all, who, as they became adept, were transferred to other machines. The other stamp girl quit because she could not afford to work with green cuppers. In great anger Cora decided to quit but instead she was transferred to Number 12. Going to work the following morning, she obtained her stamps, folded them for easy tearing, and stood ready to work at the rate of forty-four cents for each one thousand packages she stamped. But she found that the prejudiced foreman had been transferred with her and that she had green cuppers again. This proved too much and she turned in her stamps to the stamp clerk, went downstairs, and told the entire story to John Whitaker. Whitaker called in the offending foreman and accused him of favoritism. She was taken back and given an experienced cupper. But the foreman continued to annoy her in many small ways. One morning she came in to work, took a number of Camel packages made by the night force, reported her action to the busy record keeper, and began work. Evidently, in the rush of the early morning stir, the record keeper had failed to note her action and soon the foreman accused her of having stolen several packages of Camels. Leaving her machine, she started to get her coat but found the dressing room locked. As another foreman asked her where she was going, Edgar E. Bumgardner, then in training to be a foreman, approached and persuaded her to remain. He arranged for her transfer to Number 97, and there she worked happily until she had completed forty-eight years of employment with the company. There had been a time, she said, when people worked as long as they could and then starved unless they had managed to save enough for their retired years. Cora Robertson Brewer, through her persistence and longevity, had managed to accumulate enough to buy her own home.[90]

Information revealing the attitude of the higher echelon of management toward labor prior to 1916 is sketchy, but it may be revealing. In 1912 Robert E. Lasater heard of too many instances of foremen giving orders on merchants for shoes and other articles—a practice that was not allowed for any employees. It would be an excellent idea, Lasater stated, to write a letter to that effect to every foreman and subforeman "around the factories . . . and have an ironclad rule or no rule at all."[91] Two years later T. J. Noble, Jr., head of the Richmond prizery, wrote Walter Reynolds in terms that reveal a kindly attitude toward the predicament of seasonal workers:[92]

> Geo. Murphy the bearer has been a good worker in our stemmery and has helped me look up some workers. We will send him with what we get together at train tonight. George will have charge of the party as he is a native of Winston and knows where things are. He will do to use some where in the factory—he is good at covering nips and can make lumps—we will want him again next winter if he wants to come back. We allow that he has made 1/2 of his ticket cost in time so please allow him that if he does not get work at your factory he will owe the balance in cash but I think it will be better to work him at your factory.

Reynolds's reply reveals none of Noble's concern for the plight of the seasonal worker, emphasizing instead the lack of skill of many workers. The twisters referred to in this letter had a simple job—merely to arrange a few filler leaves lengthwise, surround them with a wrapper leaf, bend the resulting bundle in half, and twist the two portions into a neat twist for those who preferred this less sophisticated type of chew. Walter Reynolds wrote:[93]

> I have been away for a few days on a business trip and upon my return this morning I learned that you sent about eight men, and our Mr. Garner advises that he is unable to get any twist crews out of the lot. However, [he] is using a few of them in the Twisting Room as helpers, and we are trying to place the others in other parts of the factory so as to work the transportation out of them. Do not believe it will be possible for you to get any good twisters there, and therefore request that you do not send anymore.

Here Walter Reynolds appears interested only in obtaining from these Negroes the cost of their transportation to Winston-Salem, which would imply that labor was plentiful. Yet, in the same year, when a test was being run on the Billings stemming machine "it was (on some days) impossible to get hands to operate all the machines."[94] His attitude toward labor typifies the general outlook. Ed Blakely, an employee of many years, stated in 1950 that Walter Reynolds disliked to see an employee idle even for a few moments. When workers sat down in the packing rooms awaiting another batch of tobacco, Reynolds would invariably order them to get brooms and begin sweeping. This they always did with great stir until he left the room.[95] R. J. Reynolds, on the other hand, insisted on having many employees on hand to learn the work, regardless of their immediate value.[96]

There appears to have been little record of any protest by the employees before 1919. An undated letter from the "Strait Twist Makers" to the company during this period reveals an inequity that eventually led to the adoption of a job classification scheme—something obviously needed when this letter was written, but not implemented for a long time:[97]

> We the Twist Makers see the need of Asking the Company to Equalize the Price between other hand work. for an instant take Micky Twist (a brand) and Study how they are made. they only need one Stemmer and they does not have to forge their Roll and Cap it. therefore the Mickey and Camel (Caromel) Makers take one Stemmer and make A hundred Pounds per day at $8.75 Per Hundred. therefore they Can Pay the Stemmer $3.50 Per day and have $5.25 Per Day for them selve— Now we will Explain Straight Twist Mak-

ing. if we would undertake to make Straight Twist with one Stemmer we can not Cap and Turn up more than 65 or 70 Pounds Per day of 4 oz. 3 ply on Gravely's Choice Golden Crown Brown's Mule or Cash Balet (Value). we feel that one Dollar Raise on the hundred upon the Brands mentioned and whatever Percentage may be given Put us on about Equal Base at this Present time. In Regard to the brand Yellow Jacket we have never gotten Pay for making it. We feel that it Should be the Same Price of Cutter Twist. therefore we wont to Ask for Raise of one Dollar on Cutter, and $2.00 two Dollar Raise on Yellow Jacket thus making it a fare Break to all concerned.

Most likely this petition came from the six or seven hundred Negro operatives who went on strike during the first week of August 1914 because of the same general complaint. From the company's point of view, the difference in the work made the wages received about the same. The strike involved no demonstration and on 3 August the operatives "returned to work at the old scale of wages."[98]

Wages and Special Compensation Plans

A summary of wage changes from 1912 to 1933 (see Table 8-6) reveals a picture different indeed from the years prior to 1912 when the basic wage was $5.00 per week. Many personnel folders, however, show that $4.50 was often a starting wage. By 1914, particularly after the introduction of Prince Albert and Camels, opportunities for rising above the starting wage became more numerous. The entire matter of wages, working conditions, and labor agitation comes into clearer focus when viewed with these changes in mind. Labor became active in its own interest. Some of management's efforts to effect improvement were similar to proposals advanced by manufacturers elsewhere who sought to appease labor. A mere chronological view of the situation indicates tremendous change.

Straight hourly wages paid by the Reynolds company, discounting any attendance bonuses, are shown in Table 8-7. They reflect the extraordinary changes brought about by the events of 1919 (see Table 8-6). Data in Table 8-8 show the average yearly and weekly wages of employees in Winston-Salem at five-year intervals from 1905 to 1925, making the change that started with World War I even more apparent.[99]

After five 10 percent increases, the granting and removal of four bonuses, a raise of 25 percent, and a reduction of 20 percent, hourly earnings in 1924 were almost 100 percent over those in 1912. At nearby Dan River Mills—manufacturers of cotton cloth in Danville, Virginia, in which R. J. Reynolds, holding 3,602 shares, was the largest common

Table 8-6
Chronology of Changes Affecting Wages Paid by the Reynolds Company
During 1912–1933

Year	Change
1912	Old weekly wage (amounting to 13.9¢ per hour) established
1916	Basic wage rate increased 10%
1916 (3 Feb.)	First attendance bonus (2% of 1915 earnings) offered
1917	Shift from weekly to hourly wage rates made
1917 (1 Jan.)	Second attendance bonus (4% of 1916 earnings) offered
1917 (20 Apr.)	Basic wage rate increased 10%
1918 (7 Feb.)	First labor committee appointed
1918 (Feb.)	Basic wage rate increased 10%
1918 (Apr.)	Basic wage rate increased 10%
1918 (July)	Basic wage rate increased 10%
1918 (19 Sept.)	Overtime bonus added:
	—50% for 60 hours' work
	—25% for 30–59 hours' work
	—flat rate for less than 30 hours' work
1918 (5 Dec.)	Attendance bonus removed
1919 (8 Jan.)	Overtime bonus reduced to:
	—25% for 55 hours' work
	—10% for 30–54 hours' work
	—flat rate for less than 30 hours' work
1919 (1 Mar.)	Anthony McAndrews and James Brown (TWIU-AFL) arrived
1919 (17 Apr.)	Federal child labor law first applied
1919 (17 June)	Cooperative, waste-saving, and profit-sharing plan offered to employees
1919 (21 June)	Cooperative, waste-saving, and profit-sharing plan rejected by employees
1919 (7 July)	Bonus removed and base rate of pay increased 25%
1919 (10 July)	Union representatives requested 10 hours' pay for 8 hours' work
1919 (16 July)	Company replied to union representatives: 8-hour day, time and a half for overtime, double time for Sundays and 6 holidays
1919 (31 July)	Basic wage rate for 48-hour week increased 25%
1919 (4 Aug.)	Agreement made with TWIU-AFL

Table 8-6 (continued)

Year	Change
1920 (1 Apr.)	Contract made with TWIU-AFL: 48-hour week, same basic wage, time and a half for overtime
1920 (16 Apr.)	29 mechanics went on strike; rehired by 10 May
1921 (1 Apr.)	Union contract expired
1921 (15 Apr.)	Company established 4-day week at 8 hours per day
1921 (16 May)	Work force decreased by 1,503 employees, or 14.26%
1921 (2 June)	Basic wage rate decreased 20%
1921 (6 June)	Five-day work week of 9 hours each
1921 (6 July)	Cigarette division's work week set at 5½ days, 10 hours per day
1921 (10 Aug.)	Work force increased 6.5% over that of 8 June 1921
1933 (20 Aug.)	Basic wage rate increased 17% by National Industrial Recovery Act

Sources: R. J. Reynolds Tobacco Company: personnel department, Minutes of the Board of Directors (vols. III, p. 127, and IV, p. 122, secretary's department), contract with TWIU-AFL (file 1441, secretary's department), Announcement to Factory Employees of 19 June 1919 and Notice to Factory Employees at Winston-Salem of 4 August 1919; *Union Republican*, 26 September 1918, 9 June 1921; *Winston-Salem Journal*, 29 January, 27 December 1916, 21 April 1917, 20 September 1918; *Tobacco*, 3 May 1917, p. 27; *Southern Tobacco Journal*, 24 April 1917; *Twin City Sentinel*, 20 April, 18, 20, 21 June 1919.

stockholder—the average hourly wage in 1914 was 13.9 cents, the same wage paid by the Reynolds company at that time. But in 1924 hourly wages at the Dan River Mills were 5.1 cents an hour above those at Reynolds.[100] Meanwhile, living costs for wage earners in the United States from July 1914 to November 1919 increased from 61.3 to 109.0 and the purchasing value of the dollar declined from 163.1 to 91.7.[101] In real wages the Reynolds employees had actually lost.

The attendance bonus, an innovation introduced by R. J. Reynolds in 1916, apparently had nothing to do with the increase in wages for that year. Rather it was a special, and apparently wise, arrangement aimed at lowering absenteeism. The announcement of the offer first appeared in the factories on 1 January 1916:

Special offer to employees on our weekly
pay roll in Winston-Salem, N. C., except those
who work in the offices

Table 8-7
Average Hourly Wage Rates Paid by the Reynolds Company
During 1912–1924

Year	Hourly Rate (in cents)
1912	13.9
1916	15.3
1917	16.8
1918 (Feb.)	18.5
1918 (July)	20.4
1918 (Sept.)	20.4
1919 (7 July)	25.5
1919 (31 July)	34.4
1921 (2 June)	27.5
1924 (30 Aug.)	27.5

Source: Compiled in 1950 by Edgar E. Bumgardner, Robert N. White, and George E. Tucker of the R. J. Reynolds Tobacco Company from piecemeal records that no longer exist. The figures must be accepted as approximations.

On the last pay day before Christmas, 1916, we will, upon recommendation of your foreman, or the manager of your department, give you, in cash, two per cent on total amount of all money you received from us for any work you did in 1915, if you work regularly and faithfully during the year 1916, when we have work for you to do. This offer may be renewed in 1917, for work done in 1916, and so on from year to year, if we find that it encourages you to increase your earnings by good and steady work when we have work for you to do.

For example: under the above offer, you will receive on the last pay day before Christmas, 1916, two cents (2 c) for every dollar we paid you for any work you did for us to 1915.

January 1, 1916   R. J. Reynolds Tobacco Co.

To participate in this program an employee was required to have worked for the company at least two years. At the end of the year, the local paper announced that thousands of additional dollars had been disbursed on the last payday of 1916, that the employees had enthusiastically praised the plan, that the bonus arrangement had been decided on long before current agitation about the high cost of living, that since then several raises in

Table 8-8
*Average Yearly and Weekly Wages of Employees
in Winston-Salem During 1905–1925*

Year	Average Number of Employees[a]	Average Yearly Wage per Employee[a]	Average Weekly Wage per Employee[a]
1905	2,932	$193.40	$ 3.87
1910	4,201	243.41	4.87
1915	6,626	300.68	6.01
1920	11,237	818.22	16.36
1925	11,436	666.78	13.33

Source: Compiled in 1950 by Edgar E. Bumgardner, Robert N. White, and George E. Tucker of the R. J. Reynolds Tobacco Company from piecemeal records that no longer exist. The figures must be accepted as approximations.

[a]Includes subforemen.

wages had been granted, that the offer would be doubled for 1917, and that this profit-sharing plan, different from others over the country, had originated with the R. J. Reynolds Tobacco Company.[102]

R. J. Reynolds's own words, as the first year ended, show not only that the plan was aimed directly at absenteeism but also that work habits characteristic of earlier years constituted the basic factor in absenteeism:[103]

> It is our intention to do everything within reason for the benefit of our employees. We realize that it is a good investment to add to their comfort and happiness. We know, from actual experience, that a great many colored workers, as well as a considerable number of white workers, were in the habit of working long enough each week to obtain only sufficient money to defray the actual cost of living. They did not seem to have any idea of thrift, and never thought of saving money for a "rainy day."

> This bonus plan has demonstrated that it encouraged our employees to work full time each week. Among other benefits most of the employees have learned to put their surplus money in the savings bank, and a great many of them are buying homes with the money earned through working steadily.

That the attendance bonus benefited the company as well seems clear; for 1917 it was doubled to stand at 4 percent of 1916 earnings. By newspaper account, between $75,000 and $100,000 went to regular weekly payroll employees under the second attendance bonus plan, this time to those who had served the company for at least one year.[104] Often, however, workers could not understand their failure to receive the bonus. Further, in view of the power that the plan gave foremen, it is difficult to believe that it consistently achieved its purpose unless department managers were able to counterbalance some of the foremen's decisions.[105] At any rate, on 5 December 1918, shortly after the death of R. J. Reynolds, it was decided on motion of Robert E. Lasater, seconded by James B. Dyer, not to renew the Christmas attendance bonus offer. By that date the labor crisis had ended and the government no longer needed large quantities of tobacco products. Earlier in the same year Lasater declared that the company was "up against the real thing in material and labor cost."[106]

The four 10 percent increases in the basic wage in 1917 and 1918 resulted from a scarcity of labor. Actually, however, the labor force virtually doubled from 1915 to 1920, and 1917 found Reynolds with 40 percent of the cigarette production in the United States. Government contracts called for tremendous production and the 10 percent increases followed quickly one after another. On top of these advancements came the opportunity for laborers to draw wages at the rate of time and a half for a sixty-hour work week. The production of Camels was doubled in 1917, without benefit of advertising, just as labor became scarce as draftees departed for training camp. As early as 1916 there had been some labor scarcity when members of the National Guard began to serve on the Mexican border. The Reynolds company granted all of its employees in such service continuity of employment, regular salary or wages, the attendance bonus, and participation in profits. Wages and salaries for war service were discontinued after 1 March 1917, but continuity of employment remained. By September 1918, there was "hardly a larger industrial service flag in the South." Prepared under the direction of Mrs. Rufus E. Johnson, the flag contained 1,261 stars; one star was gold—for James Cunningham, a Negro youth who died in camp.[107] At the Richmond plant, as elsewhere at this time, it was particularly difficult to get stemmers. One of the managers was stemming leaf in January 1918, "but you can't do it all," wrote T. J. Noble, Jr., to Walter Reynolds.[108]

Insofar as surviving records indicate, the situation changed suddenly on 8 January 1919, when the overtime bonus was reduced. Anthony McAndrews, president of TWIU-AFL, had anticipated just such a drop in wages and announced that steps would be taken to unionize tobacco factories in the South, including the Reynolds plants.[109] McAndrews, intending to organize the white workers, and James Brown of Louisville, planning to do the same for the Negroes, arrived in Winston-Salem about 1 March 1919, no more than two months after the second drop from wartime wages. Within three weeks Brown signed about seventy-five Negro tobacco workers as members of the union. Membership dues included a one-dollar fee for initiation and a small weekly or monthly fee for sick benefits. A burial benefit of fifty dollars was also available through the union.

On a bench warrant sworn out by Deputy State Fire Commissioner W. A. Scott, both Brown and McAndrews were arrested on Sunday, 23 March 1919, and charged with violating state insurance regulations for operating without a license. In municipal court, they were freed on bonds of three hundred dollars each. Appearing on 26 March before Commissioner James R. Young in Winston-Salem, McAndrews and Brown secured withdrawal of the charges against them until the state attorney general could rule on the case. This he did on 19 April, declaring the TWIU-AFL to be strictly a labor union not involved in the insurance business and therefore in need of no special license. "The decision is what was to be expected," declared the editor of the *Union Republican*, because several "of the fraternal orders have similar beneficent features" and pay no such fees.[110] This unfortunate episode was the basis for organized labor's special dislike of the Reynolds company for many years. In May 1919, the TWIU-AFL began a publication in Winston-Salem called the *Labor Leader*, with M. L. Misenheimer as editor and Charles W. O'Daniel as business manager. The fight was on.[111]

The R. J. Reynolds Tobacco Company, belatedly it must be acknowledged, responded with a proposal supposed to be in line with the most progressive ideas of the period. These were the days when Harvey S. Firestone advocated profit sharing for labor, as did Champ Clark, George W. Perkins (former partner of J. P. Morgan and Company), and even Henry Ford, who wanted his employees to purchase certificates of investment. At the same time John D. Rockefeller, Jr., was pressing his creed of "Capital and Labor" on the businessmen of America.[112] It was the day of "Industrial Democracy," which sought to apply the golden rule to industrial relations in the form of company unions. Close to home there were strikes on the Norfolk and Western Railway, in the cotton mills of Albemarle, North Carolina, at nearby High Point, and in the streetcar system of Winston-Salem.[113] With the organizers of TWIU-AFL on hand and busy among the employees, company management distributed an explanation of its plan in a circular dated 19 June 1919. Shortly before, Robert E. Lasater had interviewed the president of the Passaic Metal Ware Company in New Jersey. The Passaic industrialist had made a study of training or "vestibule schools" for use with new employees. He felt that such schools were vitally important for manufacturers and quoted government figures showing that they reduced the cost of training 50 percent and the time of training 75 percent. Their use, he stated, greatly minimized the production of inadequate goods, helped place trainees advantageously, and taught them obedience, cleanliness, and the proper way to perform factory operations. They also aided in weeding out the undesirables. In conclusion he outlined the "excellent" work of James W. Russell, who had operated the New Haven Manual Training School before the war.[114]

On the day before the details of the new plan were distributed to the factory employees, Walter Reynolds accepted the invitation of George E. Hanes, director of Negro Economics in the United States Department of Labor, to attend a conference designed to promote cooperation between white and Negro workers, to stabilize labor, and to increase the productive power of Negro laborers.[115] In view of earlier but insufficient efforts to improve labor conditions, management was endeavoring to enter the twentieth century. The cooperative, waste-saving, and profit-sharing plan presented by management on 19 June 1919 indicated that a major crisis had arisen.

The plan was designed to promote cooperation between management and labor, to encourage economy in the manufacturing process, and seemingly to develop a system of profit sharing for laborers. In view of similar efforts among the leading industries of the country, the introductory statement that the plan was based on "extensive investigations through many sources" may perhaps be accepted. All details of the plan, however, had not been developed. They rested on the formation of a Factory Council for administration. Membership in the council was to consist of two equal groups, one composed of laborers selected by their fellow workers and another composed of foremen and assistant foremen selected by management. Anyone, through his representative, might present suggestions, requests, or complaints. If considered of sufficient importance by the council, such suggestions would be recommended to the directors for consideration and decision. Any ideas or plans so adopted were to be relayed to the laborers through members of the council. The financial features of the plan, possibly clear neither to the employees nor to management, rested on increased economy of operations. "After very careful investigation both in the Company's plants and in other plants of the country, the Company is fully convinced that with the full co-operation of all concerned a very substantial saving can be made in the way suggested," ran the key sentence of the plan. Two weeks from the time the plan went into effect, the amount of savings shown in operations during that period was to be determined and one-half of it paid to the employees as a percentage of increase on each employee's earnings. Plans for allotting representatives to the Factory Council were to be developed with a schedule of the division, including the number of representatives allotted to each. Representatives were required to have been in the company's employ for at least one year. So certain was management that the plan would be accepted that the date of election was set for 21 June.[116]

On the night of 17 June 1919, Samuel Clay Williams and John C. Whitaker presented this plan to five hundred foremen and subforemen at a supper in the dining room of Number 4 in the presence of local reporters. According to the *Twin City Sentinel* of 18 June 1919, it was received with unanimous approval and favorable comments even on the streets and in the factories the following morning: "The project is an innovation in this part of the country. It is in line with the co-operative spirit of the most progressive industrial institutions of the United States. Indeed, for some months the company has been making a study of similar plans now being tried out in the North and East. The proposed plan is not a model of any of the plans investigated but is rather a synthesis of the good points found in the large number studied." The proposal resembled slightly the highly praised plan presented by Julian S. Carr, Jr., to the employees of the Durham Hosiery Mills at the same time. It was based on John Leitch's plan for Industrial Democracy, which stirred industrialists in general immediately after World War I.[117]

Despite all the publicity involved, there was nothing in it. An examination of the minutes of the meeting with foremen on the night of 17 June not only shows that fact clearly but also indicates that the newspapers had given parrotlike reports. S. Clay Williams made the first speech, declaring that he had the interest of the employees at heart and that the plan was the result of much investigation to determine what could be done to lessen waste and reduce the cost of production. In reality he did little more than stress the need for saving before he turned the meeting over to John Whitaker who, like Williams, begged for cooperation. Whitaker called on the foremen to discuss the plan that was "not yet worked out," more or less in vain. Williams then interrupted to give his explanation of the plan, which clarified nothing: ". . . if this plan went into effect July 1st, or Thursday morning, two weeks from then the cost of production for that period would be determined how much less than a basic period, which would be a time just before we went into the plan, and to each hand's pay would be added turned over to him that week, the additional amount, so he would have in two weeks tangible results of his effort." T. J. Parrish asked about representatives from a room containing both whites and Negroes. Williams answered that that problem had not been worked out but that he would be glad of suggestions. Parrish had none. The climax came when foreman J. H. Nichols asked, "Every two weeks, you say, the amount would be put in the pay-envelopes provided you have a surplus. Suppose it comes under?" Williams seemed staggered and showed it by his reply: "Aren't you the man that talked about faith a while ago?" Nichols answered meekly: "Yes sir, I have got faith."[118]

Yet so certain was the editor of the *Twin City Sentinel* of acceptance that on 21 June he carried a news item stating that the plan would be introduced immediately after the voting, set for that day. The editor seemed almost regretful that the final outcome could not appear in his last issue of the week. He also stated that of the fifty-four representatives to be chosen by the employees for the Factory Council, one to each two hundred employees, twenty-one were to be whites and thirty-three Negroes. This was accurate and in itself an innovation in the South of 1919. Allotment of the representatives by room, department, or job appeared in a notice to the employees.[119]

No further recorded information about the election seems available. According to the excellent memory of Edgar E. Bumgardner, the employees rejected the plan with hoots and jeers, preferring to stand with the labor organizers.[120] At any rate, on the night of 30 June, the editor of the *Union Republican* attended a mass meeting on the courthouse square, where white and Negro employees were literally packed around the stand to hear Marvin L. Ritch, Charles W. O'Daniel, and M. L. Misenheimer address them. To the editor of the *Union Republican* the salient feature of the speeches lay in the urging of employees to join the union. Like Governor Thomas Walter Bickett, he opposed the idea of the closed shop but considered himself a friend to labor. He also regretted that the speeches gave more emphasis to grievances than to benefits, but offered no solution for the problems other than the spirit of the golden rule.[121]

Union Proposals and Management Responses

Efforts to improve working conditions stopped with the illness and death of R. J. Reynolds and were not resumed by management until after the labor disturbances just described. It may be reasonable to conclude that he would not have allowed conditions to reach that point. Yet on 7 July 1919 the company did increase the basic wage by 25 percent. Not satisfied, representatives of the TWIU-AFL conferred with company officials on the night of 10 July in Reynolds Inn regarding a union proposal for an eight-hour day with ten hours' pay. In this meeting Will Reynolds stated that his company, though facing strong competition, would pay its employees on a scale equal to any of its competitors. The company stood ready to bear the expense of sending a committee of three—two selected by the union and one by the company—to visit tobacco factories in St. Louis, New York, Jersey City, Durham, and Richmond to ascertain wages being paid for work similar to that done by Reynolds employees. If the competing companies were paying more, Reynolds would meet their scale.[122]

Six days later Will Reynolds responded to the union's proposal via a printed circular to all factory employees, calling attention to the union's failure to accept his offer to investigate wages in other plants at the company's expense. He then made his concessions:[123]

> We will go on an eight hour basis, allowing the existing rate of pay per hour for eight hours work, with time and a half for overtime and double time for Sundays and Holidays, holidays to include New Year's Day, Memorial Day, Independence Day, Labor Day, Thanksgiving Day and Christmas Day (watchmen of course excepted). This means that you get eleven hours of pay for ten hours work. When work hours close at Noon on Saturdays, piece workers as well as day workers who put in five hours or more shall be paid at the same rate per hour as is allowed on other days when ten hours are made.

On 3 August 1919, the central labor union arranged for a great Labor Day parade and speeches on the courthouse square, with James F. Barrett of Asheville and J. P. Figg of Washington, D.C., as the chief speakers.[124] James A. Gray joined Barrett and Figg in addressing the gathering, Gray stating that labor had as much right to organize as bankers or any other group. Figg praised Gray and the Reynolds organization. He also declared that in dealing with William N. Reynolds he had been received with a cordiality vastly different from receptions accorded him by some other employers with whom he had talked. Moreover, he said, "he [Reynolds] indicated to me that he wanted to do the best that he could for his employees, and upon my return later I find that he has done his best, and I hope that he may do more in the future."[125]

The following day, the company notified all factory workers at Winston-Salem of what appeared to be the first contract signed with TWIU-AFL. Effective 31 July, basic wages (prevailing just prior to 16 July) were increased 20 percent, the work week was prescribed at 48 hours (nine hours each from Monday through Friday plus three hours on Saturday), and an open shop was maintained with no discrimination against union membership. These terms were to remain in effect until 31 January 1920.[126] On 1 April 1920, the Reynolds company, its employees, and locals 145, 146, 147, 148, 151, and 152 of the TWIU-AFL signed an agreement effective from that date to 1 April 1921, incorporating the following provisions:[127]

> Forty-eight hours per week of five 9-hour days plus 3 hours on
>   Saturdays
> Time and a half for overtime
> Employees out for good reason to return to their former superintendents without going through the employment office
> Right to protest grievances to supervisors
> Right of an employee incapacitated in performance of duty to request

a transfer to another department with more congenial duties if vacancies existed

Open shop with no discrimination against union members

There is no evidence that the contract was ever signed again. Whether
the rumor was true that Robert E. Clodfelter (of TWIU-AFL) was
bought off with a farm in Forsyth County is not surely known. But there
seem to have been no further signs of union activity among the employees. Table 8-6 above shows that within just over three months after contract expiration, the Reynolds company decreased basic wage rates, the
work week (excepting the Cigarette division), and the work force.

In March 1919, during the heat of the labor disturbances, rumors
spread that the Reynolds company intended to move its plants to other
areas. The president, William N. Reynolds, refused to either confirm or
deny the rumor, but he did note that his leading competitors had found it
advantageous to locate their plants at various points. It had been his
company's policy to centralize operations in Winston-Salem—a policy
that he preferred, although from the standpoint of freight rates he could
not ignore the advantages of other locations. Moreover, on a recent trip to
the Middle West he had found surplus labor.[128] Thus it does not seem
unusual that Reynolds established branch plants in Richmond, Jersey
City, and Louisville, the latter two in 1919. Perhaps Reynolds did believe
that branch plants might prove advantageous, although it is more likely
that he was angered because of the labor disturbances. With other tobacco manufacturers, such decentralized arrangements generally had come
about not from definite planning but from combining and unscrambling
the American Tobacco Combination. The choice of Jersey City as a location freer from labor troubles than Winston-Salem seems most unlikely.

Among the reasons given for the establishment of a branch plant in
Jersey City were increased demand for Camel cigarettes, scarcity of building materials, and convenience for supplying the New York metropolitan
area with finished products. Robert E. Lasater's explanation included no
mention of labor problems. The need for expansion, he declared, could
not be met in Winston-Salem in 1919 because of the difficulty in obtaining building materials. He was sent to talk with Rufus L. Patterson, who
had built a number of munition plants in New Jersey during the war.
Lasater found, on examining the abandoned plants, especially one in
Bloomfield, New Jersey, that the task of developing one of them into a
cigarette plant would be well-nigh impossible. James B. Duke, hearing of
Lasater's problem, told him that P. Lorillard Tobacco Company owned
two plants that were empty—one in New York City and one in Jersey City.
President Thomas J. Maloney of P. Lorillard showed Lasater the Bay
Street building in Jersey City, equipped with cigarette and packaging ma-

chinery of the same make as that used by Reynolds. Maloney offered the plant to the Reynolds company at cost, less depreciation, stating that the same foremen and workers might be used. On Lasater's recommendation, the company purchased the Bay Street plant—on 6 November 1919.[129] The installation of conveyors, made in Winston-Salem and marked for assembly in New Jersey, caused considerable trouble. John Peddycord, the mechanic who built the conveyors, had many idiosyncrasies generally overlooked by the company. Determined to go to Jersey City to install the conveyors and see the world outside Forsyth County, he marked the parts with a letter code. Mechanics in Jersey City, not knowing the key word *squirrel*, could not assemble the parts and the company had to send Peddycord to do the job.[130]

The Jersey City venture proved to be temporary. The company's total production of cigarettes fell in 1920 and 1921 but increased in 1922 and 1923 by 16 and 40 percent, respectively. Additional manufacturing facilities in Winston-Salem were begun in 1922, consisting of an extension to Number 64-1 and construction of Numbers 64-2, 30 (a sweat house), 60, 64-4, 60 South, and 97—the last a cigarette factory completed in 1927.[131] Meanwhile, dealers in the Jersey City area began requesting cigarettes made in Winston-Salem. Workers in the Jersey City plant went on strike and the company closed the plant, thus completing the circuit. At any rate P. Lorillard offered the Reynolds company $2 million for the plant and all of its equipment. Reynolds accepted on 12 July 1927, granting P. Lorillard the right to use all improvements on the machinery, whether patented or not, and the privilege of purchasing replacement parts when needed.[132] P. Lorillard, late in following the lead of the Camel, doubtless needed the plant for producing Old Golds, which were designed to compete with Camels.

In Richmond the W. T. Hancock plant had been acquired by the Rucker and Witten Tobacco Company before that firm in turn was acquired by Reynolds in 1905. For a time the Reynolds company used its Richmond property for the storage of leaf, but in 1910 it began to construct a large building designed for the manufacture of chewing tobacco—probably Apple Sun Cured. Then, in 1920, it was announced that the company had purchased land adjacent to its holdings for the erection of "an immense cigarette factory in Richmond." But the manufacture of cigarettes in Richmond by Reynolds failed to materialize, though the manufacture of chewing tobacco there increased. Seven years later, in March 1927, the company's plug manufacturing was transferred to Winston-Salem, the reason given for the shift being "economy of operation, with the entire manufacturing plant of the company grouped under one roof."[133]

Many of the same factors obtained in the purchase and operation of the Strater Brothers' plant in Louisville, Kentucky. In company lore the story prevails that R. J. Reynolds sent Lasater to Louisville to investigate the value of the Strater Brothers, manufacturers of navy plug. Lasater went, took one chew of Days Work, and immediately wired back advising R. J. to buy the plant inasmuch as the name and formula of Days Work alone were worth the asking price.[134] Although the story is surely true in spirit, it cannot be true in fact because Reynolds died almost a year before the purchase. First the Greenville Tobacco Company, owned by three brothers, the firm's name was changed in 1893 to Strater Brothers. In 1912 the Burley Tobacco Company, a farmers' cooperative, purchased the Strater Brothers plant but, on 27 June 1919, sold it to the R. J. Reynolds Tobacco Company. According to the *Western Tobacco Journal*, "The labor situation in the Carolinas is such as to cause considerable anxiety to manufacturers and it is claimed this is one of the considerations in the deal."[135]

From the purchase of Strater Brothers, the Reynolds company obtained twenty-seven brands of chewing tobacco.[136]

By Joe (twist)
City Club (no identity)
Cup (plug)
Daisy (twist)
Days Work (plug)
Doctor (twist)
Drumstick or Claw Hammer
    (plug)
Full Pay Mixture (no identity)
Golden Glow (granulated Va.
    smoking)
Handspike (plug)
Harpoon (long cut smoking)
Hindoo (smoking)
Hobo (long cut smoking)

Hunkidora (twist)
Index (plug)
Kismet (plug)
Light Pressed (plug)
Natural Leaf (plug or twist)
Old Fashioned (Ky. dark
    smoking)
On the Square (plug)
Penny Post (cut plug smoking)
Roll Call (plug)
Satisfaction (no identity)
Sixteen oz. Natural Leaf (plug)
Ta Too (twist)
Torchlight (plug)
Turf (plug)

The manufacture in Louisville of these brands, or more specifically of Days Work, continued until 31 December 1928, when announcement came from Winston-Salem of the operation's transfer to the home plant:[137]

R. J. Reynolds Tobacco Company announces the transfer to Winston-Salem, as promptly as details can be worked out, of that part of its chewing tobacco manufacturing heretofore carried on at Louisville, Ky. The Louisville branch is giving work at present to approximately 300 employees. Capacity for the larger production necessary at Winston-Salem has already been developed in connection with the continued progress of the large building program which the company has had under way in this city for the past two years. This move is in line with the company's previously expressed desire to concentrate at Winston-Salem, the home of the company and its chief operating point, as many of its operations as can be advantageously located and handled here. The removal of this manufacturing operation to this city, following the removal last year of its operations theretofore carried on at Jersey City, N. J., and Richmond, Va., centralizes in Winston-Salem all of the company's manufacturing. Leaf tobacco rehandling plants will, of course, be continued in various leaf tobacco marketing centers in this and other states as now operated.

Days Work, though not a success at first, was rapidly improved until it had a tremendous lead in chewing tobaccos. As the Reynolds company's chief navy brand, it was used to reduce the lead of Star and Horseshoe, manufactured by Liggett and Myers. Reynolds began by selling Days Work in a deal of one free plug with six; as the competition grew, this was increased to two free plugs with six and finally to six free plugs with six. The competition never really relaxed and, according to one observer, became the fiercest ever known in the tobacco industry.[138] It should be noted, however, that Days Work had no great popularity until the Reynolds company took it over and improved it by the use of additional sweetening. It became and remained for decades the leading brand of chewing tobacco.

Other Strater brands did not fare so well. Cup and On the Square became fair sellers for a time, although the Masonic seal embedded on the latter caused some complaint. James K. Norfleet, a prominent Mason employed by Reynolds, was detailed to reply to all these letters of complaint. Torchlight first appeared on the Reynolds price list in 1920. At that time P. Lorillard's Beechnut, made in Middletown, Ohio, was the leading chew in the scrap tobacco category. According to well-substantiated rumors in tobacco circles, P. Lorillard then drew its heaviest revenue from this brand. Reynolds thus developed Torchlight as a scrap chew to compete with Beechnut. But Torchlight proved a failure, no doubt a bane to dealers who could be browbeaten into taking Torchlight because of the popularity of Camels. Some held that Torchlight contained too much cigar scrap, whereas others maintained that the cigar scrap was not allowed to ferment properly. In any event, Reynolds was unable to compete successfully with P. Lorillard's Beechnut.[139]

It appears fairly certain that the brief venture into the operation of branch plants in Louisville and Jersey City represented an attempt to thwart the efforts of labor to organize.[140] Once the contract with the TWIU-AFL expired, the Reynolds labor force was drastically affected by changes in number, wages, and working hours. A 6.5 percent increase in the labor force in August 1921 replaced the 14.26 percent decrease of 16 May in the same year. A decrease of 20 percent in the basic wage scale on 2 June 1921 remained in force until an increase of 17 percent in 1933 under the authority of the National Industrial Recovery Act—significant in itself. The decrease in the work week to thirty-two hours on 15 April 1921 was followed by an increase to forty-five hours on 6 June and to fifty-five hours on 6 July. These changes bore no relationship to the profits of the company during the same period.

By 1916 R. J. Reynolds, aware of dissatisfaction within the labor force, appeared ready to make some concessions on wages and working conditions. From the foregoing it is clear, however, that virtually every means for controlling the disaffections of labor had been exhausted before any marked concessions were made. Many of the changes improving the welfare of laborers from 1912 to 1924 came from the demands of society in general.

Efforts to Improve Working and Social Conditions

As early as 1906 the Reynolds company had adopted the policy of assuming the medical expenses of accident victims treated at Slater Hospital, undoubtedly to avoid litigation.[141] Certainly there were innumerable opportunities for such accidents. Above all was the employees' unfamiliarity with machinery. Unguarded gears, machines driven from overhead shafting, poor tools, electrical hazards, wet floors, lack of handrails for stairways, steampipes, and awkward stacking of supplies and equipment left the way open for many accidents. Shifting a belt from an idle pulley to the drive pulley with the open hand frequently caused lacerations and broken fingers and arms. It was not unusual for an employee to receive severe shocks and burns or to plunge down a stairway to be crippled for life. The worker from a rural area was especially liable to injury.[142] These circumstances in part led to the eventual establishment of a medical department in 1919.

The installation of free ice water and lunchrooms perhaps marked the greatest improvement in working conditions. Before 1914 workers drank water from barrels cooled with ice they purchased from their meager wages. In 1914 a drinking water system was installed for all the factories and the office. Pumped from two artesian wells, one near Number 8 and the other near Number 256, the water passed through electrically cooled pipes.[143] This system was improved in 1916 when the company contracted for a refrigerating plant that guaranteed "a duty equal to the melting of 4½ tons of ice every twenty-four hours of continuous operation when cooling water." This arrangement, which involved an ice water circulating pump and all ice water connections,[144] received wide praise although it in no way was as remarkable as the installation of lunchrooms.

A rest room for white women and a lunchroom for white employees—both in Number 256—were inaugurated in April 1915 by Robert E. Lasater. The editor of the *Union Republican* expressed gratification at these improvements in a factory "where a large number of white ladies and girls are employed." The lunchroom, seating four hundred and equipped with a kitchen presided over by an expert cook, afforded wholesome food at low prices. Wages for the patrons of the lunchroom averaged little more than thirteen cents per hour in 1915, but employees could purchase tokens at two and a half cents each in anticipation of a meal consisting of corn pone, a plate of beans, and a pickle, all for one token. If not satisfied, they could buy an additional bowl of soup with bread and crackers. A combination of these two servings, stated the *Union Republican*, at a cost of five cents, comprised a meal for an average person. Should dessert be desired, half a large sugar cake (a Moravian delicacy) might be purchased for another token.[145] Operated at cost, this new venture undoubtedly represented a great change for Lasater, long accustomed to supervising the manufacture of tobacco for a profit. Possibly no other employee benefit proved of more value for the comfort and well-being of the workers, who had been accustomed to eating cold, soggy lunches while sitting on the sidewalks, on a pile of lumber, or in a cold, barren tobacco sales house. When the decision was made to begin operating the lunchroom at cost, the editor of the *Union Republican* commended the plan, concluding: "The Republican has from time to time alluded to this need as the Local Editor has noticed time and again the employees of the R. J. Reynolds Tobacco Co., taking their noonday meal along the streets, in the warehouses or wherever they could find a convenient place and in all kinds of weather. With a place to eat their dinner or lunches furnished at cost is a good work and should be made to apply to both white and colored as we see it is proposed to do."[146]

Quickly following the lunchroom at Number 256 came another at Number 8 for Negro employees. Occupying a large part of one floor, this lunchroom was arranged with the kitchen in the center thus permitting a continuous counter and table. Meals similar to those at Number 256 were served; in addition, tables in the room provided places for those who carried their own lunches. On 29 July 1915, when this lunchroom was opened, Lenora H. Sills, a longtime civic leader, champion of improved sanitation, and friend of the Negroes in Winston-Salem, addressed the employees in the lunchroom.[147]

R. J. Reynolds took great pride in these improvements, boasting in August 1915 of the drinking water and lunchrooms that had been installed. At the same time he called attention to plans for the Reynolds estate, which his wife was developing near Winston-Salem. Intending to organize a model farm, Katharine Smith Reynolds started a church and a school, providing a minister and a teacher not only for the boys and girls on the farm but also for the adults.[148] It was in part through the influence of his wife that R. J.'s interest turned more directly to matters of social betterment for his own employees. Richard J. Reynolds, Jr., recalls a great deal of discussion between his father and mother about the installation of lunchrooms, she finally convincing him that warm, wholesome food was important for the health of his employees.[149]

Samuel Smith Stanley, manager of these earliest lunchrooms, was faced with the challenge of providing a wholesome meal at low cost; he resorted to serving black-eyed peas or beans so frequently that the lunchrooms came to be called beaneries. However, the menu did include numerous other dishes. Edward George Blakely, who cooked the first meal to be served at Number 8, recalled that they frequently served Irish stew, cabbage, and vegetable soup, along with a bakery cake if desired. He also noted that the cost of servings eventually increased to five cents per dish.[150] Floyd A. Hauser, who began work in a second lunchroom in Number 8, recalled that the lunchroom in Number 256 was closed when Reynolds Inn was opened in 1918. Later, lunchrooms were opened at Numbers 97 and 60, and many years later, in 1955 or 1956, at Tiretown. Eventually in the 1940s another was opened at Number 256. Hauser also remembered that tokens, known as "bean checks," once sold at eight for twenty-five cents and later at five for twenty-five cents. In the 1940s, there was a switch to books of meal tickets, which were frequently charged against a worker's pay check. When out of cash, employees would sometimes charge a book of tickets and then sell it at a reduced price to obtain ready cash—a practice soon stopped by John C. Whitaker.

Other troubles beset the lunchroom operation. Two apostles of free enterprise objected to the sale of lunches at cost. As one of them wrote, the operation of lunchrooms in such fashion might be good for the employees "but hard for snack sellers who have to sell for a profit or starve." Describing the venture as a case of "economic determinism," the objector declared that "R. J. R.'s scheme is a reversion to feudalism."[151] Then, there was the buttermilk dispute. Reynolds's lunchroom manager agreed to take buttermilk from the dairy of John W. Lambeth as long as it was satisfactory, but one day it was refused because it had been "churned too sweet." The dispute over the milk developed into a quarrel that eventually involved such things as the sale of butter to employees at cost and objection to one of Lambeth's employees with a German name.[152] Lunchroom service continued under the company's direction until 17 January 1958, when a professional caterer took over.[153]

Another improvement also came in 1915 with the establishment of a day nursery for children of Negro women employees. This was a cooperative effort apparently instituted by various tobacco manufacturers of Winston-Salem with the aid of Lenora H. Sills. A building at the corner of Seventh and Vine streets, formerly occupied by the Negro fire department, was being "fitted up" for the day nursery when representatives of ten of the twenty Negro churches met on 24 September 1915 to discuss the matter of a suitable matron. It was decided to prorate the matron's salary among the Negro churches. Mrs. Sills, who remained throughout the meeting, assured the group of assistance from the factories and from city officials.[154] For a time the venture was successful but quarrels in the Negro ministers' union and church committee resulted in failure to pay the matron for three months. Thereupon the nursery was closed, a budget provided, and a plan made to operate it "independent of the Negro preachers."

When the day nursery reopened on 1 February 1919, Mrs. Sills gave the preachers an ultimatum to pay the matron, make up their budget for twelve months, and obtain in advance the cash for one month's salary of the matron as conditions for taking over again. Nothing was expected from the ultimatum, although Mrs. Sills felt that the ministers were ashamed of their dereliction. Four weeks later she reported that the nursery was filling up. Mrs. Sills sent Lasater a report of the difficulties, which, she was certain, he could not even imagine:

> Nor will any of you ever know the struggles, aggravations and other knotty conditions that I have had to wade through in keeping this nursery going for four years. . . . This is the noblest work that we are doing and the dollars that we have spent in this direction will return to us more in the lives of the future citizens than any dollars that we have been spending in any direction for the betterment of the Negro. If I did not think this, I would not give the time to it that I have. I appreciate the confidence that you factory men have placed in me in the direction of all this, and have tried to see that every dollar was spent for the best.

When it reopened the board of directors for the nursery included Walter Thompson, Madison D. Stockton, Leon Cash, and the Reverend Mr. Rowe. In concluding her report, which had been requested by Lasater, Mrs. Sills noted that "the Visiting Nurses" had nothing to do with the management of the nursery.[155] Possibly the visiting nurses were concerned with the health of Reynolds's employees, though credit for this work does not belong exclusively to the company.

Interest in a day nursery for whites surfaced in 1916. It was intended to utilize a commodious house, owned by the Reynolds company, located east of the First Baptist Church on Second Street. Plans, which had been drawn up by Katharine Smith Reynolds, included supervision by Lelia Idol, a graduate nurse, "who with her colored graduate nurses [then had] charge of the health of the women employees of the company."[156] But it was not until 1919 that a white day nursery was opened under the care of a matron, Louella Suggs Burns; it was maintained only until 1922 and may be put down as a failure.[157]

During 1915–16 there was considerable agitation in Winston-Salem for the establishment of a city health department. In view of Lenora Sills's work with the Negro nursery, which the company supported, it is of more than passing interest that R. J. Reynolds and Mrs. Sills stood side by side in the matter. Both felt that extension of the city water and sewage systems should have priority over the establishment of a health department. Mrs. Sills wrote of the many houses with no water and sewage connections but with open wells and privies. At the same time Reynolds noted that many people used drinking water from wells with a privy only a few feet away. "No matter how clean the surface may be," he wrote, "there is a constant seeping of water from these privies, polluted with human excreta and the nearby well is almost invariably affected."[158] Mrs. Sills reported to the aldermen that it was almost impossible to get the merchants to use suitable garbage containers. During this campaign it was shown that Winston-Salem had the highest death rate from communicable diseases of any city in the South.[159]

Adequate housing for employees appears to have received more wholehearted effort from the company than did the provision for day nurseries. With the phenomenal growth of the cigarette business, the shortage of adequate housing became critical. From 1915 to 1919 cigarette production increased virtually tenfold. Moreover, from 1912 to 1919, the production of Prince Albert smoking tobacco doubled even the large amount of 1912. From newspaper accounts, it appears that the company's first move was to furnish relief for its Negro employees. In its plans to build fifty model homes in East Winston, the company requested the city to extend sewer and water lines for two blocks but planned to bear the cost of street and sidewalk paving itself. Upon completion the homes were to be rented at 6 percent of their value.[160] Accordingly, the company purchased a tract of 83.84 acres known as the "old Cameron land," to which a few additional lots were added.[161] About five hundred feet from the eastern terminus of the streetcar line near the City Hospital grounds, the development became known as Cameron Park. Here, according to Joseph M. Parrish, R. J. Reynolds planned to cover the creek running through the area and pull in the hills to make a rolling section of land. He also planned to sell the homes at cost but died before he could complete their development.[162]

Under the supervision of T. W. Grogan, the company's superintendent of construction, some 130 houses were built, with well-drained grounds, improved sidewalks, electric lights, and water and sewage connections. In time the area around Dunleith Avenue came to be occupied by the greatly expanding Negro population of East Winston, whereas the Cameron Avenue section went to white employees. At first these homes were leased to employees on the modest terms of 6 percent, but later they were sold to them. As early as 7 March 1918, the Real Estate Committee, then consisting of R. E. Lasater, J. B. Dyer, and J. L. Graham, proposed and obtained a contract that permitted a worker who had leased a house to apply the rent he had already paid to a down payment at the end of the lease period and thus begin buying the house. The chief provision for such an arrangement required the purchaser to maintain the property during the lease period. These houses, sold at cost, varied in price from $3,000 to $7,000. Of the 180 built, 44 were sold to white employees in a two-week period during September 1921. In the same period 16 houses on Dunleith Avenue were sold on the same terms to Negro employees.[163] The fifteen years allowed for payment and sale of the houses at cost anticipated the generous terms offered years later on federally sponsored housing.

Even more generous was the company's arrangement for certain employees who had earlier purchased or built homes in Winston-Salem, their indebtedness secured by deeds of trust or mortgages. According to board of directors minutes, many of these individuals lived under hardships because of exorbitant interest notes and attorneys' fees. Early in 1917 the directors instructed the real estate committee to advance to employees considered eligible for assistance sums of money not exceeding two-thirds of the value of their property. These loans, secured by proper deeds of trust, carried an interest rate of 6 percent and matured if the recipient left the company's employ or was discharged for cause.[164] No doubt these terms came from the generosity of R. J. Reynolds, but they were executed scrupulously by Lasater, Graham, and Dyer.

No less important was the need for housing to accommodate the influx of country girls who came into the Reynolds cigarette plants during the early days of wage increases in 1918. It is doubtful that R. J. Reynolds participated in the solution of this problem. At this time, the reformers of Winston-Salem, chief among whom were Katharine Smith Reynolds, Kate Bitting Reynolds (the wife of Will Reynolds), and Lenora H. Sills, constantly emphasized the need for better and safer housing for these young women. It was the day of the innocent country girl who required protection from the evils of city life, if indeed Winston-Salem could then be deemed a city. Just before R. J. Reynolds died, this problem was at least partially solved with the purchase of the Plaza Hotel (formerly the Webster Hotel). At the corner of Chestnut and Third streets opposite the union railroad station, the Plaza had sixty bedrooms with running water, baths, a dining room, a kitchen, and a lobby on the first floor, as well as a convenient location. On 13 July 1918 the company secured a ten-day option for $37,000. The final purchase price, approved on 2 August, amounted to $35,000.[165] After it was extensively repaired and renamed the Reynolds Inn, the young women moved in about 21 September 1918 under the care of a matron. Apparently it was first operated by Charles C. Bodenheimer, known as "Chap," and his wife as general managers and Ruth Hopkins as matron but later by W. F. Roselle and his wife. For $4.00 or $4.25 per week the new patrons received a comfortable room with two meals a day six days a week and three on Sundays.[166] Never intended as a profit-making venture, the Reynolds Inn remained a rooming place for young women at least until 1929 and was generally operated at a slight loss.[167]

Such were the efforts to improve living and working conditions for employees before the death of R. J. Reynolds: free ice water in the factories, lunchrooms operated at cost, at least one rest room for white women in Number 256, partial support for a Negro day nursery, operation of a day nursery for whites, provision of housing at cost for at least 180 families, and operation of a dormitory for white girls. Only rumors of labor troubles had preceded these improvements, although the charges aired in the 1916 campaign for the state senate seat carried ugly connotations when linked with city ordinances restraining the free movement of labor. Factory conditions, especially in the leaf department, indicated the long and rough road that lay ahead for management and labor. Then and many years later, foremen cursed employees who went to the toilet and stayed too long; they even went into the women's toilets cursing and yelling at those inside. Toilets, crude and filthy, were often without ventilation or light.[168] Such conditions seem unbelievable considering the comparative cleanliness, light, and ventilation of modern factories. Moreover, the modern foreman, expected to be polite, civilized, and well grounded in the precepts of the golden rule, would scarcely recognize his predecessor of 1918.[169]

The company's labor-oriented initiatives after 1918 were less direct and more organizational in nature. Efforts to improve employee relations and conditions of employment included establishment of an employment department, a Factory Council, and a welfare department. Health and recreational initiatives included establishment of medical and athletic departments.

Efforts to Improve Employee Relations
and Conditions of Employment

Establishment of an employment department seems closely allied to the necessity of enforcing the child labor law. Speaking before four hundred foremen and subforemen on 29 March 1919, S. Clay Williams pointed to the serious nature of the child labor law: its violation carried a penalty of 10 percent of the company's profits. Therefore, he said, the R. J. Reynolds Tobacco Company would open an employment office, "which might very properly be termed an age examination office, and a corps of employees will give their time in conducting the most complete and rigid examination of children fourteen, fifteen and sixteen years old."[170] The organization and brief functioning of the Factory Council represents the only proposal salvaged from the cooperative, waste-saving, and profit-sharing plan rejected by the employees on 21 June 1919.

The welfare department functioned briefly and quite possibly was the work of D. Rich, then near the end of his service with the company. The only available issue of its publication, the *Reynolds News*, must furnish the basis for its description. It seems likely that the welfare department attempted to unify the YWCA work, the earliest medical work, and the Factory Council, with some feeble attempts to improve relations with the employees by means of a company publication. The first issue appeared on 26 April 1918 and, judging by the numbering on the only available issue, continued to appear on schedule at least until August 1919.[171] Prosy articles by D. Rich, news from different factories and departments, a long article by John C. Whitaker entitled "Co-operation and Representation," and a substantial amount of filler occupied most of the issue for August 1919. It was published—with Miss Eva Nixon, a Reynolds YWCA secretary, as editor—at the rate of twenty-five cents per year or two cents per copy. Apparently the editor at first received assistance of a kind from six active YWCA clubs: Ever Ready (Number 256), Willing Workers (Number 12), Wide-a-Wake (Number 8), Sunshine (Number 4), Four Leaf Clover (Tin Box Shop), and Friendship (no factory indicated). These clubs had adopted the following business code, the first two items of which were goals of the cooperative, waste-saving, and profit-sharing plan:[172]

> To give the employer a full day's service
> To exercise economy on behalf of the company
> To use good, clean language
> To use no gum in public places
> To wear a neat business dress

To neither originate nor repeat slander about any girl
To make the new girl in the factory welcome

The clubs were started in 1916 by the general YWCA of Winston-Salem under the presidency of Katharine Smith Reynolds, who began the drive. Plans formulated by Nathalie Lyons Gray (wife of Bowman Gray, Sr.), Eleanor Taft (general secretary of the YWCA), and Margaret Anderson (extension secretary of the YWCA) called for the organization of YWCA clubs in various factories. In the week following 4 September 1916, two such clubs were organized in the Reynolds plants "as the YWCA of the R. J. Reynolds Tobacco factories." Kate Bitting Reynolds also assisted.[173]

Information from the factories included in the *Reynolds News* seemed to focus on employee activities such as vacations and weddings. In the available issue, word came from Perle Jones in the packing room at Number 4 that Geneva Huffman, Ruby Haigwood, and Rosa Katz had spent the Fourth of July at North Wilkesboro, where they enjoyed fishing and "*picking* blackberries." Eight girls along with Eva Nixon and "Miss Lyon" had just returned from what was evidently an industrial conference sponsored by the YWCA at Waynesville, North Carolina. Verge Apple at Number 12 had married Cathleen Sink of Woodland Avenue.

John C. Whitaker's article bore directly on personnel problems and no doubt reflected his determination to salvage something from the cooperative, waste-saving, and profit-sharing plan. Whitaker was young, ambitious, and energetic; though his chief duty lay in the problems of manufacturing, he stood foremost among those genuinely interested in the problems of employees. His purpose in writing the article was to encourage use of the Factory Council, which apparently had been started two days before rejection of the cooperative, waste-saving, and profit-sharing plan, but only with company-appointed members. He called attention to the lesson of cooperation taught by the war and declared that of the many problems to be solved during this "period of reconstruction" none was more important than that of industry. In the early days when plants were small, he wrote, it was possible for management to keep in constant touch with the employees. As industries grew into large corporations this personal relationship had gradually vanished and the door thus swung "open to differences and disputes," with the consequent development of antagonisms: "The question with which the student of industrial problems is now confronted is how to re-establish this personal relation and co-operation. The answer is not doubtful or questionable, but absolutely clear and unmistakable. It is through the establishment and operation of a proper means of close and easy communication between employer and employee on all questions touching the welfare or interest of employees." He then cited the company's recent effort to establish a plan for employee representation that would be concerned with all relations between management and its employees. In the past, he declared, the company had been remarkably free of disputes between the two groups but through misunderstanding the plan had been rejected. However, various department managers and foremen with the cooperation of the company immediately appointed a series of committees that had been meeting at the Reynolds Inn to consider and act on every suggestion called to their attention, whether complaint, suggestion, or grievance. He then listed the committees, which undoubtedly represented the beginning of the Factory Council:

Adjustment of wages and working conditions	Richard L. Dunstan and Charles M. Griffith
Economy, efficiency, and suggestions	J. H. Nichols and John Coan
Safety and accident prevention	John L. (or Vic) Putnam and R. W. Miller
Investigation of complaints	Henry A. George and Charles W. Long
Housing problems	Lewis F. Brown and W. F. Manship
Sanitation, health, and restaurants	Samuel S. Stanley and Charles C. Bodenheimer
Education and publication	C. A. Dobbins and John R. Stovall
Industrial relations	William V. Garner and George E. Tucker
Mechanical devices and inventions	Charles V. Strickland and Risden P. Reece

Whitaker felt that as soon as the employees had learned to use these committees that disaffection might be eliminated.

This one issue of the *Reynolds News* contains no reference to medical work as a function of the welfare department, but it is more than likely that the scanty benefits then available to employees did fall under this department. Reference has been made earlier to supervision of a day nursery for whites by Lelia Idol, the nurse "who . . . had charge of the health of the women employees of the company" in 1916. Lillian Louise Russell, an inspector in cigarette factory Number 4, recalled clearly that as a child she assisted Dr. Arthur de Talma Valk by holding medical instruments when he made his regular daily visits to the Number 8 office before formal establishment of the medical department.[174] Possibly the welfare department died soon after its birth for two reasons: the declining health of D. Rich before his retirement in 1923 and lack of interest on the part of other directors. Or possibly it was merged into some other department.

At any rate, the only results leading to better conditions for wage earn-ers lay in the work of the Factory Council and the employment and medi-cal departments. Something of the background of the Factory Council has been noted. It was certainly ready to function in late August 1919, but perhaps was not fully organized. On 13 July 1920, at its regular meeting, a constitution and bylaws were adopted. The purpose is frankly stated:

To promote social and cooperative feeling among the members in order to improve working, living, and social conditions among the employees

To improve the relationship between employer and employees and to discuss matters of mutual concern

To bring into one group all manufacturing executives

To prevent waste from unnecessary labor turnover

To prevent waste through lack of proper training

To prevent waste through unnecessary sickness and accident

When the constitution was adopted, membership included, in addition to those already noted, William O. McCorkle, Walter S. Lindsay, and P. Frank Hanes.[175]

No worthwhile evaluation of the work of the Factory Council can be given; possibly it served as a stepping-stone for later efforts with person-nel problems. It was the general opinion of those present at the time that Bowman Gray, Sr., objected to it on the grounds that its members fre-quently had to slight their regular duties to attend council meetings, which he did not regard as work. In other words, top management seemed to care no more for this newfangled idea than the wage earners cared for other aspects of the cooperative, waste-saving, and profit-shar-ing plan.

In Winston-Salem there was early concern over the great number of children who, while in the first three grades, quit school in order to go to work.[176] As the question was being agitated in 1916, R. J. Reynolds, in the interests of education, took the position that legislation was in-advisable:[177]

Mr. Reynolds says that a large number of colored children under the age of 16 years and not a few white children come to the R.J.R. Company's factories here early in the morning before school and stem tobacco and return in the afternoon after school for the same work. The children, he says, can earn enough to pay their board and enable them to keep in school, many of them making as high as 50 cents or more a day.

If the labor bill is enacted by Congress it would prohibit these children from working before and after school hours. And Mr. Reynolds thinks that because of this it would do more harm than good in this city.

In North Carolina in 1916 twelve-year-old children were allowed to work eleven hours a day; manufacturers generally opposed the restriction of an eight-hour-day for children under sixteen. The proposed Keating child labor law, designed to become effective nationally on 1 September 1917, limited the employment of children under sixteen to eight hours a day. It received careful analysis from the Reynolds counsel, Harry H. Shelton, who believed the proposed law would be sustained by the courts. He referred to the "great many children who are employed in the (R. J. Reynolds) factories" and promised to call attention to the matter again on 1 August.[178] Meanwhile, the North Carolina legislature enacted a child labor law that did not meet the standards of the federal law. On 19 January 1917, Shelton not only noted the penalty for violating the state law but also declared that its violation would probably deprive the company of its defenses in the event of suit for damages for personal injuries. Such an eventuality, he stated, would probably invalidate the casualty insurance with the Maryland Casualty Company.[179]

Shelton was wrong in regard to the federal law. Among those employed to fight the constitutionality of the Keating act was the firm of Manly, Hendren, and Womble of Winston-Salem, which included Colonel Clement Manly, long counsel for the R. J. Reynolds Tobacco Company. The suit that rendered the federal law invalid began in North Carolina and received a supporting decision from the United States Supreme Court on 3 June 1918.[180] During this period the editor of the *Southern Tobacco Journal* attributed the child labor law to "fanatical theorists" and claimed that the law only thrust idleness on juveniles at a time when the country was at war and in great need of labor.[181] A second child labor law, added to a federal revenue bill, received an overwhelmingly favorable vote on 8 February 1919. Two months later to the day, the *Southern Tobacco Journal* joined the "fanatical theorists" and praised the decision of the company to enforce the law by hiring no children under fourteen and none between fourteen and sixteen to work more than eight hours a day. To handle this problem, the editor continued, the Reynolds company would open an employment office, a move that should be emulated by other industrial firms.[182] On 29 March more than four hundred foremen and subforemen assembled at Number 5 to hear the provisions of the federal child labor law explained by S. Clay Williams, who urged all to comply "with the letter and spirit of the law." Should a child not appear to be sixteen, he said, the most rigid examination should be made to ascertain the true age of the applicant. Williams spoke most emphatically, stressing the heavy penalty for violation of the federal law—a fine equal to 10 percent of the total profits for a year.[183]

Compliance with this law was no easy matter; foremen and parents alike required education as to its full import. Notices in the factories on 17 April 1919 carried in special type a statement forceful enough for the supervisory force: "The attempt on the part of any employee to violate any of the foregoing instructions will immediately and without further notice work the discharge of such employee." Certain employees of the company became notaries and accompanied nurses throughout the factories to have the parents legally affirm statements regarding the ages of their children. Many years later it was often recalled that parents, especially among the Negro workers, attempted to smuggle their young children into the factories to work as stemmers.[184] All in all, application of the child labor law in the Reynolds plants amounted to a revolution, which, it should be emphasized, began while Anthony McAndrews and James Brown were organizing the employees.

The employment department, though established in part to administer the child labor law, was needed to solve other problems. Foremost was the question of the authority vested in the foremen who hired and fired at will. At some point in planning for the new department, John C. Whitaker, who became its first head, demonstrated the need for other methods of hiring by sending his trusted Negro helper, Willie Jones, to various foremen to see how many times he could be hired. With abundant native intelligence but only a first-grade education, Jones obtained eight different jobs from as many foremen.[185] The experience of Thurman Allen Porter in securing a job in 1915, though it has its ludicrous side, also indicates the slack manner of hiring employees. After leaving the University of North Carolina, Porter applied to Carl W. Harris for a job as salesman. Mistrusting Porter's youthful appearance, Harris sent him to William T. Smither, requesting that he find Porter a job in the office. Smither asked for three or four references, which Porter gave at once, one being that of a merchant in his nearby hometown. In a short time the merchant called Porter, gave him some of his stationery, and told him to write his own recommendation. When John Henry Cobb applied for a job in 1917, foremen still did the hiring, but some attempt had been made to centralize the task in Number 12 where Whitaker then had his office.[186]

A printed notice announcing the inauguration of the employment department on 11 August 1919 went to department heads and foremen on the ninth with a blank form to be signed and returned attesting that each had received the announcement and pledged his hearty support to the new department. The notice stated that the company looked to a wiser selection of employees as an important means "of stopping the waste due to irregular and unsatisfactory employment." A paragraph headed "Cooperation" acknowledged that the foremen had more responsibility than ever before in the history of industry and urged them to devote themselves solely to instruction, coordination, and increased production in order to obtain greater efficiency. If the frequently illiterate foreman of that day did not understand the text of this announcement, no doubt he soon obtained an oral explanation.

Listed were eight specific functions of the department, the last four pertaining to the Factory Council:

1. Selection and engagement of new employees
2. Follow-up of all employees, transfer of misfits, and discharge of undesirables
3. Enforcement of state and federal laws concerning minors and women
4. Analysis of labor turnover and compilation of statistics
5. Prevention of accidents and safety work
6. Supervision of washrooms, toilets, drinking water, and general sanitary arrangements for the health of employees
7. Investigation and adjustment of complaints regarding environment, conditions of work, unfair treatment, and discrimination
8. Education of all, from management down to the humblest employee, to the fact that their interests were common

Other functions were also specific: the foremen were to introduce new employees to their fellow workers in order to make them feel at home; rush orders were to be minimized in order to allow the new department time to choose satisfactory employees; workmen were to be educated to the importance of giving notice before quitting; and new applicants were to be given medical examinations in order to obtain healthier, happier, and more productive workers and in order to correct as many physical defects as possible. On the matter of quitting work, employees who gave sufficient notice were to be paid in full; those who did not must wait until the regular payday. For the new department to be successful, cooperation from the foremen was necessary. In conclusion, the initial goal lay in "developing and putting into active operation a broad labor policy that will safeguard and work for the best interests of everyone involved." This was recognized "as a task worthy of all. . . ."[187] In later years, those who watched the early development of the employment department freely acknowledged the problems involved and declared that it required virtually twenty years for the department to gain the trust and support of foremen and top management.

The department began with seventeen people, whose duties frequently led them into the factories for consultation with superintendents and foremen. For a time, at least, platitudinous and prosy semimonthly letters went from the employment office to the foremen. One, dated 5 December 1920, urged the foremen to be pleasant, to direct their workers by example, to work against a heavy labor turnover, and to emphasize economy in production. A concluding statement showed the trend that had led to the department's establishment: "Manpower, being the greatest force with which the foreman of the future has to reckon," wrote Whitaker, "means that he must continually study human nature." Another letter, dated 20 November 1921, emphasized the necessity of learning to listen: "In order to listen properly you must hold your tongue in leash."[188] From the four letters available, it is apparent that the overriding concern of the new department lay in helping to solve the labor problem by educating the foremen. The foreman's "big job," according to a letter of 5 December 1920, was to produce the right quantity and quality by the right method at a minimum cost. In a measure, good results appeared after 1921 when it was found that the 1920 absentee rate of 5.8 days per person had dropped throughout the factories to 2.8 days in 1921.[189] The establishment of the employment department during a troubled period of labor disputes and during the beginning of the administration of the child labor law paved the way for a genuine personnel department, as well as a safety department established more than twenty years later during another labor dispute.

Health and Recreation Initiatives

The medical department, started as something of an auxiliary to the employment department, was based on substantial work of earlier years, reaching as far back as 1906 when injured Negro employees went to Slater Hospital for treatment at company expense. Later such reformers as Lenora H. Sills, Katharine Smith Reynolds and Alice Gray had worked toward the same end. Some time between 1913 and 1919 Dr. Arthur de Talma Valk made regular visits to the crude first-aid stations, especially in Numbers 8 and 256, over which Alice Gray and a Miss Burke presided as nurses. Dr. Valk apparently carried on his private practice at the same time. It is likely that Dr. Wortham Wyatt also did some of this work.[190] When John C. Whitaker began efforts to establish a formal medical department as a division of the employment department, the idea provoked strong opposition from top management. Whitaker requested permission of William N. Reynolds and Robert E. Lasater for Dr. Frederic Moir Hanes to discuss his views on industrial medicine with the directors. With great aplomb Dr. Hanes performed his duty and then complimented the directors on their forward-looking decision to begin a medical department, although no such decision had been made. In his talk Hanes emphasized the fact that the company kept its machinery in good repair and was wise to plan for keeping its employees in good physical condition. Complimented and probably convinced by Hanes's reasoning, the directors soon gave the order to establish a medical department.[191]

Organized on the same day as the employment department, the medical department began its functions with Dr. Sam W. Hurdle as its head, though he also carried on his private practice. About a year later Dr. H. F. Munt joined Hurdle on the same basis, and this dual arrangement continued for some time. A Dr. Langston also served for about three months during this early period. In the latter part of August 1922, however, Dr. Edgar S. Thompson, formerly of the city health department, was employed full time and the department began to function more adequately. Soon one local newspaper pronounced the Reynolds medical system the most advanced "if not the only plan of industrial medicine in the South"—a statement far too sweeping to be strictly true. Its functions, the newspaper continued, included physical examinations to fit employment to physical capacities, prevention of the spread of contagious diseases, administration of first aid, and medical treatment in case of minor ailments.

By 1922 the medical department included not only a full-time physician but also seven trained attendants in charge of as many first-aid stations, a central dispensary, a completely equipped laboratory for physical examinations and analysis of the plant's water supply, a head nurse, clerks to keep records, a trained attendant in charge of the day nursery, and a sanitary inspector for the entire plant. Job applicants were examined and classified into three groups: those accepted, those placed in positions suited to their capacities, and those with defects rendering them unfit for work or a menace to the health of fellow workers. Of the 20,120 people examined during the first year, 17,892 were accepted as full-time workers, 1,538 were classified as special workers, and 690 were rejected. From its beginning to August 1922, the medical department administered smallpox and typhoid vaccines to more than 10,000 employees.

The contribution of the medical department to reduced turnover was proclaimed as a singular accomplishment:[192]

Since that time (August 11, 1919) the (laboring) force has become more stable, the majority of persons involved in the labor turnover being persons who remained with the company only about a month. It was found that those who remained with the company the first six months became a fixture and were either continuously employed or were among the number reinstated after having severed their connection with the company for a period. Before the inauguration of the labor (employment) department, co-operating with the medical department, the turnovers in the plant were variously estimated (there being no actual check up) to 500 per cent. It is now shown by actual records that this condition has been bettered until last year it was a small fraction of what it formerly was.

Because labor turnover stood at 87.7 percent in 1921, such exuberance over its improvement in connection with the medical and employment departments surely gives reason to assume that the situation prior to 1919 was intolerable.

Dr. Thompson, who did not retire until 15 March 1947, was undoubtedly an able administrator and must be considered the builder of the medical department. A graduate of Wake Forest College and New York University, he first came to Winston-Salem in September 1920 to work with the city health department and joined the Reynolds company two years later. In 1924 he installed a dental division in the medical department. From September through December 1924, 555 old patients and 1,088 new ones were treated free of charge. During 1925 the number rose to 3,929 old patients and 2,995 new ones.[193] Dr. Roy C. Fowler, the first dentist, remained with the department a short time and was succeeded in 1926 by Dr. Ralph C. Flowers, whose good work was later vouched for by many who sat in his chair from 1926 to 1936. Dr. Allen Heath Cash followed Dr. Flowers;[194] Cash served until 24 August 1943 when he resigned on account of ill health. Then, because of the wartime scarcity of dentists and because of management's disgust with labor troubles and consequent belief that employees felt no gratitude for the dental service, no other dentist was hired.[195]

On the retirement of Dr. Thompson in 1947, Dr. Richard Wilmot Bunn, trained at Wake Forest College and Temple University, became head of the medical department and long continued in that position. Though the combined services of Dr. Thompson and Dr. Bunn covered a forty-year period (1922–62), the assistant physicians and nurses came and went at a rapid rate. In fact, from its beginning, only two people remained in the department until retirement—Dr. Thompson and Minnie Alice Ashburn, who, after serving as a yeoman, third class, during World War I, worked continuously in the medical department from 22 March 1921 to 1 April 1959.[196] Nevertheless, in view of its beginning the growth of the department was remarkable. Measured in personnel, it advanced by the early 1960s at a greater rate than the increase of employees. The medical department provided free vaccines of various types, an X-ray department, a medical laboratory, ultraviolet equipment, technicians, many first-aid stations, two full-time physicians, and a host of nurses, maids, and clerks.[197] Its value to the company apparently has not been questioned in more recent years.

Despite the several improvements, relations with labor were not easy. In the spring of 1920, Anthony McAndrews and James Brown perfected their organization of Reynolds employees. When the company turned to a recreational program, the hope undoubtedly was to divert the workers from too much interest in the TWIU-AFL. Nevertheless, about one month after the company equipped sixteen baseball teams, a second contract with the union was signed. Apparently the director of the recreational program, Samuel Hardman, was hired about 1 January 1920. An Episcopal rector with experience in directing recreation programs in the United States Army, Hardman began the program under the auspices of the company's athletic association. Prominent among those working in the program were P. Frank Hanes, William O. McCorkle, John C. Whitaker, and Edgar E. Bumgardner.[198] There were picnics, field days, stunts, parades, bands, and dancing in addition to at least twenty-eight baseball teams, organized around workers at Number 65 (stemming), Number 12 (cigarette), Number 256 (smoking), and various other areas.[199]

Possibly the most spectacular event of the program's two-year life (1920 and 1921) was the carnival and parade to introduce it on 15 May 1920. The festivities, naturally held on a Saturday afternoon after work hours, received an enthusiastic description from a local newspaper: "One of the greatest baseball parades and carnivals ever staged in the South was pulled off by the R. J. Reynolds Tobacco Company yesterday afternoon and the event chronicles a new chapter in the history of Winston-Salem industry." Shortly after noon more than 1,000 employees gathered at Chestnut Street for the parade, which formed under the direction of Richard L. Dunstan. Included in the line of march, which went along Main Street to Piedmont Park, were eight baseball teams, employee bands, nurses, clowns, mules, and a camel, followed by two hundred automobiles filled with cheering employees. Most intriguing of the paraders was a simulated donkey with a feather duster for a tail and a banner bearing the words, "I am kicking for No. 12." At the grandstand there was much applause for the queen, Miss Lou Lawrence. Evidently an interminably long program of three baseball games followed. Stunts during intermissions included sack races, a wheelbarrow parade, a camel dance or shimmy, and a mule race between Rich and Waxy, Brown's Mule, Apple, and Humbug. William N. Reynolds served as official starter and W. W. Smoak, Jeff King, and Boris Gordon of New York as judges. It was a gala day. The Negro employees were scheduled to hold a carnival on the following Saturday.[200]

In January 1921, the recreational department purchased an amplifier to be attached to a phonograph so that music for dancing might be heard for several blocks.[201] Ultimately Will Reynolds sold seven lots to the company, to be known as Prince Albert Park, at Liberty and Twelfth streets for the use of a recreational program for Negroes.[202] By that time, however, the program had run its course. Samuel Hardman resigned his position in March 1921, and Edgar E. Bumgardner out of loyalty to the company struggled through the 1921 season as Hardman's successor.[203] Possibly the 20 percent decrease in wages on 2 June 1921 affected the life of the recreational program. At any rate its demise may be regarded as an anticlimactic symptom of the troubled years following World War I.

CHAPTER 9

New Challenges
for Management

The period begun by independence from the old American Tobacco Company and marked by the Camel revolution posed major challenges for Reynolds management. Two events had a dramatic effect: the illness and death of the company's founder and World War I. The first brought changes at the top; the second affected both demand and materials. Increased demand mandated changes and refinements in manufacturing processes. In addition, the company led efforts to lower freight rates and eliminate expensive shipping requirements. The Camel cigarette—one of the most successful tobacco products of all time—brought the firm to financial prosperity; whereas the Smokarol fiasco occasioned an aberrant failure. Such challenges begin and end with the company's leaders.

Changes at the Top

Independence from the old American Tobacco Company is dated from 22 February 1912—a day of jubilee. Quite fittingly the office force began work at the sound of a whistle, timed by Robert E. Lasater's watch, at 8:00 A.M. instead of 7:00 and 7:30 as in former years. One newspaper reported that this momentous step "on the part of the great company" had been taken "without a suggestion . . . by the employees."[1] At this time officers and directors were as follows:

R. J. Reynolds	President
William N. Reynolds	Vice-president
Bowman Gray, Sr.	Vice-president (sales)

Percy R. Masten	Vice-president (sales)
George W. Coan	Secretary
D. Rich	Treasurer
Walter R. Reynolds	General manager, manufacturing department
Joseph D. Noell	Manager, sales department
Robert E. Lasater	Superintendent, Number 256
Henry A. Oetjen	Statutory director, New Jersey

With the exception of William Reynolds, the vice-presidents apparently had few executive duties beyond the supervision of sales, although the directors had decided earlier to have each stock certificate signed by the president or one of the vice-presidents and the treasurer or assistant treasurer.[2] On 1 April 1913 James B. Dyer succeeded Noell on the board of directors and Joseph L. Graham became a director.[3] No other changes occurred among the directors until 20 November 1914, when Percy Masten resigned as of 1 January 1915, a date specifically chosen in order that he might participate in the 1914 payments accruing from his ownership of "A" stock.

Masten's resignation constituted one of the company's first crises after 1912. His letter to that effect, dated 19 November 1914 and accepted the following day, had been requested. According to resolutions passed by the directors, Masten's services were "no longer required," his former duties were to be handled "under the direction of the president" until further arrangements could be made, his duties until 1 January were those of an employee only, and he was "at the disposal of the company for such purposes as he may be called upon to perform." Apparently one reason for the directors' action was that Masten had fraternized too closely with salesmen of the American Tobacco Company.[4] In addition, many years later William T. Smither recalled that early in 1914 Masten had angered Charles A. Kent, then division manager stationed at Memphis, by discharging some of the latter's best salesmen. Consequently, on 11 July 1914 Kent voluntarily resigned and joined the American Tobacco Company. But with Masten's forced resignation, Kent returned to the Reynolds company on 14 December as manager of the southern division of the sales department, as director, and as vice-president. According to Smither and F. F. Cheek, R. J. Reynolds had offered Masten's position to Kent before Bowman Gray, Sr., could reorganize the sales department nationally.

With sales of Prince Albert and Camels increasing steadily, it was necessary to reorganize the sales department on a national basis. Gray apparently did so in 1914 by placing Kent in charge of the Memphis area,

Otho D. Reade in the Omaha area, William E. Howard in the Boston area, Egbert L. Davis in Chicago, and Mitchell Lyon in San Francisco. It thus appears that Gray's move coincided with the return of Kent, and Gray, through his dominance, emerged as head of the sales department.[5]

The minutes of the board of directors reveal other organizational and personnel changes during 1914–16. Walter Reynolds made a motion that D. Rich and George Coan be appointed as a committee to provide facilities for the storage of office stationery and other supplies and select a suitable caretaker. In March 1914, the directors resolved to allow the heads of various departments to contract for the purchase of materials, machinery, and supplies "applicable" to their departments. This proved to be an inappropriate dispersal of authority and one month later a supply or purchasing department was organized with Walter Reynolds as manager and Roy C. Haberkern as assistant manager. In 1915 Robert E. Lasater was named to the newly created position of assistant general manager in the manufacturing department.[6] Also in that year, Memory Eugene Motsinger (23 September 1874–30 March 1959) on 4 March became director and secretary, succeeding George Coan who had resigned during the previous month because of ill health. Perhaps as a portent of things to come, Bowman Gray, Sr., presided over a meeting of the board on 2 September 1915 in the absence of R. J. Reynolds. Finally, the minutes show that a bona fide advertising department was established in April 1916 (see pp. 291–92).[7]

The next series of changes in the company's management and organization were made in response to the illness and death of R. J. Reynolds. The seriousness of his illness became evident early in 1917 when, in the midst of "most pressing matters," he left Winston-Salem for a time in order to find medical help. By October he was under the care of a specialist in Baltimore and his condition was reported as greatly improved. Nevertheless, the following spring he was treated by another specialist in Philadelphia. After major surgery, he was brought home in a private car on 20 July 1918 to die nine days later from cancer of the pancreas.[8] Thus no one was surprised when it was reported that the new president, William N. Reynolds, had for the past year been "in active charge of the company."[9]

Although the evidence is scant, the use of committees seemed to emerge during this period as a means of addressing matters generally handled only by R. J. Reynolds before his illness. In 1917 the Real Estate Committee was referred to as if it had existed for some time. As of 5 April its members were James B. Dyer, Joseph L. Graham, and Robert E. Lasater. This committee experienced difficulties when it took over R. J.'s functions. Evidently R. J. had superintended all matters involving construction and repair, and Earle Mauldin, who headed that department and was a close friend of the Reynolds family, had been accustomed to receiving his orders directly from him. Mauldin made no secret of his resentment at having to report to the newly functioning committee. Ultimately, Will Reynolds as vice-president wrote him that the construction and repair department had been placed under the direct supervision of the Real Estate Committee to which he would report for instructions and approval of all vouchers, with copies going to Lasater and D. Rich. Though Mauldin responded agreeably to this reproof, he did not long remain with the company.[10]

Also on 5 April 1917 the board appointed R. J. Reynolds, D. Rich, Bowman Gray, Sr., Joseph L. Graham, and Memory E. Motsinger to its first finance committee.[11] Obviously only one member of this committee—composed of an expert salesman (Gray), a traffic manager (Graham), a secretary (Motsinger), and a treasurer (Rich)—was capable of assuming the duties of R. J. Reynolds. It will be recalled that R. J. had handled virtually all transactions relating to financing the company, which operated largely on borrowed funds. Rich, though he had been schooled by Reynolds and freely entrusted with borrowing missions in New York, had only a few more working years ahead of him. This fact concerned R. J. during his last illness.

According to his sister-in-law, R. J. Reynolds deliberated at length about the future of the company and, especially, about who would manage its finances. After discussing the question with his wife, he eventually concluded that James A. Gray, brother of Bowman Gray, Sr., and an experienced banker, was the most suitable person for the job. Gray himself later acknowledged that in the spring of 1917 Reynolds had urged him to become associated with the company.[12] Logically James A. Gray should have succeeded to R. J.'s position on the board, but only five days after the latter's death Theodore Hamilton Kirk (20 July 1875–17 September 1960) became a director and vice-president. Accordingly, way had to be made for another director. Supposedly Katharine Smith Reynolds met strong opposition in implementing the wishes of her husband. Finally, on 12 December 1919, Charles A. Kent resigned from the board and on the following day James A. Gray was formally elected a director and vice-president.[13] Just how this maneuvering was accomplished is not known. Kent may have resigned voluntarily in order to make a place for a needed financial officer. In any event, one of the obstacles to Gray's employment involved the amount of A stock that might be made available to him. Katharine Smith Reynolds is generally supposed to have taken care of that problem from her own stockholdings.[14]

However the matter was managed, it proved an excellent move for the company. Gray's own words give the best evaluation of his early work at Reynolds:[15]

On account of my banking experience and public relationships my early duties with the Company were largely confined to the fields of finance and public relations, in addition to a great deal of my time being spent in familiarizing myself with the detailed operation of the Company's business.

Early in 1920 the Reynolds Company owed about $50,000,000.00. It had grown very rapidly in preceding years and had a small capitalization, and because of that rapid growth it had been necessary to borrow very large sums of money; consequently, the question of financing was one that was uppermost in the minds of many executives of the Company and because of my previous experience I was given that as my principal responsibility. Early in 1920 I arranged for a number of new banking connections and secured large lines of credit for the Company, enabling the comfortable handling of the $50,000,000.00 debt.

Following the beginning of the deflation period in the Summer of 1920 and extending into 1921, during which time the price of leaf tobacco fell sharply, the amount of money required to carry its inventories was reduced rapidly and during the Spring, Summer and Fall of 1921 I was actively engaged in arranging for the purchase and liquidation of 6% notes of the Company due in 1922, spending a great deal of time in travel, visiting financial institutions holding these notes and arranging to purchase them. By the end of 1921, of the entire amount of $15,000,000.00 of these notes which had been outstanding, all had been purchased before maturity with the exception of $1,700,000.00, thereby resulting in a large interest saving to the Company.

After the decision of the Supreme Court of the United States in 1920 permitting non-taxable stock dividends to be issued, the Company was in a position to rearrange its capital structure which prior to that time had stood at $10,000,000.00 in Common Stock and $10,000,-000.00 in Class B Common Stock with $20,000,000.00 7% Preferred. The common stocks were selling at high premiums above par and a large part of same was held by stockholders of the old American Tobacco Company. In 1920, with other associates, I was actively engaged in working out the plans whereby $40,000,000.00 was added to the outstanding common capital of the Company through the issuance of a stock dividend in June, 1920, placing the capital structure on a much sounder basis. Then in 1921–22, I, with other members of the Staff, was engaged in arranging at the proper time for the listing of the stocks of the Company on the New York Stock

Exchange, which was effected in March 1922. This, of course, gave a much broader market for the stocks of the Company and was followed throughout succeeding years by a tremendous increase in the number of stockholders of the Company, which widened ownership had furnished a ready market for its stocks to the point that the Company had over 60,000 shareholders.

During this same period and for several years thereafter, I was active with associates in interesting the old American Company's stockholders to make available for employees of the Company their holdings of Common Stock, in many instances through the exchange of their Common for New Class B Common. This encouragement of ownership by employees of the Company in its stocks was carried out by the program initiated by Mr. R. J. Reynolds which had been begun many years before.

In attributing to Reynolds the initiation of this program, which meant so much for the development of the company, Gray reflected his own modesty and dependability. Other duties and responsibilities assigned to him during his early years with the company indicate that Gray's position was similar to that of an administrative vice-president. Successively he became supervisor of the import and export departments. In 1922 he was named a director of the Glenn Tobacco Company (a Reynolds subsidiary); somewhat later he handled matters concerning the extension of credit. The work of Gray until his death in 1952 demonstrates again the extended influence of R. J. Reynolds, who had noted the young banker's ability as early as 1917. Following Gray on the board were James Sloan in 1921; Carl Wainright Harris (22 October 1881–18 December 1937), James W. Glenn, and Roy C. Haberkern in 1923; and S. Clay Williams in 1924. Their contributions will be considered in a later phase of the company's history.

Also of concern to R. J. Reynolds was management of the company's legal and advertising functions. During 1912–24 the law department underwent numerous changes in personnel. Francis Burton Craige, though a member of the Winston-Salem legal firm of Craige and Vogler, devoted most of his time to Reynolds business. Because of poor health, however, he retired in 1916.[16] Meanwhile, much legal work for Reynolds was handled from New York City by Ambrose H. Burroughs, once with the Bonsack Cigarette Machine Company of Lynchburg, Virginia, then with the American Tobacco Company, and in private practice after 1911.[17] In 1916 the company hired Harry Howard Shelton (14 September 1874–26 October 1937) of Bristol, Tennessee, who, like Clement Manly, had been a railroad lawyer. Shelton had served as general counsel for the Virginian and Southwestern Railroad Company, which drew its main revenue from hauling coal from the mining areas of Virginia and West Virginia. At the time he agreed to join Reynolds, he held an important position with the Southern Railway.[18] The employment of S. Clay Williams, mentioned elsewhere, followed that of Shelton by six months. When Shelton resigned as general counsel on 3 March 1921, Williams succeeded him. About 1 June Richard C. Kelly became an attorney for the company, although he resigned two years later to resume private practice.[19]

Ironically, in 1902 R. J. Reynolds had persuaded his nephew Richard Samuel Reynolds, the son of Abram D. Reynolds, to abandon his legal studies at the University of Virginia and join the company. Young Reynolds is reputed to have begun work as his uncle's secretary. From time to time his name appeared as a director of the company, although inconsistently. He was listed in such fashion for the last time on 21 February 1912, near the time of his resignation.[20] In later years Richard S. Reynolds frequently maintained that it was he who originated Prince Albert and the Camel—a claim that aroused the antagonism of William N. Reynolds and possibly others in the company.[21] During 1919–24 Richard Reynolds was again allied with the R. J. Reynolds Tobacco Company in the development of a foil business.

A major departmental initiative was taken two years before the death of R. J. Reynolds. On 18 April 1916, the directors unanimously adopted a resolution to create an advertising department "for the purpose of giving general supervision to the advertising of the Company" by and with the advice and consent of other departments. Such a project had been attempted earlier on a small scale using untrained personnel to promote the production of chewing tobacco. This time there was to be more emphasis on the fine points of advertising and on the national outlook. William Martin Armistead (8 May 1873–5 November 1955), a staff member of N. W. Ayer and Son, was named head of the new department. The move formalized a relationship with Armistead that had existed for six years whereby he had supervised Reynolds advertising by means of frequent visits to Winston-Salem from his Philadelphia headquarters. Armistead directed the advertising department for less than a year; during that time he also seems to have had close ties, if not a position, with the Ayer agency. When he returned to Philadelphia at the end of January 1917, he stated that, by a new arrangement entailing frequent visits to Winston-Salem, there would be no change "in his present pleasant business relations." On 1 January 1918 he became a partner in the Ayer organization.[22] The record does not indicate why Armistead left his post at Reynolds when he did. Certainly there was no break in the company's connection with Ayer at this time. Possibly during the war years Reynolds had less need to advertise extensively, and Armistead's presence became more important in Philadelphia than in Winston-Salem. Apparently after his departure the advertising department became an arm of the sales department.

One phase of Armistead's work while in Winston-Salem ended in failure—the publication of a house organ called the *Open Door*. To edit the publication he employed J. S. Oliver, who had prepared the first issue by 25 June 1916.[23] Oliver resigned after ten months because of the directors' decision to stop publishing the *Open Door*.[24] Whatever the reason for the breakdown of the first formal advertising department, both Armistead and Oliver left at approximately the same time just as the illness of R. J. Reynolds began to affect the operation of the company. A brief analysis of the *Open Door*, which appeared seven times from June 1916 until February 1917, demonstrates the wisdom of the directors in discontinuing its publication. In format it was a four-page newspaper, 16 by 22 inches, published without date. At the time of Oliver's resignation on 22 January 1917, the last number was in press. The editor's verbosity and strong penchant for the use of adjectives was apparent in every issue. Virtually all of the first number urged the salesmen not to be lazy. It included only one item with any possible interest for salesmen, jobbers, and dealers, for whom the publication was intended. This was a reproduction of R. J. Reynolds's first advertisement as it had been published in the Roanoke *Iron Belt*. The second issue carried a long prosy list of aims concerned chiefly with spreading optimism and cheer among its readers, who would probably have preferred news of Reynolds's operations. Repeatedly Oliver explained to dealers the meaning of the title *Open Door* as it applied to the company's dealings with them. The sixth number may be judged in part by titles of articles that it contained: "A Salesman Makes an Interesting Confession," "Making Progress by Making Things Happen Yourself," "Pleasing the Customer Pays Best in the End," and "The Actual Experience of a Green Salesman." The third page of this issue contained a bird's-eye view of the plant and of some separate buildings, furnishing no doubt a happy relief to those supposed to read the publication. In the last number, which Oliver, in his letter of resignation, declared to be superior to any other issue, there were advertisements of several brands of chewing tobacco along with homilies on loyalty, successful salesmanship, frugality, and reasons for the failure of some merchants. All in all, the most interesting item to appear in any issue consisted of brief biographical sketches and pictures of the directors but these also were published in the *Twin City Sentinel* for 1 April 1916.[25]

During this unusually active period perhaps the traffic department carried the greatest burdens—burdens imposed both by the unfair freight rates prevalent in the South of that day and by necessary dependence on railway transportation.

Traffic Problems

Joseph L. Graham, who became official head of the traffic department in 1914, had joined the company eight years earlier on the recommendation of Lincoln Green (30 April 1863–19 June 1940).[26] As in other moves, it was characteristic of R. J. Reynolds to consult expert advice, and surely Lincoln Green as traffic manager of the Southern Railway was well-versed in problems of transportation. In this manner Reynolds obtained a traffic manager who served the company with great vigor and intelligence when railway freight rates were often excessive and no other means of transportation was available.

William H. Joubert states in his study of southern freight rates that the relationship of rates at Winston-Salem and Durham to rates at major Virginia cities "figured prominently in the effort to eliminate discrimination" against these North Carolina points. In 1910 rates on first-class freight from Chicago to Roanoke, a distance of 740 miles, were $0.72, whereas similar rates to Winston-Salem, a distance of 863 miles from Chicago, were $1.28. At the same time, rates from Cincinnati to Roanoke, 466 miles, were $0.62, but from Roanoke to Winston-Salem, only 122 miles, they were $0.61. North Carolina communities brought six complaints before the Interstate Commerce Commission (ICC) in a twenty-two-year period without any noticeable effect. By 1913 sentiment in the state was greatly aroused.[27]

It was during this period that Graham did much of his work for the company. He early won the allegiance of R. J. Reynolds by solving a problem relating to the shipment of smoking tobacco—one that had long baffled the American Tobacco Company.[28] Another of his early feats concerned the Reynolds company's dispute with the Pennsylvania Railroad over shipments of manufactured tobacco to Buffalo—a matter that had plagued the sales department for some time. Through the Norfolk and Western Railway, he arranged to ship goods to Cincinnati, from there to Cleveland, and finally by the back door to Buffalo at a satisfactory rate by virtue of Buffalo's favored position in relation to water rates. When officials of the Pennsylvania awoke to their loss of revenue, they made a fruitless appeal to R. J. Reynolds.[29] In addition to these early spectacular cases, Graham not only kept a careful check on correct freight rates and advised other departments in that respect during a day when shippers appeared to question all freight bills, but he also plunged into the state-wide fight to change unfair freight rates. One of his most vigorous efforts concerned shipping rates on coal.

The coal of the R. J. Reynolds Tobacco Company generally came from the Pocahontas mining district on the Virginia-West Virginia border. Winston and Salem was not on the main line of any railway. Prior to the building of the branch line of the Norfolk and Western to Roanoke, coal was delivered at Lynchburg to the Southern Railway and transported by way of Greensboro to Winston and Salem at a carrying charge of $2.55 per ton. At the completion of the Winston and Salem-Roanoke line, the haul to Winston and Salem was shortened by seventy-five miles and the rate made equivalent to that of Greensboro—apparently $2.30 per ton on coal for industrial use. In 1903 rates to all points on the main line of the Norfolk and Western and to all points on the Winston and Salem division, except to Winston and Salem themselves, were reduced by an average of $0.10 per ton; in some cases, however, the reduction amounted to $0.30 per ton.[30] At the same time rates on coal shipped to Norfolk, Virginia, over the Norfolk and Western were $1.50 per ton, although the distance of Norfolk from the Pocahontas mines was more than twice that of Winston and Salem. Moreover, in 1909 the Reynolds company used 10,000 tons of coal annually (by 1958 that amount gradually had increased to 113,000 tons).[31]

Railroads such as the Chesapeake and Ohio, running west from Newport News, Virginia, and the Norfolk and Western, running west from Norfolk, did not own coal mines in Virginia and West Virginia. Nevertheless, coal companies established by the officers, investors, and promoters of these roads and their associates purchased large holdings of the coal-bearing lands and contracted with the railroads to ship their coal. The matter was further complicated by the Pennsylvania Railroad's purchase of large holdings in the Norfolk and Western and the Baltimore and Ohio. Winston-Salem lay only slightly south of the official freight district but in the southern freight district where competitive patterns characteristic of the Old South prevailed in the lack of alleviation of rates by nearness to water transportation. Moreover, the boundary line between the official and southern freight districts fell slightly south of Roanoke.[32] Actually, as far as shipping rates were concerned, Winston-Salem enjoyed no advantages of any description. To make matters worse, the despised Southern Railway, which had penetrated all the tobacco areas of North Carolina and Virginia, also entered the coal fields.[33] Winston and Salem's only railroad connections were the Southern and the Norfolk and Western, because the Winston-Salem Southbound to Mocksville, Mooresville, and Charlotte—completed in 1910—belonged to the Norfolk and Western and the Atlantic Coast Line. The traditionally ineffective ICC offered little or no relief until passage of the Mann-Elkins Act of 1910, which made the long and short haul requirements enforceable.[34]

Nevertheless, on 22 October 1908 the Winston Board of Trade and the cities of Winston and Salem with Reynolds's lawyers and traffic manager submitted a claim before the ICC. Alleging that the shipping rates on bituminous coal in carload lots from the Pocahontas district to Winston and Salem were unreasonable, they asked not only that the Norfolk and Western be required to establish the same rates to Winston and Salem as those to Norfolk but also that reparations be allowed on earlier shipments. Before this complaint had been reviewed, the Norfolk and Western filed new rates to become effective on 1 December 1908, thereby abolishing the old rates on domestic coal and setting all rates on coal to Durham and Winston and Salem at $2.30 per ton. Letters in Graham's files for 1909 show the Winston-Salem group still awaiting the decision.[35] Eventually, however, the ICC rendered a rather peculiar decision. It held that conditions at main-line points were different from those on the branch lines to the south but that, under the circumstances shown, the rates charged Winston-Salem and Durham on soft coal were unreasonable to the extent that they exceeded $2.10 per ton. Though the commissioners refused reparations, their final judgment perhaps laid the ground for a later suit: "A reasonable reduction in rates on coal to Winston-Salem and Durham would not seriously impair the earnings of the system, and there is evidence tending to show that such reduction would increase consumption." Graham's files contain statements of surprise and disappointment at the decision.[36]

In a letter to Lincoln Green, Graham endeavored to hide his disappointment by regarding the rate of $2.10 as a maximum rate pending an anticipated readjustment to all or part of the southern freight district because of new railroad construction. He called attention to a new Reynolds factory scheduled to be in operation by the fall of 1909 and the necessity for watchfulness over "economics of operation." His colleagues, he said, had expected a material cut in the cost of steam power through a lower coal rate. "Naturally," he wrote, "the question of electric power cost will have more consideration than otherwise especially as new and ample sources of supply will be available." He then intimated that a liberal interpretation of the decision by Green might well result in great material benefit to the Southern Railway.[37] Green in his reply said he felt that the ICC had been reluctant to disturb the existing structure of rates in the Carolina territory. Furthermore, he thought that the latest adjustment had not been reduced because of the entry of the Carolina, Clinchfield and Ohio, a new coal-hauling line from the Coal Creek fields of Tennessee to Charlotte via connections with other lines.[38]

Shortly afterward Graham changed the routing of the Reynolds company's coal to the Southern Railway. He sent a detailed analysis of the situation to the traffic manager of the American Tobacco Company, requesting his opinion. But Charles S. Keene, who had once lorded it over Reynolds's shipping interests, did not feel that his assessment would be of much value because he had not studied all the factors involved. Moreover, he tended to consider the question too difficult to answer.[39] So Graham continued to work on the problem, declaring to the vice-president of the Norfolk and Western in 1912: "We cannot feel content to remain bottled up here, and pay for the short haul on your coal, on the basis of what the Southern Railway feels it should have to support the weaker line from Tennessee, or its divided haul with you, or other lines, from West Virginia."[40]

In 1912 the Winston Board of Trade through its chairman J. L. Ludlow, Graham (chairman of the freight rates committee), and the town of Martinsville, Virginia, prepared to face the ICC. This time they were determined to reduce the cost of hauling coal from the Pocahontas district to $1.50 per ton, the fee charged to eastern Virginia cities. Elaborate hearings were held in Winston on 6 and 8 April. In vain Graham made his points:

1. It was unfair to charge $1.50 per ton for all points on the Norfolk and Western except those in North Carolina where the rate remained $2.10 per ton.
2. It was unfair to increase the rate from $1.30 per ton at Roanoke to $1.75 per ton at Starkey, which was only seven miles south of Roanoke on the road to Winston and Salem but in the southern freight district.
3. It was unfair for the Norfolk and Western to make separate charges, such as for crossing a long bridge, as railroads had done in the past.
4. It was unfair to charge such a high rate for shipping a nonperishable product necessary in industrial and domestic life.
5. It was unfair to claim that a change in rates to Winston and Salem would upset all rates in North Carolina.[41]

In the oral argument that followed, Lincoln Green took exception to Graham's statement that the Southern Railway fought largely under cover of joint counsel with the Norfolk and Western as it had in past cases.[42] Graham replied that Green took the matter too seriously and added: "Perhaps we did so here, but your counsel's rough and tumble work stirred us up. . . . Of course you were the brains of the old defense, and created the Zone Miasma in that case."[43] The fact that Green and Graham were close personal friends did not restrain the latter from putting forth his best efforts in the case, which he lost. His diligence produced a remark from the Norfolk and Western division freight agent in Winston and Salem that Graham's employment with the Reynolds company "depended on getting the coal rate reduced." This Graham denied in a letter to the freight agent's superior, stating that no one in Winston and Salem would stand in the way of the freight agent's advancement to a position elsewhere. He sent copies of this letter to the division freight agent of the Norfolk and Western and to William N. Reynolds.[44]

How much further Graham went with his plans to renew efforts to obtain lower freight rates on coal in 1914 is not clear, but in that year he at least prepared an elaborate petition against the rates of the Southern Railway; the Virginian and Southwestern; the Carolina, Clinchfield, and Ohio; the Louisville and Nashville; and the Norfolk and Western—all involved in hauling or gathering coal. He made a variety of accusations: for example, that the Southern demanded higher charges in North Carolina than in far more distant points in Georgia; that competition had been suppressed by important interests working closely together; that the Southern exercised arbitrary control through its requirements for dividing rates and held coal rates in "a state of petrifaction"; that the Southern continued to maintain rates of $2.30 per ton despite the ICC order of 1909; and that the Louisville and Nashville Railway worked in collusion with the Southern in using a route of 590 miles when a shorter route of 380 miles was available via Jellico and Knoxville.[45]

Meanwhile, there is no indication that either the Norfolk and Western or the Southern failed to profit from their operations. According to the *Wall Street Journal*, in 1909 the Norfolk and Western earned between 10 and 11 percent per year but paid only 5 percent, thus assuring continuance of a higher dividend rate and additions to its property. It was no exaggeration, ran the analysis, to say that the earnings on the stock would be as much as 10 percent. The railroad had been one of the great beneficiaries of the steel works at Gary, Indiana.[46]

It is indeed a wonder that Graham, undoubtedly stirred by Reynolds, even considered fighting such a well-established company as the Norfolk and Western. This situation explains in part why the Southern Railway seemed to prosper in Winston-Salem, although its coal rates were as high as those of the Norfolk and Western. President Fairfax Harrison (13 March 1869–2 February 1938) announced in October 1915 that Winston-Salem's growth in industrial importance was phenomenal and that the business of the southern freight office there was expanding by leaps and bounds. According to him, it had become second only to Atlanta in the amount of business handled. The principal cause of this great increase lay in "the almost unprecedented expansion of the business of the R. J. Reynolds Tobacco Company." In 1917 the *Twin City Sentinel* reported that Winston-Salem stood without an equal in the amount of outgoing freight handled by the Southern. The same condition prevailed in 1922.[47]

Notwithstanding the failure of his previous efforts, the year 1924 found Graham preparing a petition for the Winston-Salem Chamber of Commerce and others requesting the North Carolina Corporation Commission to initiate proceedings before the ICC. His purpose was to prevent various railroad lines from charging higher rates for shipping coal to Winston-Salem and intermediate points to Wilmington, North Carolina,

than to Wilmington itself. This time he strongly urged the North Carolina
commission to act under the auspices of the Federal Transportation Act of
1920. Graham declared that, based on the rates established by the fiction
of water competition, the rates on coal to Wilmington were unfair to the
rest of the state. Even more discriminatory were the rates on coal passing through North Carolina bound for other states. Graham noted that
North Carolina and its various communities had long complained of being charged higher rates than neighboring states for shipments passing
through the state. When the North Carolina legislature proposed improvements for the Wilmington port, Graham rightly held that "more
wharves at Wilmington, in addition to the surplus already there, or more
boats in the tide-water section, could not reduce freight rates on coal to
North Carolina from mines in Virginia, West Virginia, Tennessee, and
Kentucky; and the use of common sense will make that plain to anyone."[48] When Lincoln Green wrote Graham that he wanted a secret meeting with him, Graham replied that he did not know what changes Green
had in mind but that he preferred remaining "on the sidelines for awhile
yet," although he was predisposed to "the distance principle with reasonable grouping or zoning and a fair basic scale modified by a differential
plan to lateral territory where distance is disregarded, as by N. & W. and
Virginian Railways, beyond Roanoke or Atlanta." Because the railroads
had established uniform and lower rates on such heavy commodities as
bricks, fertilizer, cement, and lumber, Graham felt that the same should be
done for coal.[49] Apparently this move resulted in a voluntary downward
adjustment of coal rates by the railroads themselves. Purchasers of coal in
the Winston-Salem area then realized a saving of seventeen to eighteen
cents per ton on shipping costs. According to local papers, Graham obtained this reduction by drafting a careful and factual petition to the
North Carolina Corporation Commission requesting that it take action to
secure this adjustment.[50]

Graham also moved promptly into other fields of traffic management.
One of his early complaints filed before the ICC was against the Southern
Express Company. On 2 November 1912, when a straight overcharge of
forty-two cents per hundred pounds was ordered to be repaid, the case
was dropped on Graham's motion.[51] In a 1915 complaint, Graham was
joined by the American Tobacco Company in attacking excessive charges
of the Louisville and Nashville Railway for transporting Burley leaf to
Winston-Salem and nearby locations. A ruling favorable to both companies followed elaborate hearings and argument of the case before the ICC.
Reynolds secured a reduction of approximately twelve cents per hundred
pounds for shipments from Kentucky to Winston-Salem at a time when
the company annually purchased about 25,000,000 pounds of Burley leaf,
one third of which was being transported via the Louisville and Nashville.

That railway had shipped the leaf by its longest route when it could have used one 30 percent shorter.[52] A substantial saving also resulted in 1915 from a suit against the Norfolk and Western for overcharges of six cents per hundred pounds on heavy glass jars (for smoking tobacco containers) shipped from Pittsburgh. In this case Graham won a reduction in rates and reparations with interest for three years.[53]

In another case involving the Norfolk and Western, the company diverted thirty-one carloads (1,667,733 pounds) of tinfoil from its usual water-and-rail route via the Old Dominion Steamship Company and the Norfolk and Western because of labor troubles. No commodity rate existed for the diverted shipment via the Pennsylvania Railroad and the Norfolk and Western. Graham requested a rate of fifty-five cents per hundred pounds—eight cents higher than charges by rail and water. The Pennsylvania Railroad and the Norfolk and Western, which shared the shipment, agreed on the basis of the forty-seven-cent rail-and-water charge, although the bill submitted for the shipment was made at a rate of eighty-three cents per hundred pounds. Settlement of this case found Graham and S. Clay Williams arguing before the ICC against Burton Craige who represented the Pennsylvania Railroad. Reynolds won reparations on the basis of fifty-five cents per hundred pounds at a time when tinfoil moved from New York to Richmond, Virginia, at the rate of twenty-eight cents per hundred.[54] No saving was too small to be ignored. During the same period Graham won a refund from the Southern Railway and others for unreasonable charges on four carloads of packing boxes forwarded from New Haven, Connecticut, in November and December 1916.[55] More exceptional than any of these cases was the Reynolds suit against telegraph companies for charging at the rate of one word for each figure transmitted over the wire. It was Graham's contention that single figures should be treated as letters and not as words.[56]

But far more important was the fiberboard case (*R. J. Reynolds Tobacco Company v. Abilene and Southern Railway Company*), which ended in a historic decision benefiting the entire cigarette industry. Graham, assisted by Bunyan S. Womble, presented a complaint before the ICC attacking all the major U.S. transportation lines, with some 510 railroad and steamship lines as respondents. It was a pioneering move more befitting an old, well-established cigarette manufacturer than one who had been in the business only two years.

When the Reynolds complaint was filed in 1915, with a few unimportant exceptions, first-class rates could be obtained from carriers only if cigarettes were packed in wooden boxes secured by wooden, iron, or wire straps and by a cord around the center passed in and out through every board of the four sides of the box. Moreover, the cord had to be tightly drawn and fastened with a metal seal bearing identification marks. The use of fiberboard, pulpboard, or strawboard was permitted at first-class rates only in the western freight district but requirements were strict. The combined length, breadth, and depth of such packages had to measure not less than thirty inches or they were subject to twice or three times the first-class rate of freight. Specifications in the southern freight district requiring that all fiberboard packages weigh fifteen pounds had been eliminated on complaint of the railroads.

In the period immediately following the Reynolds complaint—between 1 October 1915 and 1 January 1916—all carriers amended their regulations for the shipment of cigarettes in fiberboard containers. Among the outstanding changes, first-class rates would apply provided the package was secured with two or more metal straps "not less than 29 gauge and not less than three-eighths inch in diameter, encircling the package at least once around the end and once around the side, and drawn taut to prevent slipping." The ends of the strap were to pass through a metal sleeve and be crimped at intersections at the crossings. On fiberboard boxes exceeding twenty-four inches in length, metal straps were to be no more than twelve inches apart. To add to these expensive requirements, the western and southern freight districts demanded that first-class rates be applied to cigarettes in standard-sized containers constructed with four flaps on each end, the flaps overlapping each other two inches or more. In addition, the flaps were to be secured by staples not more than two inches apart. The ICC's Uniform Classification Committee promised to make these varying requirements uniform.

Reynolds had a definite reason for bringing suit to force changes in these requirements. Before promulgation of the new rules the company did not generally use fiberboard packing cases because of the expensive requirements involved. Earlier in 1915, however, it had made plans to use fiberboard packing cases extensively in order to economize on storage space, packing expenses, and freight charges. This decision prompted the company's effort to eliminate the burdensome restrictions on packaging. In the complaint, Graham argued that when the cigarette industry was in its infancy it was not difficult to strap, cord, and seal the few cases needed, but by 1915, with millions of cigarettes being shipped and 90 percent of them being made by four companies, the burden had become heavy. It was wrong, he declared, to require the expenditure of several thousand dollars per year in order to assure the carriers a saving of a few dollars. Attorneys representing the three freight districts contended that packing cases with mere pasted flaps might easily be opened by thieves. To this Graham replied that the Reynolds company had obtained a ruling from the North Carolina Corporation Commission permitting shipment in the state of standard fiberboard packages and that they had proved satisfactory. Moreover, smoking tobacco had long been shipped in fiberboard boxes at the same rate as in wooden boxes, and no special precautions were required for such items as liquor, candy, and firearms.

The ICC ruled on the side of common sense: fiberboard, pulpboard, and strawboard packages might be shipped without being "strapped and sealed, or fastened with staples or stitched with wire at all openings, or subjected to other such requirements" in order for the shipper to obtain first-class rates.[57] Thus by winning the suit Reynolds produced a vital change in regulations—a revolution in packing methods. One of the few valuable items to appear in the *Open Door* sums up the importance of the case: "This is a signal victory for the R. J. Reynolds Tobacco Company and forcefully illustrates the aggressive policy that has enabled them to make great progress. Other shippers of cigarettes in the United States will benefit from this decision because of the foresight and efforts of the Reynolds Company. This case, and the decision rendered, will be the means whereby cigar shippers will also soon obtain additional relief."[58]

One other accomplishment of Graham is noteworthy. In April 1916, he returned from Washington with the news that Winston-Salem would become a port of entry—the largest in the South, he estimated, except New Orleans, St. Louis, and Tampa. A subcustoms house station would also be established. With the help of Senator Furnifold McLendell Simmons (20 January 1854–30 April 1940), arrangements were completed with the Treasury Department before Graham returned home and the measures were adopted by Congress on 16 June 1916.[59] Enthusiasm over this new accomplishment produced praise for Graham, exultation over Winston-Salem's new position in the shipping world, and possibly some exaggerated claims for its future value. Approximately one year later, the editor of the *Winston-Salem Journal* reviewed the progress of the inland port in most flattering terms:[60]

When Mr. J. L. Graham, traffic manager for the R. J. Reynolds Tobacco Company, first began his efforts to have a Port of Entry and Port of Delivery established in Winston-Salem, a number of the State papers took it as a huge joke and greatly enjoyed the wit they were able to display on Winston-Salem, located on Tar Branch, being a world Port of Entry. They roared when Mr. Graham stated that he thought it would develop into a million and a half port, meaning that this amount would be paid the United States government in customs duties during a year.

That Mr. Graham spoke truer than the papers knew and that he has been enabled to get the last "laugh" has been demonstrated by recent facts, one that Winston-Salem has a million and a half dollar port, that this port heads the list of all inland ports in the United States, that this port, with the report of the first year after it was established, will take the position of seventh or eighth in the United States, either inland or seaport, and that the port in the Twin-City will pay more in customs duties than the combined revenue from the seventeen ports in all the surrounding States of Virginia, Tennessee, Georgia and South Carolina.

Although the Winston-Salem port is a branch of the Wilmington port, under Col. Walker Taylor, collector of ports of North Carolina, and probably necessarily so, because of Wilmington's location on the coast and for other reasons, according to the report of the Secretary of the Treasury for the year ending June 30, 1916, the Winston-Salem port paid in customs duties about as much duty in an average three days of last month as the Wilmington port paid all of the last fiscal year.

President Wilson signed a treasury order on April 26, 1916, authorizing the establishment of the Port of Entry, which provides for receiving goods from other ports in the United States for distribution here. On June 16, an act was passed by Congress authorizing the establishment of a Point of Delivery which allows the shipment of goods from any point in the world direct to the Winston-Salem port, where they can remain in a bonded warehouse until they are needed and called for, being delivered upon receipt of the customs duties, which are fixed and collected here.

The principal items received at the Port of Delivery in this city are sugar, licorice, foreign tobaccos and cigarette papers, most of which are used by the R. J. Reynolds Tobacco Co. in the manufacture of tobacco. Other tobacco concerns of the city have now commenced to use the port, however, and for several months the Vick Chemical Co. of Greensboro, has been using it. Other cities in this section of the State and still other firms of the city are expected to begin using the Port more than they have in the past.

The port is in charge of Deputy Collector S. F. Highsmith, who has his office in the Federal building, while C. F. Morrell is in charge of the bonded storage warehouse on East Fifth Street, at the Norfolk and Western crossing.

Mr. Highsmith's report of collections from June, 1916, during which month the port was established, up to last month, is as follows:

June	-	$ 80,885.74	December - $	119,989.01
July	-	61,925.52	January -	122,877.17
August	-	96,133.29	February -	119,073.07
September -		129,284.52	March -	128,961.73
October	-	133,505.99		
November -		134,688.20	Total -	1,071,824.24

As will be seen the collections for the last six months amount to $754,095.17, or more than half of the amount in half of a year to make a million and a half dollar port, the first three or four months during which the port was being established and beginning to receive shipments, not being a fair basis for the year. While this port is in its infancy, it is practically sure, judging by the growth of everything else in the city during the past year or two, that it will be a two million dollar port within another year.

Even with the present basis, the local port will forge fast ahead of Seattle and Galveston, probably ahead of Detroit, in close range of Baltimore, and not far behind Tampa, according to the report of the Secretary of the Treasury for these ports for the fiscal year ending June 30, 1916. . . .

An interesting side feature of this port is that during the past few months probably a hundred carloads of sugar have been loaded and sealed in cars in the interior of Cuba, brought to Havana, placed on barges for Key West, brought up the Florida East Coast railroad to Jacksonville, taken up by the Southern Railway and brought on to Winston-Salem, within six to eight days, and the original seal is broken at the Winston-Salem Port of Entry, where the sugar is unloaded, appraised, the duty fixed and it is stored until needed by the manufacturers.

Significantly, a building of the R. J. Reynolds Tobacco Company on Fifth Street by the Norfolk and Western Railway tracks served as the bonded warehouse. Although bonded by the company, it could be used by other manufacturers and businesses, apparently by a special arrangement made through Senator Simmons.[61] For the Reynolds company this move represented a great savings in warehouse and shipping charges. In addition, the payment of customs duties was not required until the seals on shipments were broken, thus enabling the company to defer payment until materials were needed—a boon to a company constantly short of capital.

It is difficult to estimate the value of Graham's work for Reynolds or even to determine his most outstanding service. Litigation over the fiber-board shipping cases appears most spectacular. On the other hand, his constant drive to reduce shipping rates on coal resulted in some success, though it was perhaps more important in arousing the business interests of North Carolina to greater effort on the problem. He steadily called attention to the fact that exorbitant freight rates discriminated against the South, a practice generally regarded as a hindrance to the development of industry in that area. It is more than likely, however, that establishment of the port of entry, copied by Durham four years later, proved of greatest advantage to the company. S. Clay Williams declared in 1943: "Joseph L. Graham was one of a number of individuals that Mr. R. J. Reynolds and others at the top of the company at the time regarded as a 'find' for Reynolds Tobacco Company. He was a natural traffic man. . . . He was one of the best informed freight rate and traffic men I have ever had any exposure to, and a man who did for Reynolds Tobacco Company an outstanding job of solving the increasingly important problems in traffic."[62] On his retirement in 1928, Graham was succeeded by Louis Franklin Owen (23 December 1871–23 May 1954). Clearly his path had been smoothed by Graham's extraordinary work, which came during a period of rapid expansion demanding improved manufacturing processes.[63]

Expansion and Changes in Manufacturing

The expansionary period of 1912–24 was marked by new acquisitions, facilities expansion, new machinery, and important patents and inventions. One striking move during these years was the acquisition of Ogburn, Hill & Company, the N. D. Sullivan Company, and Bailey Brothers. This left Reynolds in control of virtually the entire Winston-Salem tobacco manufacturing industry, which once had constituted many separate firms.

First and perhaps most important of the firms to be acquired was Ogburn, Hill & Company, which became the property of the Reynolds company on 19 September 1912 at a price to be determined by an inventory. At the time of sale it was operated by Charles Jackson Ogburn (6 May 1842–14 November 1927) and Charles DeWitt Ogburn (25 October 1861–21 August 1947). Formed in 1878 by Charles J. Ogburn of Forsyth County and William Poindexter Hill (8 October 1847–30 January 1920) of Stokes County, the firm prospered steadily on Old Town Street in Winston. When Charles D. Ogburn was admitted on 1 January 1884, the partners erected a five-story brick plant on Cherry Street and occupied it the following November. Within four years Ogburn, Hill & Company produced at least seven well-known brands: Dixie, Drummer,

Eagle, Gold Leaf, Minnie Ogburn, O. H. & Company's Choice, and Winston Leader. By that time its operations required a distinct division of labor: Charles J. Ogburn attended to the buying and prizing, Hill to the grading of leaf, and Charles D. Ogburn to the office.[64] Evidently the firm continued to prosper in a modest way until 23 August 1912, when a fire destroyed a part of the plant. Thereupon Charles J. Ogburn, the senior member, decided to retire and, because his cousin and partner (Charles D. Ogburn) did not wish to buy his interest, sold the stock of manufactured goods, brands, and goodwill to the R. J. Reynolds Tobacco Company. Of the twenty-five brands manufactured in 1903 eight were mentioned in the bill of sale, indicating perhaps that Reynolds considered them as the only ones of any marked value. Several of the Ogburn-Hill brands remained on the Reynolds price lists for many years.[65]

Reynolds purchased the N. D. Sullivan Company of nearby Walkertown in 1919. Established in 1858 by Nathan D. Sullivan (d. 14 February 1910), this firm long gave employment to a substantial number of people in the Walkertown area, but by 1919 it apparently had come to be of little importance. The Reynolds company paid only $4,000 for the firm's business, goodwill, machinery, trade secrets, and at least ten brands: Sullivan's Best, Sullivan's Free and Easy, Sullivan's 11 Inch Threes, Sullivan's Natural Leaf, Sullivan's No. 1, Sullivan's Three Break, Good Enough, Hard to Beat, Our Own, and T. C. D.[66]

Five years later Reynolds made what appears to have been its last acquisition of this type. The firm of Bailey Brothers was established in Winston in 1880 by Mumford DeJournett Bailey (18 November 1846–5 January 1929) and his brother Phillip N. Bailey (d. 22 June 1905), who came from Statesville where they had also manufactured chewing tobacco. Erecting a substantial brick building in 1882, the Baileys by 1888 manufactured some twelve or fifteen regular brands and several special brands with an annual output of 300,000 pounds. Later J. K. Bailey (d. 25 May 1890), Phillip Scott Bailey (10 February 1881–25 October 1961), and others joined the company. By 1903 Bailey Brothers produced thirty-nine different brands, but in 1924, when the firm was purchased by the R. J. Reynolds Tobacco Company, only twenty brands of chewing tobacco, two brands of smoking tobacco, and two brands of cigarettes were listed in the bill of sale. It was auctioned in a bankruptcy sale at $337,754.14; the Reynolds company became the owner on 4 September 1924.[67] Aside from several brands and other property, Reynolds obtained a power plant or boiler room containing a one-hundred-horsepower Erie City Steam Boiler, one Westinghouse generator, and power transmission equipment. This might well have been a factor in the decision to turn the Bailey factory into what has since been referred to as the Bailey Power Plant—long the company's main source of power.[68] According to one story, which illustrates the canny mind of R. J. Reynolds, he left a bricked-in door in one of his own buildings next to the Bailey plant, expecting in due time to take over that firm, remove the bricks from his factory, and thereby have a direct entry into the Bailey building.[69]

These acquisitions in many ways were of small consequence, but this was not true of increasing production. Production of chewing tobacco reached its peak about the time of R. J. Reynolds's death, but it continued to be of great importance until after the depression of 1929. Furthermore, there was scarcely any break in the rapidly increasing production of cigarettes and smoking tobacco from 1912 to 1924. Actually the problem of keeping up with demand confronted management simultaneously with the change in leadership, the scarcity of materials during World War I, and the labor problems of the same period. The situation was well described by the leading tobacco journal of the day:[70]

> Keeping pace with a progressive demand, the increase of production, in a single year, extends into billions. Camel cigarettes are so immensely popular.
>
> Presented in figures, the facts are stupendous.
>
> The number of Camel cigarettes manufactured in 1915 exceeds the output for the previous year by 1,822,455,670.
>
> Placed end on end, the Camels consumed during the past twelve months would reach from the earth to the moon and extend nearly 40,000 miles beyond.
>
> A year's production of Camels, making a ribbon of cigarettes 279,-500 miles long would girdle the globe at the equator almost eleven times.
>
> Such a tremendous output, achieved in the third year, shows the developed ability of the R. J. Reynolds Tobacco Co. But the cigarette production, amazing as it is, represents only part of the activity of the great manufacturing company in Winston-Salem. Prince Albert smoking tobacco, a brand that attained world wide distribution long ago, has gained in output, wonderfully, in recent years. For the five years following 1910, the output of Prince Albert smoking tobacco was 31,629,091 pounds more than the production for the preceding five years.
>
> The demand for the greater Reynolds products constantly increases. To supply the demand, facilities must be amplified continually.

To enumerate the buildings erected during these years would be futile. The editors of *Tobacco*, when commenting on the growth of the business in 1916, noted that ten major buildings were added to the plant from 1913 through 1916. Most important of these no doubt was Number 12 at Chestnut and Third—the center for cigarette production until completion of the Whitaker Park plant in 1961. Of reinforced concrete and steel and six stories high, the building planned "to be known as 'Number 12'" was erected by the National Fireproofing Company of Pittsburgh. One year later it was decided to double its size.[71] More intriguing, however, was the announcement in 1914 of plans for a building "to be peculiarly constructed according to scientific principles for conditioning the leaf tobacco used in the manufacture of Prince Albert smoking tobacco."[72] The nature of the scientific principles incorporated in this ten-story building with a capacity of 3,400,000 pounds of leaf tobacco is not known, but it may be assumed that something out of the ordinary had been learned about the storage and preservation of Burley leaf.

During this period of steady expansion, the editor of the *Union Republican* observed that two additional buildings, one near the union station and one at the corner of North Cherry and Seventh streets, meant more people with jobs. "Hence," he added, "the pride of Winston-Salem is its manufacturing enterprises, the greatest of which is the R. J. R. Tobacco Co., with its thousands of employees."[73] In most cases J. E. Sirrine and Company of Greenville, South Carolina, was the architect. Soon after World War I, the Libby-Owens Glass Company offered to build an experimental factory for Reynolds using glass bricks (a method developed in Germany), guaranteeing to replace them if they were not acceptable. This was Number 91. The newfangled building proved unsatisfactory at first as the bricks cracked from expansion and contraction due to extremes in temperature. At length James Thomas Solomon (b. 16 October 1888), head brick mason in Reynolds's construction department, devised a method for laying the bricks so that expansion and contraction would have no effect on them.[74]

By 1919, the area around the factories had become so congested that the Department of Public Safety closed a section of Chestnut Street between Second and Third streets during the daily lunch hour to eliminate the danger from automobiles.[75] Somewhat earlier Reynolds employed almost 10,000 people in 121 structures, the majority of which were located in downtown Winston-Salem. In the building program for these years it is evident that the company intended by 1920 to erect a new office building at Main and Fourth streets, at that time the location of the city hall. When called upon to verify this report, William N. Reynolds bitterly denied that the company had any such plans, declaring that it was unfortunate that those creating the rumor had not consulted with Reynolds officials first.[76] Nevertheless, the structure was completed only nine years later.

Meanwhile, new machinery dictated new skills and new approaches for Reynolds employees. The old-style mechanic had to know all machine jobs; he had to be able to take a machine apart, diagnose its troubles, devise needed parts, and reassemble it. During these years mechanics gradually learned to handle specific jobs and to stand idle when their particular line of work was not needed. Some felt that this shift affected morale, but the day of the specialist was coming.[77]

Symptomatic of the interest in new types of machinery was the "manufactured weather" developed by means of the Carrier equipment purchased by Reynolds in 1916. This equipment produced "automatic humidity" from the work of valves, air motors, dampers, water heaters, and the like. According to the terms of the sale, it would provide "a humidifying, air making, and ventilating system for the entire second and third floors, containing about 8,300 square feet in floor area, and the Turkish room on the fifth floor containing about 11,000 square feet in floor area. All located in our building No. 12."[78] These efforts to maintain a uniform temperature in certain areas were based on concern for the leaf—not the workers. Four years later Lewis J. Brown, the company's chief engineer, wrote that compressed air was used to remove the tobacco dust from motors and automatic machines. Gumming and clogging were ended by a fine jet of compressed air, and the machines could run with little interruption. In the same manner, compressed air helped blow away air while quick drying paste was setting. Brown also found compressed air useful for spraying liquids on leaf in order to condition dry tobacco. But its primary use was to blow the tops of Prince Albert cans off the die. As Brown put it, it was an ill wind that would not work both ways as "the sheets of tin used in making the cans are picked up by means of uncompressed air, or a vacuum."[79] Perhaps equally important as an indication of the company's growing ability to utilize advanced machinery was the work of its neighbor, the Briggs-Shaffner Company, which in 1913 obtained a license to build and sell the Quester tobacco cutter, a complicated machine.[80]

The purchase and care of machinery were not the company's only concerns at the time when consumption of chewing tobacco was near its height. When J. H. Bailey, a salesman in Georgia, sent Walter R. Reynolds a plug of Sweepstakes nine years old but in a perfectly preserved state, Reynolds acknowledged the receipt, age, and condition of the plug but urged Bailey to bear in mind that the company made tobacco to sell, not to keep. At that time Winston-Salem claimed second place as a tobacco center, with St. Louis in first. In a few years it expected to take the lead, although the Reynolds company was working "in strong rivalry with the American Tobacco Company."[81] When the Mengel Box Company prepared to begin operations in the northern part of town, R. J. Reynolds purchased 2,500 acres of timberland in eastern North Carolina to guarantee a plentiful supply of wood for caddies.[82] It did not seem that cigarettes were on his mind as he assigned various Reynolds officials the task of maintaining quality control of specific chewing tobacco brands. D. Rich, who was in charge of Reynolds Sun Cured, told Walter Reynolds that it was not up to par—but in vain. So, with R. J. in the judge's seat, the three of them chewed the brand together to determine who was right. When the case was decided in favor of Rich, all Reynolds Sun Cured made during previous days was called in from the jobbers.[83]

Walter Reynolds tried numerous plans to improve the packing of chewing tobacco in order to prevent the slick surface of the plug which touched the wood of the caddy, one being the J. H. Scott patent in which James B. Dyer owned a half interest and another, the invention of L. C. Swaim, an employee of the firm. According to John H. Peddicord, long connected with the manufacture of chewing tobacco, the problem was next attacked by using crinkled tin sheets in the pot mills—a promising plan until it was seen that final pressure in the caddies slickened the plugs again. Eventually Peddicord and Aaron W. Cornell, Jr., of the Mengel Box Company, designed a caddy with crinkles in the wood at the top and bottom. This, however, became unnecessary when plugs were wrapped in cellophane.[84] In an attempt to improve the chewing tobacco itself, Walter Reynolds in 1914 obtained a pound sample of pure chicle; he seemed disturbed that conditions in Mexico made the future supply uncertain,[85] although any combination of chicle and tobacco sounds unlikely. In the same year, as he wished to perfect the fittings for a new machine room, Reynolds sought the advice of Charles A. Penn, of the American Tobacco Company, on the use of overhead drive shafts versus direct motors for plug machines. Penn did not advise overhead drive shafts but urged Reynolds to install the Maxwell plug machines in preference to the Adams. Reynolds's reply indicates astonishing development of mechanical ability and judgment in the company: ". . . with reference to the Maxwell Plug Machines, beg to say that the cost of these would be slightly more than the cost of the Adams Machines, as we build them ourselves. . . . Furthermore, we believe that the end movement when all is closing in the Adams Machine is a desirable feature and one which it would be difficult to apply to the Maxwell machine."[86] Not only could the company's mechanics build the complicated Adams machines but they could also build their own shapes for use in prizing plug.[87]

Despite the increasing ability of the Reynolds mechanics, there was notably little change in methods of manufacturing chewing tobacco after the adoption of the Adams machine, although there were many annoyances in its production and sale. One problem concerned the ordering of labels for chewing tobacco, which was complicated by the great number of brands produced. In 1917, for example, Walter Reynolds ordered 200 million labels for Brown's Mule, 100 million for Apple Sun Cured, and only 40 million for the old favorite Schnapps. Later, however, Roy C. Haberkern purchased a few additional tags for Schnapps.[88] It is surprising that mechanics who could build machinery such as the Adams duplex press did not fabricate the simple little tin labels that were used by the millions. Possibly they lacked a knowledge of lithography, a deficiency that R. J. Reynolds at one time planned to correct in order to save money on tin for Prince Albert cans. Building Number 4, one of the earliest reinforced concrete structures if not the first erected by the company, was intended to be a lithographing plant, but because of the great demand for Camels and the scarcity of building materials during World War I it was used for the manufacture of cigarettes.[89]

Minor annoyances cropped up from time to time. In 1920 mold in the wrapped plug and poor packing of the Cup brand caused trouble in the Strater Brothers plant in Louisville. It was determined that the amount of alcohol used in the casing had been insufficient. In addition, the foreman did not know how to handle plugs already attacked by mold.[90] Because of the problem, Senator Furnifold M. Simmons could not obtain his favorite brand of plug while on his spring vacation in New Bern, North Carolina.[91] Long remembered in the company was the more spectacular but less credible complaint of a chewer in Tennessee who claimed he had found a Negro's finger in his Brown's Mule. But he was willing to forgo all the misery and horror he had experienced in return for a small box of Schnapps. Moreover, he would return the finger. Burton Craige's sedate reply emphasized the cleanliness of the Reynolds factories and suggested that the aggrieved man send the finger; the company would then send him a two-pound box of Schnapps.[92] Nevertheless, the volume of chewing tobacco produced from 1912 to 1924 rose steadily in all but four years.

Problems of the same nature accompanied the continued production of smoking tobacco. Foreign matter found in two cans of Prince Albert proved to be pistol cartridges. "How it got there nobody seems to know," wrote Richard H. Wright in 1914 when trying to sell his automatic scales to the company. As he explained:[93]

Reynolds is suspicious that some person desirous of injuring his brand managed to slip these cartridges in a can of tobacco. How he did it Reynolds has no means of knowing. It was reported to Reynolds that one of these cartridges went off in the pipe of a smoker, the smoker not having detected the cartridge going into the pipe when he was filling it with tobacco, and while smoking the heat of the fire exploded the cartridge and did considerable damage. Two instances of this kind have been reported to Reynolds, and he says if there were any means of preventing anything of this character going through our scales he would just as soon have them as Patterson's [Rufus L. Patterson of the American Machine and Foundry Company].

This was *foreign matter* of a different type, not merely the result of a fictitious complaint from a small-time cheater who wanted a free box of Schnapps.

Refinement of mechanical processes in the production of smoking to-bacco revolved largely around the work of Hans F. Richter (18 January 1878–19 March 1917). Richard Wright's chief mechanic pronounced Richter an "A. 1 mechanic, engineer and inventor" even though Richter had just made a decision opposing the mechanic's wishes.[94] When Richter died in 1917, he was described by Walter Reynolds as the manager of the tin-box shop and master mechanic for all company departments. He also "manufactured many of our special machines, and looked after the upkeep of practically all of our automatic machinery in all the plants," continued Reynolds in another letter.[95] Born at Annaberg in the Chemnitz section of Saxony, Germany, Richter arrived in New York on 12 September 1902. He lived there for five years, then joined Briggs-Shaffner Company in Winston. He was hired by Reynolds in 1910.[96] On the day of Richter's death D. Rich remarked that the company was much poorer than it had been the day before and that this tragedy had robbed the company of a very valuable man.[97] Many years later Edward Thompson Sims (b. 24 May 1888) stated that Richter had invented numerous improvements on the tin-box-making machines, built most of the Prince Albert machines, and installed all the conveyor work in the plant.[98]

Among his inventions at Reynolds were a machine for assembling bodies of cans and their tops, a match holder to be attached to the bottom of a tobacco can, a machine for affixing stamps to metal boxes, an im-proved machine for forming hinges on sheets of metal (in reality, slots for the insertion of pivot pins when attaching the top of a can to the body), and an automatic box-feeding mechanism for a bead-forming arrange-ment (that is, a machine to assure the proper position of a partially com-pleted tobacco can in relation to the beading dies). All of these machines were patented—some in foreign countries.[99] The stamping machine ap-pears to have been of no particular value to the company. But the auto-matic box-feeding device for a bead-forming machine operated with great economy. Usually such machines were fed by hand; any slight carelessness of the operator could result in improperly beaded boxes, which were then either discarded or straightened by hammering out the incorrect bead and once more put through the machine—a wasteful procedure either way. Richter's invention made improper beading impossible by ejecting—without defacement—any boxes not in proper position. The bead on the can, a running indentation near the top, strengthened the box, provided a scotch for the top, and made it easier to stack the cans for display. Of Richter's box-feeding device and cover fastener, Burton Craige wrote:[100]

> The cover fastener is the invention of Mr. Richter. The automatic feed is also his invention, but the beader was devised by a former employee of this Company whose rights have not been assigned to us, with the exception of shop rights, which I take it are incident to the employment of a mechanic whose duties are to perfect and improve our machinery.

> We wish to be completely protected on the cover fastener and on the automatic feed. The Beader has very little commercial value without the automatic device for feeding it invented by Mr. Richter.

Richter's coupon dropper evidently worked in conjunction with the cover fastener mentioned by Craige. The praise given it by the crusty Richard Wright, who seldom admired any machinery except his own, is sufficient in itself to indicate Richter's great value to the company:[101]

> . . . while in Winston yesterday I saw Reynolds' new device for dropping in coupons and closing the lids. It is simply a crackerjack. It has ours skinned a mile. He says he wouldn't have ours as a gift, and I don't blame him after seeing his. Richter got it up for him. It only takes up about 18″, no turn style, no crushing of tins, no breaking off of lids of tins, simple, accurate, positive and will probably not cost over $50.00 or $75.00 to build.

It is no wonder that, five days after the death of Hans Richter, Walter Reynolds wrote: "We have suffered a great loss in the death of our Mr. H. F. Richter." Reynolds noted that during his illness Richter was treated "by the best Doctor here" and by "a Specialist from Baltimore," the latter evidently brought in by the company. "We haven't a man in the organization whom we deem fitted to succeed him," Reynolds declared.[102] It is reasonable to suggest that the company's greatly accelerated production during the early years of Prince Albert and the Camel could not have been accomplished without Richter's help.

Walter Reynolds began his search for Richter's successor on the eve of the last illness of R. J. Reynolds and of the country's entry into World War I. The man who eventually took his place, Charles V. Strickland, though an able mechanic, was hired without any enthusiasm on the part of the company. Then fifty years old, Strickland had once worked for the American Tobacco Company; apparently while in its employ, he had contributed to the success of Rufus L. Patterson's Automatic Packing and

Labeling Machine and had developed a stemming machine of sorts. From time to time American had sent him on inspection trips to see what Reynolds was doing to improve mechanical operations.

As the new supervisor of the tin-box shop and Number 65 machine shop, Strickland was immediately assigned the task of cutting costs in the former.[103] Economy was badly needed if the 250 tons of scrap tin accumulated from April to August 1914 was a fair sample of waste in that department. Furthermore, the scrap was sold to a Rotterdam firm at $12.75 per ton with a 10 percent discount to the agent.[104] According to Strickland, this waste was eliminated by elevating the conveyor belt that ran beside the seaming machines and on which the operators, on a piece-work basis, would slide their damaged cans. Sixty people reworked those cans in the basement until Strickland elevated the conveyors and changed their direction to the floor above so that damaged cans could no longer be hidden on the conveyor. He also placed an identifying mark on the cans in order to trace them back to the operator. These changes almost eliminated the work of repairing cans. In another innovative move, he hooked three machines together so that the cans could be shaped, seamed, and have their bottoms fastened on from above almost simultaneously.[105]

To his credit, Strickland developed both a machine for inserting pivot pins to hold the top to the can, serving at the same time as a hinge, and a machine for attaching bottoms to cans. The latter permitted the operator to feed in the bodies of the cans with one hand and the bottoms with the other while moving one foot to clamp the bottom on the can. "With this machine," ran the letters patent, "the workman can fit together can bodies and bottoms of a large number of cans with ease and rapidity."[106] During the same period it appears that George H. Little (18 July 1886–3 October 1950) also contributed to the process of applying box tops to smoking tobacco cans.[107] It thus seems likely that by 1924 the arduous work of making tin boxes for smoking tobacco had become as automatic as the production of smoking tobacco itself.

Improvements in the manufacture of cigarettes between 1913, when the Camel was launched, and 1924 do not equal the number made in the smoking tobacco division. In fact, only one improvement—in the method of affixing stamps to cigarette packages—appears to have been significant. The problem was solved not by Reynolds mechanics but by Yoemel (James) N. Tzibides, a Greek who lived in the Boston area and possibly for a time in Brooklyn, New York. Apparently as early as 1914 Reynolds officials came in contact with Tzibides through Harry Hans Straus (9 January 1884–27 February 1951), then a New York agent for French firms manufacturing cigarette paper. Straus was also agent for Tzibides. In 1914 Tzibides installed a cork-tipping machine in the Reynolds plant and planned to install others.[108] His greatest contribution, however, was the invention of a machine for affixing revenue stamps to packages of cigarettes; the stamp also served as a means for sealing the package. In 1921 Tzibides transferred the title and patent rights of his "novel and useful" machine to the company. Noah E. Hartley, who joined the Reynolds company when it possessed only four packing machines each of which handled thirty packages per minute, explained the great value of Tzibides's invention: "It took a feeder, an operator, two stamp girls, and one cup girl for each machine. Then a Greek from New York or somewhere up North invented a stamping machine that could pack 63 packs per minute. Two people operated the machine, one of them feeding the machine and the other catching the packs in a carton."[109] Hartley had heard that the company paid the Greek inventor $100,000 for a patent on the machine, but, he noted: "The invention was responsible for great savings to the Company, because it allowed two operators on a machine to more than double the number of packs they could stamp in one minute."[110] Another improvement, that of automatically placing tops on cartons, came in 1921 and 1922 from the work of George Little.[111] Some years earlier the company had negotiated with the Package Machinery Company for a carton-wrapping machine that used glassine paper.[112]

By the end of 1924 cigarette manufacturing in the Reynolds plants was virtually automatic from start to finish, though still lacking a one-piece carton and a considerable amount of speed. A detailed account of cigarette making in a Reynolds factory in 1920 describes only automatic procedures from the time the prepared cigarette tobacco dropped into the hoppers to its meeting with the cigarette paper; to the printing of the word "Camel" on the paper; to the meeting of the cigarette tobacco with the printed paper; to the formation of the cigarette rod; to the buzzing cutting knife; to the cutting, scoring, printing, and forming of the cups; to the wrapping of the cigarettes in foil; and finally to the plunging of the foil-wrapped cigarettes into the cup. Unfortunately the description ends before the packages received the revenue stamp and went into the carton.[113]

World War I and Its Effects

Problems confronting Reynolds management during the war years centered around two conflicting issues: the need to produce more and the scarcity of materials. A tobacco section of the War Industries Board formed on 26 April 1918 estimated that men in the service used 60 to 70 percent more tobacco than they did in civilian life, whereas the demand of the civilian population increased 15 to 20 percent. At the same time, the use of tin had to be curtailed; more than 50 million pounds of licorice root for the entire industry had to be obtained from southeastern Europe and Persia; and saccharin, then made from toluol, which was distilled from the Tolu tree in South America, though required for tobacco was more seriously needed for TNT.[114] Under these conditions, the government had to impose restrictions. In September 1918 manufacturers of tobacco manufacturing machinery were given Class B-6 ratings; however, when the Reynolds company requested permission to buy a turbine and a condenser, which were not classified as tobacco manufacturing machinery but needed for tobacco manufacturing, the request was refused. Also in September all machinery connected with drying, packing, and storing leaf tobacco was given Class IV ratings.[115] War also meant loss of office personnel, salesmen, laborers, and in fact all types of employees. A draft board in Columbus, Ohio, told salesman Thomas Harris that selling tobacco was a nonessential occupation.[116] In July 1918 the company requested preferential treatment in distribution of coal. This was only six months after the deputy administrator at Bluefield, West Virginia, announced that the demand for Pocahontas coal for 1918 stood at 23 million tons as against 19 million that could be produced.[117] Yet, in May 1918 Walter R. Reynolds had felt that, despite the growing tendency not to put tobacco manufacturers on the preferential list, it was too soon to take any concerted action with the War Industries Board.[118]

Scarcity of manufacturing materials, which was a factor before the United States entered the war, involved rising prices as well as inconvenience. Though in 1916 R. J. Reynolds admitted that licorice was scarce, he expected to obtain an adequate supply despite poor shipping facilities.[119] Supplies of glassine paper, obtained from Germany until 1912, had become increasingly difficult to obtain by the latter part of 1914; furthermore, the price had risen from seven to ten cents per pound.[120] Likewise, the increased demand for tin plate was accompanied by a rise in cost. Before the end of 1917 Camels were packed without tinfoil. To further aggravate the situation, the fuel administration ordered the plant closed for five days in January 1918. Shipments of sugar arriving shortly thereafter carried a heavy odor of molasses. Worst of all the company was forced to inform jobbers that orders for Prince Albert were cancelled because of the increasing demand by the government.[121] At length, in September 1917 the directors decided to borrow up to $10 million for the following reasons: (1) growth of the business; (2) unprecedented cost of leaf tobacco; (3) possible doubling of internal revenue taxes; (4) a 600 percent increase in the cost of cigarette paper, a 300 to 500 percent increase in the cost of flavorings, and a material increase in the cost of other supplies; (5) an increase in the cost of labor due to the draft and the Federal Child Labor Law; (6) the necessity for making provisions for excess profits and other taxes; and (7) impending plans of the government to float an additional $5 billion in bonds—an act likely to raise interest rates on commercial loans.[122] Meanwhile, the price of Reynolds products increased and so did the excise tax, though at a greater pace, as data from price lists and the recapitulation of brands indicate for Camels alone (see Table 9-1).

Perhaps the most serious handicap of the war period in any category had to do with the procurement of cigarette paper. The company purchased its cigarette paper largely from the mills of René Bolloré in Odet and Cascadec, France, through two agents, Peter J. Schweitzer and Harry H. Straus, and possibly a third, Henry Utard. (In 1914 and 1915 Utard, a Frenchman who later represented Carenou and Tur in New York for the sale of licorice, scoured France in search of cigarette paper for Reynolds.) One problem involved the method of making payments for the paper. On 14 August 1916, the directors decided to have Peter Schweitzer, of New York, handle the matter through his Paris bank. Though approved by the stockholders on 3 April 1917,[123] this approach apparently proved unsatisfactory, because three months later the directors authorized Schweitzer to buy the Bolloré mills and one other French paper mill.[124] This too did not succeed. Though Schweitzer had recently sent his agent to France to buy paper for Reynolds, it was decided on 5 July 1917 that an officer of the company should go to France and remain there for the duration of the war and that Walter R. Reynolds should be the one to go. At the same time the directors agreed to send Schweitzer. Walter Reynolds was authorized to take whatever steps were necessary to keep the company supplied with cigarette paper—whether by purchase, by contract, or by purchasing a paper plant. The directors also authorized the treasurer to keep him supplied with funds.[125]

In view of the current difficulties in relaying funds to the Bolloré mills, it appears that Reynolds personally carried a substantial quantity of gold to France. Many stories have been told of the tremendous sum that he strapped beneath his clothing at his departure. Be that as it may, Reynolds spent five months in France, returning to New York on or about 3 January 1918.[126] While in France he signed a three-year contract with Bolloré for 165,000 bobbins of cigarette paper per quarter to replace the contract of 8 July 1917 between Peter J. Schweitzer and Bolloré on Reynolds's behalf. Later Walter Reynolds left Jean Faurant as his attorney in France and returned home because of his brother's illness. Faurant drew up an even more rigid contract with Bolloré shortly after Reynolds left. By virtue of his regard for the R. J. Reynolds Tobacco Company, Bolloré was willing to furnish the company with additional paper. In order to indemnify Bolloré for the loss of other customers, the Reynolds agent agreed to pay 10 percent of the invoice price of the goods on condition that Bolloré

Table 9-1
Selling Prices, Discounts, and Excise Taxes per Thousand Camel Cigarettes
During 1913–1922

Effective Date	Price	Discount	Excise Tax
1913 - 19 Oct.	$4.00	10% and 2%	$1.25
1916 - 13 July	4.10	10 and 2	1.25
1917 - 4 Oct.	4.55	10 and 2	1.65
1917 - 2 Nov.	5.25	10 and 2	2.05
1918 - 1 Mar.	6.00	10 and 2	2.05
1919 - 25 Feb.	8.00	10 and 2	3.00
1919 - 21 Mar.	7.30	10 and 2	3.00
1919 - 1 Nov.	7.60	10 and 2	3.00
1919 - 22 Nov.	8.00	10 and 2	3.00
1921 - 31 Dec.	7.50	10 and 2	3.00
1922 - 4 Mar.	6.80	10 and 2	3.00
1922 - 28 Oct.	6.40	10 and 2	3.00

Source: Price lists, secretary's department, R. J. Reynolds Tobacco Company.

execute the contract and that he formally agree to retain for himself and his family at least 51 percent of the business. Promise to hold 51 percent of the business intact was dependent on Bolloré's idea of bringing his factory at Odet in as a part of the Reynolds corporation.[127]

It is doubtful that Walter Reynolds intended to buy the Bolloré mills outright, although on 28 January 1920 he wrote that Bolloré had cabled for additional time in which to make a decision—evidently in regard to becoming a branch of the company. In the same letter Reynolds referred to Percival S. Hill's statement that he had taken over the de Mauduit Mills at Quimperle, France, with himself as president and "F. R. Harris, who has represented the American in France for the past several years, as Vice-President." Reynolds then declared that his company had received a cable offer from F. R. Harris of an option the latter had taken on the Champagne Mills at Troyes, France, but Reynolds wrote, "we are not interested in the purchase and operation of mills in France."[128]

Possibly the uncertainty surrounding the company's connections with French paper mills during and immediately after World War I was based on unfair dealings of the agents in France and America who took orders for cigarette paper. At some point in this period the company lost funds on purchases from Daniel Weil of France "through Schweitzer-Malmenayde." But later Walter Reynolds informed Weil that "after we understood how the deal was pulled off, we felt that you were innocent of any bad intentions in the matter."[129] From stories handed down it appears that Peter Schweitzer, an agent in the United States, and Malmenayde, his associate in France, swindled the company on both sides of the Atlantic. Yet, only eleven days before Reynolds wrote of this deal, the company bought—through Schweitzer—30,000 bobbins of cigarette paper made by the mill of Braunstein Brothers.[130] As a direct result of these difficulties the R. J. Reynolds Tobacco Company, Harry H. Straus, and others of the tobacco industry became prime movers in the successful production of cigarette paper in the United States before the source of supply was cut off by the next world war.

The Smokarol Fiasco

One problem confronting management during this period was of its own making. This involved the Smokarol fad developed by Liggett and Myers Tobacco Company to further the sale of its Velvet smoking tobacco. A Smokarol was a series of five small cylinders of smoking tobacco wrapped in cigarette paper and packed without stamps, each part designed to fit into a special Smokarol pipe. As advertised, Smokarols were supposed to prevent waste in filling pipes. According to a ruling of the Department of Internal Revenue on 29 June 1915, they were sold as smoking tobacco and taxed at eight cents per pound or about one-tenth of the cigarette tax. Evidently fearing that Velvet Smokarols would lower the sales of Prince Albert, R. J. Reynolds claimed that they should be taxed as cigarettes. William M. Armistead, then in Philadelphia, was asked to inform Charles J. Eisenlohr, a prominent cigar dealer, that the tax was unfair. Suddenly after 7 November 1915, tobacconists of all classes began receiving circulars on the unfairness of this tax. Prepared by the R. J. Reynolds Tobacco Company in the form of a letter to the Commissioner of Internal Revenue, the circular protested the tax and requested a change in the tax status of the Smokarol.

A hearing before Commissioner William H. Osborn on 2 December, at which both the Reynolds company and Liggett and Myers were well-represented by legal talent, produced no changes. But R. J. Reynolds continued to bombard tobacconists over the country with requests to protest the tax to Osborn and to send copies of their letters to his company. Of the fifty-five replies received and filed, seventeen were noncommittal and the remainder in agreement with Reynolds. In a letter to Commissioner Osborn on the eleventh, Reynolds explained what he had done, enclosing copies of the circular and the replies to it. Furthermore, he noted that some manufacturers who had not considered the question carefully would now take a different view.

Evidently the editor of *Tobacco*, then the most influential journal of its kind, did not agree with Reynolds. The issue for 16 December 1915 quoted the full text of Reynolds's circular and deemed it an effort "to harm a competitor." According to the editor, the "R. J. Reynolds Tobacco Company has neither honored nor helped itself and that there is a chorus of disapproval for the method employed." An editorial in the same issue labeled Reynolds's procedure as an "attempt on the part of one of the big companies to stab another in the back." When R. J. immediately complained at this treatment of his fight against Velvet Smokarols, the publisher of *Tobacco* apologized, stating that the writer of the attack on Reynolds had resigned. *Tobacco* then published its apology along with a letter from Bowman Gray, Sr. Gray's letter, though accepting the apology, carried on the fight.

Meanwhile, writing to R. J. Reynolds on 17 December, Armistead indicated that the Smokarol pipe was defective. His information had come from William DeMuth and Company, which manufactured the special pipes for Liggett and Myers. The pipe, something of an enlarged cigarette holder, spilled fire and ashes. Moreover, the upper edge of the bowl burned out when the rising heat struck the edge of the pipe instead of going into the air as it did in a conventional pipe. The entire matter would thus have been of little importance had Reynolds not acted so hastily and so vigorously. As it was, the question was taken to Secretary of the Treasury William G. McAdoo, who upheld the decision of the Commissioner of Internal Revenue against Reynolds's contentions.[131] Those who later recalled this incident were unable to explain R. J.'s error in judgment, especially because many of his contemporaries considered the Smokarol merely a passing fad.

Prosperity and Capitalization

Despite changes in leadership and war scarcities, the Reynolds company prospered amazingly from 1912 to 1924 as the Camel skyrocketed in sales. Net profits, slightly less than $3,000,000 in 1912, reached $23,-777,717 in 1924. Additional funds naturally became necessary during these years in order to keep pace with expanding production. From 2 July to 1 October 1917, the amount of preferred stock was raised so that the capitalization stood at $20,000,000, one-half in common and one-half in preferred stock. Because additional capital was needed, the directors considered short-term loans, the sale of debentures, an increase in the authorization of preferred stock, and the issuance of additional common stock.

They dropped the last three considerations, the last one because such a move would have injured the equities of various people holding participating stock.[132]

About this time S. Clay Williams read in the *New York Times* that the Bethlehem Steel Company had amended its charter to create the first B common stock ever known to him. Clipping the article, Williams went to work on the idea and soon solved the problem at hand by preparing for the issuance of Class B Common Stock and later New Class B Common Stock—a procedure that did not interfere with current plans for the original common or "A" stock.[133] With the creation of New Class B Common Stock in 1920 and the ruling of the Supreme Court that stock dividends were not taxable, the company from its undivided profits of $36,171,981 issued a 200 percent stock dividend. This move, though long opposed by William Reynolds, rendered the surplus less than the capitalization.[134] Nevertheless, as James A. Gray wrote later, in 1920 the company owed $50,000,000. Notwithstanding its handicaps, the net profits of the Reynolds company surpassed those of Liggett and Myers in 1916–17 and 1919–24 and those of the American Tobacco Company in 1922, 1923, and 1924 (see Table 9-2). (Appendix G shows the earnings of the company from 1912 to 1960.)

The problem of excess profits taxes during this period prevented the issuance of annual reports for 1917–19 inclusive. According to S. Clay Williams, excess profits taxes and "war taxes" for those years and for 1920 and 1921 were later adjusted, though the adjustments did not equalize the 1918 profits in a normal manner. Actually the company in that year made $18,000,000, but the "excess profits and war profits taxes" amounted to more than $10,000,000. The rebate shown in the annual report for 1927 as "Sundry Items applicable to prior periods" was $8,744,739, although there are intimations that the total refund for the years involved was approximately $20,000,000. The excess profits tax was figured on the basis of an exemption in relation to invested capital. Reynolds, with a lower capitalization than the other companies, had only a few purchased brands valued then at $1,316,691. At the same time approximate brand values of the other three major tobacco manufacturers were as follows: American, $54,000,000; Liggett and Myers, $40,000,000; and P. Lorillard, $20,000,000. Meanwhile, valuable brands of the R. J. Reynolds Tobacco Company had been made so at a tremendous cost in advertising.

For these reasons, the Reynolds company was placed at a distinct disadvantage. Relief came from "Section 210" of the Revenue Act of 1918, which ameliorated the hardships of the Revenue Act of 1916 by a formula based on a percentage of net income. Many years later it was often stated, and no doubt correctly so, that it took an act of Congress to obtain the

Table 9-2
Net Profits of the "Big Three" Tobacco Manufacturing Companies,
1912–1924

Year	American	Liggett and Myers	Reynolds
1912	—	—	$ 2,899,957
1913	$14,489,534	$ 6,459,731	2,862,567
1914	11,635,185	5,391,174	2,916,564
1915	11,234,581	6,800,276	4,729,988
1916	12,298,058	6,589,055	8,043,678
1917	13,310,685	7,363,720	10,340,345
1918	16,613,039	8,154,008	7,042,763
1919	15,972,572	5,929,036	11,272,754
1920	15,151,155	7,597,803	10,691,294
1921	18,254,664	9,854,157	16,258,323
1922	18,833,255	9,724,294	20,479,234
1923	17,808,139	9,622,397	23,039,876
1924	20,784,870	11,969,828	23,777,717

Source: Am. Tob. Co. et al. v. U.S., Record on Appeal, docket no. 9137–9139 (6th Cir., 1944), exhibits, 5:2507—after taxes. The figures have been rounded off to the nearest dollar.

rebate. But, according to S. Clay Williams, the rebate failed to eliminate all of the inequity.[135] The *Wall Street Journal* declared that Reynolds's net earnings in 1922 were "the highest ever recorded by any Company in the tobacco industry."[136] Truly, by 1924 the company had proved its ability to compete with any firm in the tobacco industry.

CHAPTER 10

Development into a Modern Industry

The meteoric rise of the Camel prior to 1925 demanded emphasis on production to fill the orders that poured in. From 1925 to 1940, however, the R. J. Reynolds Tobacco Company concentrated on other aspects of the business. Beginning in 1924, William N. Reynolds handed the presidency to Bowman Gray, Sr., and moved into the newly created position of chairman of the board. This would be followed by numerous shifts in management personnel as the company moved further away from the dominance of its founder into the less personal sphere of corporate life. It appears that advertising received the lion's share of attention because of the company's interest in exploiting its moisture-proof cellophane wrapper for cigarettes, the result of pioneer work in the industry. Modernization of cigarette production and the handling of leaf tobacco included installation of the Arenco packing machine and the Mark VI model of the Molins making machine, development of a foil-making plant, adoption of the vacuum conditioner and a mechanical method for assembling hogsheads, and, above all, support of the establishment of an American source for the production of cigarette paper. Concern for the welfare of employees led to the early adoption of a retirement plan and group health insurance. After 1937 a complete revamping of the sales department led to more harmonious working conditions for sales personnel.

Leaders in a New Era

Though working in something of a new era, the men who led the company after 1924 generally had long been associated with it. All except William Reynolds were department heads, and even he continued to keep an eye on leaf purchases. Virtually all were North Carolinians except Theodore H. Kirk, whose fierce state pride and procurement of Burley leaf generally kept him in his native state of Kentucky. Regardless of his new position as president, Bowman Gray, Sr., a merchandising expert, kept his experienced eye on sales. Money matters were the particular concern of James A. Gray, who had been hand-picked by R. J. Reynolds to manage the company's finances after his death. Employed by R. J. in 1917, S. Clay Williams entered the directorate in 1924 through the legal department. Robert E. Lasater, superintendent of manufacturing, James B. Dyer, in charge of domestic leaf, and James W. Glenn, who headed the leaf department and kept leaf inventories in balance all had worked for many years directly under R. J. Reynolds. Carl W. Harris, long with the company, handled office matters as they related to sales and advertising, and Roy C. Haberkern, trained under Walter R. Reynolds since 1909, served as director of purchasing. As traffic manager, Joseph L. Graham also continued as a director until 1928. They were working directors interested only in the business of the Reynolds company.

William Reynolds assumed the newly created position of chairman of the board in April 1924. At that time, it was decided that the president would have general supervision of property and affairs subject to the board's control. In the choice of a president the directors naturally followed the recommendation of Will Reynolds, who, on 8 April, wrote the group: "Assuming that I may take the liberty of making a recommendation as to my successor, I express my fullest confidence in Mr. Bowman Gray and unreservedly recommend him for President of the Company."[1] In reviewing Gray's qualifications for the position, the leading tobacco journal of the day called his career an excellent illustration "of the company's policy of 'building up from the bottom,' which policy has been most valuable in creating loyalty and efficiency among the officers and employees of the company." Gray, the article continued, had pioneered in the introduction of Reynolds products north of the Mason-Dixon line as well as supervising the company's entire eastern division, which included all the New England states. Gray was described as quiet and unobtrusive in his demeanor, modest in his tastes, accurate in his decisions, and indefatigable in his work.[2]

Moreover, he was basically a kind man, although his shyness earned him a reputation for brusqueness. Those who knew Bowman Gray, Sr., recalled his absolute devotion to the company. According to the sister-in-law of R. J. Reynolds, Gray was the favorite of R. J., who trusted him so completely that he sent him to his favorite location—Baltimore, the gateway for Reynolds's approach to northern markets. Gray's dogged labor induced one employee, a man-about-town from Danville, Virginia, to claim that he saw Bowman Gray only twice—both times as he returned home during the early morning hours while Gray was going to work.[3] Many years later Bowman Gray, Jr., declared that he seldom saw his father except in summer, as he customarily rose at 5:30 A.M., returned home for his evening meal at 6:30, and immediately left again for the office—a schedule he invariably maintained for six days a week and often on Sunday. When in Europe on the few vacations that he allowed himself, he frequently called on suppliers like the Bollorés of France. In the course of his work, Gray personally examined every cash order written by the Reynolds salesmen.[4] After the mushroom growth of earlier years, this careful attention to detail undoubtedly served the company well.

Beyond a doubt, Bowman Gray, Sr., was the only man in the company who could face R. J. Reynolds without loss of equanimity. According to William T. Smither, on one occasion Reynolds, upon learning of an opportunity to buy a large block of common stock, wrote Gray in Baltimore to suggest that he buy a certain number of shares. Gray, thinking that the outlay of money involved would place too great a strain on his budget, decided not to take any. Shortly afterward, when Gray had returned to the home office, R. J. told him that he had arranged a note at the bank and purchased the stock in Gray's name. Never before or after did Smither see Gray display the anger that he then showed to Reynolds in person. Nevertheless, as Smither learned later, the stock purchase was not altered. Gray's frugality with company property is best illustrated by his habit of using a pencil until it became a mere stub. Once, when a stenographer was unexpectedly called in to take dictation, she had no pencil; Gray supplied her with one about two inches long—the type he customarily used.[5] Another amusing story of Gray's unorthodox reactions came from the employment department. To obviate the confusion caused when employees had the same name, those without a middle name were given one—generally the mother's maiden name. The record of Bowman Gray, Jr., was thus distinguished from that of his father. Soon Bowman Gray, Sr., called, gruffly inquiring what the change meant and stating that he had been able to manage very well with only one name. Needless to say, the employment office eliminated this practice.[6]

The composition of the board of directors did not long remain as established in April 1924. The first break came in 1928 with the resignation of Joseph L. Graham. It was generally believed that in the election of Louis F. Owen as his successor, the board passed over Graham's recommendation of his assistant, William L. Thornton, Jr.[7] At any rate Thornton left the company in 1937 to become traffic manager for the port of New York;[8] he later held the same position with the Kimberly-Clark Corporation. It is interesting, that, in the year of his departure, Thornton appeared before the Interstate Commerce Commission on behalf of Reynolds and the Tobacco Merchants Association of the United States to argue against a 10 percent increase in shipping rates for leaf tobacco and manufactured tobacco products.[9] The next change in the board took place in 1929 upon the death of James B. Dyer, who had served the company faithfully for thirty-five years. His position fell to Robert D. Shore, the treasurer. Shore had been with Reynolds for twenty-three years.[10]

A general shift of positions within the directorate occurred in 1931 when William Reynolds asked to be relieved of his duties as chairman of the board. The bylaws were changed to permit appointment of four vice-presidents instead of three and to establish an executive committee with the committee chairman to be named each year by the board. Bowman Gray, Sr., was named chairman of the board and S. Clay Williams president. The first executive committee consisted of Will Reynolds (chairman), Bowman Gray, Sr., S. Clay Williams, Theodore H. Kirk, Robert E. Lasater, James A. Gray, and Carl W. Harris. The committee thus contained two leaf men, two from sales, one manufacturer, one lawyer, and one banker—a fair representation of the various areas of management. When the directors were not in session, this committee passed upon all business of the company except that specifically requiring the vote of the directors. Three members constituted a quorum and the committee might or might not keep minutes as it saw fit.[11] Incidentally, James A. Gray was the first to require them.

The same year witnessed another significant change—this time regarding the substance of board meetings. Roy C. Haberkern approached Will Reynolds with the suggestion that each director be required to discuss significant issues in his area of responsibility. This would broaden management's overall view of the company's activities as well as enliven the meetings. Reynolds agreed if Haberkern would compose a letter to the directors for his signature. Accordingly, the following letter was sent on 16 July 1931:

> I have been thinking about how to make the meetings of our Board of Directors more helpful and through them to keep the Directors better informed about Company business generally and to get the best use possible out of each of the Directors. I believe we can improve on what we are now, and have been, doing in the past and I make the following recommendations:

> I believe it would be good to have at each monthly meeting of the Directors a series of reports from Directors that are in touch with special phases of the business. A report from the Sales Manager giving figures for the preceding month on all important brands and by departments with comparison against preceding months and the year before would keep all Directors informed about sales. A similar report from the Manufacturing Department with respect to manu-

facture and stocks on hand, along with such report of factory operations and labor as might be included, would be interesting. I think
the Treasurer should make a report each month showing the results
of the month before as compared with preceding months and with
the year before. A similar report covering advertising and expenditures and advertising program as planned for the future would
show how the remainder of the year was set up as compared to the
year before. The Domestic Leaf Department ought to make such report each month as would give the Directors desirable information
as to stocks on hand, price, buying plans or anything else of interest.
In the same way a report from the Turkish Leaf Department would
be interesting and helpful. The Secretary's Department, including
credit work, could have an interesting report and so could the Purchasing Department and the Traffic Department.

In making these recommendations I believe that after a few meetings
are held on this plan, our Directors' meetings will come to be very
interesting discussions of the general business of the Company and
will prove very helpful to many of the Directors. At the same time, I
think this plan would bring to many Company questions the views
and ideas of some Directors whose ideas there is not now always a
chance to get.

Of course, all such reports and discussions would have to be absolutely confidential except as between Directors. Much harm could result from the failure on any Director's part to realize the importance
of keeping all such matters perfectly confidential, but I feel sure that
with this understood a great deal of good could be accomplished under this plan.

I'd like to see such a plan adopted and tried out.

The directors adopted the plan. Prior to its presentation, Reynolds obtained Haberkern's assurance that he would give the first talk—on the
functions of the purchasing department.[12] Evidently in earlier years R. J.
Reynolds had carried in his head all the information called for in this letter,
although it is doubtful that even he could have done so in 1931. If the
board required such prodding in that year, it is perhaps reasonable to assume that few directors comprehended the complex problems of the company outside their own narrow bailiwicks. Possibly Haberkern's suggestion developed from his duties as purchasing agent for all departments—a
role that gave him a wide understanding of the business.

In 1932 the role of the Real Estate Committee came under close scru-
tiny, suggesting that its performance was inadequate or possibly that it had
been undercut by the construction department. On 9 January the commit-

tee met in the office of P. Frank Hanes; Robert E. Lasater was there by invitation. Based on this meeting, Hanes reported to the directors that the company was being forced to take many losses on building projects due to the lack of supervision. To correct the situation, he said, the committee submitted the following resolutions: that Lasater be made a member of the committee; that the committee oversee all building activities; that the company architect, construction force, and engineering department "be controlled absolutely by this Committee and that they are not to order any work done unless and until authorized to do so by this Committee"; that these regulations apply to construction on all company-owned property; and that the directors hold the committee responsible for compliance. The directors unanimously adopted Hanes's report and agreed to notify all individuals and departments affected by these changes.[13] This was stern talk indeed, but there is no clear evidence that committees functioned with any degree of efficiency prior to 1950. Clearly this was the fault of the directors and possibly also the result of years of consulting with R. J. Reynolds, who had had the last word. Soon after James A. Gray assumed responsibility for financial matters, the Finance Committee was discharged, possibly at Gray's request. Years later Bowman Gray, Jr., stated that it was not until after S. Clay Williams died in 1949 that committees began to act with authority.[14]

A change in the bylaws in 1934 created a vice-chairmanship of the board of directors, a post filled by S. Clay Williams. This elevated James A. Gray to the presidency and altered the composition of the Executive Committee, which now included a chairman elected annually by the directors, the chairman and vice-chairman of the board, the president, three vice-presidents, the secretary, and the treasurer; neither of the last two had to be members of the board. Moreover, other individuals could be appointed at the board's discretion. The vice-chairman of the board thus became the second ranking executive.[15] Obviously the latter position was created as a screen for Williams's demotion. The press noted the change as a promotion for Gray,[16] as it undoubtedly was. The same officers were reelected in 1935, but the arrangement ended in July with the tragic death of Bowman Gray, Sr. while on a cruise in the North Sea.[17] Williams, by that time free of his unhappy work with the National Industrial Recovery Board (he did not like the New Deal), succeeded Bowman Gray as chairman. Williams was the only lawyer to assume the presidency or chairmanship of the company. Though he had served brilliantly in earlier years both in listing Reynolds stock on the New York Stock Exchange and in handling tax matters, he seemed at times to work at cross purposes with his colleagues. This may have been due to outside activities—when elevated to the chairmanship, he had already served on the planning and advisory board of Secretary of Commerce Daniel C. Roper, as chairman of the Industrial Advisory Board, as vice-chairman of the first National Industrial Relations Board, and as chairman of the Industrial Recovery Board.[18]

Williams's selection as chairman of the board and his outside interests had nothing to do with the crisis of 1937 involving the dismissal of Theodore H. Kirk, a director and vice-president. Kirk held those positions chiefly because he knew how to buy Burley leaf and because he had married the niece of Mrs. William N. Reynolds. Employed by the company in 1910, he was elected vice-president in 1918 upon his appointment to the board by William Reynolds. Kirk early assumed an independent attitude and, somewhat against company policy, refused to live in Winston-Salem. Apparently he was dropped for two reasons. The first related to his persistence in buying more leaf and at higher prices than authorized by the board. On occasion, these practices provoked newspaper comment, as they did one week when Reynolds buyers in Lexington, Kentucky, took about 75 percent of all leaf available, usually on the first bid.[19] The second reason had to do with a recent incident involving a casualty loss of $613,654 suffered by Reynolds during the Ohio River flood of 1937—evidently the result of Kirk's mismanagement. Burley leaf had been stored at Louisville in locations adjacent to the river even though insurance companies refused to cover the flood risk. By the end of the year the company had bought land "lying much higher above the river level" on which storage houses were built.[20] At length, S. Clay Williams asked Kirk to resign after consulting Will Reynolds, who was then in Florida. Kirk also went to Florida to plead his case, but arrived too late.[21] His letter of resignation, dated 1 April 1937, came at an unusual time. In most cases employees submitted their resignations near the end of the year in order to draw earnings from their holdings of common stock. In his rather lengthy letter, Kirk recommended that his "A" stock be placed in the hands of competent and loyal men in the leaf department whom he had trained. Appropriately, he closed on this ironic note: "I . . . have gone back to the horse and buggy days to work in single harness, where I have been told by men I loved that I really belonged."[22]

In the same year Robert D. Shore, the treasurer, and Carl W. Harris, the sales manager, died in rapid succession. Frederick Sinclair Hill (9 December 1888–27 January 1951), for many years the assistant treasurer, assumed Shore's position. Douglas Fayette Peterson (12 January 1895–27 May 1947) and Alexander Henderson Galloway were named assistant treasurers.[23] The disturbance and reorganization caused by the death of Harris late in the year attest to the burden that he evidently carried as manager of both sales and advertising. Edward Austin Darr (23 July 1889–8 October 1958), who in 1920 had been brought into the company from a Baltimore jobbing house by Bowman Gray, Sr., became sales manager. Darr's fourteen-year-apprenticeship under Harris and his brief tenure as assistant sales manager from 6 October to 18 December 1937 no doubt prepared him to some extent for the work, though many considered his personality to be against him.[24] William T. Smither became manager of the advertising department, a position created when Harris died. Thus Harris's work was split between Darr and Smither. Nor was this the only change brought on by his death. John C. Whitaker, who had replaced Bowman Gray, Sr., on the board, now succeeded to Harris's position as vice-president. Two years later, on 27 June 1939, Bowman Gray, Jr., became assistant sales manager.[25]

These shifts were of particular importance in that they brought to the fore men who would manage the company during the 1950s when Reynolds became a leader in the tobacco industry. Furthermore, they led to the creation of a permanent advertising department, which for some reason had been abandoned in 1917. In view of the company's tremendous advertising expenditures during the intervening twenty years, it is surprising that a formal, permanent advertising department was not established earlier.

As the office force expanded it outgrew the old office building, which seemed not only inadequate but also somewhat unsuitable for a company as prosperous as Reynolds after the Camel revolution. In 1927 it was decided to erect a twenty-two-story building according to the specifications of Shreve and Lamb, well-known New York architects who later designed the Empire State Building. In fact, the company's choice of architects would become a source of pride in Winston-Salem with the increasing fame of the Empire State Building. By 10 December 1927 plans for the office building received final approval, and on 1 March 1928 the contract was awarded to the James Baird Company on a bid of $1,900,000. Under the driving force of Roy C. Haberkern, completion was prompt and the transfer of personnel and furniture accomplished before the end of April 1929.[26] To Harold L. Gosselin, who joined the company in January 1929 and became manager of the office building in March, should go much of the credit for its effective supervision. By his retirement in July 1959, the Reynolds office building, visible for many miles around Winston-Salem, had earned the reputation for being one of the best-kept buildings in the United States, as well as the best kept of any designed by Shreve and Lamb.[27] Though more than a quarter of a century old when air conditioning was installed in mid-July 1956,[28] the building retained its modern appearance—from the halls of marble quarried in Belgium and France to the exterior of Indiana limestone, its original freshness preserved by occasional sand blastings. Modernity became even more apparent six years later with the installation of electronically operated elevators.

Advertising

The years 1925–40 saw a tremendous growth in advertising nationwide. In newspapers and magazines alone, the total investment had increased from $528,300,000 in 1919 to $1,120,240,000 in 1929.[29] Other advertising media used by the major tobacco companies included billboards, gratis goods, and point-of-purchase promotions such as window and counter displays. In addition, the industry had hardly begun to cautiously promote cigarette smoking among women before radio advertising became necessary in 1930.[30] The R. J. Reynolds Tobacco Company provided no exception to this expansion. Indeed, the Camel had to struggle not only with imitative rivals but also with ten-cent cigarettes, the roll-your-own vogue of the depression, and the phenomenal growth of Philip Morris. The company's advertising expenditures and those of its major rivals were extraordinary, reflecting their apparent agreement on the necessity of large-scale advertising to fuel expansion (see Table 10-1). In 1934 alone, advertising costs for the Reynolds company amounted to 81 percent of net earnings (see Table 10-2); furthermore, approximately three-fourths of this expenditure went for the advertisement of Camels.[31]

In all of these years, the Reynolds company used only three advertising agencies: N. W. Ayer and Son; Erwin, Wasey & Company; and William Esty Company, Inc. The change from one agency to another occurred in a period of little more than one year—the contract with Ayer ending in 1931, the first Erwin, Wasey advertisement appearing on 25 February 1931, and the contract with the Esty agency being signed on 30 November 1932.[32] These moves, of course, came at a critical period of the depression. Perhaps the day for Ayer's folksy advertising had passed when it was supplanted by Erwin, Wasey & Company. After taking over the Reynolds account, however, the new agency apparently did little more than handle the company's $50,000 contest in connection with the first use of cellophane as a moisture-proof wrapper for cigarettes. Possibly Erwin, Wasey's failure to furnish adequate copy led the Reynolds company to cut its funds for advertising in 1932. In a leaflet accompanying the annual report of 12 January 1933, it was broadcast to the world that Reynolds retained $4,000,000 of the money set aside for advertising in 1932 and that this unspent balance represented an additional amount available for use in 1933. It was not surprising, therefore, when Camels returned to the newspapers with a great splash in January of that year under the leadership of the Esty agency.

Undoubtedly Reynolds owed much to Ayer for transforming Prince Albert into a national product and for the successful launching of Camels, though the company's best advertising line, "I'd Walk a Mile for a Camel," came from Martin F. Reddington who first used it on billboards. In 1925

Table 10-1
Advertising Expenditures of the
"Big Three" Tobacco Manufacturing Companies, 1925–1939

Year	Reynolds	American	Liggett and Myers
1925	$10,100,027	$ 8,785,455	Not available
1926	17,639,898	7,782,288	Not available
1927	19,473,486	12,679,580	Not available
1928	12,871,532	12,191,318	Not available
1929	9,933,700	13,710,880	Not available
1930	15,137,996	19,718,071	Not available
1931	16,057,205	23,680,009	Not available
1932	5,437,304	24,815,214	Not available
1933	14,895,600	14,620,908	Not available
1934	17,400,202	12,624,160	Not available
1935	14,471,338	10,507,642	$16,646,924
1936	14,880,224	17,638,669	15,629,006
1937	14,961,767	10,190,235	16,938,990
1938	15,537,824	9,805,995	16,892,363
1939	15,363,043	9,664,381	17,749,346

Source: R. J. R. Tob. Co. et al. v. U.S., *Brief for Appellants*, docket no. 9139 (6th Cir., 1944), p. 205.

and 1926, the Ayer advertisements for Camels emphasized the proper time for smoking—*when winter's snow is falling, when on a vacation trip, when the football team is drawn up for battle, when the world series begins*, or virtually any time *when* a smoker might reach for a Camel. Interspersed with this series in 1927 was the theme of the "Smoking Refreshment That Never Ends" followed by "The Happiest Words in the World: Have a Camel." "The One Cigarette in a Million" of 1927 and 1928 emphasized the Camel's popularity. Befitting the last days of the boom period of 1928–29, the keynote turned to the pleasures of smoking. Finally in May 1929 many advertisements in fiction magazines showed a girl offering a man a Camel while he gallantly replied with the caption, "I'd Walk a Mile for a Camel—but a 'Miss' is as Good as a Mile." Then followed a slightly snobbish series highlighting the major role of the Camel at social events such as the races at Longchamps.[33]

Before the end of its contract, the Ayer agency had begun to answer the empty but effective boast of the American Tobacco Company that its Lucky Strike was toasted. In fact, all tobacco used in cigarettes was toasted

Table 10-2
Advertising Expenditures of the Reynolds Company
as a Percent of Net Earnings, 1925–1940

Year	Cost of Advertising	Net Earnings	Percent of Net Earnings
1925	$10,100,027	$25,221,579	40.04
1926	17,639,898	26,249,403	67.20
1927	19,473,486	29,080,665	66.96
1928	12,871,532	30,172,563	42.65
1929	9,933,700	32,210,521	30.83
1930	15,137,996	34,256,665	44.18
1931	16,057,205	36,396,817	44.11
1932	5,437,304	33,674,800	16.14
1933	14,895,600	21,153,722	70.41
1934	17,400,202	21,536,894	80.79
1935	14,471,338	23,896,398	60.55
1936	14,880,224	29,253,135	50.86
1937	14,961,767	27,602,372	54.20
1938	15,537,824	23,734,306	65.46
1939	15,363,043	25,645,455	59.90
1940	14,626,000	25,548,424	57.20

Source: R. J. R. Tob. Co. et al. v. U.S., *Brief for Appellants*, docket no. 9139 (6th Cir., 1944), p. 205.

because all of it went through a Proctor redryer in preparation for storage. According to one Ayer ad appearing in the spring of 1930: [34]

> Camels stand alone. If you merely want to puff, anything will do. But if you want to know the true delight of smoking—to enjoy the mild mellow fragrance of superbly blended Domestic and Turkish tobaccos, brought to perfection by the most scientific methods of manufacturers but with none of the delicacy of its natural goodness lost or spoiled by over treatment—then Camel is the cigarette for you.

The meaning of such mild copy doubtless escaped many who became enmeshed in the meaningless phrase, "It's Toasted," as it resounded from radios and repetitiously appeared in newspapers and magazines. The entire tobacco industry joined Reynolds in questioning George Washington Hill's claim that the exclusive virtues of the heat treatment belonged to

Lucky Strikes. In the spring of 1930, the company bought $300,000 worth of full-page newspaper advertisements headed: "Turning the Light of Truth on False and Misleading Statements in Recent Cigarette Advertisements." But this barrage did not check the decline of Camel sales. Reaching back to the period when many smokers were still dazzled by the distinctiveness of the Camel, Ayer relied on old themes such as "Don't Deny Yourself the Luxury of Camels," "Turn the package over and Read the Back," "The Blend that Revolutionized Smoking," and "The Luxury of Camels Costs No More."[35] What the agency seemingly failed to realize was that the Camel was no longer distinctive.

When it appeared that the company was wasting its money, Bowman Gray, Sr., and S. Clay Williams decided to cut advertising costs for 1932 from $16 million to less than $5 million. The result was a disastrous 30-percent decline in the shipment of Camels from the previous year. (During the same period Lucky Strikes declined 17 percent and Chesterfields only 10 percent.) Reynolds officials believed it was time to change advertising agencies. Before turning to what *Fortune* termed "the whizz and whoozle" of William Cole Esty (7 March 1895–21 January 1954), the company shifted its advertising account to Erwin, Wasey & Company simultaneously with the introduction of moisture-proof cellophane as a wrapper for Camels.

Although this important change in packaging did not have an immediate effect on Camel sales, it was a pioneer move that other companies were forced to copy. S. Clay Williams later captured the significance of the cellophane wrapper in the following report to the stockholders:[36]

> The year 1931 witnessed an important and outstanding development with regard to CAMEL Cigarettes. Prior to that time no cigarette manufacturer had ever been able to work out a practical solution of the industry-old problem of preserving freshness in cigarettes during the period between completion of manufacture and use by the smoker. To CAMELS, manufactured by methods designed to preserve the natural qualities of the good tobaccos of which they are made, the solution of this problem offered the maximum of benefit. This solution came early in 1931 through the discovery and development of methods for a hitherto unknown complete air-seal of moisture-proof material for the outer wrapping. This air-sealed CAMEL Humidor Pack was introduced in 1931 as capable of keeping in CAMELS until they reached the smoker practically all of that natural freshness and mildness that has always been so carefully safeguarded through our processes of manufacture. We regard this result as an accomplishment directly in line with your Company's established policy of never sparing any effort to improve its methods and the quality of its products. The impetus thereby given to the sales of

CAMELS proved, and continues to prove, the smokers' appreciation of that contribution to their enjoyment.

As in the case of numerous products used in the tobacco industry, cellophane came from Western Europe where three English chemists had done the basic work. Large-scale production, delayed by World War I, began in 1920 with the formation of a French firm, La Cellophane, which built a plant near Paris. E. I. du Pont de Nemours & Company secured the rights to manufacture the product in the United States and produced its first cellophane in 1924. Three years later moisture-proof cellophane was developed.[37] Almost immediately experimentation by a small cigar manufacturer pointed the way to the adoption of cellophane as a wrap for Camels. The new product was introduced with amazing speed. According to L. D. Long, secretary to William N. Reynolds for many years, on 3 June 1930 a vice-president of du Pont walked into Long's office and asked to see Reynolds. While he waited, he gave Long a box of cigars wrapped in cellophane. Taking one of the cigars, he demonstrated how it could be rolled underfoot on the terrazzo floor of the office without being damaged in any way. Eventually the du Pont representative saw Reynolds, but Long learned no more of cellophane until about August when he overheard Roy C. Haberkern speaking about it to Will Reynolds. Long then took out the cigars that he had received in June and gave them to Reynolds and Haberkern. Tests showed they were in excellent condition. Because the du Pont vice-president had been unable to speak with Bowman Gray, Sr., and Haberkern, it was Long's opinion that Reynolds was responsible for the use of cellophane on Camels.[38]

Apparently on 3 June 1930 Will Reynolds and his associates decided to investigate the possibility of using cellophane as a waterproof wrap for Camels. Never having adopted glassine paper for that purpose, as had some of their competitors, they immediately obtained samples of cellophane and ordered laboratory tests to determine moisture losses from different wrappings. The tests, made by Pittsburgh Testing Laboratories, furnished encouraging results. At that time no machine was ready to wrap cigarette packages with cellophane, although at least two packaging companies were struggling with the problem. At last Reynolds officials were able to find a machine that could be adapted to wrap cellophane around Camel packages at their normal rate of production, then 125 packages per minute. On 17 November 1930 the purchasing department ordered one hundred of these machines from the Package Machinery Company of Springfield, Massachusetts, and took an option on eighty others. This option, exercised on 8 January 1931, gave Reynolds the means to wrap every package of Camels in cellophane before any other tobacco company could even order the building of appropriate machinery. Under the circumstances, Reynolds hoped to market Camels for several months before competitors could follow suit and thereby answer Camel advertising. On the twenty-third all Camels went "into moisture proof cellophane wrapping," which counteracted the lack of a good seal on the foil caused by the small amount of pressure that the ends of cigarettes will withstand without damage. Here was the great opportunity. But no advertising could begin until jobbers and retailers throughout the country had depleted their stocks of unwrapped Camel packs.[39]

In February 1931 Erwin, Wasey & Company in 1,700 daily papers, 2,300 weeklies, and 400 financial newspapers and college periodicals began running announcements of a $50,000 contest sponsored by Reynolds to advertise the new cellophane wrap. Participants were asked to answer the question: "What significant change has recently been made in the wrapping of the Camel package and what are its advantages to the smoker?" In those depression-ridden years the reward seemed munificent: $25,000 for the first prize; $10,000 for the second; $5,000 for the third; $1,000 each for the next five best answers; $500 each for the next five; and $100 each for the next twenty-five. Employees, executives, or members of their families were not allowed to compete. The judges were Charles Dana Gibson, illustrator and publisher of *Life*; Roy W. Howard, chairman of the board of Scripps Howard; and Ray Long, president of International Magazine Company and editor of *Cosmopolitan*. By day and by night the public was bombarded with information on the contest slated to end 4 March 1931.[40] The response was overwhelming. As letters poured into Winston-Salem and the sacks of mail piled up, the Reynolds offices became a bedlam and space had to be rented in other parts of town. The anticipated maximum of 300,000 entries rapidly grew to 952,229. Messengers ran their earnings to high figures as they delivered as many as 5,550 special delivery letters in one day. More than 2,500 registered letters arrived on Thursday, 5 March, in contrast to 1,500 on the previous day. Contest letters, loaded onto armored trucks at the post office, remained under armed guard while being transported to the Reynolds offices. Machines split the envelopes and office girls returned at night to open and pin them to the letters enclosed.[41]

The top winners, a Boston milkman, a housewife from Brooklyn, and a real estate dealer from Duluth, were each brought to Winston-Salem in a special railroad car and welcomed by prominent businessmen. An exorbitant amount of publicity was lavished on the visitors and officials of Erwin, Wasey & Company. Local papers carried an extravagant outlay of photography, including one picture of an embarrassed looking Bowman Gray, Sr., with the contest winners.[42] An elaborate dinner, beginning with fruit cocktail in grapefruit baskets and ending appropriately with Camel cigarettes, was accorded due seriousness and the proper tinge of amusement by the toastmaster, S. Clay Williams; the neighboring Moravian bishop, Dr. Howard E. Rondthaler; and two radio stars, Morton Downey and Tony Wons. Music was provided by John H. Peddicord's orchestra of Winston-Salem. Needless to say, the beautifully printed program carried the Camel in silhouette against pyramid and palm trees.[43] All in all, it was a gaudy affair somehow out of keeping with the dignified mien of the company's chief officers.

The elaborately advertised contest was the butt of many jests, one of the most amusing coming from the *Pitt Panther*. Presented in the form of a letter from a Filipino contestant, it read:[44]

> Gentlemen Dears: Each day I have been almost an total Lucky smoker until I buy a pack of your kind for little money and wrapped by Sellufane. I like your kind cigarette. Much better since she comes from Sellufane. . . . She has smooth back, this pack and I like to rub hand over glass front. Luck she is toasted but Sellufane she is not.

Despite the sarcasm aimed at the contest, there could be no doubt that a package of cigarettes wrapped and sealed in moisture-proof cellophane was infinitely superior to the unwrapped, dry product. This move initiated by Reynolds benefited all cigarette manufacturers and gave equal pleasure to smokers in all areas of the country.

For all its notoriety, cost, and hullabaloo, it does not appear that the Camel contest had any pronounced financial benefit. Although in 1931 Reynolds experienced a gain in net earnings of approximately $2 million over 1930, the following year it suffered more than a commensurate decline. Net earnings plummeted thereafter and did not again reach the 1931 level until 1949. By November 1931 the company was spending $2 million per month to advertise Camels alone. In fact, the adoption of cellophane on Camel packages undoubtedly profited the du Pont firm more than Reynolds. Out of gratitude, du Pont on 18 November 1960 honored Reynolds officials in a special program at the du Pont Spruance plant in Ampthill, Virginia, five miles south of Richmond. The occasion was the thirtieth anniversary of the plant, established to obtain the patronage of southern tobacco manufacturers. Reynolds, as the pioneer in the use of moisture-proof cellophane in the tobacco industry, naturally received preferential treatment.[45]

Meanwhile, Erwin, Wasey & Company had combined its showy contest with an advertisement entitled "the Camels Are Coming," the old Ayer idea used eighteen years earlier in the introduction of Camels. Follow-up advertisements appeared after the contest, the most important one showing the results of experiments on cellophane-wrapped packages conducted by the Pittsburgh Testing Laboratories. Several emphasized the Camel's superiority in always being fresh but never toasted. In another, for the week of 20 April 1931, was the well-known picture of Mrs. Mabel Balfour standing by a huge mound of contest letters.[46] Evidently Erwin, Wasey could never abandon the idea of the contest and Reynolds decided to employ a new agency.

It is uncertain just how officials of the company first contacted William C. Esty, a vice-president in the advertising firm of J. Walter Thompson, Inc. prior to April 1932. According to a statement Esty made in 1938, he formed his own company on 1 April 1932 and became advertising agent for the R. J. Reynolds Tobacco Company on 1 January 1933. William T. Smither, who worked in the Reynolds sales and advertising departments from 1907 until his retirement in 1957, while agreeing that Esty left a lucrative prosition with the Thompson agency to open his own, declared that he refused to accept small accounts and operated without any for about six months. By the time he secured the Reynolds account, he was embarrassingly short of funds. This Esty explained to Bowman Gray, Sr., who then sent him monthly advances ranging from $50,000 to $100,000 for the first six months of the contract.[47] A local paper reported that Esty was joined by Edwin R. Fuller, E. H. Cummings, and John C. Esty, all of whom had left the Thompson agency with him, as well as by Donald C. Carlisle and Gerald Carson, of Batton, Barton, Durstine & Osborne, Inc. Carson would be the new agency's copywriter. The same paper noted that Esty planned to initiate an aggressive newspaper campaign for Reynolds during the week of 16 January 1933. Similar advertising would not appear in magazines until April.[48] As it turned out, Camels were advertised in 950 daily newspapers and 150 weeklies with the opening copy in full pages and later copy ranging from 850 to 1,575 lines "depending upon each paper's circulation." Papers in large cities carried copy three times a week and other papers twice a week. One person closely connected with the campaign predicted that it would furnish one of the most powerful advertising ideas for a cigarette in years.[49]

Esty, generally regarded as an unusually vigorous man who believed in aggressive advertising, began his campaign with great verve. Incidentally, as a young man he left college to become a barker for a sideshow at Coney Island,[50] and his first advertising theme for Reynolds reflected this early environment. The series, "It's Fun to Be Fooled," usually included a magician's trick and an explanation of the sleight of hand necessary for its performance. After thus demonstrating that it was more fun to know how the trick was done, the Esty copy claimed that people should also know the truth about the cigarettes they smoked: "What about heat treating?" "What about the mildest cigarette?" and "What about blending?" How much smokers actually learned about cigarettes is open to question, but they learned a surprising amount about magic. During these drab years of the depression, this last bit of knowledge became so popular that the company issued and mailed out 750,000 copies of *The Magicians Handy Book of Cigarette Tricks* and sent 250,000 to division managers. The tricks were also serialized in the colored sections of the comic strips. They ranged from Houdini's feat of escaping from a can filled with water to sawing a woman in half. Soon magicians protested that their livelihood was being undermined.[51] The advertising theme varied—for example, an explanation of the heat-treating process might be followed by the phrase, "No Tricks Just Costlier Tobacco and a Matter of Blend."

Numerous themes, equally lively, followed the magicians' tricks. They are listed below in abbreviated form as they first appeared in newspapers:

Theme	*First Appearance*
Healthy Nerves	25 June 1933
Get a Lift with a Camel	28 May 1934
They Don't Get Your Wind	6 May 1935
Try Ten Camels (Money Back Guarantee)	18 November 1935
For Digestion's Sake	20 January 1936
Largest Selling Cigarette (Costlier Tobaccos)	5 September 1937
Tobacco Growers: I Know Tobacco,	
I Grow Tobacco	2 January 1938
Camels Agree with Me	7 February 1938
Let Up, Light Up a Camel	5 September 1938
Five Extra Smokes per Pack	1 May 1939

These themes reappeared sporadically in newspaper, magazine, radio, and other advertisements for several years.

In clever fashion Esty managed to tie in his advertising with former well-known phrases relating to Camels. In the magic series, the trick changed in each consecutive advertisement, whereas the statement about Camels was varied by such phrases as "Just costlier tobaccos in a matchless blend," "Those costly tobaccos are milder," or "It's the tobacco that counts." The "Healthy Nerves" series presented a picture of and often a testimonial from some well-known athlete such as Bill Tilden, Carl Hubbell, or Mel Ott accompanied by a statement like "Camel's Costlier Tobaccos Never Get on Your Nerves, Never Tire Your Taste." So Esty's work continued to run—a combination of testimonials for Camels, different athletes with steady nerves, and a familiar old boost for Camels combined with a new one. "Get a Lift with a Camel" followed the usual plan. In this series a railroad worker, motor boat racer, secretary, college student, or some other individual obtained renewed energy by smoking a Camel. Esty got the idea for this theme from an experiment conducted by Howard W. Haggard and Dr. Leon K. Greenberg at Yale University. A report of their study indicated that a smoker received a slight increase of energy for about thirty minutes, produced no doubt by the small amount of sugar contained in tobacco. After reading the report, Esty sought testimonials from Haggard and Greenberg. They turned him down but suggested that he have a commercial firm work out the same problem. Esty followed their advice and then began his new series. Almost immediately (in 1938) Arthur Selwyn Brown unsuccessfully brought suit against Reynolds for $1,600,000 contending that he had suggested the same advertising theme in a letter to the company in May 1932. Although Reynolds had not used his idea, Brown naturally was convinced that it had been stolen. The case attracted considerable attention because of the spectacular cross-examination of Brown, who was perhaps as well-read as the company's lawyers.[52]

The Brown suit, though costly in time and legal fees, did not generate as much interest as the hearings on the Esty theme, "For Digestion's Sake—Smoke Camels." This was a strong statement often vouched for by shadowy individuals as well as by headwaiters in famous hotel dining rooms, champion baseball players, machine operators, or jungle explorers.[53] Serious questions were raised about some of Esty's themes on 26 February 1943, when the Federal Trade Commission instituted a suit against the company for false advertising. The complaint stated that, according to impartial scientific research, smoking Camels did not keep a person in good athletic condition; Camels were not made of tobacco more costly than that used in other cigarettes; Camels did not absorb the total supply of fine tobaccos produced; Camels did not burn 25 percent, or any percent, more slowly than other brands; and Camels did not contain 28 percent, or any percent, less nicotine than other brands. On at least one of these points, however, the government was in error. According to data appearing in a prospectus put out by the American Tobacco Company in connection with a proposed issue of debentures, Reynolds paid substantially more for its leaf than did its chief rival. One Reynolds official questioned the wisdom of this long-standing policy, citing prices from the company's records and the American prospectus (see Table 10-3).[54] During 1932–43 Reynolds paid an average of $0.324 cents more per hundred pounds for flue-cured leaf than did American, but $3.21 more per hundred pounds for Burley leaf. In the hearings preceding the trial, no such point-blank evidence seemed necessary; the testimony centered more on the testimonials that Esty had used. The case dragged on for some time and the court ordered a forty-day extension of the Reynolds motion to set aside the order to stop the advertising at issue. In general, the offer of rewards for testimonials had been the work of Esty, but the R. J. Reynolds Tobacco Company was implicated because it had mailed numerous cartons of cigarettes to those who gave the testimonials.[55] The most embarrassing evidence came from Margaret Bourke-White, a well-known photographer, who received $250 in cash from the Esty agency and about fifty cartons of cigarettes for her statement on behalf of Camels. Nevertheless, at the hearing she testified that she smoked Old Golds, Luckies, or Camels and had no great preference among them. Furthermore, she stated that, as she was in business, she had been delighted to make the $250.[56]

As early as 1928 a writer in *Advertisers' Weekly* attempted to classify the advertising of the different cigarette manufacturers. American and P. Lorillard, he stated, tended to emphasize that their products did not irritate the throat. Despite criticism that they were impairing the trade generally by suggesting that other cigarettes might be harmful, both companies continued to do so. Reynolds and Liggett and Myers, on the other hand, underscored pleasure and quality as the main reasons for smoking their brands. In conclusion, the writer indicated that the claims of pleasure and quality had yielded greater profits than the anticough claims.[57] It is noteworthy that the Esty agency continued Ayer's emphasis on pleasure in smoking, though to a lesser degree, at least until 1942. Possibly the T-zone claims of the decade following that year proved too suggestive. By 1948, however, Esty frequently claimed that Camels produced "not one single case of throat irritation."

Another important dimension of cigarette advertising concerned the patronage of women. The Reynolds company was unusually slow to enter this new and untapped market, though by 1927 it had become a major target of the competition. The American Tobacco Company and P. Lorillard were the first on the scene and therefore the first to benefit, followed by Liggett and Myers in 1925. According to Reavis Cox, "it was through this means that 'Lucky Strike' took the lead away from Camel."[58] It is not certain why Reynolds delayed. No doubt the directors felt that a gradual approach to such a controversial change in social habits was advisable. Even so, it is difficult to believe that they could have long permitted any bias to close their eyes to a good financial opportunity. Perhaps they were merely more conservative in their views than their counterparts in other companies. James A. Gray once remarked that he trembled to think of the time when Ayer would surely bring in copy on smoking by women.[59]

But bring it in Ayer did as early as 1928 and the approach, though gradual, was by no means shy. In the first of these advertisements, women merely gazed approvingly at men who were smoking Camels. Next came a picture of a man and a woman seated alone in a restaurant, a table between them. He is smoking but she is not, although an opened pack of Camels lies on the table, much nearer to her than to him. Actually every preparation had been made for the woman to smoke by July 1928, when a more pointed advertisement was used.[60] In the November issue of various women's magazines, including the *Junior League Magazine, Modern Priscilla, Delineator, Pictorial Review, House and Garden, Vanity Fair, Vogue,* and *Harper's Bazaar,* a woman appears at a stylish horse race. She stands in the foreground holding a cigarette in her right hand, though apparently not

Table 10-3

Average Prices of Leaf Tobacco Purchased by the Reynolds Company
and the American Tobacco Company, 1932–1943

	Flue-cured Leaf		Burley Leaf	
Year	Reynolds	American	Reynolds	American
1932	$17.61	$12.86	$19.45	$12.98
1933	20.83	18.41	17.09	13.90
1934	33.37	35.03	24.14	23.04
1935	26.45	27.49	31.70	31.28
1936	31.15	31.97	56.50	56.51
1937	29.87	30.84	32.41	27.62
1938	26.52	26.27	25.43	22.22
1939	20.14	19.86	23.85	21.49
1940	25.56	24.75	26.37	23.88
1941	34.72	35.24	40.12	32.83
1942	42.80	41.52	50.25	45.43
1943	41.50	42.39	54.28	51.91

Source: Bookman v. R. J. R. Tob. Co. et al., Transcript of Record, docket no. 129-544
(Chancery of N.J., 1946), pp. 1828, 1832, 1878–92.

quite ready to smoke it. According to the caption, she knows her way
among the good cigarettes of the world: "A good judge of horseflesh is
always a good judge of cigarettes" and obviously she is both.[61] In December the woman is having tea alone, the empty cup balanced on her lap
and a lighted Camel in her hand. In magazines such as True Story, Picture
Play, Junior League Magazine, Delineator, Pictorial Review, and Modern
Priscilla, the caption states that, after the mad but merry whirl, youth enjoys
a rest when "a really good cigarette is like the Dawn of the New Day."[62]

Yet, the new day had not fully dawned. While the lone woman smoked
after her tea in women's magazines, she made a slightly different appeal in
publications for men. Advertisements for December 1928 carried in Texas
Druggist, Tobacco Jobber, American Legion, Forbes, Outdoor Life, and Sportsman show a man and a woman both smoking. The woman tells the man
that his selection is very wise because he has chosen Camels.[63] The following month, in magazines like Modern Priscilla, People's Home Journal, and
Household Magazine, a partially concealed figure of a man is offering a
woman a cigarette, which she, standing clearly in the foreground, is accepting. The accompanying text is clear and to the point:

A man isn't safe any more ——— Not if he has Camels in his case—
For the young ladies of the land, with their usual penetration, have
discovered the excellence of this famous cigarette. . . . So that nowa-
days when a male voice is heard to say, "Have a Camel," echo answers in a soft but prompt soprano: "I'd love to."

Dawn really broke in February 1929, when many magazines and newspapers carried an advertisement showing a male clerk in a store wrapping a
carton of cigarettes for a woman who is reaching into her purse while saying: "Camels, of course, the more you demand of cigarettes, the quicker
you come to Camels."[64] For all the scruples of Reynolds officials about
smoking by women, the Rubicon was crossed with relatively little difficulty. Nevertheless, for some time the young woman in the company's advertising found it difficult to overcome her modesty about taking a real
smoke with a *real cigarette.*

Not all of the Reynolds advertising appeared in newspapers and magazines. There was a goodly amount on billboards, though there is little
about it in the company's records. One of the early billboards in New York
City was situated at Columbus Circle on a building guaranteed not to
carry the advertisement of any other firm for three years. Early in 1928 this
space cost $4,000 per month.[65] With the new emphasis on advertising in
1933, the Camel appeared on an electric sign 75 feet long and 45 feet high
atop a building at the corner of Forty-ninth and Broadway.[66] Five years
later, the Camel sign remained at the same spot; it had been enlarged by
40 square feet and its message read, in decreasing size, "Camels—Never
Get on Your Nerves—Costlier Tobaccos."[67] Prince Albert had long occupied a position of similar honor.

Like other manufacturers, Reynolds took advantage of any available advertising media and radio was no exception. Direct proof of advertising
connected with the radio industry as a whole is generally difficult to obtain
for the years prior to 1930. N. W. Ayer and Son supposedly inaugurated
one radio program as early as 1922 and later claimed to hold several firsts
in radio advertising.[68] Yet, there is no evidence (for example, records of
payment for such advertising) that Reynolds moved into radio before
1930—the last year of Ayer's contract. It appears that the "Camel Pleasure
Hour" and the "All Star Radio Revue," which began in June 1930, were
the first radio programs sponsored by Camel cigarettes. It was entirely fitting that Reynolds's best money-maker should lead the way into this new
medium of advertising. The "Camel Caravan" followed; by 2 October
1934 the new "Camel Caravan," featuring Walter O'Keefe as master of ceremonies with Annette Hanshaw (a popular singer), Ted Husing (a sports
commentator), and Glen Gray's Casa Loma Orchestra, presented a series
of two half-hour programs per week. With occasional changes in personnel

the "Camel Caravan" was aired throughout the 1930s.[69] Apparently radio advertising caused a shift from other media rather than an increase in the cost of advertising. Extreme fluctuations in these expenditures ceased after 1934, with costs remaining at the same general levels even in 1941 when they were $15,148,000.

The year 1935 ended the cigarette war, described in *Fortune* as a struggle that shook the cigarette world. American's Lucky Strikes had surpassed Camels as early as 1929. The Chesterfields of Liggett and Myers did the same in 1933 and 1934. It was this decrease in Camel sales that had prompted the company to shift its advertising to the Esty agency in January 1933. S. Clay Williams admitted that "the whizz and whoozle" of William Cole Esty returned Camels to leadership in 1936. "Whizz and whoozle" referred to Esty's advertising style, defined by *Fortune* as the "thing with power to transform wheel horses into sprinters, hoarders into spendthrifts, and sales curves into rockets."[70] So the Camel came back on the basis of advertising rather than on its merit as the first truly American cigarette. The company had no other course now that its competitors followed the teachings of the Camel and produced replicas of that revolutionary brand.

For many years advertising continued to be handled through consultation between the Esty agency and Reynolds management. As Bowman Gray, Jr., explained in 1960, the Reynolds advertising committee was conferring with two or three men from the Esty agency when the jingle "Winston tastes good—like a cigarette should" was born.[71] According to William T. Smither virtually the same method prevailed in the day of R. J. Reynolds, with R. J. himself naturally constituting management. Smither wrote:[72]

All designs and copy had to be approved by Mr. R. J. Reynolds. He insisted that all signs be clear and easily read at a distance and had a theory that the sign to be easily read must carry as much space between each letter as was used in the stroke of the letter. We had no art department or layout men and would have to go to lithographers and ask them to submit designs for ads using wording we furnished. Always when asking for these designs, we had to insist that as much space be left between each letter of every word as was used in the stroke of the letter. Mr. R. J. would spot any deviation from this method regardless of how small as soon as a design was shown him.

One time when we were working on some eight-sheet billboards for SCHNAPPS tobacco, the lithographer sent an artist from New York to work out the design right on the billboard across the street from our office in Factory #8. This was done in order that Mr. R. J. could see exactly how the sign was going to look on the boards. In that case, this lithographer got the order, but in many, many cases designs were submitted by lithographers which we could not get approved, resulting in complete loss of time and art work to the lithographer.

The difference between the signs and indoor placards of 1910 and the sponsorship of radio programs from 1930 to 1940 was merely one of media rather than procedure.

Cigarette Production and the Handling of Leaf

Vast improvements in the manufacturing and leaf divisions from 1925 to 1940 kept pace with the latest advances in the industry. It is difficult to say which of them were the most significant. Cigarette production was greatly enhanced with the installation of Arenco packing machines and the Molins making machine. Equally important in the leaf department was the adoption of vacuum conditioners and a safer type of hogshead; both alleviated drudgery, saved labor, and accelerated operations. Essential for the manufacturing process was the acquisition of a stable source for foil, previously encumbered by the monopolistic practices of its producers. The Reynolds company also played a prominent role in establishing an American source for cigarette paper. Development of the Ecusta Paper Corporation made all cigarette manufacturers independent of the ragpickers of Europe.

The Arenco packer, first developed and patented in Sweden for use in the production of matches, proved to be a marvel for cigarettes by combining cup making, packing, and stamping in one small machine. The machine's superiority was further demonstrated by its uniformity of operation and conservation of floor space occupied by each unit—only four square feet. It reduced the cost of packaging to less than one cent per thousand.[73] Reynolds was among the first cigarette manufacturers, if not the first, to install the Arenco. In experimental work in one section of Number 12, the company packed 22,644,000 cigarettes on the Arenco in 1926.[74] Other records indicate that before the end of the year testing had been completed—on 2 March Roy C. Haberkern had written that the Arenco needed a different kind of glue to replace the regular ground opaque variety then in use, and on 12 August a Reynolds mechanic had suggested four other small changes on the machine.[75] During 1927–28, however, the company's production per machine may have fallen slightly below that of the American Tobacco Company. Supposedly by 20 January 1927 the Arenco packer in American's exhibition factory at Broadway and Forty-fifth street was turning out Lucky Strikes at the rate of 97,000 per hour,[76] whereas on 3 February 1928 Richard L. Dunstan reported that each

Reynolds machine packed 75 packages per minute at an efficiency rate of 96 percent. According to Dunstan, at that time the company had twenty-four Arenco packers in operation and ninety additional machines on order.[77]

The shift to the Arenco, apparently made as easily in Winston-Salem as in New York, was but one of many progressive steps taken by the company after the death of R. J. Reynolds. This move coupled with the adoption of cellophane three years later indicates that the Gray leadership, if not as creative, was at least as fearless as that of the company's founder. With the advent of cellophane, however, a serious problem developed in joining the Arenco packer with the cellophane wrapping machine. As the story has been handed down, when pressure was put on George H. Little to work out the problem, he declared it could not be accomplished. John C. Whitaker and Dunstan won the argument by ordering Little to stay in a small room in Number 12, with mechanics but no telephone, until the two machines were joined to operate as one. Little succeeded, apparently more easily than he did in teaching his mechanics the complexities of the metric system on which the Arenco was built. Eventually he established a small school in Number 12 to provide the required instruction.[78] Keeping pace with technical changes undoubtedly improved the skills of the Reynolds mechanics.

Writing in the *Wall Street News* in 1928, a reporter stated that recent interesting developments in the tobacco industry accounted for the price reductions that had just been made. Specifically, the "R. J. Reynolds Tobacco Company, producing close to forty per cent of the total consumption of popular priced cigarettes, was the first to announce reductions." The reporter noted that approximately 50 percent of the company's entire output of cigarettes was handled on the Arenco, combining on this machine operations that inserted cigarettes in packages, applied the glassine paper wrapper, and attached the revenue stamps.[79] Though Reynolds had never used glassine paper for this purpose, the improvement was nevertheless marked. Whether the Arenco packer was partially responsible for the reduction in the price of Camels from $6.40 to $6.00 per thousand on 21 April, as the writer in the *Wall Street News* intimated, is another matter. But on the same day American reduced the price of Lucky Strikes from $6.45 to $6.00.[80] Both companies had adopted the Arenco and both were in a position to cut prices.

Almost immediately, mechanical engineers at Reynolds heard about a packing machine made by the American Machine and Foundry Company that might be even more efficient than the Arenco. Accordingly, on 30 August 1929 the company ordered a trial packer. In October 1937 it returned the machine with suggested changes to the manufacturer and a month later received one production model. By May 1942 eleven more of these packers had arrived, although they did not totally replace the Arenco until December 1948. At that time the output of the new packer was 132 packages per minute, compared with the Arenco's rate of 75 per minute.[81]

Improvements in packing were accompanied by similar advances in the making machines. Installation on 8 June 1928 of the Muller cut-off, developed in Holland, increased cigarette production from 620 per minute (on the old Standard maker) to 800 per minute. A more dramatic increase to 1,150 per minute came with the adoption of the Mark VI model of the Molins making machine manufactured at Deptford, a suburb of London. The Mark VI was tested in the Reynolds plant from May 1930 until 11 August 1936, when the first production units arrived. According to a Molins publication, Reynolds officials stirred the industry in 1936 "when they ordered 276 Mark VI machines"—a world record. Orders were repeated and eventually 279 were installed.[82]

All of these changes were made without the agony experienced by Walter R. Reynolds when he decided to use the old Ludington cup-making machine, which became obsolete with the adoption of the Arenco packer. The company now had more sophisticated methods for procuring machinery than in the years when it sought the aid of Richard H. Wright, a machinery salesman. Furthermore, notwithstanding the improvements of U.S. manufacturers, much could be said for the superiority of machine builders in Western Europe.

Almost simultaneously with the shift to Arenco packers, the company began to produce its own tinfoil. The importance of this move is underscored by earlier developments in the U.S. foil industry. The first producer on the scene was John J. Crooke, who began operations in a New York basement. Eventually one of his rollers, John C. Conley, left him and about 1883 established the firm of John Conley & Son in New York City. Meanwhile, when his own plant failed, Crooke opened a new one in Chicago. In due course some of his tin rollers moved to St. Louis and helped to found the Johnston Tin Foil & Metal Company. Next to appear was the Conley Foil Company, successor of John Conley & Son, which was incorporated on 12 December 1899 under the auspices of the American Tobacco Company. For many years the new Conley firm held a virtual monopoly over the production of tinfoil. Moreover, it acquired all the capital stock of the Johnston Tin Foil & Metal Company, whereas American held 60 percent of the Conley stock.[83] After dissolution of the American Tobacco Combination in 1911, the Conley firm, by virtue of its previously favored position, continued to dominate the foil industry. This was true even though the Johnston company had been dissolved from the Tobacco Combination on the same terms as Conley, the stock in each going to the common stockholders of the old American Tobacco Company.[84]

Another foil producer, Lehmaier, Schwartz & Company, also located in New York as early as 1899, had suffered a serious decline by 1907 after a large portion of its sales had been lost to the Conley Foil Company. During these years the two New York firms engaged in a bitter rivalry. This included accusations that former employees of one company had taken trade secrets to the other. On one occasion, a Conley superintendent was tried for buying a trade secret from an employee of Lehmaier, Schwartz but fined for violating the New York antitipping statute. Suffice it to say, the Conley Foil Company paid the fine. When Lehmaier, Schwartz began to emphasize the production of bottle caps, John Conley, Jr., insinuated that it was able to do so because of secrets stolen from his firm. Meanwhile, Lehmaier, Schwartz & Company had purchased the Patent Foil Company of Philadelphia and the Palen Tin Foil Company of Kingston, New York.[85]

Seemingly tobacco manufacturers had no choice but to buy foil from the Conley Foil Company, although it was generally disliked. Reynolds was no exception to the rule. In a letter to young John C. Whitaker, then serving in the United States Navy, Robert E. Lasater expressed his pleasure that Whitaker had seen a foil plant and become acquainted with an individual who was familiar with the machinery and the process used in making foil. Lasater added the following request:[86]

> Wish you would find out if Conley controls the factory you visited? Also keep your investigations from the Conley foil people—who possibly would resent our taking supplies from outside sources—as he has a monopoly almost of the foil business. We need more foil— as you know the shortage of last year and the class of work in manufacturing foil—which we are compelled to accept—and stand the loss— I would be delighted to be able to make our foil here in led [sic]— When this war is at an end, and you come back to help us you may be in a position to put us wise on this question— Thanking you again for your interest in our necessity—"Foil"—

In less than a year the company was presented with an alternative, though it was not exactly what Lasater had in mind. On 24 January 1919 Richard S. Reynolds, once a director of the company and later the founder of Reynolds Metals, completed the purchase of all machinery needed to manufacture foil—not an easy task, as he had discovered. *"It's one of the closest held secrets I know of,"* he emphasized in a letter to Harry H. Shelton, the company's general counsel. On the other hand, he had been fortunate to find a capable engineer who was superintendent of the Johnston Tin Foil & Metal Company from 1913 to mid-1918. Advice from this engineer, declared Reynolds, had already saved him more than $50,000 in machinery. "In addition to this," he noted, "we secured all the latest attachments and improvements, which have been added by American and Conley Foil Company, in their own shops, of which the machinery manufacturers know nothing. The Foil Companies never allow machinery manufacturers in their plants."[87] It may well be surmised that Reynolds bought his machinery from the Johnston Tin Foil & Metal Company.

The new firm of Richard Reynolds—then called the Reynolds Corporation but shortly to be known as the United States Foil Company—and the R. J. Reynolds Tobacco Company struck a deal. On 2 April 1919 Richard S. Reynolds and William N. Reynolds signed a contract confirming an earlier oral agreement. These were its terms:[88]

1. That the Reynolds Corporation at once purchase machinery for producing 20,000 pounds of standard tin foil per day.

2. That the Reynolds Corporation install this machinery in its factory in Louisville, Kentucky, and begin operations as soon as possible.

3. That as soon as the Reynolds Corporation had shown it could produce foil satisfactory for the use of the R. J. Reynolds Tobacco Company, the following agreement would become effective between the two companies:

   a. A new corporation will be jointly chartered and organized under the laws of Delaware with an authorized capital of one million dollars.

   b. Both parties agree that any part of the stock will be jointly subscribed to on the basis of 49 per cent for the Reynolds Corporation and 51 per cent for the R. J. Reynolds Tobacco Company.

   c. The Reynolds Corporation will sell and the new corporation (U.S. Foil Company) will buy for cash, on the basis of cost, all machinery, equipment, land, and factories which the Reynolds Corporation may have provided under this agreement and which can be used to advantage in the production of foil and waxed paper.

   d. The R. J. Reynolds Tobacco Company agrees to buy a minimum of 20,000 pounds of composition foil per day for ten years on the same basis of cost as outlined in the contract between the Conley Foil Company and the R. J. Reynolds Tobacco Company, dated February, 1912.

   e. The R. J. Reynolds Tobacco Company agrees also to make the new corporation an extra allowance of one cent per pound, as is now being made to the Conley Foil Company, to equalize the cost of labor until Conley shall relieve all customers of this charge.

f. In consideration of the extra effort and rush production which the R. J. Reynolds Tobacco Company will require with some of the foil contracted for, it agrees to allow the new corporation, in addition to the one cent bonus per pound already mentioned, a bonus of one cent per pound on all foil delivered by the new corporation under this agreement for the first year—this to cover the increased cost of crowded production with unskilled labor.

Two important facts emerge from this contract: the R. J. Reynolds Tobacco Company needed foil and no other tobacco company was named in the contract. June found Richard Reynolds anxious to form the new corporation and the R. J. Reynolds Tobacco Company hesitant to do so because "of the more or less acute situation . . . confronting" the company and a fear that publicity given to such a move would "aggravate the situation to the danger point."[89]

The Reynolds company soon overcame its reservations, however. On 22 August 1919 Walter R. Reynolds, Harry H. Shelton, and Richard S. Reynolds agreed on the name of the new "foil enterprise."[90] The plan was scarcely completed before the Reynolds Corporation borrowed $150,000 from the R. J. Reynolds Tobacco Company by means of three demand notes dated 22 September and 6 and 15 October.[91] In some manner not revealed in the records, William N. Reynolds contacted George Garland Allen (17 May 1874–10 October 1960) and James B. Duke, then officials of the British-American Tobacco Company. After agreeing to include the British-American Tobacco Company with the R. J. Reynolds Tobacco Company and the Reynolds Corporation in the formation of the United States Foil Company, William Reynolds discussed details of the bylaws with Duke and Allen.[92] Confirmation of the verbal understanding between the three companies is dated 30 September 1919 and signed by Walter R. Reynolds, Richard S. Reynolds, and George G. Allen. According to this agreement, the United States Foil Company was to be incorporated with an authorized capital stock of $3,000,000 of which $900,000 would be issued immediately with each participant subscribing to $300,000 worth of stock. In lieu of cash the Reynolds Corporation would transfer at cost all of its assets pertaining to tinfoil and waxed paper to the United States Foil Company. Both tobacco companies were to purchase a substantial amount of their requirements for foil and waxed paper from the new firm. Full details relating to quality were made a part of the agreement.[93]

Judging from the copies of minutes and other relevant papers, all went according to plan, although there was friction between the United States Foil Company and the R. J. Reynolds Tobacco Company shortly before the new corporation began operations. Richard Reynolds did not feel that the R. J. Reynolds Tobacco Company should participate in the profits for 1919. Walter Reynolds strongly disagreed, stating in a lengthy, formal objection that he could not reconcile the agreement of 2 April 1919 with the "present attitude" of the Reynolds Corporation. He believed that the R. J. Reynolds Tobacco Company had equity in the 1919 profits for several reasons, the chief ones being the basis on which the stock had been subscribed, the loan to the foil corporation in September and October 1919, and acceptance by the tobacco company as early as 1 September 1919 of slightly inferior foil and waxed paper made by the Reynolds Corporation.[94]

More serious disagreement eventually arose. Nevertheless, the Reynolds company on 1 January 1922, and again on 1 February 1924, contracted to buy foil from the United States Foil Company. The second contract covered a five-year period and provided extensive guarantees.[95] Yet on 3 January 1924 the directors gave Richard Reynolds thirty days in which to raise $750,000 for the purchase of 5,000 shares of stock in the United States Foil Company then held by the R. J. Reynolds Tobacco Company. Evidently Richard Reynolds saw his stock fall into other hands when the tobacco company disposed of its holdings on 5 June 1924.[96]

The fact remained, however, that the Reynolds company still had no suitable source for foil. Another opportunity was presented when two directors left the United States Foil Company: Seth Q. Kline, superintendent of manufacturing, and Walter Earl Gaines (b. 26 February 1891), production manager and treasurer. Kline, formerly with the Johnston Tin Foil & Metal Company, was a mechanical engineer of some ability. Gaines had served during World War I as government inspector of power containers made in the plant of Richard S. Reynolds. Possibly stirred by the withdrawal of the R. J. Reynolds Tobacco Company, Kline and Gaines sold their stock in Richard Reynolds's foil company and came to Winston-Salem. There they proposed to establish a foil plant to be turned over to the R. J. Reynolds Tobacco Company at the end of a specified period. During that time the Reynolds company would buy all of its foil from them at a working margin of three cents; it would also have the option to buy the business at book value of tangible assets. Reynolds, through its tin tag suppliers in Louisville, obtained an appraisal of the two men and promptly refused the offer. Kline and Gaines proceeded to Richmond, Virginia, where they founded the Tobacco Foil Company.[97]

One day in 1927, Roy C. Haberkern knocked on the door of the Tobacco Foil Company in Richmond only to find it locked. On the back door he found a notice that the plant was closed for lack of orders. Haberkern reported his discovery to James A. Gray, and on 27 June 1927 the Reynolds company drew up a contract with Kline, Gaines, and Robert B. Campbell, another officer and director of the foil company. The three men sold their business to Reynolds but agreed to operate it as soon as it could be moved to Winston-Salem.[98] A year later Gray offered to sell the real estate, buildings, and remaining machinery and fixtures of the Richmond foil plant to Liggett and Myers, which had been its chief customer. At that time he indicated his understanding that Liggett and Myers wished to retain Gaines's services. Possibly Gray did not feel they were needed in Winston-Salem. At any rate, Clinton W. Toms of Liggett and Myers curtly refused the offer,[99] and by 24 August 1928 the Tobacco Foil Company had discontinued all operations in Richmond.

Meanwhile, on 6 August 1928 Reynolds announced that it had begun to roll tinfoil in its Winston-Salem plant largely with machinery moved from Richmond. Evidently the foil division developed rapidly and continued to fill the orders of Liggett and Myers. Extensive additions were made to the plant in 1929 in order to increase output.[100]

The foil division continued to roll a combination of tin and lead until World War II intervened. During these years the more expensive aluminum product had been considered. As early as 1928 P. Lorillard wrapped its Old Golds in aluminum foil, although no special advertising accompanied the change from tinfoil. Reynolds officials carefully followed the prices of lead, tin, zinc, and aluminum and by the late 1930s decided it might be advantageous to switch to aluminum. Apparently when their technicians were unable to make this shift, Roy Haberkern sought aid from the Aluminum Company of America, whose experts designed the plant without charge—though its motives were not entirely altruistic. By December 1941, the foil division was ready to produce aluminum foil just as the Japanese bombed Pearl Harbor and ended foil production for the time being. The move to aluminum had been timely, however, for in 1944 Gaines and his men began to produce antiradar foil for the U.S. government. No cigarette foil came from the newly improved plant until late 1945—at first at a thickness of four ten-thousandths of an inch. With the advent of the Korean War and the preparedness program, when the supply of aluminum was reduced, rolling proceeded but at twenty-five ten-thousandths of an inch thick, which apparently remained the standard thereafter. Because of the expensive machinery required, the foil division did not work aluminum pig until April 1960; previously it used aluminum plate twenty-five and one-half inches wide and twenty-six thousandths of an inch thick. Incidentally, in 1951 the cost of aluminum foil amounted to one cent less per million cigarettes than the cost of lead-tinfoil in 1940. Had Reynolds purchased aluminum foil on the market in 1951, it would have cost $2 million more than that produced in its own foil division. Moreover, the company earned a modest profit from the sale of aluminum foil to Liggett and Myers, not to mention the profits it received from the production of antiradar foil.[101]

The foils division, though far overshadowed by the company's tobacco products, made considerable progress. In August 1955 the company bought the machinery, equipment, and supplies of a local firm, the Frank H. Driscoll Company and its subsidiary (Foil Products, Inc.), to manufacture laminated foil, thus making possible the development and ultimate production of improved wrapping materials. Two years later, the directors combined the foil and foil products division under the name of Archer Aluminum; it was assigned a sales manager and a department of research.[102] Thereafter the new plant, completed in 1958, was expanded into three plants with more than one-half million square feet of work and storage space. This move, while by no means a diversification in products, did represent a trend in that direction. Though the company began to produce foil well after the day of R. J. Reynolds, he had conceived the idea and, according to Roy C. Haberkern, had sent Richard S. Reynolds to Germany before 1912 to learn the foil business. To end the foil story properly, it must be said that the Conley Foil Company closed its doors in 1924, with Lehmaier, Schwartz & Company obtaining the business and the American Tobacco Company, the property[103]—a most fitting end to the Conley monopoly. Because foil was essential in packing tobacco products, the Reynolds company had been wise to develop its own source. Possibly it was the first in the industry to do so after 1911.

In 1939 Reynolds vastly improved its leaf operations by installing vacuum conditioners. This eliminated the use of sweat houses and effected great savings in the handling of leaf. To understand the importance of this move, it is necessary to analyze the function of sweat houses in the preparation of redried, stored leaf for stemming and manufacturing. Hogsheads packed with dry, unstemmed leaf were brought from storage into sweat houses, which were designed to soften the brittle leaf so that the stem could be removed with a minimum loss. An expensive investment at best, a sweat house contained numerous boilers and steam pipes constantly in operation with the temperature at 100 to 105 degrees and humidity at 90 to 95 percent. The temperature was kept even higher over the weekend, when employees did not have to enter the hot, humid sweat houses to roll out hogsheads of tobacco. Nevertheless, the steam softened only a relatively small amount of tobacco near the inside surface of the hogsheads, leaving the tobacco in the interior generally dry and brittle. Usually the bundles of leaf were then run through an ordering machine. More often than not, stemmers sat on benches surrounded by dry fragments of tobacco leaf often lying a foot deep on the floor.

Tobacco manufacturers, who had long recognized the wasteful nature of this process, naturally welcomed any improvement. According to the records available, the vacuum conditioner that partly solved the problem involved expensive but simple, rugged machinery with few moving parts.

The vacuum conditioner consisted of a large steel vacuum chamber and steam jet vacuum pumps to exhaust all air or draw a vacuum on the tobacco in the chamber and even on the hogsheads in which the tobacco was packed. Live steam was then introduced into the vacuum chamber to flow into the entire mass of tobacco. Its subsequent condensation circulated moisture throughout the hogsheads except for a very small portion at the center. With vacuum pumps, the temperature of the tobacco could be reduced to any set figure and the vacuum chamber vented in order to equalize the internal and external pressure so that the tobacco could be removed. In 1938 one Reynolds engineer reported that he had seen a unit that softened fifteen hogsheads of tobacco in one hour. Other advantages he noted were more efficient performance of stemming machines with 10 to 20 percent fewer drop leaves; a saving of 33 percent in the labor costs of the blending department; improved cigarette filler; and additional aging by virtue of the acceleration of nature's normal aging process. Possibly the least suspected benefit of the vacuum conditioner was the complete sterilization of the leaf by the destruction of the tobacco (or cigarette) beetle at all stages of life.

There were disputes over the patents for this machinery held by John H. Swisher & Sons, the Thermal Engineering Corportation of Richmond, Virginia (owners of the patent of Franklin Smith of New Haven, Connecticut), and the Guardite Corporation of Chicago (owners of the Merriam and Wiles patent—no. 2,080,179, issued 11 May 1937). The Guardite Corporation later acquired the Swisher patent, which predated the one held by Thermal Engineering by about four years. It was then a race between Guardite and Thermal Engineering, the latter backed by Carrington & Michaux, Inc., a leaf firm, and Larus & Brother Company, Inc., both of Richmond. The winner was the Guardite Corporation, which purchased the patent held by Thermal Engineering on 4 March 1940.

Meanwhile, by 1936 the R. J. Reynolds Tobacco Company, as well as the American Tobacco Company and Brown and Williamson, had begun dealing with Thermal Engineering. In April 1936, the Reynolds company bought one vacuum conditioner (known as a Thermo-Vactor), evidently for experimental purposes. According to available records, the company next purchased on 16 November 1938 three units at a cost of $320,000, plus $97,950 for installation. Confidential correspondence between Reynolds and Thermal Engineering, found when the latter was purchased by Guardite, gives some evidence of collusion involved in this equipment sale between Thermal Engineering and employees in Reynolds's leaf handling and manufacturing divisions. Moreover, the correspondence also disclosed that the three units purchased by Reynolds had actually cost Thermal Engineering only $89,000 and that the Richmond backers of that corporation had received $16,000 from the Reynolds purchase of the early vacuum conditioners. Notwithstanding, the Reynolds company began the systematic installation of vacuum conditioners in the spring of 1939.[104]

Association with the Guardite Corporation dates from the installation of a conditioner in Number 10 in December 1947. Long before the Brook Cove plant was completed in 1959 and Whitaker Park opened in 1961, this machinery had become a standard fixture. It is noteworthy that the original vacuum conditioning unit for building Number 30 could accurately add or subtract moisture within one-tenth of one percent of weight to seventy hogsheads of tobacco in two hours. Furthermore, the 70,000 pounds of leaf reached the vacuum chamber by way of forklift trucks and chain conveyors just as it had been packed for storage.

The patented hogshead adopted in 1937, while less spectacular than the vacuum conditioner, substantially improved the handling of leaf tobacco. This invention was the work of Early Lucius Snow (4 March 1893 – 19 January 1958), who joined the Reynolds company in 1908, and his assistant, Ernest Love Barkley, Jr., a Reynolds employee since 1921.[105] Originally, hogsheads for the storage of tobacco were made of unfinished timber and wooden hoops. Eventually metal hoops replaced those made of hand-riven white oak, largely because the supply of white-oak timber had been exhausted. On 8 May 1934, Snow and Barkley received a patent on a simple machine for assembling their new type of hogshead in two halves, and the company began to build them on an experimental basis. Snow's idea was to produce staves and heading material of a standard size, to use prepunched metal hoops, and to remove tobacco from the hogsheads merely by withdrawing pins to release the hoops holding the two halves together. In that way the tobacco stood free of the hogshead, though retaining its shape. By the old system the heavy, cumbersome hogsheads were smashed in with axes and the broken staves and headings generally sold for kindling. It was a wasteful procedure requiring freshly made hogsheads each year. Salvaging timber from the old-style hogsheads cost more in labor than could be saved in timber.

In 1937 Snow and Barkley gave the company the right to build an unlimited number of hogsheads according to their patent. At the same time they reserved the right to license other manufacturers and leaf dealers to make similar hogsheads.[106] Reynolds then began to manufacture them on a large scale. About the same time the cooperage shop instituted the use of plywood, cut to preset specifications and ordered from the West Coast. Shipped by water to Norfolk, Virginia, the plywood came into Winston-Salem by rail. Improvements on the hogshead-assembling machine and the use of prepunched metal bands for hoops enabled the coopers to work with ease and rapidity. This hogshead could be reused; or, if one of its thirty staves became weakened, it could be replaced and the hogshead would remain as sturdy as when new. This system had many advantages over the old method, the most important being economic. Not only could the hogsheads be reassembled and reused but also they cost less to ship—the plywood hogshead weighed only 122 pounds in contrast to 160 to 170 pounds for the older model. Moreover, the empty hogshead halves could be stored in far less space in buildings or in freight cars. They could be built the year round, whereas the old type had to be constructed just before it was used; as it became more seasoned, it fell apart. Economy and speed in packing and removing tobacco from the new hogsheads resulted from greater ease in opening the hogsheads, rapidity in reassembling them, and the absence of roughness in the wood, which in the old type injured the laborers and tore the tobacco leaves.[107]

The most obvious demonstration of the company's maturity during 1925–40, however, was its prominent role in establishing an American source for the production of cigarette paper—a move that benefited the entire tobacco industry. The hardships of U.S. cigarette manufacturers in World War I were nothing compared with what they might have been in the next war when the enemy occupied France, for many years virtually the sole source of supply. Few realized the seriousness of the situation more clearly than Roy C. Haberkern who, as purchasing agent during the First World War, had shared the anxieties of Walter R. Reynolds. In encouraging and assisting Henry H. Straus with his plans for producing cigarette paper in the United States, Haberkern became the driving force behind the company's involvement in the project.

Straus, who in 1902 had emigrated to the United States from Mannheim, Germany, soon became well-known to many tobacco manufacturers because of his work as an agent for the sale of cigarette paper and related supplies. Evidently he stood well with the Reynolds company. In 1918 he gave Walter Reynolds a confidential report on the amount of cigarette paper imported by some of the "Big Four" producers, and Reynolds replied in strict confidence one week later. Then in 1920 Straus sought Reynolds's help in connection with litigation against a French firm.[108] Nine years later Straus visited René Bolloré, Sr., in France and arranged to buy a one-half interest in the Bolloré paper mill at Troyes. At that time the Reynolds company purchased its cigarette paper almost exclusively from the Bolloré plant at Cascadec, France. Reynolds, Straus, and the Bolloré family now formed a triumvirate with cigarette paper as a unifying bond.[109] When René Bolloré visited the United States in the 1930s, Straus accompanied him to Winston-Salem. Meanwhile, as purchasing agent, Roy Haberkern maintained the close association between Reynolds and Straus.

In 1933 Straus laid his plans to produce cigarette paper in the southern United States using seed flax. In view of their long-standing relationship, it probably was natural for Reynolds and the Bollorés to become involved in the effort. Straus often sought Haberkern's advice and received much of his time. In 1941 he wrote that Haberkern "more than anybody . . . understood what [he] wanted to accomplish . . . and unceasingly inspired [him]." Other Reynolds officials also showed their interest by giving Haberkern a month's leave to help Straus find a proper location for the plant where a plentiful and pure water supply would be available, as well as study other matters. In the end, however, the Reynolds company did more than offer advice, as did the Bollorés. On 31 December 1938, they outlined with unusual care their reasons for lending Straus's Ecusta Paper Corporation $1 million for its development in North Carolina. Taken together, they constitute a page in industrial statesmanship and enlightened self-interest with the memory of Walter Reynolds's stay in Europe hovering clearly in the background:

1. It has been vitally important for many years to insure an adequate supply of cigarette paper.

2. Cigarette paper has long been purchased abroad, especially in France, and is subject to duty.

3. International disturbances, despite long-term contracts, have disrupted the company's source of supply of cigarette paper.

4. Recent experiments at home and abroad have demonstrated the practicality of manufacturing cigarette paper in the United States from domestic raw materials.

5. The persons who conducted the experiments have organized the Ecusta Paper Corporation under the laws of Delaware and have attempted to start a plant at Brevard, North Carolina, with a plan to commence the manufacture of cigarette paper.

6. The Ecusta Paper Corporation has entered into negotiations with the R. J. Reynolds Tobacco Company with a view of supplying the company a substantial part of its requirements and likewise has sought aid of the company in financing in part the establishment of the Ecusta Paper Corporation in the United States.

7. The president of the R. J. Reynolds Tobacco Company, with the approval of the Executive Committee, has executed on the part of the company a so-called Loan-Agreement dated December 1, 1938, providing for a loan of $1,000,000.00 to the Ecusta Paper Corporation.

8. The president of the R. J. Reynolds Tobacco Company has concluded negotiations for the purchase from Ecusta Paper Cor-

poration, when available, at least one-half of its requirements
of cigarette paper under terms of the agreement, dated December 22, 1938.

The resolutions that followed these conditional clauses were all routine except one—that, from the standpoints of cost and stability of supply, it was
in the best interest of the company to aid and encourage the establishment
of a plant for the production of cigarette paper in the United States.[110]
    The cooperative nature of the effort was remarkable. Liggett and Myers
also lent the Ecusta Paper Corporation $1 million and it was generally be-
lieved that the P. Lorillard Tobacco Company made a sizable loan to
Straus. Straus and the Bollorés furnished great blocks of their stock in
Ecusta as collateral for these loans.[111] Moreover, Reynolds had free use of
Ecusta's facilities for the development of reconstituted leaf tobacco.[112] Had
the source for cigarette paper remained in Europe, it is doubtful that the
American cigarette industry could have progressed as it did even without
the misfortunes of war. The ragpickers of Europe could never have found a
sufficient quantity of worn flaxen material for the industry after adoption
of the filter-tipped cigarette. Ironically, Straus's plant, named "Ecusta" for
a Cherokee word meaning rippling waters, began production on the very
day that war broke out in Europe. Had it not been for the prompt loans of
Reynolds, P. Lorillard, and Liggett and Myers, the story might well have
been different. Viewed historically, the entire project was but a continuation of the work of an early member of the Bolloré family who returned
from the Far East in 1822 with the secrets of a Chinese papermaker in his
head. In the same year he established a paper mill in Brittany.[113] That plant
as well as plants in the New World served as laboratories for Harry Straus
to test the seed flax he would use in making cigarette paper.
    As time passed and all could see the value of what had been accom-
plished, claims were made that various banks from Washington, D.C., to
Georgia had participated in the financing of Ecusta, all under the leadership of Robert March Hanes (12 September 1890–10 March 1959),
president of the Wachovia Bank and Trust Company.[114] But these claims
had to do with the expansion of the Ecusta plant, not with its initiation.
This misconception probably resulted from the Reynolds company's sale
of its Ecusta note to the Wachovia bank and Hanes's consequent appointment to the board of the Ecusta Paper Corporation. The R. J. Reynolds
Tobacco Company might well have become the owner of the Ecusta plant
had it not been for the banker's instinct of James A. Gray to give first
priority to the repayment of loans. Too, in view of the Kentucky Trail
of 1941, he may have feared charges of attempted monopoly. Other
firms subsequently manufactured cigarette paper in the United States. In

retrospect, Reynolds's failure to acquire the Ecusta Paper Corporation, which eventually went to Olin industries, seems to have been an error in judgment.

Retirement and Health Benefits

Amid the push to modernize facilities, improve production techniques, and acquire a stable source of essential materials, the R. J. Reynolds Tobacco Company did not forget its employees. In late 1929 the company established a retirement plan for all employees and arranged for them to obtain low-cost, comprehensive insurance. Perhaps no other company benefits, including the notable profit-sharing plan of 1956, contributed more to the welfare of employees. These supports came at a propitious time when encouragement was badly needed.

The company's first retirement plan, said to be the 101st such plan established in the United States, was preceded by makeshift attempts to help workers who met with illness or other misfortunes before and after retirement, especially the latter. It was generally believed that William N. Reynolds frequently made available small allocations from his personal funds to aid retired and poverty-stricken employees. In 1927 the need was formally addressed in a motion made by Robert E. Lasater. As a result, the board authorized the treasurer to honor vouchers approved by Lasater for financial assistance up to $250 per month.[115] Though a commendable move, it proved to be inadequate. Two and one-half years later, the directors launched a full-fledged retirement plan for all employees. General requirements for participation included twenty years of continuous employment by the company ending at age sixty-five for men and sixty for women. A break in employment was allowed only for service in the armed forces. Administered by the Retirement Plan Board until its termination on 31 December 1946, the plan served to cushion the retirement of 776 employees. In fact, the total amount they received exceeded that provided under the second plan, perhaps because of the company's later contributions to Social Security. Cora Robertson Brewer was one of the last to retire (on 31 December 1946) under the 1929 plan. Four years later she declared that, as a young woman, she never thought a time would come when she could quit work and be cared for by the company.[116]

The group insurance plan, scheduled to take effect on 3 December 1929 along with the retirement plan, offered group life, total and permanent disability, and accident and health insurance through the Equitable Life Assurance Society of the United States. Though its final adoption needed approval of 75 percent of the employees, 98 percent endorsed the plan. Employees were eligible to participate after only six months' employment.

Seasonal workers, however, were excluded; they received no insurance until 1962. A medical examination was unnecessary if the employee applied for the insurance within thirty days from the date of eligibility. The company evidently assumed the major cost of the plan except for a small monthly premium paid by the employee (see Table 10-4). A "slightly amended" version of the plan, which appeared after the first explanatory leaflet but with the same date, permitted retired employees to retain life insurance protection at the same premium amount. Favorable claim experiences led to a substantial increase in the amount of coverage in 1931. This change affected all wage earners, whose insurance policies now ranged from $2,000 to $20,000 at a monthly cost from $2 to $15.[117]

Possibly the most significant feature of this insurance plan was the protection it gave victims of accidents that occurred on the job. In such cases, an insured employee experiencing disability or illness before reaching the age of sixty paid no further premiums and received the principal sum in monthly installments until death "or until the full amount (was) paid." In the case of nonoccupational accidents, the employee collected indemnity payments for thirteen weeks from the eighth day of disability. The thirteen-week indemnity also applied to disabilities resulting from illnesses beginning after the age of sixty. Maternity benefits were limited to six weeks. All provisions of the plan were over and above any afforded by the compensation laws of North Carolina. There were, of course, occasional flaws in the plan's administration—apparently also by the Retirement Plan Board. In the last illness of Samuel Smith Stanley, long a faithful employee, the accident and health benefits amounted to $18 per week until 1936, though Stanley lived until 1941. When James Murphy died in 1930, the $500 due in insurance could not be paid because Louise Murphy, his widow, and Sarah Pauline Murphy, of Cleveland County, North Carolina, each claimed to be the "Rose Murphy" who had been named beneficiary. The money was left in the clerk of court's custody.[118] Nevertheless, the retirement and insurance plans of 1929 gave the employees more benefits than they had ever received before. The local newspaper bluntly described the retirement plan as a move going "far toward solving the problem of dividing the profits of the business equitably and justly so that the fruits of the enterprise shall go to those who deserve them." The same paper greeted the group insurance plan with an editorial headed: "Reynolds Takes Another Step Forward."[119]

The problem of financing the first retirement plan was not to be solved for some time. It ultimately involved the use of common stock that the company previously had bought in blocks for resale to its employees. Employee demand for the stock decreased greatly in 1929 and, as the depression continued, remained low for a number of years. At the end of 1932 the company held for resale about 100,000 shares of the common stock

Table 10-4
Partial Provisions of Group Insurance Plan
Established by the Reynolds Company, 1929

Annual Wages or Salary	Amount of Life Insurance	Amount of Weekly Indemnity	Monthly Cost to Employee
Not more than $800	$ 500	$ 6.00	$ .70
Above $800 but not more than $1,200	750	8.00	1.00
Above $1,200 but not more than $1,600	1,000	12.00	1.40
Above $1,600 but not more than $2,500	2,000	18.00	2.50
Above $2,500 but not more than $3,500	3,000	25.00	3.50
Above $3,500 but not more than $5,500	6,000	35.00	6.00
Above $5,500 but not more than $7,500	8,000	40.00	7.50
Above $7,500	10,000	40.00	9.00

Source: Leaflets: *Announcement of Group Life Insurance, Total and Permanent Disability Insurance*, and *Accident and Health Insurance Plan for Regular Full-Time Employees of the R. J. Reynolds Tobacco Company* (slightly amended), 3 December 1929—in files of J. E. Conrad, personnel department, R. J. Reynolds Tobacco Company.

valued on its books at about $67 per share. During that year the price of common stock varied on the market from $64 on 2 May to $71.37½ on 13 June. From 1931 to 1932, the amount held by employees other than directors dropped by 10,298 shares and from 1932 to 1933, by 8,336 shares. In the same periods, the number held by directors declined by 8,939 and 113,000 shares, respectively. It became evident that the 100,000 shares or more then held by the company would not soon be purchased by employees. Moreover, passage of the Securities Act in May 1933 prevented the sale of company stock to employees after a sixty-day grace period. Making no further sales to its employees after July 1933, Reynolds was left with approximately 100,000 shares of its common stock. Though this might have been disposed of on the stock market at a considerable risk, the directors instead resolved to use it as the basis for funding the retirement plan. In order to do so, the amount of stock had to be supplemented with an additional 100,000 shares. In 1943, when testifying about the common stock held in the retirement fund, S. Clay Williams explained the origin of the idea: [120]

> We had a group insurance plan and retirement plan in force for quite a few years then. We were carrying it ourselves. It was not funded. We did not have the retirement end of it covered by any insurance company. Our group policy was a policy with the Equitable Life (Assurance Society of the United States) down here, but the retirement end of that pair of propositions was not funded in any way. We had been enquiring into what the liability was under it and would be under it, were interested in actuarial studies, and had some reports made to us. One calculation that we had had the result of put before us was to the effect that, to fund that thing all the way through and carry it for the employees would require close to $10,000,000. That is, to fund it on a basis where it would carry itself through without having to run charges against the employees.

> After or during the time that was under consideration, this idea of using that 200,000 shares of common stock as a vehicle through which to carry that load, without running any additional charges against the stockholders, was suggested and came under consideration. We had been very hesitant to pick up an expense item that would run against the income of the company from year to year in any substantial amount on those things. We were very much hesitant to reach into the surplus of the company and take out a number of millions of dollars and set them aside for funding that kind of thing. Of course, under the retirement plan, when you start it there is a great deal of accumulated liability. Some men are at all but retirement age and some are younger. So the figures were big. This idea of letting that 200,000 shares of stock be set aside for that purpose and the income therefrom applied to meeting the requirements of that purpose and keep charges on that account from running against the income of the company and stockholders generally, was very appealing. We studied it, and then realized that, if we would put it in shape where each year there would be accrued to a reserve and out of the potential fund available for distribution to employees an amount that would equal on each of those shares what a participator would get on them if he held them, we would in the end and not many years down the road have that 200,000 shares of stock paid for through that reserve, without having to run any particular charges—any new charges—against the income or the stockholders of the company.

> That is the background of the appointment of the committee at September 1933 to make a study and bring in a final recommendation as to whether or not we should put that plan through. The idea had a

great deal of enthusiastic support, in our director's group, and had full acceptance with anybody who knew anything about it and whose reaction to it I knew.

This situation came about from the agreement of William N. Reynolds, Bowman Gray, Sr., James A. Gray, and S. Clay Williams to transfer 100,000 shares of their own common stock to the company in exchange for the same amount of New Class B Stock, though they did so at a loss of $30 per share. They also lost their participation rights. This exchange (30,000 shares each from Reynolds and the two Grays and 10,000 shares from Williams) brought the company's holdings of common stock to approximately 200,000 shares. Though Robert E. Lasater originally suggested using the stock to fund the retirement plan, he made no contribution to the effort.[121] On 7 September 1933 the directors appointed James A. Gray, Lasater, and Williams to study the proposal further. On 31 December the directors approved the plan to set aside 200,000 shares of company-held common stock into an account known as the "Retirement and Insurance Investment Fund."[122] Although the initial plan was terminated on 31 December 1946, 157 employees who had retired under its provisions still remained as of 11 April 1963. When participation in common stock subsequently was eliminated, these retired employees were carried on the company's payroll.[123]

Establishment of the retirement and group insurance plans, both the first of their kind in the tobacco industry, cannot be directly attributed to any pressure from legislation or labor, though many benefits paid by the company did originate in such fashion. William Reynolds, in contributing small amounts of his personal funds to the needy, showed concern for the misery that sometimes confronted him. Possibly the belief that some directors held embarrassingly large amounts of stock, the high cost of living in the 1920s, and the 20 percent cut in wages in 1921 were also factors. Lower echelons of management undoubtedly felt the situation keenly. For example, on 14 December 1926 Richard L. Dunstan wrote Charles M. Griffith of the payroll department, requesting that he not collect for three weeks any of the $35 advanced to Frazier D. Cornwall on 23 November. Dunstan then outlined the trouble Cornwall had experienced in having his mother buried in Philadelphia.[124] Such cases were probably numerous. In its reaction to announcement of the retirement and insurance plans, the local newspaper indicated sympathy for the Reynolds employees. But whatever the general sentiment may have been, the personal generosity of Bowman Gray, Sr., William N. Reynolds, James A. Gray, and S. Clay Williams was exceptional; in their concern for the welfare of the employees they were, in their geographic area, far ahead of their day.

Changes in Sales Policies

Another, more gradual move after 1937 also worked to the advantage of a large segment of employees. With the development of more dependable automobiles and the building of more and better roads, both of which contributed to the decline of country stores and a shift in buying habits, changes in the philosophy of selling and in the management of the sales force were inevitable. Other factors combined to make the years from 1925 to 1940 crucial for the sales department, including the Great Depression, the A. A. A. processing tax (designed to maintain farm commodity prices), the bank holiday, the rise of ten-cent cigarettes, and the roll-your-own vogue. An overriding concern was the successful imitation of Camels—an achievement that reversed the bitter lesson earlier taught the tobacco industry about changes in competitive patterns. Chesterfields, Lucky Strikes, and eventually Old Golds became formidable adversaries of the Camel. Always, too, a great load of chewing tobacco had to be sold, though the market for the product was slowly diminishing. As late as 1938, however, Reynolds marketed eighty-four brands of chewing tobacco, twelve brands of smoking tobacco, and only one cigarette of note.[125] In fact, it did not deemphasize the sale of chewing tobacco until 1945, whereas other major companies had done so well before then.[126] No doubt the Reynolds policy had merit, for every dollar from smoking and chewing tobacco sales yielded a greater profit than did the dollar sales from cigarettes.

In response to changing conditions in the marketplace, the company shifted to the cellophane wrapper for Camels, changed its advertising agencies, employed many more salesmen, and cut the list prices of the Camel by the greatest percentage in its history. Among the numerous other changes mentioned elsewhere in this chapter, adoption of the Arenco packing machine had the greatest impact on the price of cigarettes. So disrupted was the company's marketing during these years that George Washington Hill, testifying in 1941 about changes in list prices, declared: "I never understood R. J. Reynolds' policy until this proceeding, and if I may say so, I don't understand it now." On the question of price discrimination in favor of Camels, Hill stated: "Reynolds were the best users of pencils in the country, and Reynolds always wanted his brands sold cheaper than anybody—all of his brands."[127] It was generally a buyers' market and the company was able to hold its own only in the sale of chewing tobacco, although both cigarette and smoking tobacco sales fluctuated. Reportedly, during some of these years Reynolds had plenty of everything except money.

These were difficult times for the sales force, which was led by Carl W. Harris from 1924 until his death late in 1937. Harris worked closely with

Bowman Gray, Sr., a former sales manager. It was Gray who formulated the policy of distributing Prince Albert and Camels to all retail stores and the theory that these products sold themselves while other brands required special sales techniques. The Camel brand in particular served as a lever for forcing jobbers to handle other Reynolds products. Several brands of smoking and chewing tobacco were promoted by means of cash allotments, drop shipments, special effort brands, and pound campaigns (forcing the sale of a certain number of pounds of chewing tobacco to accompany a set number of cigarettes). In the cash allotment sale, a set number and quantity of certain brands were alloted to a division manager, who, in turn, divided the allotment among his salesmen. Securing his quota of brands from the wholesale dealer, the salesman then virtually peddled them to retailers for cash payments and turned in the proceeds to the wholesale dealer. Allotments for sales in drop shipments served the same ends, but the procedure differed. In this case, the salesman sold allotments of brands to the retailer, who received his purchases plus a small amount of free goods in drop shipments directly from the factory. When a retail dealer had insufficient brands on hand to last until a drop shipment arrived, the salesman often sold him a quantity for cash as a guarantee that his shelves would remain well-stocked during the interim. This practice also benefited the wholesalers, who received commissions on the drop shipments without having to handle or store the products involved. The various selling campaigns were changed approximately every six weeks so that the same brands were not constantly stressed. For Reynolds, this approach developed trade in many brands and blocked competitors when they failed to keep the retailers well-stocked. In other words, if a customer found a retailer out of his favorite chew, he could always secure a substitute from the Reynolds brands in virtually any category—be it Brown's Mule, Honey Cut, Reynolds Sun Cured, Black Horse, Days Work, or whatever. On the other hand, the campaigns placed intense demands on the sales force both in the home office and on the road. Furthermore, Harris and Gray had other pressing responsibilities—Harris as head of advertising and Gray as president and later chairman of the board.

Working conditions in the field became increasingly difficult as one campaign succeeded another in rapid sequence and the demand for chewing tobacco slowly declined. Moreover, because policies and procedures were decided in the home office, regional sales managers had little authority.[128] To illustrate, Larry J. Flashe, division manager at Fargo, North Dakota, in 1934 received large allotments of the following brands to be sold in drop shipments from 19 May through 23 June: Brown's Mule, Torchlight, Whale, Stud, Our Advertiser in two styles, George Washington in two styles, and OCB cigarette books. By selling a substantial quantity himself and evidently by directing a new salesman to sell what he could, Flashe was able to turn in a good report, although no single salesman sold all of his portion of the allotment. Immediately, Thurman A. Porter of the home office instructed Flashe and all other division managers to repeat the same selling campaign on 9 July.[129]

Joseph J. Stamey, who began as a Reynolds salesman on 14 July 1924, declared that prior to 1938 the sales department established quotas for brands to be sold in six or eight weeks followed by quotas for other brands to be sold in a similar period. As smoking and chewing habits gradually changed, jobbers had few or no outlets for these stocks, which sometimes remained on their shelves until they became unsalable. Quite often the division manager was overstocked and his own funds were tied up in the products. Sometimes dealers did not buy from Reynolds salesmen because the salesmen were unable to return unsalable goods to the factory for credit. According to William T. Smither, however, retail dealers could return unsalable goods by negotiating directly with the home office, though naturally such a procedure was tedious. Stamey suffered much from quotas of Torchlight and Liberty Bell, neither of which sold well in his territory in northern New York. Often a salesman would sell these slow-moving brands to a retailer, buy them back at the retail price, obtain the names of consumers from the retailer, and personally sell the goods to the consumer. Salesmen also had to sell the same brands on cash allotments as they did on drop shipments. Frequently when overloaded with a brand not readily salable in his territory, a division manager would prevail on one of his counterparts in a different geographic area to exchange it for another product. This procedure caused problems for the home office, which assumed that brands involved in such exchanges were selling in areas where the contrary was true.[130] Some division managers, who were less energetic and more prone to extravagant living than others, undoubtedly fell into financial difficulties but, on the whole, the conscientious worker fared very well.

There is no better illustration of the diligent salesmen than Francis Graves Carter (7 July 1912–16 June 1960), who joined the company as a foot salesman in the Winston-Salem area on 9 July 1934. Energetic, affable, and serious about his work, Carter too was burdened with quotas of Torchlight chewing tobacco. His method for boosting the sales of that brand became a classic example of ingenuity in the sales force. Shortly after he started selling for Reynolds, Carter came across some corncob pipes left over from an earlier promotion of smoking tobacco. In the hope of increasing sales, he tied one of these pipes to each package of his allotment of Torchlight. He soon sold his quota, although he could never fathom the connection that seemed to exist between chewers of scrap tobacco and users of corncob pipes. But Carter was an exceptional man who succeeded in any job he undertook. He became a division manager at the age of twenty-seven and a department manager ten years later. Continuing to advance rapidly in the company, he was named sales manager in 1955, vice-president and director in 1958, and president in 1959.[131]

Apparently few tasks seemed more burdensome to the sales force than preparation of the daily report. The report completed by Vernon Davis on the evening of 3 January 1938 is typical. One item called for the number of cigarettes in a package; accordingly, Davis entered the proper figure, although it was well-known to all in the home office and, indeed, the general public. Another small space on the crowded form was reserved for suggestions as well as information on the business of the company and its competitors in the territory covered. Davis duly wrote: "American have new Special poster advertising their Hollywood Hit Show." Equally troublesome was the requirement that the salesman completely itemize all advertising material he had used. Furthermore, he had to list the brands targeted for a "special effort," despite the fact that the home office had prepared the list in the first place.[132] Of course, the latter was useful in that the home office could quickly see the distribution of sales.

In view of the requirement that this report form be fully completed, the following directive to division managers in 1935 seems incomprehensible: "See to it also that your salesmen do not make entries on their reports that are meaningless and of no value. Of course, we want all entries made that the report provides for and any additional entries that we may request from time to time on some particular subject. Everything else, however, should be eliminated from the report."

In a similar letter issued on the same day, salesmen were urged to make neater reports and to stop giving duplicate information in the lower right-hand space reserved for comments on the business of Reynolds and its competitors. From the letter it appears that many salesmen contented themselves with a notation that certain Reynolds brands were best sellers—"information we can get from best seller columns of [salesmen's] reports."[133] If Carl Harris's letters sometimes seemed impulsive, hasty, and imprecise, he undoubtedly had many provocations from reports prepared by salesmen and division managers whose ability to sell tobacco products far outweighted their ability to use and interpret the English language. In any case, the daily report form of the 1930s apparently was not revised until well after 1940.

Edward A. Darr continued many of these requirements when he succeeded Harris on 1 January 1938 after serving scarcely three months as assistant sales manager. A fourteen-year veteran of the Reynolds sales department, Darr had worked in the home office as chief assistant to Harris and with sales people in the field. Nevertheless, it was not generally believed that during this time Darr received any extensive acquaintance with the more serious problems of the sales department. Soon after he became sales manager, small briar pipes were provided as premiums to promote the sales of George Washington smoking tobacco. As a result, by 1939 production of that brand, often sold by cash allotment and drop shipment, had increased by almost 1.5 million pounds. Some of this increase, however, must be attributed to a change in the package and carton as well as to improved advertising methods. During World War II the company could not continue with cash allotment sales as easily, although shortages of such brands as Brown's Mule, Stud, and Our Advertiser failed to materialize and salesmen continued to receive their quotas.[134] According to sales personnel, one department manager in Southern California refused to sell Our Advertiser smoking tobacco (7-ounce size). For that reason and possibly for noncompliance in other areas, Darr made a special trip to the West Coast and relieved him of his duties.

There were various other irritants to the sales force before the many changes begun in 1938 could be fully developed. Working conditions on the road could be unpleasant. The daily lunch allowance was rather scanty, work hours extended well beyond the eight-hour standard, and lodgings frequently did not furnish a room with a bath. Salesmen were required to stock retailers from their cars, and to tack muslin and weatherproof signs on barns and other outbuildings along country roads and highways. Furthermore, they were given a shabby canvas bag in which to carry merchandise and tools for posting advertising material. Company cars were ill-equipped for cold weather, and an inferior quality of antifreeze was supplied in all areas regardless of climate. Letters from the home office could be severely critical. There were difficulties in securing information about opportunities to buy profit-sharing stock. Division managers lacked authority. The home office had a practice of calling department sales managers to meetings in Winston-Salem during the Christmas holidays, and of failing to hold regional meetings for division managers and salesmen.

Some of these concerns naturally varied in degree from division to division.[135] Furthermore, top management was not always at fault. For example, though there may have been lags in adjustment, the daily lunch allowance was increased by 150 percent in four steps from 1929 to 1958. In some cases division managers had few if any salesmen who might be encouraged by profit-sharing allocations; on the other hand, there were managers who preferred to keep the entire allocation for themselves. One new division manager found half a basement of unused and expensive advertising supplies when he took over, a condition that an alert manager could have prevented by checking on his salesmen's use of advertising material.[136]

Other complaints also might be defended. Rooms with baths were less common in 1925 than during the 1950s. The need for heavy-duty car heaters, windshield defrosters, and a permanent type of antifreeze in such areas as Idaho and upstate New York may well have escaped those in the comfortable climate of Winston-Salem. In reality, the tedious work of stocking retailers from salesmen's cars served as a means for stocking jobbers and maintaining distribution so that the home office might be assured that the retailer had an adequate supply of goods. Some believed that Harris favored certain department and division managers whereas others thought that Darr, acting on the same principle, unfairly discharged some employees chosen by Harris. All in all, the sales policies needed extensive revision, and Carl W. Harris, who had worked so long under the policies formulated by Bowman Gray, Sr., saw no way to meet the demands of a changing life-style.

In part, the shift to new sales policies was based on a realization that the sale of cigarettes in volume offered a better means for profit than the old policy of emphasizing the odd brands no longer desired by salesmen, wholesale dealers, or customers. It was generally conceded that this change came from the work of Darr, Bowman Gray, Jr., James T. Barnes, Jr., and Frederic E. Sturmer. For a time Gray and Barnes served as the home office's representatives in the field—Gray primarily covered the northern Midwest, New England, and the Pacific Coast and Barnes, the small midwestern states and the Southwest. Meanwhile, Darr watched over sales throughout the country. Sturmer, an experienced salesman who had worked as a sales executive for the Kroger Stores and Sears and Roebuck, did not enter the picture until after the war. This imaginative and experienced team came to see the need for emphasizing brands that customers wanted.[137]

The first tangible evidence that the home office had begun to realize the futility of continued emphasis on cash allotments of unpopular brands appeared on 10 July 1939. In a letter to division managers, Darr wrote: "It certainly is a fact that there are disadvantages in overloading jobbers. However, it is no less true that there is much to be lost by not having enough goods in jobbers' stocks." Continuing to straddle the issue, he noted the dangers of shipping "excessive quantities" that might become unsalable and the importance of keeping jobbers "well enough supplied with cash goods so that the salesman will have to keep his sights high in order to keep jobbers' stocks down to a reasonable level." He ended in the same undecided key: "We hope you will get from this letter the thought that it is very important that you keep jobbers in your division plentifully supplied with cash goods and at the same time not overstock to the danger point."[138]

Twelve days later Darr referred to a letter that he had sent to department and division managers in April, asking them to think about the nature of their work. Since then, he declared, he had received many "good letters" from men in the field in response to that request. Darr then announced that he was sending them a series of messages on "Human Relations in

Business." Though these messages had not been prepared exclusively for the Reynolds sales department, Darr felt that they would help answer questions about how to deal with people. He also desired comments that might be passed along to other salesmen.[139] Previously, on 2 April, Darr had requested division managers to give all salesmen scheduled to make store sales on Saturday afternoon and evening the privilege of reporting for work at 11:00 A.M. on Saturday mornings. Because this change had proved impractical in some instances, the directive was altered to give the salesmen, in addition to the starting hour of 11:00 A.M., one full Saturday off each month.[140] This move had nothing to do with the Fair Labor Standards Act, as company and government officials did not begin to work out how the law applied to the wages and hours of salesmen until 1944.[141]

In 1940 the sales department also adopted a softened tone in regard to the sale of special effort brands by making no change in the list for August. For that month, however, the home office expected "as near one hundred per cent distribution on Special Effort brands as it is possible to get." Again, no change was made in the list for October, and contrary to the general rule, department managers were asked "to drop us a line and state how you feel about it."[142]

A form letter dated 1 January 1940 and evidently sent to the entire sales force appears to indicate for the first time the home office's desire to bring the sales into closer touch with the company. It announced the retirement of Memory E. Motsinger as secretary, the appointment of William J. Conrad, Jr., as his successor, and the election of Thomas W. Blackwell as a director.[143]

With the coming of war and decimation of the sales force, further experimentation in reshaping sales policies was halted temporarily. Many salesmen and department officials entered the armed services, including Bowman Gray, Jr., assistant sales manager. But many believed that continued evaluation of sales policies during the war years by Edward Darr and James Barnes, who became Darr's assistant on 9 January 1941, resulted in a more satisfactory program than might have been devised had the sales department been functioning with its customary staff. After Bowman Gray, Jr., returned from the Navy on 2 January 1946 and Frederic E. Sturmer, a brilliant innovator, was hired on 18 March of the same year, the changed policies became even more apparent. The most significant was the decision to allow the salesman to work with products that people wanted. That, along with changes in buying habits, essentially altered his role to that of merchandiser. The ending of drop shipments with free goods on 15 January 1949 virtually completed the transformation of the sales department, thereby making the sales force an integral part of the company.[144] Only Sturmer's outstanding work in developing the *Reynolds Tobacco Merchandiser* remains to be discussed in a subsequent chapter.

It is noteworthy that development of the R. J. Reynolds Tobacco Company into a modern industry was accomplished with little or no borrowing of capital. In fact, after 1917 or 1918 the first loan of any consequence was secured in 1938 when James A. Gray borrowed $20 million at the rate of 2.45 percent. According to S. Clay Williams, this low rate was unprecedented and all but startled the financial community in New York. It prompted another tobacco company to get its interest rate reduced on a loan obtained earlier using Gray's experience as leverage. By arranging a transfer of the Reynolds loan, Gray was able to have the rate lowered to 1.75 percent which, in 1943, Williams believed to stand "as probably the lowest rate that has ever been accorded any industrial loan of that type in this country within the period" under consideration. The loan was made to the company in return for its promissory notes to the Equitable Life Assurance Society of the United States, with the principal to mature in ten equal installments beginning on 10 April 1940 and ending on 10 April 1949. The directors approved Gray's agreement with the Equitable Life Assurance Society on 16 September 1938. At this time, however, the prime bank rate governing loans to industry was rather low, and Gray later proceeded to tie up an additional $100 million in revolving credit arrangements with the company's twelve depositary banks at similarly low rates, which had prevailed since about the end of December 1939.[145] Thereafter, it was said, bankers looked askance at James A. Gray when he appeared on Wall Street.

PART FOUR

Challenges in a Modern World, 1941–1963

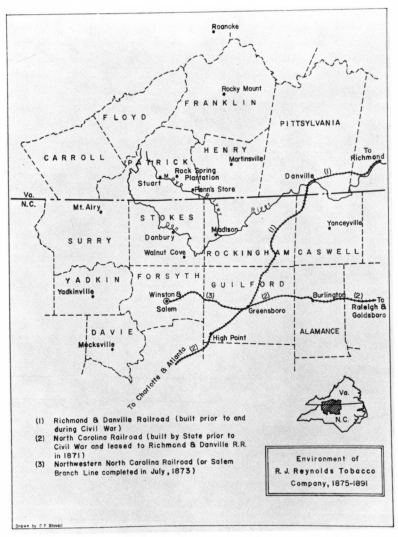

Roanoke

Rocky Mount

FRANKLIN

FLOYD

PITTSYLVANIA

CARROLL

HENRY

Martinsville

To Richmond

PATRICK

Rock Spring Plantation

Stuart

Penn's Store

Danville (1)

Va.
N.C.

Mt. Airy

STOKES

Madison

Yanceyville

SURRY

Danbury

Walnut Cove

ROCKINGHAM

CASWELL

YADKIN

FORSYTH

GUILFORD

Yadkinville

Winston & Salem

(3)

(2)

Burlington

(2)

To Raleigh & Goldsboro

Greensboro

DAVIE

ALAMANCE

Mocksville

High Point

To Charlotte & Atlanta (2)

Va.

N.C.

(1) Richmond & Danville Railroad (built prior to and during Civil War)
(2) North Carolina Railroad (built by State prior to Civil War and leased to Richmond & Danville R.R. in 1871)
(3) Northwestern North Carolina Railroad (or Salem Branch Line completed in July, 1873)

Environment of
R. J. Reynolds Tobacco
Company, 1875-1891

Drawn by C. F. Stovall

Environment of the R. J. Reynolds Tobacco Company, 1875–1891

*Birthplace of R. J. Reynolds near Critz, Virginia, generally known as Rock Spring
Plantation, was built about 1842*

*Reynolds brothers (left to right): R. J., Abram, Harbour (seated);
Walter and Will (standing)*

R. J.'s factory in 1884 taken from a letterhead

TO TAKE EFFECT ON AND AFTER JUNE 1, 1891.

PRICE LIST
R. J. REYNOLDS TOBACCO CO'S
FINE CHEWING TOBACCOS.

BRANDS.	SIZE AND WEIGHT OF PLUGS.	Weight of Package.	PRICE PER POUND.		
			One to Five Boxes	Five Boxes And Over.	As'd lots of 5 bxs 2 or More Kinds
R. J. Reynolds' Level Best, [Indented in Plug 4 Times.]	12 in. 3 ½ to lb.	12 lbs.	90	88	88
R. J. Reynolds' Double Thick, [Indented in Plug 5 Times.]	12 in. 8 oz.	30 "	65	62	62
R. J. R. 3 Break Pocket Piece, ...	3x4—7 to lb.	24 "	50	48	48
Zeb Vance, ...	9 in.—4 " "	20 & 40 "	45	43	43
Belle of N. C., ...	9 in.—5 " "	40 "	36	35	35
Caromel, ...	7 in.—5 " "	20 "	36	35	35

No rebate or payment of freight allowed, and no discount except 2 per cent. for cash.
Five original packages, if of different brands, constitute an assorted lot.

R. J.'s price list for fine chewing tobacco, 1891

D. Rich (standing), Walter Reynolds (seated at left), and R. J. before 1905

R. J.'s white work force between 1893 and 1901

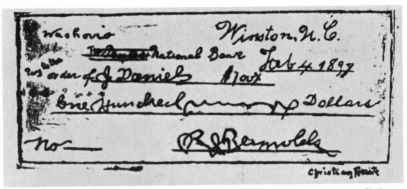

Photograph of the check sent by R. J. to Josephus Daniels when the monopolistic
Southern Railway canceled his newsman's pass in 1897

Outing of R. J.'s salesmen from New England and New York City on 27 June 1914

Clement Manly, chief of the legal department from 1890 to 1911

Francis Burton Craige, chief of the legal department from 1911 to 1916

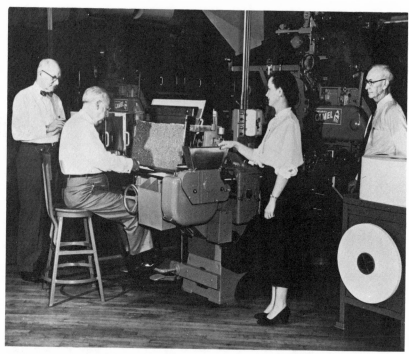

John C. Whitaker, then an inspector, at one of the five cigarette-making machines that the company used in 1913, with George Tucker (to his left); Dorothy Shaw, an inspector; and John E. Stone, chief machinist. Note the Camel sign.

Meeting of department managers in September 1948

Front row (seated on floor)	*Rear (standing, left to right)*	
W. B. Revelle	George W. Chandler	W. S. Koenig
C. R. Brooks	C. E. McKenna	B. K. Millaway
P. H. Tucker	Jack R. Scott	E. M. Fulp
J. W. McDowell, Sr.	J. W. Conyard	N. B. Correll
T. A. Porter	F. L. Hannan	Polk English
R. D. McKenzie	W. C. Osborn (?)	F. E. Sturmer
	A. H. Galloway (partly hidden)	J. K. Cone
Second row (seated)	M. L. Thompson	J. T. Barnes, Jr.
	F. G. Carter	C. W. Hines
Bowman Gray, Jr.	J. L. Cline	
S. M. Scott	T. C. Millaway	
H. H. Ramm	T. J. Voss	
R. G. Vallandingham	C. A. Burgess	
R. C. Haberkern	W. C. Osborn (?)	
James A. Gray	D. W. Sculley	
John C. Whitaker	O. J. Peard	
P. Frank Hanes	R. C. O'Bannon	
F. S. Hill	W. E. Bump	
W. T. Smither	C. T. Howard	
W. J. Conrad	F. J. Howard	
E. A. Darr	W. V. Eller	

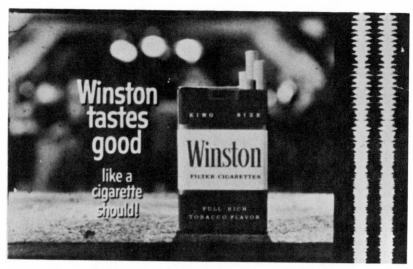

In the early 1950s, when Winston cigarettes were introduced, this was the chief advertisement

Work in the truck and storage division

Built in 1961, the Whitaker Park plant represented the last word in cigarette plants despite its art gallery appearance

Albert Cuthrell, operator of the number 3 elevator in the main office building from 1929 until automatic elevators were installed in the early 1960s, knew every employee who used the elevator in addition to knowing the floor and office number of each. Some thought he had been named for Prince Albert smoking tobacco

The handsome office building completed in 1929 was designed by Shreve and Lamb, who also designed the Empire State Building

Chairmen of the Board (left to right): William Neal Reynolds, 8 April 1924 to 6 May 1931; Bowman Gray, Sr., 6 May 1931 to 7 July 1935; S. Clay Williams, 11 July 1935 to 25 February 1949; James A. Gray, 1 March 1949 to 29 October 1952; John C. Whitaker, 5 November 1952 to 8 October 1959; Bowman Gray, Jr., 8 October 1959 to 11 April 1969

Joseph L. Graham, as head of the traffic department and a director from 1914 to 1928, worked out many improved shipping routes and, among other achievements, arranged for Winston-Salem to become a port of entry. He was also an important figure in securing the reduction of discriminatory freight rates for the entire South

Dr. Samuel O. Jones, Ph.D. in chemistry from Johns Hopkins, was largely responsible for the development of reconstituted leaf tobacco which accounted for the company's great advance in the 1950s and 1960s. This accomplishment represented a 25 percent savings in leaf tobacco by combining scrap tobacco and stems with the usable leaf.

CHAPTER 11

Labor Strife

Labor disturbances among the employees of the R. J. Reynolds Tobacco Company during the 1940s stemmed from years of neglect of economic and social problems in Winston-Salem, a temporary scarcity of labor, failure of the company to develop an adequate personnel department, installation of labor-saving machinery, and possible inequities in wages. Also a factor was the rise in prices that accompanied the relaxation of war controls after World War II. Troubled too in this decade by war scarcities and regulations as well as important legal proceedings, the company had the misfortune to produce a cigarette that proved to be a complete failure. Military requirements also affected the labor supply as well as surprisingly high levels of management. The R. J. Reynolds Tobacco Company, however, was not alone with these problems. According to Foster Rhea Dulles, the postwar struggle of American labor to maintain a wartime level of take-home pay in actual purchasing power was no less grim than in 1919.[1]

The continuous labor disturbances at Reynolds from 1943 to the early 1950s may be divided into six phases: early discontent among employees as the decade began, unionization of the company during 1941–44, changes and troubles in union leadership in the mid–1940s, the Communist exposé in 1947, the slow decline of the union in the late 1940s and early 1950s, and the aftermath of labor strife in the company.

The Seeds of Discontent

Even before 1940, widespread resentment was directed against the leadership of Winston-Salem and against the concentration of that leadership in the hands of a very few men "from an even smaller number of tightly interlocked families" who ran the city "just as surely . . . as they ran their factories." So wrote Chester S. Davis, a reporter hired by the publishing firm supporting the city's power structure. "The R. J. Reynolds Tobacco Company was the most widely cussed and discussed institution in the community," he declared. The turbulence of these years, Davis believed, came in part from ten years of depression followed by five years of war in which everything from city government to county schools had deteriorated.[2] Perhaps the most direct verification of these statements is to be found in *Just Plain Larnin'*, written by a public school teacher and published in 1934. More telling than the exaggerated picture presented in this novel is the well-substantiated belief that the author, James M. Shields, lost his job when the book appeared. The central theme, with abundant and easily identifiable references to the Reynolds company, revolves around the efforts of school personnel to work independently, the poverty and ignorance of workers—especially the Negroes—in the Reynolds factories, the abortive attempts to organize the employees against company opposition, the difficulties of children of Reynolds employees securing an education, and the accusations that labor organizers, teachers, and reformers were tinged with Bolshevism. One of the most damning statements in the novel is the accurate assessment that the only high school for whites was located conveniently for the well-to-do but not for others. It was also true that at this time the Tobacco Workers International Union of the American Federation of Labor (TWIU-AFL), through Charles W. Lakey, was trying to organize the Reynolds employees.[3]

There seem to have been other reasons for the unwholesome situation prevailing in Winston-Salem before 1940. The later improvements cited by Chester Davis point to a general lack of interest in civic and cultural affairs, an inadequate transportation system, lack of recreational facilities, shortcomings in the public school system, inadequate zoning ordinances, and unsettled race relations.[4] Davis, a former agent of the Federal Bureau of Investigation and an investigative journalist for the city's newspapers after the war, played a leading role in exposing the Communist domination of a labor union active among the company's workers during the 1940s.[5] But his analysis of the contrasting local conditions before and after 1940 indicates that Winston-Salem leadership, including the higher ranks of Reynolds management, may have been partially responsible not only for the turbulence of the 1940s but also for the entry of Communists into the most active labor union of the town.[6]

On the other hand, it is probable that lower earnings in the leaf processing department accounted for some of the trouble.

Although average wage rates for the company differed slightly from those for the industry as a whole (see Table 11-1),[7] variances within Reynolds were dramatic. Information in countless personnel folders shows that hourly wages in the leaf processing department fell substantially below those in the manufacturing division. This was true in the case of Velma Best Hopkins (b. 24 Feb. 1910) and Moranda Smith (3 June 1915–1950), both relatively unskilled leaf workers and active supporters of the Communist leaders in the union (see Table 11-2). Velma Hopkins served successively as a stemming machine operator, a drop leaf stemmer, and a strip searcher, and Moranda Smith as a stem picker, a drop leaf stemmer, and a strip preparer. But the difference in hourly wages of these two employees and *average* hourly wages for all Reynolds workers does not begin to indicate the real gap between hourly wages for workers in the leaf department and those in the manufacturing division. Below the laborers in the leaf department came the seasonal workers whose duties demanded even less skill and whose wages were also seasonal in conformity with the period for the purchase of leaf tobacco. It was to these unskilled workers rather than those in the manufacturing division that the Communist-dominated union addressed most of its efforts.

The question of paid vacations also served as an issue during the labor disturbances, although, with the exception of seasonal workers, all Reynolds employees enjoyed a paid vacation after 1 January 1940.[8] Their personnel folders show that Velma Hopkins and Moranda Smith regularly received paid vacations. This situation made the seasonal worker even more susceptible to the blandishments of organizers.

Stories of rough treatment, heavy work loads, and poor working conditions in the leaf department are numerous, although necessarily subjective. Certainly many seasonal workers who removed leaf from redrying machines worked in intense heat. Moreover, all work with leaf took place in a dusty atmosphere. The key to the disturbed period, however, seemed to be the low wages of leaf workers and the fewer benefits and lower wages of seasonal workers.

The maneuvers and organizing activities of four different unions among these employees were so commingled and multifarious as to make an orderly account difficult indeed. First to work among the employees was the Tobacco Workers International Union of the American Federation of Labor. Early in 1942 the Tobacco Workers Organizing Committee—representing the United Cannery, Agricultural, Packing, and Allied Workers of America of the Congress of Industrial Organizations (UCAPAWA-CIO)—moved into town. Known also as Food, Tobacco, and Agricultural Workers; United Tobacco Workers; Food, Tobacco, and Allied Workers; and, eventually, Local 22, this branch of the CIO fell under the sway of Communists (hereafter cited as Local 22). When it became apparent that Local 22 was Communist-dominated, a right-wing division of the same union, the United Transport Service Employees (hereafter cited as UTSE-CIO) appeared on the scene. Finally, on 20 October 1943, the secretary of state of North Carolina granted to Sam Doc Hauser, James B. Laughter,

Table 11-1
*Average Hourly Wages of Employees of the Reynolds Company
and of the Entire Tobacco Industry, 1939–1949*

Year	Average Hourly Earnings	
	Reynolds	Tobacco Industry
1939 (15 Oct.)	$ .4963	$ .4760
1940	.4963	.4940
1941 (21 Apr.)	.5459	.5200
1942 (11 May)	.5954	.5800
1943	.5954	.6430
1944 (30 Dec.)	.6294	.7060
1945 (7 June)	.6893	.7640
1946 (3 Aug.)	.8407	.8680
1947 (7 June)	.9096	.9510
1948 (15 May)	1.0473	.9950
1949 (12 Dec.)	1.1370	1.0360

Sources: Wage Increases, 1914–1950, personnel department, R. J. Reynolds Tobacco Company; *Economic Almanac, 1956*, National Industrial Conference Board (New York, 1956), p. 249.

Nannie B. Carter, and others a certificate of incorporation for the R. J. Reynolds Employees Association, Inc., a nonstock corporation and evidently also a company union.[9] Throughout the struggle it was obvious that company management intended to break the hold of any bona fide union on its employees. Undoubtedly this resolution pointed chiefly to Local 22, which was most successful in organizing.

During this turbulent decade the Reynolds directors as well as many others witnessed scenes never before known in Winston-Salem. A haunting Negro spiritual resurrected from the 1930s became the virtual theme song of the period. The chorus and first verse reveal its vigor, its applicability, its simplicity, and the source of its inspiration:[10]

I shall not, I shall not be moved,
I shall not, I shall not be moved,
Just like a tree planted by the water I shall not be moved.
When my cross is heavy, I shall not be moved,
When my cross is heavy, I shall not be moved,
Like a tree planted by the water I shall not be moved.

Table 11-2
Average Hourly Wages of Employees of the Reynolds Company Generally and of Two Employees in the Leaf Department During 1933–1947

Year	Employees Generally	Leaf Department Employees	
		Velma Hopkins	Moranda Smith
1933 (20 Aug.)	$.3222	Not available	$.15
1936	.3877	$.30–.34	Not available
1937	.4487	.38	.40
1939 (25 Sept.)	.4617	Not available	Not available
1939 (15 Oct.)	.4963	.38	.42
1940	.4963	.38	.42
1941 (21 Apr.)	.5459	.38–.41	.46
1942 (11 May)	.5954	.46	.50
1943	.5954	.46	.53
1944 (30 Dec.)	.6294	.54	.57
1945 (7 June)	.6893	.55–.58	.58
1946 (3 Aug.)	.8407	.59–.72	.68
1947 (7 June)	.9096	.77	.77

Source: Leaf department, R. J. Reynolds Tobacco Company.

Nathan M. Revel, a worker on the third floor of Number 65 where the strike first began, believed that the hymn, "I Know My God is Real," proved more effective.[11] Mrs. Flora Baitee (or Baity), a Negro stemming machine operator in a Reynolds plant who served as chairman of the "singing committee" for Local 22, reported another favorite:[12]

> The union fights the battle for freedom, freedom
> The union fights the battle for freedom
> And the bosses come tumbling down.

It was the intensity of this struggle that may have induced the company to later establish a modern personnel department and to make itself a model industrial citizen.

Unionization of the Company

Rumors of organizing activities among Reynolds employees evidently had reached some volume by 11 November 1940, when John C. Whitaker introduced Chief of Police Walter F. Anderson to the Safety Council to speak on "Fifth Column Activities in Winston-Salem."[13] No move of any importance occurred until 26 February 1941, when the TWIU-AFL unsuccessfully petitioned the National Labor Relations Board (NLRB) for the bargaining rights of production and maintenance employees. In 1942, possibly at the beginning of the year, the Reverend Owen Whitfield, a Negro minister, arrived in town to prepare the groundwork for the entry of Local 22. Whitfield appears to have made the acquaintance of several local Negro ministers, one of the first being the Reverend Frank N. O'Neal, pastor of the Union Mission Holy Church at Seventh and Vine streets. Though Whitfield's most sedulous follower proved to be O'Neal, an employee of the company, there were others, including the Reverend Robert M. Pitts, pastor of Shiloh Baptist Church, and the Reverend Edward Goldston, pastor of Trinity Baptist Church. The Reverend Mr. Pitts was known as the greatest pulpit orator among the ministers of Winston-Salem. Whitfield, said to be on the union payroll and abundantly supplied with funds, came to study the Reynolds plants. Evidently shrewd and capable, he laid the basis for an organizing drive, influencing O'Neal, Pitts, Goldston, and possibly others to organize their congregations, which contained many Reynolds employees. Later regular organizers under the leadership of Frank Hargrove came to Winston-Salem, and many white workers became interested in the drive.[14]

No notable success accompanied the work of either group until Thursday, 17 June 1943, when suddenly and dramatically the movement caught fire. At lunchtime on that day James Pickens McCardell (15 February 1905–17 June 1943), a Negro job hand who had served as draft boy or truck pusher since 26 June 1927, suddenly fell dead. Some of McCardell's fellow workers in Number 65 claimed that his death resulted from poor working conditions and an unbearable increase in his work load. His immediate superior, Samuel H. Strader, wrote more than five years later that on the previous day McCardell had complained of feeling ill and was sent to the nurse at 8:45 A.M. About three hours later he (Strader) attempted to put someone else in McCardell's place. McCardell objected, saying that he preferred to remain on the job. On the following day, Strader was summoned to return from lunch. He called the nurse and doctor who arrived about 1:00 P.M. and pronounced McCardell dead.[15]

That afternoon a sit-down strike began in Number 65, rapidly spreading to eight other buildings and departments. Sympathetic walkouts occurred in the plants of other companies in town. Conrad Espe, vice-president of UCAPAWA-CIO, arrived on the scene the next day. The sit-down strike turned into a walkout—especially of the workers in the leaf processing areas. The company immediately formed a committee, headed by Edgar E.

Bumgardner, which conferred with a committee of employees in an effort to get them back to work. Meanwhile, Espe and Frank Hargrove, taking full advantage of the situation, made regular statements to the press and directed the striking groups.[16] In addition, Donald Henderson, president of UCAPAWA-CIO, announced through the Communist *Daily Worker* that Reynolds employees had been flocking to the union since the work stoppages on 17 June—"stoppages for which even the company admits the union was in no way responsible."[17] Whatever the exact cause of McCardell's death may have been, Local 22 until that time had made no progress against TWIU-AFL.

On Monday, 21 June, all the Reynolds factories closed after more than 2,000 workers in the leaf processing department struck, demanding adjustments in wages and working conditions. They did not return until the company guaranteed in writing that it would recognize the workers' committee for discussion of grievances and that it would not penalize the workers for having participated in the strike. Accordingly, operations were resumed on the night of 22 June and by the following morning virtually all employees were back at work. Also on the twenty-second Conrad Espe announced that a petition for a representation election had been sent to the NLRB, both the TWIU-AFL and Local 22 claiming that the short strike had been unauthorized. During this period R. W. Goodrich of the United States Conciliation Service and Frank Crane of the North Carolina Department of Labor arrived in Winston-Salem.[18]

Organizing activities continued from late June until the consent election—set for 2 and 3 August—with mass meetings, newspaper advertising, radio advertising, and comprehensive newspaper publicity. The R. J. Reynolds Employees Association entered the campaign. Albert L. Lohm, field examiner for the NLRB, conferred with representatives of the company and the unions over what constituted an appropriate bargaining unit. Local 22 believed that it should include all employees except supervisors and office workers, whereas TWIU-AFL maintained that it should comprise production workers in cigarette plants. The company proposed that there be two units—one for those involved in the preparation of leaf tobacco and the other for those producing finished goods. Agreement, reached on 8 July 1943, provided for two separate bargaining units in line with the desire of the company, Local 22 having relinquished its preference in return for an early election.[19] Organizers for TWIU-AFL hit hard at Local 22 as a union run by "crack pot ex-college professors" and founded in 1936 in a rebellion from the AFL. They also implied that Local 22 admitted Communists, Fascists, and Nazis.[20] Nevertheless, Local 22 campaigned with evangelical fervor, calling for a signed contract, equal pay for equal work for men and women, guaranteed job security, increased wages, promotions based on seniority, improved vacation plans, retention and extension of hospitalization and retirement plans, and a proper grievance committee to guarantee against strikes, work stoppages, or lockouts.[21]

Meanwhile, the company undoubtedly encouraged the strengthening of the R. J. Reynolds Employees Association on the quiet. However, its open efforts were largely restricted to a letter from John C. Whitaker to production and maintenance employees. In it he explained the voting procedure; declared that the company paid wages as high as those prevailing in Winston-Salem or in the tobacco industry as a whole; summed up the employee benefits then available to all workers; referred to the wage increases of September 1939, April 1941, and May 1942, in addition to several thousand merit raises; emphasized the fact that the Office of Price Administration would not permit wage increases; called attention to the workers' job security; and stated that dividends to stockholders had been reduced. When the NLRB questioned the use of this tactic, Reynolds officials replied that the letter, which was not submitted to either of the unions, had been circulated prior to receipt of instructions from the NLRB.[22] Whitaker was no exception to southern employers in general who regarded NLRB elections as either won or lost by the company.[23]

Results of the election were somewhat inconclusive: Local 22—92 percent of leaf workers and 2,829 of manufacturing division, No union—2,856 in manufacturing division, TWIU-AFL—135 votes in both units. Officials of TWIU-AFL declared that the night before the election certain groups had told workers in the Reynolds factories that their union had given up hope for victory. The importance of the election, however, lay not so much in the aura of uncertainty as in the fact that it brought to town Donald Henderson, who served as the *bête noire* of the company for many months. At once Henderson invited supporters of the TWIU-AFL to join Local 22—an invitation immediately refused.[24] In the midst of claims and counterclaims, a short strike at nearby Taylor Brothers, a 97 percent vote of employees at the Winston Leaf Tobacco Company for Local 22 as their bargaining agent, and rumors that the R. J. Reynolds Tobacco Company had lost the election from the adverse effects of Whitaker's letter, the situation remained at a virtual standstill until 3 September 1943. On that date the NLRB voided the previous consent election. Shortly afterward it combined all regular and seasonal workers into a single voting unit and ordered a new election to be held within thirty days.[25]

With the new election set for 11 and 12 November, immediacy became a factor for Local 22 whereas delay was in the company's interest. As labor activities in other areas stirred the town, the R. J. Reynolds Employees Association went public and opened three temporary offices to accept applications for membership. Applying immediately for a place on the ballot, this union, which claimed to be independent and unaffiliated, was represented by John J. Ingle and Richmond Rucker. Though the application was denied, the attorneys were informed that workers who did not wish to have a union as bargaining agent could express their preference by voting against any union. Ingle declared, however, that the association had not been organized specifically for the November election.[26] Through a suit filed on 27 October 1943, the R. J. Reynolds Employees Association secured an order from the United States District Court restraining the NLRB and the company from holding the election as scheduled without the association's name on the ballot. Judge Johnson J. Hayes, who presided, declared that the NLRB should exercise the powers with which Congress had clothed it. Donald Henderson stated that Local 22 consented to having the R. J. Reynolds Employees Association on the ballot in order to remove difficulties raised by the restraining order "and to secure justice by proceeding with the election as scheduled." The regional director of the NLRB set 18 and 19 November as the new date for the election and notices to that effect were posted in the factories on the night of 10 November after a conference between representatives of the company, the three unions, and the NLRB.[27]

But this was not the end of delaying tactics exercised by the R. J. Reynolds Employees Association. The association and Local 22 campaigned extensively over the radio, the latter showing more acumen in the choice of programs. Furthermore, a group of fifty-two leading white and Negro citizens called for racial cooperation in a full-page newspaper advertisement. Rumors of an intended strike by the association to delay the election were met by a declaration that Local 22 would not strike under any conditions.[28] Suddenly, on 17 November 1943, the R. J. Reynolds Employees Association instituted a second judicial action—this time in the Superior Court of Forsyth County. The result was an order restraining the members of the NLRB, its regional director (W. M. Aicher), Local 22, and the R. J. Reynolds Tobacco Company from holding the election on 18 and 19 November. The order, entered about 4:00 P.M., was to remain in effect until 6 December.[29] Simultaneously, advertisements signed by the Citizens' Emergency Committee of Winston-Salem began appearing in the local papers; invariably they pointed to civic improvements that had been accomplished by cooperation between whites and Negroes.[30]

Representatives of the NLRB moved to have the suit transferred to the United States District Court. Judge F. Donald Phillips of the Forsyth County Superior Court ruled that he had no jurisdiction to hear the motion because the clerk of the court had not passed on the matter. On a technical basis the clerk in turn refused either to approve or deny the request of the NLRB. On the following day representatives of the NLRB requested Judge Johnson J. Hayes of the federal court to dissolve the order and dismiss the complaint of the R. J. Reynolds Employees Association.

Richmond Rucker immediately branded this maneuver "an abortive attempt to deprive the State court of its jurisdiction." On 24 November,
Judge Hayes intimated that he considered the restraining order of the
Forsyth County Superior Court removable but set a hearing for the thirtieth. Publicity remained merciless and the Citizens' Emergency Committee continued to stress accomplishments that had been derived from
twenty-five years of cooperation between Negroes and whites. The ruling
of the federal court to dissolve the restraining order of the Forsyth County
Superior Court made news on 2 December.[31]

Along with the announcement of Judge Hayes's ruling came the publication of a letter from William N. Reynolds to company employees. According to Reynolds, he wrote it at the request of the Citizens' Emergency
Committee. The letter contained a nostalgic appeal to the employees to
avoid outside interests aimed at creating hatred, calling attention to the
many benefits provided by the company.[32]

Meanwhile, the R. J. Reynolds Employees Association did not capitu-
late. John J. Ingle made a futile trip to Baltimore to seek an appearance
before the Fourth District Court of Appeals in an effort to have the orders
of the district court stayed. Leaders of Local 22, however, did not believe
that the NLRB would wait for the outcome of this last move before re-
scheduling the date of the consent election. According to Ingle, though
Judge Morris Ames Soper of the Fourth District Court of Appeals considered the orders of the district court technically correct, he sympathized
with the position of the R. J. Reynolds Employees Association.[33] On 7 December, Ingle indicated that he might drop plans for further court action if
the NLRB scheduled the election at a date satisfactory to the association,
although he would try to have the election deferred.[34] That day the NLRB
set 16 and 17 December as the new dates for the election, and the Citizens'
Emergency Committee placed another full-page advertisement in the
morning paper: "What Are the True Facts?" The ad stated that the Wagner-
Connery Act (National Labor Relations Act) had been misquoted and
misunderstood. As Senator David L. Walsh had said, the act did not require an employee to join a labor organization and it did not forbid the
establishment of company unions. No Supreme Court ruling made it impossible for an employee to be discharged because of failure to fulfill his
duties. "Do Not Be Decieved by Those Who Would Mislead You," the
advertisement concluded.[35]

As stronger statements were made in advertisements sponsored by the
Citizens' Emergency Committee, the R. J. Reynolds Employees Association threatened to challenge the right to vote of 900 or more seasonal
workers who had been laid off since 9 October. Meanwhile, plans were
laid for the consent election of 16 and 17 December 1943.[36] In the midst
of this excitement the War Labor Board panel recommended that mini-

mum wages for seasonal leaf tobacco workers be established at 46 cents an hour. The panel also proposed that such workers be allowed military severance pay and a paid vacation of one week for as much as twenty-six weeks of work. The latter applied to workers in independent leaf plants as well.[37] Nevertheless, the election, held in an orderly manner, gave Local 22 64.8 percent of the vote.[38] The earlier petition of the R. J. Reynolds Employees Association for postponement of the election on the grounds of subversive and coercive actions by Local 22 was denied by the NLRB while the election was in progress. Afterward both the company and the association made similar protests.[39] The regional director of the NLRB on 28 December declared that these complaints "must be traced down and will require the time and pontification of all the people involved." On 20 January 1944 the NLRB overruled these protests and certified Local 22 as the bargaining agent for Reynolds employees.[40]

Nothing in the campaign and consent election indicated that a contract would be easily arranged. Negotiations lasted from 8 February until 13 April 1944 before the first contract was signed. Despite the numerous meetings required for agreement, there remained four unresolved issues that had to be settled later. Much of this negotiating period was devoted to the contention of Local 22 that Reynolds had unfairly discharged forty-two employees during the seven months of intensive campaigning. Newspapers of the town, as with the election campaign, omitted no step or rumor emanating from the negotiations. The number of negotiators fluctuated and on occasion Local 22 had as many as forty representatives. Company representatives included John C. Whitaker (vice-president in charge of manufacturing), Edgar E. Bumgardner (assistant manager in the employment department), Haddon S. Kirk (assistant superintendent of manufacturing), Clayton Moore (associate counsel), and William P. Sandridge (an outside attorney). Most active of the negotiators for Local 22 were Frank Hargrove, Conrad Espe, Clara Hutcherson, Theodosia Simpson, and William S. Deberry, the latter a field representative of the CIO. Among the employee members of the committee were Robert Black, Crawford Shelton, Clark Sheppard, Velma Hopkins, Frank N. O'Neal, and twenty-seven others. Obviously this great host of negotiators was chosen to spur morale in Local 22. Of necessity, however, negotiations were often conducted through a subcommittee. Sharp words and threats from both sides were frequent.[41]

The contract as signed contained few provisions that had not been in effect earlier. Prominent among them were the guarantee of six unpaid legal holidays, none of which were to be observed on Saturday; seniority based on continuous and unbroken employment except for permissible absences; revision of seniority lists every sixty days; promotions based on seniority when other qualifications were equal; and a detailed grievance procedure comprising four stages and culminating in a committee of three representatives from management and three from Local 22.[42] Though the company was now obliged to observe these practices, the contract was more distinguished for the issues it left unresolved than the complaints it settled.

The unresolved issues of union security, union shop, checkoff of dues, extension of vacations, and top seniority rights for stewards were presented to a War Labor Board panel on 1–2 June 1944. Serving on the panel for the public was Dr. Albert S. Keister, professor of economics at the Woman's College of the University of North Carolina (now the University of North Carolina at Greensboro); for industry, Basil D. Browder, vice-president of Riverside and Dan River Mills, Danville, Virginia; and for labor, W. H. Crawford, regional director of the United States Steelworkers, Atlanta, Georgia. Company representatives were assisted by William F. Howe and William P. Sandridge, private lawyers. In addition to Donald Henderson, Local 22 was represented by Elizabeth Sasuly, director of UCAPAWA-CIO, and Frank Hargrove, director of Local 22. In meetings marked by controversy, sensation, strong allegations, and denials, the bitterest point at issue appears to have been the union's effort to obtain top seniority privileges for 241 shop stewards. Howe charged this number exceeded normal needs. Elizabeth Sasuly held that the company was not entitled to be the final judge of the efficiency of the CIO's shop steward system. Standards for steel plants, she declared, could not arbitrarily be applied to tobacco factories. Hargrove held that shop stewards were chosen by employees not by employers.[43] On 19 June, union representatives proposed to the War Labor Board panel that a wage structure be established for the company to divide 13,772 employees into seven grades, that wage maximums be boosted 10 to 30 percent, and that minimum wages be fixed well above existing ceilings. Company representatives denounced this proposal as an effort to break the little steel formula (the rule adopted by the National War Labor Board in 1942 permitting general wage increases to groups of employees). Specifically, Donald Henderson demanded that job ceilings be increased to $0.75 (for 2,882 employees), $0.80 (for 1,250 employees), $0.90 (for 1,486 employees), $1.00 (for 574 employees), $1.15 (for 314 employees), and $1.30 (for 179 employees). Henderson stated that as it stood the wage scale was chaotic and the merit system of raises based on favoritism.[44] Evidently becoming bored with the reading of affidavits charging Local 22 with intimidation, the panel denied the request of the company's lawyers to read others. Not to be halted so easily, attorney Sandridge read from a report of the House Committee on Un-American Activities that Donald Henderson was a Communist.[45]

The panel made its report as of 3 August 1944, over objections from both the Reynolds company and Local 22. Based on the panel's findings, the Fourth Regional War Labor Board developed the following rulings, effective 24 October:

1. *Union security*: the standard maintenance-of-membership clause with a fifteen-day escape period
2. *Seniority of shop stewards*: for purposes of layoff and recall, top seniority for one hundred shop stewards during a four-month trial period, with permission for either party to reopen the matter before the War Labor Board if desired
3. *Vacations*: for regular employees, one week after one year's service (reduced from two years) and two weeks after five years' service; for seasonal employees, one-half of a week after 1,000 hours of work and one week for employees returning the next season and working 1,000 hours
4. *Wage adjustments*: the hiring rate of 45 cents per hour to be raised after thirty days of service to 50 cents; increases of 4 cents per hour for employees being paid 50–60 cents per hour, 3 cents for those making 61–70 cents, 2 cents for those making 71–80 cents, and 1 cent for those making more than 80 cents, piece rates to be adjusted accordingly

All adjustments were retroactive to 26 April 1944, but pay for time spent by union members in negotiation was denied. Likewise, differential pay for employees in the nicotine plant and on night shift was denied. More significant was that portion of the directive stating that the company should establish a simplified wage structure and consolidate job titles with appropriate rate ranges and rates of progression within those ranges.[46]

Certain loose ends of the struggle should be noted. Before the final ruling of the War Labor Board, Local 22 filed various charges against the company with the Fifth Regional Office of the NLRB. Not until 13 September 1944, however, did the acting regional director prepare a nine-page complaint based on these charges. Of the thirty charges the most serious were that the company dominated and supported the R. J. Reynolds Employees Association, sponsored the Citizens' Emergency Committee, discharged employees associated with the union, vilified organized labor, threatened to discharge employees in Local 22, posted a regulation forbidding the solicitation of funds for membership in labor organizations, questioned employees concerning their union activities, ratified an antiunion newspaper campaign being waged by the Citizens' Emergency Committee, and increased the work load of employees. A hearing on these charges before NLRB trial examiner Josef L. Hektoen lasted only one hour on 9 October, when a stipulation presented to Hektoen brought the dispute to an abrupt end. In the agreement the company promised not to dominate or interfere with the administration of the R. J. Reynolds Employees

Association or with any organization of its employees for the purpose of dealing with grievances, labor disputes, rates of pay, and other items.[47] Earlier, however, on 25 September, the company and the union had cooperated in petitioning the War Labor Board for permission to increase the speed of cigarette machines by 3.45 percent with proportionate pay increases for the employees affected.[48]

Finally on 22 December, the company and Local 22, according to the directive of the Fourth Regional War Labor Board, signed an agreement containing additions to the contract of 13 April 1944. In it were clauses covering vacations, new wage rates with an average increase of 6.32 percent effective on 30 December, retroactive pay, rate changes, progression within rate changes, further explorations affecting simplification and consolidation of job classification, union security, and checkoff of dues. The questions of job classification and wage structure remained under negotiation until an agreement dated 16 February 1945 eliminated seventy-three former job classifications. Continuing to follow the directive of the War Labor Board, the company began the checkoff of dues for the month of January 1945. On the verified list of its membership submitted by the union to the company, 232 employees claimed that they, not being members of Local 22, were not subject to the checkoff. To handle this dispute the War Labor Board appointed Richard A. Lester, then at Duke University, who ruled in April that 216 of the 232 were not members of Local 22.[49]

The first round thus ended on the eve of the first contract's expiration.

New Contracts and Philip M. Koritz

The second round of labor disputes in Winston-Salem during 1945–47 proved more tumultuous than the first, although on the surface the Reynolds Company was not as directly involved. During this period the company and Local 22 negotiated two contracts despite the threat of a strike. Philip Milton Koritz, the new director of Local 22, and one of Reynolds's employees became involved in near physical violence with the police in connection with a strike of tobacco workers at a leaf dealer's plant adjacent to the Reynolds factories. Strikes and organizing drives in other industries of Winston-Salem and in nearby towns produced considerable tension during "Operation Dixie" staged by the CIO. The installation of SPD (strip preparation) equipment in the company's leaf department also figured in the labor turbulence of this period.

Changes in the leadership of Local 22 affected labor-management relations at Reynolds. Near the end of 1944 the Food, Tobacco, Agricultural, and Allied Workers of America of the CIO (FTAAWA-CIO) replaced Frank Hargrove with Frank Green as head of Local 22, which included all tobacco workers of Winston-Salem. Early in January 1945, Green was appointed to serve on the labor-management advisory and appeals panel of the War Manpower Commission. Because he also was a member of the advisory council of the War Labor Board and a director of the Tri-State Region of the FTAAWA-CIO, Green on 8 January 1946 handed over the leadership of Local 22 to Philip M. Koritz of New York. The following month Edwin K. McCrea became an organizer for the union.[50] Thus Green, Koritz, and McCrea figured prominently in the work leading to the second and third agreements between the Reynolds company and Local 22. Also important in these negotiations was Eugene Cleveland Pratt, a former official of the local AFL and a former employee of Brown and Williamson Tobacco Company in Winston-Salem.[51]

Attempts of Local 22 to obtain a second contract began on 7 March 1945, when Frank Green wrote John C. Whitaker proposing an early meeting for negotiations. But objections of the company delayed the first conference until 12 April. At the outset Reynolds was represented by the same group that negotiated the first contract, with the addition of Bailey Liipfert (associate counsel for the company) and William F. Howe (a consultant in labor law). Whitaker, who at first worked in the background, soon entered actively into negotiations. Howe appeared only occasionally. Negotiators for Local 22 included Donald Henderson, Frank Green, Elizabeth Sasuly, Eugene C. Pratt, and fifteen employees of whom at least seven were Negroes. Before negotiations ended J. N. Maxie and D. Yates Heafner, Department of Labor conciliators, and Frank Crane of the North Carolina Department of Labor joined the group. At the suggestion of these three officials the size of the union committee was eventually reduced to include only Donald Henderson, Elizabeth Sasuly, Frank Green, Eugene C. Pratt, Clarence O. Conrad, Velma Hopkins, Clark Sheppard, and Willie L. Grier.[52]

The second contract, effective on 28 May, was executed on 5 June 1945, subject to the Fourth Regional War Labor Board's approval of wage increases, reclassifications and job titles, and lesser matters. Other than a night shift differential of four cents per hour (except for powerhouse employees and seasonal and casual workers) and a three-percent rate increase for pieceworkers, this contract was essentially the same as the first one.[53] According to Frank Green, changes in wages included a minimum wage rate of fifty-five cents, a differential of four cents for night workers, and an increase of approximately $300,000 from adjustments in different wage classifications—in all, a wage increase of approximately $800,000.[54]

At least three disputes arose in the wake of the 1945 contract. First, Local 22 challenged the claims of several employees that they had properly resigned in writing during the escape period from 16 to 30 July. The matter was referred to Dr. Alfred S. Keister as War Labor Board arbitrator, and on 31 October it was announced that only 5 of the 116 employees disputing membership were then bona fide members of Local 22. Another controversy involved prisoners-of-war. On 20 June 1945 the union had agreed in writing to the company's use of prisoners-of-war to process green leaf tobacco because of a labor shortage. Nevertheless, Local 22 later protested their employment after considerable trouble and expense on the company's part. In a third dispute, the union sought to reopen the contract and to negotiate a new wage agreement even though the 1945 contract covered wages.[55]

Certain important events preceded the beginning of formal negotiations for the third contract. In the first place, in December 1945 the executive board of Local 22 requested early negotiations. Then came the arrival of Philip Koritz early in January to serve as the new director of Local 22. At the same time, no doubt in anticipation of the prospective negotiations, the R. J. Reynolds Employees Association started a concentrated three months' campaign for new members. Probably inspired by the example of Local 22, the association offered war bonds to those in both white and Negro divisions who signed up the most members. By April 1946 it claimed a membership of 3,000. In mid-February the NLRB, also anticipating new negotiations, established a suboffice on the ninth floor of the Nissen Building in downtown Winston-Salem. Early in February, Koritz became interested in layoffs in the leaf department when the installation of SPD machinery eliminated the need for many stemmers. On 7 March the company announced the installation of new machinery, which four days later resulted in the dismissal of 700 employees and new members for Local 22.[56] Company officials could also see the significance of new members for the R. J. Reynolds Employees Association in conjunction with the loss of employees in the leaf department.

Preliminary negotiations for the third contract were begun on 11 April 1946 by Frank Green and Philip Koritz for Local 22 and two Reynolds attorneys, who suggested an extension of the 1945 agreement. On the twenty-fifth, while Bailey Liipfert conferred with Koritz and Theodosia Simpson, Clayton Moore and Edgar E. Bumgardner, according to previous plans, appeared with an extension agreement, proposing that both sides sign it and thus extend the 1945 contract until 30 June. With minor changes, Koritz accepted the proposals and all agreed to begin negotiations on 14 May. Company records show that the union sent its proposals for the 1946 contract on 9 May.[57] According to the morning paper, as early as 26 April Local 22—through its organ, the *Workers' Voice*—had laid down the following demands:[58]

1. A union shop
2. Improved vacation plans

3. Seven paid holidays
4. Two rest periods per day
5. A wage reopening clause
6. Sick leave with pay
7. An overall wage increase of 25 cents an hour
8. A hiring-in rate of 65 cents per hour (50 cents in 1945)
9. Promotions based on seniority
10. A shorter grievance procedure
11. No loss of seniority because of absence from work

Negotiations proper began on 14 May. Clayton Moore, Edgar E. Bumgardner, Haddon S. Kirk, Bailey Liipfert, and Charles B. Wade, Jr. (administrative secretary of the Personnel Committee), represented the Reynolds Company; Philip M. Koritz, Clark Sheppard, Spencer Long, Jethro Dunlap, and Moranda Smith represented Local 22, though frequently Theodosia Simpson and Anne Matthews (a union stenographer) attended subsequent meetings. At the sixth meeting Bumgardner explained and emphasized the importance of the job and labor grade evaluation. He then made the company's first wage proposal based on acceptance of the job evaluation plan, but the union negotiators objected to the seniority clause and demanded a union shop. On 14 June, both sides agreed that conciliation was in order. Local 22 notified the Secretary of Labor of its intention to strike on 15 July unless negotiations were concluded by that date.[59] The local paper reported that Reynolds offered a wage scale beginning at 60 cents and a wage raise of 4½ cents an hour in contrast to the union demands for 65 cents and a raise of 25 cents an hour.[60] At the suggestion of the Conciliation Service of the United States Department of Labor, both parties agreed to extend the 1945 contract, and incidentally the strike date, to 30 July.

Meanwhile, in a newspaper advertisement the R. J. Reynolds Employees Association launched a bitter attack on Local 22, declaring that: "These outsiders know that all their members will flock out of C.I.O., if there is ever a new contract and another escape period." The leaders of Local 22 were labeled cowards, big talkers, liars, and foreigners who wanted to strike to bolster their own positions.[61] By 17 July, with the strike date less than two weeks away and strikes imminent at the nearby Winston and Piedmont leaf companies, no settlement on the main issues of union security, wages, and plantwide seniority appeared near at hand. Harold Lane, international CIO secretary and treasurer, arrived in town, an event that heightened interest in the situation.[62] But, on the night of the nineteenth, federal and state conciliators announced that all issues had been resolved. No announcements of the settlement came until after the contract was signed on 27 July. Though something of a compromise as a whole, the contract with respect to wages and paid holidays was retroactive to 29 May and due to expire on 1 May 1947. In brief, it provided for the following:[63]

1. An addition of $2,500,000 to $3,000,000 to the annual payroll
2. A hiring-in rate of 60 cents per hour for regular employees with an increase to 65 cents after thirty days' employment and a further increase when the employee reached the minimum of his labor grade
3. A hiring-in rate of 60 cents per hour for seasonal workers with an increase to 65 cents after thirty days
4. A night shift differential of 5 cents an hour
5. Ten labor grades and two special rated jobs for employees in the manufacturing division
6. Each worker under the labor grade plan to receive a wage increase of 18 percent or an amount sufficient to reach the minimum of his labor grade
7. Pieceworkers to receive an average increase of 10 percent
8. Three paid holidays per year
9. Retention of paid vacations
10. Broadened seniority provisions, and all layoffs and recalls to be based on job classification
11. All union employees laid off and subsequently rehired to be restored to the dues checkoff list
12. Employees to progress from the minimum rate of their labor grade at the end of specified periods of five to six months, with automatic progression in a few grades
13. A resignation period of ten days from 29 July to 7 August 1946
14. A grievance committee to consist of three representatives of the company and three of the union

Meanwhile, Philip Koritz had his fingers in other pies and labor disturbances arose on all sides in and around Winston-Salem. When Congressman Thurmond Chatham charged that a strike in the Reynolds plant in July would mean disaster to the farmers of the area, Koritz's sharp reply showed no real knowledge of the situation. Organizing activity in the nearby Hanes Knitting Company and in the Winston-Salem branch of Western Electric Company led to higher minimum rates. On 17 July Koritz filed a strike notice for workers in the Piedmont Leaf Tobacco Company, and three days later hymn-singing strikers milled around only a block from the Reynolds office building. On the day before the third contract was signed, employees of the Winston Leaf Tobacco Company also went on strike. Threats of a boycott greeted merchants in the Negro districts when Local 22 sought to establish a strike fund. Edwin K. McCrea and W. Clark Sheppard led a band of organizers to a Piedmond leaf plant only to be ordered off the property. Near the end of August, employees in a CIO union at the neighboring Thomasville Chair Factory threatened violence in the fourteenth week of a strike. In mid-October Local 22 announced its support of strikers at the Camel City Dry Cleaning and Laundry Company and at the Zinzendorf Laundry. Anger surged up two weeks later when a superior court judge sentenced nine laundry pickets to thirty days or more on the roads. When in mid-November Brown and Williamson announced minimum pay rates of 76 to 78 cents for women and 88 cents for men, many undoubtedly compared these rates with the wages paid by Reynolds. At the same time the National Electric Workers–CIO led in an election in the Winston-Salem branch of the Western Electric Company. Early in 1947 the P. H. Hanes Knitting Company and the Cone Mills of nearby Greensboro raised their minimum wages to 80 cents per hour;[64] this encouraged the strikers at Reynolds to demand more and added to the general disturbances.

Koritz, who stood in the midst of this tumult, was evidently the one who sent an exultant special to the Communist *Daily Worker* from Winston-Salem on 2 August. As published, the item carried pictures of militant Negro workers "singing their songs of struggle" at the Piedmont and Winston leaf plants and "fighting against peonage wage conditions." The pickets, ran the story, "are bolstered by hundreds of workers from the Reynolds tobacco plant." A number of claims followed. Through "Operation Dixie," the CIO planned to bring 30,000 tobacco workers into the union. New fires of enthusiasm swept through North Carolina tobacco workers when news spread of the great victory won by Local 22 over the powerful R. J. Reynolds Tobacco Company. The new contract with Reynolds raised wages an average of 12 cents per hour and eliminated the hated exemption of overtime pay for seasonal employees that had forced them to work fifty-six hours per week at regular wages. The strikes at the Piedmont and Winston plants were 100 percent "and the militant picket lines have all Winston-Salem talking." Most of these workers were Negroes who had received no more than 40 cents per hour. The writer of the item concluded, perhaps accurately: "Each day at noon the picket lines are swollen to mass proportions by Reynolds' workers who have sworn their solidarity with the leaf house workers, who are also a part of Local 22. . . . Fifteen organizers are pushing the campaign among the unorganized tobacco workers, and a number of NLRB elections are expected soon."[65]

The strike at the Piedmont plant, which started on 22 July 1946, was peaceful until swift-moving mob violence erupted late in the afternoon of 23 August. By some unfortuitous combination of circumstances, as peaceful pickets stopped a Piedmont truck there suddenly appeared about fifteen policemen, at least one reporter, and one newspaper photographer.[66] The picketing group, augmented by the arrival of about three thousand Reynolds employees, were all Negroes. When Philip Koritz arrived on the scene shortly after 5:00 P.M., the police had already arrested one man— Cal Roberson Jones, a Reynolds employee—and one woman. Noting Jones's identity, Koritz pushed his way into the melee to state that Jones was only an onlooker. But the police, ignoring Koritz's statement, shoved him into a squad car and took him to headquarters along with Jones and two Negro women. On 4 September all were convicted in municipal court on charges of having resisted arrest and sentenced to work on the roads; Jones received eight months, Koritz six, and the two women lesser terms.[67]

Shortly after his arrest, Koritz was released on his own recognizance so that he might return to the Piedmont plant and persuade the greatly enlarged and angry group to disperse. This he had promised to do at the request of Governor Gregg Cherry with whom he spoke by telephone while with the chief of police.[68] The chief, however, took the precaution to call the commander of a highway troop stationed in Greensboro. Urging quietness, peaceful procedure, and good relations, Koritz and other officials of Local 22 asked the pickets to report at the usual time.

Though the name of the R. J. Reynolds Tobacco Company barely entered into this episode, it is difficult to believe that its officials were ignorant of the details—many of which may not have appeared in the press. After appeal of the sentence imposed in municipal court by Judge Leroy W. Sams, the case went to the Forsyth County Superior Court presided over by Judge Julius A. Rousseau. In an effort to obtain at least the outward trappings of a fair trial, court officials chose five Negroes to sit on the jury. Members of the police force gave evidence against Koritz, who testified with difficulty because of frequent interruptions by solicitor J. Erle McMichael. The testimony indicated that the officers had used no guns although they had been unusually free with their nightsticks. Koritz stated that he became involved when asking an officer to give Cal Roberson Jones a break because he was only an onlooker; but he admitted seizing a policeman's arm to keep from being struck with a nightstick. On the way to the police station, Koritz declared, Officer H. E. Kelly had prodded him with his elbow and asked why he, "a damned kike," did not return to where he came from. Significant testimony was given by Frank Jones, a photographer for the *Journal and Sentinel*. Unlike the policemen, he said that none of the defendants appeared to be resisting arrest, that one of the women seemed hysterical, and that Cal Roberson Jones had tried to keep his glasses on while being hustled by the officers. Moreover, the photographer produced ten pictures he had taken at the time of the fracas. Chief of Police John M. Gold, who had been the first residential FBI agent in Winston-Salem, also testified, although there was some question as to the relevance of his account. As evidence that Koritz did not violently resist officers, the defense offered photographs showing him holding the end of an officer's nightstick while quietly dangling a cigarette from his lips.[69]

It is doubtful that the trial was fairly conducted, as it was largely the word of the policemen against that of a suspected Communist and three Negro leaf workers. Judge Rousseau sentenced Koritz to twelve months in jail instead of the six he had received in municipal court; yet, the judge appeared troubled in conscience, declaring: "I may be wrong, but I think I gave the defendant [Koritz] a fair trial . . . I'd feel bad if I knew that I had the last word on a person's liberty." Furthermore, he found it necessary to state that his sentences had not been influenced by the defendants' status as union members or pickets.[70] Koritz was transferred to Philadelphia, and rumors spread that someone in Winston-Salem had attempted to have the strikers at the Piedmont plant pronounced ineligible for unemployment compensation. The R. J. Reynolds Employees Association took on new life and urged every industrial worker in Winston-Salem to attend a meeting at the courthouse on 16 November to hear a discussion on the importance of joining the Confederated Unions of America.[71] But interest in these events faded as the struggle took another direction.

The Communist Exposé

The following year labor problems of the R. J. Reynolds Tobacco Company intensified. Negotiations for the fourth contract, which began on 4 April 1947, broke down and ended in a strike from 1 May to 9 June. Midway in the strike the local newspapers published reports that Local 22 had been infiltrated by Communists. Meanwhile, the company was aided by state and pending federal legislation.

Just before the fracas at the plant of the Piedmont Tobacco Leaf Company, the *Journal and Sentinel* on 11 August 1946 ran a feature article on communism—the first in a series written by Chester S. Davis, the paper's special "investigative reporter." It was an innocuous piece decorated with cuts of Stalin, Lenin, Earl Browder, and William Z. Foster—all, of course, far removed from Winston-Salem. Yet, it was the logical beginning of a drive to portray as Communists the leaders of Local 22.[72] In his second article, published on 18 August, Davis brought the matter of communism somewhat nearer home by analyzing the career of Alice Burke, or Mrs. Paul J. Davis, as she was known in private life. He stated that Alice Burke, as secretary of the Communist party in the Carolinas and Virginia, had publicly dissolved the party in that area and renamed it the Virginia League for Public Education to serve as a rallying point for all liberal groups. This, he declared, was merely a new method for obtaining subservience to the national Communist line as announced by Earl Browder.[73]

Davis's next article, appearing in the *Journal and Sentinel* on 25 August, focused on communism in Winston-Salem. Showing cuts of Donald Henderson and Harold Lane of the FTAAWA-CIO, Davis quoted from a report of the House Committee on Un-American Activities: "There is no secrecy about Donald Henderson's membership in the Communist Party. He has been a publicly avowed card-holding member for more than 10 years." He stated that Henderson and Lane kept close tabs on Local 22, the largest Food, Tobacco, and Alcohol (FTA) local in the United States with a membership exceeding six thousand. A United States Senate sub-committee subsequently made the same allegations regarding Henderson and the FTA, a branch later expelled from the CIO.[74] Davis also noted that Sam Hall (d. 3 January 1954), chairman of the Communist party in North Carolina, claimed two hundred party members for the state; fifty of them were affiliated with the Winston-Salem branch. The reporter referred to interviews with a number of local men who mistakenly believed Local 22 to be a Communist organization. Rather, he believed, "the top-drawer leadership," but not the rank and file members, were affiliated with the Communist party. During the August 1943 consent election campaigns, Alice Burke had been in town, registered at the Robert E. Lee Hotel from 27 July to 5 August, when she mapped out the last-minute details for the election campaign. Davis also called attention to the nature of the resolutions passed by Local 22—resolutions far beyond the ken of the general membership but always favored by the international Communist party. Both Henderson and Koritz, in replies to questions about Communist leadership in Local 22, gave identical and elaborately verbose answers. Davis noted how John L. Lewis maneuvered to bring Communists into the CIO because they were the only able organizers available, though he intended to drop them later; instead, they left the CIO. Evidently not finding pay dirt in this vein, Davis wrote no more elaborate analyses of Communist activities until the exposé—nearly nine months later.

Meanwhile, in mid-1946 the R. J. Reynolds Employee Association, claiming four to five thousand eligible voters, began rejuvenating its membership. With the Reverend A. Matthew Hicks as the only nominee for the presidency, the association planned to meet on 31 August to elect officers and hear the reports of five delegates to the Confederated Unions of America. Leaflets stressing the group's independence were distributed.[75] Evidently the company now hoped to win any consent election that might be called. Continuing their efforts, association officials scheduled a second meeting for 16 November to be held in the county courthouse in two sessions, one for whites and another for Negroes. Nevertheless, all industrial

workers in Winston-Salem were invited to hear the president and secretary
of the Confederated Unions of America. Much was made of this as an opportunity for the industrial workers to join a union free of outside bosses
and dictators.[76] Possibly near this time the Reynolds company printed and
evidently distributed widely a piece of doggerel rhyme that perhaps best
expressed the sentiments of the faithful employees. It was entitled "STOP
AND THINK" and no doubt written by Howell Robert Gwaltney (b. 28
September 1884), long a foreman in the smoking division. Three of its
fifteen stanzas are sufficient to illustrate the arguments it presented:[77]

> We must work in peace and harmony—
> Every man must try to lead,
> And help the manufacturers—
> To make the things we need.
>
> How can you trust that C.I.O. Organizer?
> He won't place his trust in you—
> Not even to let you pay your dues
> When they are coming due.
>
> But you'll better stop and think awhile,
> Before it is too late.
> You may cause yourself, and your family,
> To be locked out at the gate!

In this atmosphere negotiations for the fourth contract began on 4 April
1947. The slate of negotiators for the company remained the same. The
slate for Local 22 consisted of Etta Hobson, Etta Neal, Willie L. Grier,
W. Clark Sheppard, Jethro Dunlap, Mary Samuels, Moranda Smith, Robert
C. Black, Eugene C. Pratt, Frank O'Neal, Howard Pilcher, Spencer Long,
Edwin K. McCrea, and Josef W. Califf, the research director.[78] Union demands centered around an average increase of 24 cents per hour to establish a 90-cent minimum wage, a union shop, job security, a stronger shop
steward system, changes in grievance procedures, and seniority. The union
also planned to request a clause to provide a company-union conference
sixty days before layoffs for consideration of share-the-work programs.
Spokesmen estimated that demands for changes in existing insurance and
retirement plans would bring the average hourly increase to 30 cents.
From the statements of Califf, who called attention to the company's profit
increase of 48 percent from 1945 to 1946, it appears that the union
planned to base its arguments on ability of Reynolds to pay.[79]

Haggling in the first nine meetings resulted in the calling of a strike.
According to newspaper reports, four thousand members of Local 22
gathered on the grounds of the Woodland Avenue School on 27 April and

voted to strike unless their demands were satisfied. At this meeting McCrea declared that a union demand for an hourly increase of 24 cents had been met by an offer of a 5½-cent raise. The union negotiating committee then returned with the following counterproposals, which the company nego- tiators refused:

1. An hourly differential of 10 cents for night work (an increase of 5 cents)
2. Changes in labor grades of approximately ten thousand employees for wage purposes
3. Automatic progression to the top of the wage scale for the ten la- bor grades (then effective for the three lowest grades)
4. An across-the-board increase of 15 cents (which McCrea claimed had been arrived at in negotiations)
5. A noncontributory plan for health and group insurance
6. Overtime pay for all work over forty hours including that of leaf workers and seasonal employees
7. Union security

Believing that these demands could be won only by a stiff fight, McCrea announced a strike with picket captains standing ready for every gate of the Reynolds plants.[80] Meanwhile, the R. J. Reynolds Employees Associa- tion distributed leaflets headed: "We will work! We will not strike. We can carry on! We can carry on easily! The CIO will lose and we will become bargaining agent."[81]

The strike from 1 May to 9 June was bitter and boisterous. During that time came the final revelation of the extent of Communist control of Local 22. It is often claimed that there was no work stoppage in the manufactur- ing divisions during the strike. Accounts by numerous individuals, how- ever, indicate that operations were severely handicapped. Moreover, in Number 256, where smoking tobacco was manufactured, the strike was effective for twenty-seven working days—the duration of the conflict.[82] Nevertheless, cigarette production in 1947 increased approximately 13 per- cent over that of 1946. In the sale of surplus machinery to a leaf dealer in Kinston, North Carolina, an official of the company preferred shipment by rail, but, if the dealer wished shipment by truck, the official declared: "We suggest, in view of our present labor difficulties, that you send white driv- ers on your trucks."[83] In mid-May company officials stated that operations were about one-half normal force.[84] According to the local newspaper, al- most all the strikers were Negroes; they carried placards, sang spirituals, and picketed all seventy-three gates to the Reynolds plants, taking great care, however, to allow trucks and nonstrikers to move in and out at will.[85]

Despite the efforts of federal and state conciliators, who returned on 5 May,[86] the stalemate continued until the twenty-sixth, when Local 22—

through the Conciliation Service of the Department of Labor—requested the resumption of negotiations.[87] More than likely this sudden change of heart was prompted by the Senate's passage of the Taft-Hartley Bill, and indications that it would easily pass the House of Representatives, in conjunction with the Communist exposé.

At any rate, on 19 May 1947—only seven days before the union's request that negotiations be resumed—the Winston-Salem newspapers published startling confessions from Eugene C. Pratt, Spencer Long, and Anne Matthews of the out-and-out infiltration of Local 22 by Communists. The morning paper carried signed statements, pictures, and a front-page editorial as well as a regular editorial on the subject. In fact, it contained little else. Supposedly Pratt, softened by liquid refreshment at a party, began to unburden his conscience. According to the company record, "confidential information" reached Edgar E. Bumgardner and Bailey Liipfert, who "established contacts, gave directions to, and secretly took appropriate steps."[88] These actions undoubtedly included informing Chester S. Davis, the "investigative reporter" of the *Winston-Salem Journal*.

Pratt's confession recounted his long affiliation with the AFL; his somewhat reluctant agreement in May 1945 to become business agent for Local 22; his knowledge then that the union was dominated by Communists, including Daniel Brown Jackson, Alice Burke, and John Henry Minor; and his expectation that he would be able to throw them out. After careful observation, he had noted that questions raised for discussion by union leaders had usually been prejudged by a certain group that was always in the majority. Those who attended sessions to which Pratt was not invited included Frank Green; Theodosia Simpson (then an organizer); Robert Black, Clark Sheppard, and Velma Hopkins (all organizers); William DeBerry (an international organizer); Clara Hutcherson (a local organizer); and Eleanor Hoagland (then educational director). It was a long and detailed confession that implicated many individuals by name. Pratt, however, did not believe that the strike was Communist-inspired. In that belief he had on 15 May accompanied Spencer Long and Leon Dure, Jr., executive editor of the *Journal and Sentinel*, to Washington for a conference with Philip Murray, head of the CIO, to learn the truth about Local 22. The newspapers of Winston-Salem were thus deeply involved in the Communist exposé.

Anne Matthews, secretary of Local 22, stated that she had been a member of the Communist party for ten years and identified approximately the same people whom Pratt mentioned. About 50 persons joined the party when she was elected treasurer. She believed that there were at least 150 members of the Communist party in Winston-Salem by early 1947. The work of Philip Koritz, Velma Hopkins, and Moranda Smith especially did not cement relations between Negroes and whites and as a result many white workers failed to join Local 22, thus leaving Negro workers as the chief rank-and-file members. Like Pratt, she did not believe that the strike had been inspired by Communists.

The *Winston-Salem Journal*'s front page editorial, written by Chester Davis and headed "Communist-Union Collusion is Exposed in City; Appeal is Made to Murray for Labor Leadership," covered the entire width of the paper. He reviewed the strike, mentioned that Reynolds employees who continued to work had received harassing telephone calls, emphasized the dangers involved, and cited John M. Gold's belief that tension was increasing and that the Piedmont strike was an indication of how orderly picketing might erupt into violence. Though so far the pickets had conducted themselves admirably, he believed it was dangerous for white workers to pass through the Negro picket lines. He felt that there was no basis for assuming, as some did, that officers of the R. J. Reynolds Tobacco Company were willing to run the risk of a long and dangerous strike. Davis also listed reasons for his belief that Communists had dominated the leadership of Local 22 from the beginning. He cited the presence of Alice Burke in 1943, the arrest of Eleanor Hoagland and her husband (William Binkley, organizer of the laundry workers) for circulating seditious literature in New Orleans, the visits of Sam Hall to Koritz and to the union hall, and the contributions of Koritz on the Piedmont strike to the *Daily Worker*.[89] The reporter correctly predicted that publication of these confessions would produce charges of "Red baiting" from the Communist leadership of Local 22. He noted the statements of Pratt and Long that leaders of Local 22 were spreading the word that the police were tools of the R. J. Reynolds Tobacco Company—a charge that undoubtedly held some truth. Moreover, the strike was a powder keg, Davis declared, and the police should watch the union leaders for what they were.

The front-page editorial of the *Winston-Salem Journal* for 19 May 1947 by Leon S. Dure, Jr., called the Communist exposé complete. The Communist party, he wrote, had captured Local 22 lock, stock, and barrel. Dure repeated much of what Davis had written, though his observations showed less restraint. He reported his statement to Philip Murray that the newspapers of the town had not taken sides in the dispute, although they would be accused of having done so. He also had told Murray that anyone who stirred racial tensions in the South was an enemy of both races. Murray, he wrote, had been sympathetic.

On the same day the morning paper reported a mass rally of the strikers on the grounds of Woodland Avenue School. There William Billingsley, assistant CIO director for North Carolina, called for larger picket lines and declared that all CIO members in the state supported the strikers. Edwin McCrea warned against rumors, urged the strikers not to be provoked to violence, and assured them that almost all of the Reynolds plants had been closed. The Reverend R. M. Pitts declared that the church was supporting the strike. Throughout the meeting several persons circulated petitions to the city aldermen, requesting their help in bringing about a just settlement. Cash donations of $105.75 were received from the Twin City Barbers' Association and the St. James A. M. E. Church, and telegrams of support were read.

Reverberations from the exposé came the following day. In a full-page advertisement in the *Winston-Salem Journal* (20 May 1947), Local 22 called the exposé "Red baiting" and declared that the strike, which would help workers' families, merchants, and citizens, was in the public interest. As for the informers, both Pratt and Long had deserted Local 22 on 10 May when salaries of staff members were cut off for the duration of the strike; Anne Matthews, who had quit for maternity reasons, had been given to understand that she would not be reemployed. Soft-spoken Sam Hall stated that the Carolina district of the Communist party was being used as a scapegoat and that he had been watching to see how Gordon Gray, owner of the local newspapers and son of Bowman Gray, Sr., would use his newspaper monopoly to assist the R. J. Reynolds Tobacco Company in which he was a large stockholder.[90] William Smith, state CIO director, issued no statement but, in a telephone conversation with the *Winston-Salem Journal*, said that the CIO in North Carolina did not need the Communist party. Donald Henderson, as usual, maintained that he was neither for nor against the Communist party, but Philip Murray took a vigorous position against it. In the same issue, the editor called attention to the charges of Pratt, Long, and Anne Matthews as evidence of Communist domination of Local 22, referred to an earlier statement by David Dubinsky that the Communist party dominated twelve to fifteen of the existing forty CIO unions, stated that Philip Murray had promised an investigation, and expressed the opinion that a vast majority of Local 22 was not Communist.

Returning to the fray on 25 May, the *Winston-Salem Journal* published a front-page, boxed item listing all twenty-nine officers of Local 22, fourteen of whom were shown to be members of the Communist party. One of the fourteen, Christine Gardner, was a trustee of Local 22 and an employee of the Piedmont Leaf Tobacco Company. She had been close to the Communists as early as September 1946, though it is doubtful that she entertained any ideas beyond an increase in wages. That year, in an article published in the *Worker Magazine*, she charged that the R. J. Reynolds Tobacco Company was behind the small leaf houses' opposition to Local 22 because these dealers sold leaf to the company. She also stated that Chief of Police John M. Gold spent much time with the leaf house officials, that police had repeatedly attacked pickets on 23 August 1946, and that Reynolds had been determined to break the union ever since the first contract in 1944.[91]

These allegations doubtless explain the appearance of Christine Gardner's name on the list.

As a result of the Communist exposé, Winston-Salem became a hotbed of controversy. The *Winston-Salem Journal* displayed an excessive interest in having the leadership of Local 22 investigated by the House Committee on Un-American Activities. There were a few incidents of near violence supposedly perpetrated by members of Local 22 and futile threats of its leaders that the CIO would boycott Reynolds products. Howard P. Pilcher made a belated confession concerning leadership of Local 22. Rumors spread that strikers were being evicted from their homes for nonpayment of rent and that unemployment checks were being delayed. The Reynolds company was accused of hiring children to replace strikers. The local papers intimated that the Southern Conference for Human Welfare was dominated by Communists. Some years later many employees in the Reynolds office building still recalled an incident involving Charlotte Mock, who on 23 May was arrested for hurling a glass paperweight from the third floor and narrowly missing one of the pickets below. On arrest, she also admitted having thrown an ink bottle at a picket a few days earlier. Apparently she was fined $35 for assault with a deadly weapon.[92]

Efforts to secure an investigation by the House Committee on Un-American Activities were complicated at first by the refusal of two North Carolina congressmen to support the move and later by the haphazard work of the committee's representative, who on 2 June conferred with "several persons" but not with officials of the Reynolds company or Local 22.[93] The investigation revealed little that was new.[94] Nevertheless, on 24 July the *Winston-Salem Journal*'s Washington correspondent, in sixteen column inches on the front page of the morning paper, analyzed the testimony. Again, on the following day, Leon Dure more or less reviewed the case in an editorial, referring to J. Parnell Thomas as something of a great figure. In the piece Dure both emphasized the failure of Local 22 to submit issues to the NLRB after passage of the Taft-Hartley Act on 23 June and called attention to refusal of the top officers of Local 22 to state whether or not they were Communists.[95] In the meantime, on 24 July Local 22 had issued leaflets attacking the House committee as a "strike-breaking, union-busting agency" with no regard for the payment of fair wages, decent medical care, education, or the "gypping" of veterans.

Prior to the investigation, however, the strike had been settled. On 23 May Donald Henderson had accused the R. J. Reynolds Tobacco Company of refusing to bargain, but, according to Clayton Moore, Local 22 had not requested a conference. Henderson maintained that three requests had been made. Hopes for an end to the strike brightened on the night of the twenty-sixth when it was learned that negotiations would be resumed on the following day. Speculation in Winston-Salem revolved around the theory that pending congressional legislation had induced officials of Local 22 to bargain. No agreement was reached at the next conference on 4 June, and the situation remained deadlocked as negotiations continued. The first sign of progress appeared when a session was set for Saturday, 7 June—an unusual day for such a meeting. News of the settlement was announced on 8 June 1947 under an enormous headline covering five columns: "Agreement is Reached for Settlement of Union's Strike against Reynolds, Must Be Ratified by Local's Members."[96]

The contract, effective on 9 June, was retroactive to 5 May for wages and paid holidays. During negotiations company representatives had carefully explained that only strikers for whom jobs were available at the time would be rehired. Edwin McCrea correctly insisted that the law did not support this position. Though the union agreed to the company's handling and procedure,[97] there would be a long struggle over the rehiring of these strikers with the union insisting that seniority be the basis for rehiring. The wage increases amounted to 7 percent or about twelve cents per hour, the same figure offered by the company throughout the strike. Other provisions included the checkoff of dues at the written request of the employee, a readjustment in rating or seniority, the addition of two paid holidays, the continuation of automatic wage-rate progressions in effect before the strike, and the designation of Labor Day as a paid holiday for seasonal workers.[98]

According to Leon S. Dure, Jr., Donald Henderson's problem had been the necessity of acting swiftly in order to escape the consequences of the Taft-Hartley Act. This had led to "a quick settlement of the Reynolds strike (as) a strategic necessity." In an elaborate editorial entitled "Industrial Peace and Community Unity," Dure stated that the strike had been costly to the workers, the company, and the community. Employees in the Reynolds plants had the largest purchasing power in Winston-Salem, he continued. But the tragedy lay in the occurrence of the strike "in spite of the fact that the wage increase offered by the company on April 30 was the same as that finally embodied in the new agreement." In conclusion Dure referred to Communist leadership of Local 22 as a residual question of vital importance. The fomenters of trouble had disrupted the long-standing harmony between labor and management. Commenting on the exposé, the editor cited the courage of Eugene Pratt, Spencer Long, and Howard P. Pilcher; he did not mention Anne Matthews, whose daring undoubtedly had been greater.[99]

Reverberations from the 1947 contract pertained largely to the rehiring of the 481 strikers who had been replaced. At the union's request, a meeting was arranged for 20 June. Representatives of the company insisted that the agreement had been to reemploy only the strikers who applied between 9 and 16 June when work was available. Donald Henderson dis-

cussed the importance of good relations between management and employees, stating that even if the company had done all it had agreed to
do, it should do more. These conversations were continued on 21 June
when it was decided to meet again on the twenty-seventh. Two federal conciliators disagreed with the company's stand, but nothing constructive was
accomplished. The matter came up again when Edgar E. Bumgardner and
Bailey Liipfert met with a union committee composed of Clark Sheppard,
Velma Hopkins, and Frank O'Neal.[100] The union leaders tried a variety of
maneuvers to have the 481 strikers rehired, including applications to the
NLRB and an appearance before Senator William B. Umstead. Plans were
made in late June for the arrival of Paul Robeson, the concert singer and
Communist sympathizer, who consistently supported labor organizations
and movements for the advancement of Negroes. One purpose of this
move, according to Velma Hopkins, was to raise money for the 73 white
workers and 408 Negroes who had not been rehired. Robeson appeared at
a mass meeting on the Woodland Avenue School grounds. There he sang
for an audience of "several thousand" and in a short talk stated that he was
glad to be singing in North Carolina where his father was born in slavery
near Rocky Mount.[101]

Three months later the Reynolds company notified the 73 white workers
that jobs were available for them and most of them returned. The eventual
agreement to rehire these strikers was certainly not due to Henderson's persuasive powers.[102] In a memorandum to plant managers dated 16 September 1947, John C. Whitaker called attention to Henderson's efforts "to
negotiate the return of the striking white cigarette employees to their former jobs." No agreement had been made with Henderson or his committee before that date. The remainder of Whitaker's memorandum is
illuminating:[103]

> It seems that Mr. Henderson has timed his discussion of the Ciga-
> rette Making & Packing employees who have not been returned to
> work to coincide with the greatest need for new employees that we
> have had in a long time. Our need for new employees is occasioned
> by the necessity for some expansion in cigarette production and at
> the same time a reduction in working hours, which might effectuate
> a savings in the critical water supply in our community.
>
> After the strike, during which we had hired sufficient personnel to
> replace the strikers of the Making & Packing departments, we con-
> sidered that those strikers were no longer employees of this Com-
> pany. We have maintained that position with the Union by not ac-
> cepting grievances from this group; and up to now we have not
> found it necessary for business reasons to expand our employment.

In order to be absolutely certain that our position in this matter was legally correct, we have sought the advice of outside counsel. We are now told that we should give these employees an opportunity to return to work in our plants along with any other applicants for employment; and the Personnel Division is addressing letters to this group, giving them the opportunity to present themselves for consideration along with other applicants in this program of expanding our personnel.

I realize that there may be problems of discipline arising when these employees are returned to the plants, but I feel confident that you will understand the situation to an exent that you will handle any condition that arises within the plants in the best interests of your Company.

It appears that the number of strikers not reemployed by January 1948 was negligible.

In a speculative article in the *Winston-Salem Journal* for 28 December 1947, Marie Belk stated that the R. J. Reynolds Employees Association planned to file non-Communist affidavits in order to negotiate with the NLRB. Such an action, she claimed, might further complicate the intricate situation in Winston-Salem under the Taft-Hartley Act. She also thought Local 22 might comply with the law, though it had not then done so. Each year, at or near the time for renewal of the contract, it had been rumored that the R. J. Reynolds Employees Association might petition the NLRB for an election. But the association would have to present membership cards for one-third of the total number of company employees in order to qualify as a candidate for the position of bargaining agent. Obviously the association did not have sufficient strength to enter the contest. "Another difficulty," she wrote, "may arise from the fact that several years ago the NLRB found the Association to be company-dominated." Yet, to ensure compliance with the Taft-Hartley Act the company might refuse to deal with Local 22 on 1 May 1948, when the current contract expired. So the future was accurately foretold and the importance of the Taft-Hartley Act tacitly acknowledged. Probably, though, equally helpful labor legislation was provided by the so-called North Carolina right-to-work law, which prohibited a union shop and a simple checkoff of dues; this prohibition had certainly aided the company in negotiating the 1947 contract.[104]

The Decline and Fall of Local 22

Labor disturbances continued with hearings, conferences, lawsuits, organizing drives, elections, a split in the CIO, and reentry of the AFL—all before the downfall of Local 22 in the narrow election of 23 March 1950. Among these activities were initiation of a contract between the Reynolds company and the seasonal workers in the Greensboro redrying plant, termination of the contract with Local 22, fresh organizing drives in Winston-Salem, the important stand taken by the Reverend Kenneth R. Williams against the union, the election of 1950, and later efforts of Local 22 to make a recovery. None of these events produced commotion equal in intensity to that caused by the strike and the Communist exposé in 1947.

Organizing activities began in the company's new redrying plant in Greensboro as soon as it opened on 8 August 1947. Local 22 was first on the scene. According to Edwin K. McCrea, a work stoppage there resulted from the discharge of a union leader and from an accumulation of grievances, including lack of proper heating, inadequate wages, a recent increase in the work load, and long working hours[105]—all this in a plant that had barely begun operations. At the same time, the United Transport Service Employees, a right-wing branch of the CIO, began to organize. On 20 September 1948, a representative of this union advised the company that it spoke for a majority of the employees in the Greensboro plant. When Clayton Moore, Edgar E. Bumgardner, and Bailey Liipfert met with representatives of UTSE-CIO on 5 October, Allen R. Rosenburg, a Washington attorney, appeared, claiming to represent an independent union with ten pledged Reynolds employees. Rosenburg, of course, represented Local 22, though its leaders had not then signed the non-Communist affidavit.

Rosenburg's appearance at the conference upset all plans for determining the date for a consent election. When the question was taken before the NLRB, both unions were denied a place on the ballot on the grounds that Rosenburg's union represented a front for Local 22. The NLRB also ruled that the seasonal workers in the Greensboro plant constituted a proper bargaining unit. However, on 29 July 1949 Local 22, represented by Pressman, Witt, and Cammer of New York City, moved that it be placed on the ballot because it had become qualified on the basis of the Taft-Hartley Act.[106] Meanwhile, according to the local morning paper, Donald Henderson had attended the Communist-dominated World Peace Conference in Paris where he received an ovation from 2,244 delegates from forty-six countries for his bitter attack on the United States and his praise of the USSR.[107] As a part of Local 22's tactics it was announced early in July that the FTA branch of the CIO would comply with the requirements of the Taft-Hartley Act by filing statements on its financial condition along with non-Communist affidavits of its leaders. In a move perhaps less clever than naive, Henderson resigned as president of the FTA-CIO, claiming that the CIO board had appointed him national administrative director of the same branch. He then signed a non-Communist affidavit, stating that he was a former member of the Communist party.[108] This maneuver seemed to fool few. Nevertheless, on a strictly legal basis the NLRB permitted Local 22 to have a place on the ballot.

The election, scheduled for 27 September 1949, marked the first show of strength between the right and left wings of the CIO during the Reynolds labor troubles of the 1940s.[109] The ballot carried "United Tobacco Workers—Local 22," "No Union," and "United Transport Service Employees." Though this campaign was noisy as shifts changed at the Greensboro plant,[110] it appears that there was no violence and no opportunity for the marching and singing that had occurred earlier in Winston-Salem. Returns from the election were as follows: out of 397 votes cast, 346 went to UTSE-CIO, 26 to Local 22, and 18 to "No Union"; the remaining 7 votes were challenged.[111]

The contract covering the period from 9 May 1950 to 9 May 1951 was strictly between seasonal workers and the company. Seniority called for unbroken employment (except for permissible absences) and agreement on the part of Reynolds to prepare a revised seniority list within one week after the beginning of fall operations for 1950–51. Any seniority ruling by the company might be protested within thirty days. The contract also provided for maternity leave. When working time exceeded fifty hours per week in any of the exempted fourteen weeks, the employee received time and a half for all excess hours; otherwise, the forty-hour week was used. All eligible seasonal workers were to receive vacation pay at the end of seasonal operations. Strikes and organizational activities—either prolabor or antilabor—were prohibited, but grievances might be presented by any employee or by a shop steward. Checkoff of dues was also permitted.[112]

Before this contract was signed, the Reynolds company gave a blanket wage increase and a vacation bonus averaging 7½ cents per hour to employees in the Greensboro plant as a part of a general wage boost for all of its workers.[113] Undoubtedly the company was encouraged by the decisive defeat of Local 22 in the Greensboro election, but, in view of the rather solid entrenchment of Local 22 in Winston-Salem, any such confidence might well have been tempered with skepticism. A second and similar contract with the Greensboro workers covered the period from 14 June 1951 to 9 May 1952. On 17 April 1952 Philip McCarley, business manager of the Greensboro local of UTSE-CIO, requested that a new contract be negotiated, though he admitted that his union had no dues-paying members in the plant at that time. Possibly this resulted from an across-the-board increase of 5 cents per hour in the Greensboro plant on 3 September

1951.[114] At any rate, the company had no further dealings with the union there. In fact, whether because of labor troubles, annexation plans of the city of Greensboro, or the adoption of a more sensible real estate policy, in 1955 Reynolds decided to sell the Greensboro plant and did so in 1959.[115]

Back in Winston-Salem on 26 February 1948, during the organizing activities at the Greensboro plant, the company notified Local 22 that it would terminate its collective bargaining agreement at the close of the fourth contract, which had been signed on 30 April 1947. No doubt as a prelude to this move, the R. J. Reynolds Employees Association advertised that it would hold a business meeting in the Forsyth County Courthouse on 7 February to which the public was invited. An encouragingly large group jammed the room when Philip Weisner, vice-president, called the assembly to order at 7:30 P.M. As Weisner was about to proceed with the business, a man in the rear suggested that the meeting be opened with a prayer. Apparently surprised, Weisner asked the man to pray and he did. Then a woman asked whether an agenda had been prepared. Suddenly, Clark Sheppard, former cochairman of Local 22, stood and said: "There's only one thing R. J. Reynolds employees are interested in. That's a contract." A chorus of ayes followed. When the Reverend A. Matthew Hicks, president of the R. J. Reynolds Employees Association, requested that only dues-paying members vote, a woman shouted that the public had been invited. Association members then moved across the street while those who remained sang "I'm Like a Tree Planted by the Water. I Shall Not be Moved." Not only had Local 22 broken up the meeting but also its members stopped singing and remained in the courthouse long enough to vote the dissolution of the R. J. Reynolds Employees Association to which they did not belong! One member of Local 22—Mary Major, a packing machine inspector at Number 12—possibly more enterprising than those who remained in the courthouse, followed the retreating members of the association to their headquarters, obtained the floor, and moved that the business of the meeting be confined to discussion of the contract. After an eighty-minute filibuster during which association members struggled for control of their disrupted session, Vice-President Weisner adjourned the meeting, stating that another would be called at a future date.[116] The time and place of the next meeting were not revealed in the press, but on 5 March 1948 the R. J. Reynolds Employees Association unsuccessfully petitioned the NLRB, claiming that it represented a majority of the company's employees.[117]

Quite possibly advance information on another move influenced the company's decision to terminate bargaining with Local 22. The report of a joint committee on labor-management relations created by the Taft-Hartley Act, issued on 15 March, was filled with favorable references to the company. This report also stressed Communist infiltration of Local 22 and of the CIO generally, with special mention of the alleged efforts of Local 22 to arouse bitter racial friction.[118]

Other matters came to a head early in 1948. No doubt because of the Communist exposé, the Reynolds company's refusal to bargain with Local 22 a fifth time, and Henderson's tardy compliance with the Taft-Hartley Act, the TWIU-AFL late in February began energetic attempts to organize the Reynolds employees. The extent of the headline over the front-page item in the *Winston-Salem Journal* for 28 February probably reflected local interest in the move. S. E. Blane, vice-president of the TWIU-AFL, who announced the opening of the campaign, arrived in Winston-Salem a few hours after the company notified Local 22 of its refusal to negotiate again. The local newspaper prophesied "a repeat performance" of the campaign of 1944, when the same three unions had competed for the support of Reynolds employees. No doubt it also marveled at the synchronization of the company's refusal to bargain further with Local 22 and the reentry of TWIU-AFL. It is interesting to note that on 12 March 1948 the company received a letter from Philip Murray, president of the CIO, urging it to resume negotiations for a new contract with Local 22, although, in late November of the same year he denounced CIO unions with Communist leadership and criticized Donald Henderson from the convention floor.[119]

Promptly, after Murray's denunciation of Local 22 and its leadership, the UTSE-CIO moved into Winston-Salem. Frank Hargrove headed the drive that began on 1 December 1948.[120] Thus by the end of 1948 the Reynolds employees were faced with the choice of one of four organizing groups: Local 22, TWIU-AFL, UTSE-CIO, and the R. J. Reynolds Employees Association.

In the meantime, company officials were busy dealing with election petitions, complaints regarding the dismissal of employees, and lawsuits. Donald Henderson demanded a meeting to discuss a new contract. A portal-to-portal suit for $6,500,000, filed by Local 22 and dismissed by the Federal District Court of the Middle District of North Carolina, was taken to the United States Circuit Court of Appeals. When petitions of the company and of the R. J. Reynolds Employees Association for an election were refused by the NLRB on 2 April 1948, the association promised to appeal the decision. On 30 April, a few hours before expiration of the fourth contract, members of Local 22, carrying placards and chanting "We Want a Contract," marched outside the Reynolds office building as spectators gathered to watch. A few minutes after 5:00 P.M., as Vice-President John C. Whitaker was closing his office, several members of Local 22 entered unannounced and demanded to discuss a contract for 1948, which, they held, should include an hourly raise of 26½ cents. At the same time, word of a mass meeting to be held on the grounds of Woodland Avenue School spread through the Negro community. Crowds on Fourth Street sang "Solidarity Forever" until disbanded by Velma Hopkins. Two days later, at the mass meeting attended by some 2,000 Negroes, Local 22 apparently dropped its threat of a strike, though it empowered its executive board to authorize any united economic action necessary to enforce collective bargaining. The group also adopted a resolution demanding a raise of 26½ cents per hour.[121]

It was a riotous and troubled time in the midst of which the Reynolds company on 15 May announced pay increases totaling $1,750,000 annually for approximately 10,000 employees—to bring the average wage rate to $1.05 per hour. Immediately shop stewards of Local 22 attributed this move to "stepped up union interest and activity in all departments . . . for better wages, to make up for higher living costs and short hours." Though the raises were badly needed, they declared, organizing would be continued until the company was forced to grant not only the full 26½ cents an hour but also larger pensions and promotions by seniority instead of favoritism.[122] Haggling also continued over damages claimed to be due a number of employees who were not returned to their jobs until about four months after the strike. Officials of Local 22 wrote President Truman, senators, and congressmen demanding that the fourteen weeks of exemption from overtime payments accorded tobacconists for seasonal workers be abolished.[123]

When police, on charges of obstructing traffic, took the operators of a sound truck to police headquarters, Local 22 instructed its attorney to file an injunction against the city of Winston-Salem "to stop interference with the union's right of free speech in the use of sound equipment." The operators included Robert C. Black and Jack Frye, of Local 22, and Mike Ross of Greensboro, who was speaking for the Wallace Committee-for-President.[124] About a month later two Negro officials, Robert Black and Velma Hopkins, set up an amplifying system behind the Reynolds office building shortly after 4:00 P.M. Negroes jammed the sidewalks and office workers watched as Mary Price, chairman of the Progressive party and candidate for governor of North Carolina on that ticket, spoke to the group. Velma Hopkins then took over, declaring to the assembled workers in the words of Karl Marx: "You don't have a thing to lose but your chains." In outlining union demands, she derided the "seasonal" classification by which the company supposedly denied some workers about $300,000 in compensation for a tax saving of possibly $20,000: "Who built these great factories here? . . . We did—our mothers and fathers did, working here for 10 or 15 cents an hour. That's the reason we are uneducated and living in slums. They talk about slums. R. J. Reynolds workers are living there . . . We are only asking to be treated fair, that those working in seasonal plants be able to draw their unemployment compensation." She also noted that 250 Negro workers, who had been transferred from a plant operated the year round to seasonal work, were replaced with whites; the Negroes thus faced dismissal within six weeks. On the same day the company stated officially that it had no plans to lay off Negro workers and replace them with whites.[125] Activities of Local 22 continued more or less along these lines as the four unions dickered with the NLRB for a new election.[126]

As requests to the NLRB seesawed back and forth, it became necessary to hold hearings in Winston-Salem. Scheduled for two days, they began on 19 October 1949. The chief issue concerned the inclusion of seasonal employees: UTSE-CIO and Local 22 advocated inclusion, whereas TWIU-AFL and the company lined up against it. The TWIU-AFL and Reynolds also were in substantial agreement on other issues. (Meanwhile, by May 1948, the straight-line hourly rate of pay for Reynolds employees had been raised to a level slightly more than 100 percent above the 1940 level.)[127] Of the sixteen officials and lawyers participating in the hearings, Harold I. Cammer, Donald Henderson, Armando Ramirez, and Robert Lathan represented Local 22. As soon as the hearings were over, Local 22 began to distribute leaflets supporting Mayor Marshall W. Kurfees's demand for low-cost housing projects.[128]

To add to the confusion, the cab drivers of Winston-Salem, organized by the UTSE-CIO, went on strike from 11 November until 4 December 1949.[129] In addition, organizing activities of the unions concerned with Reynolds employees were stepped up, especially those of UTSE-CIO. On 9 February 1950, the NLRB ruled that the voting units would embrace all production and maintenance employees, including plant clerical employees and metal-finishing technicians, but not seasonal employees and a few other small groups.[130] The election was set for 8 March. The results of this election, said to be the largest labor election ever held in the state if not in the South, were inconclusive: "No Union," 3,426 votes; Local 22, 3,323; TWIU-AFL, 1,514; and UTSE-CIO, 541. The local morning paper commented that the outcome showed "a remarkable come back" for Local 22.[131]

The runoff election was scheduled for 23 March 1950. Until that date, the surprised community and undoubtedly company officials feared the outcome. Donald Henderson, in a speech over radio station WAIR on 12 March, emphasized the issue that produced so much soul-searching: namely, that the combined votes of the three bona fide unions represented a definite majority. Citing the record of Local 22 in the Reynolds plants, he claimed that, even though the union had held no contract for the past two years, its presence had restricted the company in relation to wages and working conditions. A vote against the union, he declared, would be an invitation for the company "to put the heat" on every Reynolds worker. In the news item reporting his speech, it was stated that Henderson had been correct in saying that a majority had voted for unions.[132]

This situation produced one of the most dramatic moves in this entire labor struggle. The ignominious defeat of Local 22 in the Greensboro election of 27 September 1949 obviously had been regarded as the union's downfall. But the election in the Reynolds plants on 8 March 1950 destroyed any such illusions. A survey of conditions prior to November 1948, reported by Marie Belk in the *Journal and Sentinel* for 14 November, is illuminating. In the 1946 city election, she declared, the Reverend Kenneth R. Williams, a distinguished Negro minister and educator, had been supported by Local 22 and by every Negro organization in the community. As a result, Williams led the ticket and became alderman from the third ward—evidently the first Negro to hold such a position for many years. This vote, Miss Belk believed, had also elected John H. Folger to Congress over Thurmond Chatham, who was closely connected with the Winston-Salem ruling clique. Her conclusions also bear more directly on the R. J. Reynolds Tobacco Company: "For the past several months Local 22 personnel has spent almost all of its energies in Progressive party politics. Occasionally a leaflet would be issued attacking the Reynolds Company or the Winston Leaf Tobacco Company on some point— Reynolds fifty-six hour work week without overtime during the peak season (for seasonal workers), and Winston's failure to give a wage increase for two leaf seasons." Though Local 22 had campaigned hard for Wallace, she observed, Truman apparently obtained more Negro votes. During that campaign several Negro ministers who had usually supported Local 22 became leaders in the Negro Democratic Club, including Alderman Kenneth R. Williams and the Reverend Jason Hawkins. Hawkins, she noted, had been expelled by Local 22.

With this background in mind it becomes evident that the Reverend Kenneth R. Williams, later to serve as president of Winston-Salem Teachers College, was the hero of the runoff election on 23 March 1950. He had taken his stand at a meeting of the board of aldermen on the night of 17 March in a dramatic move well-described in the news report that appeared under a four-column headline: "A resolution condemning the union was unanimously adopted after Alderman Kenneth Williams, the only Negro on the board, had stated that though he knew Local 22 would seek to wreck him for his stand, he hoped the people in Winston-Salem would 'come to their senses and send the Communists away for good.'" The resolution stated that it was common knowledge that Local 22 was communistic and that people of undesirable character controlled it. Williams declared that his conscience was his only guide. He was praised by Mayor Kurfees and applauded by the board of aldermen.[133] In reply to the resolution, Donald Henderson told some four hundred sympathizers who packed the Shiloh Baptist Church on 19 March that anyone "who throws things at us is going to have them thrown back."[134]

So the battle continued until the day of the runoff. Under a headline covering five columns, the morning paper on 24 March carried the doubtful news that Local 22 had received 4,428 votes and "No Union," 4,383; 133 votes challenged. Stating that there was no majority, the item ended with a paragraph on the vigorous campaign waged by Local 22 on the eve of the election.[135] The outcome rested on the challenged ballots, which had to be investigated by the NLRB. When the final decision came, Local 22 lost by only 66 votes.[136] In an editorial entitled "Defeat and Opportunity," the *Winston-Salem Journal* for 16 August 1950 judged the results to be the defeat of an organization that "has been dominated by Communistic elements" uninterested in the objectives of labor. In summing up the struggle the paper assumed considerable credit for this thin victory:

> The F.T.A. won the right to represent Reynolds workers and signed a contract with the company in 1944. In May, 1947, an investigation launched by the *Journal and Sentinel*, based upon the disclosure of Ann Matthews, former Communist connected with Local 22, indicated that several leaders of the local were affiliated with the Communists.
>
> Following the passage of the Taft-Hartley Act which provided that in order to be certified by the National Labor Relations Board, the officers of a labor union must sign non-Communist affidavits, the F.T.A. lost its contract with the Reynolds Company in 1948 at least in part because its officers failed to sign the non-Communist affidavit. Later, the union leaders signed the affidavits.
>
> The advent of the F.T.A. on the industrial scene here was marked by much agitation which encouraged class conflict, internal dissension and public unrest, and this situation led to a number of disturbances foreign to a community tradition of peaceful and co-operative group and interracial relations extending over a long period of years. The union local did not confine its activities to the promotion of better working hours, higher wages and other benefits for working people, but engaged in propaganda activities designed to inspire community dissension and advance the aims of the Communist Party and its foreign masters.

The statement released by Charles B. Wade, Jr., personnel manager and spokesman for the Reynolds company, was far more modest: "The company is gratified with the outcome of the election. . . . It feels that settlement of the issue is of benefit to the community, to the company's employees and to the company." To emphasize its gratitude for the outcome, Reynolds only twenty-six days later announced a wage increase affecting "more than 14,386 of its employees in Winston-Salem" at a total estimated cost of more than $2 million, effective immediately. In addition, the company indicated that effective as of 1 January 1951, all employees with one year's service would receive a paid vacation of two weeks; those with as much as twenty years' service would receive three weeks.[137]

Robert Lathan gave the official reaction of Local 22:[138]

> No matter what happens . . . we will yet remain a union in the Reynolds plants. That union is Local 22. I am sure that our membership will build a bigger and better union.
>
> The conditions inside those shops—speed-ups, wages, unemployment compensation, pensions, seniority, discriminatory practices against women, especially Negro women—require a union such as Local 22. Every union member in Reynolds can well remember the history of Local 22. I am sure they will remain loyal.

Despite these strong words the active career of Local 22 in Winston-Salem was virtually over. Shortly afterward the Reynolds company announced another increase in wages. After its expulsion from the CIO on 1 March 1950, the FTAAWA supported a move to merge with two other left-wing unions into the Distributive, Office, and Processing Workers of America, of which Donald Henderson became president.[139] James Durken assumed leadership of Local 22, then a branch of Henderson's union, and with his aides made a considerable drive to organize Reynolds employees. Other, brief attempts at such organization were of little consequence because of increases in wages, improvements in working conditions, and various employee benefits. In fact, the TWIU-AFL carried on a vigorous two-year campaign beginning in July 1953. Union members from organized plants of the company's competitors in Durham, Reidsville, Richmond, and Louisville visited Winston-Salem in relays during the campaign. These efforts culminated in an election held on 7 April 1955 in which 5,027 votes from a total of 8,069 went against the unions.[140]

The Aftermath

Oddly enough, this decade of labor strife proved beneficial to the R. J. Reynolds Tobacco Company. As discussed in Chapter 13, the company began to develop a personnel department designed to meet employee problems of the day. In other ways, too, the company began to examine itself. Beginning in August 1949, the *Management Information Bulletin* carried a series of eight articles on the importance of public relations for all segments of management. Readers were urged to exercise greater tact—not to make derogatory remarks about cigarettes made by other companies.

Seventy-five percent of the issue for 2 September 1949 dwelt on the need for Reynolds employees to be more perceptive in dealing with people. Never preface the offer of a cigarette to anyone with the statement that he should try "a *good* cigarette," wrote the editor on 6 October. The seventh article in the series encouraged managers to ask for criticism, and the last one appeared under the title of "Ambassadors of Good Will."[141] At a meeting of the Safety Council early in January 1951, Spencer B. Hanes, Jr., carefully explained that a Negro employee had been made an executive foreman.[142] Slightly more than a year later Charles B. Wade, Jr., announced to the same group that, although labor turnover in the plants had increased by a small margin in 1950, he believed that a better feeling existed among the workers.[143]

The clearest indication of a new approach, however, appeared in a printed summary of a talk made to supervisory personnel, perhaps just before the election of 1955. "During the coming days," ran the first sentence, "you are going to have a number of your employees asking you questions." When talking with their people, the supervisors were urged to be calm, collected, friendly, and by all means wise. Emphasis on the importance of *not* threatening employees pervaded the summary, which gave many examples of relatively mild threats to be avoided. Never ask a man whether he belongs to a union, admonished the writer, possibly Charles B. Wade, Jr. "It is none of our business, under the law." But should his opinion be requested, the supervisor was urged to give it privately and quietly. These very admonitions suggest the nature of previous relations between employees and foremen. Among the topics that might be safely discussed, the writer listed the great demand for Reynolds products, annual wage increases in the past seven years, adequate work for a five-day week, and the numerous benefit plans that had been established by the company.[144]

By 1962, the ten-year-old plan for desegregating white and Negro workers had been activated in the company's new Whitaker Park plant, where a *New York Times* reporter interviewed Mrs. Evelyn M. Hairston, a Negro chief inspector. Mrs. Hairston, who supervised a crew of four or five Negroes and about a dozen whites, admitted that she had been skeptical about being transferred to Whitaker Park. In October 1962, she was one of five Negro inspectors in that plant. The reporter wrote: "The Reynolds complex represents one of the most extensive programs of industrial desegregation by a home-grown Southern industry." Moreover, he stated, Reynolds had had "a program to upgrade Negroes for about a decade." Actually at this time, it had been eleven years since Spencer B. Hanes, Jr., privately announced that a Negro man had been appointed an executive foreman. After Whitaker Park was opened in April 1961, integration "spread through the rest of Reynolds' 115 acre industrial set up" in Winston-Salem. The reporter noted that, under state law, the rest rooms were still kept separate but Negroes and whites shared the same cafeterias.[145] Because this program of desegregation was emphasized as early as 1951, it cannot be attributed strictly to the requirement of government contracts.

Houston Adams, a Negro employee in Number 65, believed it was the union that made Christians out of the "Reynolds' bosses"[146]—an interpretation that furnishes the most likely explanation. It is also of interest that, when the National Association for the Advancement of Colored People in 1962 planned a program for placing Negroes in skilled jobs in the tobacco industry of the South, two leading companies were mentioned as targets, although nothing was said about the R. J. Reynolds Tobacco Company.[147]

Apparently the change in labor-management relations represented a genuine shift in policy made possible by the common sense of John C. Whitaker, who suddenly forgot his anger and began to advocate the very reforms that Local 22 had demanded. No doubt, too, Whitaker, along with others, came to realize that, though the methods of the union may have been questionable, its aims were desirable. It is not improbable that Local 22 taught the people of Winston-Salem that the Negroes of the town deserved more humane treatment. As a result, the civic leaders of both races began working together so that disturbances characteristic of some areas in the South did not develop in the Twin City.

CHAPTER 12

Litigation and Failure with a New Product

Labor disturbances and wartime restrictions on manpower and materials were not the only concerns of Reynolds management in the 1940s. During the same period the company, along with the other major tobacco manufacturers, was sued by the U.S. government on charges of violating the nation's antitrust laws and tried in Kentucky. This was a serious matter for a corporation that had never experienced any noticeable public disfavor as had the old American Tobacco Company. Moreover, the company and some of its officers were convicted, and the feeling that this judgment was unmerited did nothing to assuage the embarrassment of many of the directors. Almost simultaneously with this litigation, a derivative suit was filed against the company in New Jersey by a very small segment of its stockholders who had been influenced by a firm of unscrupulous lawyers. Though Reynolds won this case, it was also embarrassing and aggravating. Both trials meant the employment of expert legal counsel, many days spent in preparing the cases and in giving testimony, and distraction from normal business operations. The Reynolds company crowned its misfortunes by bringing out the Cavalier cigarette, which proved to be a complete failure. In doing so it lost some $30 million, almost the exact sum involved in the stockholders' suit. In the end, however, the troubled decade seemed to gird the company for new and successful ventures in the 1950s.

The Kentucky Trial

The second antitrust suit against the tobacco industry, known informally as the Kentucky Trial, got underway at Lexington in the eastern district of the state on 2 June 1941—almost thirty years after similar litigation broke the power of the old American Tobacco Company. Unlike the suit in 1911, which was brought during a period of extreme antitrust legislation, the Kentucky Trial did not attract the attention of a citizenry preoccupied with the country's probable entry into another world war. But in the U.S. tobacco industry it created nothing less than a sensation. The trial lasted twenty weeks and cost an estimated $1 million. The jury listened to thousands of words of testimony, now preserved in fourteen large volumes of transcripts and exhibits with nine additional volumes for other aspects of the case. The Reynolds company secured a court ruling that photostatic copies of its records would suffice at the trial, purchased a photostating machine, and for approximately one month operated the machine for twenty-four hours a day in three shifts. With three technicians and clerical workers on each shift, the records were copied and stacked in hogsheads for removal to Lexington.[1]

The suit was filed against eight corporations and thirty-three individuals. Included were the R. J. Reynolds Tobacco Company and six of its top officers: William N. Reynolds (chairman of the board and of the executive committee); S. Clay Williams (president); and Edward A. Darr, John C. Whitaker, Robert E. Lasater, and James A. Glenn (vice-presidents). All were highly respected, church-going models of civic virtue in Winston-Salem. In the trial of 1911 the Reynolds company had scarcely lifted a hand in defense of the old American Tobacco Company, but no such relaxed attitude could prevail in 1941. Specifically, the tobacco firms and their executives were tried and many convicted on four charges: (1) combining and conspiring in restraint of trade, (2) monopolizing, (3) attempting to monopolize, and (4) combining and conspiring to monopolize trade and commerce both in leaf tobacco and in tobacco products in violation of the Sherman Antitrust Act as amended in 1937.[2] The Department of Justice thus undertook to demonstrate that existing conditions in the tobacco industry had resulted from collusion among the big firms. Upon appeal, the Sixth Circuit Court sustained the verdict on 8 December 1944.[3]

On 10 June 1946, the Supreme Court refused to review the decision. Justice Harold H. Burton, who delivered the opinion, declared it to be an application of the law to the facts "as they were found by the jury and which the Circuit Court of Appeals held should not be set aside." Justice Felix Frankfurter agreed with the decision but wondered whether the Court should consider alleged errors in regard to jury selection. In one respect, Reynolds officials should have been amply compensated for all their grief and trouble even though the trial had momentarily damaged the company's image. Justice Burton, in his opinion, honored the Camel as no other tobacco product had ever been honored: "The fact is that Reynolds, in 1913, actually broke into the cigarette field with its Camel cigarettes, and as a vigorous competitor of American, Liggett and P. Lorillard Company revolutionized the cigarette industry."[4] Never before had outsiders of this most secretive of industries been privileged to hear so much inside information. It was reminiscent of the days when the curious read the *Report of the Commissioner of Corporations on the Tobacco Industry* in 1909 and 1911. The R. J. Reynolds Tobacco Company, had its officials not been so agitated, might also have profited from George Washington Hill's peroration on the greatness of the Camel cigarette as he testified to show that no love had been lost between the makers of Lucky Strikes and Camels. It would, indeed, be difficult to conceive of enough cooperation between the Reynolds company and Hill's company to make for concerted conspiracy. Because appeals of the verdict proved fruitless, the case was actually settled in the long proceedings in Kentucky.

This spectacular trial cannot be represented simply as a clash between agriculture and industry. In the broader sense, the case developed from two decades of exceedingly low prices received by growers of leaf tobacco, both flue-cured and Burley. Involved also was the dismal failure of the Tri-State Tobacco Growers' Cooperative Association and the accompanying success of speculative leaf dealers and owners of auction sales houses in destroying the cooperative movement in the flue-cured area.[5] As noted below, evidence was introduced at the trial that the American Tobacco Company was involved in the destruction of the same movement in the Burley area. Many other factors contributed to the deep resentment that prompted the trial, including the rise of the ten-cent cigarette, the depression, and possibly the determination of the government to assault price leadership, price uniformity, and oligopolistic practices in general.[6] For twenty-one years tobacco growers had been in a constant depression. In direct contrast to their position was that of the tobacco companies waxing rich, especially during the 1920s. Indeed, it was no secret that the R. J. Reynolds Tobacco Company had flourished in those years largely by virtue of the lower cost of leaf. In 1931—the lowest point of the depression—Reynolds and American alone poured almost $40 million into advertising; it has been estimated that the tobacco industry as a whole spent $75 million. In the same year the Reynolds company launched its spectacular campaign to exploit the cellophane-wrapped Camels, and no doubt thereby drew special attention to the contrasting economic plight of the farmers.

The R. J. Reynolds Tobacco Company was not the only firm that had profited; nor had its operations produced the economic impasse of that period. Actually Reynolds, along with the Liggett and Myers Tobacco Company, supported the growers of both flue-cured and Burley leaf in an attempt to develop cooperative methods of marketing.[7] The prosecution in the Kentucky Trial specifically noted the opposition of Charles E.

Lipscomb, Jr., to the farmers' efforts to sell leaf cooperatively when he was in charge of the western division of the Burley area for the American Tobacco Company during the 1920s. Needless to say, Lipscomb's lawyer made a valiant bid to eliminate this point but in vain,[8] thus recognizing the importance of its exclusion. Many skeptics claimed that the major tobacco companies operated in combination when buying leaf and selling manufactured goods. Price changes for the tobacco products of these companies often came at identical times and at identical figures. Many believed that the production of ten-cent, or economy brands of cigarettes, induced by the cheapness of leaf tobacco and the high price of regular cigarettes, was being sabotaged by the so-called "Big Three" (Reynolds, American, Liggett and Myers). When Hugh S. Johnson appeared before the Senate in 1935, he declared that the total amount paid to producers in the nine principal tobacco states did not equal the net profits of the "Big Four" (Reynolds, American, Liggett and Myers, P. Lorillard) cigarette manufacturers in 1932. Strange words came into the vocabularies of the speakers and writers of the day—words which by their very unfamiliarity carried more sinister connotations than did the word "monopoly"—such as "oligopoly," "duopoly," and "triopoly."[9] Were the "Big Four" combining in some devious way to plunge the tobacco farmers into serfdom and the consumers into deeper poverty? Should the government intervene and get at the root of the trouble? How could the villain be found?

In answer to congressional resolutions, the Federal Trade Commission (FTC) made several attempts to solve the mystery. In 1920 it reported the cause of distress among tobacco farmers to be the worldwide price collapse of that year. Again in 1922, it announced a continuation of the 1920 price depression but with no conclusive evidence "of buyer collusion." On a smaller scale such investigations continued. In 1925, however, in an investigation of the Tri-State Tobacco Growers' Cooperative Association, the FTC issued a biased report that not only cleared leaf dealers and all tobacco companies but also fixed responsibility for the association's decline on dishonest practices of some of the cooperative plant managers—a matter that had been corrected by the organization before the report appeared. Finally, in 1937, with its complexion greatly changed and its position made firmer by judicial ruling, the FTC issued a massive report on the prices of agricultural products, all of which were as proportionately low as those of tobacco. Its principal conclusions in regard to the prices of leaf tobacco were fourfold: (1) that cigarette prices were generally identical, (2) that the ten-cent brands should be aided by means of a lower excise tax, (3) that the snuff companies had been acting cooperatively, and (4) that the new grading system developed by the Department of Agriculture for the farmers' leaf tobacco deserved a trial. Based on this report, the Department of Justice, led by Assistant Attorney General Thurman W. Arnold, developed and filed on 24 July 1940 an Information accusing the various defendants at the Kentucky Trial of violating the Sherman Antitrust Act.[10]

Though the trial lasted twenty weeks, scarcely any of it was dull. Probably not since Patrick Henry argued in the Parson's Cause had southern tobacco growers been provided with such high drama. No lenience came from Judge Hiram Church Ford who conducted the trial. In the courtroom on the second floor of the new post office building hats of millionaires came off along with those of tobacco growers. Before the jury made its report Judge Ford warned sternly against any demonstration and instructed the marshal to arrest anyone who made a disturbance.[11] In sharp contrast to the defendants' lawyers was the chief government prosecutor, Edward H. Miller, a special assistant to the attorney general and a thirty-four-year-old graduate of the Harvard Law School. Despite his comparative youth, Miller had had considerable experience since his graduation in 1931. He had engaged in private practice in St. Louis and served for five years as representative of the Missouri state attorney general in St. Louis. He joined the antitrust division of the Department of Justice in 1939 and soon headed up the investigation of the tobacco industry.[12]

Judge Ford found the matter of jury selection problematic. All citizens engaged in the production of tobacco were excused. As finally constituted, the jury, composed of the usual number plus two alternates, included four who stated that members of their families were tobacco growers; another declared that he owned a farm on which tobacco was produced.[13] Among the fourteen jurors there were seven merchants, an oil distributor, an operator of a tourist camp, a high school principal, three insurance salesmen, and a clerk in a bus company. Both alternates became members of the regular jury in the place of two who were excused because of illness. In fact, the personnel involved in the case had more than its share of adversity. Lennox P. McLendon, one of the Reynolds company's leading attorneys, became ill before the hearings could be held on motions for a new trial. Two defendants died before the trial was over: William Washington Flowers (5 November 1874–1 May 1941), board chairman of Liggett and Myers, and Charles Fogg Neiley (1874–27 October 1941), a vice-president of the American Tobacco Company.[14] Because it was agreed at the outset that the three major corporate defendants would collaborate as much as possible in presenting their defense,[15] the jury was spared much repetitious testimony. It is noteworthy that during the trial Reynolds divulged information with far greater freedom that did the other defendants, though possibly at that time its records were more complete.

Among the Reynolds officials who appeared as witnesses and defendants, S. Clay Williams perhaps made the strongest, though not the best impression. His testimony on 2, 3, 6, 7, and 8 September was the longest given by any defendant. In printed form it fills 343 pages. In the government's opening argument to the jury, Edmund J. Ford, an assistant prosecutor, remarked not without irony: "Now, Mr. Williams has testified here at length. He was one of the last witnesses. I don't think it will be necessary for me to run through his testimony to show his interest in this company." In the closing argument for the government, Edward Miller spoke "of Mr. Williams for four days on this witness stand, with plausible explanations; an answer for everything that was asked of him." Perhaps with unnecessary sarcasm, Miller concluded: [16]

> I think Mr. Williams was on the stand longer than any defendant in this case. I think he had more answers than anybody in this case. I think he covered more ground than anybody in this case, and, gentlemen, I am willing to put it up to you this way: If you believe all the answers that Mr. Williams gave you; if you believe in their sincerity and frankness and believe that there isn't any understanding on prices, to control the price those farmers get for their leaf tobacco or to control and keep the same prices on the products of these companies; if you don't believe any such understanding exists, and you think all of Mr. Williams' explanations were frank and fair and honest and true, I would be glad to see you acquit these defendants.

Judge Ford, likewise, handled Williams roughly as he gave his very lengthy testimony, caused no doubt by his tendency to digress. When Williams was asked about the efforts of the Reynolds company to secure the voting or "A" stock left in the hands of stockholders of the American Tobacco Company by the 1911 decree, he became embroiled in giving his opinion of the objection of Louis D. Brandeis to that decree. Judge Ford noted sharply that as subject matter it was doubtless interesting to Williams but that it had no earthly bearing on the question at hand. Miller had stated that Williams was a lawyer, thereby intimating that he should know how to give testimony. Thereupon former Governor J. C. B. Ehringhaus, a lawyer for Reynolds, declared that he did not propose to be lectured by Miller. [17] With barbs such as these, the atmosphere frequently became somewhat heated.

William N. Reynolds, seventy-eight years old and attended in Lexington by his nurse, testified very briefly on 9 September. Though treated kindly by the court, he proved to be a poor witness, unable for a time to state clearly whether the company had first been chartered by the state of North Carolina in 1888 or 1908. [18] On the other hand, James A. Gray made a superb witness on 30 September. His opening words—"I live in the same house I was born in in Winston-Salem"—gave rise to a feeling of stability, which apparently was maintained throughout his testimony. Gray's analysis from his own personal knowledge of eleven changes in wholesale prices of Camels from 1920 to 1941 presumably astonished his own attorney. The only part of his testimony to raise any objection from the court was his reference to the A.A.A. processing tax, which he attempted to explain rather than to cite merely as a factor in the increase in cigarette prices. The judge, who did not object to Gray's citation of the tax measure, did object strenuously "to his dissertation on what the processing tax was, and its purpose, and its nature, and its ultimate disposition." Blame for this digression fell squarely on Gray's lawyer, Lennox P. McLendon, who deliberately stopped the testimony on price changes by asking Gray to explain the meaning of the law, how it worked, and how it applied to the R. J. Reynolds Tobacco Company. When McLendon insisted, Judge Ford answered that Gray understood what he meant, thus implying that McLendon might not. Gray then was questioned extensively on drop shipments to dealers not on the company's list of direct customers. In his answer he took special pains to show that a retail dealer received a 12 percent discount by means of the jobber's discount of 9 percent plus free goods or goods in a drop shipment worth approximately 3 percent. A direct customer likewise obtained a discount of 12 percent—that is, a combination of 10 and 2 percent. On cross-examination Miller questioned Gray sharply in regard to jobbers who wished retail prices to be higher than Reynolds did.[19]

Among the remaining defendants and witnesses, Edward A. Darr, head of the Reynolds sales department, received a long and careful examination. He explained the nature of his work and the sales organization—that it had 18 departments and 134 divisions nationwide and employed 1,166 salesmen. He introduced few new points, although he noted clearly the special attractions of drop shipments for retailers—that they paid exactly the same price on drop shipments as on goods purchased directly from the jobber, but that jobbers frequently offered a better discount rate on drop shipments to the retailer. This was because of the saving in freight when the goods were shipped directly to the retailer from the factory instead of to the jobber's warehouse. He also testified extensively on price fixing.[20] Under cross-examination Darr was cooperative, poised, and surprisingly self-controlled for one of his brusque nature. John C. Whitaker, who was not convicted in the trial, received a brief direct examination on the company's personnel work.[21] James W. Glenn, in charge of leaf purchasing, was questioned at length on points involving the marketing of leaf tobacco. Practically all of the questions covered issues that had long been connected with the failure of the farmers' cooperative associations for the sale of leaf—the grading of leaf tobacco before its storage, whether "top prices" were set before the company purchased the farmers' leaf, whether Glenn had ever belonged to the Tobacco Association of the United States (an organization of leaf dealers and owners of auction sales houses who controlled the rules governing auction sales), the efficiency of auction sales, and whether Reynolds kept its leaf buyers on the markets until the close of the marketing season.[22]

Not all of the Reynolds testimony came from high-ranking officials. A good deal of information that seemed to incriminate the company in price fixing for Camels was provided by Charles C. Roe (1896–27 October 1951), its department manager in Denver, Colorado since 5 January 1937.[23] Roe's testimony, which covered the years from 1937 to 1939, revolved around economy brands of cigarettes (generally sold for 10 cents per package), his desire to reduce the retail price of Camels from 14 cents per package (or two packages for 27 cents) to the former price of 13 cents per package (or two packages for 25 cents), and a new Colorado Unfair Practice Act (enacted in May 1937) that forbade the retail sale of articles below cost including overhead charges. Among the economy brands, then at their peak in volume of sales, were Wings and Avalon made by the Brown-Williamson division of the British-American Tobacco Company, Beechnut and Sensation by P. Lorillard, Dominos and White Rolls by Larus and Brother, Marvels by Stephano Brothers, Twenty Grand by Axton-Fisher, and Paul Jones by Philip Morris. Just as these economy brands began to multiply in 1931 during the worst of the depression, Reynolds made the great error of raising its prices. All major brands followed suit and immediately lost sales, but manufacturers of ten-cent brands surged forward, tempted no doubt by the wide range between low leaf prices and the selling prices of regular cigarettes. Though the economy brands continued to pose a threat until 1945, their sales reached a peak in 1939. Meanwhile, in 1935 the Camel surpassed its 1930 sales by four billion cigarettes and maintained its growth through the war period.[24]

This situation, coupled with the peculiarities of the new Colorado statute, was destined to produce trouble. The Unfair Practice Act allowed exceptions to meet lower prices legally set by a competitor, contained no method for distributing overhead expenses, and had no administrative machinery for its enforcement. Three self-appointed groups of retail dealers, collectively known as the Colorado Retail Dealers Association, moved into the vacuum created by the law and began its enforcement by threats of criminal prosecution. Led by Cliff Ross of Reynolds's direct retail outlet of the John D. Ross Cigar Store in Denver, these dealers then drew up a price list to their own liking with Camels retailing at the objectionable and inconvenient price of 14 cents per package (or two packages for 27 cents).

According to Roe's testimony, as the situation in Denver became more intolerable, Ross was removed from the company's direct list of customers. This rather drastic move did not deprive Ross of the opportunity to sell Reynolds goods but it did cause him to lose special and valuable discounts always accorded customers on the direct list. Roe then maneuvered to have another large retail dealer placed on Reynolds's direct list. Liggett and Myers did the same for this retail dealer but did not remove Ross from its direct list. So the bickering simmered on while one or two other direct customers were added; one of them threatened to discriminate against goods of the American Tobacco Company unless also put on its direct list of customers. About 1 January 1938, the discriminatory price structure in Denver collapsed. During the months of confusion that followed, Reynolds representatives held conversations with representatives of other companies—an unwise move and a serious offense though the circumstances may have seemed to warrant it. Of course, the company held that Ross had been the leader of price discrimination and that evidence from Denver alone did not establish a nationwide price conspiracy as charged in the Information. Reynolds submitted four-year-old correspondence showing that large retailers in Denver supported a price to the customer of 11 cents per package of Wings provided the standard brands sold for 14 cents each (or two for 27 cents). More incriminating for the manufacturers of economy cigarettes was the offer of one of them to bear all the expenses of printing a new retail price list for Denver if Wings were left at 10 cents and regular cigarettes at 14 cents per package (or two for 27 cents). Hovering over this turbulent situation in Colorado was the threat of a sales tax.[25]

Any evaluation of the charges against the R. J. Reynolds Tobacco Company for price fixing on a nationwide basis must rest on its actions in the Denver area from 1937 to 1939. According to one expert on the industry, there is no clear-cut reason for believing that Reynolds was doing anything more than engaging in "a sharp competitive struggle."[26] Judging from the evidence presented, the manufacturers of ten-cent brands worked with great vigor and doubtful tactics to keep a three-cent differential between their prices and those of regular brands. Perhaps it might be said that Roe worked in the same manner to further the interests of Camels. Furthermore, the prosecuting attorney had access to Roe's correspondence but not to that of the Colorado retailers and those representing the manufacturers of ten-cent cigarettes. In addition, at Miller's request, Judge Ford refused to admit evidence that one of the leaders in the Colorado Retail Dealers Association in the Denver division had been indicted, convicted, and fined by the federal government under the Sherman Antitrust Act for price fixing in Denver.[27]

Some years later rumors persisted among the older employees in the Reynolds office building that Edward A. Darr discharged Roe because of the evidence he gave at the trial. This would have been unreasonable indeed, as his testimony was based largely on correspondence produced in court. Other records do not bear out such suspicions. Roe remained department manager in Denver until 25 February 1944 when he became a division manager. He served in that capacity until his retirement on 1 February 1948. Moreover, Roe's successor in Denver, Norman H. Lewis, spent less than four years in that position whereas Roe had held it for more than seven years.[28] Such promotions and shifts in job were not unusual in the Reynolds sales department where the tasks demanded unremitting attention to sales prices, public relations, innumerable reports, and the like.

Other Reynolds officials and employees testified briefly in the Kentucky Trial. Among them were Charles C. Ausband, Henry S. Stokes, William J. Conrad, Jr., P. Frank Hanes, and Stuart M. Scott, the comptroller. As witnesses, however, the company had no such flamboyant figure as American's beetle-browed George Washington Hill, dressed in his customary black suit, white shirt, and bow tie. Undismayed and arrogant as usual, he gave his testimony on 2 and 3 September. For the spectators it was the highlight of the trial, with Hill emphasizing the value of his *Selling Principle of Demonstration* and paying greater deference to the influence of the Camel cigarette than to his own Lucky Strike.[29] His demeanor was in marked contrast to that of James A. Gray, John C. Whitaker, James W. Glenn, and William N. Reynolds whose photographs in the Louisville *Courier-Journal* reflected consternation at the decision of the jury.[30]

Reportedly, neither S. Clay Williams nor James A. Gray ever recovered from the humiliation of being tried, convicted, and fined by a federal court for violating a law of the United States. In any case, all of the Reynolds defendants considered themselves innocent of the charges. Williams, Gray, Edward Darr, and James Glenn were fined $15,000 each, or $5,000 for each of the counts upon which they were convicted. The company was also fined.

Some connected with the company believed that the defendants were convicted for merely having obtained the power to use monopolistic practices, and that such power had not been and would never have been used. On the other hand, it might well be argued that a substantial part of the bill of particulars filed on 2 December 1940 involved the questionable practices of leaf dealers and operators of auction sales houses, who, through the local tobacco boards of trade and the Tobacco Association of the United States, formulated the rules of the auction sales system. Historically, tobacco manufacturers have never favored the speculative practices of leaf dealers and operators of auction sales houses.

An unbiased study of the Kentucky Trial by a student of antitrust problems offers perhaps the best evaluation of the trial. Simon N. Whitney states that the simple verdict of guilt did not afford a basis for reconstructing behavior and that the defendants came home from Lexington without knowing exactly what changes had to be made in order to comply with the verdict. He also questions the wisdom of trying so complex an economic case before a jury—especially one that included six men (the five jurors and one alternate) who had been reared on tobacco farms. If the suit was aimed at breaking new ground in antitrust theory, he continues, it was unfair to brand as criminals men who had followed practices never before declared unlawful. Furthermore, the "bad blood" between executives of companies such as Reynolds and American made collusion impossible. In the past they and their agents had spied on one another freely and maintained a general attitude of mutual suspicion. Because all the defendants except those declared not guilty eventually paid fines, the British-American Tobacco Company was penalized for a strange offense "which included trying to put its subsidiary and co-defendant [Brown and Williamson] . . . out of business" for making and selling an economy brand of cigarettes (Wings). Economy brands had been produced by two other defendants: Philip Morris and P. Lorillard. Moreover, Whitney declares that Philip Morris, which had pushed its way into the industry when new firms were supposedly being frozen out by the "Big Four," was fined for its success in doing what the government presumably wished to be done. Incidentally, Judge Thomas F. McAllister of the Sixth Circuit Court of Appeals stated that American, Liggett and Myers, and Reynolds had retained positions as the three largest tobacco companies in the country since 1911[31]—a statement badly in error but perhaps of no great consequence in the case being appealed.

In a sweeping conclusion Whitney sums up the case by declaring that the prosecution in 1941 interpreted normal business actions as a conspiracy, and, because normal business actions are not easily changed, the trial had no permanent results except to scare the companies into lowering their prices. After 1941 the market itself lessened the importance of the three brands of cigarettes—Camels, Lucky Strikes, and Chesterfields—which in that year seemed so dominant. Incidentally, Whitney notes that the dissolution of the old American Tobacco Company in 1911 was "an effective application of anti-trust law which set the scene for a product revolution"—a revolution brought about, of course, by R. J. Reynolds with his Camel cigarette. It was from the Reynolds company, writes Whitney, "which did not even make cigarettes before 1912, that the idea came which swept the cigarette business through a revolution."[32]

What steps did the R. J. Reynolds Tobacco Company take to comply with the spirit of the decision in the Kentucky Trial? Reynolds and the other main tobacco manufacturers abandoned their agreements for the establishment of new markets. Thus additional auction markets began operating, although inefficiently because the warehouse facilities and export buyers were scattered. One company supposedly did not give its buyers instructions for the buying season, a move that produced erratic price movements until the buyers found ways to adjust their bids to prevailing prices. Reynolds representatives ceased attending meetings sponsored by the United States Department of Agriculture when competitors intended to be present. Drop shipments of cigarettes to retailers were eliminated and resale prices were never mentioned in connection with dealers. Reynolds no longer served as the only price leader of the tobacco industry as American began initiating some of the changes. Whether to discourage competition or to ward off government interference, prices were kept relatively low after the Kentucky Trial and the expiration of the Office of Price Administration (OPA) ceiling in 1946. Consequently profits were lower and by no means out of line with the general economic trends in 1939. In fact, this price moderation of the big cigarette companies perhaps—in the words of Simon N. Whitney—"contributed to a renewed expansion of their brands in the market." The Kentucky Trial also served as a warning against actions that might attract the antitrust division of the Department of Justice, and no doubt H. Henry Ramm kept a closer eye on such possibilities than did S. Clay Williams.

Clearly, the testimony offered during the Kentucky Trial has been of great value to economists and historians interested in the tobacco industry. That, however, was not the aim of Edward H. Miller whose work came in the wake of the disjointed times of the Great Depression.

The New Jersey Trial and Bylaw XII

On 14 November 1940, three months and twenty days after the Department of Justice filed its Information accusing the R. J. Reynolds Tobacco Company and other tobacco manufacturers of violating the Sherman Antitrust Act, another time-consuming suit was filed against the company, its directors, and its officers in the Chancery of New Jersey. In view of its possible outcome, the case of *Bookman et al. v. the R. J. Reynolds Tobacco Company et al.* (hereafter cited as the New Jersey Trial) was far more important than the antitrust suit—despite the company's conviction in Kentucky and its victory in New Jersey.

The trial was conducted over a six-year period and demanded the strict attention of Reynolds officials, especially S. Clay Williams, James A. Gray, and William N. Reynolds. It also required the retention of experienced legal talent, the diligent examination of records back to 1912, the employment of Standard and Poor's Corporation for the preparation of extensive tables and charts, numerous trips to New Jersey by various members of the office force lugging bulky records, and long searches for cancelled checks and similar items. At the time of its conclusion on 31 July 1946, the trial was believed "to be one of the longest in the history of the Chancery Court" of New Jersey, having demanded fifty days for the hearing of testimony alone.[33] The case is important for the light it shed on past difficulties of the company in maintaining the steadiness of its stock. It centered attention on the company's well-known profit-sharing common or "A" stock, and it marked an end of dependence on the ideas of R. J. Reynolds.

The suit was brought in the name of four stockholders who represented three one-thousandths of one percent of the outstanding stock in 1940 and did not indicate dissatisfaction among the remaining stockholders. Nevertheless, it involved the good name of the company and a sum of approximately $30 million. According to Reynolds's counsel, the case might conceivably have resulted "in a fantastic recovery of $100,000,000 (an amount equal to the entire outstanding capital stock of the company)."[34] More important, it was a direct attack on the officers of the company for their administration of Bylaw XII (Bylaw XIII until 1915), adopted by the stockholders on 23 August 1912 without one dissenting vote. This bylaw is generally considered to have served as the incentive for officers and employees to devote their unremitting attention to the business of the company and thereby build it into a strong organization.[35] In many ways the evidence introduced in the case furnished a recapitulation of Reynolds operations from 1912 to 1942.

Because the suit was brought by owners of only 283 shares out of a total of 9,800,000 outstanding shares, the circumstances surrounding the move are of unusual interest. The plaintiffs were Dr. Arthur Bookman, Judith W. Bookman, Ludwig Lavy, and Mary B. Healey, the last two being intervener complainants—all from the state of New York. At the outset Camillo Weiss was also a party to the suit, having—with Ludwig Lavy—filed his bill of complaint on 15 April 1941. When he saw an account of the suit in the press, however, Weiss "advised the court that he had never authorized the institution of suit against the R. J. Reynolds Tobacco Company or the individual defendants." With that action the court permitted his counsel to withdraw his name as an intervener.[36]

Another intervener, Mary B. Healey, had filed suit in the United States District Court for the Western District of North Carolina on virtually the same charges involved in the Bookman suit. There her case had been dismissed on the ground that some of the causes of action concerned the internal affairs of a New Jersey corporation and that the Bookman suit was then pending and awaiting trial. Thereupon Mrs. Healey appealed from the decision of the court in North Carolina to intervene in the Bookman suit. According to her sworn testimony given on 4 May 1943, Mrs. Healey had become acquainted with one of her lawyers in 1934, although in 1941, when he spoke to her about the R. J. Reynolds Tobacco Company, she had no factual knowledge of the matters set up in the complaint which she later filed. The lawyer who approached her first advised that she obtain additional legal aid and made the selection for her. In all she employed two legal firms in New York, one in North Carolina, one in New Jersey, and one former supreme court justice from Kentucky. They were, she testified, all working to protect her thirty-eight shares. When asked if she had paid them any fees, she replied that she had not; in response to further questioning she stated that compensation for her lawyers rested "in the lap of the gods." At that point one of her lawyers stated that her counsel's fee was "contingent upon success." In addition, the company's counsel drew from Mrs. Healey the admission that one of her lawyers had made more than one trip to North Carolina and that another had come from Kentucky to North Carolina to support her interests in the suit, although she had paid neither of them any money.[37] At the same time Arthur Bookman testified that prior to his discussion of the case with his lawyer, he had had no knowledge of the matters complained of in the suit.[38] Likewise Ludwig Lavy testified that he had not agreed to pay any expenses of the litigation.[39]

Testimony of accountants for the complainants also indicated that the suit originated with lawyers rather than with dissatisfied stockholders. The accountants were Bernard J. Reis and Company and Gray, Scheiber and Company. Bernard J. Reis testified that he and ten or fifteen assistants began to work on the case in the summer of 1940 and that together they had spent three thousand man-days examining the records of the R. J. Reynolds Tobacco Company. According to Reis's testimony he became involved with the suit at the request of Karelson, Karelson, and Rubin, the New York legal firm acting for the plaintiffs. The latter had asked Reis if his accounting firm "would undertake the job on the basis that if there were a recovery, that I (Reis) might make an application to the Court for fair compensation for my services." Should there be no recovery, Reis said, he would receive nothing. Furthermore, he acknowledged that he had received travel expenses from Karelson, Karelson, and Rubin. Gray, Scheiber and Company, in agreement with Bernard J. Reis and Company, was "to get a portion of (the) fee" if they won the case. Reis also admitted that his accounting firm had been retained before by Karelson, Karelson, and Rubin and that it had participated in many stockholders' suits similar to the Bookman case. In fact, he mentioned five such suits in which he and his firm had participated since 1936.[40]

Counsel for the Reynolds company fully recognized the speculative nature of the Bookman suit, declaring that in a very real sense it was "an effort to destroy the company rather than to benefit it." In their brief for the defendants, the attorneys described the prevalence of such suits:

> Speculative suits of this character, brought not for the benefit of the corporation, have become a widespread abuse which, happily, in the past have not been as prevalent in New Jersey as in the neighboring state of New York. The abuses involved in suits of this character caused the Chamber of Commerce of New York to appoint a com-

mittee to study the subject. As a result of the comprehensive and careful work of this committee two bills were drafted, presented to, and enacted by the Legislature, and approved by the Governor, which were designed to stop just such suits as this.

Furthermore, the brief held that no greater harm could be done the company and its sixty thousand stockholders than to support "the claims which these attorneys and accountants have made for their own benefit, in reckless disregard of the interests of the corporation and all of its stockholders."[41] Naturally, however, the Reynolds counselors would argue the case for their retainers, but their argument was based on the direct testimony of the plaintiffs, their attorneys, and their accountants.

It is also noteworthy that, while the Bookman case was pending, the New Jersey legislature enacted a statute barring such suits. The law took effect immediately and thus applied to pending suits as well as new ones. It permitted suits to be brought only when the plaintiffs were shareholders at the time of the transactions complained of.[42] Arthur Bookman and his wife, Judith W. Bookman, bought their 200 shares of Reynolds stock in July 1935; Mrs. Healey obtained her 38 shares piecemeal from January 1927 to November 1932. But the record indicates only that Lavy held his as early as 14 April 1941.[43]

The plaintiffs sued on the basis of causes of action arising from the administration of Bylaw XII, which had provided participation payments to officers and employees since 1912, and on causes independent of the bylaw. In the first category they made four charges: (1) that substantial overpayments had been made as the result of including in the net profits items that were not income and failing to deduct items that were company expenses, (2) that payments had been made to persons not entitled to receive them under provisions of the bylaw, (3) that the company had failed to include B classes of common stock for purposes of the bonus base when computing profits, and (4) that the bylaw and its 1915 amendment were invalid. The amendment in that year permitted officers and employees to share in participation payments on stock purchased at any time during the year provided the stock had been obtained from former owners entitled to share in the payments. The second category of charges related to personal gains and profits of the controlling directors and officers: (1) that the "W. N. Reynolds Special Accounts" involved the use of millions of dollars of corporate funds by the directors and officers, (2) that the directors' speculations in Class B Common Stock at the time involved the use of millions of dollars of company funds to bolster the stock market, (3) that the directors and officers used company assets and credits to obtain personal benefits, and (4) that the company had failed to deduct participation payments under Bylaw XII in its income tax returns and that it had improperly included interest from the "W. N. Reynolds Special Accounts" in the returns.[44] Because these charges covered the entire operation of Bylaw XII, the suit implicated many officers and directors who had been dead for many years.

In point number one of the first category of charges—that substantial overpayments had been made as the result of including in the net profits items that were not income and failing to deduct items that were company expenses—the plaintiffs made a variety of accusations. The directors had included dividends on stock that had never been issued and on shares that had previously been issued but reacquired by the company. The directors had improperly included so-called profits on B shares that had never been issued and on issues of reacquired B shares. The directors had improperly deducted expenses of the Retirement and Insurance Investment Fund and included interest charged on the amount paid by the company to purchase 100,000 shares of "A" stock for inclusion in that fund. Moreover, the officers and directors had improperly included interest charged to special accounts in income on which bonuses were paid; in computing the annual income on which bonuses were paid, they had failed to deduct the bonus payments as an expense of the company, thereby causing overpayments to be made to themselves and others; in computing income on which bonuses were paid, they had failed to deduct premiums paid by the company on the redemption of its preferred stock in 1925; and they had failed to include a refund from the A.A.A. processing tax in the proper years. In reference to this last item a processing tax amounting to almost $13,000,000 was levied on the company's profits for 1933, 1934, and 1935, but the refund of $2,968,099 did not come until 1941.[45] These charges impugned the officers and directors of the company in a number of actions that had been taken for the benefit of the employees.

In point number two in the first category—that payments had been made to persons not entitled to receive them—the charges became more personal. Here the complainants held that participation payments had been improperly made on shares allocated after the beginning of the participating year, that officers and employees who were not owners of record for the full twelve months had not been entitled to participation payments despite the 1915 amendment to Bylaw XII, that officers who had merely contracted to purchase shares had received participation payments on them, that such payments had been made to S. Clay Williams on 500 shares formerly owned by Katharine S. Johnston and on 1,300 obtained from Thomas Fortune Ryan, that Gordon Gray (not an employee of the company) had wrongfully received participation payments, and finally that the 1915 amendment was not valid.[46] As a result, it was claimed, all payments made under Bylaw XII from 1918 to the date of the trial exceeded the authorization of the bylaw, because Class B Common Stock and New

Class B Common Stock were both common stocks and as such were entitled to participation rights. The purpose of the bylaw could only be fulfilled by applying the 22.19 percent formula to profits from all subsequent issues of common stock regardless of class. Furthermore, according to the plaintiffs, there was no basis for the contention that the progress of the company was attributable to the functioning of Bylaw XII, which had become archaic and inequitable in operation. Among the various declarations in the second category of charges, individual defendants should be required to account for the company funds that were expended through the special accounts in W. N. Reynolds's name.[47]

In conclusion, the plaintiffs' lawyers argued that the defendants were not only liable for a tremendous sum of money but also that relief in the suit was not barred by the statute of limitations because that statute did not apply in courts of equity, that a stockholders' derivative suit was only recognized in courts of equity, and that officers and directors of the corporation acted as trustees for its stockholders. Likewise, they claimed that neglect could not figure as a factor in the defense because, in such an instance, a lapse of time must be accompanied by a full knowledge of the internal records of the corporation and that neglect or *laches* was not a defense in a continuing wrong. Nor could any other legal quibble prove effective without showing that the plaintiffs had had knowledge of this mass of wrongful acts.[48]

With its imposing list of cases cited, statutes used, and authorities consulted, the plaintiffs' brief represented a tremendous effort on the part of the legal firms involved. But the case involved a corporation that had developed without the aid of substantial capital. Its directors had fought off attempts to exploit the stock of the corporation and, in doing so, had resorted to many unorthodox measures by which control of the R. J. Reynolds Tobacco Company had been kept in the South and in North Carolina in particular. The plaintiffs' lawyers submitted their findings as "an extraordinary picture of management by directors and officers of a publicly owned corporation."[49] Three years later Vice-Chancellor Charles M. Egan, when dismissing the action, agreed with this last view of the plaintiffs by recognizing the high fidelity and exceptional skill with which the directors had managed the corporation so that its history did indeed present "an extraordinary picture of management," though not in the sense used by the prosecuting attorneys.

At the trial, the defense was led by James D. Carpenter, Jr., for the R. J. Reynolds Tobacco Company and Josiah Stryker for the thirteen directors and officers. Their brief began by emphasizing the speculative nature of the suit.[50] Moving to the validity of Bylaw XII, they stated that it was adopted by the stockholders in 1912 and accepted by all of the stockholders for more than twenty-eight years until the current suit was filed. They called attention to the inferior position of the Reynolds company in 1912 in relation to the other major companies of the tobacco industry, the annual profits of the company from 1912 to 1941, the various improvements made during those years of operation under Bylaw XII compared with similar bylaws of competitors, and in general refuted the charges made by the prosecution.

The company's counsel noted that Reynolds's invested capital of approximately $16 million in 1912 had increased to more than $160 million by 1941 notwithstanding the fact that since 1912 the stockholders had paid only $10 million into the company. Similar figures for the other major companies during that period indicated that Reynolds had not merely maintained its relative position in the industry but that forces at work in the company had been responsible for this amazing growth. Invested capital in the American Tobacco Company from 1912 to 1941 had increased from about $150 million to $250 million, in Liggett and Myers from about $70 million to slightly more than $160 million, and in the P. Lorillard Tobacco Company there had been scarcely any increase. In his testimony, S. Clay Williams attributed his company's progress to the functioning of Bylaw XII "all the way down the line as far as" it could be applied. In 1912 officials of the R. J. Reynolds Tobacco Company, realizing their weak position, were "not satisfied with the kind of [bonus] bylaw the American Tobacco Company, or Liggett and Myers Tobacco Company had adopted."[51]

More interesting and perhaps more pertinent was the explanation provided by William Reynolds of the "W. N. Reynolds Special Accounts," which amounted to no more than a continuation of R. J. Reynolds's policy of helping employees obtain participating or "A" stock as permitted by Bylaw XII. The background developed to explain this practice is of unusual interest. In his testimony on 10 June 1943, S. Clay Williams described the situation in 1917 when he first joined the company: " (D. Rich, the treasurer) was carrying a little black book in his pocket all the time in which he had listed the names of employees who had indicated to him that they wanted to buy some of the common stock of the company to participate on, and that on the basis of these inquiries and expressions of desire to buy stock, he was continuously trying to get stock and did on frequent occasions get stock and allocate it out among those on that book."[52] On the same day Williams related subsequent efforts to carry out this policy after R. J. Reynolds died, indicating at the same time the gap created by his death:[53]

> Mr. R. J. Reynolds at that time was acquiring and letting employees have that common stock in order that they might be under the incentive and spur of this bylaw. He was doing a great deal of that with his

own personal funds. . . . there was nobody in the company who felt that he was personally able to do as much of that kind of thing for employees of the company and in pursuit of the company policy in that respect as Mr. R. J. Reynolds had been doing.

Now, after his death, and some years after his death, it came to be realized that the company was not making as much headway on that policy of getting common stock from stockholders of American Tobacco Company and getting it into the hands of employees for use under the bylaw as had been hoped.

. . .(F)rom 1918 to 1919, . . . the increase in the number of employees participating was only two; 154 to 156. That was the net increase. In the year 1919 to 1920, the increase in participators was only five; 156 to 161. Those policies were not showing effective operation in that period immediately after Mr. Reynolds' death.

After 1920, when the company itself undertook to become more active in the pressing of those policies, that situation improved very definitely, under both of those policies, and in 1921 the number of participators was 308 as against 161 in 1920.

Employee participation increased when some of the directors established special accounts with company funds to obtain "A" stock from the stockholders of the American Tobacco Company so that it could be made available to Reynolds employees. An important purpose of these special funds was to assure as large a distribution as possible of the A stock among the employees in order to give them the incentives provided under Bylaw XII. The plaintiffs held that these transactions had been made primarily for the benefit of the directors themselves. But the defendants were able to demonstrate that the percentage of A stock held by the directors had declined from 61.28 in 1919 to 56.56 in 1922. Moreover, it was doubtful that the employees could have acquired large blocks of common stock without the company's help. The practice was to negotiate trades of New Class B Common Stock for common, or A stock. Actually the directors might have maintained their 1919 percentage of participation payments, invested their surplus funds in B stock, and in that way retained a larger payment per share on the holdings of A stock. What the complainants called "withdrawals from the Treasury" were in reality payments for stock acquired by the company for resale to its employees at cost plus interest less the dividends that were generally allocated for payment of the A stock. In regard to the transactions under the "W. N. Reynolds Special Accounts," James A. Gray testified on 20 October 1943:[54]

Principally they were used to record the purchase and sale of common stock ("A" stock), the common stock being bought for resale to employee, or B stock being purchased to be used to exchange for common, the common then to be resold to employees, the common stock being resold on a basis of cost plus interest less dividends, the idea being that the company did not want to make any profit out of those transactions, this acquiring of common stock for resale to employees.

They were not only used for recording that type of transactions, but throughout the years were used for a number of other recordings. For illustration, in 1927, I think it was, the company desired to purchase a piece of real estate in the central part of the city for the erection of an office building. The company arranged for a real estate company in Winston-Salem to make the purchase of that property. We advanced them the money to make the purchase. They did, and we of course had a contract for the delivery to us of title to it when we should want the title.

The investing of that money was charged to a W. N. Reynolds Special Account and was carried as an account receivable in the financial statements of the company, just as were the items covering the common stock purchases.

In the same fashion the company purchased the Tobacco Foil Company of Richmond. Likewise, seventeen years before the New Jersey Trial William Reynolds had obtained 5,600 shares of A stock from three former employees: 3,100 from Burton Craige, 1,800 from Charles A. Kent, and 700 from Thomas S. Fleshman. When the holders of this stock refused to trade at the ratio of two shares of B for one share of common, Will Reynolds worked out an agreement with them whereby, if they would trade on that basis, 5,000 B shares would be purchased for them and held one year unless they ordered its sale. Craige, Kent, and Fleshman were to receive the profit when the stock was sold. If there was any loss, Will Reynolds would personally bear it. However, by holding the 5,000 shares for a year in a safe account in order to secure the purchase price, the company ran no risk whatsoever. When the 5,000 shares were sold at a profit, it, less the 6 percent interest that the company retained, was paid by Reynolds to Craige, Kent, and Fleshman—all in William Reynolds's name without their knowledge that the arrangement had been carried out with company funds. The attorneys for the company had no difficulty in proving that the A stock had been distributed largely to employees and that the directors had not retained 40 percent of it for themselves. The defendants acknowledged that charges in the special accounts did not generally become receivables, although the accounts actually represented stock owned by the company and acquired by it for resale to its employees.[55] The question at issue involved the true ownership of the stock in the special accounts prior to its distribution to employees while they were paying for it, generally with its dividends.

The plaintiffs seemed to have a more definite point in maintaining that these special accounts had not been operated from 1928 to 1933 as they had been in earlier years. In other words, the stock acquired in the special accounts had not been resold to employees. The testimony of James A. Gray clarified that issue:[56]

> There was no demand on hand at that particular time, but our plan and contemplation was to distribute or allocate that stock to employees as soon as there was a favorable opportunity. Let me, in that connection, hesitate for a moment to call your attention to two things that made it inadvisable in our opinion to offer that stock to employees, or, to say it another way, to test our opinion that the demand might be less than the supply. Those two factors were that, April 1928 was the date at which the price of Camels was reduced, which lowered price continued until October 1929. By that time, the expiration of 1929, we ran into the stock market situation and, certainly, it was not an opportune moment, from October 1929 until 1933, to make an offer to employees to purchase stock.

After 1933, however, the demand picked up and the 75,000 shares of common stock from the estate of Bowman Gray, Sr., were heavily oversubscribed, as were the 10,000 shares of Robert D. Shore and the 15,000 shares from the estate of Carl W. Harris. From 1928 to 1933 the stock in the "W. N. Reynolds Special Account No. 2" was listed at the buying price of $67 per share, an attractive price to the employees at that time. When asked about the treatment of these items in the annual reports from 1928 to 1933—that is, whether or not the procedure should have been continued—Gray intimated that it was not changed. When asked why, he referred to items in the newspaper attributed to the president of the United States and to one or more leading economists that business recovery was right around the corner. On that basis, he claimed, he and his associates late in 1931 considered offering the stock at an early date. Nor did he think that the price of the stock inventory in the "W. N. Reynolds Special Account No. 2" was ever out of line with the market. In time of business recovery the stock might have been offered at cost price and employees would have been happy to buy it.[57]

Acquisitions of blocks of stock from particular individuals and estates were questioned. One had to do with the purchase of 86,800 shares of New Class B Common Stock from the United Cigar Stores Company in

1921. The plaintiffs held that the firm's advantageous offer to sell its holdings in Reynolds stock was made to William Reynolds in the performance of his duties as president and that the purchase of some of that stock by Reynolds, S. Clay Williams, and Robert D. Shore constituted a breach of trust. They also claimed that the board of directors had not authorized the use of corporate funds to acquire this stock. On 15 March 1943, William Reynolds explained the origin of this move:[58]

> Well, our men, department men and salesmen, were reporting that the United Cigar Stores (a chain retail outlet once closely associated with the American Tobacco Company) had a report among their competitors that they were big stockholders of Reynolds Tobacco Company and that they could sell Reynolds tobaccos at cost and then make plenty of money on the dividends from the company, and we were getting continuous letters. Just before I came up to New York (in 1921) a letter came in from our division manager in Chicago. He said some of our customers there were sore about it and were complaining considerably about the United Cigar Stores, the way they were handling the thing there, and they would publish the fact, too, that they were big stockholders of R. J. Reynolds Tobacco Company, and it didn't help us with the general trade.

Accordingly, Will Reynolds went to New York to see George J. Whelan of the United Cigar Stores in the hope of correcting the situation. He did not believe that Whelan's approach helped the cigar outlet, and he knew that it harmed the Reynolds company. Before he could make the purpose of his visit known, Whelan offered to sell the stock. When Reynolds said he did not have the money, Whelan suggested that he take it for reselling. Thinking that he might be able to sell it in New York, Reynolds asked for an option on it. Whelan proposed that Reynolds return the following day for the option, but, when he did, the retailer reported that there was already an option on the stock which he would have to buy for $35,000. Though Reynolds did not believe him, he nevertheless obtained an option himself and paid the additional $35,000. He then tried to sell the stock in New York and Winston-Salem but was able to dispose of only 22,800 shares. When it occurred to Reynolds that the company might buy the remainder, he consulted S. Clay Williams on the legality of such a move. Satisfied on that point, the directors met on 1 December 1921 and, on "full consideration of the circumstances arising out of the present ownership of this stock," adopted a resolution to purchase 64,000 shares of New Class B Common Stock owned by the United Cigar Stores in the name of Charles R. Stoddard.[59] By 1943, when Reynolds gave this testimony, one share of New Class B Common Stock, worth $33.73 in 1921, had almost doubled in value. According to evidence introduced at the trial, the company had made the initial payment for all of the stock—86,800 shares—but that certificates for the 22,800 shares sold to various individuals, including William Reynolds, S. Clay Williams, and Robert D. Shore, had been delivered to them upon payment of the purchase price to the Equitable Trust Company, the agent of the R. J. Reynolds Tobacco Company. None of these certificates were delivered to Reynolds, Williams, and Shore until they had paid for them in full with interest.

Similar accusations were made regarding 28,464 shares obtained in 1925 from the Duke family including 17,400 shares from the estate of James B. Duke. This block was sold to various employees of the company.[60]

In another complaint, the plaintiffs stated that the Reynolds company improperly handled the acquisition of 14,900 shares of A stock obtained from Thomas Fortune Ryan in 1926. This block of stock was exchanged for 19,021 shares of New Class B Common Stock. Of this amount S. Clay Williams obtained 13,000 shares. Specifically, the counsel for the plaintiffs claimed that on 1 January 1926 Williams owned only 7,000 shares of common stock; yet in 1926 he had participated in profits from 20,000 shares. To refute the charge, the company produced telegrams and copies of telegrams between Ryan on one hand and William Reynolds and Williams on the other showing that a firm contract for the sale had existed before the end of 1925.[61] This placed Williams's participation in the profits from the additional shares obtained from Ryan in line with the general practice of the company for all employees.

The accusation that Gordon Gray, son of Bowman Gray, Sr., had been improperly permitted to participate in profits under Bylaw XII because he was not an employee of the company likewise received short shrift. When Gray, a lawyer, left a New York law firm and joined the Winston-Salem legal firm of Manly, Hendren and Womble, he became a partner in that firm, which had been retained by the Reynolds company for many years. S. Clay Williams freely testified that Gray had never been "a whole-time, all-day-long employee of R. J. Reynolds Tobacco Company." His share in participation payments in 1936 had amounted to $7,018. Williams regarded the matter as routine, for the practice of permitting lawyers on a fixed annual retainer to participate under Bylaw XII had been a policy of the company for many years, even before the death of R. J. Reynolds. Williams explained Gray's participation payments in later years on the same basis.[62] He testified further that prior to 1917 Ambrose H. Burroughs, a New York attorney retained by the company, had been allotted participation payments on the basis of the small amount of A stock that he owned. Clement Manly and Harry H. Shelton—also lawyers retained by Reynolds—received similar payments. The counsel showed that their participation in profits meant no loss to the company because it did not increase the total amount paid by way of participation.[63]

So the testimony ran until 5,858 pages, not to mention hundreds of charts and exhibits, were left for Vice-Chancellor Egan to study. In addition, elaborate briefs and reply briefs were laid before the court. In view of other duties of the vice-chancellor it is no wonder that thirty-two months elapsed from the last testimony given on 30 November 1943 until the decision was rendered. The testimony covered some sad days for the Reynolds company when it made futile efforts to support the stock during the depression—a policy that left the company with an abundance of New Class B Common Stock and no doubt accounted in some measure for the decision of William Reynolds, Bowman Gray, Sr., James A. Gray, and S. Clay Williams to exchange their A stock for New Class B Common in order to place the A stock in the Retirement and Insurance Investment Fund. The testimony also registered sharp exchanges in some of the examinations and cross-examinations.

Vice-Chancellor Egan filed his opinion on 31 July 1946, only seven weeks after the Supreme Court refused to review the decision in the Kentucky Trial. His verdict furnished one bright spot for the company during the dismal and troubled 1940s. Had the lawyers in the company's own legal department written the decision, it could hardly have been more favorable.

The opinion opened with a brief history of the case including the circumstances under which the suit was brought. He then wrote: "The hearing of this suit consumed many months; the testimony covers many thousands of pages; the exhibits are voluminous; and the original and several replying briefs are very extensive. The presentation of the briefs ran into the second year after the final hearing." Vice-Chancellor Egan noted the company's temporary role as an independently operated subsidiary of the American Tobacco Company, the unhappiness of Reynolds officials during that period, the dissolution of the tobacco trust, the adoption of the bonus bylaw in 1912, its revision in 1915, and the plaintiffs' charge that it was invalid from 1912 until 1940. He stated that he had permitted the introduction of evidence to cover the early period subject to objection from the defendants but that he would rule on that point in his conclusion. He then disposed of the charges against all the directors as far back as 1912 in a statement remarkable for its support of the company's argument:

In view of the seriousness of the charges made against the directors of the defendant corporation and the long and exhaustive trial, I shall review the various matters put in issue. I find that no breach of trust has been committed by any of the defendant directors at any time. On the contrary, I find that the defendant corporation has been managed with a high degree of fidelity and exceptional skill, and with profit to the stockholders and benefit to the corporation far beyond the expectation that any stockholder could possibly have had when the bylaw was adopted in 1912.

The vice-chancellor recounted the growth of the company from its relatively low standing in the tobacco industry in 1912 to the point when new capital was needed in 1917. He noted S. Clay Williams's solution of the problem by recommending the issuance of Class B Common Stock—a maneuver that occurred to him when he read a press report that the Bethlehem Steel Company had issued a similar stock. He reviewed the amendment to the company's charter providing for the issuance of Class B Common Stock and the accompanying statement that the original common, or A, stock outstanding under the prior certificate of incorporation was to be known simply as common stock without any other designation. Observing the continued growth of the company after this change, Vice-Chancellor Egan referred to the reduction of the par value of both common and Class B Common Stock to $25, the issuance of a 200 percent stock dividend in the form of New Class B Common Stock, and the exchange of Class B Common Stock for New Class B Common Stock in reduced par value. The issuance of the 200 percent stock dividend was based on the huge sum of $36 million in undivided profits held by the company in 1920 and sentiment in Congress for laying a heavy tax on such surpluses. He noted also that neither Class B Common Stock nor New Class B Common Stock carried any voting rights and that every share of Class B Common Stock was exchanged for New Class B Common Stock. All these changes, he stated, had been duly approved by the stockholders.

Next he referred to the issuance of 7% Preferred Stock in 1913 at $100 par value subject to redemption at a premium of $20 per share. The plaintiffs contended that the payment of this premium to redeem the preferred stock in 1925—a total of $4 million—was illegal because it was not charged against the company's profits for the year in which it was paid. This, they claimed, increased improperly the participation fund under Bylaw XII for the benefit of the directors. The Vice-Chancellor ruled that the matter had been properly treated as a capital transaction, that the stockholders had approved the move on 15 January 1926, nearly fifteen years before the suit was brought, and that the action accorded with the regulations of the Federal Internal Revenue Act.

He noted that the handsome profits of the company in 1922 and 1923 permitted a further stock dividend of 33⅓ percent in New Class B Common Stock. Additional profits prompted the directors in 1927 to declare another dividend of 25 percent in New Class B Common Stock. These changes increased the company's capitalization to $100 million—$10 million in common stock and $90 million in New Class B Common Stock. This conversion of undivided profits into capital stock had cost the stockholders only $20 million, and each year since 1921 the net earnings of the corporation had exceeded the total amount paid into the corporation by the stockholders. The Vice-Chancellor then noted the last change in the capital structure of the company—on 28 December 1928—when stockholders at a special meeting reduced the par value of common stock and New Class B Common Stock from $25 to $10 per share. The proper exchange of certificates was made early in 1929. The dividends paid in 1929 were 1¼ times the total capital that the stockholders had actually contributed to the corporation. These facts, all substantiated from annual reports and the minutes, surely indicated that stockholders had not suffered from the operation of Bylaw XII.

Accordingly, Vice-Chancellor Egan ruled that Bylaw XII, which had been duly adopted by the stockholders and which had operated for thirty years, was valid. The 1915 amendment had also been valid because the bylaws permitted changes. The fact that the number of officers and individuals participating under the bylaw had increased from 27 in 1912 to 2,177 in 1928 and stood at 2,045 in 1940 indicated that the bylaw had not operated solely for the profit of the directors. He noted testimony that the R. J. Reynolds Tobacco Company had become the recognized leader in the tobacco industry because of the incentives provided by Bylaw XII. During that climb many suggestions from officers and employees had reduced costs, eliminated waste, and promoted efficiency. He cited New Jersey laws that granted the company full authority to pay executives and employees with a share of its profits. In addition, the P. Lorillard bonus suit of 1931, which the plaintiffs had used as a precedent, differed in many ways from the circumstances of this case.

The vice-chancellor also disposed of the complaint that the bonus base for Bylaw XII should have included all of the A stock plus all of the B stock rather than the common stock alone. Stockholders had approved the use of common stock in determining the bonus payments. Furthermore, stockholders had the right to call on officers for any information they desired.

As for the special accounts maintained in the names of different directors for the purchase of A stock for employees, Vice-Chancellor Egan held that they had been honestly administered, though the plaintiffs had sought—by inferences they drew from the undisputed existence of these funds—to prove charges of bad faith and self-dealing. Here he indicated the hardships suffered by the company as a result of the suit:

> It is unnecessary here to detail all of the very numerous transactions that were covered by the testimony of complainants' accountants on the one hand and that were explained in great detail, item by item, by Mr. Reynolds, Mr. Williams and Mr. Gray. Suffice it to say by way of preface that although many of these transactions went back as long as twenty years, and although many of the corporation's records sup-

porting the books were destroyed years before this suit was brought under a standing company instruction to destroy records after a certain number of years, the defendants produced before me evidence so clear and convincing of the bona fides of every transaction that I hold that there was no fraud or breach of trust whatsoever.

Nevertheless, he went into every aspect of the charge concerning the handling of special accounts, including the accusation that interest paid to the company as a part of the cost of the employee's stock was improperly credited to the earnings account. He even noted that, although 5,600 shares of common stock had been secured in a roundabout fashion from Thomas Fleshman, Burton Craige, and Charles A. Kent in William N. Reynolds's name, all company funds were properly accounted for. He concluded that these special funds were closed out in 1933 without loss to the company but, rather, to its great advantage:

> Control of the company had been removed from the stockholders of its principal competitor; the officers and employees of the corporation owned 651,703 shares of its voting stock, and from the participation fund of approximately 10% of the annual profits they were paying for 200,000 shares of common stock in the Insurance and Retirement Investment Fund which is relieving the other stockholders of contributing anything for employee retirement, health and insurance benefits. . . .

He then moved to the charge that participation payments had been made to persons not entitled to them under Bylaw XII. The old American Tobacco Company group and other old stockholders, he noted, often did not decide to sell their shares until late in the year, hoping that the market would rise. Accordingly, allocation of these shares to employees was based on the average cost of all shares acquired during the year at cost plus interest less dividends. In this way an employee obtained the stock "just as if he had owned it from the day the company first bought it." The vicechancellor held that in 1926 S. Clay Williams had not participated wrongfully in the profits of 13,000 shares of common stock obtained from Thomas Fortune Ryan because he had contracted to buy the stock just before the end of 1925. His participation had corresponded exactly to that of other employees. In the same fashion Williams was absolved from wrongdoing in another case involving the purchase of 500 shares, formerly the property of Katharine S. Johnston, from the R. J. Reynolds Memorial Auditorium Commission. Gordon Gray's participation was properly based on his membership in the legal firm of Manly, Hendren and Womble, which was retained by the Reynolds company.

The plaintiffs claimed that the company between 1929 and 1932 purchased large blocks of its New Class B Common Stock in order to protect the investment of directors in the stock of the company. Vice-Chancellor Egan declared that the defendants had proved to his satisfaction that each such purchase had been to the company's advantage. In fact, these acquisitions had netted Reynolds more than $8 million. When the market broke in 1929, the company had $12 million in cash and $17 million in government securities for which there was no immediate need. Twenty-three percent of its stock was held by brokers, and Lucky Strikes were outselling Camels. The directors, believing that the break in the market was temporary, feared a serious raid on Reynolds stock. Thus they decided to invest as much as necessary of the company's surplus in its own stock at $50 per share. This investment was shown as an asset in the annual report of 1929 and the stockholders had full knowledge of the transaction. The vice-chancellor declared: "It was common practice before 1933 for corporations to include dividends on treasury stock in company income." He also noted that the acquisition and reissuance of shares of a corporation were not capital transactions.

In the distribution of 74,045 shares of A stock acquired in 1927 from the Safe Deposit and Trust Company of Baltimore, as trustee of the estate of R. J. Reynolds, the plaintiffs charged improper methods. The directors had averaged the price of this stock with the 19,563 shares held by the company before distribution to its employees. Of this total amount, the directors bought and paid for about 20 percent while the remainder went to other employees. All paid the same price. In January 1929 all A and B stocks were converted from a par value of $25 to $10 per share. Some employees purchased theirs on the installment plan but because of deaths, resignations, and the strain of the depression many defaulted. At first the company paid the defaulting employees the difference between the market price and the amount they owed on the stock, though later it discontinued the purchase of shares at market price and bought them for the employee at cost. According to James A. Gray, the first method was adopted to preserve the morale of the employees and not to relieve William Reynolds, Bowman Gray, Sr., and himself of any liability to the Safe Deposit and Trust Company. The plaintiffs held that this stock was worth more than cost when the Retirement and Insurance Investment Fund was established. Vice-Chancellor Egan concluded that the company had benefited from the directors' arrangement.

In addition to the stock acquired from defaulting employees, the company made additional purchases that were carried in one of the Reynolds special accounts for resale to employees when there was a demand. During the years from 1929 to 1933 the company accumulated almost 100,000 shares. It was determined that the price was too high for resale. Therefore the four top officers agreed to exchange 100,000 shares of their A stock for 100,000 shares of the company's New Class B Common Stock on a share-for-share basis in order to bring the price down to $50 per share and make it readily available to the employees. For this the plaintiffs accused them of self-dealing and fraud. As shown below, each of these directors lost almost $30 per share so exchanged as well as the participation rights. Instead of offering these shares to employees, they decided to use them for the Retirement and Insurance Investment Fund. All this was recorded in the minutes. The plaintiffs also noted errors in the bookkeeping connected with these items. James A. Gray testified that these errors were caught and corrected by charging their amounts against the undistributed participation payments at the end of 1942. To the vice-chancellor there seemed no need to charge the defendants with liability when neither the directors nor the employees holding common stock had secured any gain. He noted, too, the plaintiffs' allegation that the shares placed in the Retirement and Insurance Investment Fund were not worth $50 per share, though it was proved that large blocks of A stock had sold for $60 per share. "It is also the evidence," he stated, "that the common stock before this suit was brought never sold less than 1¼ times the B stock, due solely to the participating right."

No doubt, of all the charges made, the most fruitless was that the company had failed to deduct participation payments as a business expense in its income tax returns. The vice-chancellor merely noted a letter of S. Clay Williams to the Commissioner of Internal Revenue, dated 18 December 1942, stating that the Internal Revenue Department had held that disbursements made under Bylaw XII were dividends and that the company had not been permitted to deduct them as an expense in arriving at its taxable income. Williams then listed the salaries and participation payments received by some directors and asked for advice with reference to the Salary Stabilization Law. The commissioner's reply, dated 31 December 1942, noted that participation payments were "preferential dividends, and not bonuses or additional compensation." In the face of this overwhelming evidence Vice-Chancellor Egan could find no breach of duty.

He felt the same about the charge concerning a refund from the A.A.A. processing tax covering the years 1933–35. According to the plaintiffs, it had been improper to include this refund in the corporation's income for 1941 on which bonuses were paid. The vice-chancellor merely noted the company's arrangements with the federal government by which the refund was required to be considered as 1941 income. He hardly needed to do more.

Vice-Chancellor Egan then addressed the question of salaries of the company's officers and directors. The plaintiffs maintained that the increases these officials received in 1934 and subsequent years were unauthorized and unlawful. As a matter of fact, the salaries of the top officials at Reynolds were generally considered notoriously low until adjusted in

1949. Indeed, one of the reasons for initiating Bylaw XII had been the fact that the company could not afford to pay adequate salaries. The vice-chancellor stated that the raise in 1934 had been authorized by the Executive Committee and that subsequently the board had resolved that salaries in conjunction with participation payments made in that year were not unreasonable. Nevertheless, he interpreted the complaint to mean that the salaries in dispute were exorbitant. In refuting such a claim, he declared:

> The largest salary the Company ever paid to any officer was $100,000 per year. The greatest amount that was ever paid to any officer or director was $507,999.96 paid to Bowman Gray [Sr.] in 1931 [then chairman of the board], and this included his annual salary of $33,999.96 and the remainder was participation on the common stock in which he had made a heavy investment.

He also noted that the salaries involved appeared "to have been fairly well earned," citing various charts prepared by Paul B. Coffman, vice-president of Standard & Poor's Corporation. In one chart showing the earnings of the R. J. Reynolds Tobacco Company "as against that of 131 representative American corporations for the twenty year period 1922 to 1941," the average earnings of Reynolds and the 131 representative companies were 13.83 percent and 9.53 percent, respectively. Another chart compared average earnings as a percent of invested capital, as follows: 35 corporations listed on the New York Stock Exchange with the highest average earnings, 13.95 percent; the Reynolds company, 18.64 percent; the American Tobacco Company, 11.78 percent; and the Liggett and Myers Tobacco Company, 12.95 percent. Still another chart showed the results of a hypothetical investment of about $10,000 in each of the latter three companies from January 1913 to 30 December 1942. Such an investment would have yielded the stockholders in cash income from the sale of rights, cash dividends, and value of investment the following: Liggett and Myers, $47,977; American, $56,161; and Reynolds, $150,000. Under these circumstances it appeared to Vice-Chancellor Egan that the salaries of the Reynolds officers and directors were fair and reasonable. He wrote: "The company's officers and directors by their application to the company's business have made it a successful and marvelous enterprise."

Next he cited various legal precedents bearing on the claims of the plaintiffs. In each instance his interpretation differed from that of their counsel. To quote the governor of New York, he said, a "'veritable racket of baseless law suits accompanied by many unethical practices'" had grown up in his state as a result of such stockholders' suits. The New Jersey law, passed on 10 April 1945 to stop such suits, was patterned after the New York law.

In conclusion, Vice-Chancellor Egan summarized the circumstances of the suit, describing the aim of the litigation, the plaintiffs, their lawyers, and the accounting firms that had assisted them. He also ruled that the plaintiffs could not go further back than 1927 when Mary B. Healey bought her first share of Reynolds stock. Finally, he repeated his eulogy of the officers and directors of the company:[64]

> I believe that the individual defendants discharged their duty as directors, and officers of the corporate defendant with care, integrity, and outstanding ability; that their acts, which are the object of criticism by the complainants, were undertaken for the sole aim of benefiting the corporation and its stockholders.

Many believed that the virtual wholesale destruction of the company's records ordered by President Edward A. Darr in 1953 resulted in part from the wish to avoid future searches of company records by unscrupulous lawyers and accountants. On 12 March 1953, Darr was appointed by Chairman of the Board John C. Whitaker to head up a committee to investigate the means for storing and possibly microfilming these records. With Darr on the committee were Alexander H. Galloway, Spencer B. Hanes, Jr., and Charles B. Wade, Jr. On 14 May Darr reported to the board that his committee had made a survey of the records and storage facilities for them, and that lists had been prepared of which records and correspondence should be retained permanently and which should be destroyed. These surveys, he reported, would be continued in collaboration with the heads of various departments.[65] Only deliberate disobedience of this order preserved some of the few valuable records of the company extant at the time of the author's research. When the order came, reportedly in May 1953, many records were held in various departments, though bulky ones were often stored in the Lasater Building adjacent to the office building. The former, which later housed the engineering department, was reputedly in a state of chaos most of the time. No attendant cared for the records and office help so exhausted themselves when searching for particular items that they did not always replace them with care. Some departments that retained confidential records insisted on having a wire cage built around their areas, and the credit department commandeered a rest room that could be kept under lock and key.[66]

Another phase of the work of Darr's committee produced the Records Center, primarily for the preservation of records as long as they were deemed of value in the operation of the company. Of all the divisions concerned, the legal department with its respect for precedence was the most assiduous in preserving records. Soon after Darr began his work, Lespie E. George with James V. Dorse was chosen to review the records program of the company. George was assisted by Saul Citrone, a representative of the National Records Management Council, Inc. Located on the second floor of Number 2 at 8, the Records Center was administered by James V. Dorse after April 1957.⁶⁷ Of necessity, the chief aim of the center's officials often seemed to be the destruction of records in order to make room for others. Despite this fact, the establishment of the Records Center facilitated the work of the office personnel when records were needed.

Though the New Jersey Trial centered attention on Bylaw XII and led to the establishment of the Records Center, it had little to do with the discontinuance of common, or A stock. Rather, it seems, the old standby of the company had outlived its usefulness for a variety of reasons. Perhaps the primary reason was the attitude of the Stock List Committee of the New York Stock Exchange, which regarded with distinct disfavor the listing of any new stock issue as long as the company remained under the narrow control of holders of common stock alone. In view of the manner in which A stock had been allocated and voted, Reynolds stockholders at large could not even pretend to have any voice in the control of the company. More than likely the Stock List Committee's view had become apparent by 1945 when the company issued its Preferred Stock 3.60% series, or certainly by 1948 with the issuance of the Preferred Stock 4.50% series. By 1947 the outstanding shares were as follows: ⁶⁸

Number of Shares	Type of Stock	Par Value
1,000,000	Common	$ 10
9,000,000	New Class B Common	10
490,000	Preferred, 3.60% series	100

Moreover, by New Jersey law the 200,000 shares of common stock held by the company in its Retirement and Insurance Investment Fund could not be voted either directly or indirectly. From the standpoint of capital actually invested in the company, this meant that the holders of only 5.37 percent controlled the company. While it is largely a fiction that stockholders ever actually control any company, the fiction in this case could not be maintained. Furthermore, in a number of cases much A stock had by inheritance or otherwise fallen into the hands of employees who were of no market value to the company.

There is the classic story of one employee who had inherited a substantial amount of A stock. Though tried in many capacities including that of elevator starter, he proved satisfactory in only one: he performed well and enjoyed the task of sweeping scrap tobacco from the floor in Number 8. Nevertheless, his participation payments were immense. Moreover, because of increased costs of living and high income taxes during the war years, many employees often could not afford to buy A stock; many also lacked outside resources for such purchases. In addition, the laws regulating banks made it difficult to borrow for the purchase of stock. Actually these various signs of the decreasing usefulness of Bylaw XII had been apparent for some time.[69] After almost forty years this innovation of Richard Joshua Reynolds had become archaic, though some years later many employees still did not seem to agree.

The question of devising a plan for discontinuing A stock posed some difficulties. S. Clay Williams worked on the problem for some time and arrived at a tentative plan for the exchange of the two classes of stock at the rate of one share of common, or A stock, held by employees for one and one-half shares of New Class B Common and one for one and one-fourth shares held by other stockholders. Because this seemed on the surface to be a manifestly unfair method of exchange, it was never formally presented. At Williams's death in February 1949, the problem fell to James A. Gray who developed a satisfactory plan by May 1949.[70] According to the minutes, the aim was to simplify the corporate structure of the company, to extend voting rights to holders of New Class B Common Stock, and to eliminate the current method under which officers and employees participated in profits under Bylaw XII. Under Gray's plan, the Certificate of Incorporation was amended to provide for the following:

1. Reclassifying the 200,000 shares of common in the Retirement and Insurance Investment Fund into 200,000 shares of New Class B Common
2. Decreasing thereby the authorized common from 1,000,000 shares to 800,000 shares
3. Changing the authorized New Class B Common from 130,000,000 shares to 150,000,000 shares
4. Granting holders of New Class B Common the same voting rights and privileges as those enjoyed by holders of A stock—at one vote per share
5. Stipulating that 25 percent of the number of shares of common and New Class B Common represented at the necessary stockholders' meeting would constitute a quorum, and that the company's plan for the gradual retirement of Bylaw XII should not be eliminated or altered without the affirmative vote of the holders of at least two-thirds of the outstanding shares of common and New Class B Common entitled to vote (voting separately by classes)
6. Granting holders of common the option to exchange their stock on or before 31 March 1959 on the basis of 1¼ shares of New Class B Common for each share of common; and stipulating that, upon expiration of the exchange option, each share of common remaining unexchanged should be reclassified into 1 share of New Class B Common

Obviously this move was entirely equitable, because all holders of common stock would receive 1¼ shares of New Class B Common for each share of common. Obviously, too, the voting arrangements prepared for the stockholders were virtually unbeatable.

This ingenious plan had other advantages. It eliminated the Retirement and Insurance Investment Fund and its related reserves. It extended voting rights to all holders of common stock "in line with the trend of recent years, particularly by corporations having securities listed on the New York Stock Exchange." By reclassifying the 200,000 shares of common stock held by the company into 200,000 shares of New Class B Common Stock there were sufficient shares of that class for use in exchange—in fact, the exact number needed. The plan also furnished an incentive for hastening the exchange, because failure to do so would involve a loss of one share for every four held in common stock. Of most importance perhaps was the provision for the *gradual* elimination of Bylaw XII. In 1948 1,769 officers and employees participated in a total payment of $2,370,104; many of them had invested most of their resources in common stock on which they relied for maintaining their standards of living. Had Bylaw XII been eliminated immediately, morale would have suffered. Accordingly, the amount provided for participation under Bylaw XII stood at 10 percent (full schedule) in 1949, 9 percent in 1950, and so on down to 1 percent in 1958, with none for any year thereafter.[71] This method of eliminating Bylaw XII proved effective and a different type of profit sharing (to be discussed in the next chapter) was eventually adopted.

Though elimination of common, or A stock, may have been regarded as final on 29 June 1949, when the amendment to the certificate of incorporation was adopted by the stockholders, there was still much work left for William J. Conrad, Jr., secretary of the company, in locating and persuading owners to make the exchange. His most persuasive letters emphasizing the additional profits to be obtained by the exchange for New Class B Common Stock often failed to produce results. For example, Colonel Thomas W. S. Phillips of Shadow Lake, Ossining, New York, replied on 10 June 1955: "Some years ago I turned in all of our old stock except sixty shares. These I kept for sentimental reasons as they were part of our original holdings of the old A. T. Co. break up. . . . For the same reasons I would like to retain them. . . . The number of shares is so small I know you won't be inconvenienced by my action." Conrad tried again, but on 29 December 1955 Colonel Phillips asserted: "The sentimental reason still prevails and evidently under our present tax laws Uncle Sam would be the beneficiary of most of the gain." Actually the exchange involved no taxation and Phillips would have lost nothing but his sentimental memento. Then early in February 1959, largely as a favor to Conrad, he sent in his stock certificates from the breakup "of the old A. T. Co."[72]

With others Conrad adopted a different technique in 1956, by calling attention to the new quarterly dividends due on 5 June on both classes of common stock. In 1958, he began working through the sales department to locate holders of the few shares that had not been exchanged. Finally, on 2 June 1959 he was able to write Alexander Polk English (25 April 1903–8 April 1963), department manager then stationed in St. Louis: "The New York Bank [The Chase Manhattan] has now informed us that the certificate [of Ralph Evans] has been received and we are delighted at this favorable turn in our efforts to get rid of the only two shares of the old common stock in the United States which have not been exchanged."[73]

Thus ended the life of common A—the instrument that had served so well in removing control of the R. J. Reynolds Tobacco Company from the stockholders of the old American Tobacco Company. It is not unlikely that H. Henry Ramm, who joined the Reynolds legal department on 1 January 1946 and became a director on 2 April of the same year, was hired to help eliminate Bylaw XII and broaden the company's corporate structure. He, of course, did much of the work connected with issuing Preferred Stock 4.50% series. Ramm came from the firm of Davis, Polk, Wardwell, Sunderland, and Kiendl, "counsel for the company, and representative of the New York Stock Exchange"—a firm retained by Reynolds at least as early as 27 September 1948 and possibly in 1945. Its senior partner, Leighton H. Coleman, became a director of the Reynolds company on 23 March 1959.[74]

Notwithstanding the gradual elimination of Bylaw XII and the years of paying income and excess profits taxes without deducting participation payments as business expenses, the company in 1950 petitioned the United States Court of Claims for the recovery of $8,352,851.83 plus interest. This, according to Reynolds, represented taxes improperly assessed from 1940 to 1948 inclusive. The question at issue was whether participation payments, which accrued in proportion to an employee's stockholdings, constituted compensation and were therefore deductible in arriving at the company's taxable income. One item that loomed large against allowing this claim was the allowance of participation payments to employees of the Glenn Tobacco Company, a subsidiary of the company, to which the bylaw made no reference. Judges in the Court of Claims noted two acknowledged imperfections in the functioning of Bylaw XII: some employees acquired too much stock and others not enough. Apparently the company's claims rested on a decision of the Deputy Commissioner of Internal Revenue late in 1949 that payments made under the bylaw constituted compensation for personal service. This ruling, however, was revoked after the suit was brought on the grounds that changes in Bylaw XII in 1949 were not material to the question. In the opinion the judges also referred to a tax court decision rendered on 6 July 1956, in which that court had held that bylaw payments for 1949 and 1950 were reasonable compensation and devised a formula for determining what part of the payments represented reasonable compensation. This decision, however, rested on a different bylaw and on a different record for different years. In conclusion, the claims court ruled that payments from 1940 to 1948 under Bylaw XII "were preferential dividends and not compensation such as would be deductible under the Revenue Code of 1939."[75]

The Cavalier Cigarette

Despite serious labor troubles, war shortages, extensive litigation, and financial worries, the company introduced a new cigarette in 1949. Near the beginning of the decade a number of Reynolds officials, "who were then in financial difficulties," were forced to borrow extensively from one of the daughters of R. J. Reynolds. Had they not done so, they very likely would have been forced to flood the market with Reynolds stock and thus depreciate its value.[76] Early in 1944, the company began making additions to its capital by selling debentures, by issuing new stock, and by borrowing heavily.[77] Undoubtedly funds were needed for new machinery, new buildings, the installation of SPD (strip preparation) units, and the increased cost of leaf leading to greater inventory values. Moreover, by 1949 the top leadership of the company was no longer young. The new cigarette was thus developed from a background of general discouragement.

Because of its colossal failure, however, the Cavalier cigarette deserves special consideration. Actually, when first marketed in 1949, the Cavalier was made strictly of bright, flue-cured tobacco and differed little from the old Reyno except that the Cavalier was king size. The Reyno, it will be recalled, was also a failure, although when it came out there was ample precedent for its production. More surprising is the fact that the Reyno had been discarded or "suspended for the time being" on 9 September 1946.[78] Those in charge simply dropped one failure, turned around once, and picked up the same failure in far more expensive dress. According to many who took part in the production of the Cavalier, the idea had come from S. Clay Williams. After spending considerable time in Canada, he returned to Winston-Salem enthusiastic about the Player cigarette, which he had met in his travels. He insisted that the company develop a similar cigarette. Williams was chairman of the board in addition to being a lawyer but by his own admission not a tobacco man in the sense of understanding leaf qualities.[79] The Player, an English cigarette made exclusively of bright or flue-cured leaf, was manufactured with a higher moisture content than cigarettes produced in the United States. Furthermore, immediately after production, English cigarettes were placed in a drying room so that they emerged in a hardened condition. There was also confusing talk of the use of colonial tobaccos. As a result, the Cavalier was advertised as being made from "mild tobacco of the colonial type."

Puzzled employees entrusted with the production of the Cavalier knew nothing of colonial tobaccos and little of Player cigarettes, the company possessing only one frazzled package of that brand. Accordingly Charles B. Wade, Jr., sent a friend to a special tobacco counter in the Washington Duke Hotel in Durham for a carton of Players. How much help this provided is not known, but when Robert E. Lasater sniffed the shredded leaf ready for making a trial run of Cavaliers, he pronounced it a winner. On the other hand, when John V. Hunter, Jr., told another director that it would be a failure, he received a stern lecture on the respect due directors.[80] Later the directors acknowledged the correctness of Hunter's view by changing the formula of the Cavalier.[81] The new formula made it into a cigarette of excellent quality, although this did nothing to alleviate the reputation that it had acquired earlier. Reportedly, the name Cavalier was suggested by James W. Glenn in order to emphasize the illusion of the use of tobacco typical of that produced in Virginia in the seventeenth century after that colony was supposedly made aristocratic by the influx of refugees from the reforms of Oliver Cromwell.[82] Some believed, however, that the name came from S. Clay Williams in memory of his days as a law student at the University of Virginia.

The Cavalier was first announced to the public on 4 March 1949. A few were made on 16 February and again on the twenty-second. Six days later, with four Molins cigarette machines and two packing machines built by the American Machine and Foundry Company, the making and packing of Cavaliers began in factory Number 1 on a production basis. On the afternoon of 3 March all employees received one package of the new cigarettes along with a statement that, after experimentation with different blends and much thought on the part of all the officers of the company, it had been decided to market a king-size cigarette not intended to compete with the Camel. Rather, it was designed to obtain additional business from those not then smoking Camels. According to the press the next morning, the Cavalier was to be tested only in certain areas. The Winston-Salem morning paper concluded that the Cavalier was a distinguished cigarette— apparently because the company had for many years manufactured only one brand of any marked significance.[83]

Judging from the energy exhibited by the sales department, there must have been great enthusiasm for making a success of the Cavalier. Possibly no Reynolds product has ever been introduced with so much hoopla and fanfare. At this time, of course, there were few king-size cigarettes,[84] but size is not the only important factor in marketing a new cigarette. Introduced first into Pawtucket and Providence, Rhode Island, the Cavalier, it was claimed, soon had complete distribution not only in Providence but also in Peoria and Miami. Supposedly distribution approached the 100 percent mark in San Francisco, Tampa, Flint, and Albany during the first week in April. At this time the sales department declared that methods of sale were purposely varied from city to city in order to find "the one best way which we can use in cities throughout the country."[85]

During the third week of April 1949, Charles J. Webster wrote that Reynolds salesmen were "using bold street spectacles" and advertising of all kinds in "more than ordinary promotions" of the new king-size brand. Webster then noted parades by "Cavaliercades." These involved salesmen dressed as seventeenth-century cavaliers, pretty young women in cars decorated in red and white to symbolize the Cavalier package, loud speakers, resounding automobile horns, and ceremonies with mayors presenting the keys of cities to the particular Cavalier in charge.[86] Edward F. Reid, a Reynolds salesman dressed in the Cavalier's costume, headed a twenty-car parade that conducted brief ceremonies on the steps of the city hall of Buffalo and then rode through Buffalo, Kenmore, Tonawanda, and Niagara Falls.[87] The same type of parade was engineered in Syracuse and Boston, where the first carton of Cavaliers to enter that area was presented to the flamboyant Mayor James M. Curley.[88] In June 1949 Robert C. O'Bannon (7 April 1890–12 December 1958), department sales manager in San Francisco, promoted a forty-one-car parade down Market Street where one week earlier residents had received post cards entitling them to two packages of Cavalier cigarettes for the price of one.[89] The expensive advertising campaign continued throughout the nation until March 1950, when officials of the company declared that Reynolds salesmen had made the country Cavalier-conscious. Continuing in this vein, they summed up the high-pressure advertising of the Cavalier most aptly: "The Cavaliercades are parading through the main streets of small cities and towns, led by a car equipped with a loud speaker from which comes Cavalier advertising set to music. Of course, in this lead car rides a salesman dressed in authentic Cavalier costume, complete with sword. They are still being interviewed over the radio, and continue to get free advertising newspaper stories about the parades."[90]

Two years later Vaughn W. Miller, sales manager in the Sacramento Valley, was still calling on the tobacco trade with an assistant dressed as "Mr. Cavalier."[91]

In 1953, possibly in recognition of the sad facts before them, Reynolds executives permitted the bargain sale of Cavaliers in oval tins of one hundred each for seventy-nine cents—a saving to the consumer of about eight cents per package. Sales officials declared, however, that this special price was a promotional scheme and not a new price policy. Supposedly these tins were available only on the basis of one to a customer. Rumors that this change meant a possible price war in cigarettes were quickly allayed by other companies, the American Tobacco Company stating that it had earlier done the same with Lucky Strikes and only felt an interest in the results of the outmoded use of tins for packing cigarettes. Actually what the buyer saved was the amount of the federal taxes, the eight cents corresponding to the excise tax on a pack of Cavaliers. This the company absorbed.[92]

Some feel that the efforts of radio and television comedian Garry Moore accounted for the greater part of Cavalier sales. By February 1955, however, the advertising department switched its commercials with Garry Moore and "I've Got a Secret" from Cavaliers to Winstons, which were then one of the fastest moving brands in the nation. According to a sober statement in the *Management Bulletin*, the Cavalier continued to have support on radio and television by taking over spots previously allocated to Winstons; this switch gave the Cavalier an opportunity to reach new audiences,[93] or more properly speaking it gave Winstons the favored spot formerly held by Cavaliers. Still undaunted, the company late in 1955 encased its Cavaliers in a bright new package and acknowledged a change in the blend,[94] which undoubtedly had been in process for some time.

Earlier, however, employees in the R. J. Reynolds office building had tacitly acknowledged the futility of promoting the Cavalier. When Betty Simms, a clerk accountant and the company's chief practical joker, went to the Lasater Building in search of recent records, she chanced to see some abandoned Cavalier costumes. Unable to restrain her impulse, she appropriated a costume and retired to the chapel to don the outfit. She then entered the industrial engineering department with drawn sword and bare feet to the amusement of the employees present. Though the story of this uncavalierly behavior soon reached the nineteenth floor, only laughter greeted the account of Miss Simms's interpretation of the Cavalier's role in the company. It is generally acknowledged that everything connected with the Cavalier was done wrong. Possibly this unfortunate experience constituted a valuable lesson, though an expensive one indeed as the sad career of the Cavalier represented the loss of some $30 million for Reynolds. It was soon succeeded by the filter-tipped Winston—an astonishing success from the start and a remarkable comeback for the company.

CHAPTER 13

Preparation for Expansion, 1945–1954

Labor disputes of the 1940s; shortages of manpower and materials during World War II; and changes in leadership, in the type of cigarette demanded by the public, and in sales methods all prompted a reexamination of company policies. Predominant among these changes were the organization and subsequent expansion of the personnel department and the consequent development of innovative personnel programs. During the same period a lively movement in the sales department resulted in the publication of the *Reynolds Tobacco Merchandiser*, which for sales served much as the *Management Bulletin* did for manufacturing. Two notable technical developments—the SPD (strip preparation) process and reconstituted leaf—likewise were important factors in stimulating the company's tremendous expansion of the 1950s.

The New Personnel Department

The gradual development and expansion of the personnel department resulted from changes begun in 1919. The employment department, the medical department, the Safety Council, and the Retirement and Insurance Plan thus formed the nucleus for the new venture. Over time it would also administer a job evaluation plan; a safety department to supplement the work of the Safety Council; the communications media; an employee suggestion plan; the work of a pastor-counselor; and company benefits including vacations with pay, allowances for those in the armed services, paid holidays, sick leave, free parking for employees, cafeterias, an aid-to-education plan, recognition for length of service, and the second profit-sharing plan.

Establishment of the new personnel department apparently did not come easily. On 12 July 1945, after the directors held a lengthy discussion on the advisability of such a move to improve personnel, industrial, and public relations, Roy C. Haberkern proposed that a committee be appointed to study the matter. Accordingly John C. Whitaker (chairman), Frederick S. Hill, William T. Smither, James A. Gray, and P. Frank Hanes were assigned to the task.[1] Their work culminated on 13 April 1948 in the creation of a Personnel Committee consisting of Hanes (chairman), Whitaker, Hill, and Bowman Gray, Jr. Two years later its membership included the same individuals except for the addition of Spencer B. Hanes, Jr., and the substitution of William J. Conrad, Jr., for Whitaker. On 6 April 1951 the committee consisted of P. Frank Hanes (chairman), Bowman Gray, Jr., Spencer B. Hanes, Jr., William J. Conrad, Jr., and Alexander H. Galloway.[2] These were the directors who supervised the development of the personnel department.

A few months after creating the Personnel Committee, the directors determined its responsibilities and jurisdiction. The seriousness with which the action was taken is reflected in the minutes—the preliminary remarks about this allocation of power before the resolution was introduced and the "full discussion" that followed. The first direct reference to a personnel department, as such, appeared in the resolution. With adoption of the directors' resolution, the Personnel Committee was charged with the following:[3]

1. Forming "a close co-operative relationship" with all departments of the company
2. Studying the work and personnel problems of every department
3. Consulting with the head of the personnel department and reporting to the board of directors on the work of all departments, particularly with respect to the adequacy of the staffs
4. Submitting recommendations to the directors on the staff of the personnel department
5. Making surveys and studies of the adequacy of the staffs of all departments
6. Recommending the advancement, succession, and retirement of all employees in line with current needs and expected growth of the company
7. Having the head of the personnel department arrange for the Personnel Committee and others concerned to meet with prospective and promising college graduates regarding their potential employment

8. Seeing that some of these qualified graduates were employed for work and training
9. Transferring frequently, as appropriate, developing employees to other departments for further training
10. Overseeing personnel matters of the company in view of current needs and expansion
11. Maintaining full jurisdiction over the new personnel department subject only to the final authority of the directors

On 9 September 1948, the Personnel Committee was given the authority to recommend retirements under the Employees' Retirement Plan when in the best interests of the company.[4] These moves vested great power in the Personnel Committee and, through it, in the personnel department.

Meanwhile, it appears that no one had been appointed to direct the personnel department referred to in the resolution. On 10 February 1949, the directors announced that the position of Charles B. Wade, Jr., as assistant to the superintendent of manufacturing had been terminated by his appointment on 24 January 1948 as administrative secretary to the Personnel Committee.[5] At the meeting of the board on 14 April 1949, however, it became evident that Wade was the first head of the newly formed personnel department. In implementing the resolution of 24 January 1948, the directors on the recommendation of the Personnel Committee decided that the administrative secretary of the Personnel Committee would supervise the personnel department. This included recruiting, hiring, placing, and training employees; classifying and evaluating jobs; supervising wages and salaries; handling employee relations and benefit plans; developing a system of personnel procedures and instructions; supervising employee information, which also embraced the printed media; developing personnel statistics and a personnel research library; and overseeing the work of the medical and safety departments.[6] On 14 December 1950, the board relinquished control over paid vacations and jury service for employees to the Personnel Committee.[7]

The importance of the new department is indicated by the composition of the Personnel Committee thereafter. On 11 April 1958, for example, it included Edward A. Darr (chairman), who had already served as president of the company and at that time was chairman of the Executive Committee; Bowman Gray, Jr., president of the company; Alexander H. Galloway, treasurer; Haddon S. Kirk, executive vice-president in charge of manufacturing; Spencer B. Hanes, Jr., superintendent of leaf buying; and Charles B. Wade, Jr., supervisor of the personnel department. The committee supervising insurance and hospitalization also worked closely with the personnel department. Members of that committee included William J. Conrad, Jr., (chairman), vice-president and secretary; H. Henry Ramm, vice-president and head of the legal department; Colin Stokes, superintendent of manufacturing; and Charles B. Wade, Jr.[8]

The company became interested in a job evaluation plan in 1945 simultaneously with its first move to develop a personnel department. Different conceptions and practices in different plants of the company had brought about a multiplicity of names for similar jobs. A year or two before the job evaluation plan was put into effect, there were in one department alone jobs to which as many as nineteen different wage rates were assigned, and later adjudged to be equivalent in common requirements and characteristics. Similar illustrations might be drawn from other departments. Such conditions, by no means unique in the R. J. Reynolds Tobacco Company, prevailed in varying degrees in all companies prior to the adoption of some formal plan. Job evaluation plans, though, had been prevalent in industrial organizations to some extent since the early 1920s. Actually a job classification scheme is usually prepared for the purpose of standardizing wage rates—evidently a move greatly needed in the Reynolds plants, especially during the labor disputes.

Work on the job evaluation plan apparently began in the late fall of 1945. Obviously many jobs were renamed and some order established before a job evaluation program could be undertaken. During the winter the company employed Ernst & Ernst, a firm of business consultants, to prepare a job evaluation program. Engineers of that firm spent several months working out the details with several Reynolds foremen, superintendents, and department managers. Consultation and review of the plans with representatives of different plant departments resulted in agreement as to the proper rating for all jobs.

The scheme adopted, known as the factor-point plan, involved the comparison of written job descriptions to determine the proper rank or position of each job. Based on ten labor grades and two specially rated jobs connected with the operation of the Arenco packer, the new plan was officially adopted as part of the company's wage structure on 29 May 1946. This work culminated in the establishment of a maximum and minimum pay rate for 230 jobs and the development of procedures for the program's implementation. Soon after this program went into effect for hourly paid workers, the company engaged Ernst & Ernst to develop and install a similar plan for its clerical employees. It was completed by January 1947, when the consulting firm made a final report to management. With minor exceptions, the steps taken for its installation resembled those used for hourly paid workers.[9] Until then administrative matters concerning the clerical force had been handled by Frederick S. Hill, treasurer of the company. He had, of course, through Robert D. Shore, inherited the task of supervising the office force from D. Rich to whom it was assigned early in the century because of the location of his office in Number 8.

Needless to say, the job evaluation plan was not self-perpetuating. When there was a substantial change in a job, when one became obsolete, or when a new one was created, many changes were made in records, descriptions of jobs, and schedules of rate increases. The job evaluation plan required an enormous amount of administrative and clerical work in its installation and continuation, the latter a designated responsibility of wage and salary administrators in the new personnel department. It was widely believed in the Reynolds office building that the company had instituted "Yankee" wages for employees in the factories but not for others. For that reason average hourly wage rates from 1935 to 1960 are of interest (see Table 13-1).[10]

Safety

Few projects of the personnel department, or indeed of any department, were more expertly handled in later years than safety education. The frequency and severity of injuries to employees received cursory attention for many years prior to the development of the modern safety department (or, more accurately, the safety division of the personnel department), which began on 19 May 1944 with the appointment of Wilford Graham Jones as safety engineer. But certainly as early as 1906 the matter of safety assumed some importance to Reynolds management. The company apparently had accident insurance with the Maryland Casualty Company as early as 1910, although this evidently had nothing to do with the prevention of accidents. The national safety movement, however, did not get underway until 1912. No organized effort was made to stress safety measures at the R. J. Reynolds Tobacco Company until 11 March 1929 when John C. Whitaker, then head of the employment department, organized the Safety Council. No doubt this step was prompted by the North Carolina Workmen's Compensation Act, which had just become law. In fact, the act received its final ratification on the same day the Safety Council was organized.[11]

The membership of the Safety Council was drawn from several divisions and departments, including the manufacturing, leaf processing, box shop, team and storage, medical, and legal departments. Charles V. Strickland became the first president and Haddon S. Kirk, the secretary, both serving until 8 December 1947. "Captain" Walter E. Gaines of the foil division, and later William F. Chambers of the smoking tobacco division, succeeded to Strickland's position. J. L. Putnam (chairman), Risden P. Reece, and George H. Little served on the first Inspection Committee, which regularly reported to the council. Thomas C. King (d. July 1945), a safety engineer representing the Maryland Casualty Company, also attended the monthly meetings. Over the years membership in the council increased

Table 13-1
Average Hourly Wage Rates Paid by the Reynolds Company, 1935–1960

Year	Rate	Year	Rate
1935	$.3688	1948	$1.0473
1936	.3845	1949	1.1370
1937	.4258	1950	1.1493
1938	.4617	1951	1.2205
1939	.4963	1952	1.2771
1940	.4925	1953	1.3468
1941	.5459	1954	1.4660
1942	.5954	1955	1.5288
1943	.5954	1956	1.6249
1944	.6294	1957	1.7017
1945	.6893	1958	1.7861
1946	.8407	1959	1.8543
1947	.9096	1960	1.9411

Source: Payroll department records, R. J. Reynolds Tobacco Company.
Note: Separate wages of leaf and seasonal workers were not available before 1950. Thus the table covers only the wage rates of hourly rated and piece workers; it does not include premium rates for overtime work that were received after full application of the Wages and Hours Act in 1941.

from 43 in 1929 to 129 in 1958, though the order of business remained virtually unchanged. From 1929 to 1944 the leading members included King, Putnam, William J. Fix, Sr., Dr. Edgar S. Thompson, Walter E. Gaines, Edgar E. Bumgardner, J. Paxton Davis, and P. Frank Hanes.

Regardless of regular meetings and enthusiastic reports, it does not appear that a great deal was accomplished by the Safety Council. Possibly this can be attributed to (1) failure of the company to hire a safety engineer who could work unharassed by other duties, (2) failure of the council to start a program of safety education in the plants, (3) failure of the council to interest foremen in safety education, and (4) lack of interest on the part of top management. When laying down the rules for promoting safety at a meeting of the council in February 1937, Whitaker gave first priority to the "(a)bsolute necessity of getting the ideas and information of these meetings back to foremen and employees." As a rule, the Inspection Committee looked into accidents, examined related factors, and then took the matter to the council where blame—perhaps unjustly—was duly placed on some foreman. This often made the foremen angry and bitter, at least in 1944, 1945, and 1946. The absentee rate was high, and coupled with the labor troubles of the 1940s, the situation could not be called a happy one. In addition, the Inspection Committee had no particular encouragement for building and installing guards, many of which were made of wood. J. L. Putnam, who evidently did most of the inspecting prior to 1939, was succeeded by W. E. Griffin, who resigned near 9 November 1943, and by W. E. Freel, who resigned at the meeting of April 1944. Moreover, officials of the company did not have a true picture of safety conditions because, at that time, there was a tendency to report only what top management wanted to hear.[12] Prior to 1944 the work of the Safety Council was, therefore, largely academic.

With the appointment of Wilford G. Jones as safety engineer in the early 1940s and the rise of younger men in management, the situation rapidly improved. Among those at the top who lent their assistance were John C. Whitaker, Haddon S. Kirk, Charles B. Wade, Jr., Spencer B. Hanes, Jr., Colin Stokes, and Alexander H. Galloway. Galloway, when assistant treasurer, became interested in safety from the standpoint of lowering insurance rates. Others viewed the rate and severity of accidents as a personnel problem affecting the attitude of the employees. In any case, after having had the backing of these men for ten years, Jones could proudly state that the accident frequency rate had declined significantly: in 1953, there were 1.8 accidents per million man hours at Reynolds, compared with 9.5 at the American Tobacco Company.[13] By way of comparison it is noteworthy that on 14 September 1936 Thomas C. King referred to figures provided by P. Frank Hanes "to show that R. J. R. Tob. Co. had the lowest cost of insurance of any tobacco company."

Jones's belief in his work as a vital part of human relations undoubtedly was of primary importance in the development of an outstanding safety department at Reynolds. Though he had no special training in safety (his field was construction both before and after joining the company in 1936), he immediately plunged into the promotion of preventive measures, spending much of his time in the plants. In July 1949 he planned schools for operators of fork-lift trucks. In April 1951 he held a meeting of the Safety Council on the basement floor of Number 1 Leaf House so that Charles Meecham could demonstrate the proper method for moving and stacking hogsheads and hogshead materials. In November of that year he complimented the guard crew for its excellent work in designing and installing safety measures. The safety department—with the special help of Haddon S. Kirk and the cooperation of the engineering department—had somehow created this squadron of eight or ten men who devoted all their time to producing and installing guards on machinery. Often they discarded safety devices installed by the manufacturer and replaced them with superior guards. On another occasion Jones praised Robert P. Watson, foreman at Number 1 Cutting and Drying, for his good work in an impromptu safety drill.

In October 1952 the Safety Council heard Julius H. Hart, a foreman in Number 4 Cutting and Casing, tell of a near accident on the tripper conveyor in the bulk room where James Thompson, a Negro employee, had saved the life of another worker by quick thinking. Thompson was then introduced by Edgar E. Bumgardner, who gave a history of his life and praised him highly for his action. This was a far cry from the days when foremen were blamed for unavoidable accidents.

The safety department reported in January 1955 that during the previous year 224 in-plant meetings had been held with a total attendance of 5,728 employees, the majority of whom participated in the discussions. In March Jones stressed the importance of safety practices near "our Hauni machines which cannot be guarded properly." In January 1958, however, he noted the excellence "of a preventive measure taken by installing a very simple guard . . . on (the) Max Hauni machines that will practically eliminate any further accidents at this point."[14]

Staff of the personnel department also took part in the safety program. In September 1954 Mildred Orell, as mistress of ceremonies, held a quiz program on safety measures; Mrs. Pauline Ziglar (of Number 9 Can), Foy Thompson (of Number 1 Cigarette), and Mrs. Brownie Cherry (of Number 256 Smoking) participated. In July 1956 Erwin W. Cook produced, directed, and presented to the Safety Council a play based on accidents taken from the files of the safety department. These various illustrations demonstrate Jones's ability to place others in the forefront and to actually touch the worker in the plant.

In efforts to lessen the accident rate both the Safety Council and the safety department cooperated closely with the North Carolina Department of Labor and the North Carolina Industrial Commission. Nor did the state labor agencies fail to check on the company's observation of the North Carolina Workmen's Compensation Act and its various amendments. For example, after completing his inspection of the Reynolds plants near the end of 1937, an official of the North Carolina Labor Department declared the company to have "the best spirit of good-housekeeping of any plant in N.C."[15] In December of the following year, however, an agent of the Labor Department's inspection and rating bureau was "critical of some of our toilets and dressing rooms and passageways and the conditions therein." Perhaps one result of the company's cooperation with the state labor agencies may be seen in its record for injuries at the end of 1959, which was 80 percent better than that of industry generally and 71 percent better than that of the tobacco industry.

Under Jones's leadership the company's concern for safety on the job

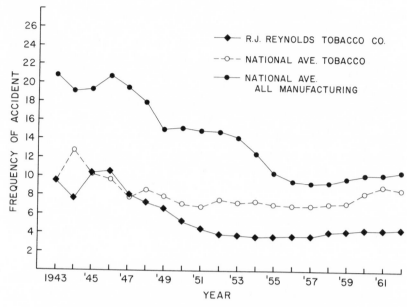

Accident Frequency for the Reynolds Company,
the Entire Tobacco Industry, and All American Manufacturers,
1943–1962

was also presented to office employees, who may have been surprised by the statement that office work was more dangerous than work in an electric power plant. They were also given a list of fourteen common causes for injuries to office workers compiled by the National Safety Council. Later in the same year Jones found another hazard—the use of ether for cleaning typewriters. Fearing ignition of the ether from a spark of static electricity created when nylon materials were rubbed together, he ordered that tetrachloride be used instead.[16]

Numerous awards and citations attest to the excellence of the safety program. In 1951 the Maryland Casualty Company presented Reynolds with a silver plaque for its "most extraordinary" safety record—a 71 percent decrease in accidents from 1945 to 1950. In the presentation, Duke C. Dorney, Jr., vice-president of the insurance company, credited individuals all the way down the line, starting with management—the spark, he declared, that gave the program vitality. Singled out for special praise was P. Frank Hanes, vice-president and chairman of the Personnel Committee, who had long promoted safety in the plants and among the drivers of the company's vehicles. Dorney also recognized the drivers themselves; they had been urged to observe safety regulations since 1929 by J. Paxton

Davis. In response to Dorney's remarks, John Whitaker referred to the five years in which more than 99 percent of all employees had maintained perfect safety records.[17] The work of Davis and his successors culminated in another award from the Maryland Casualty Company in 1952. Sixty-eight employees in the truck and storage department had driven a combined distance of 7 million miles without an accident. Again, P. Frank Hanes received special credit for this achievement but so did four truck drivers— Robert E. Reno, Elmer L. Allen, Gilbert C. Parnell, and Henry (or Joe) E. White—who together had driven 91 years (a distance equivalent to 21 trips around the globe) without a single accident.[18] Finally, in 1956 the National Safety Council announced two separate awards to the Reynolds company for its contributions to highway and traffic safety in 1955, one the Alfred P. Sloan Award and the other from the National Safety Council.[19] Many other awards and impressive records on the highway are cited in the *Reynolds Tobacco Merchandiser*, a bulletin sent to a troop of salesmen scattered over the nation.

Despite these records Wilford Jones saw no reason for complacency. In 1950 he predicted that accidents would become more severe throughout industry as the speed of machinery increased. He expressed a similar concern in 1952, though in 1953 he conceded that there had been fewer accidents and lessened severity in November than for the same month in 1952.[20] Supervisors, who had also learned to worry about accidents, asked why the rate of accidents was so high in August 1949. Jones gave his reply: the sultry weather, thoughts of vacations just passed or still to come, substitute supervisors, heavy overtime work, the employment of several hundred seasonal workers, and quite possibly a dangerous feeling of self-satisfaction after six or eight months without accidents.[21]

As a result of its improved safety record, the R. J. Reynolds Tobacco Company in 1958 adopted a retrospective rating program of insurance whereby the actual cost of losses from accidents, subject to a maximum and minimum premium, was included in the final premium at the end of the policy year. This, of course, enlarged the duties and responsibilities of Wilford Jones, who then began to handle "the claims of all Company employees throughout the United States."[22]

Communications

Just as in the development of an effective safety program, a more satisfactory method of communication between top management and supervisors was devised almost concurrently with the organization and expansion of the personnel department. This move began in 1946. Previously management had communicated with supervisors through special or occasional letters, but no real system had been developed. Usually the individuals responsible for sending these letters did not have a list of the supervisors and were forced to compile a new one each time a letter went out. With the appearance of the *Management Bulletin*, however, this haphazard method of communication ceased.

Like the new personnel department, a method for keeping the supervisory force (superintendents and foremen) conversant with company policy developed directly from the labor troubles of the 1940s. Incorporated in the change was the philosophy of John C. Whitaker, who believed that, in the eyes of employees, the foreman occupied perhaps the most important position in the company. This conviction, combined with the ideas of Charles B. Wade, Jr., fresh from a tour of duty with the armed forces, produced the *Management Information Bulletin*. As Whitaker explained in the first issue of 28 August 1946:

> For some time we have felt that you needed a larger share of the information of events and Company policy than you have been getting. The first requirement of a good supervisor or a manager is that he have good information. For this reason we will publish this bulletin as often as we have material for it. It will contain news of Company policy changes and other matters of help and interest to you.

On 16 July 1952 the bulletin began to appear under the shortened title *Management Bulletin* "in order to lighten the page and provide a more balanced layout" and no doubt also to eliminate redundancy.

It was Charles B. Wade, Jr., who, recalling the appearance of daily orders in the army, suggested the format: a single sheet, 8½ by 11 inches, or more as the situation demanded. Apparently he felt that the bulletin should be published only as needed, whereas Whitaker at first favored its regular appearance with the use of moralistic statements for inspiration and probably also for filler. Apparently Wade recommended the coding which indicated that some items might be freely discussed and others not. Though the coding continued to be used through the years, it was generally considered unnecessary. Actually Whitaker, high in management, gave the idea of a communications medium the necessary push and Wade devised the mechanics and played down the excessive use of moralistic copy.[23]

At first production of the *Management Bulletin* was largely a cooperative effort between the evolving personnel department and the print shop. Until 1952 all production facilities operated under the sales department and were limited to offset printing machines and two mimeograph machines. Thereafter, however, the print shop was greatly improved by the addition of better machinery, including a Harris printing press, and by the employment of full-time photographers. Purchase of the Harris press was long delayed for fear that local professional printers would object, as its acquisi-

tion represented a step toward professional printing. Just before these
moves the print shop was placed under the personnel department.

After 1952 the *Management Bulletin* was usually the responsibility of
one person. Wade as first editor could not devote all of his time to it and
Dell McKeithan, the second editor, became discouraged at not being able
to secure equipment necessary for expansion and improvement. Upon her
resignation Erwin W. Cook became editor, serving until succeeded by
Richard L. Dilworth in November 1959. Cook's term coincided with the
shift of the print shop to the personnel department, the employment of
photographers, and the acquisition of improved machinery.

The bulletin also experienced changes in format. It was made more read-
able in July 1949 when the first full-page lines were divided into three columns. Five weeks later the format changed again—this time to two columns. The same crowded page with little space between the lines was
continued until 1953. Similar changes may be seen from the size of the
first volume of issues extending from 28 August 1946 to 21 December
1948, evidently being closed at that point because of its excessive bulki-
ness. The second volume also covered two years, ending on 27 December
1950. In 1951, however, the editor found his bearings and the *Management Bulletin* began appearing at the rate of one volume per calendar year.
Actually its physical appearance improved with the expansion of the personnel department.

Examination of the *Management Bulletin* reveals that the labor problem
was the chief spark for its beginning. Included in the first volume are items
on a sit-down strike at Number 60 on 23 August, the wave of slowdowns
in industry nationwide, the necessity of carefully guarding gates, absenteeism, the excessive amount of time spent in toilets by employees, and the
importance of avoiding discussion of excusing employees for union meetings and personnel problems within the hearing of shop stewards. The issue for 12 December 1946 contained an item concerning a request of the
union that the company publish the Wage and Job Evaluation Supplement
to the contract and the decision to assign supervisors responsibility for job
descriptions, prices for various jobs, the automatic progression schedule,
and labor grades. On 11 April 1947, just before the Communist exposé,
the entire bulletin was devoted to contract negotiations and union demands. Coverage of labor problems continued until about mid-June 1947.
By that time, the *Management Bulletin*, well on its way, began to carry
countless items concerning company operations.

The *Management Bulletin* became an important unifying force, perhaps
second only to the profit-sharing plan. It was promptly read when delivered and often quoted in conversation. Apparently it was the only publication of its kind in the tobacco industry. In tobacco circles it was rumored
that both the American Tobacco Company and Liggett and Myers issued

to all employees a publication as an advertising device. On the other hand, the monthly *Call* of Philip Morris—sent to each employee—had somewhat broader coverage. Judging from issues for October 1954 and spring 1963, the *Call* at first was a "slick" piece, heavily illustrated and containing about eighteen pages depicting its products, advertising agency, college program, and production engineering department; the opening of its new green-leaf stemmery in Richmond and related items; and snapshots of employees on vacation. Most likely its format and content were dreamed up by an advertising agency. By 1963, however, the *Call* had become a quarterly not quite so "slick" but still generously illustrated. By contrast, the Reynolds *Management Bulletin* appeared four times in October 1954 and covered such diverse topics as the promotions of Charles W. Kirk and Jesse S. Davis, the importance of Fire Prevention Week, the winners of awards for valuable suggestions, the United Fund campaign, a memorial to the late Fred P. Flynt, service award ceremonies, Winston cigarettes, the suggestion of the month, characteristics of a good supervisor, work procedure for election day; it also included extensive news on plant safety records and a very modest amount of filler. Many of these items were liberally illustrated. All of the information could be discussed freely and, according to the philosophy behind the *Management Bulletin*, much of it was immediately passed on to employees.

Another Reynolds publication designed to draw employees closer to the company—*News for Leaf Department Men*—was put out by the personnel department. Its format resembled that of the *Management Bulletin*, though it appeared less frequently. Reportedly, the first issue—for May 1955—would have been dated earlier had Herbert Noell Hardy (b. 2 March 1894), vice-president in charge of leaf buying, taken more interest in the project.[24] According to Hardy's letter in that issue, the purpose of the news sheet was to keep leaf buyers "informed about events taking place here at the home office in Winston-Salem and wherever happenings take place that concern you and your Company," although it would also include general information about the Reynolds company. But there would be no set publication date. Much of the information came from the *Management Bulletin*; in fact, the sheet was edited first by Erwin W. Cook and later by Richard L. Dilworth, both editors of the *Management Bulletin*. Later, however, leaf department officials in the home office cooperated with the editor by submitting news items and proofreading the copy. Indeed, they began to prod the editor for more issues than he could easily handle.

The contents of *News for Leaf Department Men* appeared much as Hardy's announcement had indicated. After the first issue it was liberally illustrated. Unlike the *Reynolds Tobacco Merchandiser*, however, it carried no news of the buyers themselves, perhaps because of their greater mobility made necessary by leaf sales in several areas and a vacation period during off-season. It was generally believed in the home office that the publication served as an unusually strong unifying influence. Indeed, it is difficult to visualize any other practical means for satisfactorily cementing the interests of the leaf buyers with those of the company. No doubt, in many instances this bulletin also was of great value in informing leaf buyers of changes in regulations that affected them personally—for example, the new profit-sharing plan, which was carefully explained in the issue for 20 May 1957; changes made by the Internal Revenue Service in reporting travel expenses; the new comprehensive medical plan for all employees; changes in regulations for expense accounts; and requests for additional personnel information from the leaf buyers. In addition to items of direct personal interest to the buyers, *News for Leaf Department Men* provided abundant information about plant expansion, changes in management, and annual meetings of supervisors. The issue for 19 March 1957 contained one discordant note, political in nature, found also in the *Management Bulletin* but not in the *Reynolds Tobacco Merchandiser*. This item, which appeared under the signature of Herbert N. Hardy, though it was not necessarily written by him, lambasted the "[e]xcessive spending" and the "greater centralization of power in Washington" as threats to the nation and urged buyers to write their congressmen and senators to demand "a drastic cut in the enormous budget proposed by the Administration." Whatever the source and whoever the author, this appeal represented the standard cry of industry leaders.

In the final analysis, however, no project of the modern personnel department developed at a slower pace than *News for Leaf Department Men*. Perhaps the reluctance of officials in the higher echelons of the leaf department to support a modern communication system could be attributed to the semi-independent nature of their calling. In the earlier years of the auction sales system, the buyers, generally surrounded by admiring farmers and operators of auction sales warehouses, were often independent men-about-town who felt little need to communicate with management back in the home office. A brief analysis of the *News for Leaf Department Men* from 1955 through 1960 shows no real progress until Hardy's retirement on 1 August 1959. Members of the personnel department charged with establishing a community of interest between the company and the leaf buyers succeeded in publishing one issue in 1955 but failed to produce even that the following year. Copy for several issues awaited approval in the leaf department until it was outdated and useless for publication. Seven issues appeared in 1957 and eight in 1958.

On 2 November 1959 a new management team took over the leaf buying department: Daniel Rice Allen as manager, Fenton Drewry Royster as assistant manager, and William Stuart Leake and Cecil Roy Hatton as general leaf supervisors. At the same time, Walter Randall Rierson and

William Edward Atkinson, Jr., became supervisors of leaf buying. In addition, that year Erwin W. Cook of the personnel department conferred with several leaf buyers from the field to determine whether leaf men had any desire for news of the company. They proved to be highly interested in the publication.[25] As a result *News for Leaf Department Men* began to appear more frequently.

Not all the blame for the earlier reluctance to support the news sheet should be placed on Hardy, however. It was a new venture and Hardy, who joined the company in 1915,[26] had been a successful leaf man thoroughly devoted to the interests of the company. No doubt his difficulty lay in realizing the immensity of the company's operations in comparison with earlier years.

Employee Suggestion Plan

As part of its effort to expand and enhance the personnel department, the company adopted a suggestion plan for employees in late 1953. It was the first major tobacco manufacturer to do so. The move was sponsored by John C. Whitaker, who had been interested in improving employee relations since 1918, if not before. It is probable that a suggestion system would have been developed earlier had Whitaker been able to interest the higher ranks of management. Yet the idea had been considered as early as 1944, undoubtedly prompted by the labor disputes of that period and by the need for expanded production during the war. Many manufacturing firms had been using suggestion systems for some time, the earliest apparently dating back to the 1880s.

On Whitaker's order, preliminary work on the plan was undertaken from 1944 to 1950, though little could be done before 1946 because of the war. Specifically, Charles B. Wade, Jr., and Gordon Marshall Black conducted a survey of various companies using suggestion plans to determine the problems and benefits experienced. Among the many questions investigated were the following: interest of employees, measurable results in terms of gain for the company, availability of the plan to employees, anonymity of the suggester, difficulties that might be connected with a recent ruling of the Wage-Hour Administrator concerning the time spent on suggestions outside of working hours, a filing system, improvements made by personnel in the line of duty and later discovered to have been suggested by employees, participation of semisupervisory personnel, the length of time for keeping rejected ideas in files, and the minimum and maximum amount of awards.[27] The results of the survey were tabulated and presented to the company's Personnel Committee, then consisting of P. Frank

Hanes (chairman), Bowman Gray, Jr., Frederick S. Hill, William J. Conrad, Jr., and Spencer B. Hanes, Jr.

Except for a question raised by a stockholder at the annual meeting in April 1953, no mention of the suggestion plan appears in the minutes from 1 May 1950 until 25 November 1953, when it was adopted by the directors.[28] No doubt Whitaker's elevation to chairman of the board on 5 November 1952 expedited the action.

The detailed resolution establishing the plan gave as its main objectives "the encouragement of employees whose normal functions do not include planning or determining upon methods and means for increasing profitable operations of Company, particularly non-executive, non-administrative and non-professional employees." Specific categories of employees were exempted from participation and awards for any one suggestion were limited to $5,000. The resolution also called for a committee of five directors to act on behalf of the board in formulating, administering, and, on occasion, revising the plan. The committee was empowered to determine the amount of awards and to secure expert advice from other sources in considering the value of suggestions. On the first Suggestion Plan Committee were Alexander H. Galloway (chairman), Haddon S. Kirk, Spencer B. Hanes, Jr., William R. Lybrook, and Kenneth H. Hoover; Charles B. Wade, Jr., served as secretary. The second committee, appointed on 14 March 1957, had wide administrative authority; it consisted of William R. Lybrook (chairman), Colin Stokes, Robert W. Newsom, Jr., Edgar E. Bumgardner, and Charles W. Kirk.

Promptly on 29 November 1953, Wade, as secretary of the Suggestion Plan Committee, assembled a group known as the Suggestion Plan Unit to help Wade develop and organize the plan; its members were Christopher J. Daye, Harry H. Horton, Jr., and John T. Brandon. On the following day the Suggestion Plan Unit submitted to Chairman Galloway for his committee's review a list of practical items relating to the plan's organization—personnel and equipment, office space, ideas for suggestion boxes, bulletin boards, posters, and the like. Also included were proposals for introducing the plan to management, supervisors, and employees generally. Equally as promptly the group, from 1 to 10 December, submitted five reports on the plan's administration. From this work a leaflet was developed for presentation to all employees. It was designed to stimulate ideas most likely to produce suggestions of value, including:

1. Elimination of waste in materials and time
2. Reduction in cost of an operation
3. Reduction in time of an operation
4. Reduction in the amount of rejected work
5. Conservation of materials and supplies

6. Prevention of or reduction in wear or machinery
7. Improvement of machinery, equipment, tools, or fixtures
8. Improvement in methods of manufacture, or office procedure
9. Improvement in storage, packing, and shipping methods
10. Reclamation of materials and supplies

The leaflet and suggestion blanks necessary for administration of the plan were ready by 25 January 1954. The Suggestion Plan Unit also prepared an elaborate subject classification code.

Extreme pains were taken to introduce employees to the plan. Perhaps as important as any phase of the developmental process was the careful outlining of a method for informing supervisors. According to recommendations of the Suggestion Plan Unit, the plan was presented at the annual luncheon meeting of supervisors on 12 February 1954. In addition, all the supervisors met in small groups from 15 to 17 February for the purpose of having "every phase of the plan" explained so they in turn might explain it "to [the] employees." At least one member of the Suggestion Plan Committee attended each of these group meetings. At the annual luncheon Charles Wade emphasized the importance of the plan "in the development of better employee relations" when urging "that the supervisors . . . encourage employees . . . to express their ideas on paper and submit them." Moreover, he stated, many employees had valuable ideas. Further information on the plan appeared in the *Management Bulletin* for 12 February. On 18 February all employees received an explanatory leaflet, a suggestion blank, and a letter signed by John C. Whitaker, chairman of the board, and Edward A. Darr, president, announcing that the plan would begin on 1 March. Another detailed analysis of the plan, in the form of questions and answers, was included in the *Management Bulletin* for 2 March.[29]

Administration of the employee suggestion plan proved unusually successful. A statistical summary of the results shows that interest scarcely flagged over an eight-year period (see Table 13-2). Though many of the awards were small, some were substantial. The largest single award prior to 1959—$2,645—went to Carl S. Charles, of Number 256 filter department, for suggesting an attachment to the machines that produced filters for cigarettes. This device effected a marked reduction in the waste of materials. In 1959 the directors raised the maximum amount of a single award to $10,000 after evidence had been accumulated on the value of one suggestion. The committee, which paid Monroe B. Angel $2,035 in 1958 for the "Angel Wringer," raised his award by $7,965, thus making it the highest sum then paid for any one suggestion. Angel's invention did the work of six men and three old wringers used in the manufacture of chewing tobacco. So successful was the plan in Winston-Salem plants that on 4 November 1959, the Suggestion Plan Committee made employees in

Table 13-2
Results of Employee Suggestion Plan, 1954–1961

Year	Number of Suggestions	Number of Suggestions Adopted	Amount Paid	Estimated Annual Savings
1954	2,477	235	$ 5,745	$ 42,900
1955	2,118	313	9,840	67,791
1956	1,416	247	7,385	50,209
1957	1,510	274	11,166	71,336
1958	1,901	319	13,376	81,030
1959	1,827	388	18,944	215,085
1960	2,123	455	12,427	56,247
1961	2,366	520	11,181	38,052
Total	15,738	2,751	$90,064	$622,650

Source: *Management Bulletin* 14, no. 19, 22 February 1962.

the leaf departments at Danville, Virginia, and Lexington, Kentucky, eligible for participation.[30]

Judging from the number of responses and from the prevalence of the subject in general conversation, the suggestion plan was of decided value in unifying the interests of employees and management. It remained a matter of regret to the plan's administrator that the supervisors were unable to find more effective means for interesting a greater percentage of employees, many of whom were functionally illiterate. An effort to accomplish this became the chief goal of the Suggestion Plan Committee and the administrator of the plan.[31]

Pastoral Counseling

In another effort to improve its personnel department and no doubt also to heal the racial wounds left from labor strife, the company on 10 October 1949 hired the Reverend Clifford Hinshaw Peace to serve as pastor-counselor. According to John C. Whitaker, he and his associates had considered such a step for many years.[32] If this decision smacked of corporate piety, that idea soon disappeared with Mr. Peace's refusal to accept the position until assured that he would have complete freedom to follow his conscience when counseling an employee even when his opinion ran counter to that of management. Using a hypothetical cut in wages to illustrate this point, he stated that he would, if he thought so, tell any employee who questioned him about the justice of such a cut that he did not agree with management.[33] He also took a liberal stand on racial problems. As the featured speaker at a two-day interracial institute held in Winston-Salem under the auspices of the Forsyth Baptist Missionary Fellowship in 1956, Mr. Peace discussed a government pamphlet, *The Races of Mankind*, declaring that prejudice—the basis of all racial hatred—only led "to a scapegoat psychology in which humans blame someone else for their own shortcomings or fears."[34] Among his qualifications for the work at Reynolds were an A.B. degree from High Point College, a B.D. degree from Duke University, ten years' experience as a Methodist minister, and three and one-half years as a chaplain in the United States Army. In addition, he had grown up on a tobacco farm near High Point, North Carolina, and was thus already allied with the tobacco industry.[35]

The Reverend Mr. Peace plunged directly into his work. From the rigor and content of his orientation schedule it is evident that the company officials did not regard the new position as a sinecure. That orientation—conducted by various heads of divisions and departments—included not only introductions to supervisors and many employees but also observation of manufacturing, leaf processing, foil making, and the like. In early May 1950 Mr. Peace was still making the rounds of night shifts, which would continue until he met all supervisors and most employees. Another schedule was prepared later for his introduction to personnel in the main office.[36] It soon became company policy that employees excused for conferences with the pastor-counselor would be paid in the same manner as when they visited the medical department.[37] By 1951, according to Mr. Peace's report of 11 February 1952, he had met with eighty ministers among the employees in groups of ten to twelve. He found the Negro ministers unaware of the fact that the services of pastor-counselor were equally available to white and Negro employees.[38] After acquainting himself with his new locale the pastor-counselor determined that all visits to him would be voluntary and that his counseling would be restricted to personal problems. At no time did he force himself on any employee. From his meticulous records over a ten-year period (see Table 13-3), two conclusions may be drawn: fewer Negro employees than whites consulted him, and employees as a group most often were concerned about personality and marital troubles.

In 1949 the employment of pastors by industry was a relatively new practice. As a result, the Reverend Mr. Peace attracted considerable attention. Articles describing his unique position appeared in such publications as *Fortune*, the *New York Times*, *Forbes*, *Guideposts*, and the *North Carolina Christian Advocate*. In addition, he contributed articles on his work to the

Table 13-3
Pastoral Counseling Activities, 1951–1960

Type of Employee Problems	1951	1952	1953	1954	1955	1956	1957	1958	1959	1960
	Percentage of Counseling Sessions Devoted Primarily to These Problems									
Personality	24.0	33.0	37.0	19.3	22.6	15.4	9.9	11.4	17.4	21.9
Marital	21.0	18.0	20.0	21.0	23.4	22.7	23.7	25.3	30.0	28.8
Premarital	2.0	2.0	0.7	3.0	3.4	2.9	4.6	4.0	3.2	3.0
Alcoholism	9.0	14.0	16.0	10.0	5.3	7.8	8.7	7.7	5.8	8.1
Marital-Alcoholism	4.0	0.5	2.0	4.0	4.5	3.7	3.6	5.6	5.0	7.9
Family-Alcoholism	2.0	2.0	0.7	2.0	2.9	2.5	1.0	0.8	1.7	0.0
Job-related	3.0	4.0	2.0	7.0	5.8	5.4	4.8	3.5	4.0	4.0
Employment-related	0.0	0.0	0.0	0.0	2.7	0.7	2.9	5.1	2.3	3.0
Family	8.0	8.0	6.0	11.5	12.2	13.9	18.7	17.5	13.2	11.7
Family-Illness	0.6	3.0	0.9	2.0	1.0	1.1	1.2	2.9	3.2	2.2
Illness	0.6	0.0	0.1	0.8	0.8	0.5	0.7	0.5	1.1	0.0
Psychotic	0.3	0.7	0.1	0.8	0.8	0.7	1.4	0.5	0.4	0.2
Family-Psychotic	0.0	0.0	4.0	3.0	0.8	4.9	2.6	0.8	0.0	0.0
Financial	0.2	0.0	0.0	0.6	0.5	0.2	2.2	2.7	3.2	2.0
Grief	4.0	0.8	0.5	1.0	0.5	3.7	1.7	0.5	1.7	0.6
Miscellaneous	21.3	14.0	10.0	14.0	12.8	13.9	12.3	11.2	7.8	6.6
	Number of Employees Counseled									
Whites	174	341	353	325	343	382	361	326	421	407
Negroes	27	67	51	33	33	22	53	50	49	90
Men	115	231	223	199	164	206	206	182	235	234
Women	86	177	181	159	212	198	208	194	235	263
	Total Sessions									
	460	790	740	654	629	643	656	592	820	821

Source: Based on annual reports of the Reverend Clifford Hinshaw Peace—personnel department, R. J. Reynolds Tobacco Company.

Tri-State Medical Journal, Management Record, North Carolina Medical Journal, and *New Christian Advocate.*[39]

In connection with his duties, Mr. Peace carried out the plans of James A. Gray for the establishment of a small chapel in the main office building. Adjacent to Peace's office and only nine by twelve feet, the chapel was the smallest public room in the building. Because in-plant prayer meetings had been customary in the factories from the earliest days of the company, it was perhaps natural for management to build a chapel. In fact, both James A. Gray and John C. Whitaker told the local press that fourteen or fifteen services were held weekly and attended regularly by almost one thousand employees. The new chapel, complete with stained glass windows, was dedicated on 5 June 1951. Bishop J. Kenneth Pfohl, of the Moravian Church, officiated. He was assisted by the Reverend Charles B. Adams, president of the Winston-Salem Ministerial Association, and the Reverend J. A. Davis, president of the Interdenominational Association, who read alternate verses of the Psalm beginning: "The earth is the Lord's, and the fulness thereof; the world and they that dwell therein." James A. Gray presented the chapel for dedication.[40]

Company Benefits

In contrast to the chapel, which affected only some of the workers, the many benefits provided by the company touched the lives of all Reynolds employees. After 1945 those benefits were improved substantially. The retirement and group insurance plans of 1929 were revised to broaden coverage; hospital service was expanded; vacations with pay were increased, as were the number of paid holidays; and other benefits were added including pay for excused absences, supplemental pay for jury duty, and free parking facilities. The company offered a plan for aiding the education of employees, matching grants to educational institutions, various service awards, and, perhaps of most importance, the profit-sharing plan of 1956. In addition, it distributed the publication *Guideposts* to all employees, whether of any value or not.

Concern about liability of the company for retirement benefits under the 1929 plan led to the adoption of a funded plan, effective on 1 January 1946. This permitted the adjustment of retirement benefits with the old-age benefits provided under the Social Security Act as of 1 January 1937. Previously, the company was paying double benefits in part. It was the outlook for the growth of this burden that prompted the adjustment in 1946. Funds and assets for the new plan, including the company's annual contributions, investments, and reinvestments, were deposited with the trustee, the Mellon Bank and Trust Company of Pittsburgh, Pennsylvania. The new Retirement Plan Board consisted of P. Frank Hanes, John C. Whitaker, Frederick S. Hill, Edward A. Darr, and Herbert N. Hardy. Every Reynolds employee, including those in the armed forces, began to participate after 31 December 1946, as there was no twenty-year waiting period. The plan was amended subsequently so that typical employees after forty years of credited service, the full period covered by retirement benefits, might expect monthly pensions ranging from $123.03—the amount drawn by a retired elevator operator—to $267.07 (see Table 13-4).[41] By 31 December 1960, Reynolds had $70,972,850 in trust for the payment of retirement allowances; at the time, this was believed to be the largest investment in a retirement plan by any tobacco company.[42]

Table 13-4
Typical Benefits Resulting from the
Reynolds Company's 1946 Retirement Plan

Place of Work	Typical Retirement Allowance	Social Security Benefits
Office Building	$123.03	$107.30
43 and 65 Blending	124.32	106.30
97 Factory Service	131.53	112.90
Smoking Division	139.98	116.40
No. 1 Machine Shop	248.17	123.00
64 Casing and Cutting	249.27	123.00
Leaf	267.07	123.00

Source: Selected from a list of retired employees filed in the office of J. E. Conrad, personnel department, R. J. Reynolds Tobacco Company.

Group life insurance, first instituted in 1929 at a nominal monthly cost to employees along with the first retirement plan, likewise underwent many changes. These changes eventually led to family group insurance and later to coverage by a noncontributory plan, for which employees with as much as six months' service were eligible when not insured under the contributory plan. All employees hired after 1 July 1952 were covered by the noncontributory plan. Finally, effective 1 August 1962, seasonal workers became insured under the noncontributory life insurance plan generally at $1,500 for the first two years of employment (after having worked a qualifying season) and $3,000 thereafter. These plans, with detailed payment schedules for injuries of various kinds, represented a tremendous improvement over the first free treatments in 1906 at the Slater Hospital, which, compared with modern standards, was little more than a shack.

Another important benefit provided at small cost in cooperation with the Hospital Savings Association of North Carolina was the Hospital Service Plan, which on 15 June 1939 became available to office, factory, and plant employees. It covered all hospital expenses except those for attending physicians, specialists, surgeons, and special nurses. The company's announcement of the plan included the following statement: "With good hospital facilities for white citizens available in the City, and with the new Kate Bitting Reynolds Memorial Hospital for Negroes in operation and found to have adequate capacity for this additional use, it is not expected that the operation of this plan will unduly strain existing hospital facilities and it is hoped that all Members will, whenever appropriate, take full advantage of the service provided."[43] Possibly it might have been launched earlier had there been adequate hospital facilities in Winston-Salem for both races. On 15 December 1948 this plan was replaced by the Hospital and Surgical Service Plan, which provided for additional expenses incurred for long periods of hospitalization by granting substantial amounts toward the cost of surgery. For a nominal sum an employee might have family members covered. Amendments in 1955, 1958, and 1960 offered further material advantages for the employee and the employee's family.

From a chronological point of view the next benefit accruing to employees was perhaps more remarkable. Characterized in the announcement of 15 February 1940 as a means for providing rest and recreation for eligible hourly and piecework employees, a plan for vacations with pay became effective on 1 January 1940. At this time such a practice, though growing in favor among business organizations, was far from common.[44] At the R. J. Reynolds Tobacco Company there was little open pressure from labor and no decline in production; rather, production was considerably higher than in 1939. On the surface, at least, the company's reason for establishing the new policy must be accepted as stated. Under the plan each employee who had completed two years of continuous service was entitled to one week's vacation at Christmastime plus one-fiftieth of the wages paid him during the previous calendar year. Employees who had completed five years of continuous service received a similar amount plus an additional week's vacation. Amendments effective on 1 January 1951, 1 January 1953, 31 December 1953, and 31 December 1956 generally reduced the qualifying period of continuous service until employees received a Christmas vacation of one week provided they had been with the company since 1 July of the calendar year. The second vacation period eventually was increased to two weeks for those employed more than one calendar year and to three weeks for those employed more than nineteen continuous years. An amendment effective on 14 March 1963 further liberalized the vacation plan by granting a second vacation of three weeks after ten years of continuous service and four weeks after twenty-five years of service. Salaried employees fared as well, although their vacations were scheduled somewhat differently.

None of these provisions applied to seasonal workers. In fact, they obtained vacation pay only as a result of negotiations for a union contract in 1944. Previously, the company had refused the union's demand for such a policy. As one of the unresolved issues of the negotiations, the matter was referred to the War Labor Board which ruled in favor of the workers. According to a directive issued over the signature of Chairman M. T. Van Hecke, if a seasonal employee worked one thousand hours he must receive as vacation pay an amount equivalent to wages for twenty hours of work at his prevailing wage scale. If he worked twice as long his vacation pay was doubled.[45] Later this arrangement was changed so that all seasonal workers, regardless of how long they worked, received vacation pay based on a percentage of their total earnings—2 percent for the first three consecutive years of employment and 4 percent thereafter.

Employees entering the armed services also received a number of benefits, beginning on 23 December 1940 and continuing into the 1960s. By 1955 some of these benefits were extended to employees in military reserve training programs. Those called to duty by virtue of the Universal Military Training and Service Act also received a number of benefits under a plan that became effective on 10 October 1957. It should be noted, of course, that some of these allowances were in accord with the Selective Service Act of 1948. By that time, however, the company's plans were well-established. A recapitulation of the plan made available on 23 December 1940, when one year of military service was mandatory, reveals the extent of the company's concessions to draftees. By a decision of the Executive Committee of the board of directors, an enlisted employee (1) incurred no break in service if he returned to the company within forty days after an honorable discharge, (2) received credit for continuous service equivalent to the length of his military service plus forty days of leave, (3) retained his family membership in the Hospital Service Plan, (4) kept his vacation rights and payments as if continuously in the employ of the company, (5) continued his group life insurance with the premiums paid by the company, and (6) received as supplemental compensation a sum equivalent to two weeks of his wages or salary. Changes in 1941 and 1943 pertained to the lengthening of the period of required military service, with the company continuing to maintain at its own expense family membership in the Hospital Service Plan and the employee's group life insurance. As amended in 1957 the plan for employees entering the armed services or Universal Military Training included the following:

1. Supplemental compensation amounting to two weeks' pay for those employed as long as six months
2. Vacation pay in lieu of vacation for one year
3. Accumulation while in the armed forces of credited service for retirement
4. Restoration of membership in the profit-sharing plan on the same basis as on return from an authorized leave of absence
5. Continuation of group life insurance (and family life insurance) for thirty-one days following entry into the armed forces; reinstatement of all insurance plans and hospital and surgical service plans when reemployed

Other benefits of less importance but of value in removing minor irritants became available in the 1940s and 1950s. The policy of granting paid holidays developed from union negotiations. In accordance with the executive order of the president of the United States, the 1945 contract allowed six legal holidays, although none of them were paid. In the 1946 contract Easter Monday, the Fourth of July, and Labor Day were specified as paid holidays; New Year's Day and Thanksgiving Day were also included in the contract for 1947. To this list the company in 1956 added Christmas Day not only for hourly and piecework employees but also for seasonal workers.[46] The policy of excused absences with pay, equivalent to sick leave, was established in 1948. At the outset an employee on the weekly payroll might be excused five days during the second and third calendar years of his employment, ten days during the fifth and sixth years, and fifteen days in one calendar year thereafter. In 1956 these regulations were greatly liberalized. Supplementary pay to equal the amount lost by jury duty or summons as a witness was granted to hourly and piecework employees in 1948. But perhaps that year free parking in the crowded areas of downtown Winston-Salem seemed more important to them. Steadily expanded over the years, the parking facilities for company employees eventually included 4,888 spaces acquired at a cost of virtually a quarter of a million dollars. Incidentally, the numerous cafeterias provided for the convenience of all employees always operated at a substantial loss to the company.

The Education Plan for Eligible Employees, which became effective on 5 April 1957, constituted another valuable benefit. Under this plan the company refunded to its employees one-half of the cost of tuition for courses taken and passed during nonworking hours in an accredited institution or in an institution approved by the administering committee. Although the courses were supposed to be related to the employee's current job, or one the company contemplated for him, it appears that any course leading to a degree was approved. By 1963, 736 employees had taken advantage of the education plan, and the committee appointed to administer the program contained six of the original ten members—largely from the personnel department. Most of these employees took courses at liberal arts colleges, but some pursued studies in business schools. Salesmen were inclined to enroll in leadership training programs offered by the Dale Carnegie organization.[47]

A later benefit—and to some, the most appreciated—was made available in conjunction with the company's Aid-to-Education Program. Effective on 1 June 1962, Educational Matching Grants permitted the company to match the gift of any employee to his alma mater provided it was a recognized degree-granting institution or a junior college with credits transferable to a recognized degree-granting institution. No contribution by an employee could be less than $10 nor greater than $1,000. Significantly, the Reynolds Company did not match contributions for the support of intercollegiate athletics or for athletic scholarships. Though the program started late in the year, eighty-one employees contributed to their alma maters in 1962.[48] Regardless of the tax-exempt status of the company's contributions, the channeling of aid into such worthwhile projects demonstrated a high degree of corporate citizenship.

As an adjunct to the many benefits available to employees during this period, the company established two practices that undoubtedly contributed to morale. In November 1947 Norman Vincent Peale's *Guideposts* was distributed to supervisors on an experimental basis. At the instigation of James A. Gray, it was given to all employees beginning in March 1949. Management insisted that supervisors read the publication before distributing it so that they could call attention to its supposed excellence. An admonition to supervisors in 1949 ran: "Take a little time when you pass it out. *GUIDEPOSTS* makes sense." Its value as a moral influence was often the subject of facetious remarks in the office building, although *Guideposts* continued to be delivered every month to every Reynolds employee at an annual cost to the company of almost $25,000. Certainly of more importance was the awarding of a Reynolds pin in recognition of long service, a practice that began in May 1941. Accompanied by a certificate indicating years of service, the pin, which showed the Reynolds office building against a background of three tobacco leaves, was awarded first at the end of twenty years of service and thereafter, with appropriate changes in symbols, at intervals of five years. Beginning in January 1961, additional awards of silver were given, ranging from a bonbon dish for twenty years of service to a handsome tray for fifty years. In the beginning the foreman simply handed an award to a factory employee and offered his congratulations, but in 1951 the presentation became more elaborate. Each month ceremonies arranged by the personnel department were held in honor of the recipients all the way from the tenth floor conference room to the outermost plant. An attempt to present distinguished service awards apparently ended in failure. Shortly after thirteen men were so recognized in 1954—the first and only time distinguished service awards were made— the directors decided to postpone further action until the plan had been studied in greater detail.[49]

Purposely, the profit-sharing plan of 1956 has been reserved as the last benefit to be considered. No doubt this plan, which replaced the one initiated by R. J. Reynolds, served more than any other benefit to bind the interests of employees and management. It was more democratic than the first profit-sharing plan in that all employees were eligible to participate after three years of continuous employment regardless of stock ownership. Moreover, participation continued until retirement or a break in service. Leaves of absence in the armed forces or the Red Cross were authorized if the employee returned to the company within a specified time after release. A committee composed of H. Henry Ramm, William J. Conrad, Jr., Alexander H. Galloway, and Stuart M. Scott worked for two years to develop the plan in frequent consultation with other directors. Accordingly, each year Reynolds set aside the equivalent of 5 percent of the amount by which the operating income exceeded 8 percent of the net value of operating assets, excluding income from subsidiaries. Roughly estimated, this represented nearly 15 percent of an employee's total annual compensation. As trustee, the Wachovia Bank and Trust Company held and invested the amount allocated for profit sharing and provided an annual report to all participating employees. Usually benefits were paid either as a cash lump sum, in a combination of cash and company stock, in monthly installments over any period up to fifteen years, or in an annuity from an insurance company. Benefits paid in one year were taxed as a capital gain, as the company learned when the plan was submitted to the Internal Revenue Service for approval. Employees leaving voluntarily were paid on the basis of accrued vested rights; ten full years in the plan entitled an employee to 100 percent of the balance of his account. The full amount in profit-sharing accounts was paid in four cases: (1) at retirement under the company's retirement plan, (2) upon total and permanent disability, (3) upon layoff or discharge (except for dishonesty, willful destruction of company property, or disclosure of trade secrets), or (4) at death at any time for any cause.[50]

It was generally understood that increased profits for the company meant an increase in the employee's profit-sharing account. Nevertheless, older employees in the office sometimes yearned for the old plan of participating stock, claiming that a lump sum at retirement came too late in life to afford them any pleasure. When this writer attended an orientation program for new employees, the explanation of the profit-sharing plan received the greatest interest among employment benefits. It was possible for the lowest paid individual in the company to accumulate almost $25,000 in a normal working life. This, however, was contingent on business conditions remaining as they were when the plan was instituted.

Sales

A significant change in the sales department also accompanied the organization and expansion of the personnel department. For many years communications between the home office in Winston-Salem and salesmen in the field were restricted primarily to instructions for handling "deals" or combinations of brands arranged with the aim of distributing all of the brands. Prior to 1938 letters from the head of the sales department often were caustic; they always demanded greater returns from the sales force but seldom offered any ideas for producing them. Improvements started in 1938 were soon interrupted by the war and little was accomplished until after 1945. One important move was to emphasize ideas for selling, which were soon communicated through the *Reynolds Tobacco Merchandiser*. The first issue, which appeared on 5 November 1946, plainly stated this purpose.

The idea for this publication was undoubtedly conceived by Frederic Ernest Sturmer, who was brought to the company by Edward A. Darr, himself responsible for many improvements in the sales department. Sturmer, a graduate of the University of Michigan with considerable experience in selling, had worked for William Esty Company, Inc., for five years before entering the navy. Evidently Darr became acquainted with Sturmer's qualifications through the company's long association with the Esty agency. When Sturmer joined the Reynolds company on 18 March 1946 as manager of the merchandising section of the sales department,[51] he lost little time in gaining approval to publish the *Reynolds Tobacco Merchandiser*. In some ways the new publication was handled like the *Management Bulletin*; certainly the physical setup was virtually the same, including the utilization of mimeographing facilities until the issue for 26 May 1952. Sturmer edited the first few issues himself. Beginning with the issue for 25 February 1947, George Wallace Chandler took over as editor. Chandler, who joined the company in 1936, had worked in the billing department in the shipment of goods to warehouses over the country. From this experience he thoroughly understood an important phase of the sales department— that shipment to these warehouses constituted the heart of the company's rapid system of delivering goods throughout the nation.[52]

Though primarily a vehicle for the exchange of new selling ideas, the *Reynolds Tobacco Merchandiser* also served as a unifying agency. In pursuit of this secondary goal the editor, on 23 January 1948, began and continued for some time a series entitled "Let's Get Acquainted." The series began with a sketch and a picture of Edward A. Darr, then vice-president and sales manager. Other sales officials in the home office so featured were Bowman Gray, Jr., John T. Barnes, Jr., Frederic E. Sturmer, Thurman A. Porter, Norman F. Matthews, Beverly K. Millaway, and W. Archie Sugg. Men in the field—especially department managers—also appeared, including Peter H. Tucker (8 November 1889–6 January 1959) of Chicago, James R. Haston of Tampa, and John K. Cone of Los Angeles. When significant changes occurred in the company's top management or in the sales department, the officials involved received similar but more pretentious treatment. Frequent lists of salesmen with long service records or accident-free driving records served the dual purpose of giving the readers a sense of working together and of the importance of observing safety regulations.

Another feature addressed the question of sales resistance from retail dealers. In the issue for 21 November 1947, the editor asked all salesmen to note briefly in the space provided three irrefutable arguments used by retail dealers when they resisted buying Reynolds products. In due time 374 ambitious salesmen submitted 1,122 replies containing 33 arguments. By careful analysis it was found that only 7 of them accounted for 71 percent of all replies. As listed in the *Reynolds Tobacco Merchandiser*, they were:

1. Unsatisfactory margin of profit on tobacco products (a prevailing misconception later corrected in the company's trade advertising)
2. Inability of retailers to meet prices of competitors
3. Lack of requests for specific brands
4. Lack of display space
5. Reluctance to stock new or additional items
6. Previous unfavorable experience with specific brands (plug brands)
7. Slow turnover of specific brands

The editor then requested answers that salesmen found most effective in combating any of these arguments. He was, he declared, working on the premise "'that somebody's smarter than anybody—and that's everybody.'" A number of answers were submitted. Whether this maneuver to overcome sales resistance produced the merchandising revolution that followed is highly debatable. At any rate, the revolution began immediately after the publication of these seven arguments seemingly in response to some of them.

Examination of the *Reynolds Tobacco Merchandiser* from its inception reveals that in 1948 the sales department suddenly shifted from merely stocking the dealers to helping them make greater sales. The motto on the masthead changed seven times from 5 November 1946 to 28 January 1949. The last three changes demonstrate the steady move toward giving the retailer service:

Motto	*Date*
Merchandisers Develop Know-How and then Show-How	27 February 1948
The Dealer is Your Business Partner— Help Him Sell	17 December 1948
A Merchandiser Sells through Serving	28 January 1949

This shift to promoting sales through service to the retail dealer rather than combating sales resistance accompanied a number of other changes in concepts for merchandising tobacco products. Before World War II, drug store managers had a traditional hold on the sale of cigarettes, but, because they regarded them as items of convenience, they did not pay much attention to merchandising. This situation generally prevailed until the growth of supermarkets. About this time the company began to emphasize in its cigarette advertising the importance of turnover as well as markup. This led the Reynolds sales force to introduce floor displays of cigarettes in cartons.

The mechanisms for displaying and selling cigarettes by the carton were largely based on a scheme devised by Wayne Leonard Tibbets, a salesman in Seattle, Washington, who joined the company in 1925. Indeed, the work he began served to make the R. J. Reynolds Tobacco Company a pioneer in modern methods of merchandising cigarettes. No doubt his contribution was of sufficient value to offset the cost of producing and distributing the *Reynolds Tobacco Merchandiser* many times over.

Tibbets's method required no fancy equipment. The idea came to him one day after entering a retail store in Seattle. Overloaded with the paraphernalia of a tobacco salesman, Tibbets rested a small cardboard Camel display rack on an upended orange crate as he talked to the manager. He then began explaining the advantages of displaying cigarettes on a self-service basis. Suddenly noticing how neatly the Camel display rack fitted atop the orange crate, Tibbets saw new possibilities. Why not cover the raw sides of the crate with attractive Camel posters and use it as a base to support his Camel display stand? Too, because he wished to help the dealer increase his total cigarette sales, why not stack cartons of competitive cigarette brands on and beneath the central divider of the upended crate to form an all-brand display? The dealer agreed that the idea was worth testing—and a new method of displaying cigarettes had its beginning.

Amazing success when he further developed and tested the innovation locally induced Tibbets to send a picture and description of it to the *Reynolds Tobacco Merchandiser*. They appeared in the issue for 30 April 1948:

> This photograph shows how I use an orange crate, CAMEL posters and CAMEL rack #785 (cardboard Camel carton display stand) to make a floor display stand for cartons of cigarettes. Staple the CAMEL rack to top of crate, fill it with CAMELS (in cartons) and fill the lower part of the crate with other items from the dealer's stock (cigarettes of other companies). When placed on floor, this makes CAMELS easiest to pick up . . . *The display requires just one square foot and will sell 200 cartons a week in the average store.* Some dealers want more than one display as soon as they find out how much faster their cigarettes sell.

Tibbets, of course, was aided by the coincidence that Camel rack number 785, of cardboard, measured eleven by twelve inches on the base and had slanted sides and a high back. It was, in fact, perfectly constructed for the use that he made of it. Reputedly, in Seattle cigarette retailers "were out on the streets" in search of Tibbets whom they wished to build orange crate displays for their stores. Plans for displaying the brands of rival firms were unheard of at this time.[53] It must be recalled, however, that Tibbets placed Camels on the most advantageous spot of the orange crate display. On 15 March 1963 he wrote that Reynolds made "real progress" when it instituted the *Reynolds Tobacco Merchandiser*, thereby giving salesmen the opportunity to put their ideas to use when selling *through* the dealer instead of *to* him.[54]

Tibbets's idea led to other changes. Soon the Reynolds company developed a cardboard display stand to replace the improvised orange crate arrangement. This was followed by the construction of metal racks, and then by the manufacture of handsome wooden fixtures. By March 1953, if not earlier, the company offered retailers—free of charge—hardwood carton racks holding 150 or 250 cigarette cartons and occupying one square foot of floor space. Thereafter it built various modes and sizes of racks, including a counter display stacker that held only 15 cartons. The type advertised in June 1954 was described as "fully adjustable to accommodate a complete assortment of brands in proportion to actual sales."[55] From this statement it is clear that some time earlier Reynolds had pioneered in the inventory control method, or the Reynolds dealer-service plan. This enabled retailers to stock and display various cigarette brands according to their sales volume. Meanwhile, the sales department devised a small vertical stand for displaying packages of cigarettes. Occupying less than one-third of a square foot, this rack was designed for a space near the cash register— the area known among cigarette salesmen as the "hot spot." As an extension of this idea, the department developed and offered free to cigarette retailers a number of handsome package display fixtures completely designed for the "hot spot." This move led to a change in the method of displaying cigarettes by the package—a method quickly imitated by other tobacco companies.[56]

Advertisements in trade journals began to reflect the company's move to fully adopt the concept of service to retailers. Clearly, the *Reynolds Tobacco Merchandiser* had initiated a sharp break with the immediate past. But in his first advertisement, written in 1892, R. J. Reynolds had expressed virtually the same regard for the jobber and the retailer with whom he wished to enjoy good business and a satisfactory profit. Seventy-one years later George W. Chandler unknowingly expressed R. J.'s early views when he declared that the idea of service to the retailer could not be mere lip service. It was instead a matter of determining specific services that would really benefit cigarette retailers, of deciding which of those services the company was qualified to perform, and of developing detailed plans for providing them.

Leaf Processing

Important changes were not restricted to sales methods. In its gradual development of the "SPD process," the R. J. Reynolds Tobacco Company became one of the pioneers in the long search for a satisfactory method to remove the stems from tobacco leaves. The initials "SPD," which also represented the strip preparation department, referred to a process for stemming leaf using a series of complicated machines known as tippers, softeners, thrashers, and separators. This procedure replaced the few hand stemmeries and the stemming machine department (SMD). Closely allied with the shift to the SPD process was the adoption, as early as the mid-1930s, of green stemming for Georgia leaf. In green stemming, the stem was removed as soon as the leaf was purchased from the farmer; the leaf was ready for storage once the stem had been removed. Both the SPD process and green stemming eliminated much hand labor. They also eliminated dust and scrap in workrooms, provided a saving in tobacco leaf, reduced maintenance costs, increased the volume of production, caused a marked saving in floor space, improved strips, and generally increased efficiency.

A brief description of the SPD process will perhaps clarify its role in the development of the company. The so-called green leaf, really a yellowish brown cured leaf, came from the farmer in bundles of eight, ten, or more leaves held closely together by a tie leaf, which was wrapped securely around the butts of the leaves with the butt end of the tie leaf itself tucked carefully into the leaves comprising the bundle. Through a conveyor the bundles of leaf reached a tipping machine, which snipped off a portion of the tip end of each leaf, the amount varying with the type of tobacco. These tip ends, still somewhat closely packed as they came in bundles, went by conveyor to a tumbling cylinder, which loosened them. Because the small proportion of stem left in this part of the leaf did not need to be removed, the tips, after the elimination of foreign matter, were blended with other strips from the SPD process. Shorn of their tip ends but still remaining in bundles, the leaves then went by conveyor to a tie leaf cutter, which loosened the tie leaves.

At this point the loosened bundles reached a butt cutter, which sheared off the butt end of each leaf, leaving two portions—the center and the butt end. Both portions of the leaf then proceeded to a softening or ordering cylinder before coming to the thrasher, which literally slipped the leaf off the softened stem. After thrashing, the mixture of strips and stems reached the separator, which, by the utilization of air and gravity, separated the leaf from the stems. After appropriate searching, screening, and drying, the strips were ready for storing, aging, and subsequent blending. Except for additional runs through thrashing and separating units, the butt ends, which contained the heaviest part of the stems, were treated like the centers. Usually the strips were packed in hogsheads by automatic strip packers, thus demonstrating another remarkable development in the leaf processing department. This department also handled the blending of different types of tobaccos necessary for the various brands.

The pneumatic separation of leaf from the stem occurred over a number of years. Early in 1935 an experimental SPD unit was developed on the top floor of Number 43 using thrashers, Muller separators, and searching tables. Further study led to two major advances in 1943 and 1944: (1) development of the tipping operation on which, according to word of mouth, experimentation had been conducted from time to time since 1917 (in the ell between numbers 43 and 65), and (2) expansion of SPD operations in Number 43, where intensive experimentation involving thrashers and pneumatic separators had been in progress since 1935. In July 1944 installation of small SPD units in Number 8 to handle drop leaves from stemming machines resulted in the elimination of twenty-two stemmers. On 28 October 1944 the first complete SPD production unit, known as Number 43 SPD-1, was established with a single cutter belt, a three-stage thrasher, and a separator line. Equipment included Sprout-Waldron thrashers, a Landrum and Hammack straight line separator, Landrum and Hammack pneumatic separators, necessary searching tables, ordering drums, dust collectors, and finished strip conveyors to Number 12 Casing and Drying and to the basement of Number 43 for packing. With about 40 employees, Number 43 SPD-1 handled only the Georgia strips that went into the Camel blend; by contrast, the machine and the hand stemmeries previously performing this task had required about 250 people. In 1944 production in the various hand and machine stemmeries was similar to that of 1940, although costs had risen slightly because of increased hourly rates. On the other hand, the cost of labor for producing strips in Number 43 SPD-1 fell to slightly less than one dollar per hundred pounds of strips. Even better, automation now permitted the production of approximately 4,000 pounds of strips per hour. The experimentation of at least twenty-seven years had at last borne fruit, and SPD units were rapidly spread to other leaf handling areas, although there were difficulties in obtaining machinery and material during and immediately after World War II.

The company actually developed much of the first machinery used in the SPD process. In an unsigned memorandum of 23 March 1944 headed "Comparison of Stemming Methods," reference is made to "the Tail Cutting Device we developed." In 1947 a new separator developed by the American Machine and Foundry Company was found to be inferior to the "RJR Separator" when tested by the leaf processing department. The RJR pneumatic separator, developed by James E. Chilton, Horace P. Harrington, William W. Rike, and Jay Giles Smith, was compact; it also spread the tobacco over a greater area and permitted better air flow than did the Landrum separator. Chilton contributed an important device known as the *seal*, which allowed an even, steady flow of tobacco and eliminated the intake of air at the discharge point. Though used for some time, these RJR separators were gradually replaced by models from the American Machine and Foundry Company.

Few developments were more important for the company than the SPD process. Because of high volume in the production of strips, it made green stemming possible; in fact, without it green stemming could never have been adopted. Strange as it may seem, however, the SPD process reduced the number of skilled laborers, because the operation of stemming machines required greater skill than did the SPD line. A far more serious result involved the decreasing need for labor. According to a memorandum dated 3 February 1948, there were 3,533 employees in the stemming division in July 1944 but only 1,415 in February 1948. It is not clear what happened to the 2,118 stemmers displaced by automation. Persons interviewed much later reported that many left Winston-Salem. Another explanation appeared in the *Winston-Salem Journal* for 8 March 1946:

> The R. J. Reynolds Tobacco Company yesterday announced installation of new machinery, resulting in a layoff of certain Leaf Processing Department employees to be effective next Monday, March 11.
>
> A company official said that approximately 700 Negro workers in the Stemming Departments would be affected—ultimately 500 at Plant 60 and 200 at Plant 65. The company official explained that this change had been brought about by the installation of new machinery which would result in a better stemming operation for its tobacco and would provide better working conditions for its employees.
>
> The installation of this new machinery has been contemplated for some years, but it was delayed due to the shortage of certain materials during the war, the company official said. It was stated that the making of this installation at this time will greatly facilitate the company's handling of its constantly expanding business.
>
> The company official emphasized that all workers who are laid off will register for re-employment with the company. . . .
>
> Workers who had been notified of a release were registering at Local 22 headquarters. A meeting in which the situation was discussed was held Wednesday (March 6, 1946), with about 800 in attendance, the union spokesman said.

Further savings in labor resulted from the installation of more efficient separators in October 1948, though generally these displaced employees were given other jobs.[57]

As late as 1957 the R. J. Reynolds Tobacco Company believed that it had certain advantages over other tobacco manufacturers in its techniques for stemming, drying, and packing tobacco in hogsheads—virtually all of which pertained to the SPD process:[58]

1. Specialized methods for unloading sheet and bundle tobacco from trucks and conveying it to stemmeries
2. Methods of feeding leaf tobacco to tipping tables in the tipping operation
3. Methods of conditioning tobacco for stemming
4. Combination, arrangement, and type of machinery for stemming and separating
5. Conveyors as a part of the stemming and separating process
6. Drives and controls on feeders and conveyors as part of the stemming process
7. Methods and conditions for cleaning strip tobacco
8. Methods and conditions for conditioning strip tobacco for storage
9. Methods of packing strip tobacco for storage
10. Stem processing
11. Methods for handling materials peculiar to all of these processes

When tobacco growers became agitated over the possibility of reductions in acreage because of the introduction of reconstituted leaf in the 1950s, they evidently did not know the effects of the SPD process.[59] Its installation permitted green stemming, which accounted for an increased yield of tobacco suitable for manufacturing. On the other hand, the volume of cigarette production at Reynolds virtually doubled from 1944 to 1958—years that included the wholesale introduction of the SPD process and reconstituted leaf. Had the company clung to old methods and practices, it would have been outdistanced to the extent that it undoubtedly would have purchased less tobacco. The company had no choice, the farmers had little, and the tobacco stemmers had none at all.

Research

Few if any developments in the tobacco industry were more important than the fabrication of reconstituted leaf, or "processed tobacco," as it was generally referred to by employees of the R. J. Reynolds Tobacco Company. Reconstituted leaf, which involves the highly satisfactory utilization of stems, scrap tobacco, and tobacco dust in manufacturing, represented a

great saving in leaf tobacco, always the single most expensive item connected with the making of tobacco products. All the major companies no
doubt began working on this problem quite early. Nevertheless, the Reynolds company pioneered not only in the production of reconstituted leaf
but also in a method for its fabrication.

The stem itself constitutes from 25 to 35 percent of the weight of the
leaf. Certainly R. J. Reynolds had this in mind as early as 1910 when he
ordered that a greater proportion of G-7, then the code name for crushed
stems, be included in Red Bird chewing tobacco. It is possible that similar
thoughts in 1916, 1917, and 1922 produced an interest in dust conveyors
and machinery for scrap cleaning.[60] In fact, the idea of using stems in the
manufacture of tobacco products generally may well have received strong
impetus from the example of the cigar industry. As early as 1921, the Universal Tobacco Machine Company produced a machine that flattened "the
stem to the same thinness as the leaf, removing the gum moisture, and de-
liver(ing) the entire leaf (stem included) ready to be 'worked.'" In the notice advertising this machine appeared the statement that hand stemming
caused the loss of 15 to 25 pounds in stems and scrap for every 100
pounds of leaf.[61]

Just when the company became actively engaged in the pursuit of reconstituted tobacco is not absolutely clear. According to Edgar E. Bumgardner
work began in the early 1920s when William N. Reynolds and John C.
Whitaker, in an attempt to salvage loss from stems, rolled them into a flat
sheet for cutting and subsequent inclusion in smoking tobacco and plug
filler. In the 1930s Whitaker spent considerable time trying to develop a
reconstituted tobacco to use as a wrapper for chewing tobacco.[62] Possibly
then, however, his chief motivation was the scarcity of wrappers caused by
the farmers' long concentration on leaf suitable for cigarettes. At any rate,
the problem of salvaging stems and scrap was recognized as far back as the
days of R. J. Reynolds.

For a time the company turned to the utilization of stems to produce
nicotine sulphate for use in insecticides, particularly black leaf 40, a move
rendered futile by the development of synthetics during World War II. At
best this attempt to salvage waste from stems and scrap provided little financial return. Apparently at the behest of John C. Whitaker the company
during the early 1930s planned an attack on the stem problem of a less
empirical nature. Its principal investigator was Samuel O'Brien Jones.
After a year at Davidson College Jones transferred to North Carolina State
College, where he studied engineering for a year and chemistry for three.
When he graduated in 1932, he received an R. J. Reynolds fellowship for
four years of study at the Johns Hopkins University. On 3 June 1933,
Jones became a temporary employee in the research department under the
direction of Edgar Hoskins Harwood. He worked in the same position

each summer until he received the Ph.D. degree in chemistry from Johns Hopkins in 1936. On 31 March of that year he was employed by Reynolds on a permanent basis. The company's investment in Jones's education was destined to yield manifold returns. In 1935, he wrote Whitaker:[63]

> By the end of this school year I shall have completed the work required of me by the University for my dissertation. Next year I shall be able to work on any problem I wish. I have talked with Dr. Reid (Professor E. Emmett Reid), who is head of the Organic Research department here, and he said he would be very glad for me to work on some problems of interest to you. As you know, you suggested the problem of stems to me last fall. I believe some work has been done on that at our laboratory there (R. J. R. Research dept.), but I do not know how much was accomplished. However, I am sure that you are able to suggest some specific problem which I can work out here next year.

Earlier, on 19 November 1934, Jones had informed Edgar E. Bumgardner, always closely associated with Whitaker: "I am trying to find a simple and inexpensive method for the chemical treatment of stems which will enable them to be rolled flat and cut as tobacco is—I have succeeded in treating the stems in such a way that, after being rolled and cut, the stems do not dry up and powder—I have not attacked the problem of flavoring them, but I believe that can be worked out."[64]

The important role of John Whitaker in convincing his fellow workers of the importance of research in general is even more apparent in his letter of 17 October 1934 to Jones:[65]

> In my opinion we have reached the point in the tobacco business, when much attention should be paid to research work. With the growth of the complexity of certain processes, and the more exacting requirements demanded of the finished product, it is becoming increasingly true that decisions relating to changes in materials or processes require reference to the men in the laboratory. These men should become more dependent upon the knowledge of the properties of materials, the discoveries of new methods of treatment, new methods of test, and the elaboration of new processes discovered and perfected in the laboratory. We have great hopes that each succeeding year will find the laboratory in the lead for reducing manufacturing costs without sacrificing quality.

Though in the development of reconstituted tobacco Jones and his associates carried out Whitaker's desire "for reducing manufacturing costs without sacrificing quality," it would take many years to do so. Not until 7 June 1950 was reconstituted tobacco first used in cigarettes, and not until 27

October 1950 did Reynolds produce as much as one million pounds of the leaf.

For several years much of the experimental work on converting fragmented tobacco and stems into sheets for reblending with natural leaf was conducted at Shed 112, Number 202 at Whitaker Park where the pilot plant was eventually located. It should be kept in mind that reconstituted leaf was developed three years before the company built the first part of its modern research building. Furthermore, one million pounds of reconstituted leaf suitable for making cigarettes were ready for blending only three days after Kenneth Harry Hoover, director of the research department, arrived to plan the modern building and its equipment.[66] It is thus ironical that the most notable work of the research department up to that time grew from the limited arrangements in the old Reynolds Inn. Some believe that the success with reconstituted leaf revealed the importance of research to top management and thus produced the modern research department; others think that failure of the Cavalier cigarette paved the way for the new expenditures on research. Possibly it was a combination of the two.

The efforts leading to the development of a satisfactory reconstituted tobacco involved much trial and error, though all the while a single aim remained in focus. Jones worked at Reynolds approximately two years before launching (in 1938) a program directly aimed at the conversion of scrap and stems into sheets of tobacco that could be used with ordinary leaf. The first phase involved rolling and cutting the stems of flue-cured tobacco. Only a small portion of this was used in cigarettes. Another method tried in 1941 was known as the MMM process, so named for three men who worked on the project—Robert Murray Lybrook (23 July 1918–26 October 1957), Frank Voorhies Miller, and Lindsay Price Morris. In the MMM process a mixture of tobacco dust was steamed and rolled into a sheet. Though suitable for smoking tobacco, the processed leaf could not be used in cigarettes because it lacked sufficient tensile strength and shattered when cut.

Taking a different tack in February 1946, Ernest Elias Kapp, Jr., John Edwards Holland, and Jones attempted to make plug wrappers from stems. Though they had no experience in making paper, they concluded that a likely method for forming reconstituted leaf might well be based on the paper-making process. Accordingly, they borrowed a book on paper making from the public library, and, by following the procedures it described, eventually devised their own plans for making sheets of reconstituted leaf from tobacco pulp. Kapp and Holland pulverized flue-cured stems in an old-fashioned, hand-operated coffee mill, drained the resulting pulp on a wire screen to form a sheet, and pressed it with a felt mat. Then they made additional sheets, using scrap as well as stems. Jones prepared an extract from water heated to 140 degrees Fahrenheit and cigarette scrap and sprayed it on the sheets. When the sheets were dry, the investigators cut some of them and rolled a few cigarettes. Evidently encouraged, they made more sheets—this time from stems and cigarette scrap. These they cut and mixed with tobacco cut for cigarettes, using six parts of their product with ninety-four parts of the other. John C. Whitaker and Robert E. Lasater smoked some of them with great relish and the real campaign began.

Between 24 June and 5 August 1946, Kapp, Holland, and Jones worked out the basic procedure for making sheets of reconstituted tobacco for use in cigarettes. It involved the extraction of tobacco flavoring derived from water, stems, and scrap. To form the sheet of tobacco fibrous materials, stems were pulped and used with fines (unusually small pieces of scrap). After it was pressed, dried, and tested, tobacco extract was sprayed on the sheet. Again they made cigarettes, this time a greater number, which were tested by Whitaker, Lasater, George E. Tucker, James A. Gray, James W. Glenn, and Henry S. Stokes.

Early in August 1946, Gray authorized Jones and his group to establish a pilot plant. Kapp, Wilson Clark Lamb, and Fred P. Flynt purchased secondhand equipment such as pumps, pulp-refining equipment, and a crude papermaking machine generally known as a wet machine. Though none of these items had been designed for the specific task of producing reconstituted tobacco, they represented the best that could be found and were made to work. The wet machine, for example, was used to make tobacco fibers into a sheet. When the pilot plant was ready in January 1947, operations began, though not without difficulty. The researchers were convinced that a method for obtaining the extract should be mastered first; this was confirmed by the troubles they met. They soon recommended the purchase of an Oliver filter for cleaning the extract and the construction of an extractor, which was built in the company's own sheet metal and millwright shops. Realizing that the pulp-refining equipment, which pulled the fibers apart in order to reform them into sheets, would limit the rate of production, top management recommended that Lamb and Jones be sent to the Ecusta plant to investigate the possibility of using other papermaking machinery. Through the good offices of Roy C. Haberkern, always on close terms with the Ecusta Paper Corporation, this move was easily arranged. Based on their findings, Lamb and Jones recommended that a Hydrafiner be borrowed from Ecusta and installed in the pilot plant at Winston-Salem. This machine doubled the tensile strength of the sheets, giving them the elasticity so badly needed for the cutting process. By early 1948 sheets of reconstituted tobacco could be cut as easily as the natural, strong-bodied, and elastic leaves from the storage sheds.

Yet, another problem confronted them. Jones, in doing some work for

Chemical Abstracts, discovered that on 6 January 1946 the International Cigar Machinery Company had received a patent for a machine to make reconstituted sheets of tobacco from fines. When he told John C. Whitaker about it, the latter became disturbed that the Reynolds method infringed on the cigar patent. On 5 February Jones informed Whitaker that this was not the case and that some features of the Reynolds process could be patented. But Robert S. Dunham, a patent lawyer who studied the matter for the company, recommended that a patent not be considered because it would give away more than it could protect.

Though success seemed near, the research team led by Jones encountered additional problems. The extractor, installed by late June 1948, worked well with stems and large scrap but proved ineffective with tobacco dust. Fred P. Flynt, a near mechanical genius, solved the problem by having a two-screw type extractor designed and built. In another phase of the process, it was found that sheets of reconstituted tobacco were frequently torn as they passed through the drying machine. When an apron dryer in Number 256-1 operated satisfactorily with sample sheets, management authorized the construction of an apron drying machine. Accordingly, on 14 October 1948 Jones rolled twelve square feet of reconstituted leaf in aluminum foil and took them to the Ross Laboratory in New Brunswick, New Jersey, where a suitable dryer was designed and built. Successfully installed by 17 January 1950 the machine worked perfectly and the first continuous sheet of reconstituted tobacco was run through the dryer on 9 March. In view of the different burning qualities of stems and leaf, the conversion of stems, fragmented leaf, and tobacco dust into strips of even and excellent quality represented a significant accomplishment. On 13 July 1949, Reynolds management approved the construction of a plant to produce 10,000 pounds of reconstituted leaf per day.

Strange as it may seem, it was the last test run on the last day of the experiential period that revealed some of the details in the preparation of reconstituted tobacco. Thereafter it was necessary to train people to operate machinery with which they had had no previous experience; in fact, the training of workers was one of the most difficult tasks involved in achieving a high degree of plant efficiency. Various features of the Reynolds process continued to be improved, including the type of solvents for extracting flavoring from the dust of Turkish leaf and the substitution of better machinery. Though some Burley stems could not be used in the production of reconstituted leaf because of insufficient tobacco flavor and inadequate burning properties, the R. J. Reynolds Tobacco Company went far to emulate the example of Armour and Company, which reputedly used all of a porker except the squeal. Indeed, the manufacturing division utilized all of the leaf purchases except a portion of Burley stems and the heavy tobacco aroma that generally hovered over Winston-Salem.

Later other tobacco manufacturing companies also began to use reconstituted leaf. Liggett and Myers was the first, in 1955, though its production process differed considerably from that of Reynolds.[67] Philip Morris was next, in 1957, followed by P. Lorillard, in 1959. Apparently both companies likewise developed a process unlike that of the Reynolds company, as did the American Tobacco Company.[68]

In addition, by the end of 1950 the American Machine and Foundry Company had developed a method for producing reconstituted leaf. According to the firm's prospectus, its process had been in preparation for "the last few years" and would "make tobacco history." Its methods for making "microflake tobacco strips," as the nomenclature ran, involved placing finely ground waste and scrap on a stainless steel belt, which was then "sprayed with an atomized film of adhesive dispersion." The "adhesive dispersion" consisted of sodium carboxymethyl cellulose, commonly used in ice cream and salad dressings. Apparently the idea was to grind the fragmented leaf along with stems and dust. In May 1951 Morehead Patterson, president of American Machine and Foundry, arranged to present his plan for reconstituted leaf to John C. Whitaker along with a specially printed estimate of costs for installing a plant to produce "microflake tobacco strips." Whitaker recalled that when Patterson's representatives examined a sample of the Reynolds reconstituted tobacco, they congratulated him on its excellence and declared it was better than theirs. Incidentally, Whitaker refused to give them samples of the Reynolds product. In fact, in view of the great curiosity shown by the American Tobacco Company, all Reynolds personnel were warned not to discuss the new product and for some time it remained top secret.[69]

This remarkable achievement, though chiefly the work of Jones and his associates, could not have been accomplished without the contributions of other departments and individuals. The project was instituted by John C. Whitaker, who no doubt knew of R. J. Reynolds's interest in salvaging waste from stems. James A. Gray and James W. Glenn approved it and Haddon S. Kirk spurred on the work after Whitaker became president on 1 July 1948. Other members of the research department contributed valuable information, and the engineering department cooperated in the designing and building of necessary equipment. Members of the purchasing and leaf processing departments made helpful suggestions. The legal department investigated the patentability of the process, and various other departments assisted in the establishment and operation of the pilot plant. All in all, the development of reconstituted leaf represented the highest degree of cooperation within the company.

CHAPTER 14

Expansion of the Company and Its Enhancement of Life in the Area

The company quickly rebounded from its blunder with the Cavalier cigarette by introducing the Winston and the Salem, both highly successful from the outset. Success with these new filter-tipped brands did not eliminate attention to the Camel, which remained the best-selling cigarette of the industry until the beginning of 1960. The growth in sales of these three products demanded extensive expansion of leaf storage and manufacturing facilities. This led to construction of the company's Whitaker Park plant, a large industrial complex consisting of many storage sheds, leaf processing facilities, and a modern cigarette plant located on the edge of town with ample parking facilities. Along with this move, Reynolds built three storage and leaf processing centers, one each in nearby Stokes and Davie counties and a third in Lexington, Kentucky. In making these moves, officials of the company adopted a new policy in relation to its real estate holdings by acquiring sufficient land to support further expansion in the same areas. The new facilities inspired numerous other changes including the establishment of an industrial engineering department, a remarkable expansion of research facilities and enlargement of the engineering department, the purchase of airplanes, and the adoption of new advertising methods. During this period the company also began a systematic approach to its contributions for community improvement, restricting them chiefly to projects emphasizing health and education and thereby continuing the practices of R. J. Reynolds, who made his first noteworthy contribution to an educational institution in Winston-Salem.

The Filter-Tipped Cigarette

By its introduction of the Winston cigarette, both filter-tipped and cork-tipped, the company in 1954 recognized changes that occurred in the cigarette industry after World War II. With considerably less vision, of course, Reynolds had introduced the Cavalier in 1949 for the same basic reason. Seven years later, however, Cavaliers amounted to little in sales, though it cost approximately 52.9 cents per carton to advertise them. In contrast, during the same year the cost of advertising Camels amounted to only 2.5 cents per carton. Also in that year approximately 40 billion Winston cigarettes were sold at an advertising cost of 5.8 cents per carton. By then the Winston had already surpassed its chief rival, the Viceroy. Moreover, in 1956, 25.4 billion Viceroys were sold at an advertising cost of 8 cents per carton.[1] During its first year of full production the Winston attained national leadership in the filter-tipped field.[2] Early in 1954, as the Winston was readied for marketing after two years of rigorous research and experimental tests, Brown and Williamson could not meet the demand for its filter-tipped Viceroy. Meanwhile, the American Tobacco Company had no filter-tipped cigarette.[3] Clearly the Winston was introduced at a most propitious time.

Success of the Winston was more fortuitous than planned. Edward A. Darr, then vice-president in charge of sales, happened to spend his vacation of 1951 in Europe where he learned that filter-tipped cigarettes accounted for approximately one-half the market in Switzerland. Despite the initial opposition of the other directors, the company had its filter-tipped cigarette ready for the market less than four months after Dr. Ernest L. Wynder, of the Sloan-Kettering Institute for Cancer Research, announced in December 1953 that he had induced skin cancer in mice by painting them with tobacco tar.[4] By that time cigarette smokers had begun turning to the filter tip. Moreover, Darr had become president of the Reynolds Company on 5 November 1952.

Little was accomplished in developing a filter-tipped cigarette until Darr became president. Possibly failure with the Cavalier inspired some caution. A few months before, the current interest in filter-tipped cigarettes had been reported by Percy J. Bartle in the Richmond branch of the Molins Machine Company. Bartle's comments were passed on to Haddon S. Kirk, a director in charge of manufacturing, by Joseph H. Sherrill, an assistant in the manufacturing department but later a director. According to Bartle, William H. Ogsbury, of the American Tobacco Company, was then in Europe investigating equipment for filter-tipped cigarettes, and the Liggett and Myers Tobacco Company was interested in the mouthpiece type of cigarette. Approximately a month later Sherrill told Kirk about the machinery needed to produce filter-tipped cigarettes.[5]

After the directors' luncheon following his appointment as president, Edward A. Darr instructed Kirk to "start experimenting again with filter-tip cigarettes to develop a blend." In the style of all tobacco manufacturers, Kirk then sent for a carton each of three brands of filter-tipped cigarettes before meeting with Kenneth H. Hoover, Edgar H. Harwood, and Peter C. Markunas—all of the research department—"to discuss the development of a filter-tip blend." Giving Hoover three packages of each brand, Kirk requested that a complete blend analysis of each be made by Josiah L. Keaton, also of the research department. At the meeting, Kirk learned that the department had already analyzed "the six different filter-type CAVALIER cigarettes delivered to them some weeks" earlier; these had been made at the request of John C. Whitaker. Hoover felt that the sales department should indicate the strength of the filter and various types of leaf to be included. This would enable Harwood to more easily and quickly develop various blends than could the manufacturing department by having the leaf processing department deliver a proposed blend for a factory test. The group then wisely decided that the type of filter used would depend on the blend adopted and that the two items should be worked out together. Agreement was also reached that a strong, harsh, flavorless tobacco could not produce a good cigarette but that a full-bodied tobacco blend could "probably" be made "somewhat milder by the use of the proper filter." After the meeting, Kirk took samples of the cigarettes made of Cavalier-cut tobacco with the six types of filters to Darr's office, where he also found Bowman Gray, Jr. Kirk asked for their help "in developing the proper type of filter-tip cigarette" by smoking some of the sample cigarettes. Darr wanted one with taste and aroma like the Camel rather than the Cavalier because the public liked the Camel better than any other cigarette on the market. Bowman Gray agreed. They then decided to prepare immediately, and have the sales department thoroughly test, a filter-tipped cigarette of Camel type tobacco using all six types of filters on hand. In addition, Kirk left one set of filter-tipped cigarettes of the Cavalier blend for Whitaker to test.[6]

Undoubtedly there was much searching of souls before the final decision was made. Reliable evidence indicates that the Winston was to be marketed first on 11 March 1954, although the company did not accept orders for the brand until about two weeks later. In fact, the Winston made its first public appearance on 17 March,[7] but not without difficulty. Twenty-four thousand pounds of machinery for making the filter plugs in quantity, apparently of special design and manufactured by the Molins Machine

Company of Deptford, England, came into New York Harbor on 11 March aboard the *Queen Mary*. Because of a longshoremen's strike, the ship returned to England on the thirteenth with the machinery still on board. Meanwhile, the Reynolds traffic department attempted to have the cargo transferred at an English port from the *Queen Mary* to a vessel scheduled to unload at some Atlantic port not involved in the strike.[8]

Despite these seemingly rapid decisions to enter the filter-tipped market, the directors had wavered considerably on the question. In commenting on changing conditions throughout the cigarette industry induced by "switched smoking, king-size cigarettes, and various types of filter-tip cigarettes," Haddon S. Kirk in September 1953 declared that the smoking public was becoming more critical. He noted that the general lack of enthusiasm for the king-size Chesterfield, Philip Morris, and Old Gold had made top management very cautious about producing an 85-millimeter Camel or a filter-tipped cigarette. Probably he was also thinking of the Cavalier. Nevertheless, on 10 June 1954, three months after the Winston appeared, the directors ordered the acquisition of all materials needed to manufacture a filter-tipped Camel of 85 millimeters "including the procurement of necessary equipment, advertising, wrapping material, and supplies." Although this was done at considerable expense, the plan was scrapped before production could actually begin.[9] Obviously these moves and countermoves reflect the uncertainty that prevailed in the tobacco industry during the early 1950s.

Behind all this lay the difficulty of obtaining adequate machinery to assemble and connect filter plugs with the cigarette tobacco. Apparently, at that time the only machine available for such work was the Molins Filter Tip Attachment. Not particularly satisfactory, the Molins FTA, as it was known, formed the tobacco rod for the cigarette under compression, cut the rod, left a space for insertion of the filter plug, and wrapped the filter and the tobacco rod in paper. In the beginning the jointure of the filter with the tobacco was not firm—a condition that gave rise to the term "loose necks." So marked was this characteristic of the early Winstons that when a letter of complaint arrived addressed to the "vice president in charge of goose necks," the mail and file department immediately forwarded it to Kirk.[10]

As a result of the problem it became necessary to either improve the Molins FTA or find more effective machinery. The company acted with unusual alacrity. Eleven days before the first official Winston cigarette was manufactured on the Molins machine,[11] Joseph H. Sherrill was in Hamburg, Germany, investigating the Hauni KFZ Filter Tip Cigarette Assembling Machine produced by the Hauni Maschinenfabrik Körber and Company. According to the prospectus this machine had outstanding qualities—among them, the output of more than one thousand cigarettes per minute, linkage with any cigarette rod-forming machine, guaranteed uniform length of filter, perfect sealing of tobacco and filter, ease of operation, and small space requirements. Sherrill obtained a test machine, "the first of the new and improved lot which he [Kurt A. Körber] started assembling this week." This was "a confidential deal" because Körber did not wish others to know about it. Shipped from Hamburg on 6 March 1954, the Hauni machine was not then equipped with all the improvements desired by Sherrill. The Hauni company also sent its own erector and later one of its directors, Ulrich Riegger, to Winston-Salem. On 6 May, Riegger and Edward A. Darr signed a purchase agreement for 114 Hauni machines. Because time was "of the essence" to the Reynolds company, a schedule guaranteed shipment of the machines with the accompanying compressed air plans in varying lots from June 1954 to May 1955. Furthermore, thirty of the first forty-two models shipped to the United States after the date of the contract were to come to Reynolds. In addition, the machines were to have incorporated in them thirty-one changes listed by Sherrill. One of these changes called for redesign of the feed drum to eliminate friction so that the cigarette would not tend to climb and be torn when fed into the drum. This was the point where the greatest number of cigarettes had been damaged on experimental runs.[12] Notwithstanding the inclusion of "limber necks," the runaway sales of Winstons account for the extreme haste to obtain a more satisfactory machine.

Though Winstons were produced by the Molins attachment for some time, especially in factory Number 1 at 6, in November 1954 Kirk wrote of plans to discontinue using it as soon as the company had enough Hauni machines to meet the production demands of the sales department. He estimated that date to be not later than March 1955. In referring to the rapid growth of filter-tipped cigarettes and the race of the Molins Machine Company, the Hauni Maschinenfabrik Körber and Company, and the American Machine and Foundry Company to develop improved filter-tipping machines, Kirk estimated the life of the Hauni machine to be no more than seven years. In fact, he declared, he would not be surprised if it became obsolete in less than seven years.[13] Actually improvement in the form of the Hauni Max machine came within two years. Meanwhile, the Winston division of cigarette production operated at top capacity to meet "the constantly increasing demand." By 27 September 1954, though on the market for only six months and ten days, the Winston was sold in every state of the Union and in several countries in Europe, South America, Asia, and Africa.[14]

As early as October 1954, the American Machine and Foundry Company believed it had the improved machinery at hand in an attachment to be ready for distribution early in 1955.[15] The Molins Machine Company also produced an improved filter-assembly attachment for its Mark VI

Making Machine.[16] Meanwhile, at Reynolds Haddon S. Kirk, Colin Stokes, and George E. Tucker of the manufacturing division with Dr. Samuel O. Jones, Edgar H. Harwood, and Luther J. Upton of the research department struggled to make a better filter plug to run on the Hauni machine. During this time a representative of the Tennessee Eastman Company visited the cigarette factories while the Reynolds force was working on an experimental machine. This machine, a Hauni 17, had been equipped with a device for handling estron, the trade name for cellulose acetate used in making the filters. In a secretive fashion characteristic of the tobacco industry, machine 17 was shut down and certain employees were cautioned not to discuss with the Eastman representative anything "about the improvements that we have worked out for machine No. 17."[17] Reynolds employees headed by Kirk obtained additional equipment made by Hauni, the Molins Machine Company, and the American Machine and Foundry Company; made comparisons; and studied the output of all of them.[18]

This rush to obtain machinery to keep up with the demand for Winston cigarettes was reminiscent of the tumultuous years that had accompanied the procurement and installation of machinery to produce Prince Albert and Camels. On 9 December 1955, for instance, Kirk called a meeting in the office of James E. (or Bill) Thomas to discuss factory space for expanding the production of Winstons. Eventually the space was found and, on 9 February 1956, the directors ordered the purchase of a variety of cigarette machines, including 46 Hauni Max Filter Tip Assemblers. This move was intended not only to make up for a current shortage of equipment but also to eliminate "the excessive overtime pay in the cigarette division" caused largely by the growing sales of Winstons. The results were highly successful. The Hauni assemblers could be attached to any making machine, and they enabled the company to save three people per machine in operation.[19] A month later the directors ordered the purchase of 114 additional assemblers to replace the Hauni machines originally acquired.[20] The company continued to use them in the early 1960s.

Demand for Winstons continued to be so great that during 1956 the Hauni Max models of filter-tip assemblers had to be flown from Hamburg, Germany, to New York by air freight. They were assembled and prepared for shipment in Hamburg—bolted to wooden frames and wrapped in polyethylene. They generally left Hamburg one day, arrived in New York the next, and were transported immediately by truck to Winston-Salem. Within four days of leaving Hamburg they began turning out Winstons. At that time air freight on these shipments amounted to seven and one-fourth times the amount of ocean freight.[21] In view of the probable loss in production during the longer period required for shipment by sea, the cost of air freight actually represented a saving.

Entry of the company into the filter-tipped market paid off despite the expenses to which some directors are supposed to have objected. With Camels leading all cigarette brands in sales for the eleventh consecutive year, the end of 1959 found the Winston holding third place and ahead of Lucky Strikes. That year Winston's total production reached more than 46 billion and no doubt contributed heavily to Reynolds's share of the market, 29.6 percent, the largest of any company in the tobacco industry.[22]

This phenomenal reception of the Winston cigarette reflected in a large measure the demand for filter-tipped cigarettes—a demand that had grown since the beginning of the cancer scare in 1952 with the republication of "Cancer by the Carton" from the *Christian Herald* by *Reader's Digest*.[23] Nevertheless, the Winston prospered and its advertising proved quite effective. The first newspaper advertisement appeared in the New England area on 30 March 1954. As each new territory was opened for distribution, advertising support was provided through newspapers, radio, television, posters, and other media. Prominent among the Winston-sponsored programs was Walter Cronkite's "Morning Show," which began on 12 July 1954.[24] As has been noted, early in 1955 Winstons replaced Cavaliers as sponsor of the Garry Moore television show. Supposedly because of advertising, requests for Winstons came from various army and navy installations in foreign countries.[25]

In most newspaper and magazine advertising, the accent was on youth. The first version of Winston's prize line, so offensive to those who guard the purity of the English language, appeared during the week of 6 September 1954 in the newspapers of Pittsburgh, Pennsylvania, as "Winston tastes real good—like a cigarette should." It was subsequently refined, but still ungrammatical: "Winston tastes good—like a cigarette should." This final wording was carried first in *Life* on 4 October and used steadily thereafter. Although the phrase seemed to be defended only by Bergan Evans, who called himself a descriptive grammarian, it was generally accepted and highly effective. Evans held that those who complained about the use of the word *like* as a conjunction should also explain how Shakespeare, Keats, and the translators of the King James version of the Bible "came to be in the employ of the R. J. Reynolds Tobacco Company."[26] Curiously, no one claimed credit for this line, which Bowman Gray, Jr., chose to describe as "colloquial" rather than ungrammatical.[27] One thing was certain: it made no health claims. Nor did the other line so widely used in advertising Winstons—"it's what's up front that counts." The latter came in for more jocular remarks among Reynolds employees than the phrase that offended the purists. At one annual meeting of the supervisors, as the chairman of the board extolled the audience for making the company what it was, a sibilant whisper reached the ears of many in the rear of the hall: "It's what's up front that counts."

Notwithstanding jests about its advertising phrases and the difficulties experienced in its production, the Winston constituted a landmark in the history of the company. Along with substitution of the 1956 profit-sharing plan for the ownership of "A" stock by employees, it represented a distinct movement away from the ideas of R. J. Reynolds and indicated that the company at last could move ahead independently of its founder.

Just as Camels appeared on the heels of Prince Albert so the Salem menthol, filter-tipped cigarette followed the successful Winston. There were differences, however. The time lapse between the introduction of Winstons and of Salems amounted to little more than two years. Furthermore, all matters relating to the production of Salem cigarettes were well-guarded secrets. Even some of the directors were in the dark. Eleven days after Salems were introduced to the public, Bowman Gray, Jr., declared: "Of all the new brands in the past thirty years of the tobacco industry, I think SALEMS were the best-kept secret. This was another achievement of the team-work process. People went ahead with their work and said nothing, and we had a real jump on competition. Orders are coming in very, very gratifyingly."[28] Nevertheless, it is more than likely that ability to maintain such secrecy was based on the fact that the company had already assembled and learned to use machinery and cellulose acetate for the Winston filter-tipped cigarette. When it was decided to manufacture Salems, only the menthol had to be obtained because Winstons and Salems are identical in form.

When Salems were introduced, the mentholated market had long been dominated by Brown and Williamson's Kools, which, by 1955, accounted for about 4 percent of total cigarette sales. The Salem, heavily laden with Burley tobacco but only slightly flavored with menthol, was scheduled to be brought out in January 1957. According to a trade rumor, Philip Morris was then about to introduce its reworked Spud cigarette. Bowman Gray, Jr., immediately moved up the date for Salems by nine months, declaring at the time: "Why not take the cream off before you get to the milk?"[29]

Accordingly, on 12 April 1956 when Frederick Carter, head of the sales department, requested $2 million to introduce, promote, and advertise Salems, his appeal was granted. On 19 April the executive committee decided to give a package of the new Salem cigarettes to all active and retired employees on the twenty-third and to release an account of its new king-size, filter-tipped, menthol-fresh Salem cigarette to the *Winston-Salem Journal* for publication on the twenty-fourth. It was scheduled to go on sale in Winston-Salem on 30 April and in Philadelphia and other northern points on 7 May.[30] Carter believed, and correctly so, that the Salem would be generally accepted because it combined "the trend of king size, improved filter, and a new idea in menthol freshness." Indeed, it was the first filter-tipped menthol cigarette on the market.[31]

The Salem proved to be as successful as the Winston. By advancing its introductory date, the company was ahead of its competition—the Philip Morris mentholated and revamped Spud—by one month. A sales task force flew out of Winston-Salem near the end of April and immediately held meetings with salesmen in New England, New York, Cleveland, and other areas in the East. Wholesale dealers poured orders in so promptly that by 3 May 1956 the manufacturing department had to add 180 temporary employees and start a third shift to expand the production of Salems. No doubt there was much truth in the boast of the *Management Bulletin*: "With all the other problems to be worked out in planning, scheduling, and coordinating, Supervision had just that very short time (Thursday afternoon to Sunday night) to inform the people about the situation and condition them for the changes to come. That job was done so well, and our people responded with such understanding and enthusiasm, that there were more volunteers for the third shift than could be used."[32]

On 29 June 1959, the company announced in a large number of the nation's newspapers a "revolutionary" development for Salem cigarettes. This was the high porosity paper so often noted in the springlike scenes characteristic of Salem advertisements. Devised by the research department, it was described as "an amazing and exclusive cigarette paper." "SALEM has scooped the cigarette industry again," ran the boast in the *Management Bulletin* for 29 June 1959. Furthermore, the company planned "to push hard and wring every possible advantage from our lead before competitors try to copy this discovery." For those who consider the "high porosity paper" an advertising phrase, it should be kept in mind that almost all cigarettes are now made with high porosity paper. It is even rumored in the trade that P. Lorillard developed and patented a machine for punching infinitesimal holes in its cigarette paper.[33] This change marked a shift in the advertising of Salems to emphasize air that softened every puff. Reportedly, by 1961 the Salem cigarette ranked fifth in sales of all brands in the United States.[34] Of the twenty-five menthol cigarettes introduced up to that time, the Salem was the only brand of any importance. The American Tobacco Company tested its Riviera cigarette on the market for three years before abandoning it. In 1962 it introduced the Montclair, which differed from other menthol brands by carrying flavor in the filter rather than in the tobacco.[35]

Still in the expansive mood, the Reynolds company resolved to counter American's fast-growing, king-size, nonfilter Pall Mall with the Brandon, a cigarette of the same class. It was first introduced in the New England states, Southern California, and the Winston-Salem area on 22 January 1962[36] and later tested in New York State (except for the metropolitan area), Northern California, and parts of Alabama and Pennsylvania beginning in June. Advertising supported the salesmen in all these areas.[37] By March 1963, when it became evident that the Brandon was not appealing to the smoking public, Reynolds decided not to expand distribution to other areas. William S. Smith, Jr., manager of the sales department, explained the company's position: "Non-filter king size brands, notably Pall Mall, were growing during the months before the introduction of BRANDON. As it turned out, however, this growth began to weaken early in the year. Since that time, the entire category has sustained losses as the switch to filter brands has gained momentum."[38] This reasoning may seem plausible, though Pall Malls led the list of cigarette sales in 1962 by a greater margin over Camels than in 1961.[39] Neither was filter tipped.

Whether from elation over the fine showing made by Winstons and Salems or from the need for a new smoking brand, Reynolds in August 1956 announced its newest product—Carter Hall Smoking Tobacco. Advertised as "an aromatic smoking tobacco with a new distinctive flavor," Carter Hall appeared in an attractive laminated foil pouch packed in a cardboard box wrapped in printed cellophane. National distribution began on 1 January 1957, though advertising was generally limited to sports and men's magazines such as *Argosy, Outdoor Life,* and *Field and Stream.*[40]

Apparently, however, no startling sales were expected from Carter Hall, because for some years there had been a gradual decline in the use of both smoking and chewing tobacco. Statements in numerous annual reports had called attention to this trend in the tobacco industry. In 1955, the year before Carter Hall was introduced, sales of Reynolds chewing and smoking tobacco products declined 4 percent from the previous year.[41] The dominance of cigarettes and their increasing share of the company's net sales are illustrated in Table 14-1.

None of these new products did much to dim the brilliance of the Camel whose formula continued to stand as a guide for the entire tobacco industry. Nevertheless, changes were made, or attempted, in minor areas of the Camel's personality. No doubt Reynolds officials at the Kentucky Trial in 1941 noted George Washington Hill's testimony that, though Reynolds had been first to wrap packages in cellophane, it had not gone all the way. Hill stated that American, P. Lorillard, and Liggett and Myers had already placed a tear strip, or "one of those little red openers," on their cigarette packages for ease in opening the cellophane wrapper. But "Camels has [*sic*] not as yet followed that competition."[42] In the spring of 1940, when Lucky Strikes first appeared with a "zipper opener," the Reynolds sales department was concerned enough to prepare a written statement of the disadvantages of such an opener for distribution to all of its division managers. A zipper opener, the sales department claimed, destroyed the effectiveness of cellophane as a moisture-proof wrapping. Possibly hoping to avoid the expense of a strip opener, the company did not make a change until 3 June 1947. On that date the directors authorized Roy C. Haberkern to buy the machinery needed to provide a "strip opener" on packages

Table 14-1
Percent of the Reynolds Company's Net Sales
Attributable to Cigarettes, 1940–1960

Year	Percent
1940	83.09
1941	84.19
1942	86.13
1943	88.10
1944	86.67
1945	85.25
1946	91.33
1947	92.88
1948	92.73
1949	92.74
1950	93.12
1951	93.60
1952	94.29
1953	94.57
1954	94.41
1955	94.97
1956	95.68
1957	95.79
1958	95.77
1959	95.80
1960	96.19

Source: Cost records, comptroller's department, R. J. Reynolds Tobacco Company.

of Camels.[43] By April 1948, fifteen machines had been installed. This change might well have been made earlier because it was more or less inevitable.

Another change was attempted in 1955 when John C. Whitaker objected to omission of the comma between "N.C." and "U.S.A." on the Camel package. According to Haddon S. Kirk, the insertion of a comma in that position would run the last of the lettering into the tower shown on the package. But to move the printing to the left to permit insertion of the comma would throw the page off balance. Therefore, wrote Kirk, the punctuation on the Camel package should be left in its incorrect form.[44]

Still another effort to improve the dress of the Camel proved more serious. Word leaked out in 1946 that the company had started making a new design for the Camel package—one much clearer and simpler with the Camel itself reduced in size and the name in larger type. Not until October 1958, however, did any official note appear concerning the change. At that time it was considered up to the minute according to the best packaging standards. But, on 7 November, members of the executive committee, including John C. Whitaker, Haddon S. Kirk, H. Henry Ramm, and Herbert N. Hardy, met to consider public reaction against the new package. Before the meeting Whitaker had talked by long distance to sales executives Bowman Gray, Jr., and Frederick G. Carter, and found them gravely concerned. Reaction against the more stylish package, which *Tobacco* termed "violent," seemed on the verge of seriously impairing sales. The company had received numerous complaints from Camel smokers indicating they thought the blend had been changed. There was evidence that this idea was being circulated by salesmen of competitors because the words "Turkish & Domestic Blend" had been omitted from the package. Other smokers felt that the Camel looked pale and sick, somewhat like a candy cigarette. After conferring with the executive committee and other Reynolds officials, Whitaker ordered that production on the new package be halted and that supplies of the old style be obtained as quickly as possible. His actions were approved with alacrity by the directors on 13 November 1958. Possibly to draw smokers more closely to the old revolutionary brand, officials of the company planned to thank Camel users in newspaper advertisements for helping them "not to change the label of the best-liked cigarette of them all." It was rumored that R. J. Reynolds, Jr., became so angry over the change in the package that his father had designed and for which his mother had prepared the blurb that he sold most of his Reynolds stock.[45]

Obviously, in some respects the Camel now belonged to the public domain. Perhaps, too, it was the only cigarette capable of exciting so much loyalty: No such public uproar greeted a new and more loudly decorated carton in 1959.[46] Though the Camel has been honored by a justice of the United States Supreme Court as a revolutionary force in the tobacco industry, it has also achieved a kind of spiritual honor. In an audience with the Pope in 1950, Congressman Thurmond Chatham accidentally held in his hand a package of Camels along with some medals. The kindly Pope smiled tolerantly and continued with his duties as Chatham heard something like "Benedictus."[47]

Meanwhile, during the early 1950s cigarette advertising reached a near record level. Bruce Robinson, of the American Newspaper Publishers Association, reported that such advertising was 28.3 percent greater in the first quarter of 1952 than for the same period in 1951. For the first time in the history of the cigarette industry the five leading brands were advertised concurrently in newspapers nationwide. Plans were made to advertise lesser brands in the same manner. With the frequent appearance of new brands Robinson felt that additional fuel was being added to the hot competition characteristic of the cigarette business. Among the most intensive campaigns was that being waged for Camels; at the end of 1952 Reynolds had "just completed a concentrated five month newspaper program" of advertising.[48] The Camel continued to hold first place in the sales of all brands, though in July 1960 Bowman Gray, Jr., acknowledged that it was becoming "a close horse race."[49] Despite a substantial gain in 1959 while other regular brands were declining, a king-size, nonfilter cigarette was gaining on the Camel. The "close horse race" involving the old standby in 1960 demonstrated again the wisdom of launching the Winston and the Salem. Even the editor of the *Twin City Sentinel* conceded at the end of 1959 that "Camels cannot be expected to hang onto the top spot forever, even though they continue to gain in sales."[50]

Expansion of Facilities

With top selling brands in three categories—regular sized, filter tips, and menthol cigarettes—the R. J. Reynolds Tobacco Company could not continue to operate without expanding its manufacturing and leaf storage facilities. The final step in the expansion program, the building of the Whitaker Park plant, was not taken until the North Carolina legislature amended its tax formula in 1957, giving corporations substantial concessions as an inducement to locate in the state. The new construction, along with other building projects already underway, was expected to amount to a capital outlay of $50 million in the Winston-Salem area.[51] According to Governor Luther H. Hodges, who had worked vigorously to have the tax formula revised, the company's decision to expand in the Winston-Salem area resulted almost exclusively from the tax change. In fact, Governor Hodges announced the new Reynolds expansion before the company did. At the time, however, Reynolds was already spending about $15 million to enlarge its facilities for leaf processing, research, and aluminum foil making in the Winston-Salem area. Moreover, at the same time it was expanding its leaf processing and storage facilities in Lexington, Kentucky, at a cost of $5 million, and it was rumored that new manufacturing facilities would also be established there. All this was due to expansion of sales. "It's a happy problem we're faced with," declared Bowman Gray, Jr., then executive vice-president in charge of sales.[52] Beginning in 1954, the company purchased on the edge of Winston-Salem 65 acres of land where the new cigarette plant was built plus 183.74 acres for future expansion.

Ground for the cigarette plant was broken on 17 October 1958, and the first cigarettes produced there—Winstons—rolled off the line on 4 April

1961, although the first shipment of 700 cases, each containing 60 cartons, bound for the Metropolitan Distributing Warehouse in Jersey City did not leave until the twenty-sixth.[53] Planning for the new factory began in 1956 with the appointment of a committee representing the manufacturing, engineering, research, and industrial engineering departments. The committee reported on 12 September 1957, but actual construction did not begin until March 1959. The site, which housed numerous storage sheds of old Tiretown as well as new ones, a leaf processing plant, and the spacious factory, more like an art museum than an industrial plant, was named for John C. Whitaker who, at the time of the ground breaking, had been connected with the manufacturing department for forty-five years. At completion, the Whitaker Park plant undoubtedly was the world's largest, newest, and most modern cigarette factory. The air-conditioned factory covered approximately 14 acres—large enough to accommodate 20 railroad cars at one time under the covered loading area, parking space for 900 automobiles, 2,000 employees working in two shifts, and a cafeteria with a seating capacity of 375. Beautiful Howardi holly trees and a fountain adorned the front entrance. Equipped with Hauni Garant Making Machines, Hauni Tipping Machines, giant Legg cutters, Molins box-making machines, packers made by the American Machine and Foundry Company, and like items, the plant produced Winstons at the rate of 1,400 per minute without a "loose neck" in the lot. Perhaps most unusual was the shipping area; it boasted an electric counting and routing machine—among the most modern of its day. Camels and Winstons traveled on the same conveyor, which automatically sent the regular brand to one car and the filter tips to another. Surely the Old Red Factory was forgotten in all this elegance of modernity. Possibly the outstanding achievements in the construction of the Whitaker Park plant were the ability of the engineering department to design and construct the entire building and the success of the directors in correctly evaluating the total cost of the project.[54]

Concurrently with the building of the Whitaker Park plant, the company was wrestling with the problem of providing additional room for handling leaf tobacco. As early as June 1953, the directors had appointed a committee to consider the feasibility of establishing leaf storage facilities and developing redrying and stemming operations outside North Carolina. Three years later the problem had become one of obtaining a more equitable rate of taxation on leaf stored in Winston-Salem and Forsyth County. Another committee, consisting of John C. Whitaker, Bowman Gray, Jr., Robert M. Hanes, Alexander H. Galloway, Stuart M. Scott, and William R. Lybrook, was appointed in February 1956 to "continue negotiations with the Board of County Commissioners of Forsyth County in an effort to work out a satisfactory solution of this matter."[55]

Approximately a month later a long feature article entitled "Tax Relief on Stored Tobacco—Should Forsyth County Grant It to Reynolds," by Chester S. Davis, appeared in a local paper. It centered on four issues: (1) that Forsyth County was unhealthily dependent on stored tobacco as a source of income, (2) that the county taxed stored tobacco with a heavier hand than any major tobacco manufacturing county in the South, (3) that Reynolds had asked for substantial relief on taxes then levied on approximately $320 million worth of leaf stored in 1955, and (4) that if tax relief were not granted, "Reynolds, in response to certain plain economic facts, will *shift the bulk of its leaf storage out of Forsyth County and, in all probability, out of North Carolina.*" Davis noted that the company's taxes on stored tobacco in Forsyth County had risen from $425,260 in 1939 to $1,700,271 in 1955. Rates were much lower in states such as Kentucky, South Carolina, Alabama, and Virginia, as they were in Durham and Rockingham counties, both tobacco manufacturing areas. Reynolds officials quietly presented these statistics to the county commissioners of Forsyth County.[56] Four days later William Lybrook reported that apparently for inventories reported on 1 January 1956 the commissioners would accept as a method of evaluation the acquisition price of leaf, without costs of redrying, handling, insurance, and other expenses, less 10 percent for estimated shrinkage. Lybrook noted that for future years an even more satisfactory formula might be obtained.[57] That arrangement, however, did not come to pass.

Against this background the company moved to expand its leaf operations and storage facilites by establishing a center in nearby Stokes County—a shift that reverberated locally. When a bill was introduced in the North Carolina legislature to exempt from ad valorem taxation for one year all tobacco stored in Stokes County for shipment to other areas, State Senator Calvin Graves of Forsyth County told the senate that he believed that R. J. Reynolds Tobacco Company was attempting to pressure Forsyth County into granting tax relief by helping sponsor the Stokes bill. This, of course, was promptly denied by President Edward A. Darr, who declared that as far back as March 1957 the company had been attracted by Stokes County's efforts to obtain industry. Furthermore, Stokes County was near Reynolds's manufacturing plants and, in the interest of the company, he had to consider every alternative that might increase efficiency and economy.[58]

Shortly afterward the directors approved a recommendation of the Real Estate, Buildings, Machinery, and Equipment Committee to buy twenty-four prefabricated steel tobacco storage houses as "the first stage in the program for developing the Stokes County leaf storage and processing facilities." Numerous objections to the original site of 270 acres caused the Real Estate, Buildings, Machinery, and Equipment committee to purchase an additional adjacent tract. The engineering department desired land that was more level in contour in order to construct forty-eight storage sheds in groups of sixteen each so that each group would be 500 feet apart. In supporting this stand, the leaf processing department did so on the grounds that the cost of fencing, grading, railroad sidings, access roads, pump houses, and fire protection would create additional expenditures of at least $100,000. All these factors and possibly others induced the directors to buy 80 additional acres, already under option, at $800 per acre. When equipped with storage sheds, a steam generating plant, redrying facilities, an unloading building, a garage, roads, a railroad spur truck, and a fire protection system, the Brook Cove plant cost an estimated $21,484,006. This parklike area was named Brook Cove in honor of William R. Lybrook and Walnut Cove, a nearby town in Stokes County.[59]

Soon after completion of the Brook Cove plant, a celebration was held on Sunday, 13 December 1959. Attended by 5,500 persons chiefly from Stokes County, it was an elaborate event with sight-seeing tours over the plant, compliments for the modern appearance of the buildings, and refreshments served by the company. The speaker for the occasion, a small-town banker from Walnut Cove, praised the new plant for the jobs and the payroll that it would provide. Moreover, Brook Cove would help shoulder the tax burden of Stokes County. Eventually consisting of fifty-six storage sheds, as well as other buildings, the Brook Cove area had a storage capacity of 260 million pounds of leaf. The leaf processing building alone contained more than 2,350 tons of structural steel. There the observers from Stokes saw 12 miles of paved roads, parking space for two hundred cars and seventy tractor trailers, 2.3 miles of railroad track in the plant area, the company's own engine for shuttling railroad cars, and seven drilled wells to maintain an ample water supply. Though there were fork-lift trucks capable of handling eight hogsheads of tobacco at one time, the citizens of Stokes undoubtedly were more interested in the 150 year-round jobs and the 500 seasonal jobs created by the new plant. As the main speaker declared, Stokes County was in love with the R. J. Reynolds Tobacco Company.[60]

Similar expansion of redrying and storage facilities occurred in the Burley area at Lexington, Kentucky, where taxes on stored leaf were lenient. Apparently in 1952, when the company began to construct its fifth 500-hogshead storage warehouse in Lexington, it had no further plans for any notable expansion in that area. But in 1956 it was rumored that the company would build a major "stemming and re-drying tobacco plant" in Lexington at an expected cost of $15 to $20 million. Reynolds had been looking for a suitable site for such a plant since 1953.[61] With the adoption of long-range plans involving large tracts of land for future expansion, the company sold scattered tracts in Kentucky used largely for storage.[62] On 10 May 1956 Stuart M. Scott, chairman of the Real Estate, Buildings, Machinery, and Equipment Committee, presented his report recommending the initial work on a site of approximately 270 acres three miles south of Lexington between Clay's Mill Road and Nicholasville Pike. The directors allocated $2,250,000 to begin the project, which at that time included twelve storage sheds. On 14 November 1957, they approved an additional $10,865,670 to complete the stemming and redrying plant to include a total of twelve storage sheds.[63]

Considerable effort went into locating and building the Lexington plant. There were difficulties with zoning, labor conditions had to be investigated, and the possibility of expansion had to be considered. In fact, the company later bought an additional tract of 200 acres adjacent to the first purchase so that its holdings of almost 500 acres might suffice beyond the foreseeable future. Finally, through the cooperative efforts of various departments, particularly the engineering department, the plant was ready for initial operation in the late fall of 1959.[64]

Meanwhile, plans on the drawing board called for the immediate construction of sixteen additional storage sheds on an 800-acre tract in nearby Davie County to be completed early in 1963.[65] The Davie plant along with all other storage sheds by mid-1963 gave the company roughly 8,768,276 square feet of storage space in 223 sheds, or, in other words, 201.29 acres with hogsheads of leaf standing four deep in many sheds.[66] Ordinarily a hogshead of stemmed leaf contained from 900 to 950 pounds of tobacco but a hogshead of unstemmed leaf, as used in the manufacture of chewing tobacco, held about 1,000 pounds.

These vast changes in the storage of leaf tobacco plus changes in the SPD (strip preparation) process and the adoption of green stemming caused a reorganization of the work of the leaf processing department in the Winston-Salem area. All stemming and redrying of green leaf tobacco became the function of the Winston-Salem Leaf Division consisting of Number 1 Redrying, Whitaker Park Processing, and Brook Cove Processing under the supervision of Charles M. Davis. The stemming division became the blending division charged with stemming and blending redried leaf tobaccos and strips for manufacturing operations. Included in this division were all downtown plants, Number 43-65 SPD, Number 60 SPD, Number 256 SPD, and Number 8 SPD, with Jesse S. Davis as superintendent. Blending facilities in the new Whitaker Park plant later became a part of this division.[67]

The expansion of the 1950s eventually reached into a foreign country. In March 1960, the company announced the formation of the Reynolds-Neuerburg G.m.b.H. to manufacture cigarettes, the most important being the Overstaltz and the Guldenring. The newly formed subsidiary held a 51 percent interest in the German firm of Haus Neuerburg K.G., with plants in Trier, Baden-Baden, and West Berlin and headquarters in Cologne. In

September Joseph H. Sherrill left Winston-Salem for Germany to serve as comanager of the Reynolds-Neuerburg operations.[68] During 1961 Haus Neuerburg not only increased its advertising and marketing activities but also introduced a menthol-flavored, filter-tipped cigarette called the Reyno, in reality the Salem. Company personnel also aided its affiliate in developing a new filter-tipped cigarette, the Gordon, which was ready to be tested in 1960.[69] Reynolds's aim in expanding to West Germany, of course, was to establish a base within the European Common Market in order to take advantage of its expanding economy.

Changes Accompanying the Expansion of the 1950s

Expansion of manufacturing and leaf facilities during the 1950s produced changes in a variety of areas. Some were more important than others.

A minor change in office work had to do with the handling of payrolls and checks. On 12 November 1953 Alexander H. Galloway, treasurer and chairman of the Finance Committee, reported that his committee recommended the purchase of a Todd check-writing, adding-listing machine and a Todd check signer connected as one unit "for use in signing all Regular Accounts Payable checks drawn on accounts maintained with the Company's depositary banks known as Regular Accounts, with one facsimile signature in lieu of the present method of requiring two written signatures on each check." Though James A. Gray repeatedly had opposed this move, he evidently had made no objection to the payment of all employees in Number 4 Cigarette Factory by IBM checks early in 1949. It was well after Gray's day, however, that the company obtained its "Small Brain"—an IBM 650 magnetic drum data-processing computer. A series of classes, sponsored by the International Business Machine Company but under the direction of the comptroller's department, initiated personnel from eight departments into the mysteries of handling the "Small Brain."[70] These items, of course, merely indicate the beginning of a movement toward the acquisition of such devices.

The industrial engineering department seldom had access to the 650 computer because it was primarily for accounting and billing purposes. When it was replaced by two 1401 models, however, the industrial engineering employees began using one of them from 12:00 to 8:00 five days per week. The work of this department, however, had its roots in John C. Whitaker's appointment of Wilson C. Lamb to contrive a method for grading tobacco automatically in order to select wrappers of varying colors. In a measure this department took over some of the work formerly assigned to the research department. This prototype of the industrial engineering department existed in 1944 when Whitaker requested Ernst and

Ernst to suggest ways to improve productivity. The firm recommended three moves: (1) a job evaluation plan, which was completed in 1945, (2) manpower budgets for determining the number of hours of work needed to produce a given quantity, and (3) a system of wage incentives. The industrial engineering department was never able to devise a method of wage incentives acceptable to management. As a result the accomplishments of this department, headed by Robert W. Newsom, Jr., were chiefly in the area of earned hour control at least until 1953. Newsom, the first industrial engineer hired by the company, began his work in 1948.

The company created a formal industrial engineering department on 12 July 1950 with five trained engineers. By the early 1960s fifty-five people worked in the department; twenty-seven of them had been trained at such institutions as North Carolina State College, Clemson College, Georgia Institute of Technology, the University of Tennessee, and Virginia Polytechnic Institute. So far as can be determined, no other tobacco company had such a department as early as 1950. In addition to its regular staff, the department leaned heavily on two consulting mathematicians—Dr. John W. Sawyer and Dr. Robert Johnson. Studies in the handling of materials, which became popular during World War II, immediately received emphasis because of increases in labor rates. Accordingly, for some time the industrial engineering department concentrated on material-handling equipment such as pallets and fork-lift trucks. Success in this area may be deduced from the company's investment of more than $1 million in fork-lift trucks and similar equipment. The department also took advantage of later developments resulting from the war, especially in the area of linear programming. For example, by describing the problems of making cigarettes in mathematical terms, studies could be made to determine the proper location for manufacturing different types of cigarettes. The number of trucks needed to handle demand economically was derived after systematic collection of data and their processing by computer. Studies involving earned hour control resulted in the saving of more than 600,000 man-hours per year in the manufacture of 100 billion cigarettes. On occasion the industrial engineering department discovered operations that were unnecessary. Before introduction of the vacuum conditioner, hogsheads of leaf were naturally left in the sweat houses for ordering. After that time, however, possibly from habit, the leaf continued to physically pass through the sweat houses. Through study, the industrial engineers eliminated the sweat house from the route of the leaf. This reduced the number of hogsheads for temporary storage and saved almost $125,000 per year. In a slightly different manner they achieved gross savings of $96,220 per year in the operation of cooper shops. The company maintained two of these shops—one for repair work and the other for assembling new patent hogsheads. By developing a fixture for use in repairing the hogsheads, the engineers combined the operations of both shops into one. The department also spent a good deal of time on building projects and had its own shop (in Number 1 at 8) for constructing models. So extensive was the one constructed for the Whitaker Park plant that the table holding it was 24 feet long.[71]

Expansion of the engineering department necessarily accompanied other developments of the 1950s. It so happened that Norman T. Buddine succeeded Risden P. Reece as head of the department on the eve of the expansion period—1 August 1950. Buddine, a mechanical engineer with three degrees from Columbia University, assumed responsibility for engineering, maintenance, construction, air conditioning, architecture, power, electricity, and mechanical operations under the authority of the Real Estate, Buildings, Machinery, and Equipment Committee.[72] Illustrations of the expansion of this department are abundant. In June 1950, for example, its chief offices were moved from the second floor of the main office building to the newly renovated three-story Lasater Building adjacent to the office building.[73] Shortly afterward the department announced a new method for handling maintenance work. By dividing the entire plant area, including out-of-town locations, into maintenance zones and establishing an office with personnel and equipment for a wide variety of maintenance jobs in each zone, all repair orders could generally be handled with greater dispatch. When the zone chief could not manage a request, it was referred to the proper shop in the engineering department.[74]

Another indication of the department's growth comes from an analysis of the electric shop in the construction and maintenance division and of the shops building. In July 1959, the electric shop was moved from Number 12, where it occupied 8,000 square feet of floor space, to Number 38 (the old office building) where it was allocated 36,000 square feet of floor space. Up to that time electric supplies had been scattered in a number of storage areas, making it difficult to work efficiently. In 1930 the company used about 2,500 electric motors, but by 1959 the number had grown to 12,000. In 1959 weight controllers for cigarette machines, X-ray gauges, D C drives, photoelectric cells, and other materials greatly swelled stock levels over those of 1930. In the same span of years the staff of the shop grew from 25 to more than 270 people.[75] Further consolidation in the engineering department came with the new engineering shops building, Number 91-2, between Vine Street and Patterson Avenue, which was started in 1961 and completed late in 1962. The two-million-dollar, three-storied structure contained 144,000 square feet of floor space and roof-top parking for 160 automobiles. It housed a service and storage room, a machine design unit, and electric and woodworking shops. Connected with Number 91-1, it was thus consolidated with the pipe, millwright, and sheet metal shops already housed in that building. Through this move the work of the department's construction and maintenance division was far better coordinated.[76]

The same expansion produced problems in communications for the engineering department. Trucks hauling men and supplies shuttled constantly from downtown Winston-Salem to the Kernersville storage area, to Whitaker Park, to Brook Cove, and ultimately to the Davie storage area. Economical use of these vehicles posed a major challenge. Primarily because of the rapid increase in activity within the engineering department generated by expansion of the company, there was a shortage of trucks in the early 1950s. The idea of using radio as a means for obtaining greater service from the trucks available belonged to Clarence Eugene Stephenson (25 May 1909–11 January 1963), holder of a B.S. degree in electrical engineering from the Georgia Institute of Technology. At the time, Stephenson was assistant superintendent in charge of mechanical shops, though he later became superintendent of the construction and maintenance division of the engineering department. At its inception in 1952, the two-way radio communication system controlled three trucks from station KIF-547 with antennae atop 256-1, the old building erected by R. J. Reynolds in 1891. Approved by the Federal Communications Commission (FCC), the radio station operated on a frequency of 152.87 megacycles. After 1952 the company bought two-way radio communications for 25 vehicles and 24 portable two-way radios for engineering department personnel. Further expansion of the system included fifty-seven radio paging units, which permitted contact with many employees in maintenance within two minutes. A high-powered selective paging transmitter was installed in the downtown area and a lesser one at Whitaker Park. Used customarily by people whose duties took them to ten or twelve places in one day, the system had a potential expansion to 455 receivers. Moreover, the two-way transmitter was moved from the 256-1 tower to the top of the Reynolds office building. Numerous areas other than those connected with the operation of vehicles benefited from this system. It was of special aid in preventing long shutdowns and in calling for medical assistance for workers occasionally injured on the job. The truck drivers, in reporting their arrivals and departures, frequently used colorful names such as "Cow Palace" for a building the company purchased from a meat-packing firm or "Ponderosa" for Whitaker Park. In order to attend to the diversity of duties performed by the engineering department, to keep in touch with similar systems in the vicinity, and to observe federal regulations, the company retained a lawyer in Washington to keep abreast of FCC changes in the Winston-Salem area.[77]

The stirring 1950s likewise produced a new emphasis on research. Considerable progress in that area had been made since the days of William O. McCorkle, R. J. Reynolds's flavorer hired before 1911, and E. Wright

Noble, who could do a few simple analyses. Edgar H. Harwood, a graduate of North Carolina State College and the company's first bona fide chemist, was employed on 16 June 1930 to work in the flavoring department in Number 64. Later he moved to Reynolds Inn, and by 1949 he was superintendent of the chemical department where he was assisted by Charles M. Sprinkle. At that time, with 51 employees and one clerk-typist, the chemical department was part of the manufacturing division. It was organized into sections consisting of chemical engineering—the largest— instrument development, glass shop, research project development, moisture control, analytical laboratory, organic research laboratory, metallurgy, chemical manufacturing, and 200 by-products where nicotine sulphate was developed.[78]

Motivated by the success in developing reconstituted leaf, the failure of Cavalier cigarettes, or the desirability of keeping up with the times, the directors about 1950 began to expand research work. Liggett and Myers, for example, organized a strong research program with elaborate facilities well before the R. J. Reynolds Tobacco Company began to move in that direction. Sometime before October 1950, James A. Gray asked Roy C. Haberkern and John C. Whitaker to investigate the problem of developing a modern research department. Accordingly, they visited the research departments of other companies such as the Corn Products Refining Company and Standard Oil of Indiana.[79] On 23 October 1950 the Reynolds company announced the appointment of Kenneth H. Hoover, then in charge of research and development for Commercial Solvents Corporation, as director of research. More than seven months later the directors authorized the Real Estate, Buildings, Machinery, and Equipment Committee to proceed with the construction of a research laboratory to cost approximately $1,750,000.[80] Complete with offices, laboratories, a model shop, a glass-blowing shop, a conference auditorium, a fireproof vault, and a library, the new research building was dedicated on 5 February 1953 with great fanfare. Evidently the new research plant had proved itself by April 1954, when the directors ordered additions valued at $1,900,000, furniture at $200,000, and equipment at $250,000 to more than double the facilities of the department.[81]

The newly organized research department consisted of six specialized divisions: chemical, biochemical, analytical, chemical engineering, agricultural, and research information service. The department eventually employed 187 people including 71 scientists, 32 of whom held advanced degrees. With a library of more than 10,000 volumes, photographic dark rooms, a chemical pilot plant, and a tobacco processing plant, the department expanded rapidly. Among its various contributions, the most outstanding were the development of blends for Winston and Salem cigarettes and high porosity paper. Also important was the department's work in quality control. It became routine to use automatic controls in testing and checking the firmness, size, and burning qualities of cigarettes; establishing the quality of the filter; guarding against air pockets; studying moisture control; inspecting the machinery daily for proper performance; checking cellophane for complete sealing; and seeing to numerous other tasks.[82] Reputedly, the research department began an all-out attempt to solve the problem of aging leaf but, shortly after the cancer publicity appeared, switched to basic research in order to explore the chemistry of tobacco.[83]

Expansion in the 1950s produced enthusiasm for a project of a different nature. In 1946 a committee composed of Frederick S. Hill, Edward A. Darr, and William J. Conrad, Jr., considered the purchase of a company airplane impractical, as did the directors who unanimously supported the committee's decision. But circumstances had changed by 10 December 1953, when the directors voted to buy a DC-3 for approximately $140,000.[84] On 9 May 1957 Bowman Gray, Jr., executive vice-president in charge of sales, secured prompt approval for the purchase of a Beechcraft two-engine plane at an approximate cost of $152,000.[85] Again, on 12 February 1959, Gray, then president but still watchful of the sales department, reported that studies and conferences indicated the need for an F-27, estimated to cost $750,000. This twin-engine, turboprop jet liner with Rolls Royce engines was fully pressurized and air-conditioned. Built to carry sixteen passengers, equipped with tables and several reclining chairs, and manned by a crew of two, it had a cruising speed of 300 miles per hour.[86] Later the DC-3 and the Beechcraft were sold and another Fairchild turboprop jet was purchased. These planes were used primarily by the sales department, which handled the dispatching service. Thus it became possible "to cover the country with more people faster," a matter of particular help "to Company personnel traveling to the Midwest and Pacific Coast."[87] According to *Tobacco*, the company believed so strongly in advertising that the DC-3 was painted cream and brown, the colors of the Camel package and carton, and the Beechcraft, green and white in deference to the Salem cigarette. Always true to its chief money-maker, company officials had the Fairchild decorated with the Camel motif.[88]

From the secretary's department came a noteworthy move undoubtedly inspired by the general enthusiasm characteristic of the period. William J. Conrad, Jr., director, vice-president, secretary, and chief of credit arrangements, conceived the idea of writing what became known as goodwill letters to customers on the direct list long regarded for paying their bills promptly and correctly. When the owner of E. W. Schmidt & Company of Ann Arbor, Michigan, acknowledged Conrad's second letter in 1956, he declared that he had not received more than four such letters in his twenty-three years of business. Moreover, he stated, the first letter from Conrad in

1949 had been framed and hung in his office. A wholesale grocery company in Rockford, Illinois, made copies of a similar letter to accompany a financial statement to its banking connections and to Dun & Bradstreet, Inc. *Tobacco Leaf* carried a copy of Conrad's letter to the Pittsburgh Candy and Cigar Company and a comment by the reporter who had heard of letters from manufacturers "asking for the do-re-mi in language plain and explicit"; Conrad's message, however, was the first ever brought to his attention. Roy Graham of El Queeno Distributing Company in Chisholm, Minnesota, wrote that he had heard from one of the company's "Top Brass" that all clocks at Reynolds were set by the time his checks arrived each week. Responses of this kind were numerous and equally enthusiastic.[89]

The advertising department, also made more alert by the new expansion, seized onto an idea that evidently had been practiced by other companies—the offer of cigarette lighters decorated to resemble packages of Winstons, Salems, and Camels. First intended to promote the sale of cigarettes by the carton, the lighters could be obtained by mailing in ten empty Winston or Salem packages with fifty cents. The project was thus self-supporting. By late 1957 the lighters had become so popular that for a time the company was unable to supply the demand. During the last week of May 1959, 320,000 lighters were sent to customers but still there was a shortage.[90] The success of this promotional drive surprised even Reynolds officials.

No doubt the visitors' program, formally established in 1918, was an even more effective method of advertising. This involved guided tours through the company's manufacturing plants. The first daily count of visitors was made on 10 November 1930; from then until the end of the year 276 persons toured the plants. Thereafter the number increased every year except 1933 and a period in the 1940s. The great surge forward, however, began in the 1950s and continued into the next decade. In 1962 alone 101,013 visitors were counted; they came from every state in the Union and fifty-nine foreign countries, particularly Canada and France. At first the tours were handled through the employment office. In 1955, however, a visitors' reception room, decorated with a tobacco motif including a growing tobacco plant, became the central point for coordinating the increasingly complicated program. There Goldston H. Dalton and Mrs. Dorothy J. Shaw served as host and hostess in the grand southern manner. It was often stated that letters from visitors and stockholders showed more interest in Dalton and Mrs. Shaw than in the chairman of the board. Dalton took over the program in 1919 immediately after returning from World War I. Needless to say, the guides who conducted the tours were not only carefully trained but also thoroughly conversant with the machinery and the manufacturing processes. Possibly the most distinguished visitor ever entertained by the company was William Howard Taft, who observed the manufacture of Prince Albert and Camels in 1920 when in Winston-Salem to deliver an address on "Americanism and Bolshevism." No doubt the most notorious devotee to Camels was Bonnie Parker who, with Clyde Barrow, toured what was evidently the Reynolds factory in the early 1930s.[91]

Every visitor was presented with gifts, generally tobacco products for adults and pencils and pens for children, not to mention postcards, ashtrays, and a short history of the company. Bread-and-butter letters that poured in as a rule stressed the cleanliness of the plants and the excellence of Camel cigarettes. The value of the program may be seen from a letter of Dr. Choop Jatiskasthira of Bangkok, Thailand: "I smoke Phillip Morris but now that I have tried this fresh Camel maybe I change. I will give Camels a good try for all your kindness to me today."[92]

But the changes that sparked the entire expansion of the 1950s came from management, which in 1945 began transforming itself into a cooperative working unit more suitable for the coordination of a complex organization than for the domination by one man characteristic of earlier years. The board of directors, generally consisting of fifteen members during the 1940s and 1950s, underwent numerous changes after 1945. The retirement of James W. Glenn in 1948 and the death of S. Clay Williams on 25 February 1949 elevated John C. Whitaker to the presidency and James A. Gray to chairman of the board. Gray's death in 1952 sent Whitaker to the chairmanship and Edward A. Darr to the presidency. From 1945 to 1955 thirteen new directors replaced older members of the board at their death or retirement. Some attributed certain shifts in company policy to these changes. Yet, three prominent moves during these years—adoption of the SPD process, development of reconstituted leaf, and the building of a modern personnel department—began well before many of the changes occurred. Nevertheless, numerous innovations in the work of the directors came simultaneously with the expansion of the 1950s.

The first such shift in procedure must be attributed directly to S. Clay Williams, who often was regarded as a one-man administrator. This was the institution of Monday luncheon meetings for directors, which permitted them to confer far more frequently than had been customary in the past. Minutes were not kept until April 1960, though reportedly these meetings were conducted by and large according to the plan for directors' meetings established by Roy C. Haberkern and William N. Reynolds in 1931. Judging from the copy of a voucher issued on 28 May 1945 for $140.77 to reimburse Williams for "directors luncheons," it is evident that he started the luncheons on 23 April and paid for them himself. He probably adopted this policy as a result of his experience as a director with the American Telephone & Telegraph Company (AT&T).[93] Prompt and regular exchange of information at the meetings undoubtedly led to more active responsibility on the part of all directors. It was frequently stated, however, that at first Williams spent much time discussing the Kentucky Trial.

Another change, which may well have developed from the weekly luncheon meetings, was to have committees function in more than name only. Though some have maintained that little was accomplished until after Williams's death,[94] there is evidence that the policy of greater dependence on committees may have begun earlier. On 13 May 1948, the directors initiated a comprehensive definition of the duties and responsibilities of standing committees, beginning with the Real Estate, Buildings, Machinery, and Equipment Committee and then the Personnel Committee. This allocation of power clearly represented an effort to ensure more vigorous performance, at least of the Real Estate, Buildings, Machinery, and Equipment Committee.[95] Not until April 1949, however, was the membership of standing committees regularly listed in the minutes. At that time there were six: Group Insurance and Hospitalization; Advertising; Blends and Formulas; Personnel; Leaf; and Real Estate, Buildings, Machinery, and Equipment.[96] In July duties and responsibilities similar to those outlined for the Personnel and Real Estate, Buildings, Machinery, and Equipment committees were listed for the remaining committees.[97] It thus appears that allocation of more rigorous duties for the six committees in preparation for greater dependence on them started in 1948 when Williams was chairman of the board and ended in July 1949 while James A. Gray served as chairman. The same six committees were listed with their membership in 1950 and 1951. In April 1952 the Finance Committee was established, or more, accurately, reinstated.[98] The seven standing committees reported to the board in 1952 and 1953 but increased to eight in 1954 with the creation of the Suggestion Plan Committee. Again, these committees reported in 1955 and 1956.[99]

But in the spring of 1957, when the expansion of company activities became more marked, the system of standing committees was drastically changed. Five of them became administrative committees and were charged with broad duties. Moreover, all prior actions of the board relating to the standing committees were rescinded. If they may be graded in importance according to the number of directors required on each, they ranked as follows: the Blends and Formulas, and Real Estate, Buildings, Machinery, and Equipment committees with three each; the Advertising and Leaf committees with two each; and the Suggestion Plan Committee with one. This left three original standing committees: Group Insurance and Hospitalization, Personnel, and Finance. A fourth, the Business Diversification Committee, was appointed the same year.[100] As an indication of its importance, all five members of the Business Diversification Committee were directors, namely Bowman Gray, Jr. (chairman), Alexander H. Galloway,

Spencer B. Hanes, Jr., Kenneth H. Hoover, and Charles H. Babcock. Incidentally, in 1963 this same committee contained nine directors with Spencer B. Hanes, Jr., as chairman.

In line with these general changes in top management came the introduction of directors from outside the company, beginning with the election of Robert M. Hanes (president of the Wachovia Bank and Trust Company) in 1955 and followed by Charles H. Babcock (financier and son-in-law of R. J. Reynolds) in 1957, Leighton H. Coleman (senior partner in the law firm of Davis, Polk, Wardwell, Sunderland & Kiendl) in 1959, and Gordon Gray (lawyer, educator, government official, and brother of Bowman Gray, Jr.) in 1961. Though distinguished in many areas, these new directors were not far removed from the company.

Bowman Gray, Jr., was credited with a statement that the addition of outside directors proved helpful, especially in making the switch from the average cost method of inventory valuation to the LIFO (last in, first out) accounting technique. Gray regretted that the change had not been made earlier, because that would have meant "a materially lower debt today."[101] The LIFO plan was adopted on 31 December 1957, effective from the beginning of the year, thus making Robert Hanes and Charles Babcock the only outside directors who might have influenced the vote. The fight to use the LIFO technique lasted at least seven years; in the end it was adopted by a majority vote rather than unanimously.

First presented in detail to the Executive Committee on 16 November 1950 by Stuart M. Scott, comptroller and director, assisted by H. Henry Ramm and William R. Lybrook at the request of James A. Gray, the LIFO plan met a cool reception; yet its legality as a part of the Revenue Code of 1920 and its potential for extensive tax savings for 1950 received careful attention. Analysis of the effects of the upward movement of leaf tobacco prices beginning in 1940 in relation to inventory values as of 31 December 1949 and acquisition prices of leaf tobacco for 1950 did not overbalance objections to the LIFO plan. They were fivefold: (1) adoption of the LIFO plan in 1950 would freeze inventory values of the company "with the consequent possibility of tax losses for future years"; (2) the LIFO plan had not been used by other companies in the tobacco industry; (3) the average cost method of inventory valuation had been approved by the Treasury Department in 1920; (4) in the past, despite variations in leaf prices, the average cost method had permitted stable profits; and (5) earlier use of the LIFO method would not have led to such profits. A lengthy deliberation ended with a negative vote.[102] Again, on 20 December of the following year, adoption of the LIFO method was the chief topic of discussion at a meeting of the directors, but the final note of the minutes read: "no action was then taken pending further study." About four months later at the annual meeting of stockholders, James A. Gray called on Albert D. Berning, an accounting specialist, to explain certain questions regarding the LIFO inventory method. When the matter was raised at directors' meetings in 1952 and 1953, it again met rejection. Four years later, however, the plan received a majority vote and immediately went into effect.[103]

As an adjunct to the expansion of the 1950s the capital structure of the company was simplified. This shift, as discussed earlier, eliminated the old common, or "A" stock, and left the company with two classes of stock, common and Preferred 3.60% series, the Preferred 4.50% series issued in 1948 having been redeemed on 1 October 1958. The company gradually bought up the Preferred 3.60% series at favorable rates until, as of 14 August 1963, it owned 252,385 shares of the original 490,000 shares authorized and issued in 1945 at $100 par value. Meanwhile, in April 1959 the par value of common stock was reduced from $10 to $5. Later, by an almost unanimous vote, the stockholders increased the authorized 30 million shares of common stock, par value $5, to 60 million shares and split the outstanding 20 million into 40 million shares, thus leaving 20 million authorized but unissued shares at the end of 1961. In the two-for-one split of the common stock in September 1961, $100 million was transferred from "earnings retained" to the common stock capitalization account, which was thereby raised from $100 million to $200 million. Until this time the common stock capital had remained at $100 million since 1927. As an indication of the company's growth, in 1927 its "total undivided profits" were $40,696,775, but in 1961 the "earnings retained for the requirements of the business" were $363,305,246 despite the transference of $100 million to the common stock capitalization. According to *Fortune*'s directory, R. J. Reynolds's original capital of $7,500 had enabled his company to rank 51st among industrial corporations in the United States at the end of 1961.

Community Development

The R. J. Reynolds Tobacco Company has done more than provide bountiful dividends for its stockholders. Industry in many instances may claim direct benefits to humanity as in the cases of steel, clothing, food, or fuel. A tobacco company, however, provides direct benefits in the form of simple pleasure for millions as well as funds for other items. When Western Europeans first met the tobacco plant, they derived pleasure from its use in far cruder forms than those made available by manufacturers who have studied and worked for the improvement of their products. The good accomplished by the R. J. Reynolds Tobacco Company certainly goes far beyond the simple pleasures derived from the use of its products. It has been instrumental in the social and economic development of North Carolina and the Winston-Salem area. It has provided opportunities for hundreds of employees who have used their wages, salaries, and dividends to educate their children and raise their standard of living. Its operations have drawn into the purview of the people of North Carolina and Winston-Salem individuals from all parts of the United States and from many foreign countries. The journey of Walter R. Reynolds to France in 1917 in search of cigarette paper has been duplicated many times by others under different circumstances. Did Joseph L. Graham not successfully fight all the railroad interests of the United States in 1915, and did he not make Winston-Salem an important inland port in 1916 and thereby aid the entire area? Such broadening influences as these could not have been provided by the blackberry pickers of the 1870s. The bases for these conclusions, however subjective, are found in the preceding chapters. It remains to note objective evidence of the company's role in community and statewide development.

In doing so it may be well to consider the standards suggested in 1959 by Lawrence L. Lavengood, a business historian. When writing of the enviable position of businessmen in American democracy, Lavengood held that they should dedicate themselves to the objectives which in the past had made them great. These he declared to be (1) the ingenious production of goods and services of high quality at the lowest possible price, (2) the search for and exploitation of new frontiers of economic opportunity, (3) the provision of assistance and support to (but not prescription of) the community's institutions of learning and artistic refinement, and (4) the staunch use of prestige in guarding the individual's civil liberties.[104] Measured against these standards, the R. J. Reynolds Tobacco Company has already been shown to excel in the first two. Certainly, after the troubles of the 1940s, the company appears to have assimilated and adopted the fourth standard. In viewing its role as a supporter of institutions concerned with human betterment, the contributions of individuals who have profited from the operations of the company cannot be excluded. It should be kept in mind that the company as a business organization under New Jersey law was never free to assert its full responsibility to the community until 1953. On 25 June of that year, the New Jersey Supreme Court ruled that "the corporate power to make reasonable charitable contributions exists under modern conditions even apart from express statutory provision."[105] When the company's executive committee on 23 February 1953 considered the feasibility of a contribution to Old Salem, Inc., its members decided to await the outcome of this litigation then pending concerning the rights of New Jersey corporations to make such donations.[106]

As in many other areas, R. J. Reynolds himself set the example and the pace for the support of community projects in the Winston-Salem area, though he did so at a time when earnings and goals were relatively limited. His first cash donation of this nature, so far as can be determined, came early in 1891 when he needed all the funds that he could muster to build his new brick factory. When Simon Green Atkins (11 June 1863–28 June 1934) appeared before the local Board of Trade on 30 January 1891 to request assistance for establishing a Negro college in Winston-Salem through state aid, the board appointed a committee to study the matter. Meanwhile, Negro citizens had raised $2,000 of the $2,500 required to get action from the state legislature. When no report from the committee of the Board of Trade was forthcoming, R. J. Reynolds contributed the needed $500. The Slater Industrial and State Normal School (now Winston-Salem State University) was incorporated on 28 September 1892.[107] Later Reynolds participated in a move to buy an experimental farm for the Slater State Normal and Industrial College to be named in memory of Lieutenant William E. Shipp, of the Tenth Colored Cavalry, who lost his life at the Battle of Santiago in 1898. Shipp had been interested in the work of the Slater college. Messages praising this action came from such prominent Americans as President William McKinley, former President Grover Cleveland, Governor-elect Theodore Roosevelt, and Daniel C. Gilman of the Johns Hopkins University.[108] Reynolds made another generous move to aid the college on 11 November 1899 when he proposed to give $5,000 toward the establishment of a hospital and nurses training department provided Professor Simon G. Atkins raised a similar amount by 1 January 1901, as he declared he could. This gift, Atkins stated, was "the most liberal contribution that has been made for such a purpose by a Southern white man." William A. Blair at once wrote an official of the Southern Education Board:[109]

> In connection with our work for the proper training of the colored people here, I am sure you will be glad to hear that one of our citizens, Mr. R. J. Reynolds who had not appeared to take much interest in the work which we have been attempting to do, has been observing it in a quiet and careful way without our knowledge, and now he comes to us and offers a cash donation of $5,000 provided we will raise a like amount, to establish a hospital for colored people and a training school for colored nurses in connection with our school.

Because Reynolds obtained no indirect benefits from the operation of the Slater Hospital until 1906, his contribution undoubtedly was altruistic. Shortly afterward he made a similar offer to the Ladies Hospital Association for the establishment of the Twin-City Hospital.[110]

R. J. Reynolds also made many less spectacular gifts during the 1890s and early 1900s. Among them were a prize for an athletic contest in 1893, aid to a student in the Oxford Orphanage in 1897, a donation of more than $1,000 to the orphanage from 1894 to 1897, and many small contributions to local churches of various denominations.[111] Gifts of $1,000 to the Baptist Orphanage in nearby Thomasville in 1901 and a similar amount to Guilford College in 1903 also mark him as a liberal contributor to worthwhile causes.[112] Always interested in agricultural progress, Reynolds in 1910 furnished prizes for a corn-growing contest.[113] His wife Katharine Smith Reynolds made the first contribution ($100) toward building a monument in memory of Charles Duncan McIver, founder of the Woman's College of the University of North Carolina (now the University of North Carolina at Greensboro) where she had been educated.[114] So unusual were these gifts in a period of general poverty in the South that Reynolds, as early as 1901, was called a benefactor to the Winston-Salem area.[115]

His personal contributions to civic, charitable, and educational institutions continued until his death. When a group sought funds for a YWCA building in 1914, Reynolds promised to give a sum equivalent to one-seventh of what it might raise. His portion amounted to $5,000. Two years later, in order to finish the building, he offered to donate an additional $5,000 if the leaders of the project would raise an equivalent sum. When on 31 March 1916, a whirlwind campaign failed to realize this goal, Reynolds at once extended the time allowed them for matching his offer. Though completed in 1917, the YWCA building had an indebtedness of $10,000. The directors of the company, in a meeting called for that purpose, voted to contribute the $10,000 if the YWCA agreed to accommodate the company's employees economically and to work generally "to uplift and strengthen the character of such employees." Significantly, and no doubt at R. J.'s request, the motion for this unusual gift was made by William N. Reynolds and seconded by Walter R. Reynolds. Yet, it was necessary to obtain approval from the stockholders for the contribution, which evidently was the first of any consequence made by the company.[116] R. J. Reynolds's interest in this area undoubtedly stemmed from the pioneer work of Katharine Smith Reynolds in local YWCA activities; possibly he also was motivated by the benefits it promised his employees.

For Negro employees of the company R. J. Reynolds led the drive to build homes that would rent at 6 percent on the investment as an alternative to the shacks they then rented from private owners, who charged three to six times as much.[117] He also contributed $5,000 and the site for a Negro church called, in his honor, the Reynolds Temple Methodist Church. When it was formally opened on 25 November 1917, the congregation and friends such as Mayor Robert W. Gorrell, D. Rich, and Lenora H. Sills joined in a "special prayer for the speedy recovery of Mr.

R. J. Reynolds, who has so liberally aided in the erection of the church, that he may soon return home to continue his great work in the interest of humanity and Winston-Salem." In the end, however, a memorial service for Reynolds, planned to be held at the church on 9 November 1918, was attended by a large congregation of both races.[118] The contributions of R. J. Reynolds thus generally went for projects intended to help the most neglected segment of the Winston-Salem population.

In many ways R. J.'s personal aid in upbuilding Winston-Salem continued after his death. In a nuncupative will made in the presence of George W. Orr and Clement Manly on 23 July 1918, Reynolds, "in bed propped up with pillows, . . . ill, feeble in body but mind sound and clear," declared he wanted them to see that his estate paid for additions to the Negro and white sections of the Twin-City Hospital. According to a newspaper report, the amount spent in making additions for each race reached $120,000.[119] In continuing his work, Katherine Smith Reynolds endowed a Chair of Biology at Davidson College, gave $50,000 for the purchase of a site on which to build a high school, and was responsible for building the handsome R. J. Reynolds Auditorium—all as personal memorials to him.[120] Perhaps, in the long run, the R. J. Reynolds High School proved the most valuable of all the contributions inspired by Reynolds. Almost forty years after its doors were first opened its students won more National Merit Competition Scholarships than did students from any other high school in the country.[121] R. J.'s contributions to human betterment continued through the foundations established by his children after their patrimonies had been greatly increased by the successful operations of the company.

With the exception of the $10,000 appropriated for the local YWCA, the Reynolds company is known to have made only three minor contributions for social betterment before World War I. They were $100 for St. Luke's Hospital, located in the state capital, in 1899; a small sum for prizes offered by the agricultural department of the Forsyth County Fair in 1905;[122] and possibly one other. After the 1916 flood in the mountains of western North Carolina, the company sent Charles A. Dobbins into Wilkes County to investigate the damage and then offered to match any amount raised in Winston-Salem to aid the victims.[123] Naturally, the company contributed to the war effort. Donations were made to such organizations as the Red Cross, the YMCA, and the United War Work Fund. In addition, the company regularly supported subscriptions to Liberty Loan drives and campaigns to interest employees in the purchase of savings stamps. During the war years, however, it apparently made only one contribution to civic improvement—a gift of $500 to the local chamber of commerce.

From the end of the war until the 1940s contributions to welfare projects came largely from individuals who had profited from operations of the company. Contributions from the company during this period were limited to $1,000 for the Associated Charities in 1920, a like sum for residents of New Bern, North Carolina, who were made homeless by a fire in 1922, a gift two years later of real estate in Cameron Park for use as a street or playground, and $5,000 to the Red Cross for aid to drought-ravaged areas in the 1930s.[124]

Among the major personal contributions was Joseph L. Graham's gift of $1,000 in 1919 to the Winston-Salem Foundation, created in that year by Francis H. Fries to build a fund for charitable, religious, and educational institutions. More than half a million dollars was given to the Oxford Orphanage in Oxford, North Carolina, and the Methodist Children's Home in Winston-Salem from the estate of John Neal, a division manager who had been stationed in Omaha, Nebraska. William N. Reynolds was the benefactor of the Prince Albert Playground for use of the Negro population and a $20,000 school building in the Quaker Gap section of Stokes County, North Carolina. D. Rich offered $125,000 or one dollar for every two raised by the congregation of the First Baptist Church of Winston-Salem; he also was responsible for erection of the Carrie Rich Memorial Library and the D. Rich Memorial Administration Building at Buie's Creek Junior College (later Campbell College). Other contributions included a printing press for the Barium Springs Orphanage donated by James Sloan in 1923; a highly prized radio receiving set for the State School for the Blind and pews for the Presbyterian Church in Mount Airy by Katharine Smith Reynolds; a substantial quantity of radium for the City Memorial Hospital for the treatment of both white and Negro patients and 242 front feet of valuable real estate for the new Centenary Methodist Church on Fifth Street by Bowman Gray, Sr., and his wife; the Miller Municipal Airport, funded by a gift of $100,000 to the Winston-Salem Foundation by Robert E. Lasater; and an organ for Constitution Hall (in Washington, D.C.), owned by the Daughters of the American Revolution, which was purchased with a $50,000 donation by Mrs. William N. Reynolds.[125]

More substantial contributions were made during the 1930s. The most outstanding came from William N. Reynolds and his wife, who gave funds to build the Louisa Wilson Bitting Dormitory at Salem College and to accredit the Nancy Reynolds Memorial School, a high school named for his mother; $5,000 to help buy Stratford Hall, the ancestral home of Robert E. Lee; and $200,000 toward the construction of a new hospital for whites in Winston-Salem. Apparently, they also donated money for a Negro hospital, later named the Kate Bitting Reynolds Memorial Hospital but generally known among its patrons as "the Katie B."[126] In 1937, S. Clay Williams donated $50,000 to Wofford College for the William A. Law Scholarship Fund. In the same year the Bowman Gray family contributed $100,000 to match funds of the Work Projects Administration (WPA) to build the Bowman Gray Memorial Stadium, owned by the city of Winston-Salem. Also in 1937 the Z. Smith Reynolds Foundation gave $100,000 to help fund a state campaign against venereal disease, the first of its numerous donations.[127]

Although by 1940 the directors of the Reynolds company seemed inclined to aid substantially in community development, they were still somewhat constrained by their concern that stockholders would object. The long-debated issue of a building fund for the Winston-Salem and Forsyth County Hospital, which came to a head in 1945, is a case in point. The city had authorized a bond issue of $1,500,000 for the hospital, and a substantial amount had already been raised by subscription. The company then paid about 40 percent of the property taxes levied by Winston-Salem and Forsyth County. Because 40 percent of the bond issue was exactly $600,000, Robert E. Lasater finally moved that if a contribution were made, it should be for that amount. After considerable investigation, the other directors agreed. Accordingly, the company offered to give $600,000 if other corporations and individuals raised a like amount and the city avoided a bond issue—to Reynolds, the perferable course. The directors' rationalization of this action for the stockholders was twofold: (1) in relation to the federal tax situation, the stockholders' interests would be best served by a contribution, and (2) additional hospital facilities were needed to administer the company's hospital plan.[128]

Nevertheless, during the 1940s the company made numerous contributions to various war funds and to the Community Chest. In addition, it gave a total of $30,000 to the United Negro College Fund, the American Cancer Society, the American Heritage Foundation, and Friends of the Land. When asked to contribute to the Better Business Foundation of North Carolina, Inc., to be administered by the School of Commerce of the University of North Carolina, the directors were hard pushed until James A. Gray recalled that since 1912 the company had owned a number of shares of stock issued by MacAndrews and Forbes. Until the directors began considering some way to solve this problem without offending the stockholders, ownership of the MacAndrews and Forbes stock apparently had been virtually forgotten. When sold in 1946, it yielded $63,609 for the Better Business Foundation.[129] Two years later a request from North Carolina State College (now North Carolina State University) for a contribution to its Agricultural Foundation led to a donation of $10,000.[130] The building of the War Memorial Coliseum in Winston-Salem posed a problem that could not be solved with small contributions or odd holdings of stock. As a result the directors agreed to contribute $150,000 on condition that $600,000 be raised from other sources. When called upon to announce the company's gift at a dinner meeting at the Robert E. Lee Hotel,

S. Clay Williams declared: "I am reluctant to stand and acknowledge applause, because this is the gift of more than 62,000 stockholders of the R. J. Reynolds Tobacco Company."[131] No doubt this statement indicated the natural reaction of an attorney who had been unable to find a precedent for the fait accompli.

After Williams's death in 1949 but before 25 June 1953, the company became bolder in making donations to community projects. Eight sums ranging from $2,500 to $41,600 went to organizations such as the National Fire Protection Association, the American Red Cross, the National Fund for Medical Education, and the United Fund.[132] During the same period the company made substantial contributions to the Salvation Army, Salem College, City Memorial Hospital, William N. and Kate B. Reynolds Memorial Park, and Winston Lake Park.[133] A gift of $65,000 toward the construction of a building for the Salvation Army represented genuine charity for the unfortunate. Equally as public-spirited was the company's pledge to give $150,000 toward the construction of new facilities for a public library in Winston-Salem. A contribution of $200,000 (plus an additional $25,000) was made for the erection of a YMCA and YWCA building for Negroes. A like amount was given for a wing to the Baptist Hospital in Winston-Salem,[134] thus helping to pave the way for bringing Wake Forest College to Winston-Salem—in which the company was to play a prominent role.

Before considering the extensive contributions of the company to routine organizations and to libraries, research facilities, and colleges made after 25 June 1953, what is perhaps the most notable cultural accomplishment derived from the profits of the R. J. Reynolds Tobacco Company should be noted. This was the establishment of Wake Forest College (now Wake Forest University) in Winston-Salem. The move and subsequent improvements called for extensive aid from the company and from the Reynolds and Gray families. Wake Forest, a liberal arts college operated by the Baptist church, was originally situated in the eastern part of the state in the town of its name. In the mid-1930s the continuation of its two-year medical school became endangered when the American Medical Association decided to reduce the number of physicians in the country either by reducing the size of classes in four-year medical schools or by eliminating all two-year schools. When the dean of the Wake Forest two-year medical school heard that the trustees of the Bowman Gray Foundation wished to establish a medical school in Winston-Salem, he contacted the foundation. On 2 August 1939 the trustees offered the Wake Forest School of Medicine Science the principal and interest of the foundation. Trustees of the Baptist Hospital in Winston-Salem joined the program and the Baptist church agreed to raise funds for enlarging the hospital. The funds that it raised plus the $750,000 donated by the Bowman Gray Foundation became the nucleus for building the four-year Bowman Gray School of Medicine, a branch of Wake Forest University. Practicing physicians in Winston-Salem also provided valuable assistance. The first students began to arrive in September 1941, although the position of the medical school remained insecure. Eventually James A. Gray, Bowman Gray, Jr., Gordon Gray, and the widow of Bowman Gray, Sr., poured funds and property into the school until, with federal funds and aid from the Ford Foundation, its position became secure.[135] Despite the unsettled status of corporate gifts before 1953, the company contributed $475,000 to the Bowman Gray School of Medicine and to the establishment of Wake Forest College in Winston-Salem. Between late 1953 and 1959, however, the company donated more than $1.5 million to these two institutions.[136]

During this period various individuals who had profited from the operations of the R. J. Reynolds Tobacco Company made generous donations to civic and educational institutions. Among them were the 186-acre Reynolds Park with an 18-hole golf course, tennis courts, a swimming pool, and other recreational facilities—a gift of the children of R. J. Reynolds; extensive improvements to the local airport funded by the Z. Smith Reynolds Foundation; a sponsor's fund of $20,000 given by James A. Gray for the development of a recreational area for Negroes to be constructed by the WPA; a gift of $100,000 by Mary Reynolds Babcock toward the construction of a coliseum on the campus of North Carolina State College; endowment of the Craige Chair of Jurisprudence and History at the University of North Carolina with a $150,000 contribution from Burton Craige; a gift of $10,000 to the Thomas V. Blackwell Memorial Fund, preferably for the education of young men and women of the First Baptist Church in Winston-Salem; the Rondthaler Chair of Practical Theology at the Moravian Theological Seminary of Bethlehem, Pennsylvania, endowed by Louis F. Owen; securities sufficient to yield an annual income of $5,000 to help promote research in agriculture at North Carolina State College and a lot valued at $100,000 to be used as a site for the Public Library of Winston-Salem and Forsyth County—both donated by Richard J. Reynolds, Jr.; and a considerable sum given by Roy C. Haberkern and others for the Colored Baptist Orphanage, later called the Memorial Industrial School.[137]

In addition, two other extensive donations came from the estate of Kate Bitting Reynolds and from an endowment established by James A. Gray. Kate Bitting Reynolds left an estate of $8,000,000, of which she placed $5,000,000 in a perpetual trust fund. The income of the trust fund was earmarked for the poor and needy of Winston-Salem and Forsyth County; for the most part, the remainder was for schools, colleges, and hospitals primarily in North Carolina.[138] The James A. Gray Endowment Fund of

$1,700,000 generally went to Methodist colleges of North Carolina, though substantial amounts were given to other colleges, including $100,000 to Winston-Salem State College. Previously Gray had contributed more than $1,000,000 to various churches, playgrounds, and orphanages.[139]

Meanwhile, in 1946 the North Carolina Baptist Convention accepted as a recurring annual gift the income from $10,000,000 in the Z. Smith Reynolds Foundation on condition that Wake Forest College be moved to Winston-Salem.[140] In 1959, in addition to its annual gift, the foundation gave the college $750,000 for the construction of a dormitory.[141] Mary Reynolds Babcock, the older daughter of R. J. Reynolds, and her husband, Charles H. Babcock, donated 300 acres of land within the city limits of Winston-Salem as a site for the campus of Wake Forest University and made numerous other contributions to the college. In fact, in her relatively short life, Mary Reynolds Babcock gave a total of $7,000,000 to civic, educational, artistic, and charitable projects that indirectly affected the Winston-Salem community.[142]

During the 1950s the Reynolds company began a systematic approach to the support of community projects. Indeed, after 25 June 1953 its direct contributions to civic, educational, and charitable projects became too numerous to describe. Not all were confined to North Carolina. Donations to community chests soon expanded beyond Winston-Salem to include many areas where the company owned warehouses for manufactured products, redrying plants, or branch offices. In 1955, for example, the company gave $200 to the Community Chest of Mason County, Kentucky, and $500 to the United Bay Area Crusade, Inc., which included most of the charitable agencies in San Francisco and adjoining areas. Three years later $500 was donated to the Jersey City YMCA.[143] In fact, after June 1953, it appears that all areas having a definite connection with the R. J. Reynolds Tobacco Company received donations for some civic project.

The following list of company donations to educational projects during the mid-1950s is perhaps typical but certainly not complete:

College Foundation, Inc	$ 50,000
Friends of Kentucky Libraries	15,000
4-H Clubs of North Carolina	300
National Fund for Medical Education	1,000
North Carolina Foundation of Church-Related Colleges	180,000
North Carolina State College	169,000
Ohio Northern University	500

Old Salem, Inc.	75,000
Salem College and Academy	340,000
Triangle Research Association	106,000
United Negro College Fund	15,000
University of Kentucky	20,000
University of North Carolina	5,130 (annually)
	5,400
University of Tennessee	15,000
Winston-Salem Art Center and Council	149,500

These donations, though generally made with the tax exempt status of such gifts in mind, might easily have gone to less worthy causes.

By July 1959, it became necessary to appoint a special contributions committee to keep records and to adopt rules of procedure. Specifically, the committee was to formulate policy on contributions as donations or as membership fees, and to review such policy and recommend changes; to prepare each year a proposed budget for donations and membership fees; to consider and act upon all applications for contributions not exceeding $10,000, as well as proposed memberships or renewal of memberships in organizations with annual fees of less than $1,000; and to prepare an annual statement of all contributions and membership dues. H. Henry Ramm (chairman), Alexander H. Galloway, and Colin Stokes served first on the committee.[144]

Certain other notable private and corporate gifts made in the 1950s continued the pattern laid down by R. J. Reynolds. In 1950 William N. Reynolds gave $100,000 for a combined school gymnasium and community center at Critz, Virginia, for the use of the Hardin Reynolds Memorial School. In the following year, he donated $340,000 to North Carolina State College to supplement the salaries of outstanding professors. Around the same time, in addition to the site given by Richard J. Reynolds, Jr., the Public Library of Winston-Salem and Forsyth County received $250,000 from other members of the Reynolds family, $110,000 from the Bowman Gray family, and $150,000 from the R. J. Reynolds Tobacco Company. Shortly afterward Robert E. Lasater left funds for the Old Hickory Boy Scout Council, St. Paul's Episcopal Church, and the community chest of Winston-Salem. Later the Mary Reynolds Babcock Foundation granted $375,000 to Sweet Briar College as well as another gift. During her lifetime Mary Reynolds Babcock had given an earlier donation to improve the library of Sweet Briar College. Members of the Reynolds family contributed $175,000 toward erection of the R. J. Reynolds–Patrick County Memorial Hospital at Stuart, Virginia.[145]

A fund donated by Willian N. Reynolds to Duke University in 1935 and used for student aid eventually permitted the simultaneous support of sixteen students at a maximum of $2,400 per year. Out of this grew a program of four-year scholarships, known as the William Neal Reynolds Memorial Scholarships, with priority given first to the children of employees of the R. J. Reynolds Tobacco Company and second to children of families living in Forsyth County. Under the leadership of Richard J. Reynolds, Jr., the Z. Smith Reynolds Foundation in 1962 established an outstanding scholarship program at the Woman's College of the University of North Carolina in memory of Katharine Smith Reynolds. Assuming the full expenses of twelve scholars each year until a maximum of forty-eight scholarships were awarded each year, the program covered the state of North Carolina by drawing students from each of twelve designated geographic areas. When this program was established, the Z. Smith Reynolds Foundation also made numerous other grants to North Carolina colleges, and hospitals and related causes. Perhaps the most outstanding single gift to any local educational institution was the $2,000,000 left to the Winston-Salem Foundation by the widow of Bowman Gray, Sr.; both principal and income were earmarked exclusively for the Bowman Gray School of Medicine. Taxes on the gift were borne by the other heirs of her estate.[146] Smaller but probably more promising for the future was the annual sum of $25,000 first set aside by the company in 1960 for public school teachers of Winston-Salem and Forsyth County to use for summer travel or study.[147] The record shows that during 1960, 1961, and 1962 the company donated a total of $4,215,180, of which educational institutions received 50–52 percent and hospitals approximately 20 percent.[148]

Incomplete as this account may be, it nevertheless reveals the continuing interest of the company, its principals, and their families in the social and economic improvement of North Carolina. For the company's part, need for technical skill was not the only factor that influenced Reynolds officials to emphasize the importance of education. They apparently realized that the progress of their business in a large measure had depended on the brains of Western Europe. Without such materials and equipment as tin foil, glassine paper, and the Hauni filter-tip assembler developed in Germany; the Rose packing machine, the Mark VI making machine, and cellophane from England; the Arenco packer from Sweden; and cigarette paper from France, it would have been impossible for the company to develop as it did. Perhaps the path lay clearer after World War II and the consequent danger of the disappearance of Western Europe as a source for outstanding ideas. No one can prophesy the future course of the R. J. Reynolds Tobacco Company, but the pattern for its support of the community's institutions of learning and artistic refinement was clearly fixed. It all came from the work started by Richard Joshua Reynolds, whose

tombstone in Salem Cemetery carries an epitaph written by Clement
Manly:

> Original in thought, natural in act,
> Justice to all men his guide,
> Energy in boundless measure
> Made up this workman of the world.

APPENDIXES

A P P E N D I X   A
Ancestral Line of Richard Joshua Reynolds

Christopher Reynolds, first known of the family, born about 1530 in County Kent, England, married and settled in London, where he and his sons engaged in trade and commerce. Known children: *George*, Christopher, Mary.

George Reynolds, born 1555 in County Kent, England, died in 1634 in London, married Thomasyn Church on 20 January 1585, settled in London. Children: Thomas, John, Robert, Anne, *Christopher*, and others.

Christopher Reynolds, born 1611 at Gravesend, England, and died Isle of Wight County, Virginia, married Elizabeth (surname unidentified), arrived in Warwick County, Virginia, in 1622 aboard the *Francis and John* and settled on 450 acres patented on 15 September 1636. Children: *Richard*, Christopher, John, Abbasha, Elizabeth, Jane, Thomas.

Richard Reynolds, born 1641 in Isle of Wight County, Virginia, died 27 July 1711 in Newport Parish, Virginia, married Elizabeth Sharpe. Children: *Richard*, Christopher, Sharpe, Elizabeth, John.

Richard Reynolds, born in 1669 in Isle of Wight County, Virginia, married Mary Anderson in 1694 and settled in King William County, Virginia. Children: William, James, Thomas, *David*, Barbara, John.

David Reynolds, born in 1720 and settled in Pittsylvania County, Virginia. Children: Joseph, Richard David, *Abram David*, Jesse, Alexander.

Abram [Abraham] *David Reynolds*, married Mary Harbour and settled in Patrick County, Virginia. Children: *Harden William*, David.

Harden [Hardin] *William Reynolds*, born 20 April 1810 in Patrick County, Virginia, and died in 1881 [1882], married Nancy Jane Cox. Children: Katherine, Mary Jane [Mary Joyce], Agnes Cox, Abram David, *Richard Joshua*, Harden [Hardin] Harbour, Lucy B., William Neal, Walter R.

Richard Joshua Reynolds, born 20 July 1853 [1850] in Patrick County, Virginia, married Mary Katherine [Katharine] Smith on 27 February 1905, and settled in Winston-Salem, N.C. Children: *Richard Joshua*, Mary Katharine, Nancy Susan, Zachary Smith.

Source: Based on "Christopher Reynolds and His Descendants" by S. F. Tillman, 3212 Cummings Lane, Chevy Chase 15, Maryland, 1 April 1959; lithographed by the Goetz Company, Washington, D.C., 1959.

Note: This record is believable from a geographic point of view—the slow migration of the Reynolds family from Warwick County, Virginia (in the extreme eastern part of Virginia and now consolidated with the city of Newport News), westward to Isle of Wight County and farther westward to Pittsylvania County, which once contained Patrick County. Except for a few known minor errors, listed below and generally made in other publications, the facts after 1785 correspond with those that have been fairly well authenticated from other records and given in the text of this work. The errors noted in this genealogical work are as follows: Hardin William Reynolds (not Harden William), the death of Hardin William

Reynolds on 30 May 1882 (not 1881), omission or error of name of Hardin W. Reynolds's oldest child (Mary Joyce Reynolds), the date of the birth of Richard Joshua Reynolds on 20 July 1850 (not 20 July 1853), and the misspelling of Mary Katharine Smith (not Mary Katherine Smith). Some of the other dates may be questionable, but the genealogical line seems authentic.

APPENDIX B
Personal Property and Farming Operations of Hardin W. Reynolds

Table B-1.
Selected Items from the Personal Property of Hardin W. Reynolds, 1832–1882

| Year | Slaves | Livestock | | Money, Bonds, and Interest | Value of Personal Property | Taxes on Personal Property |
		Horses and Mules	Other			
1832	—	2	—	—	—	$ .12
1833	—	2	—	—	—	.12
1834	—	1	—	—	—	.06
1835	—	2	—	—	—	.12
1836	—	3	—	—	—	.18
1837	—	0	—	—	—	.00
1838				Not listed		
1839	8	8	—	—	—	3.04
1840	9	10	—	—	—	3.50
1841	10	9	—	—	—	5.13
1842	11	·10	—	—	—	5.65
1843	12	10	—	$ 227	—	7.51
1844	17	10	—	1,500	—	12.10
1845	18	10	—	—	—	6.88
1846	18	11	—	60[a]	—	7.88
1847	19	11	—	180[a]	—	10.03
1848	19	10	—	200[a]	—	10.43
1849	23	17	—	150[a]	—	11.44
1850	37	13	—	200[a]	—	11.47
1851	20	Not listed		250[a]	—	13.89
1852	40	13	173[b]	5,107	$21,034	37.87
1853	44	13	229	250	17,530	51.06
1854				Not listed		
1855	54	16	250	16,000	17,700	53.80
1856	53	18	250	12,000	1,365	91.40
1857	52	21	245	10,000	11,780	83.92
1858	59	20	290	10,000	11,835	87.75
1859	58	24	285	20,000	23,160	131.84
1860	59	18	240	22,000	24,900	140.00
1861	54	18	240	22,000	25,080	131.72

1862	80	24	255	15,000	42,990	259.14
1863	88	24	224	35,000	—	1,139.20
1864				Not listed		
1865	—	—	—	260	—	2.15
1866	—	10	105	2,000	—	6.85
1867	—	11	178	—	—	6.72
1868	—	15	150	500	—	35.71
1869				Not listed		
1870	—	9	145	—	1,665	9.32
1871	—	8	120	—	1,615	9.08
1872	—	10	118	1,000	3,100	79.25
1873	—	11	102	—	2,298	12.49
1874	—	12	84	—	16,142	96.32
1875	—	10	79	4,000	11,000	68.94
1876	—	13	83	1,556	12,605	63.03
1877	—	11	77	4,700	4,710	46.07
1878				Not listed		
1879	—	10	69	8,800	15,950	53.97
1880	—	10	54	7,820	15,950	88.68
1881	—	12	53	5,116	12,346	62.73
1882	—	12	53	5,116	12,346	49.39

Source: Based on Personal Property Tax Lists, Patrick County, Virginia (Microfilm, Virginia State Library).

Note: The inconsistencies seemingly indicate changes in methods of handling taxable property and the frequent but inconsistent inclusion of figures relative to Reynolds's tobacco factory. The state auditor wrote on the Patrick tax list for 1851: "This compiler . . . has also made numerous mistakes." It appears also that Reynolds occasionally shifted property from taxable to nontaxable categories. This table therefore merely reflects an approximation of Reynolds's position. The columns headed "Slaves," "Livestock," and "Taxes on Personal Property" are the most reliable indices.

[a] Interest only.

[b] Indicates cattle, sheep, and hogs.

Table B-2.
Farming Operations of Hardin W. Reynolds, 1850 and 1860

	1850	1860
Land and Machinery		
Improved land (acres)	200	250
Unimproved land (acres)	2,000	600
Cash value of farm	$7,000	$8,000
Value of implements and machinery	$200	$175
Livestock		
Horses	6	0
Mules	0	4
Milk cows	15	7
Working oxen	4	2
Other cattle	70	17
Sheep	30	0
Swine	100	50
Value of livestock	$1,800	$1,068
Farm Production		
Wheat (bushels)	300	200
Rye (bushels)	150	100
Corn (bushels)	2,500	1,000
Oats (bushels)	600	100
Tobacco (pounds)	18,000	4,000
Wool (pounds)	60	—
Peas and beans (bushels)	20	5
Irish potatoes (bushels)	100	Not included
Sweet potatoes (bushels)	100	Not included
Flax (pounds)	100	Not included
Butter (pounds)	300	Not included
Flax seed (pounds)	6	Not included
Beeswax (pounds)	125	Not included
Other Values		
Value of homemade manufactures	$200	Not included
Value of animals slaughtered	$700	Not included

Source: Based on Original MS. Census Returns, Patrick County, Virginia, Agriculture, 1850, p. 581; 1860, p. 3 (microfilm, Virginia State Library).

APPENDIX C
Brands Introduced and Acquired by the Reynolds Company, 1899–1924

The following tables list (1) chewing tobacco brands made by the R. J. Reynolds Tobacco Company just prior to entry into the American Tobacco Combination, (2) chewing brands made by manufacturing companies acquired by the Reynolds company, and (3) smoking tobacco brands acquired after 1911. Although these lists cannot be called complete or accurate, they, with other brands mentioned in the text, present a reasonable picture of the company's brands during the period covered. Except for some of Reynolds's earlier purchases, these generally have been taken from 1903 listings, as brands were more numerous at that time.

Table C-1.
Chewing Tobacco Brands of R. J. Reynolds Tobacco Company, 1899

---

1. A. A. A. A.	27. City Stock
2. Advertiser	28. City Talk
3. Aggie Twist	29. Clara Twist
4. Ambrosia	30. Cleopatra
5. Arlington Twist	31. College Select Twist
6. Autumn Peach	32. Comet Twist
7. B. 4 Any Twist	33. Crescent Twist
8. Banana	34. Cricket Twist
9. Beacon Light	35. Crown of Diamonds
10. Belle of North Carolina	36. Daisy Girl
11. Bessie F.	37. Dixie's Delight
12. Big Jim	38. Domino
13. Black Crook	39. Double Thick
14. Bloomingdale	40. Druid Hill Twist
15. Blue Blazes	41. Drummitt Grove Twist
16. Boss	42. Eclipse
17. Bridal Wreath	43. Eleanor Calhoun
18. Bright Mollie Twist	44. Elsinore
19. California Twist	45. Emma Virginia
20. Calvert Twist	46. Enterprise
21. Capitol	47. Extra North Carolina Chew
22. Caramel	48. F. X. J. Twist
23. Cash Value	49. Farmers' Leader
24. Center Shot	50. Flanagan
25. Charter Oak	51. 4 A Naturally Sweet
26. Chief Justice	52. Gen. Hancock

53. George Washington Twist
54. Gold Cord Twist
55. Golden Crown
56. Golden Hair
57. Golden Leaf
58. Golden Rain Twist
59. Golden 7's
60. Gypsie Girl
61. Handful
62. Henry Clay
63. Hermit
64. Hickory Wythe
65. High Standard
66. Holly Grove
67. Honest
68. Honey Dew
69. Ida G
70. Jeannie Winston
71. Jockey Club
72. June Apple
73. Leatherwood
74. Legal Tender Twist
75. Level Best
76. Little Albert Twist
77. Little Hattie Twist
78. Little Idol Twist
79. Little Nutie
80. Lottie
81. Lucy Reynolds
82. Lula Hurst
83. Lula Tatum
84. Luxury
85. Magnolia Twist
86. Maid of Athens
87. Maltese Cross Twist
88. Mayflower
89. Metropolitan
90. Mild Naturally Sweet
91. Monarch Twist
92. Monumental
93. Mountain Eagle
94. My Pet
95. National
96. Naturally Sweet
97. Nerveless Light Pressed
98. Nickel Twist
99. Novelty Pocket Piece
100. Nutmeg
101. Occabot
102. Old Cabin
103. Old Joe
104. Old North State
105. Old Reliable
106. Olive Branch
107. Opera Twist
108. Ophir Twist
109. Orange
110. Orange Blossom
111. Orinoco Pounds
112. Our Advertiser
113. Our Idea
114. Our Joy
115. Our President
116. Our Pride
117. Patapsco
118. Peerless
119. Perfection
120. Plantation Twist
121. Planters' Choice
122. Premium Twist
123. Purity
124. Quartette Twist
125. Queen Ann's
126. Quick Seller
127. R. E. X.
128. R. J. R.
129. R. J. Reynolds
130. Rare Bit Twist
131. Raspberry
132. Razor Back
133. Ready Cash
134. Red Brick
135. Rex
136. Rocket Twist
137. Rod
138. Romeo
139. Rose Bud Twist
140. Rosenfeld's Natural
141. Rough Diamond
142. Sand Road
143. Sapphire
144. Saratoga R. & R.
145. Schnapps
146. Seal

147. Snipe Twist
148. Solace
149. Split Silk
150. St. Claire
151. Standard Twist
152. Strawberry
153. Sunny South
154. Sweep Stakes
155. Syndicate
156. Tar Heel
157. Thistle Dew
158. Thomas Jefferson Extra Fine
     ½ Pounds
159. Town Talk
160. Triplets
161. Trumps Twist
162. Uncle Ned
163. Walter Raleigh Fine Golden
     Twist
164. Watt Slaton
165. White Rose
166. World's Choice
167. Yellow Rose
168. Zeb Weaver
169. Zulu

Source: From J. W. Connorton, ed., *Connorton's Tobacco Brand Directory of the United States for 1899* (Chicago, 1899), pp. 27–274.

Table C-2.
Chewing Tobacco Brands of T. L. Vaughn and Company of Winston, N.C., 1899; Purchased by R. J. Reynolds Tobacco Company, 30 April 1900

1. Anabel
2. Annie Harrold
3. Baltimore Beauty
4. Big Sandy
5. Breckinridge
6. Bridal Wreath
7. Cable
8. Carrie Hoyt
9. Charcoal
10. Cherokee
11. Consolation
12. Danube
13. Dew Drop
14. Doctor's Prescription
15. Eagle
16. Early Rose
17. Elegant
18. Enterprise
19. Favorite
20. G. C.
21. Gem
22. Ginsang
23. Gold Bug
24. Gold Dust
25. Gold Seal
26. Gold Wedge
27. Grand Jury
28. Gray Jacket
29. Hazel Wood
30. Home Rule
31. Home Run
32. Honest George
33. Honey Cup
34. Huellen
35. Jess Lovely
36. Jim Dandy
37. Jumbo
38. Key Note
39. King of North Carolina
40. Legal Tender
41. Life Boat
42. Lillie's Pride
43. Little Gypsey
44. Little Robin
45. Lord Byron
46. Lullaby
47. M. M. M. M.
48. Mascot
49. Mayflower
50. Mock Turtle

51. Monroe
52. Morning Glory
53. Morocco
54. Napoleon's Sword
55. Narrow Gauge
56. Natural Leaf
57. New Boot
58. New Broom
59. Nutmeg
60. Oakdale Twist
61. Old Rover
62. Orient
63. Our Boss
64. Our Boy
65. Our Dark Horse
66. Perfection
67. Pilot
68. Plow Boy
69. Pot Rack
70. Potrack
71. Racket
72. Red Apple
73. Red Snapper
74. Safety
75. Sambo

76. Shotwell
77. Sky Lark
78. Southern Light
79. Spinner
80. Spot
81. Stampede
82. Standard
83. Steam Engine
84. Sterling
85. Sweet Home
86. T. L. Vaughn & Co.'s Natural Leaf
87. T. L. Vaughn & Co.'s Very Fine
88. Tip Top
89. Tom Jefferson
90. Trophy
91. Tug Fork
92. Tugaloo
93. Uncle Dan
94. Vaughn's Best
95. Vaughn's Leader
96. Violet
97. Whaler
98. Wide Awake
99. Wine Sap
100. Winston Exchange

Source: From J. W. Connorton, ed., *Connorton's Tobacco Brand Directory of the United States for 1899* (Chicago, 1899), pp. 27–274.

Table C-3.

Chewing Tobacco Brands of Brown Brothers and Company of Winston, N.C., 1899;
Purchased by R. J. Reynolds Tobacco Company, 30 November 1900

1. Alabama
2. Anchor
3. Artillery
4. Autumn Leaves
5. Big Nickel
6. Bill Nye
7. Black Nancy
8. Blue Points
9. Brer Rabbit
10. Brick Factory
11. Bridal Cake
12. Broad Smile
13. Brown Bros. Fine 8-oz.
14. Brown's Mule
15. Bully Chew
16. Bumble Bee
17. Carolina Gem
18. Centennial Twist
19. City Talk
20. Cloth of Gold
21. Cottage Home
22. Creole Girl
23. Cross Tie
24. Crystal Flake
25. Current Events
26. Deep Rock
27. Dexter
28. Dixie
29. Drum
30. Flap Jacks
31. Fox King
32. French Flats R. & R.
33. G. G. G. G. Twist
34. Gem
35. Gold Bar
36. Golden Link Twist
37. Golden Rod
38. Halcyon Days
39. Home Comforts
40. Honest 7's
41. Honest Trade
42. Horn
43. Irish Twist
44. Kettledrum
45. Little Joker
46. Little Horn
47. Little Neck
48. Long Horn
49. Loyalty
50. Lunch
51. Maginty Twist
52. Mahogany Twist
53. Mule (Brown's)
54. Odd Trump
55. Old Oaken Bucket
56. Old Reb
57. Old Rip Van Winkle
58. Oliver Twist
59. Our Pet
60. Our Q
61. Passion's Solace
62. Peace and Plenty
63. Peace Maker
64. Phoenix
65. Plantation
66. Plantation Joys
67. Planter's Chew
68. Premium
69. R. & R. Chips
70. Reaper
71. Red Elephant
72. Red Fox
73. Rough and Tough
74. Round Top
75. Ruby
76. Sailor Boy
77. Slap Jacks R. & R.
78. Standard
79. Stonewall
80. Stonewall Brigade
81. Swamp Angel
82. Tar Heel
83. Top
84. Twin City

85. W. W. W. W. Twist	88. Wedding Cake
86. Waverly	89. Wild West
87. Web of Life	90. Wit and Humor

Source: From J. W. Connorton, ed., *Connorton's Tobacco Brand Directory of the United States for 1899* (Chicago, 1899), pp. 27–274.

Table C-4.
Chewing Tobacco Brands of P. H. Hanes and Company of Winston, N.C., 1899;
Purchased by R. J. Reynolds Tobacco Company, 30 November 1900

1. Apple Jack	34. Lock Out
2. Bread and Meat	35. Magnolia
3. Bridge of Lodi	36. Mamie
4. Brigham Young	37. Man's Pride
5. Bright Jewels Twist	38. Missing Link
6. Capt. Jack Twist	39. Monarch Twist
7. Centre Shot Twist	40. Mountain Boy
8. Cotton States	41. Mown Hay
9. Cricket	42. Nickel Twist
10. Crowned Heads	43. O. I. C.
11. Cyclone	44. O. N. T.
12. Dandy Jim	45. Osceola
13. Early Bird	46. Our Charlie
14. Extra Heavy	47. P. H. Hanes & Co.'s Natural Leaf
15. Farmers' Alliance	48. Pic Nic
16. Florence Twist	49. Planters' Choice
17. Forest Flower	50. Possum Hollow
18. Gertrude	51. Queen Bee
19. Gilt Edge	52. Seal
20. Golden Egg	53. Seal Twist
21. Government 4's Twist	54. Shell Mound
22. Greek Slave	55. Solid South
23. Hard Times	56. Speckled Beauty
24. Hebrew Children	57. Standard A. A. A.
25. Honey Suckle Twist	58. Stella Twist
26. Hornet	59. Sultan
27. I. X. L.	60. Supreme
28. Ida May	61. Sweep Stakes
29. Imperial	62. T. T. T.
30. Inflation	63. Wade Hampton
31. Just Out	64. Water Lily
32. Kate Claxton	65. World for a Dime
33. Lillian Russell	

B. F. Hanes Branch of P. H. Hanes and Company

1. Alpine
2. B. F. Hanes Best
3. B. F. Hanes Natural Leaf
4. Benjamin Franklin
5. Black Warrior
6. Carolina Boss
7. Carolina's Favorite
8. Double Thick
9. Frog
10. Gilded Age
11. Golden Chain
12. Hot Stuff
13. Josie
14. Little Susie
15. Norfolk & Western
16. Our Senator
17. Owl
18. Pan Electric
19. Red Rabbit
20. Scattered Nation Twist
21. Telephone
22. Tom Boy

Source: From J. W. Connorton, ed., *Connorton's Tobacco Brand Directory of the United States for 1899* (Chicago, 1899), pp. 27–274.

Table C-5.
Chewing Tobacco Brands of Pegram and Penn of Madison, N.C., 1899; Purchased by R. J. Reynolds Tobacco Company, August 1902

1. Cabinet
2. Fair Rebel
3. Maggie
4. Magic Tobacco
5. Nigger Baby
6. Our Favorite
7. Our Leader
8. P. & P.
9. Pegram & Penn's Best
10. Red Jacket
11. Sally Jay
12. Seven Up
13. Supreme Judge
14. Tug of War
15. Whole Chunk

Source: From J. W. Connorton, ed., *Connorton's Tobacco Brand Directory of the United States for 1899* (Chicago, 1899), pp. 27–274.

Table C-6.
Chewing Tobacco Brands of Lüpfert-Scales Company of Winston, N.C., 1903;
Purchased by R. J. Reynolds Tobacco Company, 1903

1. Acme	19. Old Reliable
2. Bertie	20. Our Ideal
3. Big Apple	21. Our Peach
4. Black Mammy	22. Our Tom
5. Brown Jug	23. Piedmont Daisy
6. Corn Tassel	24. Quaker City
7. Crack a Jack	25. Red Letter
8. Duckie	26. Red Meat
9. Elk	27. Rolling Pin
10. Fat Back	28. Rule of Three
11. First Step	29. School Girl
12. 5 Points	30. Snapper Jack
13. H. L. & Co.	31. Ten Center
14. Half Shell	32. Thoroughbred
15. High Grade	33. 20th. Century
16. Jack Snapper	34. Wild Duck
17. National Chew	35. Winston Boom
18. Old Plantation	

Source: From J. W. Connorton, ed., *Connorton's Tobacco Brand Directory of the United States for 1903* (Chicago, 1903), pp. 7–232.

Table C-7.
Chewing Tobacco Brands of T. A. Crews of Walkertown, N.C., 1903; Acquired by
R. J. Reynolds Tobacco Company, Through the Purchase of
Lüpfert-Scales Company, 1903

1. Big 4	11. Garden Gossip
2. Companion	12. Honest Money
3. Crews Big 4	13. Netted Gem
4. Crews Eleven Inch 3's	14. Paragon
5. Crews Netted Gem	15. Pride of America
6. Crews Paragon	16. Solid Meat
7. Crews Pride of America	17. Tolu
8. Crews Solid Meat	18. Triumph
9. Crews Yellow Jacket	19. Yellow Jacket
10. Eleven Inch 3's	

Source: From J. W. Connorton, ed., *Connorton's Tobacco Brand Directory of the United States for 1903* (Chicago, 1903), pp. 7–232.

Table C-8.
Chewing Tobacco Brands of Reynolds Tobacco Company of Bristol, Tenn., 1899;
Purchased by R. J. Reynolds Tobacco Company, c. 1904

1. AAAA		39. Katydid	
2. A. D. R.		40. Knights of Labor Pancake	
3. All Good		41. Lady Randolph	
4. Annie Clare		42. Little Lula Twist	
5. Anno Domini		43. Major (The)	
6. B		44. Mamie Anderson	
7. BB		45. Maud S.	
8. Big Mogul		46. Mayflower	
9. Black Warrior		47. Minnie Lee 3 ply Twist	
10. Blue String Twist		48. Miss Lucy	
11. Big Ton		49. Mogul	
12. Border City Twist		50. Moss Rose	
13. Bright Mollie		51. My Queen [May Queen]	
14. Bristol Bell		52. Natural Twist	
15. Clarence		53. Nickel Navy	
16. Combination Twist		54. Nickel Pancake	
17. Competition Twist		55. Nickel Twist	
18. Creole		56. No. 10	
19. Daisy Girl		57. Old Hickory	
20. Dixie		58. Our Joe	
21. Eunika Twist		59. Our Pet	
22. Fig		60. Pig Tail Twist	
23. "Frisco"		61. Possum	
24. Gold Tap		62. Queen Bess	
25. Golden Pancake		63. Ring Leader	
26. Golden 7 oz. Twist		64. Royal Twist	
27. Golden Twist		65. S. S. S.	
28. Grover		66. Sailor Knot Twist	
29. Ham Meat		67. Seal	
30. Heel Tap		68. Silver Bells	
31. Hero		69. Silver Dime	
32. Honest Chew		70. Sky Blue	
33. Honest John		71. Standard	
34. Hope		72. State Line Twist	
35. Huckleberry Twist		73. Sun Cured	
36. Hunkidori Twist		74. Texas Pony	
37. Jo Jo		75. W. J. Northern	
38. Justice Twist		76. XXXX	

Source: From J. W. Connorton, ed., *Connorton's Tobacco Brand Directory of the United States for 1899* (Chicago, 1899), pp. 27–274.

Table C-9.
Chewing Tobacco Brands of Rucker and Witten Tobacco Company of Martinsville, Va.,
1903; Purchased by R. J. Reynolds Tobacco Company, December 1905

1. Big Three	10. Old Pioneer
2. Black Buster	11. Old Vet
3. Double Thick (Rucker & Witten's)	12. Pulaski
4. Electric Light	13. R & W's Double Thick
5. Gladstone	14. R & W's Natural Leaf
6. Henry County Dude	15. Red Bird
7. Liberty Bell	16. Skinner
8. Long Pole	17. Stone Fence
9. Nickleby	18. Willie Brown

Source: From J. W. Connorton, ed., *Connorton's Tobacco Brand Directory of the United States for 1903* (Chicago, 1903), pp. 7–232.

Table C-10.
Chewing Tobacco Brands of W. T. Hancock of Richmond, Va., 1903; Acquired by
R. J. Reynolds Tobacco Company, Through the Purchase of
Rucker and Witten Tobacco Company, December 1905

1. A. No. 1 Chew	25. Blended
2. A. No. 1 Smoke	26. Blind Billy
3. Above All	27. Blind Tiger
4. All the Go	28. Blue Bird
5. All the Rage	29. Blue Eye (special)
6. Alliance Boy	30. Blue Jay
7. Amazon Eagle	31. Blue Ridge
8. Angelica	32. Boss
9. Any Time	33. Brag Twist
10. Apex	34. Brass Tack
11. Apple Twist	35. Break Away
12. Atlantic Cable Coil	36. Broad Gauge
13. Banner	37. Bucket Twist
14. Beer	38. Buckshot
15. Bell's Life	39. Buzz Saw
16. Belle of Richmond	40. C. A. B.
17. Ben Trovato	41. Call Again
18. Berkshire	42. Capital Chew
19. Big Hunk	43. Caramel (special)
20. Big J	44. Celestial
21. Big Nickel	45. Centennial
22. Big Run	46. Charlotta Twist
23. Big State	47. Cinderella
24. Black Boy	48. City Belle

49. City of Westbrook
50. Clincher (special)
51. Clover Club
52. Cow Horn Twist
53. Craps
54. Crescent
55. Dandy
56. Dewberry Twist
57. Dice Box
58. Dublin Thick
59. Dwarf Roses
60. Economy
61. Edna
62. Electric
63. Elkanna Twist
64. Essex
65. Eureka
66. Eye Opener
67. Fairfax
68. Far West
69. Farmers' Girl
70. Finest
71. Flip
72. Fog Horn
73. For Business Only
74. 44
75. 42
76. Four Seasons
77. Free Pass
78. Garfield
79. Gold Fish
80. Gold Seal
81. Golden Fleece
82. Golden Nugget
83. Golden Prize
84. Golden Seal
85. Good Article
86. Good Times
87. Grab
88. Granger
89. Greased Lightning
90. Gum
91. H. O. B.
92. Hancock
93. Hancock Tag
94. Hancock's Best

95. Hancock's Fig
96. Handy
97. Handy Boy
98. Happy Dreams
99. Hi Ho!
100. Home Rule
101. Honey Shuck
102. How Is This?
103. Humbug
104. Irish Lad
105. Jack Bass
106. Jackson's Best
107. James Russell
108. Jamestown
109. Jay Cure
110. Joe Jefferson
111. K. M. Q. (special)
112. Knights of Pythias
113. Labor Man's Day
114. Leader
115. Liberty Bell
116. Little Annie
117. Little Giant
118. Little Helen
119. Lone Ranger
120. Long Fives
121. Lowmor
122. Lucy Long
123. Luray
124. Magic
125. Magnolia
126. Mahomet
127. Manie
128. Maritana
129. Mayflower Twist
130. McGinty
131. Merrimac
132. Monarch
133. Montrose
134. Move On
135. My Size
136. No. 1
137. No Trust
138. Nobby Twist
139. Oh Yes
140. Old Hickory

141. Old Judge
142. Old Port
143. Old Rip
144. Old Sport
145. Old Vet (special)
146. Old Veteran (special)
147. Oliver Twist
148. On Tap
149. On Time
150. On Top
151. Opera
152. Orange Blossom
153. Oriental Twist
154. Osceola
155. Ouida
156. Our Black Boy
157. Our Delight
158. Our Dime
159. Our Hustler
160. Our Leader
161. Our Mack
162. Our Standby
163. Out of the Sea
164. Padlock
165. Palma
166. Paragon
167. Peerless Twist
168. Pig
169. Pilot Boy
170. Pine Apple
171. Pink Ribbon
172. Pride of Canada
173. Pride of Vicksburg
174. Racket
175. Ranger
176. Reaper
177. Red Hot Cakes
178. Red Stone
179. Red, White and Blue
180. Riel (special)
181. Rose Bud Twist
182. Royal
183. Rustic
184. Ruth
185. Salmon's
186. Samson
187. Sensation
188. Shield Tag
189. Shin Dig
190. Silver Key
191. Slipper
192. Something New
193. Spot Cash
194. Spring
195. Stand By
196. Sugar Cured
197. Sunset
198. Sunshine
199. Surprise Twist
200. Sweet Chimes
201. Sweet Gum
202. Sweet Mash
203. Talledega
204. Ten Pins
205. Texas Pride
206. They're After Me
207. "33"
208. Tom Cat
209. Tom, Dick and Harry
210. Tri-Color
211. Tolley
212. Trumps
213. 29
214. Twin Sisters
215. Twist I Like
216. 215
217. 2 Johns
218. U. & I.
219. Vanilla Cream
220. Vega
221. Victor
222. Vinet
223. Viola
224. Voice (The)
225. War Governor
226. Warrior
227. Way Up
228. What Next
229. Whistler
230. White Fawn
231. White Mountain
232. White Rose

233. Winesap
234. X-Rays
235. Yellow Jacket

236. Yosemite
237. Yum Yum
238. Zuleika

Table C-11.
Chewing Tobacco Brands of Hadley and Smith of Mount Airy, N.C., 1903; Acquired by R. J. Reynolds Tobacco Company, Through the Purchase of Rucker and Witten, December 1905

1. Battle Ship
2. Free Silver
3. Little Bantam
4. Little Grady
5. Old Times
6. Our Birdie
7. Our Reliance

8. Ready Cash
9. Red Bird
10. Red June
11. Silver Quarter
12. Tar Heel
13. Willie G

Table C-12.
Chewing Tobacco Brands of Sparger Brothers of Mount Airy, N.C., 1903; Acquired by R. J. Reynolds Tobacco Company, Through the Purchase of Rucker and Witten, December 1905

1. Advance
2. Ben Hill
3. Bessie Birch
4. Best 9-4's
5. Bomb Shell
6. Buster Twist
7. Carolina Belle
8. Champion Dime
9. Cotton Exchange
10. Cream of N.C.
11. Dan River
12. Dove
13. Farmer's Pride
14. Free Delivery
15. Grover Cleveland
16. Levi

17. Natural Beauty
18. Natural Leaf
19. New Dip
20. Old Indian Chief
21. Orange Leaf
22. Our Best
23. Our Favorite
24. Queen of Georgia
25. Satisfaction
26. Sparger's Bros. Very Best
27. Surry
28. Triumph
29. U. & I.
30. Wheel Horse
31. World's Wonder
32. Ye Winning Plug

Table C-13.

Chewing Tobacco Brands of B. F. Gravely and Sons of Leatherwood, Va., 1903;
Purchased by R. J. Reynolds Tobacco Company, 1906

1. B. F. Gravely's Latest 6 Inch
2. B. F. Gravely's Superior
3. B. F. Gravely & Sons' AAAA
4. B. F. Gravely & Sons' Cabinet
5. B. F. Gravely & Sons' Choice
6. B. F. Gravely & Sons' Companion
7. B. F. Gravely & Sons' Diamond
8. B. F. Gravely & Sons' Extra 9 Inch
9. B. F. Gravely & Sons' Golden Rule 9 Inch
10. B. F. Gravely & Sons' Golden Swan
11. B. F. Gravely & Sons' Old Coon
12. B. F. Gravely & Sons' Our Brag Brand 9 Inch
13. B. F. Gravely & Sons' Special
14. B. F. Gravely & Sons' Treco 9 Inch
15. Berta G
16. Cabinet
17. Carrollton
18. Champion
19. Comet Twist
20. Diamond
21. Eagle, 3-ply Twist
22. Extra Nine Inch
23. Fine 3-ply Twist
24. Flue Cured Twist
25. Gravely Extra Twist
26. Gravely's Choice Twist
27. H. T. & H. Clay
28. Hartford Twist
29. I. X. L.
30. J. T. & H. Clay Fine lbs.
31. Leatherwood Twist
32. Moss Rose
33. My Maryland
34. Special
35. Star of Henry
36. Treco

Source: From J. W. Connorton, ed., *Connorton's Tobacco Brand Directory of the United States for 1903* (Chicago, 1903), pp. 7–232.

Table C-14.

Chewing Tobacco Brands of Spencer Brothers and Lee [or Spencer Brothers] of Martinsville, Va., Purchased by R. J. Reynolds Tobacco Company, 1906

1. Amazon
2. Baltimore Beauty
3. Clean Cut
4. Daily Bread
5. Extra Golden
6. Extra Pounds
7. Fatted Calf
8. Gold Brick
9. Grand
10. Grand 3-ply Twist
11. Grape Juice
12. Henry County Twist
13. Hickory
14. Hickory Nut
15. Intrinsic
16. J. H. Spencer's Best
17. Jeb Stewart
18. Little Beauty
19. Little Queen
20. Merit
21. Mintmore
22. North America
23. Northern Beauty
24. Oriole
25. Our Charlie
26. P. D.
27. Peach and Honey
28. Perfection
29. Red Bird
30. Red Fox
31. Red S
32. Rewarder

33. Rose Bud
34. Shorthand
35. Silver Dimes
36. Sly Coon
37. Spencer Bros. 4's
38. Stolen Kisses

39. Sun Cured
40. Superior
41. Tally Ho
42. Telegraph
43. Will of the People

Source: From J. W. Connorton, ed., *Connorton's Tobacco Brand Directory of the United States for 1903* (Chicago, 1903), pp. 7–232.

Table C-15.
Chewing Tobacco Brands of Ogburn, Hill and Company of Winston, N.C., 1903;
Purchased by R. J. Reynolds Tobacco Company, 19 September 1912

1. Belle of York
2. "Boot Black"
3. Crown
4. Dixie
5. The Drummer
6. "Eagle"
7. Gold Leaf
8. Good as Gold
9. "Good Value"
10. Jeff Davis
11. Little Joe (special)
12. "Mild and Mellow"
13. Minnie Ogburn

14. "Monarch"
15. "Natural Leaf"
16. New Broom
17. O. H. & Co.'s Choice
18. O. H. & Co.'s Dixie
19. Ogburn, Hill & Co.
20. Red Fox (special)
21. Rich and Waxy
22. Sallaphone
23. Snake Root
24. Tar Heel
25. Winston Leader

Source: From J. W. Connorton, ed., *Connorton's Tobacco Brand Directory of the United States for 1903* (Chicago, 1903), pp. 7–232.

Table C-16.
Chewing Tobacco Brands of Strater Brothers of Louisville, Ky., 1903; Purchased by R. J. Reynolds Tobacco Company, 27 June 1919

1. Argo
2. Bandit
3. Barbecue
4. Bitter Sweet
5. Black Cross
6. Black Grape
7. Black Hawk
8. Blazer
9. Brandy
10. Breaker
11. Buckle
12. Buckshot
13. Bugle
14. Butter Scotch
15. Caboose
16. Capstan
17. Cash
18. Casino
19. Checker Board
20. Chips
21. Claw Hammer
22. Clover Leaf
23. Cocktail
24. Coon
25. Coon Skin
26. Crescent
27. Crown
28. Cup
29. Cup Greenville
30. Daisy Twist
31. Days Work
32. Dictator
33. Diver
34. Doctor Twist
35. Dog Leg Twist
36. Echo
37. Fishback
38. Flute
39. Fox
40. Future
41. Gold Flake
42. Good Will
43. Green Ribbon Twist
44. Gridiron
45. Hammer
46. Handspike
47. Harpoon
48. Head Light
49. Heart
50. High Ball
51. Hobnob
52. Hunkidora
53. Index
54. Index Natural Leaf
55. Index Twist
56. J. H. T.
57. Jack Pot
58. Jibboom
59. Kentucky Club
60. Kentucky Pride
61. Kildeer
62. Kismet
63. Ladder
64. Landslide
65. Lasso
66. Leader
67. Lemon Pie
68. Leopard
69. Let-Her-Go
70. Lightning
71. Mastodon
72. Moonlight
73. New Moon
74. None Such
75. Old and New
76. Old Fashioned Kentucky
77. On the Square
78. Our Own Twist
79. Owensboro Light Pressed
80. Padlock
81. Pansy
82. Peach
83. Pet
84. Pirate
85. Poker
86. Pony

87. Pride of Kentucky
88. Rabbit Foot
89. Red Ribbon Twist
90. Roll Call
91. Sagamore
92. Sangaree
93. Silver Dime
94. Slipper
95. Social Club
96. Spigot
97. Sport
98. Strater's Light Pressed
99. Strater's Natural Leaf
100. Strater's Natural Leaf Twist
101. Sucker
102. Sunlight
103. Sure Crop
104. Swivel
105. Ta Too
106. Tip Top
107. Torchlight
108. Trinket
109. Trombone
110. Trumpet
111. Turf
112. Veteran
113. Victor
114. Vindex
115. White Jack
116. Woodsman
117. Workman's Friend
118. X. L.

Source: From J. W. Connorton, ed., *Connorton's Tobacco Brand Directory of the United States for 1903* (Chicago, 1903), pp. 7–232.

Table C-17.
Chewing Tobacco Brands of N. D. Sullivan Company of Walkertown, N.C., 1903;
Purchased by R. J. Reynolds Tobacco Company, 6 October 1919

1. Cool Chew
2. Essie Hall
3. Free and Easy
4. Good Enough (Sullivan's)
5. Natural Leaf (Sullivan's)
6. No. 1 (Sullivan's)
7. Number One
8. Our Own (Sullivan's)
9. Sullivan's Best
10. Sullivan's Natural Leaf
11. Sullivan's Three Break
12. Sullivan's 11 in. 3's
13. T. C. D. (Sullivan's)
14. Three Break
15. Tube Rose
16. Tulee Rose

Source: From J. W. Connorton, ed., *Connorton's Tobacco Brand Directory of the United States for 1903* (Chicago, 1903), pp. 7–232.

Table C-18.

Chewing Tobacco Brands of Bailey Brothers of Winston, N.C., 1903; Purchased by
R. J. Reynolds Tobacco Company, 16 July 1924

1. Bailey's Choice	23. Liver Regulator
2. Big Nick	24. Natahala
3. Big 20	25. No. 5
4. Big Whistle	26. No. 10
5. Bill Arp	27. O. K.
6. Brag (Sikes)	28. Old Bob
7. Broad Gauge	29. Our Charlie
8. C. C. C.	30. Planters' Choice
9. Carrie B.	31. Queen
10. Cock Spur	32. Rebel Spry [Spy]
11. Crusher	33. Red C
12. Dora	34. Renown
13. Eli	35. Rock and Rye
14. Ellen Fisher	36. Rough and Ready
15. Eula	37. Same All Through
16. Farmer's Pride	38. Silver Moon
17. Flossie	39. Solid
18. Gatling Gun	40. Spring Chickens
19. Kicker	41. Sweet Carolina
20. Lilac	42. Top Rail
21. Little Giant	43. Zoe
22. Little Irene	

Source: From J. W. Connorton, ed., Connorton's Tobacco Brand Directory of the United States
for 1903 (Chicago, 1903), pp. 7–232.

Table C-19.

Smoking Tobacco Brands, 1903, of Plants Purchased by R. J. Reynolds Tobacco
Company After 1911

1. Ambrosia	13. Bourbon
2. Assembly	14. City Club Mixture
3. B–Z	15. Cock of the Cock
4. Best and Cheapest	16. Cock of the Walk
5. Big Five	17. Cock Spur
6. Big Four	18. Co-operative
7. Bird Eye	19. Corker
8. Bitter Sweet	20. Crack
9. Black Diamond	21. Daily Bread
10. Blue Ridge	22. Delicious Puff
11. Bonanza	23. Delight
12. Boss	24. Dude's Delight

25. Emblem
26. Extra
27. Eye Opener
28. F. C. B.
29. Farmers' and Mechanics'
30. 15 Puzzle
31. Fireside
32. Flower of Durham
33. 4 for 5
34. Fresh Co. B
35. Full Pay Mixture
36. Gold
37. Golden Seal
38. Grand Mogul
39. Grand Pa's
40. Honest Toil
41. Jersey
42. Let Her Go
43. Lion
44. Master Workman Long Cut
45. Medal
46. Mine Workers
47. Morning Puff
48. None Such
49. North Star
50. North Star Shorts
51. Old Fashioned Kentucky
52. Old Kentucky
53. Our Daily Bread
54. Our Emblem
55. Our Own Cut and Dry
56. Owl Friend
57. Photo
58. Rose Bud
59. Royal Arms
60. Sagmore
61. Satisfaction
62. Spanish
63. Spanish Mixed
64. Stripped
65. Stylish
66. Surprise
67. Sweet Shrub
68. 3 for 5
69. Triple Mixture
70. Trump
71. Union Seal
72. United Labor
73. United Mine Workers
74. Virginius
75. White Mule
76. Wonderful
77. XX Extra No. 1 Chewing and Smoking
78. Yankee Navy

Source: From J. W. Connorton, ed., *Connorton's Tobacco Brand Directory of the United States for 1903* (Chicago, 1903), pp. 321–492.

Note: All of these brands were made by Strater Brothers except one, Cock Spur, which was made by Bailey Brothers. Reynolds acquired four firms after 1911: Ogburn, Hill & Company, Strater Brothers, N. D. Sullivan Company, and Bailey Brothers.

A P P E N D I X   D
Private Brands Manufactured for Jobbers
by the Reynolds Company, 1925

Jobber	Brand	Comparable Reynolds Brands
Neudecker Tobacco Co. Baltimore, Md.	Big Schooner	ONT
	Big N Tobacco	Cutter
	Big Plug	Cutter
	Per Cors	Cutter
	Johns' 7's	Cutter
	Neudecker's Own Tobacco	Gold Wedge
	B. F. Gravely & Sons Champion	Star of Henry
	B. F. Gravely & Sons Diamond	Star of Henry
	N. T. Co's Mellow Lbs.	Star of Henry
William Deiches & Co. Baltimore, Md.	Gravely's Choice 3 Ply	[Special Work]
	B. F. Gravely & Sons Cabinet	Star of Henry
	B. F. Gravely's Henry County Pounds	Star of Henry
	Daisy Extra Fine	Daisy
F. A. Davis & Sons Baltimore, Md.	Old Crow	Top
	Pine Apple	Rough & Tough
	Honey Cut	Schnapps
	B. F. Gravely & Sons Latest	Star of Henry
	B. F. Gravely & Sons Extra Fine Pounds	Star of Henry
	B. F. Gravely's Special "Bright"	[Special Work]
	Spencer's AAAA	AAAA
	B. F. Gravely & Sons Extra	Gravely's Fine
	OD	Daisy
	Peach & Honey	ONT
	Broadway	Cutter
	Five Ounce Twist	Cutter
J. F. Obrecht & Co. Baltimore, Md.	Shady Grove 3's	Red Meat
	Shady Grove 4's	Red Meat

Jobber	Brand	Comparable Reynolds Brands
Washington Tobacco Co. Washington, D.C.	Island of Cuba	Gold Wedge
D. Loughran Co., Inc. Washington, D.C.	D L Twist	ONT
A. B. Cunningham & Sons Philadelphia, Pa.	B. F. Gravely & Sons Golden Swan Black Nancy	Star of Henry ONT
S. Shepherd's Sons Philadelphia, Pa.	Clara Emma	Twist Cash Value Twist Cash Value
A. W. Condon Frederick, Md.	Superior Barrow Oronoko Tobacco[a]	Apple Apple
B. Walls Milledgeville, Ga. [Owner of Bonner's Daisy]	Bonner's Daisy	Early Bird
B. H. Merck Gainesville, Ga.	Merck's Plug	Thoroughbred

Source: Based on a List of Private Brands Accompanying R. J. R. Price List No. 41, Effective on and after 1 January 1925, comptroller's department, R. J. Reynolds Tobacco Company.

[a] The Reynolds company paid one cent per pound to Joseph Williams for the privilege of making Barrow Oronoko.

A P P E N D I X   E
Division Managers in the Reynolds Sales Force, 1914

Name	Location	Number of Salesmen
Allison, J. Phillip	Buffalo, N.Y.(?)	6
Alspaugh, John W.	Winston-Salem, N.C.	6
Bailey, Junius H.	Macon, Ga.	6
Batchelor, George F.	Rochester, N.Y.	3
Batchelor, John J.	Syracuse or Albany, N.Y.(?)	7
Benson, John S.	Chicago, Ill.	11
Birchfield, W. V.	Marion, Va.	8
Brannock, Robert L.	Seattle, Wash.	4
Brinkley, Cleveland D.	Jackson, Miss.	4
Cook, Fred E.	Charleston, W.Va.(?)	8
Cornell, George P., Jr.	Birmingham, Ala.	9
Cornett, Eli, Jr.	Winchester, Ky.(?)	4
Counts, F. B.	Hagerstown, Md.(?)	4
Cox, J. Porter	Muskogee, Okla.(?)	7
Davis, Paul P.	Louisville, Ky.(?)	12
Dawson, Asa B.	Pittsburgh, Pa.	8
Dobson, Lucian P.	Springfield, Mo.	3
Doughty, Madison B.	New York, N.Y.	13
Duling, Charles H.	Charleston, W.Va.	11
Durham, M. W.	Portland, Oreg.	5
Ethridge, William B.	St. Louis, Mo.	12
Flynn, J. H.	Buffalo, N.Y.(?)	6
Fogg, S. S.	Portland, Maine(?)	2
Gaither, Floyd J.	Montgomery, Ala.	6
Gilbert, Thomas B.	Philadelphia, Pa.	9
Goldwire, L. E.	Memphis, Tenn.	11
Harrison, J. R.	Fayetteville, N.C.	4
Hendrix, C. W.	(?)	3
Hobson, L. C.	Nashville, Tenn.	7
Johns, Ferdinand P.	Richmond, Va.	10
Johnson, D. T.	(?)	3
Jones, R. Conrad	Minneapolis, Minn.	8
Kelley, F. P.	Portland, Maine(?)	3
King, John E.	Providence, R.I.(?)	4
Lasater, N. Everette	Altoona, Pa.	3
Lawson, Ellis P.	Newark, N.J.	8

Name	Location	Number of Salesmen
Lewitz, F.	(?)	5
Lupton, John	Syracuse, N.Y.	3
McBee, W. P.	(?)	(?)
McCann, Ed A.	(?)	3
McCarthy, G. C.	Oklahoma City, Okla.	6
McCoin, Elmer G.	Greenville, S.C.	5
McCraney, W. M.	Natchez or Hattiesburg, Miss.(?)	10
McEwen, William W.	Lake Charles, La.(?)	7
McFadden, Benjamin R.	Cleveland, Ohio(?)	9
McGrady, Charles W.	Albany, Ga.(?)	5
McKee, Carl E.	Columbus, Ohio	3
Machen, Jesse L.	Abilene, Tex.	4
Madison, Albert F.	Little Rock, Ark.	8
March, A. Hume	Dallas, Tex.	10
Martin, C. B.	Milwaukee, Wis.	6
Maxwell, Earle S.	Cincinnati, Ohio	5
Meredith, G. T.	Columbus, Ohio(?)	5
Miller, W. G.	Greenville, S.C.(?)	4
Modlin, Herman L.	Shreveport, La.	7
Moody, J. T.	(?)	4
Moore, F. C.	Duluth, Minn.	5
Mueller, William H.	Baltimore, Md.	16
Neal, John	Helena, Mont.(?)	5
Nunn, George L.	Des Moines, Iowa	5
O'Bannon, W.	Davenport, Iowa	3
Osborne, Houston J.	San Antonio, Tex.(?)	12
Osborne, James H.	Louisville, Ky.(?)	12
Paylor, John H.	Raleigh, N.C.	5
Phillips, J. W.	(?)	3
Porcher, Artemus D.	Columbia, S.C.	13
Reade, Otho D.	Omaha, Nebr.	(?)
Roach, Charles H.	Harrisburg, Pa.	10
Ross, John W.	Jacksonville, Fla.	4
Scott, Claude E.	Peoria, Ill.	8
Scott, W. B.	Sioux Falls, S.Dak.	3
Shannon, John K.	Butte, Mont.(?)	4
Shores, Walter	(?)	5
Simpson, Charles J.	(?)	3
Smith, Reynolds	Detroit, Mich.	7
Steers, George L.	Boston, Mass.	11
Steffner, George U.	Atlanta, Ga.	7
Stultz, W. Z.	Charlotte, N.C.	5

Name	Location	Number of Salesmen
Sweeney, Timothy E.	Worcester, Mass.(?)	4
Wagnon, Arthur B.	Indianapolis, Ind.(?)	9
Waldrep, O. P.	(?)	5
Walker, E. B.(?)	Spokane, Wash.(?)	2
Waller, Charles L.	Mobile, Ala.	5
Williard, C. H.	Salt Lake City, Utah	3
Woodruff, Edwin H.	(?)	3
Worley, Chapman A.	Denver, Colo.(?)	6
Yates, A. B.	Paducah, Ky.	12

Sources: Compiled from the following records of the R. J. Reynolds Tobacco Company: a list of sixty-six division managers on the reverse side of Circular D-M-16 1/2-F.A., Winston-Salem, N.C., 25 Sept. 1914 (sales department); Authorized Sales Force, 1914–1931; Resignation and Employment Bulletins, 1 Jan. 1917–31 Dec. 1941; and Sales Book vol. II (sales accounting department). Many of the first names came from lists of stockholders in Minutes of the Board of Directors, vol. IV, passim.
Note: Because of shifts in personnel, some divisions appear with more than one manager.

A P P E N D I X F
Stock Data of the Reynolds Company, 1922–1963

	Par Value	Volume	Range for Year		
1922					
Common B	$ 25	755,020	$ 43.750 (27 Mar.)	to	$ 63.750 (21 Nov.)
7% Preferred	100	14,438	111.125 (11 Apr.)	to	118.750 (19 Oct.)
1923					
Common B	25	811,900	47.000 (10 Jan.)	to	75.000 (31 Dec.)
7% Preferred	100	9,755	114.000 (9 July)	to	118.000 (9 Feb.)
1924					
Common B	25	440,400	61.625 (31 Mar.)	to	79.375 (2 Dec.)
7% Preferred	100	16,150	115.250 (26 Mar.)	to	121.000 (17 June)
1925					
Common B	25	616,300	72.250 (24 Mar.)	to	95.875 (15 Dec.)
7% Preferred[a]	100	11,300	119.875 (8 Jan.)	to	122.000 (29 Apr.)
1926					
Common B	25	727,200	90.000 (30 Mar.)	to	121.875 (19 Nov.)
1927					
Common A	25	630	134.250 (7 May)	to	200.000 (28 Dec.)
Common B	25	1,068,520	98.500 (24 Feb.)	to	162.000 (15 Dec.)
1928					
Common A	25	640	165.500 (19 Mar.)	to	195.000 (7 May)
Common B	25	1,092,900	128.000 (24 Apr.)	to	165.500 (28 Nov.)
1929					
Common A	10	4,720	70.000 (24 Apr.)	to	89.500 (14 Oct.)
Common B	10	2,504,600	39.000 (14 Nov.)	to	66.000 (11 Jan.)
1930					
Common A	10	9,070	70.000 (3 June)	to	80.000 (2 Jan.)
Common B	10	2,152,232	40.000 (27 Dec.)	to	58.625 (11 Mar.)
1931					
Common A	10	7,830	69.000 (25 June)	to	75.500 (19 Feb.)
Common B	10	2,030,150	32.500 (28 Dec.)	to	54.500 (24 June)
1932					
Common A	10	8,995	64.000 (2 May)	to	71.375 (13 June)
Common B	10	2,382,500	26.500 (30 June)	to	40.250 (14 Jan.)

	Par Value	Volume	Range for Year		
1933					
Common A	10	6,297	60.000 (5 Jan.)	to	62.750 (24 Jan.)
Common B	10	3,127,200	26.500 (3 Jan.)	to	54.250 (15 Sept.)
1934					
Common A	10	3,260	57.000 (5 Jan.)	to	62.875 (26 Nov.)
Common B	10	1,041,900	39.750 (21 Mar.)	to	53.750 (5 Dec.)
1935					
Common A	10	2,780	55.250 (22 Apr.)	to	67.000 (12 Nov.)
Common B	10	833,300	43.125 (26 Mar.)	to	58.625 (23 Nov.)
1936					
Common A	10	3,560	58.875 (16 Sept.)	to	65.625 (10 Feb.)
Common B	10	575,600	50.000 (29 Apr.)	to	60.500 (17 Nov.)
1937					
Common A	10	2,910	55.000 (19 Oct.)	to	67.000 (26 Jan.)
Common B	10	522,000	40.250 (7 Dec.)	to	58.000 (8 Jan.)
1938					
Common A	10	3,470	51.250 (31 Jan.)	to	58.500 (11 Jan.)
Common B	10	409,600	33.750 (30 Mar.)	to	46.500 (8 Jan.)
1939					
Common A	10	990	52.000 (25 July)	to	58.000 (7 Jan.)
Common B	10	434,300	35.000 (21 Sept.)	to	45.000 (4 Jan.)
1940					
Common A	10	1,110	52.000 (22 May)	to	56.000 (3 Oct.)
Common B	10	514,700	30.500 (23 Dec.)	to	44.000 (8 May)
1941					
Common A	10	2,260	49.750 (30 Dec.)	to	53.500 (12 Jan.)
Common B	10	577,550	22.125 (23 Dec.)	to	34.250 (7 Jan.)
1942					
Common A	10	1,750	31.750 (9 Nov.)	to	54.000 (27 Jan.)
Common B	10	412,600	20.000 (23 Apr.)	to	27.500 (27 Jan.)
1943					
Common A	10	2,333	34.375 (4 Feb.)	to	39.250 (21 July)
Common B	10	502,200	25.250 (2 Jan.)	to	32.250 (2 June)
1944					
Common A	10	2,250	36.000 (3 May)	to	39.625 (7 Nov.)
Common B	10	356,700	28.000 (3 Jan.)	to	35.875 (10 July)
1945					
Common A	10	4,980	37.125 (13 Mar.)	to	46.500 (8 Nov.)
Common B	10	521,200	31.375 (2 Jan.)	to	40.000 (18 Oct.)
Preferred 3.60[b]	100	28,600	99.375 (21 Sept.)	to	106.000 (13 Dec.)

	Par Value	Volume	Range for Year		
1946					
Common A	10	5,900	43.000 (18 Feb.)	to	50.875 (31 July)
Common B	10	571,500	36.250 (11 Sept.)	to	46.875 (6 June)
Preferred 3.60	100	42,020	100.000 (25 Nov.)	to	108.750 (25 Feb.)
1947					
Common A	10	8,820	45.000 (29 May)	to	50.500 (11 Dec.)
Common B	10	350,200	36.125 (20 May)	to	44.125 (4 Feb.)
Preferred 3.60	100	37,100	85.000 (26 Dec.)	to	104.000 (6 Feb.)
1948					
Common A	10	3,015	43.000 (18 Dec.)	to	50.000 (8 Jan.)
Common B	10	559,900	33.125 (28 Dec.)	to	41.250 (2 Jan.)
Preferred 3.60	100	32,210	80.000 (14 Oct.)	to	94.000 (1 June)
Preferred 4.50[c]	100	20	103.750 (31 Dec.)	to	103.750 (31 Dec.)
1949					
Common A	10	2,580	42.500 (7 Mar.)	to	50.000 (19 Sept.)
Common B	10	367,900	34.375 (21 Apr.)	to	39.875 (6 Oct.)
Preferred 3.60	100	17,000	85.250 (3 Jan.)	to	98.000 (16 Aug.)
Preferred 4.50	100	35,800	102.375 (4 Jan.)	to	108.250 (23 Nov.)
1950					
Common A	10	8,200	39.500 (27 Dec.)	to	50.000 (10 Jan.)
Common B	10	659,800	32.000 (15 Dec.)	to	39.875 (7 Jan.)
Preferred 3.60	100	20,900	94.500 (5 Jan.)	to	99.500 (31 Mar.)
Preferred 4.50	100	15,160	104.750 (9 Dec.)	to	108.750 (2 June)
1951					
Common A	10	750	40.000 (26 Feb.)	to	45.000 (31 Mar.)
Common B	10	711,455	31.750 (26 June)	to	36.000 (4 Jan.)
Preferred 3.60	100	24,600	83.000 (13 Dec.)	to	98.500 (23 Jan.)
Preferred 4.50	100	20,260	101.250 (29 Dec.)	to	108.500 (19 Mar.)
1952					
Common A	10	310	40.500 (5 Jan.)	to	47.000 (28 Oct.)
Common B	10	727,276	32.125 (2 Jan.)	to	43.250 (8 Dec.)
Preferred 3.60	100	22,680	85.000 (3 Jan.)	to	92.250 (25 Apr.)
Preferred 4.50	100	16,510	101.250 (2 Jan.)	to	107.000 (30 Dec.)
1953					
Common A	10	1,272	48.000 (31 Dec.)	to	58.500 (21 July)
Common B	10	1,021,000	36.750 (22 Dec.)	to	49.000 (7 Aug.)
Preferred 3.60	100	23,600	80.250 (5 June)	to	90.750 (5 Jan.)
Preferred 4.50	100	16,570	98.875 (1 June)	to	107.000 (5 Jan.)
1954					
Common A	10	710	46.000 (16 Mar.)	to	54.000 (3 Dec.)
Common B	10	2,138,800	33.625 (2 July)	to	44.250 (28 Dec.)
Preferred 3.60	100	33,800	78.000 (2 Jan.)	to	88.000 (10 Feb.)
Preferred 4.50	100	38,330	95.750 (1 July)	to	105.000 (9 Nov.)

	Par Value	Volume	Range for Year	
1955				
Common A	10	500	51.000 (14 Mar.) to	62.000 (2 Nov.)
Common B	10	1,440,400	40.000 (14 Mar.) to	54.875 (5 Dec.)
Preferred 3.60	100	27,830	82.000 (12 Jan.) to	91.000 (5 Dec.)
Preferred 4.50	100	21,920	101.000 (26 Jan.) to	106.000 (17 Oct.)
1956				
Common A	10	10	70.000 (26 Apr.) to	70.000 (26 Apr.)
Common B	10	773,900	49.000 (1 Oct.) to	57.750 (7 May)
Preferred 3.60	100	17,400	81.000 (12 Sept.) to	89.750 (16 Jan.)
Preferred 4.50	100	20,500	91.000 (26 Dec.) to	105.250 (11 Jan.)
1957				
Common A	10	60	68.125 (6 June) to	73.500 (19 Sept.)
Common B	10	789,800	52.125 (22 July) to	66.250 (5 Dec.)
Preferred 3.60	100	22,100	72.125 (24 June) to	82.250 (22 Jan.)
Preferred 4.50	100	19,660	87.250 (6 Sept.) to	99.000 (4 Mar.)
1958				
Common A	10	70	83.125 (7 Feb.) to	100.00 (5 Sept.)
Common B	10	923,400	64.000 (10 Jan.) to	90.750 (31 Dec.)
Preferred 3.60	100	18,900	80.000 (9 Jan.) to	87.750 (22 May)
Preferred 4.50[d]	100	—	94.750 (9 Jan.) to	102.500 (12 May)
1959				
Common A[e]				
Common B (old)[f]	10	230,500	92.000 (2 Jan.) to	116.250 (29 Apr.)
New Common	5	727,600	47.875 (15 June) to	65.000 (24 Nov.)
Preferred 3.60	100	30,500	76.000 (8 Oct.) to	84.500 (26 Mar.)
1960				
New Common	5	1,083,800	55.125 (21 Jan.) to	94.500 (6 Dec.)
Preferred 3.60	100	18,100	76.500 (5 Jan.) to	85.000 (2 Aug.)
1961				
New Common				
Before split on				
7 Sept.	5	810,600	91.250 (3 Jan.) to	149.875 (23 Aug.)
When issued	5	146,500	69.000 (26 Sept.) to	75.250 (7 Sept.)
After split	5	604,100	73.625 (17 Oct.) to	89.500 (11 Oct.)
Preferred 3.60	100	22,500	83.000 (8 Mar.) to	90.500 (6 Oct.)
1962				
Common	5	4,390,400	34.500 (23 Oct.) to	80.675 (16 Feb.)
Preferred 3.60	100	19,500	86.875 (8 Nov.) to	90.000 (4 Jan.)
1963				
Common	5	5,156,800	36.750 (17 July) to	47.375 (14 May)
Preferred 3.60	100	18,500	84.250 (23 Sept.) to	88.250 (8 Feb.)

Sources: Compiled from records of the R. J. Reynolds Tobacco Company and the *Commercial and Financial Chronicle*. In some years figures for volume of trade from these sources do not absolutely agree, though it is believed that they provide as accurate a picture as may be given.

[a] Redeemed 31 December 1925.
[b] Admitted to trading 21 September 1945.
[c] Admitted to trading 13 October 1948.
[d] Redeemed 1 October 1958.
[e] Exchanged for New Class B Common on 31 March 1959.
[f] Reclassified as New Common $5 par on 9 April 1959.

A P P E N D I X   G
Invested Capital and Earnings:
The Reynolds Company vs. Other Tobacco Companies, 1912–1960

(Excluding Goodwill and Contingency Reserves in All Years)

Year	Invested Capital (in millions of dollars)				Total	Amount Earned	% Earned	R. J. Reynolds Tobacco Company (in millions of dollars)		
	American	Liggett and Myers	P. Lorillard	Philip Morris				Invested Capital	Amount Earned	% Earned
1912	90.3	31.1	28.1	Not available	149.5	30.2	20.20	12.7	2.9	22.83
1913	84.0	36.3	30.2	Not available	150.5	28.4	18.87	14.7	2.9	19.73
1914	80.6	38.1	31.7	Not available	150.4	23.5	15.63	16.7	2.9	17.37
1915	77.4	36.7	31.8	Not available	145.9	24.8	17.00	19.1	4.7	24.61
1916	77.0	38.8	31.0	Not available	146.8	26.7	18.19	22.5	8.0	35.56
1917	78.0	39.2	32.1	Not available	149.3	29.6	19.83	28.0	10.3	36.79
1918	80.1	48.9	34.5	Not available	163.5	34.2	20.92	42.6	7.0	16.43
1919	118.4	71.8	42.6	Not available	232.8	33.5	14.39	56.8	11.3	19.89
1920	122.2	72.7	43.7	Not available	238.6	35.4	14.84	90.0	11.6	12.89
1921	126.7	85.9	52.0	Not available	264.6	40.4	15.27	95.8	17.2	17.95

(Excluding Goodwill and Contingency Reserves in All Years)

Year	Invested Capital							R. J. Reynolds Tobacco Company		
	American	Liggett and Myers	P. Lorillard	Philip Morris	Total	Amount Earned	% Earned	Invested Capital	Amount Earned	% Earned
			(in millions of dollars)					(in millions of dollars)		
1922	126.0	70.6	53.8	Not available	250.4	40.0	15.97	90.7	20.5	22.60
1923	117.6	75.4	55.8	Not available	248.8	35.6	14.31	103.5	23.0	22.22
1924	120.4	79.7	55.8	Not available	255.9	41.0	16.02	115.7	23.8	20.57
1925	125.8	94.2	53.3	1.3	274.6	46.3	16.86	128.4	25.2	19.63
1926	128.6	110.9	56.3	1.5	297.3	47.5	15.98	117.9	26.2	22.22
1927	132.2	118.2	56.6	1.8	308.8	48.3	15.64	130.2	29.1	22.35
1928	136.7	125.7	73.7	3.9	340.0	50.4	14.82	142.6	30.2	21.18
1929	143.0	130.1	73.0	4.3	350.4	57.6	16.44	146.7	32.2	21.95
1930	197.8	137.4	83.8	4.3	423.3	75.0	17.72	153.4	34.3	22.36
1931	208.8	157.9	85.3	4.5	456.5	78.2	17.13	157.6	36.4	23.10
1932	224.5	163.9	74.4	4.5	467.3	74.3	15.90	164.6	33.7	20.47
1933	236.2	170.5	70.4	4.5	481.6	39.7	8.24	174.1	21.2	12.18
1934	226.8	170.1	61.0	4.6	462.5	50.9	11.01	160.2	21.5	13.42
1935	221.3	173.2	57.5	5.7	457.7	49.7	10.86	152.4	23.9	15.68
1936	199.9	165.1	56.4	7.6	429.0	54.3	12.66	144.8	29.3	20.23
1937	190.6	165.8	54.8	13.9	425.1	58.5	13.76	145.2	28.2	19.42
1938	187.5	166.7	54.2	16.4	424.8	59.7	14.05	145.2	23.7	16.32
1939	182.6	170.0	54.9	26.6	434.1	61.5	14.17	166.8	26.0	15.59
1940	200.6	173.4	55.2	29.4	458.6	63.5	13.85	168.4	25.9	15.38
1941	195.6	176.5	56.2	46.6	474.9	56.3	11.86	170.3	23.6	13.86

(Excluding Goodwill and Contingency Reserves in All Years)

| Year | Invested Capital (in millions of dollars) | | | | | Amount Earned | % Earned | R. J. Reynolds Tobacco Company | | |
	American	Liggett and Myers	P. Lorillard	Philip Morris	Total			Invested Capital (in millions of dollars)	Amount Earned	% Earned
1942	190.9	177.1	56.7	49.3	474.0	55.0	11.60	163.1	20.2	12.39
1943	263.8	178.0	57.6	74.0	573.4	55.0	9.59	164.6	19.1	11.60
1944	268.2	181.6	78.5	74.9	603.2	52.7	8.74	166.6	18.7	11.22
1945	359.4	175.5	77.7	76.6	689.2	54.7	7.94	168.4	20.6	12.23
1946	355.3	218.0	78.0	80.8	732.1	69.2	9.45	217.4	29.6	13.62
1947	362.9	297.3	78.6	102.1	840.9	81.5	9.69	284.6	35.2	12.37
1948	419.4	304.6	79.8	102.8	906.6	106.7	11.77	323.7	39.3	12.14
1949	505.4	316.8	80.8	108.7	1011.7	113.5	11.22	420.2	45.4	10.80
1950	516.7	364.8	82.4	115.7	1079.6	110.1	10.20	433.1	45.1	10.41
1951	523.0	360.0	83.7	152.1	1118.8	90.2	8.06	445.7	36.8	8.26
1952	521.3	360.7	97.5	156.1	1135.6	93.0	8.19	450.1	36.5	8.11
1953	620.6	361.1	98.2	158.4	1238.3	106.3	8.58	454.4	39.1	8.60
1954	621.6	363.1	129.8	168.3	1282.8	104.0	8.11	460.9	49.5	10.74
1955	622.7	362.3	130.0	169.7	1284.7	116.3	9.05	472.8	57.5	12.16
1956	629.9	366.1	140.5	175.4	1311.9	116.4	8.87	490.2	66.9	13.65
1957	633.1	365.9	139.1	176.8	1314.9	136.4	10.37	511.8	71.1	13.89
1958	644.1	367.4	141.6	190.2	1343.3	153.8	11.45	533.1	83.8	15.72
1959	653.3	372.2	178.4	194.5	1398.4	155.2	11.10	537.2	97.0	18.06
1960	666.1	371.5	189.3	239.1	1466.0	156.4	10.67	575.6	113.8	19.77

Source: Compiled by the R. J. Reynolds Tobacco Company.

APPENDIX H
Officers and Directors of the Reynolds Company

The R. J. Reynolds Tobacco Company did not come into corporate existence until chartered by the state of North Carolina on 11 February 1890. The business was a proprietorship until Reynolds, on 2 January 1888, formed a partnership known as R. J. Reynolds and Company with William N. Reynolds and Henry Roan; this lasted only one year. When the R. J. Reynolds Tobacco Company of North Carolina became a subsidiary of the American Tobacco Company on 4 April 1899, the company received a New Jersey charter under which it has since operated. Many prefer to call 1 January 1912 the beginning date because it marks the resumption of independent operations after the dissolution of the old American Tobacco Company. Because the company could never have existed without the work begun by R. J. Reynolds on 19 October 1875, when he purchased a lot in Winston for his factory, it seems logical to include the names of all officers and directors regardless of the status of the business at any particular time.

Directors

R. J. Reynolds	19 October 1875–29 July 1918
William N. Reynolds	12 February 1890–14 May 1942
Henry Roan	12 February 1890–13 February 1893
Thomas L. Farrow	7 March 1892–13 February 1893
Walter R. Reynolds	13 February 1893–6 March 1921
John F. Parlett	6 February 1897–4 April 1899
Robert Critz	29 May 1893–4 April 1899
John B. Cobb	4 April 1899–2 April 1902
George W. Watts	4 April 1899–16 August 1905
Benjamin N. Duke	4 April 1899–16 August 1905
James B. Duke	4 April 1899–16 August 1905
Caleb C. Dula	2 April 1902–16 August 1905
George W. Coan	16 August 1905–10 February 1915
D. Rich	16 August 1905–15 March 1923
Robert B. Horn	16 August 1905–8 April 1907
C. A. Hopman	16 August 1905–2 February 1912
Richard B. Reynolds	8 April 1907–21 February 1912
Henry A. Oetjen	21 February 1912–3 April 1923
Percy R. Masten	2 April 1912–20 November 1914
Bowman Gray, Sr.	2 April 1912–7 July 1935
Joseph D. Noell	2 April 1912–22 November 1912
Joseph L. Graham	2 April 1912–2 February 1928

Robert E. Lasater	2 April 1912 – 1 April 1947
James B. Dyer	1 April 1913 – 19 August 1929
Memory E. Motsinger	4 March 1915 – 1 January 1940
Charles A. Kent	3 December 1914 – 1 January 1920
Theodore H. Kirk	2 August 1918 – 1 April 1937
James A. Gray	1 January 1920 – 29 October 1952
James Sloan	30 March 1921 – 1 May 1923
Carl W. Harris	3 April 1923 – 18 December 1937
James W. Glenn	3 April 1923 – 1 July 1948
Roy C. Haberkern	3 April 1923 – 1 February 1955
S. Clay Williams	8 April 1924 – 25 February 1949
Louis F. Owen	2 February 1928 – 31 December 1947
Robert D. Shore	1 April 1930 – 1 October 1937
John C. Whitaker	11 July 1935 – 13 July 1961
Henry S. Stokes	1 April 1937 – 1 June 1947
P. Frank Hanes	5 October 1937 – 8 April 1953
Edward A. Darr	23 December 1937 – 8 October 1958
Thomas W. Blackwell	1 January 1940 – 24 August 1943
Richard J. Reynolds, Jr.	14 May 1942 – 1 April 1947
Frederick S. Hill	9 September 1943 – 27 January 1951
William J. Conrad, Jr.	2 May, 1945 – 1 April 1960
William T. Smither	2 May 1945 – 1 February 1957
Marion A. Braswell	2 May 1945 – 11 October 1945
Raymond G. Vallandingham	2 May 1945 – 1 April 1957
Herbert N. Hardy	2 May 1945 – 1 August 1959
H. Henry Ramm	2 April 1946 – 29 June 1970
Bowman Gray, Jr.	12 June 1947 – 11 April 1969
Haddon S. Kirk	8 January 1948 – 1 April 1962
Spencer B. Hanes, Jr.	1 July 1948 – 27 September 1966
Stuart M. Scott	24 June 1948 – 1 March 1959
Alexander H. Galloway, Jr.	31 January 1951 – 20 April 1973
William R. Lybrook	5 November 1952 – 29 June 1970
Kenneth H. Hoover	8 April 1953 – 31 December 1964
Charles B. Wade, Jr.	13 April 1955 – 15 October 1975
Robert M. Hanes	1 February 1955 – 10 March 1959
Colin Stokes	10 April 1957 – 14 July 1976
Charles B. Babcock	10 January 1957 – 8 October 1964
Frederick G. Carter	15 October 1958 – 16 June 1960
Leighton H. Coleman	23 March 1959 – 20 June 1968
David S. Peoples	10 September 1959 – 15 October 1975
Joseph H. Sherrill	13 April 1960 – 31 August 1976
William S. Smith, Jr.	21 June 1960 – 15 October 1975
Gordon Gray	13 July 1961 – 29 June 1970
D. Rice Allen, Jr.	11 April 1962 – 4 May 1964

Chairman of the Board

William N. Reynolds	8 April 1924–6 May 1931
Bowman Gray, Sr.	6 May 1931–7 July 1935
S. Clay Williams	11 July 1935–25 February 1949
James A. Gray	1 March 1949–29 October 1952
John C. Whitaker	5 November 1952–8 October 1959
Bowman Gray, Jr.	8 October 1959–

President

R. J. Reynolds	19 October 1875–29 July 1918
William N. Reynolds	2 August 1918–8 April 1924
Bowman Gray, Sr.	8 April 1924–6 May 1931
S. Clay Williams	6 May 1931–16 April 1934
James A. Gray	16 April 1934–11 April 1946
James W. Glenn	11 April 1946–1 July 1948
John C. Whitaker	1 July 1948–5 November 1952
Edward A. Darr	5 November 1952–14 November 1957
Bowman Gray, Jr.	14 November 1957–8 October 1959
Francis G. Carter	8 October 1959–16 June 1960
Alexander H. Galloway	21 June 1960–

Vice-President

William N. Reynolds	12 February 1890–2 August 1918
Benjamin N. Duke	4 April 1899–16 August 1905
Richard S. Reynolds	15 April 1911–21 February 1912
Percy R. Masten	9 April 1912–20 November 1914
Bowman Gray, Sr.	9 April 1912–8 April 1924
Charles A. Kent	3 December 1914–1 January 1920
Walter R. Reynolds	2 August 1918–6 March 1921
James A. Gray	1 January 1920–16 April 1934
Theodore H. Kirk	9 April 1923–1 April 1937
S. Clay Williams	8 April 1924–6 May 1931
Robert E. Lasater	6 May 1931–1 April 1947
Carl W. Harris	6 May 1931–18 December 1937
James W. Glenn	1 April 1937–11 April 1946
John C. Whitaker	23 December 1937–1 July 1948
P. Frank Hanes	11 April 1946–8 April 1953
Roy C. Haberkern	11 April 1946–5 November 1952
Edward A. Darr	11 April 1946–5 November 1952
Herbert N. Hardy	7 April 1949–15 October 1958
Bowman Gray, Jr. *	7 April 1949–14 November 1957
Haddon S. Kirk *	5 November 1952–8 October 1959

William J. Conrad, Jr.	5 November 1952–1 April 1960
Alexander H. Galloway, Jr.*	13 January 1955–21 June, 1960
H. Henry Ramm	14 November 1957–29 June 1970
Spencer B. Hanes, Jr.*	15 October 1958–27 September 1966
Francis G. Carter	15 October 1958–8 October 1959
Colin Stokes*	8 October 1959–29 June 1970
Kenneth H. Hoover	12 November 1959–31 December 1964
Charles B. Wade, Jr.*	12 November 1959–20 September 1973
William S. Smith, Jr.*	10 November 1960–29 June 1970
William R. Lybrook	12 January 1961–29 June 1970
Joseph H. Sherrill	10 January 1963–31 August 1976
David S. Peoples*	4 May 1964–29 June 1970
Willard M. Bright	4 May 1964–

*Executive vice-president or senior vice-president during part of term.

Chairman of Executive Committee of Board of Directors

William N. Reynolds	6 May 1931–14 May 1942
S. Clay Williams	8 April 1943–11 April 1946
James A. Gray	11 April 1946–29 October 1952
Roy C. Haberkern	5 November 1952–1 February 1955
John C. Whitaker	1 February 1955–14 November 1957
Edward A. Darr	14 November 1957–8 October 1958
Herbert N. Hardy	15 October 1958–1 August 1959
John C. Whitaker	1 August 1959–8 October 1959
Haddon S. Kirk	8 October 1959–1 April 1962
Alexander H. Galloway, Jr.	13 April 1962–

Secretary

Henry Roan*	1 December 1882–13 February 1893
William N. Reynolds*	13 February 1893–29 May 1893
Robert Critz*	29 May 1893–4 April 1899(?)
George R. Lybrook*	4 April 1899–26 January 1902
George W. Coan**	2 January 1902–10 February 1915
Memory E. Motsinger	4 March 1915–1 January 1940
William J. Conrad, Jr.	1 January 1940–1 April 1960
William R. Lybrook	1 April 1960–

*Also treasurer.
**Also treasurer until 15 April 1911.

578 Appendixes

Treasurer

Henry Roan*	1 December 1882–13 February 1893
William N. Reynolds*	13 February 1893–29 May 1893
Robert Critz*	29 May 1893–4 April 1899
George R. Lybrook*	4 April 1899–26 January 1902
George W. Coan**	2 January 1902–15 April 1911
D. Rich	15 April 1911–15 March 1923
Robert D. Shore	15 March 1923–1 October 1937
Frederick S. Hill	5 October 1937–27 January 1951
Alexander H. Galloway, Jr.	31 January 1951–10 April 1959
Edward C. Peterson	10 April 1959–

*Also secretary.
**Pro tempore until 26 January 1902.

Assistant Secretary

Memory E. Motsinger	5 October 1912–4 March 1914
Arthur M. Strauss	12 April 1917–19 October 1948
William T. Smither	12 April 1917–5 February 1920
Edward A. Darr	1 April 1920–9 April 1923
Robert W. Sills	9 April 1923–11 November 1948
William J. Conrad, Jr.	9 April 1923–1 January 1940
Louise A. Peterson	11 November 1948–31 December 1970
Charles F. Benbow, Jr.	14 June 1956–14 December 1961
Oscar F. Hege	8 November 1956–28 February 1973
Jeremiah R. Marion, Jr.	15 December 1958–30 April 1971
John W. Dowdle, Jr.	10 May 1962–

Assistant Treasurer

Memory E. Motsinger	12 May 1909–5 October 1912
Frank J. Liipfert	3 October 1912–31 July 1915
Marion G. Follin	3 March 1915–1 February 1917
Edward B. Hastings	12 April 1917–9 April 1923
Robert D. Shore	12 April 1917–15 March 1923
J. Porter Stedman	1 March 1923–4 April 1927
G. Ellis Ashburn	15 March 1923–31 December 1956
Frederick S. Hill	14 April 1927–5 October 1937
Alexander H. Galloway, Jr.	5 October 1937–31 January 1951
Douglas F. Peterson	5 October 1937–27 May 1947
Watson G. Scott	9 December 1948–2 June 1955
Edward C. Peterson	31 January 1951–10 April 1959

Bahnson Gray	9 October 1952–3 February 1955
Byron B. Mason	8 November 1956–30 September 1974
Robert D. Shore, Jr.	8 November 1956–12 September 1961
Charles F. Benbow	14 December 1961–31 May 1968
Zachary T. Smith	10 January 1963–

Source: Compiled by the R. J. Reynolds Tobacco Company.

ABBREVIATIONS

In the notes that follow, RJR refers to the files of the R. J. Reynolds Tobacco Company. In reference to interviews that took place in Winston-Salem or documents with a Winston or Winston-Salem dateline, the name of the city has been omitted in the interests of brevity. (Winston and Salem were consolidated in 1913.)

Ashe	Samuel A. Ashe, Stephen B. Weeks, and Chas. L. Van Noppen, eds., *Biographical History of North Carolina*, 8 vols. (Greensboro, N.C., 1905–17)
Connorton's	J. W. Connorton, ed., *Connorton's Tobacco Brand Directory of the United States* (Chicago, 1886–93)
Fries	Adelaide L. Fries and associates, *Forsyth: A County on the March* (Chapel Hill, 1949)
J&S	*Journal and Sentinel*
MB	*Management Bulletin*
MIB	*Management Information Bulletin*
Minutes	Minutes of the Board of Directors, RJR, vols. I through X. Numbered chronologically beginning 4 April 1899 and filed as of 1964 in the secretary's dept.
N&O	Raleigh *News and Observer*
NYT	*New York Times*
OD	*Open Door*
PP	*People's Press*
RCCTI	*Report of the Commissioner of Corporations on the Tobacco Industry*, 3 vols. (Washington, D.C., 1909–15)
Sent.	*Sentinel*
STJ	*Southern Tobacco Journal*
TCS	*Twin City Sentinel*
Tilley	Nannie M. Tilley, *The Bright-Tobacco Industry, 1860–1929* (Chapel Hill, 1948)
Tob.	*Tobacco*
UR	*Union Republican*
WS	*Western Sentinel*
WSJ	*Winston-Salem Journal*
WTJ	*Western Tobacco Journal*

NOTES

Chapter 1
Background and Training of R. J. Reynolds

1. Max Lerner, *America as a Civilization: Life and Thought in the United States Today* (New York, 1957), pp. 280–82. Note the same conclusion in Frederick L. Allen, *The Big Change: America Transforms Itself, 1909–1950* (New York, 1952), pp. 234–58. An attempt to place portraits of William N. Reynolds and Bowman Gray, Sr., in the boardroom in 1942–43 resulted in failure—Minutes, vol. VII, pp. 266, 271, 309.

2. Mrs. J. S. Dunn, interview with author, 8 Dec. 1959.

3. According to the testimony of James W. Glenn, Maryland tobacco was not added to the Camel cigarette blend until early in 1916—*Am. Tob. Co. et al. v. U.S., Record on Appeal*, docket no. 9137–9139 (6th Cir., 1944), transcripts, 6:4731.

4. Virginia G. Pedigo and Lewis G. Pedigo, *History of Patrick and Henry Counties Virginia* (Roanoke, Va., 1933), pp. 263–67; *Patrick County Virginia: Its Resources and Advantages*, issued by Board of Supervisors (Roanoke, Va., 1907), pp. 3–5; Maynard Conner and William B. King, *An Economic and Social Survey of Patrick County*, University of Virginia Extension Series, vol. 21, no. 6, ed. Leland B. Tate (University of Virginia, 1937), pp. map (frontispiece), 7, 19; Historical Marker, U 30, on courthouse grounds, Stuart, Va.

5. Patrick County, Virginia, Deed Book, vol. IV, p. 89, Patrick County Clerk's Office, Courthouse, Stuart, Va. (hereafter cited as Patrick County Deed Book).

6. To Walter C. Reynolds (of 357 West 25th Street, New York, N.Y.), 10 Oct. 1918—Correspondence of Walter R. Reynolds, purchasing dept., RJR. Note Appendix A for indications that Reynolds may have been correct. Note also a statement that the Reynolds were Scotch highlanders—W. A. Blair, "Richard Joshua Reynolds," in Ashe, 3:334.

7. To E. E. Reynolds (of Phoenix, Ariz.), 19 May 1914—Correspondence of Walter R. Reynolds. Hardin William Reynolds's brother, David Harbour, died unmarried—Pedigo and Pedigo, *History of Patrick and Henry Counties*, p. 231.

8. Miss Irene Smith, interview with author, Mount Airy, N.C., 1 Nov. 1959.

9. Patrick County Personal Property Taxes, 1813 (alphabetically arranged; MS volume, Virginia State Library—hereafter volumes in this series will be cited by name and date). Land Book, 1850–55, p. 30, shows that Abraham Reynolds's estate in 1852 contained 1,077 acres—Patrick County Clerk's Office, Courthouse, Stuart, Va.

10. Patrick County Personal Property Taxes, 1831–40.

11. Gravestones in the Reynolds family cemetery at Rock Spring, the family's old home near Critz, Va.; Patrick County Marriage Register, 1791–1822 (microfilm, Virginia State Library); Pedigo and Pedigo, *History of Patrick and Henry*

Counties, p. 158. During the years 1791–1822, twenty-six individuals by the name of Reynolds were married in Patrick County.

12. List of supplies furnished Abe and Jack Reynolds (freedmen), 1865–66; contract with Abe Reynolds (freedman), 15 Jan. 1866; unpaid note for fifty cents due Abraham Reynolds signed by Elijah Spencer on 8 May 1833—Papers of Hardin William Reynolds, in possession of Nancy S. Reynolds, Greenwich, Conn. On the land once owned by Abraham Reynolds, about a quarter of a mile from his house, there still exists the foundation of a dam and a mill house—a further indication of enterprise on the part of Abraham Reynolds.

13. *Hardin W. Reynolds, Adm. of David H. Reynolds, Decd. v. James M. Smith, Exr. of James M. Redd, Decd.*—Roanoke Circuit Court of Law and Chancery, 1839–52, consisting of items in the Chancery Order Book, vol. I (Aug. 1838–1 Mar. 1866), depositions, briefs, excerpts from account books, articles of agreement, and other evidence all filed in the office of the Clerk of Roanoke County, Salem. Va. The case is generally referred to as *Reynolds v. Redd*.

14. A. D. Reynolds in Pedigo and Pedigo, *History of Patrick and Henry Counties*, p. 26. An entirely plausible story was told by J. S. Kuykendall, who knew R. J. Reynolds intimately. By this account, Hardin W. Reynolds, when about eighteen years old, lived at Rock Spring with his father Abraham, who owned a good-sized tract of land and engaged in general farming with tobacco as a money crop. Hardin, anxious to succeed in the world, attended an administrator's sale and bid on a tract of land. His neighbors, expecting to enjoy the results, allowed the land to go to him at a reasonable figure. Upon going home to get money for the first payment, he received a scolding from his father, who felt that they had all the land that they could cultivate. His mother encouraged him, however, and on the following morning Abraham set him free to manage his new purchase. When trying to sell his first crop of tobacco, young Reynolds found only one purchaser and he offered but three cents per pound. Because he needed more money to finance the next payment on his farm, Hardin refused the offer and decided to manufacture his crop. With encouragement from his parents, he stemmed his leaf, worked it into twists, and obtained pressure from a wooden lever bearing a basket of rocks on one end. With a six-horse load of manufactured tobacco, he then set forth on a selling trip into North and South Carolina and thereby obtained sufficient funds to pay the entire sum due on his land. Hardin then decided to buy tobacco and manufacture it. This he did, selling his product in North and South Carolina, Tennessee, and Kentucky for about three years. Eventually finding his chewing tobacco less favored than formerly, he discovered that his product was being outsold by a man from Stokes County, N.C., who had used honey as a sweetening agent. Adopting this same idea, Hardin Reynolds manufactured his tobacco with honey until licorice came into use, as many others did. J. S. Kuykendall in *STJ*, reprinted in *TCS*, 27 June 1919. Like honey, licorice combined flavor, sweetness, and hygroscopic qualities.

15. *A New and Comprehensive Gazetteer of Virginia and the District of Columbia* (Charlottesville, Va., 1835), pp. 257–58.

16. Note also Abram D. Reynolds's reference to a letter from his father (Pedigo and Pedigo, *History of Patrick and Henry Counties*, pp. 34–35) that may have been written by his mother. The Papers of Hardin William Reynolds show that

he wrote with great difficulty and many inaccuracies, but he could convey his meaning and keep accurate records.

17. Hardin W. Reynolds (nephew of R. J. Reynolds), interview with author, 11 Apr. 1962. Apparently Joshua Cox was stirred to anger when the Tories killed five of his horses in one night—"I. J. B." in *Danbury Reporter-Post*, reprinted in *UR*, 24 Jan. 1894. With his friend Colonel John Martin, Cox raised a small force for attacking Tories. Of one skirmish, John H. Wheeler, the historian, wrote: "old Joshua . . . was shot and left for dead, and his horse shot also lying by him. Much joy was caused among the Royalists; but it was subdued when they learned that both man and horse had recovered so far as to be able to reach the camp." —*Historical Sketches of North Carolina, from 1584 to 1851* (Philadelphia, 1851), p. 405. Proof that Nancy Jane Cox, the daughter of one Joshua Cox who had married his first cousin (Agnes Cox), was the granddaughter of the revolutionary Joshua Cox rests on a sketch of R. J. Reynolds that is generally replete with minor errors—*Cyclopedia of Eminent and Representative Men of the Carolinas of the Nineteenth Century with a Brief Historical Introduction of South Carolina by General Edward McCrady, Jr., and of North Carolina by Hon. Samuel A. Ashe*, 2 vols. (Madison, Wis., 1892), 2:550. See also Blair, "Richard Joshua Reynolds," in Ashe, 3:335.

18. Jonathan Daniels, *Tar Heels: A Portrait of North Carolina* (New York, 1941), pp. 171–72. The coin is now owned by Richard Joshua Reynolds III.

19. Compare her handwriting and spelling in records among the Papers of Hardin William Reynolds (payment from John Tuder, 16 June 1833; from Andrew M. Lybrook, 17 Apr. 1884; from Mrs. Martin, 7 May 1884; from Mary Joyce Lybrook, 11 Aug. 1884; and for various other sums from Andrew M. Lybrook) with letters in her husband's name but in her handwriting regarding her son's entrance to Virginia Military Institute; these letters, preserved in the archives of the Virginia Military Institute, Lexington, began on 29 Dec. 1862 and were generally addressed to General Francis H. Smith, superintendent of the institute.

20. Patrick County Deed Book, vol. IX, pp. 262–63.

21. Patrick County Land Tax List, 1882 (alphabetically arranged; MS volume, Virginia State Library—hereafter cited as Patrick County Land Tax List, by date). Deed books in the Patrick County Clerk's Office, Courthouse, Stuart, Va., reveal the accuracy of the tax list: vols. XIII, pp. 65, 86, 207, 238, 456, 486; XIV, p. 512; XV, pp. 86, 112, 281; XVI, pp. 40, 46, 61, 430, 465, 472; XVII, pp. 179, 203, 298, 408, 411–12; XVIII, pp. 345, 402–3, 435–36; XIX, pp. 339, 567; XX, p. 459; XXI, p. 64; XXII, pp. 219, 304. Deed books in the office of the Register of Deeds, Stokes County, Danbury, N.C.: vols. XVII, pp. 232–33, 565–66; XVIII, pp. 312, 467–68, 626; XX, pp. 47, 394–95. One transaction (Deed Book, vol. XVIII, p. 626) does not include acreage.

22. Patrick County Deed Book, vol. XXII, p. 445.

23. See table entitled "Selected Items from the Personal Property of Hardin W. Reynolds (Tax Records)" in Appendix B.

24. See, for example, a receipt for the purchase of a boy named Jack for $550 on 21 June 1849; a slave named Jim from the estate of David B. Hatcher for $765 on 10 Nov. 1858; and a slave woman named Milley about 23 years old,

sound and healthy "accept a bad burn Scarr," for $700 on 29 July 1859—Papers of Hardin William Reynolds.

25. Register of Births, Patrick County, Va., 1853–96 (microfilm, Virginia State Library, reel 24).

26. Abram D. Reynolds (son of Hardin William) upon returning from Confederate service was greeted by his father as follows: "My Son the Yankees have been here and torn up Evry thing and my Negro men have all gone with them. . . ."—Recollections of Abram D. Reynolds, p. 16, in possession of Nancy S. Reynolds, Greenwich, Conn. See *War of the Rebellion: A Compilation of the Official Records of the Union and Confederate Armies* (128 vols. [Washington, 1880–1901], ser. 1, vol. 49, pt. 1), p. 332, for the record of Palmer's stay in Taylorsville.

27. To Hardin William Reynolds, Greensboro, N.C., 16 Nov. 1865—Papers of Hardin William Reynolds.

28. Rent bond of Joel Tuggle to Hardin William Reynolds, 15 Sept. 1855—ibid.

29. In ibid.

30. Ibid. The accounts about tanning hides during and just after the Civil War are in possession of Nancy S. Reynolds, Greenwich, Conn.; specific items relating to kips bear dates of 18 Nov. 1861, 19 Dec. 1862, and 24 Dec. 1865.

31. See tables in Appendix B entitled "Selected Items from the Personal Property of Hardin W. Reynolds (Tax Records)" and "Farming Operations of Hardin Reynolds, 1850 and 1860 (Census Returns)."

32. Papers of Hardin W. Reynolds, passim; Sale Bill of Hardin William Reynolds's Estate, Patrick County Will Book, vol. VIII, pp. 55–65, Patrick County Clerk's Office, Courthouse, Stuart Va.

33. Recollections of Abram D. Reynolds, pp. 37–43. For additional proof of Reynolds's activities as a banker, see *U.S. Tobacco Journal*, 3 Aug. 1918—Prince Albert Scrapbook, vol. VII, advertising dept., RJR.

34. Reynolds's factory does not appear in the returns for 1880, but he continued to work for the rest of his life—Inventory of Hardin William Reynolds's Estate, Patrick County Will Book, vol. VIII, p. 49; Papers of Hardin William Reynolds, passim.

35. [R. J. Reynolds] to "Dear Pa," 26 Mar. 1881—Papers of Hardin William Reynolds.

36. W. Russell Critz, interview with author, Critz, Va., 12 Feb. 1960.

37. Inventory of Hardin William Reynolds's Estate, Patrick County Will Book, vol. VIII, p. 49–65.

38. Recollections of Abram D. Reynolds, pp. 29–30.

39. J. C. Robert, *The Tobacco Kingdom: Plantation, Market, and Factory in Virginia and North Carolina, 1800–1860* (Durham, N.C., 1938), p. 175.

40. The author has no unequivocal proof that Reynolds served in the militia as captain, but his papers show over and over that he enjoyed that title. In Pedigo and Pedigo, *History of Patrick and Henry Counties*, facing p. 232, his portrait is captioned "Captain Hardin W. Reynolds of Patrick County, Virginia." In 1875 a news item in a North Carolina paper carried a reference to "Capt. Reynolds of Va."—*UR*, 27 May 1875. Note also Blair, "Richard Joshua Reynolds," in Ashe,

3 : 335. Even more convincing is the use of the title in 1856 and 1857 in court records—Patrick County Court Order Book, vol. VII, pp. 292, 312, Office of Clerk of Court, Patrick County Courthouse, Stuart, Va.

41. Patrick County Court Order Book, vols. VI, p. 16; VII, pp. 45, 103, 137.

42. Recollections of Abram D. Reynolds, pp. 1–5. Among the Papers of Hardin William Reynolds there is a receipt of Paul C. Pigg for three bushels of salt received on 20 June 1864, evidently repayable in kind.

43. Receipts for subscriptions and donations—Papers of Hardin William Reynolds; Recollections of Abram D. Reynolds, p. 7.

44. Receipt of Thomas Shelton for Reynolds's payment for carriage harness, 12 June 1852—Papers of Hardin William Reynolds.

45. Personal Property Interrogatories, 1882—ibid.

46. *UR*, 8 June 1882.

47. *UR*, 27 May 1875, 6 Apr. 1876, 4 Apr., 17 May 1877; *PP*, 8 June 1876; *WS*, 31 May 1877, 2 May 1878 (quotation). See *UR*, 14 Aug. 1890, for a sketch of McCanless. For reviews before the state supreme court see *North Carolina Reports: Cases Argued and Determined in the Supreme Court of North Carolina*, 67 (June term, 1872): 193–96; 74 (Jan. term, 1876): 256–58; 90 (Feb. term, 1884): 652; 91 (Oct. term, 1884): 231–32. See Stokes County (N.C.) Deed Book, vol. XX, p. 47, for a description of the 475 acres sold by Cox to Reynolds in 1864.

48. Primarily from the Bible of R. J. Reynolds, in possession of Nancy S. Reynolds, Greenwich, Conn.

49. Indirect proof of this is in the Recollections of Abram D. Reynolds, pp. 7–8.

50. Itemized and receipted account for Catherine Reynolds at Salem Female Academy, 1 June 1859; receipt for $75 for board and tuition of Hardin William Reynolds's two daughters at Danville Female College, 29 Aug. 1859—Papers of Hardin William Reynolds; *Bristol Herald Courier*, 29 May 1915.

51. E. P. Zentmeyer to Hardin William Reynolds, Mayo Forge, Va., 31 Dec. 1880; receipt of estate of Hardin William Reynolds for "$84.31 the amt. due me for my services as governess for Katie," 2 June 1882, signed Alice B. Crenshaw— Papers of Hardin William Reynolds.

52. Receipt of B. A. Anthony for tuition of the Reynolds children, 22 Mar. 1860; receipt of Nannie Walker for tuition of Lucy and Harbour, [1866?]; receipt of W. H. Shelton for tuition of Lucy and Harbour, 28 January 1867; receipt of Thomas T. Allen for tuition of Harbour and Willie, 20 July 1872; receipt of Mollie E. Williams for tuition of Willie, Walter, and Katie, 5 Aug. 1878.

53. Scrapbook of Robert P. Dalton, pp. 73, 77, in possession of Miss Ethel Dalton, Winston-Salem, N.C., as of 12 June 1960.

54. Records from Alumnae Office, Salem College, Winston-Salem, N.C., supplied by the secretary, Miss Lelia Marsh, on 4 Mar. 1961; receipts of payment by Hardin William Reynolds of $75 for the board and tuition "of his two daughters in D. F. College" on 29 Aug. 1859, and of $25 for "the board and tuition of his daughter in Danville Female College" on 16 Oct. 1860, both signed by Jas. Jameson—Papers of Hardin William Reynolds; *Bristol Herald Courier*, 29 May 1915.

55. Pedigo and Pedigo, *History of Patrick and Henry Counties*, p. 184; Papers of Hardin William Reynolds, passim; *WS*, 22 Oct. 1896; *UR*, 5 Jan. 1899; Nelson M. Blake, *William Mahone of Virginia: Soldier and Political Insurgent* (Richmond, Va., 1935), pp. 164, 216, 219n, 224; Charles C. Pearson, *The Readjuster Movement in Virginia* (New Haven, 1917), pp. 63–64. In 1930 a portrait of Lybrook and three fellow senators was unveiled in the Virginia capitol in the room once occupied by the Confederate senate.

56. Recollections of Abram D. Reynolds, passim; Papers of Hardin William Reynolds, passim; letters relative to Abram D. Reynolds, Archives, Virginia Military Institute, Lexington.

57. *Catalogue of Officers and Students of the Virginia Agricultural & Mechanical College, First Session, 1872–1873*, p. 10; *1873–'74*, p. 9. In one account of the golden jubilee celebration at Virginia Polytechnic Institute (VPI) in 1922, Hardin Harbour Reynolds was listed as one of "the original eleven who took their diplomas in 1875"—*Richmond News Leader*, 20 May 1922, courtesy of officials of the VPI archives. Judging from the census enumeration made 30 July 1870, Hardin Harbour was away from home at the age of seventeen, probably at some academy for preparation to enter college—Original MS Census Returns, Patrick County, Va., 1870, Schedule 1: Inhabitants, p. 83 (microfilm, Virginia State Library, reel 16).

58. Records from Alumnae Office, Salem College, Winston-Salem, N.C., supplied by the secretary, Miss Lelia Marsh, on 4 Mar. 1961. When old Sullins College was burned in 1915, all records were destroyed—Amelia Baskervill Martin to author, Bristol, Va., 22 Mar. 1961. Mrs. Martin's husband, Dr. W. E. Martin, served as president of Sullins from 1904 to 1910. A receipted account for expenses of Lucy Reynolds advanced by Abram D. Reynolds in the fall of 1875 in Bristol indicates that Lucy may have attended Sullins at that time—Papers of Hardin William Reynolds.

59. See below.

60. Receipted account with Abram D. Reynolds for "Willie and Walter" including tuition for their attendance at King College, 1882—Papers of Hardin W. Reynolds; Record Book N, p. 800, and Book O, p. 49 (in Registrar's Office, Duke University) contain the records of both. The editor of the *UR* (15 May 1884) received an invitation to the Trinity College commencement showing that William N. Reynolds was one of the marshals.

61. Esp. in Papers of Richard H. Wright, Flowers Collection, Duke University Library, Durham, N.C.

62. See below.

63. See below; Recollections of Abram D. Reynolds, pp. 29–31, 33–34, 45–49.

64. Hardin Harbour Reynolds to "Dear Ma," 4 June 1880—Papers of Hardin William Reynolds.

65. *UR*, 16 June 1892, 1 June 1893, 6 Feb. 1896, 16 July, 4 Oct. 1900; *Tob.*, 2 June 1893, p. 5; *WTJ*, 29 May 1893, p. 4; Fries, p. 173; R. J. Reynolds Ledger, 1881–89, pp. 132, 363—secretary's dept., RJR; *STJ*, 1 Apr. 1893.

66. Hardin William Reynolds, interview with author, 11 Apr. 1962. Probably

his addiction to alcohol was also a factor—William N. Reynolds to Andrew M. Lybrook, 6 Jan. 1892, Papers of Hardin William Reynolds.

67. Recollections of Abram D. Reynolds, pp. 33–34; W. Russell Critz, interview with author, Critz, Va., 12 Feb. 1960. See also below.

68. *Bristol Herald Courier*, 29 May 1915.

69. Miss Ethel Dalton, interview with author, 19 Sept. 1959. Miss Dalton stated that her grandmother, who taught in Patrick County during the Civil War, told this story from the time of its occurrence until her old age. Georgia L. Tatum, in *Disloyalty in the Confederacy* (Chapel Hill, 1934), pp. 160–61, writes that "many of the best people in parts of Bedford, Botetourt, Roanoke, Montgomery, Giles, Floyd, Franklin, Patrick, Henry, and parts of Pittsylvania were said to be 'completely demoralized'" by the ravages of the deserters. This fact is more fully accounted for by Robert P. Dalton—Scrapbook of Robert P. Dalton, p. 183. Note also the efforts of R. J. Reynolds's own brother to destroy a lawless band of deserters in Patrick—Abram D. Reynolds in Pedigo and Pedigo, *History of Patrick and Henry Counties*, pp. 32–37; Recollections of Abram D. Reynolds, pp. 17–24.

70. Original MS Census Returns, Patrick County, Va., 1860, Schedule 1: Free Inhabitants, p. 95 (microfilm, Virginia State Library).

71. *Catalogue of Emory and Henry College* (Wytheville, Va.), *1868–69*, p. 8, *1869–70*, p. 7. Most of the records of the college were destroyed in two devastating fires (President Earl G. Hunt, Jr., to author, 2 Oct. 1959) so that the official catalog record of enrollment is the only available proof that Reynolds attended Emory and Henry. His attendance at school at that time is verified by the Original MS Census Returns, Patrick County, Va., 1870, Schedule 1: Inhabitants, p. 83 (microfilm, Virginia State Library, reel 16). This enumeration, made 30 July 1870, lists "Harbour H. 17" and "Richard J. 19, going to school." The Emory and Henry yearbook, the Sphinx for 1913, was dedicated to R. J. Reynolds. Blair ("Richard Joshua Reynolds" in Ashe, 3:336) states that Reynolds attended Emory and Henry but that he left in 1870 before graduation. Both the census date and Blair's are slightly incorrect. On the date of the census enumeration Reynolds was twenty years old, and, according to the Emory and Henry catalogs, he was not at the college in 1871. In the Recollections of Abram D. Reynolds, p. 30, it is stated that R. J. attended Emory and Henry.

72. *Bristol Herald Courier*, 29 May 1915.

73. "Richard Joshua Reynolds," in Ashe, 3:335–36.

74. Pedigo and Pedigo, *History of Patrick and Henry Counties*, p. 233.

75. P. 30. Abram D. Reynolds was an able and a devout man, and, as his Recollections and the Papers of his father reveal, truthful and in no way given to bombast as R. J. was on occasion.

76. *WS*, 17 Dec. 1885. Also late in life William N. Reynolds stated that he was about eight when he began to work in his father's factory, although he conceded that it was only "a little" work—*Am. Tob. Co. et al. v. U.S., Record on Appeal*, transcripts, 6:4860. Abram D. Reynolds declared in 1915 that he and each of his brothers were put to work in the father's factory at "an early age"—*Bristol Herald Courier*, 29 May 1915.

77. *WSJ*, 25 Apr. 1915. See also *STJ*, 30 July 1918; *OD* 1, no. 2 [Sept. 1916?].
OD was the official publication of the R. J. Reynolds Tobacco Company for a
short time.

78. Recollections of Abram D. Reynolds, pp. 29–30. In later years, when referring to his work at Rock Spring, Reynolds described the season for manufacturing as follows: "In those days tobacco factories only ran four months in the
year and the other eight months I was engaged as a tobacco salesman"—*Bristol
Herald Courier*, 23 May 1915.

79. *STJ*, 17 June 1919. This story was told in 1917 by R. J. Reynolds to the
late J. S. Kuykendall, who later vouched for its accuracy as told to him—J. S.
Kuykendall, interview with author, 16 Sept. 1959.

80. *OD* 1, no. 2 [Sept. 1916?]. Of the various other somewhat similar accounts, the following are typical: *WSJ*, 25 Apr. 1915; *STJ*, 30 July 1918; Archibald Henderson et al., *North Carolina: The Old North State and the New*, 5 vols.
(Chicago, 1941), 4:21; *Tob.*, 1 Aug. 1918; Blair, "Richard Joshua Reynolds," in
Ashe, 3:336. For evasion of taxes see Tilley, pp. 538–40.

81. Recollections of Abram D. Reynolds, pp. 1–5.

82. Various dates for Reynolds's enrollment in the Bryant & Stratton Business
College have been given, but 1873 appears to be correct. *Bryant & Stratton's
Commercial Arithmetic* was written by H. B. Bryant and H. D. Stratton ("found-
ers and proprietors of the 'National Chain of Mercantile Colleges'"), E. E. White
(superintendent of public schools, Portsmouth, Ohio), and J. B. Meriam (cashier
of City Bank, Cleveland, Ohio). When it was reprinted in 1871, Bryant and
Stratton's chain had branches in eight large cities of the United States. Reynolds
stated in 1915 that in 1872 he "felt the need of a more thorough business education and gave up this work [manufacturing tobacco at Rock Spring for Abram D.
Reynolds] to take a course at a business college"—*WSJ*, 25 Apr. 1915. All records of the Bryant & Stratton Business College prior to 1904 were destroyed in
the famous Baltimore fire of 7 Feb. 1904—Mrs. Mary Belle Walker (director
of Strayer College) to author, Baltimore, Md., 25 Sept. 1959; *World Almanac,
1959*, p. 160; John C. Whitaker, interview with author, 27 Oct. 1959. Whitaker
wrote his name and the date, 1917, in the textbook when he received it. Mrs.
Senah Critz Kent and Mrs. Nannie Critz O'Hanlon, nieces of R. J. Reynolds,
declared it to be a well-known fact in their family that R. J. always intended to
prepare an arithmetic textbook—Mrs. Kent and Mrs. O'Hanlon, interview with
author, 4 Feb. 1962.

83. *Baltimore American* in *STJ*, 22 Feb. 1909. Reynolds personally gave this
information to a reporter of the *Baltimore American* in 1909.

84. *OD* 1, no. 2 [Sept. 1916?]; *STJ*, 30 July 1918.

85. *Bristol Herald Courier*, 23 May 1915.

86. *WSJ*, 25 Apr. 1915; photostatic copy of passport no. 45,489, in the office
of Edward J. Hickey, deputy director, Passport Office, Wash., D.C.—courtesy of
Zachary T. Smith.

87. These anecdotes (from Harrison C. Berkeley of 5 Jack Jouett Apartments,
Charlottesville, Va., 24 Sept. 1959) were obtained through the intermediation of
Mrs. Burton Craige of Winston-Salem. Reynolds told the stories to Berkeley in
1912 on the porch of the Marlborough-Blenheim Hotel, Atlantic City, N.J., as

both recovered from illnesses.

88. *OD* 1, no. 6 [Jan. 1917?]. William Neal Reynolds was thirteen years younger and Walter Robert sixteen years younger.

89. Recollections of Abram D. Reynolds, pp. 17, 24; *Bristol Herald Courier*, 29 May 1915; *TCS*, 1 Apr. 1916. Note also *WSJ*, 25 Apr. 1915. Possibly the most direct and certainly the most detailed account of R. J.'s desire to work rather than attend school came from Harrison C. Berkeley (of 5 Jack Jouett Apartments, Charlottesville, Va., 24 Sept. 1959), who personally heard it from Reynolds in 1912.

90. Robert S. Galloway, interview with author, 14 Oct. 1959. Galloway, then aged ninety-three, knew R. J. well and stated that this experience made a vivid impression on the fifteen-year-old youth.

91. W. E. Snyder, interview with author, 30 Oct. 1959.

92. William Watts Ball Diary, MS. vol. IV (17 June 1918–8 June 1919), pp. 94–95—Flowers Collection, Duke University Library, Durham, N.C., courtesy of Dr. Mattie Russell.

93. (New York, 1941), p. 195. Note a far more drastic indictment of the Reynolds family for lack of education and refinement by Vincent Sheean in *New Republic*, 2 Nov. 1932, pp. 320–22. Sheean, with all the dogmatic ignorance of a journalist making his sensational point on hearsay, actually wrote that the Reynolds family was illiterate, that R. J. Reynolds was prejudiced against education, and that he admitted to his organization "nobody who had undergone the disgrace of a term in college."

Chapter 2
Laying the Foundation

1. Fries, p. 170; Tilley, pp. 11–18, 135–36. Reynolds said in 1915 that he came to Winston in part "on account of the town being located in the center of the belt in which the finest tobacco in the world is grown"—*Bristol Herald Courier*, 23 May 1915.

2. Fries, pp. 69, 170; Tilley, pp. 210, 260; *WSJ*, 18 July 1914, 13 Mar. 1921, 28 Sept. 1930; *UR*, 23 Jan., 11 Sept. 1890.

3. Receipted bill of A. C. Young, Winston, N.C., 19 May 1883—RJR museum.

4. *The State*, 31 Oct. 1942, p. 2. Other than the quotation, this account is based on *Danbury Reporter* in *WSJ*, 8 Aug. 1918; *STJ*, 8 Aug. 1929; Bill East in *WSJ*, 9 Sept. 1941; Chester Davis in *J&S*, 5 Feb. 1950; Mrs. J. Spott Taylor (Danbury, N.C.) and Ernest Fulp, interviews with author, 24 Apr. 1960. Mrs. Taylor, then aged ninety-three, stated that Captain Spottswood B. Taylor, of Danbury, advised Reynolds to come to Winston. Mr. Fulp said Lash refused to sell land near the proposed rail line.

5. See above; *Bristol Herald Courier*, 23 May 1915.

6. Forsyth County Deed Book, vol. 8, pp. 47–48, office of Register of Deeds, Forsyth County Courthouse, Winston-Salem, N.C. See Fries, p. 59, for purchase of land by the commissioners.

7. *WS*, 17 Dec. 1885. Note also ibid., 18 Jan. 1877, and Edward Rondthaler

in *TCS*, 18 Oct. 1919. See *UR*, 4 Oct. 1883, for a sketch of Edward F. Belo. William N. Reynolds in 1950 told an improbable story that R. J., miffed because his father took in one of his younger sons (probably Hardin Harbour) as a full partner, decided to leave Rock Spring. At any rate, as Will Reynolds recalled, the father offered R. J. a farm in Stokes County called the Moore place. R. J. liked it and considered building a tobacco factory there until persuaded by Spottswood B. Taylor to go to Winston because of the railroad, tobacco factories, and auction sales houses there. William N. Reynolds, interview with Dell McKeithan and W. S. Koenig, 26 July 1950—personnel dept., RJR. R. J.'s immediate purchase of land contiguous to the railroad makes it doubtful that he ever considered locating on an isolated farm. Furthermore, Will Reynolds, in his recollections, always downgraded R. J. For another evaluation of the Salem Branch Line, see *Asheville Citizen* in *WTJ*, 24 Sept. 1888, p. 10. A detailed account of the building of the Northwestern North Carolina Railroad is in Charles Lewis Price, "Railroads and Reconstruction in North Carolina, 1865–1871" (Ph.D. dissertation, University of North Carolina, 1959), pp. 499–508.

8. Forsyth County Deed Book, vol. 14, pp. 464–65.

9. Fries, pp. 64, 81; Edward Rondthaler, *The Memorabilia of Fifty Years, 1877–1927* (Raleigh, 1928), p. x.

10. *WS*, 1 Mar. 1877; *UR*, 12 Apr. 1877; Fries, p. 70; *TCS*, 31 Mar. 1916.

11. *New York Sun* in *WS*, 26 Apr. 1877. Edward Rondthaler, later to become bishop of the Moravian church, declared that on his arrival in Winston and Salem in 1877 he was struck "most forcibly" by "the big bales of dried blackberries" which were "almost legal tender . . . comprising in many cases the current money owing to the low conditions in finance." He also stated that Joseph H. Stockton and his brother-in-law, Alexander Pfohl, operated a berry shipping and general merchandising business on the site of the Wachovia Bank and Trust Company at that time—*TCS*, 18 Oct. 1919.

12. *WS*, 1 July 1880. Note also ibid., 9 Mar. 1882.

13. Ibid., 16 July 1885; *PP*, 25 Aug. 1887; *UR*, 5 July 1888 (circular of Hinshaw and Medearis), 14 May 1896, 4 July 1907, 21 July 1910.

14. *STJ*, 17 June 1919. One speculator in leaf tobacco, when telling of his first visit to Winston in 1873, declared that he reached the town "in a wagon, a lone passenger" by way of High Point "[s]kinned and scarred by rough riding"— William E. Dibrell in *Southern Tobacconist and Manufacturers' Record*, 19 Apr. 1898.

15. J. D. Cameron, *A Sketch of Tobacco Interests in North Carolina* (Oxford, N.C., 1881), p. 18; *WS*, 5 June 1884. See also *UR*, 23 Jan., 11, 23 Sept. 1890.

16. *N&O*, 5 Apr. 1896; *WS*, 5 June 1884, 17 Dec. 1885.

17. *N&O*, 5 Apr. 1896. Some accounts list the Hanes's arrival in Winston as 1874, but the more reliable ones agree on 1873. Cameron, in *A Sketch of Tobacco Interests in North Carolina* (p. 17), gives 1874; *WS*, 17 Dec. 1885, gives 1873 or 1874.

18. Note esp. *STJ*, 29 Nov. 1909.

19. *Bristol Herald Courier*, 23 May 1915.

20. *WS*, 24 Oct. 1878. The additions of 1877 (given as 1878 in Table 2-1) were undoubtedly those noted by Dr. Henry A. Brown, long pastor of the First

Baptist Church in Winston, who stated that the factory was built of brick halfway up and finished with wood when he first saw it on 14 Dec. 1877—*TCS*, 13 Dec. 1919.

21. *WS*, 8 May 1879.

22. Note also *UR*, 3 Mar. 1881; *WS*, 2 Dec. 1880, 10 Mar. 1881. Apparently Reynolds had his factory completely faced with brick in 1881—*WS*, 8 Dec. 1881.

23. *PP*, 28 Nov. 1878.

24. *UR*, 27 July 1882. See also *WS*, 17 Aug. 1882.

25. *WS*, 28 June 1883 (R. J. R.); *UR*, 30 Nov. 1882 (twenty-three factories).

26. *Winston Leader*, 21 Nov. 1882.

27. Goldston H. Dalton, interview with author, 29 Oct. 1959. Mr. Dalton heard this account from his father Alexander Scales Dalton (12 Feb. 1862–15 Oct. 1931), who began to work for Reynolds in the fall of 1880 and did not retire until Sept. 1922.

28. *PP*, 6 May 1875. See J. C. Robert, *The Tobacco Kingdom: Plantation, Market, and Factory in Virginia and North Carolina, 1800–1860* (Durham, N.C., 1938), p. 217, for the prevalence of summer work in antebellum years. This practice was continued until about 1885—Tilley, p. 489.

29. *UR*, 5 May 1881; *PP*, 17 Oct. 1878.

30. *UR*, 2 Dec. 1886. See the following for evidence regarding the continuing practice of seasonal work: *PP*, 12 Apr., 10 May, 8 Nov. 1877, 17 Oct. 1878, 11 Mar. 1880; *UR*, 4 May 1882, 4 Oct. 1883; *WS*, 22 Feb., 26 Apr., 20 Dec. 1883.

31. *UR*, 3 Feb. 1887. On 26 Sept. 1889, the *UR* carried this item: "A number of firms speaks [*sic*] of continuing operations the year round."

32. John Q. Adams, Jr., interview with Dell McKeithan and Erwin W. Cook, 29 Sept. 1950—personnel dept., RJR. Adoption of the Proctor Redrying Machine permitted changes in the handling of leaf tobacco and consequent year-round work. For its importance see Tilley, pp. 313–15.

33. *PP*, 8 Nov. 1877.

34. *Winston Leader*, 11 Mar. 1879.

35. Ibid., 4 May 1880.

36. MS Census Returns, 1880, Forsyth County, N.C., Schedule 3: Manufacturers (microfilm, N.C. Division of Archives and History, Raleigh).

37. *Winston Leader*, 4 Sept. 1883; *WSJ*, 27 Sept. 1911; *TCS*, 26 Sept. 1911; Mrs. Stella Farrow Paschal, interview with author, 16 Dec. 1959.

38. Roan (*WSJ*, 14 June 1925; *American Biography: A New Cyclopedia*, 42: 245–47; R. J. Reynolds Ledger, 1881–89—secretary's dept., RJR, p. 183; William N. Reynolds, interview with Dell McKeithan, 30 May 1951—personnel dept., RJR); Rich (*WSJ*, 22 Oct. 1924; R. D. W. Connor, W. K. Boyd, J. G. de Roulhac Hamilton, et al., *History of North Carolina*, 6 vols. [Chicago, 1919], 4:42–44).

39. William N. Reynolds, interview with Dell McKeithan, 26 July 1950—personnel dept., RJR.

40. J. R. Dodge in *Tenth Census*, 3:908.

41. *WS*, 6 Mar. 1879 (quotation), 28 Oct. 1880.

42. *PP*, 30 Jan. 1890. *UR*, 15 Apr. (workers from Richmond and Danville), 22 Apr. 1886; *PP*, 4 May 1882; William P. Hairston, interview with author, 29 Nov. 1960. Mr. Hairston declared that in 1889, at the age of eight, he walked from Henry County to Winston.

43. Miss Ruth Poindexter, interview with author, 11 Jan. 1960; Mary C. Wiley in *TCS*, 28 Nov. 1945; *American Biography: A New Cyclopedia*, 42: 183–85. Poindexter came to Winston in 1871 and began operating his own store in 1878.

44. *UR*, 20 Jan. 1887.

45. Ibid., 11 Nov., 23 Dec. 1886, 24 Mar. 1887.

46. *WS*, 4 Apr. (quotation), 11 Apr. 1889. Note *WTJ*, 29 Apr. 1889, p. 8, for an account of a similar strike in Danville, Va.

47. See Robert, *Tobacco Kingdom*, pp. 213–16, and Tilley, pp. 490–93, for general descriptions of the manufacture of chewing tobacco from 1820 to 1885. Note R. J. Reynolds Ledger, 1881–89, esp. pp. 277, 351, 437, 483, for evidence of the use of brandy.

48. *WS*, 7 Sept. 1882, 24 Apr. 1884; R. J. Reynolds Ledger, 1881–89, p. 594; *Federal Reporter*, 1st ser., 21: 433–58.

49. *UR*, 31 May, 7 June 1883; Tilley, p. 367.

50. *PP*, 15 Sept. 1887; *UR*, 15 Sept. 1887; R. J. Reynolds Ledger, 1881–89, passim; Tilley, pp. 440, 524.

51. R. J. Reynolds Ledger, 1881–89, passim, esp. pp. 712, 719.

52. *Winston Leader*, 22 July 1884.

53. *UR*, 3 Apr. 1884; *Winston Leader*, 8 Apr., 8 July 1884.

54. *WS*, 28 Mar. 1882 (skating rink), 17 Dec. 1885 (leaf on hand); *UR*, 3 June 1886; Forsyth County Deed Book, vol. 26, pp. 122–23.

55. *WS*, 30 Mar. 1882; *UR*, 30 Mar. 1882; *PP*, 16, 23 Mar. 1882; *Winston Leader*, 14 Mar. 1882.

56. Based generally on William N. Reynolds, interviews with Dell McKeithan, 26 July 1950, 30 May 1951—personnel dept., RJR. Unclaimed letters for Willie Reynolds, as young Reynolds was known, held in the Winston post office on 30 June and 8 Sept. 1883 (*UR*, 5 July, 13 Sept. 1883) indicate that Will Reynolds spent the summer of 1883 in Winston. In 1885 it was also stated that "As nearly as possible all the leaf used [in his factory] is bought upon this market by Mr. [R. J.] Reynolds personally"—*WS*, 17 Dec. 1885. Note Will Reynolds's account of his career; he worked in every department but in later years had charge of the leaf dept.—*Am. Tob. Co. et al. v. U.S., Record on Appeal*, docket no. 9137–9139 (6th Cir., 1944), transcripts, 6: 4860–61.

57. *Tob.*, 15 July 1892, p. 3. In 1884 the editor of a Winston newspaper noted that P. W. Dalton's departure with a wagonload of manufactured tobacco "looked like a return to the old covered-wagon trade days" (*Winston Leader*, 5 Feb. 1884), thus indicating that peddling had become obsolete.

58. William N. Reynolds, interview with Dell McKeithan, 26 July 1950. See also *Am. Tob. Co. et al. v. U.S., Record on Appeal*, transcripts, 6: 4862. Here Will Reynolds referred to "twist tobacco for the jobbers," which R. J. made principally when he first came to Winston using the "tags and brands" of the jobbers.

59. R. J. Reynolds Ledger, 1881–89, pp. 653, 670.

60. *WS*, 17 Dec. 1885. One firm with which Reynolds dealt as early as 1881 was F. A. Davis and Company of Baltimore, Md. (R. J. Reynolds Ledger, 1881– 89, p. 5); it was still a Reynolds customer in 1964. Founded in 1876, it became F. A. Davis and Son in 1885 when E. Asbury Davis joined the firm—Joseph Kolodny, *4000 Years of Service: The Story of the Wholesale Tobacco Industry and Its Pioneers* (New York, 1953), p. 140. Among Reynolds's other Baltimore customers during 1881–89 were Hornthal & Dieches, W. S. Floyd, S. Rosenfeld & Company, Jacob Adler & Company, H. L. Durrall & Company, and Nachman, Ash & Company. According to testimony given in 1908 by George W. Coan, then secretary and treasurer of the Reynolds company, "the bulk of its business was in Baltimore, Md." as late as 1899, when the company was reorganized under the laws of New Jersey—*U.S. v. Am. Tob. Co. et al., Record: Testimony of Witnesses*, 5 vols., docket no. 660–661 (C.C. of Sou. Dist. of N.Y., 1907), 3: 644.

61. Robbins, *Descriptive Sketch of Winston-Salem*, p. 35.

62. Scrapbook, 1891–99, advertising dept., RJR.

63. State license, 10 Sept. 1886, signed by the treasurer of North Carolina and issued to R. J. Reynolds—file 00, secretary's dept., RJR. Note also *UR*, 16 Sept. 1886.

64. *Baltimore: Its History and Its People* (various contributors), 3 vols. (New York and Chicago, 1912), 2: 170, 171 (quotations). For the remainder of this account see Tilley, p. 687; R. J. Reynolds Ledger, 1881–89, pp. 180, 516, 658; *Baltimore Sun*, 15 Oct. 1908. Reynolds had connections with the Parletts as early as 1881. See also R. J. R. Tob. Co. to the Trade, 5 Jan. 1898, stating that "our tobacco business in Baltimore and Washington territory" prior to 1 Jan. 1898 was a distinct division under the management of John F. Parlett—Scrapbook, 1891–99, advertising dept., RJR.

65. *WS*, 22 Dec. 1887. Of additional interest on this point is a premium award to B. F. Parlett and Company—made in 1878 by the Maryland Institute for the Promotion of the Mechanic Arts—for chewing tobacco, pasted carefully in Reynolds's Scrapbook for 1891–99. No doubt Parlett won this premium on tobacco manufactured by Reynolds.

66. *UR*, 23 June 1887.

67. R. J. Reynolds Ledger, 1881–89, pp. 330, 629, 630(2), 723, 741.

68. *WS*, 22 Oct. 1885.

69. William N. Reynolds, interview with Dell McKeithan, 26 July 1950—personnel dept., RJR.

70. Ibid.; *Connorton's for 1886 and 1887* (entered according to act of Congress, Feb. 1886), p. 46 (Maid of Athens). Schnapps spelled "Snaps" appeared first in *WS*, 17 Dec. 1885.

71. Assignment of trademark "R.J.R." from R. J. Reynolds to the R. J. R. Tob. Co. of New Jersey, 11 Aug. 1916—file 25, secretary's dept., RJR. In 1907 it was R. J. Reynolds's firm belief that he had begun making Schnapps about 1880—*R. J. R. Tob. Co. v. Allen Bros. Tob. Co., Federal Reporter*, 1st ser., 151: 819–34.

72. Entered according to act of Congress, Feb. 1887, pp. 39–163.

73. R. J. Reynolds Ledger, 1881–89, pp. 638, 642, 649, 683, 687; advertise-

ment in *Connorton's for 1887*, between pp. 101 and 102.

74. Forsyth County Credit Ledger of Dun, Barlowe & Co., p. 517 and passim—courtesy of Glenn L. Johnson, Dun & Bradstreet, Inc.

75. Turner's *Winston-Salem Directory*, 1889–90, p. 18.

76. William N. Reynolds, interview with Dell McKeithan, 26 July 1950—personnel dept., RJR. According to *WS* (26 May 1898), Charles A. Fogle (d. Oct. 1892) formed a copartnership with J. G. Sides shortly before 1871 and established a small contracting business. In 1871 Christian H. Fogle (30 Aug. 1846–22 May 1898) bought Sides's interest and shortly thereafter the firm of Fogle Brothers was established. Fogle Brothers is generally supposed to have built Reynolds's first factory.

77. *WSJ*, 25 Apr. 1915; Roy G. Booker in *Manufacturers' Record*, 1 June 1916 (reprinted in *WSJ*, 4 June 1916).

78. R. J. Reynolds Ledger, 1881–89, pp. 24, 535, 759. Apparently, though, close financial connections with Lybrook continued as late as 1 Sept. 1882, when Reynolds wrote the following note to the Wachovia National Bank: "You will please pay any check signed by A. M. Lybrook of Lybrook & Reynolds and charge same to my account"—letter of R. J. Reynolds in possession of Meade Willis, Jr., Wachovia Bank and Trust Company, as of 1964. Note *Tob.*, 30 Mar. 1922, p. 91, for a statement that Lybrook was Reynolds's silent partner during the first year of operation.

79. William N. Reynolds, interview with Dell McKeithan, 26 July 1950—personnel dept., RJR; R. J. Reynolds Ledger, 1881–89, passim; Fries, p. 183.

80. *UR*, 29 June 1882; *WS*, 22 Dec. 1887; R. J. Reynolds Ledger, 1881–89, p. 658; information supplied by Mary Parlett, 88 Main St., Concord, Mass. See also above.

81. Minutes of Meetings of Stockholders, 1890–99, p. 31—secretary's dept., RJR. Parlett at that time was undoubtedly a bona fide stockholder, because Reynolds and his associates had discovered as early as 4 Mar. 1892 that directors must be stockholders—ibid., p. 15.

82. R. J. Reynolds Ledger, 1881–89, pp. 170, 755, 759; Forsyth County Deed Book, vol. 17, pp. 463–66; Tilley, p. 598.

83. *WS*, 17 Dec. 1885.

84. Stuart (Va.) *Press* in *WS*, 24 Nov. 1887. William N. Reynolds (interview with Dell McKeithan, 26 July 1950—personnel dept., RJR) stated that R. J. had resolved to pay for the 1888 addition to his factory, get the $100,000 and retire, and leave the business to him. He also stated that R. J. abandoned the idea of retirement just before building Number 256; this would have been in 1891—in many respects a crucial year for R. J.

85. *UR*, 1, 22 Dec. 1881.

86. Tenement house (*WS*, 10 Aug. 1882); Lafayette Mills (R. J. Reynolds Ledger, 1881–89, p. 727); Merchants' Hotel (*WS*, 27 Jan. 1887); *UR*, 23 Dec. 1886; *PP*, 3 Feb. 1887); Mock's Mill (*WS*, 19 May 1887); Gadsden investment (William J. Conrad, Jr., interview with author, 4 Sept. 1959; *RCCTI*, 1: 104); Barringer Hotel (*WS*, 27 Nov. 1890).

87. Forsyth County deed books, vols. 8 (pp. 47–48), 11 (pp. 478–80), 14 (pp. 68–70, 340, 463–67), 15 (pp. 181–83), 16 (pp. 167–68, 576–78), 17

(pp. 384–85, 463–66), 18 (pp. 420–21, 599–600), 19 (pp. 278, 405–6, 416, 535–36), 21 (pp. 261–62), 22 (pp. 557–58), 26 (pp. 114–17, 120–23, 182–83, 583–85), 28 (pp. 329–31, 558–59), 29 (pp. 17–18, 199, 404–5).

88. Forsyth County Deed Book, vol. 14, pp. 539–52. Whitaker served as first president of the first streetcar system of Winston, in 1887.

89. *WS*, 22 Dec. 1887.

90. City commissioner (*Winston Leader*, 13 May 1884); sanitary and fire committees (*UR*, 15 May 1884, *Winston Leader*, 13 May 1884, *WS*, 15 May 1884); road supervisor (*PP*, 5 Aug. 1886, *WS*, 10 July 1890); 1890 election (*UR*, 20 Feb. 1890); Cleveland and Fowle (*PP*, *UR*, *WS*, all 21 June 1888).

91. Marian Revelle in *TCS*, 3 Aug. 1912.

92. *WS*, 15 Apr. 1880; A. D. Mayo in *New England Journal of Education*, reprinted in *UR*, 5 Mar. 1885.

93. *UR*, 8 Mar., 24 May 1888, 25 July, 29 Aug. 1889; *WS*, 8 Mar. 1888. Eventually the Forsyth Five-Cent Savings Bank was transferred to the Wachovia Loan and Trust Company. Note *PP*, 23 Apr. 1885, for Immigration Society.

94. *UR*, 20 Mar. 1884 (St. Patrick); *Winston Leader*, 15 July (Mother Goose Dance), 26 Feb. (Polly Pepper) 1884.

95. *UR*, 11 Dec. 1879; *Winston Leader*, 27 Feb. 1883; *PP*, 26 Feb. 1885.

96. See, for example, *WS*, 14 June 1888, 9 May 1889; *UR*, 31 May 1888. For the quotation, note Hardin Harbour Reynolds to "Dear Ma," 4 June 1880—Papers of Hardin William Reynolds, in possession of Nancy S. Reynolds, Greenwich, Conn.

97. Robert S. Galloway, interview with author, 14 Oct. 1959.

98. Gray N. Leinbach and Pleas H. Grubbs, interview with author, 12 Apr. 1961. Mr. Grubbs listed O. B. Grubbs, Wade H. Yarborough, Francis Pratt, and Thomas Thacker whose taxes were so paid by Reynolds. Note also R. J. Reynolds Ledger, 1894–98, p. 224, for additional evidence regarding the farms of Wade H. Bynum and W. H. Matthews.

99. *Plant and Plug*, June 1881 (a waggish monthly paper published in Winston during the 1880s by R. D. Moseley). See also *WS*, 30 Mar. 1882.

100. *UR*, 13 Jan. 1887.

101. R. J. Reynolds Ledger, 1884–94, p. 521. Note a description of his horses including Young Matador in *WS*, 24 May 1894.

102. John C. Reich, interview with Dell McKeithan and Erwin W. Cook, 31 Aug. 1950—personnel dept., RJR.

Chapter 3
Growth and Transition

1. *Lynchburg Daily Virginian*, 10, 21 Apr. 1857; *Journal of N.C. Senate*, 1854–55, p. 220; *Journal of N.C. House of Commons*, 1854–55, pp. 374, 379, 383–86.

2. Albert W. Atwood, "John Pierpont Morgan," *Dictionary of American Biography*, 13: 176.

3. Marian Revelle in *J&S*, 8 Dec. 1929. For the charter of the Northwestern North Carolina Railroad Company to build a line via Salem from Greensboro to

Lexington, N.C., see *Constitution of the State of North Carolina, together with the Ordinances and Resolutions of the Constitutional Convention Assembled in the City of Raleigh, Jan. 14th, 1868* (Raleigh, 1868), pp. 57–61. Before the line was completed, the citizens of Winston protested the statement that it was to be built to Salem; rather, they maintained, it was to be built to the "Winston Depot," as indeed it was—*Greensboro Patriot,* 23 July 1873.

4. *UR,* 21 Aug. 1890; Forsyth County Deed Book, vol. 6, pp. 347–57—Office of Register of Deeds, Forsyth County Courthouse, Winston-Salem, N.C.; *Greensboro Patriot,* 28 Mar. 1872, 23 July 1873. The mortgage was satisfied in 1888 by another mortgage covering the railroad from Salem Junction to Wilkesboro. By court compromise Forsyth County eventually received stock certificates for $75,000 in lieu of the $100,000 contributed to the building of the road. For a general sketch of the Richmond and Danville, see John F. Stover, *The Railroads of the South, 1865–1900: A Study in Financial Control* (Chapel Hill, 1955), pp. 233–53.

5. William A. Whitaker to John T. Moore, Augusta, Ga., 12 Apr. 1873—courtesy of John C. Whitaker. See Stover, *Railroads of the South,* p. 111, for the lease of the North Carolina Railroad for thirty years by the Richmond and Danville on 11 Sept. 1871.

6. *Roanoke News* in *WS,* 18 Mar. 1886. For the statement of a Winston correspondent that his town "labors under the disadvantage of the want of more railroad facilities," see *N&O,* 29 Mar. 1887; for Winston's bitter experience at the hands of the Richmond and Danville, see *UR,* 11 July 1889.

7. *UR,* 11 July 1889; *WS,* 11 July 1889. See also *PP,* 17, 24 Feb., 7 July, 3 Nov. 1887, 18 Oct. 1888; *WS,* 29 Aug. 1889; *UR,* 28 Nov. 1889. The Richmond and Danville obtained the Virginia Midland from Alexandria to Lynchburg and Danville by 1883 and thus stood ready to extend its main line to Charlotte by way of Greensboro—Stover, *Railroads of the South,* p. 236.

8. William P. Hairston, interview with author, 7 May 1961; *Encyclopedia of Virginia Biography,* 5 vols., ed. Lyon G. Tyler (New York, 1915), 4: 228–29. See *WSJ,* 20 June 1916, for a concise summary of railroads entering Winston-Salem.

9. *Roanoke News,* in *WS,* 18 Mar. 1886.

10. *UR,* 15 Apr. 1886; *WS,* 15 Apr., 3 June 1886; *PP,* 6 May 1886.

11. *PP,* 3 Feb., 23 June 1887; *UR,* 23 June 1887. For incorporation of the Roanoke and Southern, see *Laws and Resolutions of the State of North Carolina passed by the General Assembly at its Session of 1887,* pp. 157–66; *Acts and Joint Resolutions passed by the General Assembly of the State of Virginia, 1887–1888,* pp. 265–67.

12. *PP,* 7 July 1887.

13. *Roanoke Times* in *PP,* 3 Nov. 1887, 5, 26 Jan., 3 May 1888; *UR,* 5 Jan., 23 Feb., 26 Apr. 1888. For Articles of Consolidation of the Virginia and North Carolina sectors of the Roanoke and Southern, see Forsyth County Deed Book, vol. 42, pp. 486–96. Note also *Acts and Joint Resolutions . . . of the State of Virginia,* pp. 265–67.

14. *WS,* 29 Mar. 1888.

15. *UR,* 14 June 1888. Whether or not from the force of Reynolds's argument, Sauratown township carried its bond election for $10,000—ibid., 21 June

1888. R. J. generally kept well informed on current affairs. See, for example, R. J. Reynolds Journal—Day Book, 1894–98, p. 307, for his subscription to the *Atlanta Journal* for 1897—in possession of Charles H. Babcock as of 1963.

16. *UR*, 28 Mar., 4 Apr. 1889, 3 Sept. 1891.

17. Ibid., 11 Apr. 1889.

18. *WS*, 16 May 1889.

19. Ibid., 3 Mar. 1892. Joseph T. Lambie, in *From Mine to Market: The History of Coal Transportation on the Norfolk and Western Railway* (New York, 1954), pp. 150–53, notes losses on operation of the Roanoke and Southern line in the 1890s but great prosperity for the Norfolk and Western as a system.

20. Edward Rondthaler, *The Memorabilia of Fifty Years, 1877–1927* (Raleigh, 1928), p. 103.

21. Stover, *Railroads of the South*, pp. xvii, 234–36; Hugh T. Lefler, *History of North Carolina*, 2 vols. (New York, 1956), 2: 627.

22. *N&O*, 6 Feb. 1897.

23. Ibid., 7 Feb. 1897; Minutes of Winston and Salem Chamber of Commerce, 1889–1922, office of Winston-Salem Chamber of Commerce.

24. Josephus Daniels, *Editor in Politics* (Chapel Hill, 1941), p. 214.

25. *N&O*, 13 Feb. 1897.

26. Ibid., 18 Feb. 1897—published again on 19, 20, 21 Feb. 1897. For Daniels's account of this episode see *Editor in Politics*, pp. 210–18.

27. R. D. W. Connor, W. K. Boyd, J. G. de Roulhac Hamilton, et al., *History of North Carolina*, 6 vols. (Chicago, 1919), 5: 3.

28. D. P. Robbins, *Descriptive Sketch of Winston-Salem, Its Advantages and Surroundings, Kernersville, Etc.* (Winston, N.C., 1888), pp. 34–41; *UR*, 17 Apr. 1890, *Connorton's for 1894*, p. 552; *North Carolina and Its Resources* (publication of N.C. Department of Agriculture [Raleigh, 1896]), passim.

29. *STJ* in *UR*, 12 Jan. 1893; Tilley, p. 589.

30. Comptroller's dept., RJR.

31. Fries, pp. 95–96.

32. *UR*, 1, 22 Jan. 1891; *PP*, 22 Jan. 1891. The *STJ* long appeared from Winston-Salem, though not in the excellent form of its early years.

33. *WS*, 20 Mar. 1890.

34. *UR*, 24 Apr., 28 Aug., 29 May 1890, 5 May 1892, 10 May 1894. The hotel involved was the first Zinzendorf, designed as a summer resort; it burned in 1892 and was not rebuilt—ibid., 11 May 1893; Fries, p. 92.

35. *PP*, 2 Apr. 1891.

36. In *UR*, 6 Oct. 1892.

37. Partnership agreement, 2 Jan. 1888—filed with balance sheets, secretary's dept., RJR. Reynolds's "own tobacco" evidently concerned his activities as a leaf dealer for the firm of A. A. Smith and Company, which was dissolved in 1889 because of Reynolds's increasing duties in manufacturing—*WTJ*, 14 Jan. 1889, p. 1.

38. William N. Reynolds, interview with Dell McKeithan and W. S. Koenig, 30 May 1950—personnel dept., RJR.

39. Minutes of Meetings of Stockholders, 1890–99, pp. 230–36—secretary's dept., RJR.

40. Ibid., pp. 2–7.

41. Minutes of Board of Directors, 1890–99, pp. 2–3—secretary's dept., RJR.

42. *UR*, 3 Jan. 1889.

43. Ibid., 25 Apr. 1889.

44. Ibid., 9 May 1899 (B. F. Hanes), 15 May 1890; *PP*, 15 May 1890; *Tob.*, 29 Nov. 1889 (p. 5), 16 May 1890 (p. 5).

45. *UR*, 30 Oct. 1890.

46. *PP*, 25 June 1891; *Tob.*, 24 July 1891, p. 5; advertising leaflet of Lucile Tobacco Works—courtesy of John C. Whitaker (son of William A. Whitaker).

47. *Tob.*, 8 July 1892, p. 4.

48. *WS*, 22 Aug. 1889; *UR*, 10 Oct. 1889.

49. William N. Reynolds, interview with Dell McKeithan, 26 July 1950—personnel dept., RJR.

50. *UR*, 5 Mar. 1891; Minutes of Board of Directors, 1890–99, pp. 4–5; *WSJ*, 25 Apr. 1915.

51. *WS*, 9 Apr. 1891, 14 Apr. 1892; *UR*, 16 Apr. 1891; *PP*, 2 Apr. 1891; *Tob.*, 18 Mar. 1892, p. 5.

52. Survey of R. J. Reynolds Chestnut Street Factory, 7 Mar. 1900—RJR museum, *WTJ*, 12 Dec. 1892, p. 2; *WS*, 28 Apr. 1892.

53. Survey of R. J. Reynolds Chestnut Street Factory, 7 Mar. 1900.

54. *WS*, 25 July 1895; *UR*, 25 July 1895.

55. *UR*, 4 Mar. 1897.

56. R. J. R. Tob. Co. to The Mutual Fire Insurance Companies, 30 Mar. 1897—Scrapbook, 1891–99, advertising dept., RJR. See also *Tob.*, 9 Apr. 1897, p. 8.

57. *UR*, 26 Jan. 1899.

58. *UR*, 25 May 1893; *Gold Leaf*, 25 May 1893.

59. Scrapbook, 1891–99; R. J. R. Tob. Co. to "Dear Sirs," 3 June 1892—papers from the desk of Robert E. Lasater, file 2653, secretary's dept., RJR.

60. A search and requests at the Roanoke Public Library, the Virginia State Library, and headquarters of the Norfolk and Western Railway revealed no knowledge of the *Iron Belt*.

61. From handbill in Scrapbook, 1891–99. The handbill, 6 by 9 inches, carries Reynolds's version on one side and the editorial on the other. At the bottom of Reynolds's version there appears in his handwriting: "Above 1st ad written by R. J. Reynolds." This is also reprinted in *OD*, no. 1 [August (?), 1916] as an extract from the "March Edition of the Iron Belt, Roanoke, Va."

62. *WSJ*, 25 Apr. 1915. Actually Reynolds's statement was virtually correct because in 1894 his business increased by 209,227 pounds and in 1895 it increased from 1,215,328 to 2,126,767 pounds.

63. This was no idle bet, as Reynolds and his brother Will certainly disliked the free silver policy of William Jennings Bryan—Daniels, *Editor in Politics*, p. 248; William N. Reynolds to editor of *WSJ*, 14 Oct. 1950—Santford Martin MSS, Duke University, Durham, N.C. On a petition of businessmen of Winston and Salem to Congress requesting repeal of the silver purchasing clause of the Sherman act and the appointment of "an expert commission to consider and rec-

ommend a scientific plan of currency," R. J. Reynolds's name appeared as first signer—*WS*, 3 Aug. 1893.

64. *UR*, 24 Dec. 1891; *WTJ*, 26 Dec. 1892, p. 18.

65. *STJ*, 11 Nov. 1893.

66. *WS*, 24 Oct., 11 Nov. 1895. See also *UR*, 8 Aug., 5 Sept. 1895; *WTJ*, 21 Oct. 1895 (p. 2), 2 Dec. 1895 (p. 3).

67. See *STJ*, 15 Apr. 1893 to June 1894, passim. See ibid., 17 Feb. 1894, for Reynolds's empty space.

68. *Tob.*, 3 Aug. 1894, p. 8; *UR*, 6 Sept. 1894.

69. *Tob.*, 7 Feb. 1896, p. 5. Mahood had displayed a Reynolds advertisement at a similar tragedy in Feb. 1893 at Richlands, [S.C.?].

70. *WSJ*, 25 Apr. 1915.

71. *UR*, 14 Apr., 12 May 1892; *WSJ*, 22 Jan. 1931. In 1904 Stedman, described as sales manager of the R. J. Reynolds Tobacco Company, became sales manager for Liipfert-Scales and Company. This occurred after Reynolds purchased Liipfert and Scales.

72. *TCS*, 8 July 1935; Salesmen's Record Book, vol. I—sales dept., RJR; *National Cyclopaedia of American Biography*, 39: 485; R. J. R. Tob. Co. to L. M. McKenzie, 30 June 1893—courtesy of James L. McKenzie; *WSJ*, 27 July 1915. It appears that the Salesmen's Record Book was begun well after 1900, although it contains a few earlier dates evidently supplied by salesmen still with the company when the record was started. The mortality rate among these salesmen appears to have been rather high. Bowman Gray, Sr., came home from the University of North Carolina at the age of seventeen to serve as teller in the Wachovia National Bank and remained in that position until joining Reynolds—*PP*, 10 Sept. 1891; clipping in scrapbook of Bowman Gray, Jr., from *WS*, [Sept.?] 1895.

73. *UR*, 21 Oct. 1897.

74. Scrapbook, 1891–99.

75. See *Connorton's for 1894*, pp. 24–290, for similar brands listed by the Reynolds and Parlett firms. The remainder of this discussion is drawn from Scrapbook, 1891–99. According to one reference John T. Parlett resigned as Reynolds's agent effective 31 Dec. 1897, and was succeeded by Bowman Gray— R. J. R. Tob. Co. to the Trade, 5 Jan. 1898, Scrapbook, 1891–99. See Appendix D for a list of private brands being manufactured as late as 1925.

76. A drop shipment is a competitive device involving delivery to the retailer of a quantity of free goods in return for a substantial order. When an order for a drop shipment is taken by a manufacturer's salesman, the retailer chooses the jobber through whom he wishes the order to go—*R. J. R. Tob. Co. et al. v. U.S., Brief for Appellants*, docket no. 9139 (6th Cir., 1944), pp. 212–13. Apparently the first use of the term "drop shipment" by the company did not occur until 1 Mar. 1889. Drop shipments other than for cigarettes were still used by Reynolds in 1964.

77. Except for citations already shown, this account is based on materials in Scrapbook, 1891–99.

78. Ibid. The law was induced by action of the American Tobacco Company in regard to "EE-M" medicated cigarettes manufactured in Georgia by Arnold and McCord. American notified wholesale dealers in Georgia that by handling EE-M

cigarettes they were violating their contract with American and that they could no longer be allowed its best discounts. Wholesale dealers discontinued the handling of EE-M cigarettes because American's goods meant more profit. Arnold and McCord secured copies of correspondence bearing on these points and thus aided in persuading the Georgia legislature to pass an act nullifying all contracts of firms outside the state doing business in Georgia under methods designed to prevent free and full competition by controlling prices. Many tobacco firms were affected. *N&O*, 17 Jan. 1897; *Acts and Resolutions of the General Assembly of the State of Georgia, 1896*, no. 122, pp. 68–70. This law was considered comprehensive and quite drastic—*St. Louis Globe-Democrat*, 2 Jan. 1897.

79. In the case of chewing tobacco, the company on 15 June 1898 hoped to have its new weights ready by 25 June—Scrapbook, 1891–99.

80. *Am. Tob. Co. et al. v. U.S., Record on Appeal*, docket no. 9137–9139 (6th Cir., 1944), transcripts, 6: 4862.

81. Loose sheet, dated 19 Feb. 1891, in handwriting of R. J. Reynolds, listing his personal property—R. J. Reynolds Ledger, 1888–94, secretary's dept., RJR.

82. See p. 409 for 4A Naturally Sweet Cut Plug, a smoking tobacco, and p. 106 for 4A Naturally Sweet, a chewing tobacco.

83. Smoking Tobacco Price List, Number 1—Scrapbook, 1891–99. About this time Duke's Mixture sold at forty cents per pound—*St. Louis Post-Dispatch*, 9 Jan. 1895.

84. *Connorton's for 1895*, pp. 367–514.

85. Scrapbook, 1891–99; *Connorton's for 1899*, pp. 372, 470.

86. Tilley, pp. 580–81. Note esp. p. 508, n. 65. For advertisement of the Adams press, see *Connorton's for 1894*, p. 4.

87. Tilley, p. 580; circular (28 Feb. 1896) and order blank (Sept. 1897), Scrapbook, 1891–99; contract: Adams Tobacco Press Co. and R. J. R. Tob. Co., 27 Mar. 1896—file 64½, secretary's dept., RJR. When the Reynolds company was incorporated under the laws of New Jersey, this contract was canceled and Reynolds received four Adams machines. As a part of this shift, the Adams Tobacco Press Company agreed to sell the R. J. Reynolds Tobacco Company of New Jersey twenty duplex presses at $275 each—contract: R. J. R. Tob. Co. of N.J. and Adams Tobacco Press Co., 20 June 1899, file 49, secretary's dept., RJR. Liggett and Myers and the Drummond Tobacco Company were first to use the Adams press.

88. *UR*, 20 Oct. 1898; Tilley, pp. 313–15.

89. Contract: R. J. R. Tob. Co. with Cleveland Electric Manufacturing Co., 12 Dec. 1891—file 00, secretary's dept., RJR.

90. *WS*, 22 Mar. 1894.

91. *Manufacturers' Report* in *WSJ*, 4 June 1916.

92. The only Winston manufacturer to use Burley in the early years apparently was Brown Brothers and Company—*UR*, 29 June 1882. For the discovery of saccharin see Tilley, pp. 588–89, 619. For early advertising of saccharin in connection with tobacco see *Connorton's for 1894*, p. 572. This advertisement was by E. L. Prussing & Co. (Ltd.) of Chicago.

93. *WTJ*, 5 Feb. 1900, p. 3.

94. Ibid., 19 Dec. 1898, p. 4. This issue (p. 9) lists J. T. Farrish, of Winston

and H. N. Frankel, of St. Louis and Louisville, as agents for Merck & Co., owners of saccharin in the United States and Canada.

95. *Charlotte Daily Observer*, 23 Oct. 1898 (special edition on the Winston Tobacco Fair—courtesy of Miss Mary C. Wiley). According to the recollections of Joseph M. Parrish (interview with Dell L. McKeithan and Erwin W. Cook, 4 Aug. 1950—personnel dept., RJR), Reynolds began factory Number 256 in 1891; before then the number of workers was small, operations by hand, and equipment simple, consisting chiefly of a little steam boiler and some forty to fifty casing kettles. Lump making was farmed out to a contractor who worked in a corner of the factory and R. J. himself frequently helped to knock out shapes.

96. *OD* 1, no. 1 [August, 1916?].

97. Reynolds's own brand book stamped "February 26, 1909," is marked on the outside in bold black letters, "R. J. Reynolds. Private." Moreover, virtually every brand of chewing tobacco contained saccharin. Reynolds's brand book in possession of John C. Whitaker as of 1964. At that time saccharin was unknown to the average person who had not yet learned to use it in his coffee.

98. *Tob.*, 10 Nov. 1893, p. 8. In 1893 Reynolds also advertised other brands as being made of naturally sweet flue-cured leaf—*WTJ*, 12 June 1893, p. 8.

99. Apparently Naturally Sweet was first registered in 1893—*Connorton's for 1894*, p. 178. This directory was entered according to act of Congress in Jan. 1894; hence, he must have registered his new brand in 1893.

100. Scrapbook, 1891–99.

101. Confirming letter of C. C. Speiden of A. Klipstein & Co. to R. J. Reynolds, New York, 16 Jan. 1899—file 37, secretary's dept., RJR. The composition of Heyden Sugar is given in a letter of E. T. Jester to Walter R. Reynolds, New York, 23 Dec. 1903—Correspondence of Walter R. Reynolds, purchasing dept., RJR. The cost of saccharin on 11 Oct. 1960 was $1.40 per pound—E. M. Harwood, interview with author. The rush of tobacco manufacturers to use saccharin had evidently reached its crest by 1900 when Reynolds's contract called for 1,000 pounds at $2.75 per pound—contract: A. Klipstein & Co. with R. J. R. Tob. Co., New York, 21 June 1900, file 96, secretary's dept., RJR.

102. *WSJ*, 17 Mar. 1920; *TCS*, 17 Mar. 1920; *WS*, 30 Nov. 1893; Mrs. J. S. Dunn, interview with author, 8 Dec. 1959.

103. Minutes of Meetings of Stockholders, 1890–99, pp. 8–9.

104. Minutes of Board of Directors, 1890–99, pp. 4–7.

105. Minutes of Meetings of Stockholders, 1890–99, p. 10.

106. Ibid., p. 11; *WS*, 11 June 1891.

107. Minutes of Meetings of Stockholders, 1890–99, pp. 15–16.

108. These three letters were placed in R. J. Reynolds Ledger, 1888–94.

109. Minutes of Meetings of Stockholders, 1890–99, p. 18.

110. R. J. Reynolds Ledger, 1888–94, pp. 112, 328.

111. *WSJ*, 16 Mar. 1913, 19 Feb. 1937; *N&O*, 5 Apr. 1896. W. Ernest Dalton was also a member of the firm of Dalton, Farrow and Company, organized in 1892. By 1898 the firm consisted of three Daltons, R. I., R. E., and W. E., with Farrow—*UR*, 6 Jan. 1898.

112. *N&O*, 5 Apr. 1896.

113. Minutes of Board of Directors, 1890–99, p. 9.

114. Minutes of Meetings of Stockholders, 1890–99, pp. 20–22.

115. *Complete Tobacco Directory*, (Philadelphia, preface dated 1 Mar. 1889), p. 349.

116. *Connorton's for 1890*, p. 431; *for 1891*, p. 449; *for 1892*, p. 479; *for 1893*, p. 530. This firm appeared in addition to the firm of Abram D. Reynolds in Bristol. Doubtless Critz and Reynolds turned their brands over to the R. J. Reynolds Tobacco Company. Note also *Tob.*, 10 Mar. 1921, p. 3.

117. *UR*, 3 Aug. 1893.

118. These balance sheets reveal a much less cheerful account than Reynolds's letter of 15 Dec. 1897, which summarized conditions from 1892 through 1897 in terms of production—*Eleventh Annual Report of the Bureau of Labor Statistics of North Carolina, 1897*, p. 226.

Chapter 4
Affiliations, Acquisitions, and Consolidations

1. *RCCTI*, 1: 3. Duke claimed that he accepted the presidency because of a controversy between Frank H. Ray, Harry Drummond, and Pierre Lorillard, each of whom wanted the position—*U.S. v. Am. Tob. Co. et al., Record: Testimony of Witnesses*, 5 vols., docket no. 660–661 (C.C. of Sou. Dist. of N.Y., 1907), 4: 357–58.

2. Forsyth County Deed Book, vol. 55, pp. 567–68, Office of Register of Deeds, Forsyth County Courthouse, Winston-Salem, N.C.; *Charlotte Daily Observer*, 23 Oct. 1898.

3. Tilley, pp. 267–78, 415–27.

4. *RCCTI*, 1: 71–72, 94–97; *U.S. v. Am. Tob. Co. et al., Record: Testimony of Witnesses*, 3: 403; John W. Jenkins, *James B. Duke: Master Builder* (New York, 1927), p. 94.

5. Josephus Daniels, *Tar Heel Editor* (Chapel Hill, 1939), p. 473.

6. *RCCTI*, 1: 99, 469.

7. Ibid., 1: 99–103; Jenkins, *James B. Duke*, pp. 107–8.

8. *RCCTI*, 1: 3, 103, 222. James B. Duke declared in 1908: ". . . I think that is one of the mistakes the American Tobacco Co. made in the beginning that we didn't keep a separate organization for all of the principal businesses we bought. . . . Because we would have got better service and better management; we would have had competition and would have built and extended the business"—*U.S. v. Am. Tob. Co. et al., Record: Testimony of Witnesses*, 4: 394.

9. *U.S. v. Am. Tob. Co. et al., Record: Testimony of Witnesses*, 4: 385.

10. Robert S. Galloway (14 Oct. 1959) and J. S. Kuykendall (16 Sept. 1959), interviews with author.

11. William N. Reynolds, interview with Dell McKeithan and W. S. Koenig, 30 May 1951; L. D. Long, interview with author, 2 Nov. 1959. Long served for many years as secretary to Will Reynolds.

12. See *RCCTI*, 1: 117 , for Cobb's position. Cobb may have been the intermediary, because about two years later Reynolds sent him "a fine pair of his own

bred horses" (Tilley, p. 642n), a favor apparently not shown for any other officer of the American Tobacco Company.

13. *R. J. R. Tob. Co. et al. v. U.S., Brief for Appellants*, docket no. 9139 (6th Cir., 1944), p. 69 (R. J. R.). Note also the testimony of William Reynolds in *Am. Tob. Co. et al. v. U.S., Record on Appeal*, docket no. 9137–9139 (6th Cir., 1944), transcripts, 6: 4865–66.

14. Josephus Daniels, *Editor in Politics* (Chapel Hill, 1941), pp. 598–99.

15. Tilley, pp. 262–69; *WS*, 27 June 1889.

16. *WS*, 16 Jan. 1890, 27 Oct. 1892.

17. *STJ* in *UR*, 9 Feb. 1899.

18. *UR*, 9 Mar. 1899.

19. Ibid., 23 Mar. 1899.

20. Minutes, vol. I, pp. 29–31. The Certificate of Organization of the R. J. Reynolds Tobacco Company under New Jersey laws was signed 3 Apr. and filed 4 Apr. 1899.

21. *UR*, 6 Apr. 1899. Note a similar report in *Tob.*, 7 Apr. 1899, p. 5.

22. Minutes of Meetings of Stockholders, 1890–99, pp. 37–47—secretary's dept., RJR.

23. Minutes, vol. I, pp. 29–32; *RCCTI*, 1: 274; General Conveyance of R. J. R. Tob. Co. of North Carolina to the R. J. R. Tob. Co. of New Jersey, 11 Apr. 1899—file 1, secretary's dept., RJR; Certificate of Organization and By-Laws, 3 Apr. 1899, passim—secretary's dept. R. J. Reynolds held 13,446 shares; William N. Reynolds, 2,048; Walter R. Reynolds, 573; Lucy Reynolds Critz, 562; John F. Parlett, 573; and Robert Critz, 11.

24. Minutes, vol. I, pp. 15–35.

25. Minutes of Board of Directors, 1890–99, p. 25, secretary's dept., RJR; Minutes, vol. I, pp. 37–38.

26. R. J. R. Tob. Co. to "Our Salesmen," 11 Apr. 1899—secretary's dept., RJR.

27. Quoted in *UR*, 13 Apr. 1899.

28. Forsyth County Deed Book, vols. 57 (pp. 404–6), 58 (pp. 236–38); *UR*, 20 Apr., 18, 25 May, 6 July 1899; contract with C. R. Makepeach & Co. of Providence, R.I., 9 May 1899—file 41, secretary's dept., RJR; Minutes, vol. I, pp. 41–42, 44; William P. Hairston, interview with author, 29 Nov. 1960; Ed Blakely (2 June 1950) and Henry E. Enochs (29 July 1950), interviews with Dell McKeithan and Erwin W. Cook—personnel dept., RJR.

29. The extent of office space in Number 256 is shown on a plat of R. J. Reynolds Tobacco Company, Chestnut Street Factory, 7 Mar. 1900—RJR museum. The clearest description of offices in Number 8 came from John Needham (31 Oct. 1951), Frank George (25 Oct. 1951), and Ed Blakely (2 June 1950), interviews with Dell McKeithan and Erwin W. Cook—personnel dept., RJR. For other aspects of the building see *Tob.*, 9 June 1899, p. 5; Edward Rondthaler, *The Memorabilia of Fifty Years, 1877–1927* (Raleigh, 1928), p. 174. At this time new leaf storage houses arose in Winston and Danville, Va.—Minutes, vol. I, pp. 69, 70, 73.

30. In order as described above, contracts with Davenport, Morris and Co.,

Richmond, Va. (file 33), Watt Martin, Agent for Scioto Sign Col, 27 Apr. 1899 (file 40), Adams Tobacco Press Co., 20 June 1899 (file 49), Talbott and Sons, 14 Nov. 1899 (file 72), Mayo-Hysore and Co., 14 Aug. 1899 and 9 Mar. 1900 (file 66), Kester Manufacturing Co., 1 July 1899 (file 50), and Philadelphia Textile Machinery Co., 10 Jan. 1900 (file 76); order from Husker, Marcuse Manufacturing Co., 12 Jan. 1900 (file 77); letter from Electrical Engineering Co., Charlotte, N.C., 12 July 1900 (file 103)—all in secretary's dept., RJR. These actions generally received approval of the resident directors—Minutes, vol. I, pp. 40–43. Two other directors, George W. Watts and Benjamin N. Duke, were present, however, when approval was given for Reynolds to take up the option on the lot for Number 8—ibid., p. 44.

31. *Tob.*, 9 Nov. 1900, p. 1. Apparently production in Number 8 began in July 1901—ibid., 26 July 1901, p. 5.

32. *UR*, 17 Sept. 1903.

33. *RCCTI*, 2: 56.

34. Ibid., 1: 104.

35. Ibid., 2: 191.

36. William N. Reynolds, interview with Dell McKeithan and W. S. Koenig, 30 May 1951.

37. *RCCTI*, 1: 106, 370, 372.

38. T. L. Vaughn & Co. to R. J. Reynolds, 20 Apr. 1900—file 88, secretary's dept., RJR; *UR*, 3 May 1900; *WTJ*, 7 May 1900, p. 4. Vaughn lived until 5 Feb. 1932—*TCS*, 6 Feb. 1932.

39. Based on letter of Williamson W. Fuller of Continental Tob. Co. to R. J. R. Tob. Co., New York, N.Y., 26 Apr. 1900, contract of sale and supplement between T. L. Vaughn and Co. and R. J. R. Tob. Co., 30 Apr. 1900, and inventory of T. L. Vaughn and Co., 9–11 May 1900—file 88, secretary's dept., RJR; *RCCTI*, 1: 189 (on p. 106 the sales figure is given, erroneously the author believes, as $190,506). In Minutes, vol. I, p. 73, the sale is merely approved—on 5 July 1900—without comment. See *WSJ*, 1 Sept. 1937, for a sketch of William V. Garner's career. Reynolds also obtained the services of Luther Swaim, who in 1950 recalled that he had been "bought" along with Vaughn's machinery and brands and that he had helped move machinery from the Vaughn factory to Number 8, where he became a general handyman before becoming a foreman— Luther Swaim, interview with Dell McKeithan and Erwin W. Cook, 13 Oct. 1950, personnel dept., RJR.

40. Inventory of T. L. Vaughn and Co., 9–11 May 1900—file 88, secretary's dept., RJR. Appendix C shows a listing of one hundred brands claimed by Vaughn in 1899.

41. William J. Conrad, Jr., interview with author, 25 July 1961.

42. *N&O*, 5 Apr. 1896; *UR*, 12 Oct. 1893, 3, 10 Dec. 1896, 23 Mar. 1899, 29 Nov. 1900; contract: Brown Brothers and Co., 13 Feb. 1894—file 152, secretary's dept., RJR; *RCCTI*, 1: 372 (production in 1900).

43. *Tob.*, 14 Dec. 1900, p. 5. For comments of the local editor see *UR*, 29 Nov. 1900.

44. Minutes, vol. I, pp. 75–78, 86. The same purchase price is listed in *RCCTI*, 1: 189.

45. *UR*, 29 Nov. 1900. See Appendix C for a list of chewing tobacco brands made by Brown Brothers and Company in 1899.

46. P. H. Hanes and Co. to R. J. Reynolds, 22 Nov. 1900—file 167, secretary's dept., RJR; Minutes, vol. I, pp. 75–81.

47. R. D. W. Connor et al., *North Carolina: Rebuilding an Ancient Commonwealth, 1584–1925*, 4 vols. (New York and Chicago, 1929), 3: 467–68; contract and bill of sale: B. F. Hanes and Co. to R. J. R. Tob. Co., 22 Dec. 1900—file 167, secretary's dept., RJR.

48. *Tob.*, 14 Dec. 1900, p. 5. See also *UR*, 29 Aug. 1895, and *WTJ*, 10 Dec. 1900, p. 3.

49. Pleasant H. Hanes to Benjamin N. Duke, 20 June 1899—Benjamin N. Duke MSS, Duke University, Durham, N.C. Hanes asked Duke's advice concerning the purchase of stock in Continental.

50. Proposal of sale: P. H. Hanes and Co. to R. J. Reynolds, 22 Nov. 1900; inventory of P. H. Hanes and Co., 18–26 Dec. 1900, and of B. F. Hanes and Co., 27–29 Dec. 1900; contract and bill of sale: P. H. Hanes and Co. to R. J. R. Tob. Co., 22 Dec. 1900—all in file 167, secretary's dept., RJR; Minutes, vol. I, pp. 80–81, 88–89. According to *RCCTI*, 1: 189, the sale was made for $671,950. In real estate Reynolds obtained a substantial part of both sides of Chesnut Street between Second and Third streets.

51. Note Appendix C for brands listed by Hanes in 1899.

52. *WSJ*, 5 Dec. 1945; *J&S*, 17 Feb. 1946—courtesy of Fred D. Hauser.

53. *UR*, 23 Nov. 1899.

54. It is so stated in *WTJ*, 10 Dec. 1900, p. 3. See also *Tob.*, 14 Dec. 1900, p. 5; *UR*, 6 Dec. 1900.

55. William J. Conrad, Jr., interview with author, 25 July 1961.

56. *UR*, 6 Dec. 1900, 21 Mar. 1901.

57. Ibid., 4 Apr. 1901.

58. *N&O*, 5 Apr. 1896; *UR*, 15 May 1902; contracts: T. J. Teague (receiver) and R. J. Reynolds, 14 Aug. 1902, and T. J. Teague (receiver) and R. J. R. Tob. Co., Aug. 1902—file 262, secretary's dept., RJR; R. J. Reynolds Tobacco Company's price list of Pegram and Penn brands, in effect on and after 10 July 1902—Scrapbook of Robert E. Lasater, RJR museum. See Appendix C for all chewing brands listed in 1899 by Pegram and Penn.

59. *WTJ*, 19 July 1897, p. 2; *WS*, 22 July 1897.

60. Sullivan County, Tenn., Trust Deed Book, vols. 66, pp. 105–10, 385–86; 69, pp. 366–67. For a detailed sketch of Benjamin L. Dulaney see *Bristol Herald Courier*, 17 Sept. 1961—courtesy of E. M. Rollins.

61. *RCCTI*, 1: 389.

62. *U.S. v. Am. Tob. Co. et al., Record: Testimony of Witnesses*, 2: 268–70.

63. Ibid., 2: 314–21 (quotation, pp. 320–21).

64. *RCCTI*, 1: 184, 389.

65. *U.S. v. Am. Tob. Co. et al., Record: Testimony of Witnesses*, 2: 386–88.

66. *RCCTI*, 1: 13.

67. Agreement: Robert C. Norfleet with Chesley Hamlen and Melvin S. Hamlen, Feb. 1897—file 537, secretary's dept., RJR; *TCS*, 24 Jan. 1916.

68. History of active brands owned by Liipfert, Scales and Co., 20 Sept. 1907—

file 537, secretary's dept., RJR.

69. *WSJ*, 23 Jan. 1916; *WS*, 29 Oct. 1885; *UR*, 27 Jan. 1916.

70. Liipfert, Scales and Co. to R. J. R. Tob. Co., 24, 26 June 1903—file 537, secretary's dept., RJR. See also Minutes, vol. I, pp. 205–6, for approval of the contract on 20 June 1904. Apparently Reynolds had entered negotiations with Liipfert, Scales and Co. by 18 Aug. 1903.

71. Agreement: Liipfert, Scales and Co., partners in Liipfert, Scales and Co. and R. J. R. Tob. Co., 18 Aug. 1903—file 537, secretary's dept., RJR.

72. New York, 26 Aug. 1903, on stationery of the Continental Tobacco Company—ibid.

73. *UR*, 3 Sept. 1903, 4 Feb. 1904.

74. Bill of sale: T. A. Crews and James W. Crews (trading under the name of T. A. Crews) and Liipfert, Scales and Co., 1 June 1904—file 537, secretary's dept., RJR. The T. A. Crews business was started about 1892 soon after completion of the Roanoke and Southern Railway—Gowan H. Caldwell in *J&S*, 9 Apr. 1933. See Appendix C for the Crews brands.

75. *RCCTI*, 1: 111, 271, 2: 193–94; *U.S. v. Am. Tob. Co. et al., Record: Testimony of Witnesses*, 3: 632–34.

76. See Appendix C.

77. *UR*, 4 Jan. 1912; contract: F. J. Liipfert, J. K. Norfleet, R. C. Norfleet, J. S. Scales, and P. O. Leak with R. J. R. Tob. Co., 13 Dec. 1911—file 537, secretary's dept., RJR.

78. Virginia G. Pedigo and Lewis G. Pedigo, *History of Patrick and Henry Counties Virginia* (Roanoke, Va., 1933), pp. 136–43, 250–52; Tilley, pp. 513, 523–24, 686, 688; Minutes of Stockholders for 23 July 1906 (D. H. Spencer and Sons [Inc.])—file 355, secretary's dept., RJR.

79. Memorandum of Agreement between D. H. Spencer and Sons, Spencer Brothers, and R. J. R. Tob. Co.; indenture covering sale of B. F. Gravely and Sons to D. H. Spencer and Sons (Inc.), 4 Mar. 1904—all in file 355, secretary's dept., RJR.

80. Sales agreement: D. H. Spencer and Sons (Inc.) with R. J. R. Tob. Co., 23 July 1906, and Ambrose H. Burroughs to R. J. R. Tob. Co., 111 Fifth Avenue, New York, N.Y., 20 June 1906—ibid.; *RCCTI*, 1: 190, 191n, 275.

81. J. H. Spencer, president of D. H. Spencer and Sons (Inc.) to R. J. R. Tob. Co., Martinsville, Va., 12 Mar. 1907—file 355, secretary's dept., RJR. John W. Carter of Martinsville, attorney-at-law and owner of five shares of preferred and five shares of common stock in D. H. Spencer and Sons (Inc.), wrote Reynolds's attorney, Clement Manly, on 18 Jan. 1907, in reply to Manly's letter of 15 Jan.: "You can not regret more than I that we have been unable to bring about a final determination of the matter now in dispute between R. J. Reynolds Tob. Co. and D. H. Spencer & Sons, Inc." Carter had consulted with D. W. Spencer, J. H. Spencer, and H. C. Gravely, who felt that their interpretation of the contract was correct; they did not fear litigation but wished to avoid it; they believed that if arbitrators were chosen, they should be men of high character—not local men who might unconsciously be influenced by the local situation. Ibid.

82. Minutes, vol. I, p. 220; *RCCTI*, 1: 275.

83. *U.S. v. Am. Tob. Co. et al., Record: Testimony of Witnesses*, 2: 741. See ibid., 3: 632–33, for the secrecy of American's bookkeeper.

84. Ibid., 2: 494.

85. *RCCTI*, 1: 139.

86. *N&O*, 5 Apr. 1896; *UR*, 13 Dec. 1900, 3 Jan., 10 Oct. 1901; *J&S*, 29 Sept. 1946.

87. *N&O*, 5 Apr. 1896; *UR*, 22 May 1902, 14 July 1904.

88. *RCCTI*, 1: 187n; *Tob.*, 4 Jan. 1906, p. 15; *UR*, 21 June 1906.

89. Caleb C. Dula to R. J. Reynolds, New York, 31 July 1905—file 305, secretary's dept., RJR.

90. [R. J. Reynolds] to Ambrose H. Burroughs, 9 Sept. 1905—ibid.

91. Hancock was employed and apparently managed the production of Refined, a smoking tobacco, but, by putting too much water in the rum casing, caused the tobacco to mold and thousands of cans had to be recalled from dealers. Hancock was fired and a new brand, Prince Albert, was developed to replace Refined—Sam Mitchell (17 July 1950) and John C. Reich (31 Aug. 1950), interviews with Dell McKeithan. Pannill Rucker held 250 shares of Reynolds stock as of 3 Apr. 1906—Minutes, vol. I, p. 279. By 7 Feb. 1907, however, Rucker, who had been Reynolds's agent in Virginia, severed his connections with the company—Minutes, vol. I, p. 302.

92. Extract from Minutes of Rucker and Witten Tob. Co., 15 Aug. 1905—file 305, secretary's dept., RJR.

93. The Commissioner of Corporations reported the purchase price as $512,898—*RCCTI*, 1: 186.

94. *Tob.*, 5 Oct. 1905, p. 6. It was generally believed in Richmond that Rucker's letter resulted from orders issued by the American Tobacco Company— *Tob.*, 12 Oct. 1905, p. 4.

95. Minutes, vol. I, p. 104.

96. Agreement of Neudecker Tob. Co. and Continental Tob. Co., 3 Sept. 1902, assigned to R. J. R. Tob. Co. on 24 Mar. 1904—file 264, secretary's dept., RJR; Minutes, vol. I, pp. 210, 222.

97. John C. Reich, interview with Erwin W. Cook, 31 Aug. 1950—personnel dept., RJR. A firm, Walker Brothers, manufactured plug tobacco in Winston in 1894—Fries, p. 171. M. A. Walker became a leaf buyer for Reynolds in 1900— *WTJ*, 20 Aug. 1900, p. 7.

98. *U.S. v. Am. Tob. Co. et al., Record: Testimony of Witnesses*, 3: 144–45. Pickett manufactured twenty-two brands of chewing tobacco in 1903—*Connorton's for 1903*, pp. 7–232.

99. *U.S. v. Am. Tob. Co. et al., Record: Testimony of Witnesses*, 3: 612.

100. Ibid., 2: 426–27, 476, 582; 3: 594, 611–12, 618.

101. Ibid., 2: 425.

102. Ibid., 3: 613–14. The Hanes in Reynolds's letter referred to either Pleasant H. Hanes or John W. Hanes or both of them, as each owned 1,000 shares in the R. J. Reynolds Tobacco Company at this time—Minutes, vol. I, p. 93. Two days later Cobb replied to Reynolds that it is "not necessary, and in fact is inadvisable, to put anything on your minute book other than a resolution as follows."

He then gave the wording of a resolution transferring the smoking brands acquired from Vaughn, Brown, and Hanes to the American Tobacco Company. On 19 Mar. Reynolds wrote Cobb expressing pleasure that Cobb did not require "agreement in regard to our own brands of smoking, and sale of scrap to be recorded on our books"—*U.S. v. Am. Tob. Co. et al., Record: Testimony of Witnesses*, 3: 616–17. The resolution, exactly as worded by Cobb, appeared in due time in the minutes of the R. J. Reynolds Tobacco Company—Minutes, vol. I, pp. 104–5. Incidentally, only granulated smoking tobacco was manufactured from scrap.

103. Price lists, comptroller dept., RJR. This collection of price lists is not complete.

104. *U.S. v. Am. Tob. Co. et al., Record: Testimony of Witnesses*, 3: 628. Possibly Duke intended to start a rival to Our Advertiser.

105. Ibid., 2: 380–81.

106. Ibid., 3: 640–44, 652–53.

107. *Am. Tob. Co. v. U.S. et al., Record on Appeal*, 6: 4880.

108. *U.S. v. Am. Tob. Co. et al., Record: Testimony of Witnesses*, 3: 622–24. Reynolds began sending the information but the first report on purchases of leaf apparently did not leave Winston until 20 Feb. 1903.

109. Ibid., 2: 116–19; 3: 592–93, 622–24. When Reynolds received extensive advice from the Continental Tobacco Company regarding the purchase of sun-cured leaf on the Richmond market, he sent Will Reynolds to look into the matter—ibid., 3: 624–25.

110. Ibid., 2: 216; 3: 592–94, 610, 622, 630–31. Frank George, who came with the company on 1 Oct. 1906, stated that reports on the company's business were being sent to the American Tobacco Company at that time—interview with Dell McKeithan, 25 Oct. 1951.

111. *U.S. v. Am. Tob. Co. et al., Record: Testimony of Witnesses*, 3: 631–32.

112. Ibid., 3: 632–33.

113. William J. Conrad, Jr., interview with author, 28 Sept. 1961.

114. *U.S. v. Am. Tob. Co. et al., Record: Testimony of Witnesses*, 3: 610–11. See Minutes, vol. I, p. 83, for this resolution.

115. *U.S. v. Am. Tob. Co. et al., Record: Testimony of Witnesses*, 3: 629.

116. *RCCTI*, 3: 239.

117. Ibid., 3: 10n. See also pp. 216, 240.

Chapter 5
Management and Labor under the Tobacco Combination

1. Clement Manly to Benjamin N. Duke, 19 June 1899, preceded by a telegram—Benjamin N. Duke MSS, Duke University, Durham, N.C. The meeting was held 22 June with Watts and Duke present—Minutes, vol. I, p. 44.

2. H. J. Blauvelt to Benjamin N. Duke, Winston, N.C., 31 Jan. 1900—Benjamin N. Duke MSS.

3. Josephus Daniels, *Editor in Politics* (Chapel Hill, 1941), p. 599.

4. *U.S. v. Am. Tob. Co. et al., Record: Testimony of Witnesses*, 5 vols., docket no.

660–661 (C.C. of Sou. Dist. of N.Y., 1907), 2: 138, 3: 222–30, 613, 621–22, 627–28, 650–51.

5. Ibid., 3: 255–59, 266; *RCCTI*, 1: 25, 310.

6. *U.S. v. Am. Tob. Co. et al., Record: Testimony of Witnesses*, 3: 617, 620, 626–27.

7. Minutes, vol. I, pp. 35, 121–23; *UR*, 19 Dec. 1901, 30 Jan. 1902.

8. Archibald Henderson et al., *North Carolina: The Old North State and the New*, 5 vols. (Chicago, 1941), 5: 59–60; *WSJ*, 24 Nov. 1939; *U.S. v. Am. Tob. Co. et al., Record: Testimony of Witnesses*, 3: 587, 589. Coan was elected on 24 Feb. 1902—Minutes, vol. I, p. 123.

9. Minutes, vol. I, p. 164.

10. *RCCTI*, 1: 11, 131–32; Minutes I, p. 230; *U.S. v. Am. Tob. Co. et al., Record: Testimony of Witnesses*, 4: 356–57.

11. Minutes, vol. I, pp. 242–45.

12. *U.S. v. Am. Tob. Co. et al., Record: Testimony of Witnesses*, 3: 612–13, 644–45.

13. Reid A. Nunn, interview with author, 16 Oct. 1959.

14. *UR*, 2 July 1896, 19 June 1902, 14 Mar., 18 July 1907, 21 Aug. 1913, 10 Dec. 1914, 14 Jan. 1915; Salesmen's Record, vol. I—sales dept., RJR; Robert B. Horn to R. J. Reynolds, 8 Jan. 1907—file 350, secretary's dept., RJR; *WSJ*, 20, 24 Aug. 1913, 2, 25 Sept. 1918. George F. Dwire managed the premium dept. in 1904—Memoirs of Charles M. Griffith, personnel dept., RJR.

15. Salesmen's Record, vols. I, II, III; William T. Smither, interview with author, 24 Mar. 1960; *U.S. v. Am. Tob. Co. et al., Record: Testimony of Witnesses*, 3: 644–45.

16. *STJ*, 6 July 1902.

17. Contract: N. W. Ayer & Son and R. J. R. Tob. Co., 1 Oct. 1918, replacing the contract of 11 Feb. 1910—file 1274, secretary's dept., RJR; *UR*, 22 Sept. 1910 ("Cross-tie Philosophy"); *WSJ*, 4 May 1941; *U.S. v. Am. Tob. Co. et al., Record: Testimony of Witnesses*, 3: 640. Richard Samuel Reynolds, of Bristol, Tenn., the son of Abram D. Reynolds, attended law school at the University of Virginia in 1901–2 before joining the R. J. Reynolds Tobacco Company—E. W. Lautenschlager (registrar) to author, University of Virginia, Charlottesville, 14 Apr. 1960. He later founded Reynolds Metals—Richard S. Reynolds, Jr., *Opportunity in Crisis* (New York, 1956), passim.

18. Salesmen's Record, vol. I, passim; William T. Smither, interview with author, 13 Oct. 1960.

19. *RCCTI*, 1: 104–5; *UR*, 2 July 1903.

20. C. T. Dixon (29 Nov. 1951) and Noah E. Hartley (10 July 1950), interviews with Dell McKeithan and Erwin W. Cook; John Petree, interview with Dell McKeithan, 4 Aug. 1950; Roy C. Haberkern, interview with author, 23 Jan. 1960; Minutes, vol. I, pp. 321–22; *WSJ*, 3, 4 Aug. 1943; death certificate of William O. McCorkle—payroll dept., RJR; personnel file of William O. McCorkle—box 1749C, Records Center, RJR; R. J. Reynolds Private Brand Book—in possession of John C. Whitaker as of 1963.

21. R. J. Reynolds to Walter R. Reynolds, Baltimore Md., 12 Apr. 1910; E. T. Jester to Walter R. Reynolds, New York, 20 June 1903—in possession of E. M.

Harwood, research dept., RJR as of 1963. This collection contains five letters of Jester (evidently in charge of flavorings for the American Tobacco Company) to Walter R. Reynolds on the subject of flavorings. Roy C. Haberkern once saw G3 in a factory of the American Tobacco Company—Roy C. Haberkern, interview with author, 29 Sept. 1960.

22. *WSJ*, 20 Apr. 1915, 27 Nov. 1928; *J&S*, 19 Oct. 1941. Possibly the canny Reynolds was moved to employ Manly partly because in 1885 he had married Emily Buford, the daughter of Algernon S. Buford, president of the Richmond and Danville Railroad Company.

23. *UR*, 5 Jan. 1911. For sketches of Craige's career see R. D. W. Connor, W. K. Boyd, J. G. de Roulhac Hamilton, et al., *History of North Carolina*, 6 vols. (Chicago, 1919), 5: 114–15; Archibald Henderson et al., *North Carolina: The Old North State and the New*, 4: 29–32. For the attempted hiring of Brooks see Aubrey L. Brooks, *A Southern Lawyer: Fifty Years at the Bar* (Chapel Hill, 1950), pp. 90, 189.

24. *U.S. v. Am. Tob. Co. et al., Testimony of Witnesses*, 3: 607–8.

25. *TCS*, 4 Nov. 1931. See also *WSJ*, 5 Nov. 1931; *UR*, 8 Apr. 1908; *Tob.*, 3 Aug. 1916, p. 28.

26. Bessie Lleweylln (Raleigh, 31 Mar. 1960) and William J. Conrad, Jr. (22 Apr. 1960), interviews with author.

27. Memoirs of Charles M. Griffith—personnel dept., RJR; personnel file of Charles M. Griffith—manufacturing personnel, RJR.

28. Memoirs of Charles M. Griffith; notice of 27 Nov. 1907 from desk of Robert E. Lasater—file 2653, secretary's dept., RJR; *UR*, 28 Nov. 1907, 9 Jan. 1908.

29. Memoirs of Charles M. Griffith.

30. *RCCTI*, 1: 92–93; penciled note "Motion GWC W RR"—file 306, secretary's dept., RJR; *U.S. v. Am. Tob. Co. et al., Record: Testimony of Witnesses*, 3: 279–81 (Reed's testimony), 600 (Coan's testimony); Minutes, vol. I, p. 276.

31. *U.S. v. Am. Tob. Co. et al., Record: Testimony of Witnesses*, 2: 45–46, 3: 600; Walter R. Reynolds to Am. Tob. Co., 27 Apr. 1905, and M. M. Whedbee to R. J. R. Tob. Co., New York, 21 Nov. 1905—Correspondence of Walter R. Reynolds, purchasing dept., RJR.

32. Minutes, vol. II, p. 64; Marian Revelle in *J&S*, 15 Dec. 1920; Frank George, interview with Dell McKeithan, 25 Oct. 1951—personnel dept., RJR.

33. Contract with Chas. E. Pless (dealer in office supplies), 14 Dec. 1909—file 438, secretary's dept., RJR; *UR*, 25 Jan. 1906 (Victoria Hudson); Frank George (25 Oct. 1951) and C. P. Burchette (8 June 1950), interviews with Dell McKeithan; Roy C. Haberkern (23 Jan. 1960) and Mrs. John C. Walker (10 Dec. 1962), interviews with author.

34. Memoirs of Charles M. Griffith; H. Floyd Hauser, interview with Dell McKeithan and Erwin W. Cook, 11 July 1950; *Valuable Presents Given for Tobacco Tabs for the Entire Year of 1902*—Plug Scrapbook No. 3, advertising dept., RJR; *Catalogue of Presents, Good Until January 1, 1907*—RJR museum; Minutes, vols. I (pp. 210–11), II (pp. 87–88); William J. Conrad, Jr., interview with author, 22 Mar. 1960; *UR*, 5 Dec. 1901, 13, 20 Dec. 1906. Reynolds gave premiums as early as 1899—memorandum for ordering supplies, 1 Jan. 1900, RJR museum.

35. *U.S. v. Am. Tob. Co. et al., Record: Testimony of Witnesses*, 2: 581–83, 695, 3: 650; *RCCTI*, 1: 90; William J. Conrad, Jr., interview with author, 1 Aug. 1961. In 1910 the Reynolds company was described as "the largest handler of strictly sun cured tobacco on earth"—*UR*, 16 June 1910.

36. *Am. Tob. Co. et al. v. U.S., Record on Appeal*, docket no. 9137–9139 (6th Cir., 1944), exhibits, 6: 1096–1275, 3253–54.

37. H. Floyd Hauser, interview with Dell McKeithan and Erwin W. Cook, 11 July 1950; personnel folder of H. Floyd Hauser—Records Center, RJR. See *UR*, 22 Mar. 1900, for injury of one Candler.

38. These totals, the only ones available for these years, are on record in the payroll dept., RJR.

39. Ed Blakely (2 June 1950) and Adam Gill (13 July 1950), interviews with Dell McKeithan; Charlie W. Wells, interview with author, 13 Jan. 1960; various personnel files in Records Center, RJR.

40. *UR*, 22 Jan. 1903 (Hunt), 30 July 1903 (Jones), 6 June 1907 (Loggins).

41. Ibid., 13 Dec. 1900; Charlie W. Wells, interview with author, 13 Jan. 1960.

42. William L. Brown to Walter R. Reynolds, 22 Feb. 1900—in possession of E. M. Harwood, research dept., RJR, as of 1963. The earlier part of this sketch is drawn chiefly from John Needham (31 Oct. 1951), C. T. Dixon (29 Nov. 1951), L. M. Craver (30 June 1950), Arless Hauser (11 July 1950), Jacob A. Berrier (1 June 1950), Katie Foy (12 Jan. 1951), and Joseph M. Parrish (4 Aug. 1950), interviews with Dell McKeithan. Assistance also came from J. C. MacLachlan, personnel dept., RJR; W. S. Buchanan and John H. Peddicord, plug div., RJR.

43. Thomas F. Bryant (8 June 1950) and John Q. Adams (29 Sept. 1950), interviews with Dell McKeithan.

44. Joseph M. Parrish (4 Aug. 1950), Sam Mitchell (17 July 1950), John C. Reich (31 Aug. 1950), Adam Gill (13 July 1950), C. T. Dixon (29 Nov. 1951), John Petree (4 Aug. 1950), and Edward T. Sims (26 Oct. 1951), interviews with Dell McKeithan—personnel dept., RJR.

45. Based partly on information from Ed Blakely (2 July 1950), Joseph M. Parrish (4 Aug. 1950), Thomas F. Bryant (8 June 1950), Arless Hauser (11 July 1950), and Cora Brewer (17 July 1950), interviews with Dell McKeithan. On 20 Feb. 1903, Willie Thrift died after a threshing administered by Henry Jackson Stultz (d. 28 Feb. 1943), "a boss in the factory," but evidence given at the trial exonerated Stultz who was superintendent of the pressroom at the time of his death—*UR*, 26 Mar., 2 Apr. 1903; *Tob.*, 4 Feb. 1943, p. 17.

46. Winston, N.C., 25 May 1909—scrapbook material, RJR museum.

47. For the fourteen listed buildings see Description of Company Properties, secretary's dept., RJR. For references to other buildings see, for example, Minutes, vols. I (pp. 116, 159, 179, 208, 210, 316), II (pp. 49–51, 88–89, 110); *STJ*, 13 June 1910, 10 Apr. 1911; *UR*, 17 Feb., 14 Apr., 5 May 1910. Note also an account of Reynolds's proposed factory to be built in Richmond, Va.—*Tob.*, 18 Aug. 1910, p. 4.

48. Minutes, vol. II, pp. 49–51; *UR*, 14 June 1906; *WSJ*, 22 Jan. 1913.

49. *MB* 11, no. 70, 30 Oct. 1959. See *MB* 11 (no. 60, 18 Sept. 1959) for an account of a Bates-Corliss engine generator installed in number 256-4 in 1909

and not dismantled until 1959. A Hamilton-Corliss generator installed in Number 12 not too many years after 1909 remained under the loving care of Emanuel R. Luper, engineering foreman, who not only helped install the machine but also operated it from the beginning, kept it in perfect condition until 1935 when the Bailey Power Plant was made adequate, and until 1958 ran the machine at least once a week, keeping it ready for an emergency.

50. *UR*, 8 Mar. 1906 (reduction of hours); *Tob.*, 30 May 1902, p. 3 (10 percent raise for 400 workers); C. T. Dixon, interview with Dell McKeithan, 29 Nov. 1951; statistics from payroll dept., RJR (average wages).

51. *UR*, 30 Mar. 1911.

52. *Southern Tobacconist and Manufacturers' Record*, 1 Feb. 1898.

53. *UR*, 23 Nov. 1899, 21 June 1900; *N&O*, 22 Nov. 1899; *Southern Tobacconist and Manufacturers' Record*, 28 Nov. 1899, 26 June 1900.

54. *UR*, 11 Oct. 1900, 22 May 1902, 21 May 1908.

55. Ibid., 23 May 1901.

56. Ibid., 23 May 1901 (children under 12), 1 Mar. 1906 (Dempsie Archie).

57. *North Carolina Reports: Cases Argued and Determined in the Supreme Court of North Carolina*, 141: 248–60. A similar case in the same year involving an adult, *Jones v. R. J. Reynolds Tobacco Company*, also reached the North Carolina Supreme Court. The company was adjudged guilty at the December term of the Forsyth Superior Court for 1905. Jones's injury came from slipping on tobacco strips on the factory floor, falling onto an unguarded saw, and losing two fingers—ibid., pp. 176–78. In 1907 a similar case (*Cora Nelson v. R. J. Reynolds Tobacco Company*), originating in the Forsyth County Superior Court in 1905 or 1906, was appealed from the North Carolina Supreme Court—*Southeastern Reporter* 57, pp. 127–28. In an interview with the author, Edgar E. Bumgardner (2 Feb. 1962) declared that Manly advised Reynolds to send all injured workers to a hospital.

Chapter 6
A National Product and Financial Stability

1. *Baltimore American* in *STJ*, 22 Feb. 1909.

2. Supplemental Petition re. Excess Profits Taxes, 1917—secretary's dept., RJR.

3. *WSJ*, 26 Jan. 1940.

4. Certificate of Registration, 2 Mar. 1906—file 307, secretary's dept., RJR.

5. *Connorton's for 1887*, p. 78; *for 1903*, p. 77.

6. Assignment of George Washington label to R. J. R. Tob. Co., signed by Caleb C. Dula, 27 Apr. 1910; Ambrose H. Burroughs to R. J. R. Tob. Co., New York, 27 Apr. 1910—both in file 457, secretary's dept., RJR.

7. Richard H. Wright to R. J. R. Tob. Co., Durham, N.C., 4 Dec. 1912; Robert E. Lasater to Richard H. Wright, 9 Aug. 1913; E. L. Bracy to R. J. R. Tob. Co., Baltimore, Md., 2 Oct. 1913—all in papers of Richard H. Wright, Flowers Collection, Duke University Library, Durham, N.C.

8. Certificate of Transfer of Stud Turner to the R. J. R. Tob. Co., 7 Dec. 1909—file 444, secretary's dept., RJR.

9. *U.S. v. Am. Tob. Co. et al., Record: Testimony of Witnesses*, 5 vols., docket no. 660–661 (C.C. of Sou. Dist. of N.Y., 1907), 3: 641–42, 4: 397; Descriptive Price List No. 16, 3 Jan. 1910—in possession of Francis Day, leaf dept., RJR, as of 1963. Reynolds also made other brands during this period including Cotton Bale (which became Cotton Bag in Oct. 1907), Hot Sausage, Old North Carolina Mixture, and Split Silk. These were started earlier and did not receive the attention bestowed on Refined, Prince Albert, B. F. Gravely & Sons Special Stud, and George Washington.

10. Of interest, too, is P. Lorillard's production of smoking tobacco in 1897—5,910,000 pounds.

11. Descriptive Price List, 18 Dec. 1907. At this exposition the R. J. Reynolds Tobacco Company distributed a handsome booklet of thirty-two pages (*Souvenir Booklet: Jamestown Exposition* [1906]) showing a full-page advertisement of Refined as well as other brands—advertising dept., RJR.

12. Sam Mitchell (17 July 1950), John C. Reich (31 Aug. 1950), and William N. Reynolds (1 June 1950), interviews with Dell McKeithan—personnel dept., RJR. Hancock came with the company in 1906 from or with the Rucker and Witten Tobacco Company—*UR*, 21 June 1906.

13. Circular letter to division managers, salesmen and jobbers, 2 Feb. 1911—Correspondence of Walter R. Reynolds, purchasing dept., RJR.

14. Ernest W. Fulton to Colin Stokes, 15 May 1953—scrapbook material, RJR museum; descriptive price lists dated 28 Oct. 1922 and 1 June 1933—in possession of John H. Peddicord as of 1963.

15. John C. Whitaker, interview with William N. Reynolds, 1 June 1950—personnel dept., RJR.

16. This letter is part of a file that was in the possession of the late Roy C. Haberkern, Winston-Salem, N.C., who joined the company in 1909. Haberkern's sense of history prompted him to save this file when an order came to destroy papers of the company not then current. He kindly lent the author the entire file on which this section is based. The company museum, however, contains a faded photograph of King Edward VII by Underwood and Underwood stamped with the stipulation that it not be used for advertising purposes.

17. On the death of King Edward VII in 1910, a suggestion that "Now King" be replaced with "Now Dead" met refusal when some wag in the company suggested that such a statement would indicate the end of Prince Albert smoking tobacco; accordingly "Now King" appeared on no labels after 1910—William J. Conrad, Jr., interview with author, 27 Oct. 1961. Woodward and Tiernan Printing Company, listed in *Gould's St. Louis Directory for 1907* (p. 1976), became Simmons Woodward, Inc.—Marie H. Roberts, Reference Dept., St. Louis Public Library.

18. William N. Reynolds (1 June 1950), Sam Mitchell (17 July 1950), and C. T. Dixon (29 Nov. 1951), interviews with Dell McKeithan. James W. Glenn, in *Am. Tob. Co. et al. v. U.S., Record on Appeal* (docket no. 9137–9139 [6th Cir., 1944], transcripts, 6: 4727), stated that Prince Albert was made of Burley. R. J.

Reynolds Private Brand Book, stamped 26 Feb. 1909—then in possession of the late John C. Whitaker.

19. Clipping from *Saturday Evening Post*, 2 Sept. 1911, p. 55—Prince Albert Scrapbook, vol. I: Magazines, advertising dept., RJR; patent 862,115, 30 July 1907.

20. *UR*, obituary, 18 Feb. 1904.

21. Quoted by John C. Pennie (of Pennie and Goldsborough) to Clement Manly, Wash. D.C., 23 Mar. 1904—file 334, secretary's dept., RJR.

22. Pennie and Goldsborough to Manly and Hendren, Wash. D.C., 30 July 1907—ibid.

23. *U.S. v. Am. Tob. Co. et al.*, docket no. 118–119 (United States Supreme Court, Oct. term, 1910), 62nd Cong., 1st sess., doc. no. 40, p. 3; *Tob.*, 18 (pp. 4–5) and 25 (p. 3) July 1907.

24. Correspondence of R. J. R. Tob. Co. with F. A. Davis and Sons, 8 Oct. 1907–7 Nov. 1907—file 380, secretary's dept., RJR.

25. R. J. Reynolds Tobacco Company's *Illustrated Price List* (accompanying the descriptive price list for 3 Jan. 1910), p. 9—in possession of Francis Day, leaf dept., RJR, as of 1963.

26. Contract: N. W. Ayer & Son and R. J. R. Tob. Co., 1 Oct. 1918, replacing contract of 11 Feb. 1910—file 1274, secretary's dept., RJR; *Tob.*, 7 July 1910, p. 14. Note also the sketch of a paper read by R. J. Reynolds before the Western Association of Retail Cigar Dealers in Seattle, Wash., in Jan. 1917—*Tob.*, 25 Jan. 1917, p. 8.

27. H. Floyd Hauser, interview with Dell McKeithan and Erwin W. Cook, 11 July 1950—personnel dept., RJR.

28. Thomas F. Bryant, interview with Dell McKeithan and Erwin W. Cook, 8 June 1950—ibid.

29. Louis Fischer to J. Martin Umstead [secretary to R. H. Wright], 12 June 1909—Papers of Richard H. Wright; contract: R. J. R. Tob. Co. and A. E. Heekin Can Co., 18 June 1909—file 441, secretary's dept., RJR. This first contract was supplemented a number of times.

30. *STJ*, 20 Feb., 3 Apr., 5 June 1911.

31. Edward T. Sims, interview with Dell McKeithan and Erwin W. Cook, 26 Oct. 1951—personnel dept., RJR.

32. Walter R. Reynolds to Richard H. Wright, 14 Jan., 1 Feb. 1909; Richard H. Wright to R. J. R. Tob. Co., Durham, N.C., 15, 29 Jan. 1909—both in Letterpress Book, 22 Sept. 1908–8 June 1909, pp. 425, 472, Papers of Richard H. Wright. See Tilley, pp. 500–501, for a sketch of the Lawrence machine.

33. Richard H. Wright to R. J. R. Tob. Co., Durham, N.C., 8, 11 Feb. 1909—Letterpress Book, 22 Sept. 1908–28 June 1909, pp. 507, 527; Walter R. Reynolds to Richard H. Wright, 9, 27 Feb. 1909—all in Papers of Richard H. Wright.

34. Richard H. Wright to Louis Fischer, Durham, N.C., 10 Apr. 1909; Walter R. Reynolds to Richard H. Wright, 14, 21 Apr., 10 May 1909—both in ibid.

35. Walter R. Reynolds to Richard H. Wright, 13 May 1909; Richard H.

Wright to R. J. R. Tob. Co., Durham, N.C., 28 May, 1 June 1909—both in Letterpress Book, 22 Sept. 1908–28 June 1909, pp. 861, 893, ibid.

36. Louis Fischer to J. Martin Umstead, 12 June 1909—ibid.

37. Walter R. Reynolds to Richard H. Wright, 2 July 1909—ibid.

38. Walter R. Reynolds to Richard H. Wright, 6 July 1910—ibid.

39. Richard H. Wright to R. J. R. Tob. Co., Durham, N.C., 2 Feb. 1911—Letterpress Book, 2 Nov. 1910–21 Mar. 1911, p. 754, ibid.

40. Richard H. Wright to R. J. R. Tob. Co., Durham, N.C, 31 Mar. 1911—Letterpress Book, 22 Mar.–6 Sept. 1911, p. 69, ibid.

41. Richard H. Wright to R. J. R. Tob. Co., Durham, N.C., 5 Apr. 1911; Richard H. Wright to Rose Brothers, 5 Apr. 1911—both in Letterpress Book, 22 Mar.–6 Sept. 1911, pp. 113–14, ibid.

42. Richard H. Wright to R. J. R. Tob. Co., Durham, N.C., 6 May 1911—Letterpress Book, 22 Mar.–6 Sept. 1911, p. 294, ibid.

43. Richard H. Wright to R. J. R. Tob. Co., Durham, N.C., 30 May 1911—Letterpress Book, 22 Mar.–6 Sept. 1911, p. 442, ibid.

44. Louis Fischer to Richard H. Wright, 8 July 1911; Richard H. Wright to Louis Fischer, 4 July 1911—both in Letterpress Book, 22 Mar.–6 Sept. 1911, pp. 744–45, ibid.

45. Louis Fischer to Richard H. Wright, 8 July 1911—ibid.

46. Walter R. Reynolds to Richard H. Wright, 9 Aug. 1911—ibid.

47. R. J. Reynolds to Richard H. Wright, 10 Aug. 1911—ibid.

48. Louis Fischer to Richard H. Wright, 19 Jan. 1912; Richard H. Wright to Louis Fischer, Durham, N.C., 19 Jan. 1912—both in ibid.

49. Louis Fischer to Richard H. Wright, 7 Feb. 1912—ibid.

50. Richard H. Wright to R. J. R. Tob. Co., Durham, N.C., 20 Feb. 1912; Walter R. Reynolds to Richard H. Wright, 24 Feb. 1912; Richard H. Wright to R. J. R. Tob. Co., Durham, N.C., 26 Feb. 1912—all in ibid.

51. Richard H. Wright to R. J. R. Tob. Co., Durham, N.C., 5 Mar., 1, 3 Apr. 1912—ibid.

52. Richard H. Wright to R. J. Reynolds, Durham, N.C., 6 Apr. 1912—ibid.

53. Contract: Wright's Automatic Tobacco Packing Machine Co. and R. J. R. Tob. Co., 10 Apr. 1912—file 545, secretary's dept., RJR.

54. R. J. Reynolds to Richard H. Wright, 30 Apr. 1912; Walter R. Reynolds to Richard H. Wright, 10 May 1912; Richard H. Wright to R. J. R. Tob. Co., Durham, N.C., 11 May 1912—all in Papers of Richard H. Wright.

55. Richard H. Wright to R. J. R. Tob. Co., Durham, N.C., 6 June 1911—Letterpress Book, 22 Mar.–6 Sept. 1911, p. 498, ibid.; Joseph M. Parrish, interview with Dell McKeithan, 4 Aug. 1950—personnel dept., RJR.

56. Richard H. Wright to E. L. Bracy, Durham, N.C., 22 June 1912—Papers of Richard H. Wright; Noah E. Hartley, interview with Dell McKeithan and Erwin W. Cook, 11 July 1950—personnel dept., RJR.

57. Richard H. Wright to Clinton W. Toms, Durham, N.C., 19 Mar. 1912; T. T. Anderson to Richard H. Wright, St. Louis, Mo., 29 Apr. 1912; Richard H. Wright to Robert E. Lasater, Durham, N.C., 2 May 1912; Robert E. Lasater to Richard H. Wright, 3 May 1912—all in Papers of Richard H. Wright.

58. Memorandum of Carl W. Harris to Burton Craige, 18 Nov. 1912—file 672, secretary's dept., RJR; Wright's Automatic Tobacco Packing Machine Co. to R. J. R. Tob. Co., Durham, N.C., 6 May 1911—Letterpress Book, 22 Mar.–6 Sept. 1911, p. 285, Papers of Richard H. Wright.

59. A. E. Heekin to R. J. R. Tob. Co., Cincinnati, Ohio, 13 Feb. 1912; Egbert L. Davis to William H. Muller, 22 Nov. 1913—both in file 672, secretary's dept., RJR.

60. Burton Craige to H. Lewis Brown [of the A. H. Burroughs firm], 21 Aug. 1914—ibid.

61. Correspondence of Burton Craige, esp. Letters Patent to R. J. R. Tob. Co., 12 Aug. 1913—ibid.

62. Noah Hartley, interview with Dell McKeithan and Erwin W. Cook, 11 July 1950—personnel dept., RJR. Information on injuries from B. F. Harrison and Fred W. Mays, interviews with author, 22 Feb., 22 Mar. 1960. Ernest W. Fulton stated in 1957: "Our Company decided to manufacture its own cans, and the Metal Can Division was established in 1909"—*MB* 9, no. 36, 28 June 1957.

63. Thomas F. Bryant, interview with Dell McKeithan and Erwin W. Cook, 8 June 1950—personnel dept., RJR; Fred W. Mays, interview with author, 22 Feb. 1960; memorandum of William F. Chambers to Edgar E. Bumgardner, 13 Nov. 1961.

64. W. E. Snyder, interview with author, 30 Oct. 1959.

65. In correspondence of Walter R. Reynolds.

66. *RCCTI*, 3: 251.

67. Borden, *Economic Effects of Advertising*, p. 248.

68. Prince Albert Scrapbook: Magazines, vol. I. In *Babbitt* (Signet Classic: New American Library, 1963), pp. 100–101, Sinclair Lewis uses Prince Albert advertising as a sample of "poetry" greatly admired by the "average man."

69. *WSJ*, 24 Jan. 1912.

70. Richard H. Wright to Louis Fischer, Durham, N.C., 20 Dec. 1912—Papers of Richard H. Wright.

71. Minutes, vol. I, pp. 62 (1899), 97 (1900), 133 (1901), 169 (1902), 195–96 (1903), 233 (1904), 286 (1905), 309–10 (1906), 341–42 (1907), and vol. II, pp. 21 (1908), 60 (1909), 106 (1910), 158–59 (1911); *RCCTI*, 2: 191 (goodwill).

72. *RCCTI*, 3: 78 (Schnapps, etc.).

73. Minutes, vol. I, pp. 88–91, 149–50, 260–62, 273–75; Report of Committee on Stock List, N.Y. Stock Exchange, 15 Mar. 1922—box 1236C, Records Center, RJR.

74. Minutes, vol. I, p. 154.

75. Ibid., vol. II, p. 191.

76. *RCCTI*, 2: 190.

77. Minutes, vols. I, passim; II, p. 116, passim.

78. Ibid., vol. I, pp. 83, 149–50, 156–57, 186–87, 224–25, 255–56.

79. Ibid., vol. II, pp. 73–74.

80. Ibid., vol. I, pp. 93–94.

81. Ibid., pp. 278–79. It should be noted that five stockholders listed in 1906 held much smaller allotments in 1905 and that others listed in 1901 held larger

amounts. Also included in the 1906 list are the wives of Bowman Gray, Sr., William N. Reynolds, and Clement Manly, whose names do not appear in this table. See Minutes, vol. I, pp. 305–6.

82. Miscellaneous papers re. Increase in R. J. R. Tob. Co.'s Capital Stock, 1906—file 306, secretary's dept., RJR; Minutes, vol. I, pp. 273–75.

83. Miscellaneous papers re. R. J. Reynolds's Capital Stock, 1906—file 306, secretary's dept., RJR.

84. R. J. Reynolds to Caleb C. Dula, 13 Mar. 1906—ibid.

85. William E. Brock to R. J. Reynolds, 13 Mar. 1906; Charles A. Kent to R. J. Reynolds, 8, 12 Mar. 1906; L. A. Myers to R. J. Reynolds, 19 Mar. 1906; R. J. Reynolds to L. A. Myers, 20 Mar. 1906—all in ibid.

86. R. J. Reynolds [by C. B.] to Bowman Gray, 20 Mar. 1906; R. J. Reynolds [by C. B.] to Joseph D. Noell, 20 Mar. 1906; Bowman Gray to George W. Coan, Baltimore, Md., n.d. [but written in 1906]—all in ibid.

87. George W. Coan to Robert B. Horn, 23 Feb. 1906—ibid.; Minutes, vol. I, p. 279.

88. Ambrose H. Burroughs to R. J. Reynolds, New York, N.Y., 21 Dec. 1905; R. J. Reynolds to Ambrose H. Burroughs, 23 Feb. 1905—both in misc. papers re. R. J. Reynolds's Capital Stock, 1906, file 306, secretary's dept., RJR.

89. Ambrose H. Burroughs to George W. Coan, New York, N.Y., 15 Feb. 1906—ibid.

90. Junius Parker to R. J. Reynolds, New York, N.Y., 17 Feb. 1906—ibid.

Chapter 7
Independence and New Directions

1. Meade Willis, Sr., interview with author, 8 Feb. 1961.

2. In Correspondence of Walter R. Reynolds—purchasing dept., RJR. This was the decision that directed the circuit court to determine a plan for dissolving the Tobacco Combination—see *Tob.*, 1 June 1911, p. 4.

3. R. J. R. Tob. Co. "To Our Salesmen," 15 Nov. 1911, initialed by D. Rich and "EPM" and evidently preserved as an important historical record of the company—file 3070, secretary's dept., RJR. Reprinted in *Am. Tob. Co. et al. v. U.S., Record on Appeal*, docket no. 9137-9139 (6th Cir., 1944), transcripts, 6: 4867–70.

4. Circular S-26-C in *Am. Tob. Co. et al. v. U.S., Record on Appeal*, transcripts, 6: 4867–68.

5. *R. J. R. Tob. Co. et al. v. U.S., Brief for Appellants*, docket no. 9139 (6th Cir., 1944), p. 74.

6. *RCCTI*, 3: 12.

7. Exhibits Introduced, *R. J. R. Tob. Co. v. U.S.*, docket no. 254–54 (U.S. Court of Claims), p. 12—legal dept., RJR.

8. *RCCTI*, 3: 217.

9. *R. J. R. Tob. Co. et al. v. U.S., Brief for Appellants*, p. 35.

10. *Tob.*, 30 Nov. 1911, p. 3; R. J. R. Tob. Co. Financial Statement for 1912, 6 Mar. 1913.

11. Minutes, vol. II, pp. 172–73, 223–31.

12. *Tob.*, 30 Nov. 1911, p. 3.

13. Minutes, vol. II, pp. 120–22, 129–32, 133–41, 214–20; *U.S. v. Am. Tob. Co. et al., Decree* (C.C. of Sou. Dist. of N.Y., 16 Nov. 1911), pp. 14–15; *U.S. v. Am. Tob. Co. et al., Federal Reporter*, perm. ed., 191: 422.

14. Minutes, vol. II, p. 125.

15. *R. J. R. Tob. Co. et al. v. U.S., Brief for Appellants*, pp. 75–77.

16. *Am. Tob. Co. et al. v. U.S., Record on Appeal*, transcripts, 5: 3950–54.

17. Certified copy of Bylaw XII of the American Tobacco Company with amendments, Exhibits Introduced, *R. J. R. Tob. Co. v. U.S.*, docket no. 254–54 (U.S. Court of Claims).

18. Certified copy of Bylaw XII of Liggett and Myers Tobacco Company—legal dept., RJR.

19. Certified copies of Bylaws XII and XIII of the P. Lorillard Tobacco Company—ibid.

20. Minutes, vol. II, p. 221. Note also p. 179 for Reynolds's first bylaw. Many years later, when asked whether James B. Duke had suggested the adoption of Bylaw XII, William N. Reynolds did not know, although he did not think so—*Am. Tob. Co. et al. v. U.S., Record on Appeal*, transcripts, 6: 4877.

21. About 1913, R. J. Reynolds told Charlie Wells, one of his favorite hands in the shipping dept., that he would help him buy some stock, and Wells intended to do so until laughed out of the idea by his fellow workers. His failure to follow Reynolds's advice became one of Wells's deep regrets, for he knew "Mr. R. J." would have helped him—Charlie Wells, interview with author, 13 Jan. 1960.

22. W. A. Armfield, interview with author, 29 Jan. 1960.

23. Mrs. Joseph R. Fletcher, interview with author, 16 Apr. 1960.

24. *Am. Tob. Co. et al. v. U.S., Record on Appeal*, transcripts, 7: 5311.

25. R. J. Reynolds to stockholders of R. J. R. Tob. Co., 8 Aug. 1912—secretary's dept., RJR.

26. In 1944, when the number of shares held by employees other than directors stood at the highest point, a total of 1,906 persons including directors held participating stock. In discussing this question on 2 Oct. 1941, S. Clay Williams declared there were then more than 2,000 employees holding participation stock; later on the same day, he estimated the figure to be around 2,000—*Am. Tob. Co. v. U.S., Record on Appeal*, transcripts, 7: 5068, 5071. Changes in total number of shares resulted from the reduction of par value first to $25 and then to $10 per share.

27. George W. Coan, Secretary, to "Dear Sir," 30 Aug. 1912—secretary's dept., RJR.

28. Two telegrams, both dated 24 Apr. 1912, from Burton Craige to Frank P. McDermott (N.J. agent, d. 3 Jan. 1921)—copies, no. 785, box 1242, Records Center, RJR. Slight errors in spelling and position as director have been corrected and checked by consulting *RCCTI*, 1, 2, passim. Others on the list may possibly have held official positions in the old American Tobacco Company.

29. Copy of letter of R. J. Reynolds to Harry H. Shelton [Philadelphia, Pa.], 6 June 1918—secretary's dept., RJR; Will of Richard Joshua Reynolds, Clerk's

Office, Forsyth County Courthouse, Winston-Salem, N.C. By 1918 preferred stock had declined from $123 in 1916 to par because stockholders had so much Class B Common to take up that they sold preferred in order to take care of subscription rights in Class B Common. Thus the price of preferred was forced down, a circumstance that probably affected common or A stock—Walter R. Reynolds to J. Walter Lemkau, 21 June 1918—Correspondence of Walter R. Reynolds.

30. R. D. W. Conner et al., *North Carolina: Rebuilding an Ancient Commonwealth, 1584–1925*, 4 vols. (New York and Chicago, 1929), 4: 21; Minutes, vol. II, pp. 172–73, 223–24; *Tob.*, 31 May 1917, p. 4.

31. Minutes, vol. IV, pp. 47, 73.

32. Ibid., pp. 79, 109.

33. *Am. Tob. Co. v. U.S., Record on Appeal*, transcripts, 7: 5071–72.

34. Will of Richard Joshua Reynolds.

35. Minutes, vol. IV, pp. 195, 232.

36. C. Vann Woodward, *Origins of the New South, 1877–1913*, vol. 9 of *History of the South*, eds. Wendell H. Stephenson and E. Merton Coulter (Baton Rouge, La., 1951), pp. 291–320, esp. p. 318. For additional information on participation stock and its final elimination, see Chapter 12, p. 817.

37. Ben Dixon MacNeill in *North American Review* 232 (Aug. 1931): 101–10.

38. Exhibits presented in *Bookman v. R. J. R. Tob. Co. et al.*, docket no. 129–544 (Chancery of N.J., 1946)—legal dept., box 806C, Records Center, RJR; *J&S*, 19 Dec. 1937; William J. Conrad, Jr., interview with author, 19 Dec. 1961. Because there was so little time, Robert E. Lasater withdrew his offer for the sale of his stock in favor of Harris's stock—George E. Tucker (to those concerned), 21 Dec. 1937, miscellaneous folder, 1925–38, box 696, Records Center, RJR.

39. Rice Gwynn to William N. Reynolds, Danville, Va., 13 Feb. 1924, in Exhibits Introduced, *R. J. R. Tob. Co. v. U.S.*, docket no. 254–54 (U.S. Court of Claims).

40. F. G. Marburg (of Alex. Brown & Sons) to Vernon Davis, Baltimore, Md., 27 Apr., 25 May, 3 June (telegram) 1942; Vernon Davis to Alex. Brown & Sons, Butte, Mont., 3 June (telegram), 6 June 1942; memorandum of William C. Smith to dividend disbursing dept. of Chase Manhattan Bank—all courtesy of Vernon Davis; Vernon Davis, interview with author, 12 Jan. 1962.

41. D. Rich to stockholders of R. J. Tob. Co., 30 Oct. 1914—secretary's dept., RJR. See also Minutes, vol. II, p. 385.

42. William C. Smith, interview with author, 3 May 1961. See below.

43. S. Clay Williams to Committee on Stock List, N.Y. Stock Exchange, 14 Mar. 1922; memorandum of S. Clay Williams re. Listing on the N.Y. Stock Exchange, dictated on 18 Mar. 1922—both in box 1236C, Records Center, RJR.

44. John W. Hanes, Jr., to James A. Gray, New York, 24 Jan. 1922—ibid.

45. Memorandum of S. Clay Williams to Memory E. Motsinger, 24 Jan. 1922—ibid. Note also the decision of the directors on 2 Mar. 1922 to apply for listing—Minutes, vol. IV, p. 283.

46. Memorandum of S. Clay Williams re. Listing on the N.Y. Stock Exchange,

18 Mar. 1922. The memorandum is thus dated only two days after the stock was listed. Incidentally, this ticker-tape symbol was changed to "R.J." in 1939 and back again to "R.J.R." on 28 June 1960—*WTJ*, 14 July 1960, p. 9.

47. Scrapbook, 1891–99—advertising dept., RJR.

48. William P. Hairston, interview with author, 29 Nov. 1960. William T. Smither declared that he had read many letters from Bowman Gray, Sr., on this point—interview with author, 29 Nov. 1962.

49. This last interpretation was given by a local newspaper when Reynolds ordered five cigarette machines on 6 Feb. 1913—*WSJ*, 7 Feb. 1913. This was also the opinion of Reynolds's friend, Josephus Daniels—*Tar Heel Editor* (Chapel Hill, 1939), pp. 476–77. Measured in pounds, the per capita consumption of tobacco in cigarettes increased slightly more than fourfold from 1900 to 1913—Neil H. Borden, *The Economic Effects of Advertising* (Chicago, 1947), p. 216.

50. William N. Reynolds, interview with John C. Whitaker, 1 June 1950—personnel dept., RJR. For the general belief relative to cigarettes, see Tilley, pp. 273–74, 608–9.

51. Rufus L. Patterson to Walter R. Reynolds, New York, 4 Mar. 1912; Walter R. Reynolds to Rufus L. Patterson, 2 Apr. 1912—Correspondence of Walter R. Reynolds.

52. *STJ*, 8 Apr. 1912.

53. Richard H. Wright to R. J. R. Tob. Co., Durham, N.C., 12 Nov. 1912—Papers of Richard H. Wright, Flowers Collection, Duke University Library, Durham, N.C.

54. *STJ*, 18 Nov. 1912.

55. Minutes of Winston-Salem Chamber of Commerce, 1889–1922, p. 115—office of Winston-Salem Chamber of Commerce that succeeded the Winston Board of Trade; *WSJ*, 11 Feb. 1913.

56. Sales dept. to salesmen, 12 Feb. 1913—sales dept., RJR.

57. *STJ*, 10 Feb., 8 Apr. 1913.

58. Ibid., 22 July 1913.

59. *Connorton's for 1903*, p. 512; *Am. Tob. Co. et al. v. U.S., Record on Appeal*, transcripts, 5: 3860 (testimony of George Washington Hill); John E. Stone, interview with Dell McKeithan and Erwin W. Cook, 1950—personnel dept., RJR; J. C. Robert, *The Story of Tobacco in America* (New York, 1949), p. 231.

60. Walter R. Reynolds to Richard H. Wright, 23 Dec. 1912, 3 Jan. 1913—Papers of Richard H. Wright.

61. Edgar E. Bumgardner, interview with author, 8 Dec. 1959. The man in question was Pinkney Sheppard Preston of the Briggs and Shaffner firm, which manufactured cigarette machinery.

62. Personnel folder of Richard L. Dunstan—inactive files of manufacturing personnel dept., RJR; *TCS*, 27 Nov. 1947; *MIB* 1, no. 61, 30 Dec. 1947; John E. Stone (1950) and Noah E. Hartley (10 July 1950), interviews with Dell McKeithan and Erwin W. Cook—personnel dept., RJR; contract: American Machine and Foundry Co. with R. J. R. Tob. Co.—file 615, secretary's dept., RJR.

63. Miscellaneous folder, 1925–38—box 696, Records Center, RJR.

64. John E. Stone, interview with Dell McKeithan and Erwin W. Cook, 1950—

personnel dept., RJR; personnel folder of John E. Stone—manufacturing dept., RJR.

65. Personnel folder of Henry L. Lorraine, Jr.—inactive files of manufacturing personnel dept., RJR. Lorraine stated, however, that he would report to Dunstan on 24 Feb. 1914—Henry L. Lorraine, Jr., to Walter R. Reynolds, Richmond, Va., 19 Feb. 1914, Correspondence of Walter R. Reynolds.

66. Based on a series of letters in the Papers of Richard H. Wright between Wright and Walter R. Reynolds dated as follows: 3, 4 Dec. 1912; 13, 14, 20, 21, 24 May, 16, 21, 23 June, 2 July 1913; 3 Jan. 1914. See Tilley, p. 627, for development of the Quester machine, which was built and sold in the United States by Briggs-Shaffner Company of Winston-Salem—*Tob.*, 30 Mar. 1922, p. 106. The Legg cutter, long a favorite, was an English machine made by Robert Legg, Ltd., which merged with the American Machine and Foundry Co. in 1960—*WTJ*, 14 July 1960, p. 17.

67. Richard H. Wright to R. J. R. Tob. Co., Durham, N.C., 12 Nov. (two letters), 19, 4 Dec. 1912; Burton Craige to Richard H. Wright, 16, 27 Nov., 2 Dec. 1912—all in Papers of Richard H. Wright.

68. Richard H. Wright to R. J. R. Tob. Co., Durham, N.C., 29 Dec. 1913; Walter R. Reynolds to J. Martin Umstead, 14 Aug. 1914—both in ibid.

69. Walter R. Reynolds to Richard H. Wright, 19, 20 Dec. 1912—ibid.

70. Walter R. Reynolds to Richard H. Wright, 14 Jan. 1913—ibid.

71. Walter R. Reynolds to Ludington Cigarette Machine Co., 16, 22 Jan. 1913—ibid.

72. Walter R. Reynolds to Richard H. Wright, 8 Feb. 1913—ibid.

73. Walter R. Reynolds to Richard H. Wright, 15, 17 Feb. 1913—ibid.

74. Walter R. Reynolds to Richard H. Wright, 17 Feb., 3 Mar. 1913; Richard H. Wright to E. L. Bracy, Durham, N.C., 28 Mar. 1913—both in ibid.

75. Walter R. Reynolds to Richard H. Wright, 11, 15, 19 July 1913—ibid.

76. Walter R. Reynolds to Richard H. Wright, 8 Feb. 1913—ibid. The Standard Cigarette Machine, first developed in 1908, was capable of producing three hundred cigarettes per minute; it is generally considered the greatest contribution of the American Machine and Foundry Company to the cigarette industry—*Tob.*, 27 July 1950, p. 65.

77. Walter R. Reynolds to Richard H. Wright, 13 Feb., 28 July 1913—Papers of Richard H. Wright.

78. Walter R. Reynolds to Richard H. Wright, 23, 26 July 1913—ibid.

79. Walter R. Reynolds to Richard H. Wright, 12 Sept. 1913; Roy C. Haberkern to Richard H. Wright, 27 Sept. 1913—both in ibid.

80. A Reyno slide box, a 1913 Camel cup, and a Red Kamel hinged box were in the company museum, but there was no package for the Osman, a Turkish blend, which was described early in 1914 as being thoroughly wrapped in tin foil and packed in "a rich, distinctive looking package . . . richly lithographed in sepia and gold"—*Tob.*, 5 Mar. 1914, p. 29—apparently a cup package. Richard L. Dunstan referred to Osman twenties in 1939—to Haddon S. Kirk, 24 Feb. 1939, box 696C, Records Center, RJR. The name "Reyno" was suggested by Joseph L. Graham—Reid L. Nunn, interview with author, 14 May 1963.

81. *R. J. R. Tob. Co. et al. v. U.S., Brief for Appellants*, p. 78.

82. *Am. Tob. Co. et al. v. U.S., Record on Appeal*, transcripts, 6: 4729–30. An article, "Camels of Winston-Salem" (*Fortune*, Jan. 1931, pp. 45–55), credits the Camel with being revolutionary in blend, esp. pp. 45, 49.

83. *Am. Tob. Co. et al. v. U.S., Record on Appeal*, transcripts, 5: 3853–62. Note a discussion of these same points in Tilley, pp. 609–10, where some emphasis is placed on the scarcity of Turkish leaf because of war conditions. When Hill gave this flattering testimony, the president of Liggett and Myers (James W. Andrews) showed less enthusiasm for the role of the Camel in the cigarette industry where-as the sales manager for the New York district showed no knowledge in this respect—*Am. Tob. Co. et al. v. U.S., Record on Appeal*, transcripts, 6: 4490–93, 4574–77.

84. *Tob.*, 25 Dec. 1913, p. 29. See also *Tobacco Leaf*, Dec. 1913. The American Tobacco Company, with its customary attitude of proprietorship toward the city of New York, permitted a questionable statement to be published later, namely that, like Prince Albert, the Camel was introduced outside the big-city markets—American Tobacco Company, *"Sold American!" The First Fifty Years* (New York, 1954), p. 44. As a matter of fact, the Camel appears to have been marketed early in Cincinnati—*Tob.*, 12 Feb. (p. 22), 12 Mar. (p. 23), 19 Mar. (pp. 16–17), 7 May (p. 19) 1914—but perhaps first in Cleveland where Vincent Riggio first saw Camels sell rapidly while his cigarettes remained on the counter—*Am. Tob. Co. et al. v. U.S., Record on Appeal*, transcripts, 5: 3958. Julian L. Watkins, in *The 100 Greatest Advertisements, Who Wrote Them and What They Did*, new Dover ed. (New York, 1959), p. 27, on excellent authority states that Camels were first marketed in Cleveland. Note also *Am. Tob. Co. et al. v. U.S., Record on Appeal*, transcripts, 6: 4730.

85. Winston-Salem, N.C., 4 Dec. 1914—Papers of Richard H. Wright.

86. R. J. R. Tob. Co. to Charles E. Hughes and Co., 3 Oct. 1913. Burton Craige wrote on 1 Nov. 1913 ". . . we made sale of Camel cigarettes in Virginia. This sale was made on Oct. 3, 1913."—Burton Craige to Arthur S. Brown, 1 Nov. 1913, file 720, secretary's dept., RJR. Notes of Roy C. Haberkern on the Camel Cigarette, 26 Feb. 1947, state that Gwynn made the first sale—personnel dept., RJR.

87. See, for example, a picture of the Reyno box in Cigarette Supplement to Price List No. 20, effective 1 Sept. 1913, and a Reyno box preserved in the RJR museum.

88. Calendar notebook of R. J. Reynolds for 1913, 1914, 1915—in posses-sion of the late Roy C. Haberkern as of 1962. Notes of Roy C. Haberkern on the Camel Cigarette, 26 Feb. 1947, with Hoen's label of 24 Sept. 1913 attached—personnel dept., RJR. Charles H. Babcock, son-in-law of R. J. Reynolds, stated in an interview with the author (19 Jan. 1963) that Katharine Smith Reynolds aided considerably in these decisions.

89. Notes of Roy C. Haberkern on the Camel Cigarette, 26 Feb. 1947. A photostatic copy of the transcript of Katharine Smith from the Woman's College of the University of North Carolina, 9 May 1961, shows that she studied En-glish, French, and Spanish—courtesy of Zachary T. Smith.

90. Notes of Roy C. Haberkern on the Camel Cigarette, 26 Feb. 1947. Note a

slightly different account in *Cosmopolitan*, Feb. 1960, p. 133. The story was repeated essentially in this form a number of times in the local press. Apparently "Ferrell" was Andrew J. Farrell, a Winston-Salem photographer in 1913—*Winston-Salem, N.C. City and Suburban Directory*, 1913, pp. 184, 583. Barnum and Bailey's Circus performed in Winston-Salem on Monday, 29 Sept. 1913—*UR*, 2 Oct. 1913. The company museum contained a framed photograph of "Old Joe," the camel, with an attendant.

91. To Ambrose H. Burroughs, 26 Apr. 1913—file 720, secretary's dept., RJR.

92. Kremer and Strasser to R. J. R. Tob. Co., New York, 3 July 1913—ibid.

93. Burton Craige to Ambrose H. Burroughs, 25 July 1913—ibid.

94. Ambrose H. Burroughs to Burton Craige, New York, 26 July 1913—ibid.

95. Burton Craige to Arthur S. Brown, Wash., D.C., 11, 17 Nov. 1913; Thomas B. Gilbert to R. J. R. Tob. Co., Philadelphia, Pa., 3 Dec. 1913—all in ibid.

96. Burton Craige to Arthur S. Brown, 12 Dec. 1913—ibid.

97. B. R. McFadden to R. J. R. Tob. Co., Cleveland, Ohio, 13, 19 Dec. 1913; Burton Craige to B. R. McFadden, 16 Dec. 1913; Salvatore Ragona to Burton Craige, New York, 15, 22, 26 Dec. 1913—all in ibid.

98. Salvatore Ragona to Burton Craige, New York, 22 Dec. 1913—ibid.

99. Telegrams; Burton Craige to R. J. R. Tob. Co., Philadelphia, Pa., 27 Dec. 1913—all in ibid. This file contains the actual assignment to the R. J. Reynolds Tobacco Company of all claims to the Red Kamel by the Turco-Russian Cigarette Co. and by its proprietors (J. and B. Friedberg and S. Cohen), Philadelphia, Pa., 29 Jan. 1914.

100. Richard L. Dunstan to Haddon S. Kirk, 24 Feb. 1939—box 696C, Records Center, RJR.

101. Percy R. Masten to C. L. Waller (division manager at Mobile, Ala.), 2 Nov. 1914—sales dept., RJR.

102. Bowman Gray, Sr., to F. C. Moore, 19 Aug. 1913—ibid.

103. R. J. R. Tob. Co. to division managers, filed with material dated 12, 25, 28 Sept., 11 Nov. 1914—ibid. Note price list for 20 Aug. 1914 for cork tips.

104. Richard L. Dunstan to Haddon S. Kirk, 24 Feb. 1939—box 696C, Records Center, RJR.

105. Reyno price list, 1 Sept. 1913; Percy R. Masten to Artemus D. Porcher, 4 Oct. 1913—sales dept., RJR.

106. B-1 to division managers, 27 Oct. 1913—ibid.

107. R. E. Johnson to division managers to be given to salesmen, 28 Oct. 1913; Percy R. Masten to division managers, 7 Nov. 1913; Percy R. Masten to A. F. Madison, 7 Nov. 1913; B. C. (?) to T. P. Ledbetter, 5 Dec. 1913; unsigned letter to division managers, 13 Dec. 1913—all in ibid. The story of Reynos and John W. Alspaugh came from Bowman Gray, Jr.—interview with author, 30 Apr. 1963.

108. R. J. R. Tob. Co. to division managers, 23 May 1914; Percy R. Masten to John W. Alspaugh, 3 Sept. 1914—sales dept., RJR.

109. R. J. R. Tob. Co. to division managers, 19 Sept., 2 Oct. 1914—ibid.

110. Price lists for 1928 show the Reyno but it is absent from the list for

1931—lists in comptroller's office and sales dept., RJR. No price lists for 1929 and 1930 appeared to be available.

111. Recapitulation of Cigarettes Shipped Each Year—cost records, comptroller's dept., RJR.

112. *Am. Tob. Co. et al. v. U.S., Record on Appeal*, transcripts, 7: 5221–23.

113. Watkins, *The 100 Greatest Advertisements*, pp. 26–27; Ralph M. Hower, *The History of an Advertising Agency: N. W. Ayer & Son at Work, 1869–1949* (Cambridge, 1949), pp. 308, 313. Watkins failed to describe the first advertisement. A statement by Bowman Gray, Sr., in 1931 lends credence to Watkins's account: "Camels will not be disconcerted by the advance of a competitor so long as advertising is mainly responsible for it; but when a cigarette moves up without a maximum of advertising we will take serious notice"—"Camels of Winston-Salem," *Fortune*, Jan. 1931, p. 55.

114. *United States Tobacco Journal*, 5 Dec. 1914.

115. Camel Scrapbook: Newspapers, vol. I, 1914–16—advertising dept., RJR.

116. *Tob.*, 4 Feb. 1915; *WTJ*, 8 Feb. 1915; *Printer's Ink*, 18 Feb. 1915; *Saturday Evening Post*, 3 Apr. 1915—all in Camel Scrapbook: Newspapers, vol. I, 1914–16, advertising dept., RJR.

117. Based on the following: Camel Scrapbook: Magazines, vols. I (1916–17), II (1919), III (1920), IV (1920–23); Newspapers, vols. I (1914–16), II (1919), III (1920), IV (1921)—advertising dept., RJR.

118. Camel Scrapbook: Newspapers, vol. I, 1914–16. Camel Scrapbook: Magazines, vol. I (1916–17) shows repeated versions of this advertisement in various trade journals—ibid.

119. In Correspondence of Walter R. Reynolds. For reproductions of the wording see, for example, Camel Scrapbook: Magazines, vol. I (1916–17)—advertising dept., RJR, and *Tob.*, 5 Apr. 1917, p. 19.

120. There are five different bills of different dates entitled "Papers from Pinkerton Detective Agency re. Injurious Rumors"—file 1113, secretary's dept., RJR. Note also Minutes, vol. IV, pp. 3, 28.

121. In Correspondence of Walter R. Reynolds. Billings regretted that he had not written earlier.

122. Roy C. Haberkern, interview with author, 29 Sept. 1960.

123. James P. Wood, *The Story of Advertising* (New York, 1958), p. 373.

124. Typed Memoirs of William T. Smither—advertising dept., RJR. See no. NA 1921, Camel Scrapbook: Newspapers, vol. IV, for the earliest use of the slogan in advertising other than on billboards. Wood in *The Story of Advertising* (p. 268) credits the origin to the remark of a stranger to a billboard worker. Some credit Theodore Cramer, a copywriter of N. W. Ayer and Son, though it seems likely that he only adapted Reddington's billboard slogan for use in newspaper and magazine advertising. As of 1960 Mrs. Annette Reddington Fennell owned the original of the poster that her father painted—Mrs. Fennell to author, New York, N.Y., 31 Oct. 1960.

125. *Am. Tob. Co. v. U.S., Record on Appeal*, transcripts, 6: 4338, 4746–50.

126. Framed certificates signed by A. D. Watts, Collector of Internal Revenue for the Fifth District, Statesville, N.C.—RJR museum.

Chapter 8
Effects of Expansion on Leaf Handling and Labor

1. Personnel Book, leaf dept., RJR. At one point Blackwell served as the company's legal representative in Kentucky—Minutes, vol. II, p. 232.

2. Tilley, pp. 234–36.

3. See, for example, *TCS*, 24 Nov. 1909.

4. Minutes of Winston Board of Trade, 1889–1922, for 8 Oct. and 5 Dec. 1890. For activities of the Farmers' Alliance in the Old Bright Belt, see Tilley, pp. 405–21.

5. *UR*, 17 Oct. 1912. For the Farmers' Union's establishment of cooperative sales houses, see Tilley, pp. 445–48.

6. *UR*, 20 June 1912.

7. Reavis Cox, *Competition in the American Tobacco Industry, 1911–1932* (New York, 1933), p. 173. For accounts of large sales of Burley leaf by the Burley Tobacco Growers' Cooperative Association to the R. J. R. Tob. Co., see *Tob.*, 23 Feb. (p. 3), 12 Oct. (p. 3), 23 Nov. (p. 27), 14 Dec. (p. 3) 1922, 18 Jan. 1923 (p. 3); *UR*, 26 Oct. 1922.

8. Note Tilley, pp. 449–86, for a survey of this association.

9. For profits of the three companies see *Am. Tob. Co. et al. v. U.S., Record on Appeal*, docket no. 9137–9139 (6th Cir., 1944), exhibits, 5: 2507.

10. Minutes of Executive Committee of Board of Directors, Tri-State Tobacco Growers' Cooperative Association—box 3 of the association's Papers, N.C. Division of Archives and History, Raleigh.

11. *Tri-State Tobacco Grower*, Mar. 1926. See also ibid., Dec. 1922, for a picture of Richard R. Patterson, manager of the association's leaf department, holding a check for $1,127,443.06 paid by the R. J. Reynolds Tobacco Company. This check was given wide publicity. A complete file of *Tri-State Tobacco Grower*, possibly the only one in existence, is preserved in box 100 of the association's Papers, N.C. Division of Archives and History, Raleigh.

12. William N. Reynolds to Richard R. Patterson, 26 Apr. 1924—box 22, Papers of Tri-State Tobacco Growers' Cooperative Association. This collection contains considerable correspondence between the association and the R. J. Reynolds Tobacco Company.

13. William N. Reynolds, interview with Dell McKeithan, 30 May 1951—personnel dept., RJR. Double sales began on the Danville market by 1892 (Tilley, p. 232) and no doubt soon afterward in Winston. For a brief account of Eaton's record see *WSJ*, 19 Sept. 1937. According to the recollection of Sam Mitchell, John Simpson succeeded Eaton as head buyer perhaps in the Virginia-Carolina area—Sam Mitchell, interview with Dell McKeithan, 17 July 1950, personnel dept., RJR.

14. Spencer B. Hanes, Jr., interview with author, 2 Feb. 1962; *J&S*, 18 Sept. 1960.

15. Minutes, vol. I, pp. 70, 73, 116–17, 119; *UR*, 5, 12 Apr., 19 July 1900. Apparently Rice Gwynn, long head buyer in Danville, assumed leadership on that market where Eugene Hester managed the redrying—Notes of Roy C. Haberkern on the Camel Cigarette, 26 Feb. 1947, personnel dept., RJR; *UR*, 8

Aug. 1918. By one account Reynolds had "several buyers" and "one of the largest leaf factories in Danville" in 1897 (*Southern Tobacconist and Manufacturers' Record*, 16 Nov. 1897), although it is doubtful that this leaf factory was more than a rehandling plant where tobacco purchased in Danville was readied for shipment to Winston.

16. Minutes, vol. I, pp. 116, 159–60, 189, 207–9.

17. Ibid., p. 210.

18. *UR*, 14 June 1906.

19. Ibid., 4 Apr., 6 June 1907; Minutes, vol. I, p. 316.

20. Minutes, vol. I, p. 189; *STJ*, 13 June 1910. In 1910 it was known as the Tenth Street Prizery—M. M. Whedbee to R. J. R. Tob. Co., New York, 21 Nov. 1905, Correspondence of Walter R. Reynolds, purchasing dept., RJR. In 1920 the company purchased land at Byrd and Tenth streets along with two factories and other buildings—contract: Atlantic Land and Improvements Co. and R. J. R. Tob. Co., 4 May 1920, file 1500, secretary's dept., RJR.

21. *UR*, 10 Mar., 14 Apr. 1910.

22. Minutes, vol. II, pp. 88, 92. Note also *STJ*, 10 Apr. 1911, for plans of what appears to have been yet another storage warehouse—264 by 140 feet—near the Norfolk and Western Railway.

23. *Tob.*, 18 Aug. 1910, p. 4; *STJ*, 10 Feb. 1913, 2 July 1914; *UR*, 9, 16 June 1910, 2 July 1914; contract: Southern Bell Telephone and Telegraph Co. with R. J. R. Tob. Co., 28 Oct. 1912—file 588, secretary's dept., RJR.

24. *WSJ*, 8 July 1915, 14 June 1916; Joseph M. Parrish, interview with Dell McKeithan and Erwin W. Cook, 4 Aug. 1950—personnel dept., RJR; contract: Southern Railway Co. with R. J. R. Co., 15 Jan. 1922—file 1575, secretary's dept., RJR; *TCS*, 19 July 1919 (Ziglar sheds). Tiretown is so called because of an effort to manufacture automobile tires there during World War I . Note esp. *TCS*, 10, 17 May 1919, for accounts of the Hanes Rubber Co. and its model village. In 1921 the Reynolds company purchased fifty-nine acres "just above the Hanes Rubber Company"—*UR*, 25 Aug. 1921; Minutes, vol. IV, p. 278.

25. J. S. Cobb to Walter R. Reynolds, Durham, N.C., 8 May 1916—Correspondence of Walter R. Reynolds.

26. *WSJ*, 8 July 1915.

27. Ibid., 29 Apr. 1917. See also *OD*, no. 7 [Feb. 1917?].

28. Minutes of Danville Tobacco Association, vol. IV, pp. 25–26, 33–34, 51—Office of Danville Tobacco Association, Danville, Va.

29. Contract: W. K. Anderson and R. J. R. Tob. Co., 6 Sept. 1918—file 1269, secretary's dept., RJR.

30. In *STJ*, 3 June 1913.

31. *Tob.*, 1 Jan. 1920, p. 28. Note also a proposal to buy a Proctor dryer for the Louisville plant on 28 Feb. 1920—file 1434, secretary's dept., RJR.

32. *WSJ*, 27 Feb. 1920.

33. Report of Committee on Stock List, N.Y. Stock Exchange, 15 Mar. 1922—box 1236C, Records Center, RJR. Data compiled from Trial Balances for 1917 (box 281C, Records Center) by the leaf-processing dept. reveal fifteen redrying plants, thirty-nine storage houses in Winston-Salem, and sixty-six storage houses in other towns. These trial balances carry no names of towns, nor do the

data compiled from them by the leaf-processing dept. agree with those given in the Report of Committee on Stock List.

34. Purchases and Prices of Leaf *as Made*—box 1579C, Records Center, RJR.

35. Trial Balances for 1917—box 281C, Records Center, RJR.

36. Edgar E. Bumgardner, interview with author, 2 Feb. 1962.

37. Minutes, vol. II, p. 376.

38. Ibid., vol. I, pp. 179, 208–9.

39. *UR*, 27 Apr. 1916.

40. Contract: R. J. R. Tob. Co. with the Garford Co., 29 Aug. 1913, with Reynolds's attached order of 27 June 1913—file 644, secretary's dept., RJR; H. Floyd Hauser, interview with Dell McKeithan and Erwin W. Cook, 11 July 1950—personnel dept., RJR; *TCS*, 21 Nov. 1959. Reynolds, a motoring enthusiast, had owned a chain-driven automobile as early as 1910 when he chugged through the Sandy Ridge section of Stokes Couny, astonishing the inhabitants—Arthur Shelton in *WSJ*, 21 Feb. 1951.

41. *MIB* 3, no. 24, 20 July 1951; *WSJ*, 20 July 1951; *MB* 5, no. 15, 16 Apr. 1953; Edgar E. Bumgardner, interview with author, 29 Jan. 1960.

42. Walter R. Reynolds to H. W. Vanderpoll, 5 June 1919; Walter R. Reynolds to James Matthews, 12 June 1919—both in Correspondence of Walter R. Reynolds; notes on the career of William J. Conrad, Jr.—courtesy of Louise Peterson, a former assistant secretary of the Reynolds company. Incidentally, William Conrad's task, a trying one, became necessary when quantities of Prince Albert fell into the hands of speculators who were sending it back to the United States, affixing revenue stamps, and selling it as a fresh product notwithstanding its damaged condition. This assignment indicated extreme confidence in young Conrad, who found the tobacco in Germany, Belgium, France, and, to his surprise, 26,000 cases in Spain. Farrish, by his marriage to Lil Bitting, was connected to the Whitaker family—*TCS*, 9 Sept. 1916.

43. Agreement: Standard Commercial Tobacco Co. with R. J. R. Tob. Co., 30 Jan. 1924—file 1712, secretary's dept., RJR.

44. Agreement: P. Lorillard Co. and R. J. R. Tob. Co. with Glenn Tob. Co. and Alston Tob. Co., 19 June 1923—file 1678, secretary's dept., RJR; S. Clay Williams to J. M. B. Hoxsey, 8 Mar. 1928, and press release of R. J. R. Tob. Co., 11 Apr. 1946—box 1236C, Records Center, RJR. For general information on Turkish-type leaf see Frederick A. Wolf, *Aromatic or Oriental Tobaccos* (Durham, N.C., 1962).

45. On 31 Dec. 1940, for example, the company held in bond, duty paid, Turkish-type leaf as follows by origin and storage plus 12,369 pounds allowed for shrinkage: Macedonia (8,647,699 lbs.), Smyrna (14,333,595 lbs.), Sukhum (1,911,811 lbs.), Latakia (10,508 lbs.), German lots (345,022 lbs.), Class 8 warehouse (546,735 lbs.), and blending room (534,043 lbs.)—a total of 26,329,413 pounds. Sukhum is a district surrounding the city of Sukhumi in the southern area of the USSR more than a hundred miles north of the Turkish border on the Black Sea where the Samsun type of Turkish leaf is produced—Wolf, *Aromatic or Oriental Tobaccos*, p. 100. "German lots" were merely the amounts purchased from German dealers in the Near East. In 1940–41 more than 2,000,000 pounds were lost on the SS *Petalli*. Turkish-type leaf is shipped

one year after its purchase in order to allow for additional drying in preparation for the sea voyage. This small leaf, not stemmed or redried as are domestic variations, also requires a different type of storage house with racks to permit further drying. (Information also drawn from Trial Balance, 31 Dec. 1940—box 282C, Records Center, RJR; L. G. Travis, leaf-processing dept., 16 Feb. 1962.)

46. *WSJ*, 8 May 1921.

47. Ibid., 17, 18 Aug. 1921. Prices of flue-cured or Bright leaf for farmers declined more than 50 percent in 1920—Tilley, pp. 356–57.

48. *WSJ*, 19, 20 Aug., 5 Oct. 1921.

49. Reynolds's exact words are supposed to have been: "I think it is a fine thing. The income tax is the fairest tax that can be levied. If I don't have it, I don't have to pay it. If I've got it, I don't mind paying it"—*J&S*, 14 May 1950. Santford Martin, Jr., recalled hearing this story from his father many times— Santford Martin, Jr., to author, Wash. D.C., 22 Aug. 1963. Josephus Daniels (*The Wilson Era: Years of War and After, 1917–23* [Chapel Hill, 1946], p. 238) declared that Reynolds was determined to charge the government for tobacco sold the United States Navy at the excessively high rates permitted by a group of tobacconists for sales to the army during World War I.

50. Henry S. Stokes, interview with author, 4 Apr. 1960.

51. Jesse S. Davis, interview with author, 3 June 1960; *MB* 6, no. 36, 1 Oct. 1954. Lee R. Salmons, of the leaf-processing dept., in a typed account entitled "History and Development of the Leaf Stemming and Blending Process at the R. J. Reynolds Tobacco Company," p. 23, gives 13 July 1953 as the date for the discontinuance of the last hand stemmery at Number 43. This sketch, compiled from verbal accounts of old employees and plant records, was in the possession of Mr. Salmons, leaf-processing dept., RJR, as of 1963.

52. Burton Craige to Edward N. Rich, 21 Feb. 1914—file 757, secretary's dept., RJR. Of the 285 employees in the Strater branch in Louisville, Ky., on 25 Sept. 1928, 107 were stemmers. Names and addresses of employees in the Strater plant were in the possession of Walter E. Gladstone, R. F. D. 2, East Bend, N.C.

53. *RCCTI*, 1: 268.

54. Contracts: R. J. R. Tob. Co. with Virginia-Carolina Chemical Co., 16 Dec. 1912, and with Tobacco By-Products and Chemical Corp., 24 Apr. 1924— files 645, 1726, secretary's dept., RJR; Tilley, pp. 356–57.

55. Burton Craige to Edward N. Rich, 21 Feb. 1914—file 757, secretary's dept., RJR.

56. Richard H. Wright to Clark Dulaney, Durham, N.C., 18 Nov. 1913— Papers of Richard H. Wright, Flowers Collection, Duke University Library, Durham, N.C.

57. *RCCTI*, 1: 267, 277.

58. Contract: Peter P. Shouse and R. J. R. Tob. Co. under contract to Briggs-Shaffner, 14 July 1909—files 420, 421, secretary's dept., RJR.

59. Louis Fischer to Richard H. Wright, 19 Jan. 1912—Papers of Richard H. Wright.

60. Walter R. Reynolds to Richard H. Wright, 13 May 1913; Richard H. Wright to R. J. Reynolds, Durham, N.C., 27 Apr., 1, 18 May 1912; R. J. Reyn-

olds to Richard H. Wright, 30 Apr. 1912—all in Papers of Richard H. Wright. Scovill's machine evidently fell into the hands of the successor to the Standard Tobacco Stemmer Company—*WTJ*, 28 July 1913, p. 2.

61. Contract: Continental Tob. Stemming Co. (merged with Tob. Stemming Machine Co.) and R. J. R. Tob. Co., 7 July 1913; Twenty-Six Day Experiment with Billings Stemmers, 9 Dec. 1913–31 Jan. 1914; Edward N. Rich to Burton Craige, Baltimore, Md., 13 Feb. 1914; Burton Craige to Edward N. Rich, 21 Feb. 1914—all in file 757, secretary's dept., RJR.

62. Edward N. Rich to Burton Craige, Baltimore, Md., 13 Feb. 1914—ibid.

63. Charles I. James to R. J. R. Tob. Co., Baltimore, Md., 27 Feb. 1914—ibid.

64. Charles I. James to R. J. Reynolds, Baltimore, Md., 24 Nov. 1914; B. E. Williams to Harry H. Shelton, Lynchburg, Va., 1 Oct. 1920—both in file 516-D, box 1243, Records Center, RJR.

65. Harry H. Shelton to Ambrose H. Burroughs, 27 Oct. 1920; Ambrose H. Burroughs to Burton Craige, New York, 11 Mar. 1915; Rufus L. Patterson (president, Standard Tob. Stemmer Co.) to R. J. Reynolds, New York, 11 May 1914; Burton Craige to Arthur S. Brown (partner of Burroughs), 8 Dec. 1914—all in ibid. See also Minutes, vol. III, pp. 64–65.

66. Letters Patent for Richter Tob. Stemming Machine transferred to R. J. R. Tob. Co., 20 July 1920—file 1361, secretary's dept., RJR. The administrator made the transfer.

67. Agreement: Thomas E. Pasley and George W. Agee with R. J. R. Tob. Co., 19 Nov. 1929; S. C. Markley (president, Comas Cigarette Machine Co. of Salem, Va.) to Leaf Dept. of R. J. R. Tob. Co., 22 June 1931—both in file 1998, secretary's dept., RJR. According to the city directory, in 1921 Agee was a coal dealer in Winston-Salem.

68. Salmons, "History and Development of the Leaf Stemming and Blending Process at the R. J. Reynolds Tobacco Company."

69. Ibid., pp. 1–9; memorandums of agreement: Wachovia Bank and Trust Co. (administrator of estate of Hans F. Richter) and Mrs. Hans F. Richter with R. J. R. Tob. Co., 8 Sept. 1924, and Hans F. Richter and R. J. R. Tob. Co., 8 Nov. 1912—file 2514, secretary's dept., RJR.

70. Roy C. Haberkern, interview with author, 26 Nov. 1961.

71. Noah E. Hartley, interview with Dell McKeithan and Erwin W. Cook, 11 July 1950—personnel dept., RJR; *WSJ*. 17 Sept. 1951.

72. *WSJ*, 10 Dec. 1916.

73. Ibid., 7 Oct. 1916.

74. Ibid., 7 Dec. 1916, 24 Jan., 26 Apr. 1917.

75. Archibald Henderson et al., *North Carolina: The Old North State and the New*, 5 vols. (Chicago, 1941), 3: 428–29.

76. *WSJ*, 1, 3 Oct. 1916. The bitterness of the campaign no doubt resulted from the fact that Holton was thrown out of his position as United States District Attorney through partisan politics. In the contest Holton had written the Department of Justice that he would not resign. Thereupon senators Simmons and Overman from North Carolina conferred with Attorney General James C. McReynolds to lay plans for removing "obstinate officials"—ibid., 11 Nov.

1913. Continuing on his campaign theme, Holton aroused considerable bitterness, as manifested in *TCS*, 28, 29 Aug., 6, 11 Sept., 2, 19, 20, 24, 26 Oct. 1916.

77. *WSJ*, 17 Oct. 1916. Because in 1915 Reynolds's average weekly wages, including those of subforemen, amounted to $6.01, Holton obviously exaggerated to some extent. Although denied by Liggett and Myers, a rumor had persisted as far back as 1912 that this company intended to establish a large branch in Winston-Salem—*TCS*, 29 July 1912. Prices received by tobacco farmers in 1916 were unusually high.

78. *WSJ*, 20 Oct. 1916.

79. Ibid., 21 Oct. 1916.

80. Ibid., 29 Oct. 1916.

81. *UR*, 9 Nov. 1916. Note also ibid., 19, 21, 26 Oct., 2 Nov. 1916, for reprintings of letters and other items referred to in this discussion.

82. *Compilation of the General Ordinances and Charter of the City of Winston-Salem, North Carolina*, comp. Philip Williams (Winston-Salem, 1916), sec. 64, subsec. E (p. 18), sec. 725, subsec. 2 (p. 272); *Revisal of North Carolina*, comp. Geo. P. Pell, 2 vols. (Charleston, S.C., 1908), 2 (ch. 110, sec. 5180): 2473. Italics mine. Under this ordinance, in Nov. 1917 Russell Wimbish was fined $500 and the costs in municipal court for merely telling some of his Negro friends about the need for cooks at Camp Meade. Wimbish had no license. *TCS*, 3 Nov. 1917.

83. Minutes, vol. IV, pp. 45–46.

84. Ibid., p. 79.

85. Foster Rhea Dulles, *Labor in America: A History* (New York, 1949), p. 228.

86. John Needham, interview with Dell McKeithan and Erwin W. Cook, 31 Oct. 1951—personnel dept., RJR.

87. Edgar E. Bumgardner, interview with author, 27 Oct., 7 Dec. 1959. Note Robert S. Smith, *Mill on the Dan: A History of Dan River Mills, 1882–1950* (Durham, N.C., 1960), pp. 104–5, for similar conditions in Stokes County and other areas near Winston-Salem.

88. Records of employment dept.—in possession of the late John C. Whitaker as of 1959.

89. John C. Whitaker, interview with author, 27 Oct. 1959; Ed Blakely, interview with Dell McKeithan, 2 June 1950—personnel dept., RJR.

90. Cora R. Brewer: interview with Dell McKeithan, 17 July 1950, and personnel folder, Records Center, RJR.

91. Robert E. Lasater to "Mr. Walker," 8 Jan. 1912—Correspondence of Walter R. Reynolds.

92. T. J. Noble, Jr., to Walter R. Reynolds, Richmond, Va., 23 June 1914—ibid.

93. Walter R. Reynolds to T. J. Noble, Jr., 25 June 1914—ibid.

94. Edward N. Rich to R. J. R. Tob. Co., Baltimore, Md., 3 Mar. 1914—file 757, secretary's dept., RJR.

95. Ed Blakely, interview with Dell McKeithan, 2 June 1950—personnel dept., RJR.

96. John C. Reich, interview with Dell McKeithan, 31 Aug. 1950—ibid.

97. Petition of Strait Twist Makers to R. J. R. Reynolds Tob. Co.—Correspondence of Walter R. Reynolds. The three-ply twist involved a slightly more intricate process than the two-ply twist.

98. *UR*, 6 Aug. 1914.

99. The increase shown in Table 8-7 is approximately the same as that shown from 1915 to 1925 in Table 8-8.

100. Smith, *Mill on the Dan*, pp. 133, 283.

101. *Economic Almanac for 1946–47*, National Industrial Conference Board (New York, 1946), pp. 276–77. See also Paul H. Douglas, *Real Wages in the United States, 1890–1926* (Boston, 1930), pp. 305–6.

102. *TCS*, 29 Jan., 26 Dec. 1916.

103. *WSJ*, 27 Dec. 1916.

104. For the second bonus plan see *Tob.*, 18 Jan. 1917, p. 4. For the distribution under the plan see *TCS*, 22 Dec. 1917.

105. Edgar E. Bumgardner, interview with author, 10 Apr. 1962.

106. Minutes, vol. IV, p. 122; Robert E. Lasater to John C. Whitaker, 19 Apr. 1918—in possession of the late John C. Whitaker as of 1959.

107. Minutes, vols. III (pp. 115–16), IV (pp. 1–2, 27); *WSJ*, 8 Sept. 1918.

108. Richmond, Va., 11 Jan. 1918—Correspondence of Walter R. Reynolds.

109. *Tob.*, 28 Feb. 1918, p. 24. McAndrews, a native of Cincinnati, served as an official in TWIU-AFL as early as 1899 and became its president in 1908, remaining in that office at least until 1919—*WTJ*, 1 May 1899 (p. 5), 17 Feb. 1908 (p. 12), 13 Oct. 1919 (p. 4).

110. *UR*, 27 Mar., 24 Apr. 1919; *TCS*, 24, 25 Mar. 1919. In an account of labor in North Carolina, Chester Davis mistakenly calls Brown, John Brown—*J&S*, 3 Sept. 1950.

111. *UR*, 8 May, 3 July 1919.

112. *TCS*, 23, 26 Sept., 16 Oct., 31 Dec. 1919.

113. Ibid., 13, 14 June, 11, 30 Aug., 6, 15, 16, 18, 22 Sept. 1919.

114. I. W. England to Robert E. Lasater, Passaic, N.J., 14 Jan. 1919—Correspondence of Walter R. Reynolds. Reynolds purchased metal signs from the Passaic Metal Ware Co. as early as 1915—contract: R. J. R. Tob. Co. with Passaic Metal Ware Co., 22 Apr. 1915, file 853, secretary's dept., RJR. The company also sought aid from Lee Welling Squier, whose letterhead carried his specialty: "Industrial Cooperation on Scientific Lines"—L. W. Squier to R. J. R. Tob. Co., Philadelphia, Pa., 1 Dec. 1919—file 603, box 1237C, Records Center, RJR.

115. George E. Hanes to Walter R. Reynolds, Wash., D.C., 18 June 1919—Correspondence of Walter R. Reynolds.

116. In files of personnel dept. Except for a few changes in capitalization, this plan was reproduced verbatim in *TCS*, 20 June 1919, and in *WSJ*, 20 June 1919. Note also *UR*, 26 June 1919; *Tob.*, 26 June 1919, p. 6.

117. Carr's plan involved Industrial Democarcy as proposed by John Leitch in his nostrum for solving industrial friction by the organization of legislative bodies modeled on the federal Constitution. Carr died before results could be obtained—*TCS*, 18 June 1919; W. K. Boyd, *The Story of Durham: City of the New South* (Durham, N.C., 1927), pp. 131–35; John Leitch, *Man to Man: The Story of Industrial Democracy* (New York, 1919), passim, esp. chap. 7, pp. 133–68. In

nearby Danville, Industrial Democracy, introduced in Riverside and Dan River Mills in 1919, functioned only until 1930—Smith, *Mill on the Dan*, pp. 262–76, 306–7, 310. Harold U. Faulkner, a noted economic historian, regards "Industrial Democracy" as a grandiose term and John Leitch, its leading proponent, as something of a fake. Few such plans appeared before 1917 and they, as well as the ones that came later, merely permitted the formation of company unions "initiated, nursed, protected and financed by the employers." He also describes the plan introduced by John D. Rockefeller, Jr., in 1915 as the one receiving the greatest publicity—*The Decline of Laissez-Faire, 1897–1917*, vol. 7 of *Economic History of the United States* (New York, 1959), pp. 273–74. Winston-Salem newspapers were not the only ones in North Carolina to be impressed with Leitch's high-sounding terms. See, for example, an editorial in *N&O*, 20 June 1919.

118. Minutes of meeting of foremen of the R. J. R. Tob. Co. in dining room of Factory No. 4, 17 June 1919 (15 typed pages)—file 603, box 1237C, Records Center, RJR. In this same file is a copy of a letter of the company to Professor Simon Green Atkins (11 June 1863–28 June 1934) urging him, as an associate member of the Negro Ministerial Association and one interested in the welfare of his race, to use the "enclosed copies" of the cooperative, waste-saving, and profit-sharing plan to further that association's understanding.

119. *TCS*, 21 June 1919; notice to factory employees headed "Attention all Factory Employees," 20 June 1919—personnel dept., RJR. The subhead read "Notice of Allotment of Employee Representatives to be Elected to the Factory Council, June 20, 1919."

120. Edgar E. Bumgardner, interview with author, 2 Mar. 1962.

121. *UR*, 3 July 1919.

122. *TCS*, 12 July 1919. Note also *UR*, 17 July 1919, for the same account except that Walter R. Reynolds made the proposal for the company.

123. Printed circular: William N. Reynolds to all factory employees, 16 July 1919—personnel dept., RJR.

124. *TCS*, 3 Aug. 1919.

125. Ibid., 1, 2 (quotation) Sept. 1919.

126. Notice to all factory employees at Winston-Salem, 4 Aug. 1919—personnel dept., RJR.

127. Poster dated 1 Apr. 1920; contract with TWIU-AFL: locals 145, 146, 147, 148, 151, and 152, 1 Apr. 1920—file 1441, secretary's dept., RJR. The contract was signed by W. H. Strowd for Local 145, Frank H. Martin for 146, R. L. Coles for 147, Sam Nelson for 148, Coley Cureton for 151, and Wade Bitting for 152; by S. Clay Williams for the Reynolds company; and by A. McAndrews, E. Lewis Want, George L. Allen, John F. Allen, R. E. Clodfelter, and J. B. Murphy for the TWIU-AFL committee. Seemingly the union had requested an increase of 20 percent in wages, but, when it was shown that Reynolds was already paying more than any other large tobacco company, President Anthony McAndrews advised the locals to accept the contract and be satisfied. This they promptly did. *Tob.*, 15 Apr. 1920, p. 33. Note also copies of the contract in *TCS*, 4 Aug. 1919, and *UR*, 7 Aug. 1919.

128. *WSJ*, 11 Mar. 1919.

129. Robert E. Lasater, interview with Dell McKeithan (?), 2 Feb. 1951; Minutes, vol. IV, p. 161. News of this proposed purchase became public in late Aug. 1919—*WTJ*, 25 Aug. 1919, p. 1.

130. Noah E. Hartley, interview with Dell McKeithan and Erwin W. Cook, 11 July 1950; Edgar E. Bumgardner, interview with author, 2 Mar. 1962.

131. Report of Risdon P. Reece, 22 Dec. 1950—personnel dept., RJR. Number 60 was the first reinforced concrete building designed, built, and equipped by the engineering and construction dept.

132. Sam Mitchell, interview with Dell McKeithan, 17 July 1950—personnel dept., RJR; Minutes, vol. V, pp. 202–3; S. Clay Williams to Committee on Stock Exchange, 20 Aug. 1927—box 1236C, Records Center, RJR; William J. Conrad, Jr., interview with author, 26 Apr. 1960; *Tob.*, 26 May 1927 (p. 62), 21 July 1927 (pp. 14, 23).

133. *Tob.*, 18 Aug. 1910 (p. 4), 22 Apr. 1920 (p. 8—rumor of cigarette plant), 19 May 1927 (p. 21), 26 May 1927 (p. 62); *WSJ*, 11 May 1920; R. J. R. Tob. Co. to American Surety Co., 1 Apr. 1920, 24 May 1927—file 1822, secretary's dept., RJR.

134. Edgar H. Harwood, interview with author, 11 Oct. 1960.

135. *WTJ*, 22 Dec. 1919, p. 3 (quotation). See also ibid., 26 June 1893 (p. 10), 1 June 1908 (p. 2), 7 July 1919 (p. 4), 22 Sept. 1919 (p. 14).

136. Deeds and other papers concerning the purchase of Strater Brothers from the Burley Tobacco Company—files 1351, 1495, secretary's dept., RJR.

137. *Tob.*, 29 Nov. 1928, p. 48. Actually the Strater plant employed 285 people as of 25 Sept. 1928—names and addresses of employees in Strater plant were in the possession of Walter E. Gladstone, R.F.D. 2, East Bend, N.C.

138. Testimony of Edward H. Thurston, vice-president of Liggett and Myers, in *Am. Tob. Co. et al. v. U.S., Record on Appeal*, transcripts, 6: 4512–13. William J. Conrad, Jr., recalled Walter Reynolds's statement that Strater Brothers had to be sold because the strength of their brands had killed off many chewers—William J. Conrad, Jr., interview with author, 31 Aug. 1960.

139. Bowman Gray, Jr., (tape-recorded) interview with Dudley Doust, 18 Mar. 1960; Edgar E. Bumgardner (21 Feb. 1962), Roy C. Haberkern (29 Oct. 1961, 18 May 1962) and William J. Conrad, Jr. (12 Mar. 1962), interviews with author.

140. Roy C. Haberkern (18 May 1962) and Edgar E. Bumgardner (2 Mar. 1962), interviews with author. Both Haberkern and Bumgardner declared that labor was the key to the moves.

141. Clement Manly advised the adoption of this policy.

142. Memorandum of Edgar E. Bumgardner, 15 Sept. 1959.

143. *UR*, 27 Aug. 1914.

144. Contract: Arctic Ice Machine Co. (of Canton, Ohio), with R. J. R. Tob. Co., 10 Aug. 1916—file 1064, secretary's dept., RJR.

145. *UR*, 29 Apr. 1915; *WSJ* in *STJ*, 23 Feb. 1915.

146. *UR*, 25 Feb. 1915.

147. *WSJ*, 30 July 1915.

148. *UR*, 19 Aug. 1915.

149. Richard J. Reynolds, Jr., to author, Ettlingen, Germany, 8 Oct. 1962.

150. Goldston H. Dalton, interview with author, 25 Feb. 1960; Edward G. Blakely, interview with Dell McKeithan and Erwin W. Cook, 2 June 1950—personnel dept., RJR; personnel folder of Samuel S. Stanley—Records Center, RJR. Four lunchrooms were open by June 1916—*TCS*, 3 June 1916.

151. *WSJ*, 28 Apr. 1915.

152. J. W. Lambeth to Walter R. Reynolds, Thomasville, N.C., 16 Aug. 1918; Walter R. Reynolds to J. W. Lambeth, 22 Aug. 1918—Correspondence of Walter R. Reynolds.

153. *MB*: 9, 1957: no. 23 (29 Apr.), no. 43 (9 Aug.), no. 66 (20 Dec.); 10, no. 3 (17 Jan. 1958).

154. *WSJ*, 25 Sept. 1915.

155. Mrs. J. E. (Lenora H.) Sills to Robert E. Lasater, 27 Feb. 1919—Correspondence of Walter R. Reynolds. One account (*WSJ* in *Tob.*, 28 Dec. 1916, p. 7) states that the Negro day nursery, which provided for twenty-five children, was partly financed by "the tobacco manufacturers." By December, according to a report of Mrs. Sills, "an operating corner" at the nursery was equipped in preparation for treating "students of the schools at prices anyone can pay. The colored people are taking hold of this work with an intelligence and earnestness that means permanent progress"—*WSJ*, 9 Dec. 1915.

156. *WSJ* in *Tob.*, 28 Dec. 1916, p. 7.

157. Edgar E. Bumgardner, interview with author, 2 Mar. 1919; personnel folder of Louella Suggs Burns—Records Center, RJR. Possibly this day nursery was begun by the medical dept.—*TCS*, 2 Sept. 1922.

158. *WSJ*, 29 July (R. J. Reynolds), 30 July (Mrs. Sills) 1915.

159. *WSJ*, 1 Apr. and 2 July (Mrs. Sills), 4 June (death rate) 1915. Incidentally, Lenora Sills became the first sanitary inspector for Winston-Salem (ibid., 10 June 1915) and the following year found her urging the removal of the "filthy cow stalls" (ibid., 12 Jan. 1916).

160. *WSJ*, 14, 17 Oct. 1916; *TCS*, 8 Sept., 14, 26 Oct. 1916.

161. Forsyth County Deed Book, vol. 145, p. 240—Office of Register of Deeds, Forsyth County Courthouse, Winston-Salem, N.C.; Minutes, vol. IV, pp. 36, 121; *TCS*, 19 May 1917.

162. Joseph M. Parrish, interview with Dell McKeithan, 4 Aug. 1950.

163. Minutes, vol. IV, pp. 82–83, 154; *WSJ*, 11 Sept. 1921; *TCS*, 10 May, 7 Dec. 1919.

164. Minutes, vol. IV, pp. 33–34.

165. Agreement: C. W. Barbee with R. J. R. Tob. Co., 13 July 1918, on stationery of the Plaza Hotel—file 2653, secretary's dept., RJR; Minutes, vol. IV, pp. 117, 147. See also *Tob.*, 22 Aug. 1918, p. 29.

166. Edgar E. Bumgardner, interview with author, 8 Mar. 1962; *Reynolds News*, Aug. 1919. When discontinued as an inn, the building for a time housed a cafeteria with white employees served on the first floor and Negroes in the basement; it later housed the research dept.; still later as 80-1 it was generally used for storage until razed in 1960 to make way for a parking lot.

167. Cost Production Book, 1923–30—RJR museum.

168. Roy C. Haberkern, interview with author, 29 Oct. 1961.

169. These same ideas were emphasized for inspectors. In a list of twelve

points on "How a Department Inspector Can Be of Great Help to Her Foreman and to the Company" sent to inspectors in 1952, the final point urged that the golden rule be observed so that the remaining eleven points would follow naturally—personnel records, box 142C, Records Center, RJR.

170. *WSJ*, 30 Mar. 1919. The federal law, which prohibited employment of children under fourteen and limited the time and hours for employment of those aged fourteen to sixteen, imposed a penalty of 10 percent of a firm's profits for violation. The law, approved 24 Feb. 1919, was a part of the revenue act of that year—*Statutes-at-Large of the United States of America*, 40: 1138.

171. *WSJ*, 5 May 1918; *Reynolds News*, Aug. 1919. This issue (vol. 2, no. 5) was in the possession of Marie Merritt Rich Shore of Winston-Salem as of 4 Sept. 1962.

172. This code appeared in the first issue of *Reynolds News*—*WSJ*, 5 May 1918.

173. *TCS*, 11 Sept. 1916.

174. Lillian Russell, interview with author, 31 Jan. 1962. She also recalled that this was about 1916 or 1917 and that Dr. Wortham Wyatt possibly did some of this early work. For the work of Lelia Idol see *WSJ* in *Tob.*, 28 Dec. 1916, p. 7.

175. Signed constitution of the Factory Council of R. J. R. Tob. Co.—personnel dept., RJR.

176. *WSJ*, 11 Feb. 1913.

177. Ibid., 30 Jan. 1916. See also *UR*, 3 Feb. 1916.

178. Elizabeth H. Davidson, *Child Labor Legislation in the Southern Textile States* (Chapel Hill, 1939), pp. 259–63; Harry H. Shelton to R. J. Reynolds, Walter R. Reynolds, and Robert E. Lasater, 18 Jan. 1917—Correspondence of Walter R. Reynolds.

179. Harry H. Shelton to R. J. Reynolds, Walter R. Reynolds, and Robert E. Lasater, 19 Jan. 1917—Correspondence of Walter R. Reynolds.

180. Davidson, *Child Labor Legislation in the Southern Textile States*, pp. 263–65.

181. *STJ*, 28 Aug. 1917.

182. Ibid., 8 Apr. 1919.

183. *WSJ*, 30 Mar. 1919.

184. William J. Conrad, Jr. (one of the notaries in 1919), interview with author, 15 Nov. 1960; notice re. Child Labor, 17 Apr. 1919—personnel dept., RJR. This notice indicated three actions prohibited to all employers: (1) to employ or permit any child under fourteen years to enter or work in a factory; (2) to employ any child under sixteen or anyone who seemed to be sixteen "until such child present an Employment Card, issued by one of the Company's Child Labor Examiners, showing the child's approved age"; (3) to permit the child between fourteen and sixteen to work more than eight hours in any day or before 6:00 A.M. or after 7:00 P.M.

185. John C. Whitaker, interview with author, 27 Oct. 1959.

186. Thurman A. Porter, interview with author, 2 Mar. 1962; John H. Cobb, interview with Dell McKeithan and Erwin W. Cook, 26 June 1950; personnel folders of Thurman A. Porter and John H. Cobb as of 16 Jan. 1962.

187. Announcement of employment dept., R. J. R. Tob. Co., "to Department Superintendent [*sic*] and Foremen," 9 Aug. 1919—personnel dept., RJR. Note

John C. Whitaker's explanation of these facts in *Am. Tob. Co. et al. v. U.S., Record on Appeal*, transcripts, 7: 5048–49.

188. Size of the department is given in "Notice to Employment Department," 16 Aug. 1919—personnel dept., RJR; Semi-Monthly Letter from Employment Department to Foremen, 5 Dec. 1920—in possession of John Q. Adams in Number 8, RJR, as of 6 Aug. 1963; ibid., 5, 20 Nov., 5 Dec. 1921—Correspondence of Walter R. Reynolds.

189. *TCS*, 2 Sept. 1922.

190. *WSJ*, 28 Mar. 1913; Floyd A. Hauser (25 Feb. 1960) and Lillian Russell (31 Jan. 1962), interviews with author. Albert Cuthrell (b. 5 Aug. 1895) recalled having his finger dressed by Dr. Valk well before 1919.

191. Brief Sketch of Medical Department—medical dept., RJR.

192. *TCS*, 2 Sept. 1922.

193. Brief Sketch of Medical Department; Cost Production Book, 1923–30—RJR museum.

194. *TCS*, 7 Jan., 21, 22, 26, 27, 28 Oct. 1936; personnel folder of Dr. Ralph C. Flowers—Records Center, RJR. Dr. Flowers, also prominent for connections with the Exchange Club and a magician of considerable renown, unfortunately became involved in the theft of gold from a dental supply house.

195. Personnel folder of Dr. Allen H. Cash—box 1667C, Records Center, RJR; Dr. Richard W. Bunn, interview with author, 27 Jan. 1960.

196. Personnel folder of Minnie Alice Ashburn; *MB* 8, no. 11, 13 Apr. 1956; Dr. Richard W. Bunn, interview with author, 27 Jan. 1960.

197. Brief Sketch of Medical Department; North Carolina To-Day (N.C. Dept. of Conservation and Development), Dec. 1937.

198. Edgar E. Bumgardner, interview with author, 8 Mar. 1962; *WSJ*, 16 May 1920.

199. Scrapbooks of clippings kept by John C. Whitaker—personnel dept., RJR.

200. *WSJ*, 16 May 1920.

201. Ibid., 21 Jan. 1921.

202. Deed: William N. Reynolds and wife to R. J. R. Tob. Co., 11 Apr. 1922—file 1599, secretary's dept., RJR. It was given as a token to the "thousands of colored employees" who have "stood by the company" and made it one of the largest and best known—*UR*, 29 Sept. 1921.

203. Edgar E. Bumgardner, interview with author, 8 Mar. 1962; *UR*, 31 Mar. 1921.

Chapter 9
New Challenges for Management

1. *WSJ*, 23 Feb. 1912. See also *UR*, 29 Feb. 1912. William J. Conrad, Jr., referred to this day as one of great rejoicing—interview with author, 26 June 1960.

2. Minutes, vol. II, pp. 119, 164.

3. Ibid., p. 286.

4. Ibid., pp. 398–400; Roy C. Haberkern, interview with author, 2 Mar. 1962.

5. Minutes, vol. III, p. 18; William T. Smither, F. F. Cheek, C. L. Jordan, and B. K. Millaway, interviews with author at various times. Kent's career in Salesmen's Record Book, vol. II.

6. Minutes, vols. II (pp. 342, 376–79), III (pp. 66–67, 105, 118); an undated notice signed by Reynolds and Haberkern to all departments, by action of the board of directors on 20 Apr. 1914, soliciting information and cooperation—sales dept. RJR.

7. Minutes, vol. III, pp. 22–23, 63.

8. Harry H. Shelton to Ambrose H. Burroughs, 12 Feb. 1917—file 757, secretary's dept., RJR; *UR*, 25 Oct. 1917, 18 Apr., 25 July, 1 Aug. 1918.

9. *WSJ*, 3 Aug. 1918.

10. Vice-president (William N. Reynolds) to Earle Mauldin, 8 Feb. 1918; Earle Mauldin to William N. Reynolds, 8 Feb. 1918—file 2653, secretary's dept., RJR. See *WSJ*, 27 Aug. 1916, for indications of closeness of Mauldin to the Reynolds family. J. N. Tucker stated that Mauldin left the company and eventually joined J. E. Sirrine of Greenville, S.C.—interview with author, 5 Oct. 1960.

11. Minutes, vol. IV, pp. 33–34.

12. Autobiographical sketch of James A. Gray—box 1579C, Records Center, RJR.

13. Minutes, vol. IV, pp. 116, 165–66; Mrs. J. S. Dunn, interview with author, 8 Dec. 1959.

14. Mrs. J. S. Dunn, interview with author, 8 Dec. 1959. As of 6 Apr. 1920, James A. Gray owned 2,650 shares but one year later his holdings amounted to 12,000 shares (Minutes, vol. IV, pp. 175, 251), an increase not explained by the 200 percent dividend.

15. Autobiographical sketch of James A. Gray. Many of Gray's statements are verified elsewhere in this study. A special meeting of the directors was called on 3 May 1920, soon after the Supreme Court decision making possible the distribution of tax-free stock dividends, and the plan was presented for rearranging the company's capital structure—Minutes, vol. IV, pp. 195–96. See Eisner V. Macomber, in *United States Reports* (252: 189–238), for the decision against taxation of stock dividends on 8 Mar. 1920.

16. *UR*, 5 Jan. 1911; R. D. W. Connor, W. K. Boyd, J. G. de Roulhac Hamilton, et al., *History of North Carolina*, 6 vols. (Chicago, 1919), 5: 114–15; Burton Craige to R. J. R. Tob. Co., 1 Dec. 1916—file 1107, secretary's dept., RJR.

17. *WTJ*, 18 Apr. 1892, p. 3. See, for example, Ambrose H. Burroughs to Burton Craige, New York, N.Y., 7 July 1917—file 1107, secretary's dept., RJR; *NYT*, 20 June 1929.

18. *WSJ*, 29 Sept. 1916; *Tob.*, 12 Oct. 1916, p. 14. Shelton's brother, P. M. Shelton, was also supposed to begin on the same date as R. J. Reynolds's private secretary.

19. *UR*, 14 June 1923; Minutes, vol. IV, p. 245; *Tob.*, 19 May 1921, p. 14.

After his resignation Shelton moved to Wash. D.C., where he represented the
Reynolds company until his death—Mrs. Paul Weston, of Bristol, Tenn., sister of
Shelton.

20. Minutes, vol. II, p. 128. Richard S. Reynolds was a first-year law student
at the University of Virginia during the 1901–2 session—letter of E. W. Laugh-
tenschlager to author, registrar of the University of Virginia, Charlottesville, 14
Apr. 1960.

21. For repetition of this claim see *WSJ*, 4 May 1941. It was sometimes stated
that Richard S. Reynolds, realizing that R. J. Reynolds's sons would have preference in the company, decided to leave—Richard S. Reynolds, Jr., *Opportunity in
Crisis* (New York, 1956), passim. Whenever it was mentioned that Richard S.
Reynolds helped develop Prince Albert or the Camel, Will Reynolds struggled to
contain his anger—William J. Conrad, Jr., interview with author, 8 Apr. 1960.

22. *TCS*, 13 Jan. 1917; Ralph M. Hower, *The History of an Advertising Agency:
N. W. Ayer & Son at Work, 1869–1949* (Cambridge, 1949), p. 124; Minutes, vol.
III, p. 105. Armistead, who had had considerable advertising experience in his
native state of Tennessee and in Georgia, joined the Ayer advertising agency in
1909. His name (with a Winston-Salem address) first appeared as a stockholder
(200 shares) in the Reynolds company in 1916; the same information still applied one year later—Minutes, vols. III (p. 78), IV (p. 11). In his Memoirs dictated in 1954, Armistead made no reference whatever to his stay in Winston-
Salem, although one of his colleagues recalled that he spent one year with Reynolds—excerpts from Memoirs of William M. Armistead on his association with
the R. J. R. Tob. Co., selected by Warner S. Shelly, president, N. W. Ayer & Son,
Inc.; Warner S. Shelly to author, Philadelphia, Pa., 24 Oct. 1960.

23. *WJS*, 25 June, 10 Oct. 1916.

24. Ibid., 24 Jan. 1917; Minutes, vol. IV, pp. 3–4; J. S. Oliver to R. J. Reynolds, 22 Jan. 1917—file 1124, secretary's dept., RJR.

25. All seven issues of the *Open Door* were preserved in the advertising dept.
and several issues were scattered in other departments.

26. Arthur S. Kennickell, Jr. (8 June 1962), and John S. Graham (14 June
1962), interviews with author; personnel form of Lincoln Green—courtesy of
W. Mason King, vice-president, Southern Railway System. Green, as general
freight agent for the Southern in Atlanta in 1904, surely knew Graham, who at
that time worked with the Central of Georgia.

27. *Southern Freight Rates in Transition* (Gainesville, Fla., 1949), pp. 149–55.

28. Arthur S. Kennickell, Jr., interview with author, 8 June 1962. Mr. Kennickell recalled only the importance of this move.

29. John S. Graham, interview with author, 14 June 1962.

30. *Decisions of ICC*, 16: 12–19.

31. Joseph L. Graham to J. J. Campion (traffic manager, Carolina, Clinchfield
and Ohio Railway), 9 Apr. 1909—file I, box 213C, Records Center, RJR; information from comptroller's office, RJR.

32. Edward C. Kirkland, *Industry Comes of Age: Business, Labor, and Public
Policy*, vol. 6 of *Economic History of the United States* (New York, 1961), pp. 77,
83, 92.

33. C. Vann Woodward, *Origins of the New South, 1877–1913*, vol. 9 of *History*

of the South, eds. Wendell H. Stephenson and E. Merton Coulter (Baton Rouge, La., 1951), pp. 292–93.

34. Harold U. Faulkner, *The Decline of Laissez-Faire, 1897–1917*, vol. 7 of *Economic History of the United States* (New York, 1959), pp. 188–90.

35. *Decisions of ICC*, 16: 12–19; W. E. Lamb to Winston-Salem Board of Trade, Wash. D.C., 25 Mar. 1909; F. M. Simmons to Clement Manly, Wash., D.C., 10 Apr. 1909—file I, box 213C, Records Center, RJR.

36. *Decisions of ICC*, 16: 12, 17–18; file I, box 213C, Records Center, RJR. A clipping in Graham's files from the *Charlotte Observer*, 19 Apr. 1909, contains a severe castigation of the ICC for not having given Durham and Winston relief "from the exorbitant coal rates now exacted from them by the Norfolk & Western Railroad."

37. Joseph L. Graham to Lincoln Green, 21 Apr. 1909—file I, box 213C, Records Center, RJR.

38. Lincoln Green to Joseph L. Graham, Wash., D.C., 23 Apr., 27 July 1909—ibid.

39. Joseph L. Graham to Charles S. Keene, 1 May 1909; Charles S. Keene to Joseph Graham, New York, N.Y., 11 May 1909—ibid.

40. Joseph L. Graham to T. S. Davant, 4 Apr. 1912—ibid.

41. *WSJ*, 29 Mar. 1912; Brief of Joseph L. Graham and Hearings in docket no. 4717—files I and 71, box 213C, Records Center, RJR.

42. Lincoln Green to Joseph L. Graham, Wash., D.C., 14 Sept. 1912—ibid.

43. Joseph L. Graham to Lincoln Green, 20 Sept. 1912—ibid.

44. Joseph L. Graham to T. S. Davant, 13 Apr. 1912—ibid.; *Decisions of ICC*, 26: 146–51.

45. Copy of petition to ICC, 4 Apr. 1914—box 213C, Records Center, RJR.

46. *Wall Street Journal*, 14 Dec. 1909.

47. *WSJ*, 29 Oct. 1915; *TCS*, 14 Feb. 1917; *Tob.*, 30 Mar. 1922, p. 101.

48. Joseph L. Graham to Corporation Commissioner of North Carolina, 3 June 1924—file III, box 213C, Records Center, RJR; *WSJ*, 4 June 1924; *TCS*, 13 Oct. 1924 (quotation). With his argument Graham helped to kill the ship and terminal bill.

49. Joseph L. Graham to Lincoln Green, 12 Mar. 1925—file III, box 213C, Records Center, RJR.

50. Joseph L. Graham to Allen J. Maxwell, 27 May 1925—ibid.; *WSJ*, 12 June 1925; *TCS*, 11 June 1925; Lincoln Green to Allen J. Maxwell, Wash., D.C., 11 June 1925—file III, box 213C, Records Center, RJR.

51. *Decisions of ICC*, 19: 608.

52. *WSJ*, 10 Nov., 14 Dec. 1915, 17 June 1916; *Decisions of ICC*, 39: 600–608.

53. *WSJ*, 5 Nov. 1915. The author was unable to find this case in the *Decisions of ICC*, although the local paper quoted directly from the decision.

54. *Decisions of ICC*, 55: 33–34; *Tob.*, 30 Jan. 1919 (p. 4), 21 Aug. 1919 (p. 3).

55. *Tob.*, 1 Nov. 1917, p. 4.

56. *UR*, 10 Jan. 1918; *Tob.*, 24 Jan. 1918, p. 16.

57. *Decisions of ICC*, 39: 371–77.

58. Vol. I, no. 3 (Oct. 1916?). For other information on this case see *WSJ*, 8

Jan., 8 June 1916; *UR*, 15 June 1916. Officials of the company in Graham's day would scarcely understand a later debate of two Reynolds employees on the question of abolishing the ICC "after 75 years of (its) burdensome regulation of an industry that is no longer a monopoly"—*TCS*, 7 June 1962.

59. *WSJ*, 23 Apr. 1916; *TCS*, 24 Apr. 1916; *Statutes-at-Large of the United States of America*, 39, pt. 1, p. 232.

60. *WSJ*, 29 Apr. 1917. Graham's prophecy of a port of entry to yield $1.5 million for a complete year was more than realized, as shown by the following statistics from the *Annual Report of the Secretary of the Treasury on the State of the Finances* for the port of entry of Winston-Salem: *1917*—first full year of operation—(p. 348), $1,661,585.52; *1918* (p. 537), $1,673,307.45; *1919* (p. 702), $2,778,739.25; *1920* (p. 851), $3,797,415.88. Durham, an older and for many years more important tobacco manufacturing town than Winston-Salem, was listed for the first time in *1920* (p. 851), with receipts of only $490,877.01.

61. *WSJ*, 26 May 1916. For additional comments see *TCS*, 7 July 1916; *STJ*, 2 May 1916.

62. *Bookman v. R. J. R. Tob. Co. et al., Transcript of Record*, docket no. 129–544 (Chancery of N.J., 1946), pp. 1952–54.

63. For a short complimentary sketch of Graham on the occasion of his appointment to the traffic department of the Tobacco Merchants Association, see *Tob.*, 3 Aug. 1916, p. 28; for a short summary of his career, see *OD*, vol. 1, no. 2.

64. D. P. Robbins, *Descriptive Sketch of Winston-Salem, Its Advantages and Surroundings, Kernersville, Etc.* (Winston, N.C., 1888), p. 39.

65. Bill of sale: Ogburn, Hill & Co. to R. J. R. Tob. Co., 19 Sept. 1912—file 592, secretary's dept., RJR; Minutes, vol. II, pp. 238–39; *UR*, 29 Aug., 26 Sept. 1912; Connor, Boyd, Hamilton, et al., *History of North Carolina*, 4: 51–53; *WSJ*, 22 Aug. 1947; undated clipping and information from Judge Oscar Efird of Winston-Salem, N.C.; *Connorton's for 1903*, pp. 7–232. Other members of the Ogburn family had also manufactured tobacco, including Sihon Alexander Ogburn and Matthew Lewis Ogburn (b. 1 June 1832). Sihon A. Ogburn, who manufactured chewing tobacco in 1887, had at least one traveling salesman—*UR*, 18 Aug. 1887. He originated the well-known Cannon Ball brand. Matthew L. Ogburn originated Bull of the Woods, later purchased by Taylor Brothers but eventually sold to the British-American Tobacco Company. Actually the Ogburn family, through the work of James Edward Ogburn (d. 6 May 1895), appears to have been the first to engage in the modern manufacture of tobacco in the Winston-Salem area—about four miles north of the original site of the town at what became Pine Brook Country Club.

66. File 1403, secretary's dept., RJR. Robbins, *Descriptive Sketch of Winston-Salem*, p. 44; *WSJ*, 27 Dec. 1949; *UR*, 17 Feb. 1910. Sullivan listed only fifteen brands in 1903—*Connorton's for 1903*, pp. 7–232.

67. Robbins, *Descriptive Sketch of Winston-Salem*, pp. 36–37; deeds and bill of sale, 18, 28 Aug. 1924—file 1750, secretary's dept., RJR; Minutes, vol. IV, p. 425; *WTJ*, 2 June 1980, p. 9; *UR*, 29 June 1905, 29 June 1922; *J&S*, 6 Jan. 1929, *TCS*, 25 Oct. 1961.

68. See *MB* 14, no. 51 (25 May 1962), for additions to the Bailey Power Plant.

69. William J. Conrad, Jr., interview with author, 21 Sept. 1959.

70. *Tob.*, 2 Nov. 1916, p. 8.

71. Minutes, vol. III, pp. 66, 68; contract: National Fireproofing Co. and R. J. R. Tob. Co., 12 Oct. 1915—file 948, secretary's dept., RJR; *UR*, 13 Feb. 1913; *WSJ*, 21 Oct. 1916. In the spring of 1913 the first of this series was started on the corner of Church and Fourth streets and was to be connected with Number 5—*WSJ*, 16 Mar. 1913.

72. *Tob.*, 9 July 1914, p. 4.

73. *UR*, 15 July 1915.

74. Edgar E. Bumgardner, interview with author, 22 Jan. 1962. Apparently Solomon's supervisor blocked every attempt of the Libby-Owens Glass Company to reward him.

75. *TCS*, 10 Dec. 1919.

76. *WSJ*, 13 Mar. 1920.

77. Edward T. Sims, interview with Dell McKeithan and Erwin W. Cook, 26 Oct. 1951—personnel dept., RJR.

78. Contract: Carrier Engineering Corp. and R. J. R. Tob. Co., New York, 26 Oct. 1916—file 1091, secretary's dept., RJR.

79. *Compressed Air Magazine* in *Tob.*, 10 June 1920, p. 37.

80. *Tob.*, 29 Mar. 1922, p. 106.

81. Walter R. Reynolds to J. H. Bailey, 10 Apr. 1914—Correspondence of Walter R. Reynolds, purchasing dept., RJR; *UR*, 4 July 1912.

82. *UR*, 10 Apr. 1913; *WSJ*, 13 Jan. 1917.

83. William J. Conrad, Jr., interview with author, 15 Nov. 1960.

84. Walter R. Reynolds to Henry Turner, 22 Dec. 1913, 17 Sept. 1914; Walter R. Reynolds to Ullman Bros., 22 Dec. 1913; Burton Craige to Ambrose H. Burroughs, 27, 29 May 1915; Ambrose H. Burroughs to Burton Craige, New York, N.Y., 5 June 1915—all in file 919, secretary's dept., RJR; John V. Hunter, Jr. (7 Aug. 1963) and John H. Peddicord (14 Aug. 1963), interviews with author.

85. Walter R. Reynolds to J. Turner Farish, 18 June 1914—Correspondence of Walter R. Reynolds.

86. Walter R. Reynolds to Charles A. Penn, 3 Apr. 1914; Charles A. Penn to Walter R. Reynolds, New York, N.Y., 9 Apr. 1914; Walter R. Reynolds to Charles A. Penn, 14 Apr. 1914 (quotation)—all in ibid.

87. Walter R. Reynolds to W. P. Mayo, 11 May 1920—ibid.

88. George C. Weldon to Walter R. Reynolds, Louisville, Ky., 19 Mar. 1917; Walter R. Reynolds to George C. Weldon, 24 Mar. 1917; George C. Weldon to Walter R. Reynolds, Louisville, Ky., 9 May 1917—Correspondence of Walter R. Reynolds.

89. Edgar E. Bumgardner, interview with author, 2 Mar. 1962.

90. Walter R. Reynolds to A. M. Clement, 15 Jan. 1920—Correspondence of Walter R. Reynolds.

91. Frank A. Hampton to S. Clay Williams, Wash., D.C. 28 Apr. 1923;

Egbert L. Davis to J. H. Paylor, 30 Apr. 1923—file 521, box 1247, Records Center, RJR.

92. G. W. Kelley to R. J. R. Tob. Co., Knoxville, Tenn., 11 June 1914; Burton Craige to G. W. Kelley, 16 June 1914—Correspondence of Walter R. Reynolds.

93. Richard H. Wright to Automatic Weighing Machine Co., Durham, N.C., 10 Jan. 1914—Papers of Richard H. Wright, Flowers Collection, Duke University Library, Durham, N.C.

94. Louis Fischer to Richard H. Wright, Philadelphia, Pa., 28 Feb. 1914—ibid.

95. Walter R. Reynolds to B. T. Buchardi, 24 Mar. 1917; Walter R. Reynolds to George C. Weldon, 24 Mar. 1917—both in Correspondence of Walter R. Reynolds.

96. Burton Craige to Ambrose H. Burroughs, 3 Apr. 1913—ibid.; *TCS*, 19 Mar. 1917; *WSJ*, 20 Mar. 1917.

97. William J. Conrad, Jr., interview with author, 1 Mar. 1962.

98. Edward T. Sims, interview with Dell McKeithan and Erwin W. Cook, 26 Oct. 1951.

99. Patents 1,136,555; 1,209,759; 1,096,863; 1,274,600; and 1,105,840—files 685, 1106, and 1650, secretary's dept., RJR.

100. Burton Craige to Ambrose H. Burroughs, 28 Jan. 1913—file 685, ibid.

101. Richard H. Wright to Louis Fischer, Durham, N.C., 23 May 1914—Papers of Richard H. Wright.

102. Walter R. Reynolds to George C. Weldon, 24 Mar. 1917—Correspondence of Walter R. Reynolds. See esp. *TCS*, 13 Jan. 1917.

103. Charles V. Strickland, interview with Dell McKeithan and Erwin W. Cook, 2 Nov. 1951—personnel dept., RJR.

104. Contract with Philip Bauer & Co. of New York City, 9 Apr. 1915; memorandum: Philip Bauer & Co. to R. J. R. Tob. Co., New York City, 9 Apr. 1914—file 753, secretary's dept., RJR.

105. Charles V. Strickland, interview with Dell McKeithan and Erwin W. Cook, 2 Nov. 1951—personnel dept., RJR. Strickland paid tribute to the work of Edward T. Sims for his improvement of the George Washington packing machines and to William O. Morgan, one of the most expert diemakers he had ever known.

106. For inserting pivot pins see assignments of Pintle-Inserting Machine to R. J. R. Tob. Co., 24 July 1919 (file 1408), 22 June 1921 (file 1604), and 7 June 1921 (file 1559); letters patent for Strickland's Pintle-Inserting Machine, 5 Apr. 1922, and assignment of the same machine by Strickland to R. J. R. Tob. Co., 24 Apr. 1923 (file 1670)—all in secretary's dept., RJR.

107. Contract: R. J. R. Tob. Co. and George H. Little, ? Feb. 1922 (file 1585); assignment: George H. Little to R. J. R. Tob. Co., 1921 (file 1553)—both in secretary's dept., RJR; *WSJ*, 5 Oct. 1950.

108. Contract: Yoemel (James) N. Tzibides and R. J. R. Tob. Co., 25 Mar. 1914—file 739, secretary's dept., RJR; sketch of Harry H. Straus by Isabella Palais of Asheville, N.C. Miss Palais was Straus's secretary.

109. Noah E. Hartley, interview with Dell McKeithan and Erwin W. Cook, 10 July 1950—personnel dept., RJR.

110. Ibid. Note several assignments of patents for stamp-affixing machines and

other devices from James N. Tzibides to the R. J. R. Tob. Co.—in files 1569 and 1693, secretary's dept., RJR—generally dated from 1921 to 1923. Insofar as records indicate, the directors authorized the payment of $50,000 to Tzibides and his partner on 25 July 1921—Minutes, vol. IV, p. 276. For a full description of Tzibides's inventions secured by Reynolds, see *Tob.*, 27 Sept. 1923, pp. 41, 64.

111. Contract: R. J. R. Tob. Co. and George H. Little, ? Feb. 1922 (file 1585), and assignment: George H. Little to R. J. R. Tob. Co., 1921 (file 1553)—secretary's dept., RJR; *WSJ*, 5 Oct. 1950; Noah E. Hartley, interview with Dell McKeithan and Erwin W. Cook, 10 July 1950—personnel dept., RJR.

112. Contract: Package Machinery Co. and R. J. R. Tob. Co., 8 Sept. 1914 and 2 Oct. 1917—files 800 and 1198, secretary's dept., RJR.

113. *Tob.*, 25 Mar. 1920, pp. 208–10.

114. Bernard M. Baruch, *American Industry in the War: A Report of the War Industries Board* (Washington, 1921), pp. 208–10. Joseph L. Graham represented the Reynolds company on the advisory committee for the tobacco industry established by the War Industries Board.

115. A. P. Bender to Harry H. Shelton, Wash., D.C., 24 Aug. 1918; War Industries Board to Tobacco Manufacturers, 3 Sept. 1918—file 588, box 1244C, Records Center, RJR.

116. C. E. McKee to R. J. R. Tob. Co., Columbus, Ohio, 13 Sept. 1918—ibid.

117. H. G. Phillips (of War Industries Board) to R. J. R. Tob. Co., Wash., D.C., 5 July 1918—ibid.; Harman Woodward to Walter R. Reynolds, Charleston, S.C., 20 May 1918, and Walter R. Reynolds to Harman Woodward, 18 May 1918—Correspondence of Walter R. Reynolds.

118. Walter R. Reynolds to G. B. Dudley, 23 May 1918—Correspondence of Walter R. Reynolds.

119. *WSJ* in *STJ*, 2 May 1916.

120. Roy C. Haberkern to Richard H. Wright, 24 Dec. 1914—Papers of Richard H. Wright.

121. Walter R. Reynolds to Louis Muench, 14 Apr. 1917, and J. Walter Lemkau to Walter R. Reynolds, New York, N.Y., 29 Apr. 1918—Correspondence of Walter R. Reynolds; *WSJ*, 18 Jan. 1918.

122. Minutes, vol. IV, pp. 45–46.

123. Ibid., vols. III (pp. 120–21), IV (p. 28); Walter R. Reynolds to Henry Utard, 18 Jan. 1920—Correspondence of Walter R. Reynolds.

124. Minutes, vol. IV, pp. 39–40.

125. Ibid., pp. 42–43.

126. Walter R. Reynolds to C. B. Richard & Co., 19 Jan. 1918, and to W. I. Tuttle, 2 Feb. 1918—Correspondence of Walter R. Reynolds; *WSJ*, 10 Jan. 1918.

127. Contracts with René Bolloré, 27 Sept. 1917 (at Odet), and 5 Dec. 1917 (at Paris)—file 2142, secretary's dept., RJR; Walter R. Reynolds to Lt. Gregory N. Graham, 20 Nov. 1918—Correspondence of Walter R. Reynolds.

128. Walter R. Reynolds to Henry Utard, 28 Jan. 1920—Correspondence of Walter R. Reynolds. E. T. Jester in writing about Hill and cigarette paper added: "Hill is becoming more inflated as he grows older and does not appear to profit by experience. Mr. J. B. Duke tried some years ago to negotiate control of the Regie (French government monopoly in tobacco) for the A. T. Co. and could

not. What chance has P. S. H.?"—E. T. Jester to Walter R. Reynolds, New York, N.Y., 6 Feb. 1920, ibid. See *Wall Street Journal*, 26 Jan. 1920, for Hill's announcement of his purchase of a paper mill "from the son of Count de Maudet [Mauduit] who was the father of the cigarette making industry in France. The factory is one of the most important in France." Note also Reynolds's reply to the cable sent by F. R. Harris and Reynolds's reply to Henry Drucklief for 27 Jan. and 13 Feb. in Correspondence of Walter R. Reynolds.

129. Walter R. Reynolds to Daniel Weil, 27 Jan. 1920—Correspondence of Walter R. Reynolds.

130. Contract: Peter J. Schweitzer and the R. J. R. Tob. Co., New York, N.Y., 16 Jan. 1920—file 1415, secretary's dept., RJR.

131. Discussion of the Smokarol fiasco is based on file 800, box 1231, Records Center, RJR; *Tob.*, 16 Dec. 1915 (pp. 3, 10–11), 30 Dec. 1915 (pp. 3, 18); *WSJ*, 24 Feb. 1916.

132. *Bookman v. R. J. R. Tob. Co. et al., Transcript of Record*, pp. 1598–1605.

133. Ibid., pp. 1606–14, 1621.

134. Ibid., pp. 1697–99, 4381; Macomber, in *United States Reports*, 252: 189–238. This decision was rendered on 8 Mar. 1920.

135. *Statutes-at-Large of the United States of America*, 40, pt. 1, chap. 63, sec. 201, p. 303, and chap. 18, sec. 210, p. 1062; *Bookman v. R. J. R. Tob. Co. et al., Transcript of Record*, pp. 2430, 2436–37, 2501, 2510–14. Experts employed by the American Tobacco Company early in 1917 estimated that the excess profits tax on an 8 percent basis would cost that company $118,000 per year—*Tob.*, 3 May 1917, p. 16.

136. In *Tob.*, 26 Apr. 1923, pp. 54–55.

Chapter 10
Development into a Modern Industry

1. Minutes, vol. IV, pp. 418–19. See also *Tob.*, 17 Apr. 1924, p. 5.

2. *Tob.*, 17 Apr. 1924, p. 5. S. Clay Williams gave essentially the same evaluation in 1943, stating that Gray, a sales genius, was of enormous value to the company—*Bookman v. R. J. R. Tob. Co. et al., Transcript of Record*, docket no. 129–544 (Chancery of N.J., 1946), pp. 1959–62. William T. Smither described Gray as a driver who expected all to work as he did, although few, if any, were able to do so—William T. Smither, interview with author, 16 Sept. 1963.

3. Mrs. J. S. Dunn, interview with author, 8 Dec. 1959.

4. Dudley Doust, (tape-recorded) interview with Bowman Gray, Jr., 18 Mar. 1960; typed Memoirs of William T. Smither, advertising dept., RJR.

5. Mrs. Ethel McGee, interview with author, 1 June 1960.

6. Edgar E. Bumgardner, interview with author, 8 Feb. 1962.

7. Minutes, vol. V, p. 213.

8. *J&S*, 19 Dec. 1937.

9. *WSJ*, 23 Sept. 1937.

10. Minutes, vol. V, p. 397; *WSJ*, 20, 24 Aug. 1929; *Tob.*, 29 Aug. 1929, p. 27.

11. Minutes, vol. VI, pp. 109–11; *WSJ*, 7 May 1931; *Tob.*, 14 May 1931, p. 14.

12. Minutes, vol. VI, pp. 117–18; Roy C. Haberkern, interview with author, 26 Nov. 1961. No doubt Reynolds kept well the secret of his inspiration, because Haberkern, brusque, capable, and too often right on points at issue, was not generally appreciated. Lasater usually referred to him as "Lord Haberkern."

13. Minutes, vol. VI, pp. 126–27. No Real Estate Committee had been listed since 1917 when it consisted of Lasater, James B. Dyer, and Joseph L. Graham.

14. Dudley Doust, (tape-recorded) interview with Bowman Gray, Jr., 18 Mar. 1960. See Minutes, vol. IV, p. 419, for a change in the bylaws removing the powers of the Finance Committee.

15. Minutes, vol. VI, pp. 357–58.

16. *Tob.*, 19 Apr. (p. 3) and 26 Apr. (p. 15) 1934; *WSJ*, 17 Apr. 1934; *TCS*, 16 Apr. 1934.

17. Minutes, vol. VI, pp. 439–40; *WSJ*, 9 July 1935; *Tob.*, 11 July 1935, pp. 3–4.

18. *Am. Tob. Co. et al. v. U.S., Record on Appeal*, docket no. 9137–9139 (6th Cir., 1944), transcripts, 7: 5059. For Williams's evaluation to chairman of the board see *WSJ*, 12 July 1935; Minutes, vol. VI, p. 446; *Tob.*, 18 July 1935, p. 11. Arthur M. Schlesinger, Jr., in *The Coming of the New Deal* (Boston, 1959), p. 164, characterizes Williams as an unhappy failure when chairman of the National Industrial Recovery Board.

19. Undated clipping from a Lexington, Ky., newspaper, in possession of the late Roy C. Haberkern, Winston-Salem, N.C.

20. Letter of James A. Gray to the stockholders, 31 Dec. 1937—Minutes, vol. VII, p. 130. The *World Almanac, 1959*, p. 159, lists a severe flooding along the Ohio on 22 Jan. 1937.

21. William J. Conrad, Jr., interview with author, 2 May 1960. Conrad said that a short while later the company's operations were hindered because its supply of Burley leaf had been exhausted.

22. Minutes, vol. VII, p. 98. Note ibid., p. 99, for the unanimous acceptance of Kirk's resignation. See also *Tob.*, 8 Apr. 1937, p. 5; *WSJ*, 2 Apr. 1937.

23. Minutes, vol. VII, p. 117; *J&S*, 28 Jan. 1951; *Tob.*, 7 Oct. 1937, p. 7; *WSJ*, 6 Oct. 1937.

24. Minutes, vol. VII, pp. 124–25; *Tob.*, 23 Dec. (p. 3) and 30 Dec. (p. 28) 1937; *Am. Tob. Co. et al. v. U.S., Record on Appeal*, transcripts, 6: 4936–38, 7: 5014–47; *MB* 9, no. 58, 14 Nov. 1947; miscellaneous records, box 696, Records Center, RJR; Bessie Lleweylln, interview with author, Raleigh, N.C., 1 Mar. 1960.

25. Minutes, vol. VII, pp. 125, 176.

26. Ibid., vol. V, pp. 215–26; *Tob.*, 15 Dec. 1927, p. 3; *J&S*, 28 Apr. 1929. According to the *World Almanac, 1959*, p. 251, the Empire State Building was completed on 1 May 1931. Reynolds made final purchase of the old City Hall property on 5 Oct. 1927—Forsyth County Deed Book, vol. 287, pp. 31–34, Office of Register of Deeds, Forsyth County Courthouse, Winston-Salem, N.C. Note also Minutes, vol. V, p. 210.

27. William J. Conrad, Jr., interview with author, 26 Apr. 1960. The latter

statement was made by an agent of Shreve and Lamb, who sent out a survey team to inspect all the buildings they had designed. For a history and description of the building see Roy Thompson in *J&S*, 16 June 1963.

28. *MB* 11, no. 45, 2 July 1959; Edgar E. Bumgardner to Harold L. Gosselin, 17 July 1956—personnel folder of Harold L. Gosselin, Records Center, RJR.

29. Ralph M. Hower, *The History of an Advertising Agency: N. W. Ayer & Son at Work, 1869–1949* (Cambridge, 1949), p. 128.

30. *Tob.*, 10 July 1930, p. 20.

31. *R. J. R. Tob. Co. et al. v. U.S., Brief for Appellants*, docket no. 9139 (6th Cir., 1944), p. 205.

32. Hower, *The History of an Advertising Agency*, p. 124; Camel Scrapbook: Newspapers, vol. XIX—advertising dept., RJR; *WSJ*, 13 Dec. 1932.

33. Camel Scrapbook: Magazines, vols. VI, VII, VIII, IX, passim.

34. Ibid., vol. XI.

35. Ibid., Newspapers, vol. XVIII; *Fortune*, Aug. 1938, pp. 29–30. Ayer's last advertisement was filed for 20 May 1931.

36. Minutes, vol. VI, p. 152. From 1930 to 1946, this type of information appeared on a separate printed sheet with the annual reports; some of the sheets, including the one for 1931, have been lost. Beginning in 1946 Secretary William J. Conrad, Jr., at his own personal expense and somewhat against the sentiment of at least one high official, secured a composite arrangement for the annual reports (William J. Conrad, Jr., interview with author, 15 June 1962), the only significant improvement in the format since early in 1931. The practice of sending all stockholders an annual letter accompanying the financial statement of the preceding year, at the time a vast improvement, was initiated by Bowman Gray, Sr., on 14 Jan. 1931—*Bookman v. R. J. R. Tob. Co. et al., Brief on Behalf of All Defendants*, docket no. 129–544 (Chancery of N.J., 1946), p. 94.

37. An Englishman received a patent on viscose in 1898, but not until 1911 did Dr. J. E. Brandenburger, of Switzerland, design a machine for continuous production of strong transparent cellophane—J. L. Brill, research director (film dept.) for E. I. du Pont de Nemours & Company, in *Encyclopaedia Britannica*, 1963 ed., 5: 141. A garbled account appears in *MIB* 2, no. 46, 26 May 1950.

38. L. D. Long, interview with author, 2 Nov. 1959. Much of Long's account is substantiated by other evidence.

39. R. Bruce Clodfelter, interview with author, 17 Sept. 1962; Kardex Record, purchasing dept., RJR; *R. J. R. Tob. Co. et al. v. U.S., Brief for Appellants*, pp. 394–95; *Am. Tob. Co. et al. v. U.S., Record on Appeal*, transcripts, 7: 5230–33, 5368–69. One interesting problem involving the use of cellophane had to do with its sealing. No one knew how to seal it, and the task of finding out was delegated to Roy C. Haberkern. When Rose Brothers of Gainsborough, England, claimed they could handle the matter, Haberkern contracted with them to deliver the machine only to Reynolds. The Englishmen came, but it appeared they could not seal the cellophane. The Package Machinery Company also arrived with the same claim based on the accidental discovery of a sealing method. One of its mechanics, reaching for cleaning fluid to wash his grimy hands, had allowed a few drops to fall on the hot soldering iron along with scraps of cellophane, thus discovering that he had developed a method for sealing cellophane. Haberkern,

not wishing one company to know of the other's presence, put the Rose experimenters in Number 4 and the representatives of the Package Machinery Company in Number 12. As it turned out, the latter not only had a better wrapping machine but also a method of sealing which was being reported to Haberkern for the first time. Haberkern wished to rescind his contract with the Rose Brothers and proceeded to do so by insulting them in fine style—Edgar E. Bumgardner, interview with author, 31 Jan. 1962.

40. Camel Scrapbook: Newspapers, vol. XIX; *Tob.*, 20 Aug. 1931, p. 24; *WSJ*, 25 Feb. 1931.

41. *Modern Packaging* 25 (Oct. 1951); 78; *WSJ*, 6 Mar. 1931; Jane McIver and Minnie Rierson, interview with author, 14 Oct. 1960; *Tob.*, 19 Mar. (p. 31), 21 May (pp. 3–4) 1931.

42. See, for example, *TCS*, 18 May 1931; *Tob.*, 21 May 1931, pp. 3–4.

43. Program of Dinner for Mr. James Thomas Sharkey, Boston, Mass.; Mrs. Walter Sweet, Brooklyn, N.Y.; and Mr. Julius M. Nolte, Duluth, Minn., 18 May 1931—courtesy of John H. Peddicord, Winston-Salem, N.C. In May 1931 one disappointed claimant to the first prize filed an attachment against Sharkey's funds in the National Shawmut Bank of Boston, and caused the company considerable trouble before relinquishing his claim in 1935—file on *E. W. Hasbrouck v. R. J. R. Tob. Co., James T. Sharkey, and National Shawmut Bank as Trustee*—box 945C, Records Center, RJR.

44. *Pitt Panther*, May 1931, in Clipping Scrapbook, vol. I, p. 66—advertising dept., RJR.

45. Program of the Thirtieth Anniversary of the du Pont Spruance Plant, 18 Nov. 1960—courtesy of William S. Smith, Jr. Note also Richmond *News Leader*, 2 Oct. 1930, for the beginning of the cellophane production at the Spruance Plant. For the cost of advertising Camels in Nov. 1931, see *R. J. R. Tob. Co. et al. v. U.S., Brief for Appellants*, p. 395. Du Pont retained the Reynolds account until about 1951.

46. Camel Scrapbook: Newspapers, vol. XIX; Magazines, vols. XII, XIII, XIV, XV. S. Clay Williams's account of the introduction of cellophane is in *Am. Tob. Co. et al. v. U.S., Record on Appeal*, transcripts, 7: 5230–33, 5368–69.

47. Typed Memoirs of William T. Smither, 11 Aug. 1959; *Arthur Selwyn Brown v. R. J. R. Tob. Co., Transcript* (U.S. Dist. Ct., Middle Dist. of N.C., May term, 1938, Winston-Salem), 2: 3–5.

48. *Editor and Publisher* in *WSJ*, 13 Dec. 1932. For information on Esty see *R. J. R. Tob. Co. v. F.T.C., Transcript of Record*, 2 vols., docket no. 4795 (7th Cir., 1950), 2: 1486–92.

49. *WSJ*, 16 Jan. 1933; *Tob.*, 2 Feb. 1933, p. 25.

50. Typed Memoirs of William T. Smither, 11, 24 Aug. 1959.

51. Camel Scrapbook: Newspapers, vol. XX; *Sphinx* (organ of Society of American Magicians) in *Editor and Publisher*, 4 Feb. 1933; Clarence S. Johnson, interview with author, 17 Nov. 1960.

52. Camel Scrapbook: Newspapers, vol. XXII; *R. J. R. Tob. Co. v. F.T.C., Transcript of Record*, 2: 1471–86; Bunyan S. Womble, interview with author, 18 May 1960; *Tide*, 15 June 1938—Scrapbook, vol. II, advertising dept., RJR. Hearings before the United States District Court, Middle District of North Carolina, were

extensive and lively. The typed transcript and correspondence on the case are in box 953C, Records Center, RJR.

53. Camel Scrapbook: Newspapers, vols. XXIV, XXV.

54. Memorandum of Edward A. Darr—file 521, box 2660, Records Center, RJR. S. Clay Williams, in sworn testimony given in 1943, stated that average prices per pound paid by the "Big Three" tobacco companies from 1927 through 1939 were as follows:

Flue-Cured Leaf		*Burley Leaf*	
Reynolds	22.39 cents	Reynolds	22.42 cents
American	20.45	American	21.05
Liggett and Myers	20.35	Liggett and Myers	17.22

Bookman v. R. J. R. Tob. Co. et al., Transcript of Record, pp. 1828, 1832, 1878–92.

55. *R. J. R. Tob. Co. v. F.T.C., Transcript of Record*, passim.

56. Ibid., 1: 474–80. An account of this case by Blake Clark (*Reader's Digest*, July 1943, pp. 17–21) is unfavorable to the company.

57. *Advertisers' Weekly*, 3 Mar. 1928—Scrapbook, vol. I, p. 6, advertising dept., RJR.

58. *Competition in the American Tobacco Industry, 1911–1932* (New York, 1933), pp. 223–24.

59. William J. Conrad, Jr., interview with author, 6 Sept. 1962.

60. Camel Scrapbook: Magazines, vol. IX, p. 756-D.

61. Ibid., p. 763-D.

62. Ibid., pp. 776-D, 787-D.

63. Ibid., pp. 791-D, 796-D, 798-D.

64. Ibid., p. 832-D.

65. Contract: Outdoor Advertising, Inc., and R. J. R. Tob. Co., 29 Mar. 1928 and supplements—secretary's dept., RJR.

66. *Tob.*, 2 Nov. 1933, p. 23.

67. Contract: R. C. Maxwell Co. and R. J. R. Tob. Co.—file 2084, secretary's dept., RJR.

68. Hower, *The History of an Advertising Agency*, p. 138.

69. Camel Scrapbook: Newspapers, vol. XVIII, p. 49; *Tob.*, 10 July 1930 (p. 17), 13 Sept. 1934 (p. 4), 17 Oct. 1935 (p. 13), 25 June 1936 (p. 41); *WSJ*, 28 Apr. 1936; *J&S*, 24 Apr. 1938.

70. *Fortune*, Aug. 1938, pp. 25, 30, 96.

71. Dudley Doust, (tape-recorded) interview with Bowman Gray, Jr., 18 Mar. 1960.

72. Typed Memoirs of William T. Smither, 11 Aug. 1959.

73. *Tob.*, 20 Jan. 1927, p. 13. When giving testimony in 1943 on improved techniques for packing cigarettes, S. Clay Williams credited "a Swedish machine" for the combination of three operations—*Bookman v. R. J. R. Tob. Co. et al., Transcript of Record*, pp. 1865–66.

74. Cost Production Book, 1923–1930, no pagination—RJR museum.

75. Memorandum of "J. L.," 12 Aug. 1926; Roy C. Haberkern to Richard L. Dunstan, 2 Mar. 1926—miscellaneous folder, box 696, Records Center, RJR.

76. *Tob.*, 20 Jan. 1927, p. 13.

77. Richard L. Dunstan to Roy C. Haberkern, 3 Feb. 1928—miscellaneous folder, box 696, Records Center, RJR.

78. Edgar E. Bumgardner, interview with author, 31 Jan. 1962. See testimony of S. Clay Williams for an account of joining the two machines, which he describes as an independent move by a man "enthusiastically devoted" to the reduction of costs in the Reynolds plants—*Bookman v. R. J. R. Tob. Co. et al., Transcript of Record*, p. 1867.

79. In *Tob.*, 3 May 1928, p. 23.

80. Cox, *Competition in the American Tobacco Industry*, p. 199.

81. John V. Hunter, Jr.: memorandum of 9 Dec. 1959; interview with author, 8 Oct. 1962.

82. John V. Hunter, Jr., interview with author, 8 Oct. 1962; R. J. R. Tob. Co. to C. J. Schuster, 21 Apr. 1939—file 780, box 1234C, Records Center, RJR; *Molinsmo*, 1960, no pagination. Richard L. Dunstan advised the sale of the old Muller cut-offs in 1939—miscellaneous file, box 696C, Records Center, RJR. J. E. (Bill) Thomas referred to the 279 machines purchased during 1936, 1937, and 1938—J. E. Thomas to Haddon S. Kirk, 9 Oct. 1952, file labeled "Cigarette Machines," box 137C, ibid. See *Tob.*, 26 May 1927, p. 64, for a description of the Muller cut-off.

83. *RCCTI*, 1: 24, 183, 265, 276; *U.S. v. Am. Tob. Co. et al., Record: Testimony of Witnesses*, 5 vols., docket no. 660–661 (C.C. of Sou. Dist. of N.Y., 1907), 3: 149–64; Walter E. Gaines, "Some Remarks on the Foil Industry" before directors of R. J. R. Tob. Co., 25 Feb. 1952—file entitled "History and Interesting Points on Tin, Lead, and Aluminum," office of Archer Aluminum.

84. *U.S. v. Am. Tob. Co. et al., Decree* (C.C. of Sou. Dist. of N.Y., 16 Nov. 1911), p. 15; *U.S. v. Am. Tob. Co. et al., Federal Reporter*, perm. ed., 191: 418–19.

85. *U.S. v. Am. Tob. Co. et al., Testimony of Witnesses*, 3: 296–308.

86. Robert E. Lasater to John C. Whitaker, 1 June 1918—courtesy of John C. Whitaker; John C. Whitaker, interview with author, 3 Feb. 1962. Reavis Cox understood the monopolistic position of the Conley Foil Company but not the circumstances in which the Reynolds company found itself—*Competition in the American Tobacco Industry*, pp. 132–35.

87. Richard S. Reynolds to Harry H. Shelton, Bristol, Tenn.-Va., 24 Jan. 1919—file 600, box 1237C, Records Center, RJR.

88. Agreement signed in Louisville, Ky., on 2 Apr. 1919—ibid.

89. Harry H. Shelton to R. J. R. Tob. Co., 10 June 1919—ibid.

90. Memorandum of Harry H. Shelton, 22 Aug. 1919—ibid.

91. Harry H. Shelton to National Bank of Kentucky, 16 Feb. 1920—ibid.

92. Richard S. Reynolds to Harry H. Shelton, Louisville, Ky., 3 June 1920—ibid.

93. Confirmation of a conversation accepted by George G. Allen, Walter R. Reynolds, Richard S. Reynolds, 30 Sept. 1919—ibid.

94. Walter R. Reynolds to Harry H. Shelton, 26 Jan. 1920—ibid.

95. Agreements: U.S. Foil Co. of Louisville, Ky., and R. J. R. Tob. Co., 1 Jan. 1922 (file 1565) and 1 Feb. 1924 (file 1707)—secretary's dept., RJR.

96. Minutes, vol. IV, pp. 380, 423. Later in the 1920s, the British-American

Tobacco Co. apparently sold its stock in the U.S. Foil Co.—Richard S. Reynolds, Jr., *Opportunity in Crisis* (New York, 1956), pp. 15–16. Roy C. Haberkern declared that Bowman Gray, Sr., made this move because of difficulties in dealing with Richard S. Reynolds.

97. Seth Q. Kline to R. J. R. Tob. Co., Louisville, Ky., 10 Feb. 1925; Seth Q. Kline and Walter E. Gaines to R. J. R. Tob. Co., 2 Apr. 1925, with attached plan; W. R. Cobb to Geo. C. Weldon, Louisville, Ky., 8 Apr. 1925; Geo. C. Weldon to Roy C. Haberkern, Louisville, Ky., 9 Apr. 1925; Roy C. Haberkern to Seth Q. Kline, 14 Apr. 1925—all in file 1105, box 1212C, Records Center, RJR. In a letter of Richard S. Reynolds to Harry H. Shelton, Louisville, Ky., 20 Jan. 1920 (file 600, box 1237C, in ibid.), Gaines's name appears on the letterhead as treasurer of the Reynolds Corp.

98. Roy C. Haberkern, interview with author, 26 Nov. 1961; contract: Seth Q. Kline, Robert B. Campbell, and Walter E. Gaines with R. J. R. Tob. Co., 3 June 1927—file 1943, secretary's dept., RJR. Immediately after establishment of the Tobacco Foil Co. its officers borrowed $25,000—Minutes of Tobacco Foil Co., secretary's dept., RJR.

99. James A. Gray to Clinton W. Toms, 16 July 1928; Clinton W. Toms to James A. Gray, New York, 11 Aug. 1928—both in file 1105, box 1212C, Records Center, RJR.

100. Walter E. Gaines, "Some Remarks on the Foil Industry"; Herbert J. Privette to Colin Stokes, 18 May 1953—scrapbook material, industrial engineering dept., RJR; *Tob.*, 9 Aug. 1928 (p. 21), 15 Aug. 1929 (p. 3). Parts of this account are also based on a file containing letters of Campbell, Kline, and Gaines while in the process of transferring the Tobacco Foil Co. to Winston-Salem—file labeled "Tobacco Foil Co., Inc.," office of Archer Aluminum.

101. Roy C. Haberkern, interview with author, 26 Nov. 1961; Walter E. Gaines, "Some Remarks on the Foil Industry."

102. Minutes, vol. IX, pp. 163–64; bill of sale, 15 Aug. 1955—file 87, secretary's dept., RJR; *MB 7*, no. 37 (18 Aug. 1955), 9, no. 65 (12 Dec. 1957); Bowman Gray, Jr., and Alexander H. Galloway to employees, 23 Oct. 1963—Records Center, RJR. The foil div. could not be named Gaines because of Gaines dog food. Gray was not suitable. Because Archer is another name for Bowman, it was called Archer Aluminum for Bowman Gray, Jr., with John W. McDowell, Jr., as manager, Seba J. Collins, Jr., as production manager, and John J. Hibbits as sales manager.

103. Clippings filed with material dated Nov. 1924—file 600, box 1237C, Records Center, RJR.

104. This discussion is based on a memorandum of Roy C. Haberkern to James A. Gray, 23 May 1940, and on a letter of John M. Baer to R. J. R. Tob. Co., Chicago, 15 Apr. 1939, with specifications for the Guardite Tobacco Tempering Unit attached—courtesy of Roy C. Haberkern; file 780, box 1242, Records Center, RJR, esp. report of Mebane E. Turner to Robert E. Lasater, 10 Jan. 1938; a typed booklet entitled "'Thermo-Vactor' Tobacco Processing Cycle"—engineering dept., RJR; and Mebane E. Turner, interview with author, 25 Sept. 1962.

105. Mrs. Early L. Snow and C. M. Davis, interviews with author, 22 Oct. 1962; Personnel Book, leaf-processing dept., RJR.

106. Agreement: Early L. Snow and Ernest L. Barkley, Jr., with R. J. R. Tob. Co., 3 June 1957—file 2160, secretary's dept., RJR. Their patent number was 1,958,353.

107. C. M. Davis, interview with author, 22 Oct. 1962.

108. Harry H. Straus to Walter R. Reynolds, New York City, 2 Nov. 1918; Walter R. Reynolds to Harry H. Straus, 9 Nov. 1918; Harry H. Straus to Walter R. Reynolds, New York City, 22 Mar. 1920—all in Correspondence of Walter R. Reynolds, purchasing dept., RJR.

109. Contracts: René Bolloré with R. J. R. Tob. Co., 5 Dec. 1933, 18 Dec. 1934, 13 Nov. 1935, 8 June 1938—file 2142, secretary's dept., RJR. At the end of 1923, when the company shipped more than 56 million pounds of cigarette tobacco, it decided to register its "OCB" brand of cigarette paper. The initials were derived from the names of paper mills owned by Bolloré in Odet and Cascadec, France—Registration of Trademark, OCB, 29 May 1923, file 1697, secretary's dept., RJR.

110. Minutes, vol. VII, pp. 161–62. Straus's tribute to Haberkern was inscribed in the latter's copy of Don Wharton's *America's White Paper* (New York, 1940).

111. Agreements: René Bolloré and R. J. R. Tob. Co. re. Loans from Tobacco Companies, Nov. 1938; Harry H. Straus re. Loan from Tobacco Companies, 9 Dec. 1938—both in box 3040, Records Center, RJR. Note also René Bolloré to Ecusta Paper Corp., 21 Nov. 1938, sworn to before Gaston Thubé—file 1382, box 1238C, ibid. In reply to a letter from Owen D. Young requesting information on the Ecusta Paper Corp., S. Clay Williams reviewed the Reynolds's experience with cigarette paper during World War I and stated that Straus had solved the problem. Williams concluded: "To make a long story short, this Company and Liggett and Myers Tobacco Company were both prevailed upon by Mr. Straus to back him financially to substantial extent . . ."—S. Clay Williams to Owen D. Young, file 1282, box 2670C, ibid. *Time* (8 Apr. 1940, pp. 74, 76), with its usual enlarged bump of perspicuity, stated that part of the capital for Ecusta came from Straus's "well lined pockets," part from his two French companies including René Bolloré, part from the Irving Trust, and part from cigarette manufacturers who put in $1 million each. This last statement, however, is not borne out by any of the information available to the author. Only Reynolds, Liggett and Myers, and P. Lorillard aided in the venture. Other than the items already cited, information for this sketch has been drawn from various interviews with Roy C. Haberkern and from a revealing typed sketch, "Harry H. Straus, 1884–1951," prepared for the author by Isabella Palais. Helpful information also came from *The Fifth Anniversary Record of a New American Industry: Ecusta Paper Corporation* (Pisgah Forest, N.C., 1944) and Wharton, *America's White Paper*.

112. Dr. Samuel O. Jones, interview with author, 25 Sept. 1962. Note S. Clay Williams's account of the company's cooperation in the development of the Ecusta plant—*Bookman v. R. J. R. Tob. Co. et al., Transcript of Record*, pp. 1869–73.

113. *Réalitiés*, Dec. 1958.

114. *J&S*, 6 July 1947. For additional and similarly questionable information see *WTJ*, Dec. 1963, p. 41.

115. Minutes, vol. V, p. 199. As superintendent of manufacturing, Lasater had ample opportunity to become cognizant of such cases.

116. Ibid., pp. 402–5; *WSJ*, 29 Nov. 1929; Cora R. Brewer: personnel folder, Records Center, RJR, and interview with Dell McKeithan, 17 July 1950. According to older employees, the first Retirement Plan Board consisted of P. Frank Hanes, John C. Whitaker, and Robert D. Shore.

117. Minutes, vols. V (pp. 404–5), VI (p. 125); typed notes of H. F. Preston; *Twenty-Fifth Anniversary of the Group Insurance Plan of the R. J. Reynolds Tobacco Co.*; leaflets: *Announcement of Group Life Insurance, Total and Permanent Disability Insurance*, and *Accident and Health Insurance Plan for Regular Full-Time Employees of the R. J. Reynolds Tobacco Company* (slightly amended), 3 Dec. 1929—in files of J. E. Conrad, personnel dept., RJR.

118. Personnel folder of Samuel S. Stanley—Records Center, RJR; *WSJ*, 22 Jan. 1931.

119. *WSJ*, 29 Nov. (quotations), 4 Dec. 1929. In the nearby Dan River Mills at Danville, Va., no retirement plan for employees was adopted until 1 May 1948—Robert S. Smith, *Mill on the Dan: A History of Dan River Mills, 1882–1950* (Durham, N.C., 1960), pp. 517–18.

120. *Bookman v. R. J. R. Tob. Co. et al., Transcript of Record*, pp. 2400–2402. Note also in ibid. (pp. 4607–9, 4637–39) the testimony of James A. Gray.

121. Ibid., pp. 4608–9, 4635A, 4648–49.

122. Minutes, vol. VI, pp. 282, 309–10; Consolidation of Registration Statement . . ., form A-Z, Pfd. Stock, 3.60 Series, S.E.C., no. 2, 7 July 1945—secretary's dept., RJR.

123. H. F. Preston and I. J. Miller, interviews with author, 11 Apr. 1963.

124. Miscellaneous folder, 1925–1938, box 696, Records Center, RJR.

125. List of Active Brands, 1 Apr. 1938—in possession of Sanford B. Fitts, Jr., research dept., RJR, as of 1963.

126. F. F. Cheek, interview with author, 18 Sept. 1963.

127. *Am. Tob. Co. et al. v. U.S., Record on Appeal*, transcripts, 5: 3910.

128. William T. Smither (16 Sept. 1963), F. F. Cheek (18 Sept. 1963), Bowman Gray, Jr. (20 Apr. 1963), and G. W. Dobbs (11 Oct. 1963), interviews with author.

129. Allotment Sheet of Larry J. Flashe; Thurman A. Porter to Larry J. Flashe, 5 July 1934—courtesy of Larry J. Flashe.

130. Joseph J. Stamey (12 Nov. 1962), Bowman Gray, Jr. (1 Nov. 1963), and William T. Smither (16 Sept. 1963), interviews with author.

131. Personnel folder of Francis G. Carter with clippings from the *NYT*, *New York Herald Tribune*, and *WSJ*, all dated 17 June 1960—Records Center, RJR.

132. Carbon copy of daily report of Vernon Davis for 3 Jan. 1938—courtesy of Vernon Davis.

133. DM-21-A to division managers and S-21-A to salesmen, 12 Aug. 1935—courtesy of Vernon Davis.

134. Vernon Davis (6 Nov. 1962) and Bowman Gray, Jr. (1 Nov. 1963), interviews with author.

135. Instructions to Salesmen—sales accounting dept., RJR. High winds and flimsy ladders often caused salesmen to swallow flat-headed tacks when nailing muslin signs for advertising.

136. William T. Smither, interview with author, 16 Sept. 1963; Joseph W. Conyard to Vernon Davis, Portland, Ore., 27 Nov. 1962—courtesy of Vernon Davis.

137. William T. Smither (16 Sept. 1963), F. F. Cheek (18 Sept. 1963), and Bowman Gray, Jr. (20 Apr., 1 Nov. 1963), interviews with author.

138. In files chronologically arranged, sales dept., RJR.

139. R. J. R. Tob. Co. to department and division managers, 22 July 1940—sales dept., RJR.

140. R. J. R. Tob. Co. to division managers with copies to department managers, 15 July 1940—ibid.

141. H. Henry Ramm, interview with author, 15 Oct. 1963.

142. R. J. R. Tob. Co. to department and division managers, 19 July, 16 Sept. 1940—sales dept., RJR.

143. It was the opinion of Bowman Gray, Jr., that the presence of this notice in the files of the sales dept. indicated that it was sent to every member of the sales force.

144. Minutes, vol. VIII, p. 257. This move was made under protest as the result of insistent criticism from the Justice Department. Note Minutes, vol. VII, p. 223, for Barnes's appointment as assistant to Darr.

145. *Bookman v. R. J. R. Tob. Co. et al., Transcript of Record*, pp. 1874–76; Minutes, vol. VII, pp. 152–53, 272–73, 334–35; *Am. Tob. Co. et al. v. U.S., Record on Appeal*, transcripts, 6: 4927–28.

Chapter 11
Labor Strife

1. Foster Rhea Dulles, *Labor in America: A History* (New York, 1949), pp. 354–55. By the end of 1942, 1,183 employees were in the armed forces—Letter to Stockholders accompanying Annual Report for 1942, RJR.

2. Chester S. Davis in *J&S*, 8, 15 Apr. 1962.

3. Undated paper signed by Lakey and filed with materials for 1933—file 1114, box 1212C, Records Center, RJR. Brown and Williamson Tobacco Co. (in Winston-Salem) was organized by the TWIU-AFL as early as 1935—*J&S*, 15 Dec. 1935. Note also *WSJ*, 10 July 1942. A committee representing Local 217 of TWIU-AFL asked the company for a closed shop on 16 Jan. 1941—*Thursday*, 16 Jan., 31 July 1941. See also ibid., 15 May, 5 June 1941; *WSJ*, 29, 30 May, 11 Dec. 1941. John C. Whitaker's long mimeographed note to supervisors, dated 3 Nov. 1939, advising promptness and fair dealing in the settlement of grievances (to R. L. Dunstan in miscellaneous file, box 696C, Records Center, RJR) indicates that all was not smooth sailing in 1939.

4. *J&S*, 8, 15 Apr. 1962.

5. *WSJ*, 28 Apr. 1951.

6. Chester S. Davis also stated that the North Carolina labor movement with

few exceptions was headed by men "who militantly oppose communism"—*J&S*, 10 Sept. 1950.

7. Wage Increases, 1914–1950—personnel dept., RJR; *Economic Almanac, 1956*, National Labor Conference Board (New York, 1956), p. 249.

8. See below.

9. *Tob.*, 28 Oct. 1943, p. 76.

10. John D. Hawkins, *Daily Food in Negro Spirituals* (n.p., n.d.), p. 141—courtesy of Effie J. Adams. The repetitive portion comes from Psalms 1: 3 and Jeremiah 17: 8.

11. Nathan M. Revel, interview with author, 1 Feb. 1963.

12. *Daily Worker*, 17 May 1947.

13. Safety Council Minutes, 11 Nov. 1940—safety dept., RJR, filed chronologically.

14. *WJS*, 7 Mar. 1941; "History of Union Activities Since 1941" (a typed booklet), pp. 1–2—personnel dept., RJR; *Labor Relations Reference Manual*, 8: 292; *Report of the Joint Committee on Labor-Management Relations*, 80th Cong., 2nd sess., 1948, S. Doc. 986, pp. 181–82. Whitfield was not listed as a minister in 1947 but as vice-president of the FTAAWA-CIO and chairman of the Political Action Committee from the deep South—*Daily Worker*, 17 Jan. 1947. A caption under his photograph in the *Worker Magazine* (2 Feb. 1947) states that Whitfield was from Missouri.

15. "History of Union Activities Since 1941," pp. 2–3; *TCS*, 18 June 1943; personnel folders of James P. McCardell and Samuel H. Strader—box 1748C, Records Center, RJR. The cause of McCardell's death was belatedly given by Dr. Edgar S. Thompson as a cerebral hemorrhage. A check of his medical record from his employment to his death shows that McCardell in that time visited a company physician eighty-one times, twenty-three of which resulted from minor lacerations suffered while in the factory. It also indicates that McCardell frequently visited his family physician. McCardell was rated as reliable and his wages were increased from twenty-six cents per hour when first hired to fifty-four cents. An account of his death given by Velma Hopkins in 1947 appeared in the Communist *Worker Magazine* (15 June 1947): "'A man died. . . . A man in Plant 65 asked for permission to go see the company's medical department. But they said no, and he died; he died right there on the job.'"

16. *WSJ*, 22 June 1943; *TCS*, 22 June 1943; "History of the Union Activities Since 1941," p. 3; notes from smoking division kept by J. O. Saunders, p. 57.

17. "History of Union Activities Since 1941," pp. 2–3; *Daily Worker*, 26 June 1943. Donald Henderson (b. 4 Feb. 1902) received A.B. and M.A. degrees from Columbia University after he was employed as a farm worker and telegraph operator prior to 1920. He was an instructor at Rutgers University from 1926 to 1928 and at Columbia University from 1928 to 1933. Leaving the teaching profession, Henderson served as a labor leader in agriculture for the AFL from 1934 to 1937. He then became international president of the FTAAWA-CIO, a position he held during the labor disturbances in Winston-Salem—*Who's Who in America, 1950–1951*, 26: 1206.

18. *WSJ*, 23 June 1943; "History of Union Activities Since 1941," p. 4.

19. *WSJ*, 2, 3, 4, 6, 9 July 1943; "History of Union Activities Since 1941," p. 5.

20. *WSJ*, 25, 26, 27, 31 July, 3 Aug. 1943.

21. Ibid., 25, 27, 30, 31 July, 2, 3, Aug. 1943.

22. Ibid., 30 July 1943. Commencing with the second quarter of 1942, dividends were cut from fifty to thirty-five cents per share, although a year-end dividend of fifteen cents was declared—*Annual Report* for 1942, RJR.

23. Frank de Vyver, "The Present Status of Labor in the South," *Southern Economic Journal* 16 (July 1949): 16.

24. *WSJ*, 5, 6, 7 Aug. 1943; "History of Union Activities Since 1941," p. 5.

25. *WSJ*, 8, 13 Aug., 1, 5 Sept. 1943; "History of Union Activities Since 1941," p. 6; *Labor Relations Reference Manual*, 13: 79.

26. "History of Union Activities Since 1941," p. 7; *WSJ*, 10 Nov. 1943.

27. "History of Union Activities Since 1941," p. 7; *WSJ*, 10, 11 Nov. 1943; *Tob.*, 11 Nov. 1943, p. 11.

28. *J&S*, 14 Nov. 1943; *WSJ*, 17 Nov. 1943.

29. "History of Union Activities Since 1941," pp. 7–8; *WSJ*, 18 Nov. 1943. Various details of the restraining order filed on 17 Nov. 1943 may be found in *R. J. Reynolds Employees Association v. Harry A. Millis, Gerard Reilley, and John M. Houston, Tobacco Workers Organizing Committee, UCAPAWA-CIO, and R. J. Reynolds Tobacco Co.*—file docket no. 17,041, Office of Clerk of Court, Winston-Salem, Forsyth County, N.C. Houston represented the NLRB.

30. See, for example, *WSJ*, 18 Nov. 1943; *J&S*, 21 Nov. 1943.

31. *WSJ*, 24, 25 Nov., 1, 2 Dec. 1943. A copy of Judge Hayes's order preventing the R. J. Reynolds Employees Association from taking any further proceedings in the Forsyth County Superior Court is in *R. J. Reynolds Employees Association v. Harry Millis et al.*

32. *WSJ*, Dec. 2, 1943.

33. Ibid., 6, 7 Dec. 1943.

34. Ibid., 8 Dec. 1943.

35. "History of Union Activities Since 1941," p. 8; *WSJ*, 12 Dec. 1943.

36. *WSJ*, 13, 14, 15 Dec. 1943.

37. Ibid., 16 Dec. 1943.

38. Ibid., 17, 18 Dec. 1943; "History of Union Activities Since 1941," p. 8.

39. *WSJ*, 21, 22, 23 Dec. 1943; "History of Union Activities Since 1941," p. 8.

40. *WSJ*, 28 Dec. 1943, 11, 16, 22 Jan. 1944; "History of Union Activities Since 1941," p. 8.

41. "History of Union Activities Since 1941," p. 9; *WSJ*, 5, 16 Feb. 1944.

42. Agreement: UCAPAWA-CIO on behalf of the Tobacco Workers Organizing Committee and the R. J. R. Tob. Co., 13 Apr. 1944—file 2332, secretary's dept., RJR.

43. "History of Union Activities Since 1941," pp. 10–11; *WSJ*, 25 May, 2 June 1944.

44. *WSJ*, 20 June 1944.

45. Ibid., 21 June 1944.

46. "History of Union Activities Since 1941," pp. 11–12; *WSJ*, 25 Aug. 1944.

47. *WSJ*, 7 July, 16 Sept., 10, 13 Oct. 1944; "History of Union Activities Since 1941," pp. 12–13.

48. *WSJ*, 30 Sept. 1944; "History of Union Activities Since 1941," p. 12.

49. "History of Union Activities Since 1941," pp. 14–15. The agreement between the company and the union made near the end of December is given in detail in *WSJ*, 28 Dec. 1944.

50. *WSJ*, 20 Jan. 1945; "History of Union Activities Since 1941," pp. 12, 19.

51. "History of Union Activities Since 1941," p. 15; personnel folder of Eugene C. Pratt—Records Center, RJR. Pratt had been briefly employed by Reynolds as a young boy.

52. "History of Union Activities Since 1941," pp. 15–17; personnel folders of various employees mentioned—Records Center, RJR.

53. "History of Union Activities Since 1941," p. 17; Agreement: R. J. R. Tob. Co. and FTAAWA-CIO, 5 June 1945—personnel dept, RJR.

54. *WSJ*, 30 May 1945; *Tob.*, 7 June 1945, p. 16.

55. "History of Union Activities Since 1941," pp. 17–19. For a slightly different account of Keister's arbitration, see *WSJ*, 1 Nov. 1945.

56. *WSJ*, 4 Dec. 1945 (request of executive board), 13 Apr. (R. J. Reynolds Employees Association), 2 Feb., 15 Feb. (suboffice of NLRB), 8, 9 Mar. (SPD process) 1946. See also Chapter 13 for effects of SPD.

57. "History of Union Activities Since 1941," pp. 19–20; *WSJ*, 14, 15 May 1946.

58. *WSJ*, 26 Apr. 1946. Note also *Tob.*, 2 May (p. 22) and 23 May (p. 8) 1946. Only two issues of the *Worker's Voice* (Dec. 1946 and Feb. 1947) were available to the author—in box 1191C, Records Center, RJR.

59. "History of Union Activities Since 1941," pp. 20–21; *WSJ*, 17 June 1946.

60. *WSJ*, 17 June 1946; *Tob.*, 4 July 1946, p. 4.

61. *WSJ*, 21 June 1946.

62. Ibid., 17 July 1946.

63. Agreement: R. J. R. Tob. Co. and FTAAWA-CIO, 29 July 1946. See also *J&S*, 28 July 1946; *Tob.*, 15 Aug. 1946, p. 4.

64. *WSJ*, 20 June (Chatham), 25 July (Hanes to 73 cents), 8 Aug. (Western Electric; 60-cent minimum wage), 24 Aug. (strikes at Piedmont and Winston leaf plants; threatened boycott of merchants; McCrea), 28 Aug. and 5 Nov. (Thomasville Chair Factory), 27 Oct. and 15 Nov. (laundry strikers), 15 Nov. (Brown and Williamson), 19 Nov. (Western Electric election) 1946; 21, 28 Feb. 1947 (raises by Hanes and Cone).

65. *Daily Worker*, 3 Aug. 1946. The issue for 18 Jan. 1947 contains an item entitled "Sparking Dixie Drive," showing Koritz, Donald Henderson, and Theodosia Simpson.

66. *WSJ*, 24 Aug., 15, 16 Oct. 1946. It was later stated that the police, anticipating trouble, arrived by 4:30 P.M. Evidently the entry of the truck into Piedmont's grounds had been prearranged. Eugene C. Pratt, testifying in 1947, stated that Koritz did not adhere to the understanding between the police and the union—*Hearings Before the Un-American Activities Committee, Feb. 27, July 23, 24, 25, 1947*, H.R., 80th Cong., 1st sess., 1947, p. 91. Evidence by Pratt (p. 91) indicates that the understanding could have been connected with the staging of

mass meetings or parades. None of this explains the presence of so many police-men and reporters at the same split second.

67. *WSJ*, 24 Aug., 7 Sept. 1946. Bail for Jones and Koritz was set at $1,000 each. In an account of this episode in the *Daily Worker* (18 Feb. 1947), Koritz's eyes were said to sparkle as he told the story, though at that time he faced a year's sentence on a North Carolina road gang unless saved by the state supreme court. He claimed that he and the Negroes were held in jail two hours before charges were filed against them. Soon, however, the chief of police thought up charges: resisting arrest and obstructing justice.

68. *WSJ*, 24 Aug. 1946. A full record of this case, including a copy from the municipal court and the verdict of the North Carolina Supreme Court, is in For-syth County Superior Court records—file docket no. 30,935, Office of Clerk of Court, Forsyth County Courthouse, Winston-Salem, N.C.

69. *WSJ*, 15, 16, 17 Oct. 1946. See *TCS*, 17 Jan. 1964, for a sketch of Gold's early career.

70. *WSJ*, 18 Oct. 1946. An editorial in this issue stated that the similar actions of the municipal and superior courts emphasized the supremacy of the law in Winston-Salem, that the jury had contained good Negro citizens, and that the community would not tolerate force on picket lines. Note accounts in two Com-munist publications: *Daily Worker*, 17 Oct. 1946; *Worker Magazine*, 20 Oct. 1946. In the appeal to the state supreme court, the defendants argued that the number of Negroes selected for possible jury service (225) as opposed to whites (10,367) and the use of separate tax lists were discriminatory to both races— *North Carolina Reports: Cases Argued and Determined in the Supreme Court of North Carolina* 227: 552–58. The sentence of Judge Rousseau was upheld. See also "History of Union Activities Since 1941," pp. 21–22; *WSJ*, 6 June 1947.

71. *WSJ*, 30 Oct., 15 Nov., 15 Dec. 1946. Koritz's efforts to obtain a review of the case by the United States Supreme Court were refused—ibid., 14 Oct. 1947. In a column adjacent to another item on Koritz's sentence, it was stated that food costs in Winston-Salem had almost doubled since 1940—ibid., 1 Nov. 1947.

72. Communist publications openly backed the CIO's "Operation Dixie" in its efforts to organize tobacco workers in North Carolina and Virginia—*Daily Worker*, 3 Aug. 1946; *Worker Magazine*, 20 Oct. 1946.

73. Alice Burke, candidate for the United States Senate against Senator Harry F. Byrd in 1946, joined the Communist party in 1930 and in May 1940 became secretary of the party in Virginia. Born on a Montana homestead, she had re-mained there until forced off by the farm crisis that followed World War I—*Daily Worker*, 3 Oct. 1946; *Worker Magazine*, 3 Nov. 1946. The sharp-featured cuts shown in these publications bear no resemblance to her picture as published in *J&S*, 18 Aug. 1946.

74. "Communist Domination of Certain Unions," *Report of the Subcommittee on Labor and Labor-Management Relations of the Committee on Public Welfare, United States Senate*, 82nd Cong., 1st sess., 1951, S. Doc. 89, pp. 19–30.

75. *WSJ*, 30 Aug. 1946.

76. Ibid., 15 Nov. 1946.

77. This call exemplifies the strong paternalistic bent long prevalent among officials and foremen of the company. Gwaltney wrote an abundance of such

doggerel, much of which was included in his personnel folder, though this one was not. A copy of "STOP AND THINK!" was in possession of Erwin W. Cook, personnel dept., RJR.

78. "History of Union Activities Since 1941," pp. 23–24; *J&S*, 23 Mar. 1947; *WSJ*, 26 Mar. 1947.

79. "History of Union Activities Since 1941," p. 25; *WSJ*, 3, 5 Apr. 1947.

80. *WSJ*, 28 Apr. 1947. Actually the company on 17 Apr. offered the negotiators of Local 22 an increase of approximately seven cents in all labor grades—*MIB* 1, extra no., 18 Apr. 1947.

81. *WSJ*, 30 Apr. 1947. The actual leaflet was filed under Local 22, Bulletins, box 1191C, Records Center, RJR.

82. Notes kept by J. O. Saunders, p. 67—office of smoking tobacco div., RJR.

83. Spencer B. Hanes, Jr., to L. B. Jenkins Tobacco Co., 3 June 1947—box 798, Records Center, RJR.

84. *Tob.*, 15 May 1947, p. 9.

85. *WSJ*, 2 May 1947. According to company records, operations continued from the beginning of the strike with practically all whites working but with most blacks on strike—"History of Union Activities Since 1941," p. 27.

86. *WSJ*, 6 May 1947.

87. Ibid., 27 May 1947.

88. "History of Union Activities Since 1941," p. 27.

89. There seems to be no proof of this last charge, although the victory of Local 22 at the Winston and Piedmont leaf houses was fully detailed in the *Daily Worker*, 29 Sept. 1946.

90. Gordon Gray controlled the two Winston-Salem newspapers and James A. Gray was the second largest stockholder—*Time*, 12 Sept. 1949, pp. 64–65.

91. *Worker Magazine*, 15 Sept. 1946.

92. *WSJ*, 24, 25 May 1947. Charlotte Mock was not an employee of the company. For accounts of similar provocations to pickets by the hurling of bottles and firecrackers from windows of Number 12 and the Zinzendorf Hotel, see ibid., 21 May 1947.

93. Ibid., 30 May, 3, 11, 12, 13 June 1947.

94. Ibid., 10, 12, 18, 24 July 1947. Note *Report of the Joint Committee on Labor-Management Relations*, pp. 178–98, for a resumé of the situation in Winston-Salem and *Hearings Before the Committee on Un-American Activities*, pp. 63–123, for the testimony of Anne Matthews, Eugene C. Pratt, Spencer Long, Robert C. Black, W. Clark Sheppard, and Edwin K. McCrea. Note also *Tob.*, 31 July 1947, p. 125, for a resumé of the hearings.

95. *WSJ*, 24, 25, July 1947.

96. Ibid., 24, 26, 27, 29 May, 5, 6, June 1947; *J&S*, 8 June 1947.

97. "History of Union Activities Since 1941," p. 29.

98. Agreement: R. J. R. Tob. Co. and FTAAWA-CIO, 9 June 1947—personnel dept., RJR; *J&S*, 8 June 1947; *Tob.*, 12 June 1947, pp. 8, 17. The *Daily Worker* (9 June 1947) hailed the settlement as a great victory, although in the next issue called attention to the needs of strikers who were faced with delays and stumbling blocks in returning to work. The *Daily Worker* continued to refer to the strikers' problems until near the end of June when the matter was suddenly

dropped. No doubt the drastic change in the checkoff of union dues resulted from the so-called North Carolina right-to-work law passed on 18 Mar. 1947—North Carolina, *Session Laws and Resolutions Passed by the General Assembly for 1947*, chap. 328, pp. 381–82.

99. *WSJ*, 10 June 1947.

100. "History of Union Activities Since 1941," pp. 30–32; *WSJ*, 21, 25 June 1947.

101. *WSJ*, 25, 30 June 1947.

102. Ibid., 27 Sept. 1947.

103. *MIB* 1, no. 48, 16 Sept. 1947. Note Minutes, vol. VIII, pp. 116–17, for mention of an acute water shortage as of 11 Sept. 1947.

104. *MIB* 1, extra, 18 Apr. 1947; North Carolina, *Session Laws and Resolutions Passed by the General Assembly for 1947*, chap. 328, pp. 381–82.

105. *WSJ*, 24 Dec. 1947; Official Report of Proceedings Before the National Labor Relations Board, docket no. 34-RC-95, Greensboro, N.C., 20 Nov. 1948, passim. William A. Haney, manager of the plant, reported 175 out of 550 employees absent on the night of 22 Dec. only.

106. *Labor Relations Reference Manual*, 24: 1072–74; "History of Labor Activities Since 1941," pp. 40–42; *WSJ*, 6 May 1949.

107. *WSJ*, 23 Apr. 1949. By another and possibly a more dependable account, at the World Congress of Partisans for Peace Henderson stated only that American workers would not allow themselves to be pushed into war—*NYT*, 23 Apr. 1949.

108. *WSJ*, 8, 27, 28 July, 18 Aug. 1949. Henderson's affidavit was referred to the Department of Justice—*NYT*, 18 Aug. 1949.

109. *WSJ*, 9, 10 Sept. 1949.

110. *J&S*, 25 Sept., 4 Dec. 1949.

111. "History of Union Activities Since 1941," pp. 42–43; *WSJ*, 28 Sept. 1949. The newspaper account listed 28 votes for Local 22 and 2 that were adjudged void.

112. Contract: R. J. R. Tob. Co. and UTSE-CIO, East Market Street Extension, near Greensboro, N.C., 9 May 1950—box 798C, Records Center, RJR; *WSJ*, 10 May 1950; *MIB* 2, no. 44, 15 May 1950.

113. *WSJ*, 14 Dec. 1949.

114. "History of Union Activities Since 1941," pp. 52–54.

115. Minutes, vols. IX (p. 167), X (pp. 143–44); C. C. Johnson to Southern Bell Telephone Co. of Greensboro, N.C., 25 May 1959—box 798C, Records Center, RJR.

116. Roy Thompson in *J&S*, 8 Feb. 1948. Discharged for the unusual reason of "passing bad work," Mary Major left the company's employ on 6 Mar. 1948—personnel folder, Records Center, RJR. See "History of Union Activities Since 1941" (pp. 35–36) and *Tob.* (4 Mar. 1948, p. 14) for the company's termination of the bargaining agreement.

117. "History of Union Activities Since 1941," p. 38; *WSJ*, 5 Mar. 1948; *Tob.*, 8 Apr. 1948, p. 12. Attorneys for the association planned to appeal the decision—*Tob.*, 22 Apr. 1948, p. 19.

118. *Report of the Joint Committee on Labor-Management Relations*, pp. 178–98;

"History of Union Activities Since 1941," p. 33.

119. "History of Union Activities Since 1941," p. 43; *WSJ*, 28 Feb., 1 Dec. (Murray's denunciation of Henderson) 1948; *J&S*, 14 Mar. 1948 (Murray's letter). On 1 Mar. 1950, the CIO expelled the FTAAWA and the United Office and Professional Workers of America, which Henderson later joined.

120. *WSJ*, 1 Dec. 1948.

121. Ibid., 6, 20 Mar. (Henderson), 17 Mar. (portal-to-portal suit), 3 Apr. (R. J. Reynolds Employees Association), 1, 3 May (demonstrations) 1948; *Tob.*, 13 May 1948, p. 17 (in Whitaker's office). The portal-to-portal suit was first filed in Jan. 1947 on charges that Reynolds employees were required to arrive on company premises early and to remain after quitting time; this, it was claimed, should constitute working time according to the Fair Labor Standards Act— *Tob.*, 23 Jan. 1947, p. 3.

122. *WSJ*, 19 May 1948; *Tob.*, 27 May 1948, p. 3.

123. *WSJ*, 15 June, 19 July 1948.

124. Ibid., 22 July 1948.

125. Ibid., 19 Aug. 1948.

126. During this period Local 22 began to show special venom toward William Smith, director of the CIO in North Carolina—*Tob.*, 6 Jan. (p. 21), 24 Mar. (p. 14) 1949.

127. *WSJ*, 23 July, 6 Oct. 1949; "History of Union Activities Since 1941," pp. 46–47; Official Report of Proceedings Before the National Labor Relations Board, docket no. 34-RC-157, Winston-Salem, N.C., 19, 20 Oct. 1949, passim.

128. *J&S*, 30 Oct. 1949.

129. *WSJ*, 10, 11, 12 Nov. 1949; *J&S*, 4 Dec. 1949.

130. "History of Union Activities Since 1941," pp. 47–48; *Tob.*, 16 Feb. 1950, p. 18.

131. *WSJ*, 8, 9 (quotation), 10 Mar. 1950. Note also "History of Union Activities Since 1941," pp. 47–48; *Tob.*, 2 Mar. (p. 3) and 16 Mar. (p. 3) 1950.

132. *WSJ*, 13 Mar. 1950.

133. Ibid., 18 Mar. 1950. Sometime after his election, Williams was given royal treatment in New York by the Communists, including a reception in the offices of Alderman Benjamin J. Davis. There Williams attributed his election to support from labor, liberal whites, Negroes, and local newspapers—*Worker Magazine*, 22 June 1947. Evidently this flattery did not affect him.

134. *WSJ*, 20 Mar. 1950.

135. Ibid., 24 Mar. 1950. In the company's record the vote is given as 4,428 for Local 22 and 4,381 for "No Union," with 134 ballots challenged and 164 void—"History of Union Activities Since 1941," p. 48. In *Tob.*, 13 Apr. 1950, p. 12, the vote agrees with that of the company record.

136. *WSJ*, 15 Aug. 1950. This vote was certified by the NLRB on 22 Aug.— "History of Union Activities Since 1941," p. 50.

137. *WSJ*, 15 Aug., 12 Sept. 1950; *Tob.*, 21 Sept. 1950, p. 15.

138. *WSJ*, 15 Aug. 1950.

139. Ibid., 21 Sept. 1950; *Brief History of the American Labor Movement*, bulletin no. 1000, United States Department of Labor (Washington, 1950), pp. 50–51.

140. "History of Union Activities Since 1941," pp. 55–56; *Tob.*, 15 Apr. 1955, p. 7.

141. This series is in *MIB* 2, 1949, as follows: no. 17 (19 Aug.), no. 18 (26 Aug.), no. 19 (2 Sept.), no. 20 (15 Sept.), no. 21 (22 Sept.), no. 23 (6 Oct.), no. 24 (14 Oct.), no. 25 (20 Oct.).

142. Safety Council Minutes, 8 Jan. 1951—safety dept., RJR.

143. Ibid., 11 Feb. 1952.

144. "Summary of a Talk Made to Supervisory Personnel"—personnel dept., RJR. The copy made available to the author was stamped "Confidential" in heavy black letters.

145. *NYT*, 15 Oct. 1962; *Time*, 3 Jan. 1964, p. 24. In conformity with a change in North Carolina law, the company in July 1963 ordered the removal of all "White" and "Colored" signs over toilets.

146. Houston Adams, interview with author, 19 Apr. 1960.

147. *WSJ*, 8 June 1962.

Chapter 12
Litigation and Failure with a New Product

1. Erwin W. Cook and Sidney J. Walters worked on the photostating project— Erwin W. Cook and Sidney J. Walters, interviews with author, 26, 27 June 1963.

2. *Am. Tob. Co. et al. v. U.S., Record on Appeal*, docket no. 9137–9139 (6th Cir., 1944), transcripts, 1: 4–34. According to the more direct phrasing of a Kentucky newspaper, three companies, including the R. J. Reynolds Tobacco Company, one subsidiary, and thirteen executives were convicted of violating the antitrust act by (1) fixing prices and suppressing competition, (2) conspiring and combining to monopolize the tobacco industry, (3) attempting to achieve a monopoly, and (4) achieving it—Louisville *Courier-Journal*, 28 Oct. 1941.

3. *Am. Tob. Co. et al. v. U.S., Federal Reporter*, 2nd ser., 147: 93–120.

4. *Am. Tob. Co. et al. v. U.S., Cases Argued and Decided in the Supreme Court of the United States*, 328: 780–816 (tribute to Camel, p. 791).

5. Tilley, pp. 293–98, 449–86.

6. Simon N. Whitney, *Antitrust Policies: American Experience in Twenty Industries*, 2 vols. (New York, 1958), 2: 22–23. William H. Nicholls, in his *Price Policies in the Cigarette Industry: A Study of "Concerted Action" and Its Social Control, 1911–50* (Nashville, Tenn., 1951), p. 423, considered the case a legal milestone in "the social control of oligopoly." Note also his brilliant essay on the legal and economic implications of the case in chap. 28.

7. See above.

8. *Am. Tob. Co. et al. v. U.S., Record on Appeal*, exhibits, 5: 3011; transcripts, 5: 3830–36. In 1941 Lipscomb had charge of all of American's purchase of domestic leaf tobacco except cigar leaf.

9. J. C. Robert, *The Story of Tobacco in America* (New York, 1949), pp. 260–61.

10. Whitney, *Antitrust Policies*, 2: 28–30; Tilley, p. 480. For the Information see *Am. Tob. Co. et al. v. U.S., Record on Appeal*, transcripts, 1: 4–34. Roy C. Haberkern recalled that well before the case was filed the Department of Justice

wrote each of the so-called "Big Four" tobacco companies asking for their comments on the charges. Other companies replied, but the request to Reynolds, turned over to P. Frank Hanes for reply, was ignored because he considered it unnecessary. Some believed that this failure accounted for the rather rough treatment accorded the company's witnesses during the trial. Roy C. Haberkern, interview with author, 26 Nov. 1961.

11. *Lexington Herald*, 28 Oct. 1941; Robert, *The Story of Tobacco in America*, pp. 261–64.

12. *Lexington Herald*, 28 Oct. 1941.

13. *Am. Tob. Co. et al. v. U.S., Record on Appeal*, transcripts, 1: 280–443; appendix, 1: 1–81.

14. Ibid., transcripts, 8: 6404; Louisville *Courier-Journal*, 28 Oct. 1941; *Tob.*, 6 Nov. (p. 19), 4 Dec. (p. 4) 1941.

15. *Liggett & Myers v. U.S., Brief of Appellants*, docket no. 9138 (6th Cir., 1944), p. 3.

16. *Am. Tob. Co. et al. v. U.S., Record on Appeal*, transcripts, 7: 5056–5399, 8: 6338–39.

17. Ibid., 7: 5063–65.

18. Ibid., 6: 4860–81. William J. Conrad, Jr., stated on 30 Oct. 1962 that Reynolds had his nurse at Lexington.

19. Ibid., 6: 4882 (residence), 4902–18 (changes in cigarette prices), 4912–15 (processing tax), 4894–96 and 4924–27 (drop shipments).

20. Ibid., 6: 4936–39 (organization of sales forces), 4952–54; 7: 4961–74 (drop shipments), 4977–5006 (price fixing).

21. Ibid., 7: 5048–55.

22. Ibid., 6: 4724–4859.

23. For the testimony of Roe see ibid., 5: 3325–3479.

24. Richard B. Tennant, *The American Cigarette Industry: A Study in Economic Analysis and Public Policy* (New Haven, 1950), p. 88.

25. *Am. Tob. Co. et al. v. U.S., Record on Appeal*, transcripts, 5: 3343, 3345, 3413 (sales tax). Rumor had it that when the directors first learned of the situation in Denver they ordered Edward A. Darr to keep out of it and to destroy any correspondence he might have on the matter. This he did not do, thereby involving the company in an embarrassing situation.

26. Tennant, *The American Cigarette Industry*, pp. 311–12.

27. *Am. Tob. Co. et al. v. U.S., Record on Appeal*, transcripts, 5: 3477.

28. Ibid., 5: 3325; Sales Record Book, vol. V—sales dept., RJR.

29. *Am. Tob. Co. et al. v. U.S., Record on Appeal*, transcripts, 5: 3836–3955.

30. Louisville *Courier-Journal*, 28 Oct. 1941. For the outcome of the case note also *NYT*, 28 Oct. 1941.

31. Whitney, *Antitrust Policies*; *Am. Tob. Co. et al. v. U.S., Federal Reporter*, 2nd ser., 147: 100. Brown and Williamson had been a wholly owned subsidiary of the British-American Tobacco Company since 1927.

32. Whitney, *Antitrust Policies*, 2: 14–56. Note pp. 27 and 56 for reference to the revolution wrought by the Camel.

33. *NYT*, 2 Aug. 1946. Note a long resumé of the case in *WSJ*, 2 Aug. 1946.

34. *Bookman v. R. J. R. Tob. Co. et al., Brief on Behalf of All Defendants*, docket no. 129–544 (Chancery of N.J., 1946), p. 5.

35. For a discussion of the origin and functioning of Bylaw XII, see Chapter 7, pp. 350–62.

36. *Bookman v. R. J. R. Tob. Co. et al., Brief on Behalf of All Defendants*, p. 1.

37. *Bookman v. R. J. R. Tob. Co. et al., Transcript of Record*, docket no. 129-544 (Chancery of N.J., 1946), pp. 1283–89.

38. Ibid., p. 1272.

39. Ibid., pp. 1277–78.

40. Ibid., pp. 1131–55a.

41. *Bookman v. R. J. R. Tob. Co. et al., Brief on Behalf of All Defendants*, pp. 8–9.

42. The act was approved and effective on 10 Apr. 1945—*New Jersey Statutes Annotated, Official Classification, Title 14, Corporations* (Cumulative Annual Pocket Part for use in 1963), p. 17. It was applicable to any suit "instituted or maintained."

43. *Bookman v. R. J. R. Tob. Co. et al., Transcript of Record*, pp. 1271, 1273, 1283.

44. *Bookman v. R. J. R. Tob. Co. et al., Brief on Behalf of Complainants and Interveners-Complainants*, docket no. 129–544 (Chancery of N.J., 1946), pp. 1–3. Note Minutes, vol. III, pp. 70–71, for the 1915 amendment to Bylaw XII.

45. *Bookman v. R. J. R. Tob. Co. et al., Brief on Behalf of Complainants and Interveners-Complainants*, p. 7; Annual Report of the R. J. R. Tob. Co., 1941.

46. *Bookman v. R. J. R. Tob. Co. et al., Brief on Behalf of Complainants and Interveners-Complainants*, p. 93.

47. Ibid., pp. 134, 182, 193.

48. Ibid., pp. 447–99.

49. Ibid., p. 500.

50. *Bookman v. R. J. R. Tob. Co. et al., Brief on Behalf of All Defendants*, pp. 4–9.

51. Ibid., pp. 11–12.

52. *Bookman v. R. J. R. Tob. Co. et al., Transcript of Record*, pp. 3078 (quotation), 3088–89.

53. Ibid., pp. 3078–80.

54. Ibid., pp. 4451–52.

55. *Bookman v. R. J. R. Tob. Co. et al., Brief on Behalf of All Defendants*, pp. 246–49.

56. *Bookman v. R. J. R. Tob. Co. et al., Transcript of Record*, p. 5053.

57. Ibid., pp. 5053–61.

58. Ibid., p. 5529. See also *Bookman v. R. J. R. Tob. Co. et al., Brief on Behalf of Complainants and Interveners-Complainants*, pp. 362–67.

59. Minutes, vol. IV, pp. 279–80; *Bookman v. R. J. R. Tob. Co. et al., Transcript of Record*, pp. 5529–37.

60. *Bookman v. R. J. R. Tob. Co. et al., Transcript of Record*, pp. 2710–11.

61. *Bookman v. R. J. R. Tob. Co. et al., Brief on Behalf of All Defendants*, pp. 166–74.

62. *Bookman v. R. J. R. Tob. Co. et al., Transcript of Record*, pp. 2746–63.

63. *Bookman v. R. J. R. Tob. Co. et al., Brief on Behalf of All Defendants,* pp. 176–78.

64. This discussion of Vice-Chancellor Egan's ruling is based chiefly on *Atlantic Reporter,* 2nd ser., 48: 646–700. The blocked quotations are from pp. 650, 651, 659, 663, 691, 700, respectively.

65. Minutes, vol. IX, pp. 12, 34. Darr was elected president of the company on 5 November 1952.

66. Oscar F. Hege, interview with author, 30 May 1963.

67. *MB* 9, no. 14 (20 Mar. 1957), no. 22 (26 Apr. 1957); James V. Dorse, interview with author, 20 May 1963. George also spent some time in New York studying the problem, evidently with the National Records Management Council, Inc. Plans for housing the engineering dept. in the Lasater Building began in 1956 when the building was purchased for $200,000. The necessary alterations were started in 1957. Minutes, vol. IX, p. 297.

68. Minutes, vol. VIII, p. 113.

69. William J. Conrad, Jr. (28 May 1963) and William R. Lybrook (27 May 1963), interviews with author. The stock listing application of the company for recalling "A" stock and other factors connected with it (No. A-13264, 30 June 1949) mentions only two of these reasons: high rates of income taxes and restrictions on borrowing for the purchase of listed stocks.

70. William J. Conrad, Jr., interview with author, 28 May 1963.

71. Minutes, vol. VIII, pp. 304–22; Stock Listing Application No. A-13264, 30 June 1949 (quotation)—secretary's dept., RJR.

72. Special Stock Exchange of Reynolds A for B—mail and file dept., RJR. The letters in this file are arranged chronologically.

73. Ibid.

74. *MB* 9 (no. 58, 14 Nov. 1957), 11 (no. 17, 23 Mar. 1959); Minutes, vol. VIII, p. 232; H. Henry Ramm, interview with author, 4 June 1963. Two other members of the company's legal dept., Henry C. Roemer, Jr., and Robert D. Rickert, who joined Reynolds later, also came by way of Davis, Polk, Wardwell, Sunderland, and Kiendl.

75. *R. J. R. Tob. Co. v. U.S.,* docket no. 254–54 (United States Court of Claims, 1957), *Federal Supplement* 149: 889–98. It is of interest that Davis, Polk, Wardwell, Sunderland, and Kiendl constituted part of the battery of lawyers for the company in this case.

76. *Reports of the Tax Courts of the United States* 7 (1 Jan.–30 June 1947): 130–36.

77. Minutes, vols. VII (pp. 345, 350, 370–71, 387–88, 397, 468–69), VIII (pp. 213, 220–27, 245); *Tob.,* 21 Nov. 1946, p. 14.

78. Minutes, vol. VIII, p. 3.

79. *Am. Tob. Co. et al. v. U.S., Record on Appeal,* transcripts, 7: 5075; Henry F. Snow, interview with author, 12 Dec. 1962. Edgar H. Harwood stated that the research dept. developed an excellent blend for the Cavalier but that top management refused it—Edgar H. Harwood, interview with author, 2 July 1963. Bowman Gray, Jr., described the Cavalier as "a gigantic blooper" which he attributed to top management—"R. J. Reynolds' King-Size Profits," *Fortune,* Dec. 1957, p. 130; *Time,* 11 Apr. 1960, p. 110.

80. Roy C. Haberkern (23 Jan. 1960), John V. Hunter, Jr. (29 Apr. 1963), and Charles B. Wade, Jr. (30 Apr. 1963), interviews with author. Note *Tob.*, 24 Mar. 1949, p. 5, for a statement that Cavaliers were made of "mild tobaccos of the original Colonial type." Note also a press release of 18 Mar. 1949, in Cavalier Scrapbook: Magazines, vol. I (advertising dept., RJR), for a statement that the Cavalier was "a distinctive cigarette specially blended for those who find enjoyment in the natural flavor and aroma of extremely mild tobaccos of the original Colonial type." Colonial tobaccos, of course, were not mild.

81. Minutes, vol. IX, p. 206. At this time the package was also changed.

82. H. Henry Ramm, interview with author, 3 May 1963.

83. Memorandum initialed by Haddon S. Kirk in scrapbook material—industrial engineering dept., RJR; *WSJ*, 4 Mar. 1949.

84. P. Lorillard introduced a king-size cigarette, the Embassy, about one week before the Cavalier appeared; other king sizes at the time were Pall Mall and Herbert Tareyton by American and Fatima by Liggett and Myers—*WSJ*, 4 Mar. 1949.

85. *MIB* 2, no. 8, 8 Apr. 1949 (quotation); *Tob.*, 24 Mar. 1949, p. 5.

86. *Tob.*, 21 Apr. 1949, p. 8.

87. Ibid., 12 May 1949, p. 6.

88. Ibid., 16 (p. 12) and 30 (p. 42) June 1949.

89. Ibid., 19 May (p. 14), 23 June (p. 16) 1949.

90. *MIB* 2, no. 36, 7 Mar. 1950. On 11 Oct. 1951, the Advertising Committee recommended that the budget for advertising Cavaliers be increased over that of 1951 by $450,000—Minutes, vol. VIII, p. 444.

91. *Tob.*, 17 Jan. 1952, p. 21.

92. *Wall Street Journal* in *Tob.*, 6 Aug. 1953, p. 4. Apparently Cavaliers were sold in tins for only a short time. The company museum contains the first tin made on 15 July 1953, the five millionth tin made on 5 Oct. 1953, and the ten millionth tin made on 27 Jan. 1954. Incidentally, Cavaliers in oval tins were hand packed—John V. Hunter, Jr., interview with author, 29 Apr. 1963. The entire move was recommended by the sales dept. in order to stimulate consumer interest, first on 9 July 1953 and again on 13 Aug. and 24 Sept. 1953—Minutes, vol. IX, pp. 40, 42–43, 48.

93. *MB* 7, no. 7, 9 Feb. 1955.

94. Ibid., 7 no. 49, 9 Nov. 1955; 8, no. 12, 19 Apr. 1956.

Chapter 13
Preparation for Expansion, 1945–1954

1. Minutes, vol. VII, pp. 410–11.

2. Ibid., vol. VIII, pp. 174, 378, 423.

3. Ibid., pp. 193–94.

4. Ibid., p. 212.

5. Ibid., p. 272.

6. Ibid., pp. 298–99.

7. Ibid., pp. 399–400.

8. Ibid., vol. X, p. 23.

9. This sketch is based largely on notes preserved by Gordon M. Black, of the personnel dept., who participated in the development of the job evaluation plan including the conduct of studies and the preparation of materials essential for its administration; and on the typed evaluation booklet that resulted from the work of the personnel dept. and Ernst & Ernst. Note *MIB* 1 (no. 4, 7 Oct. 1946) and 2 (no. 19, 2 Sept. 1949) for instructions to foremen on the new rules for making changes in the jobs of employees that might affect their labor grades. Note also Minutes, vol. VIII, pp. 76–77.

10. The company maintained the wages and hours put into effect in 1933 under the cigarette manufacturing code of the National Industrial Recovery Act—*Tob.*, 6 June 1935, p. 29. Of the 725 new workers hired in May 1934, some were chosen from a list of applicants in the employment dept. and others from names supplied by the Winston-Salem Relief Commission. Officials stated at the time that it had been the company's policy "to employ workers from families most in need of a regularly employed member"—ibid., 14 June 1934, p. 3.

11. *Public Laws and Resolutions . . . of North Carolina, 1929*, chap. 120, pp. 117–47.

12. Minutes of Safety Council, 1929–1959 (arranged chronologically)—safety dept., RJR; Wilford G. Jones, interviews with author, 26 Jan. 1960, 21 June 1963. The minutes will frequently be cited by date in the text.

13. Minutes of Safety Council, 10 May 1954; Wilford G. Jones, interviews with author, 26 Jan. 1960, 21 June 1963.

14. Minutes of Safety Council, passim; *MIB* 3, no. 13, 18 Apr. 1951.

15. Minutes of Safety Council, 13 Dec. 1937.

16. *MIB* 2, no. 60, 9 Nov. 1950.

17. *Tob.*, 1 Mar. 1951, p. 6.

18. Ibid., 15 May 1952, p. 21.

19. Ibid., 18 May 1956, p. 15; *MB* 8, no. 16, 16 May 1956.

20. Minutes of Safety Council, 20 Dec. 1950, 14 Dec. 1953, 13 Dec. 1954.

21. *MIB* 2, no. 27, 29 Nov. 1949.

22. *MB* 10, no. 2, 10 Jan. 1958.

23. Based on *MIB*s; *MB*s; Erwin W. Cook, interview with author, 28 Feb. 1963.

24. Erwin W. Cook, interview with author, 28 Feb. 1963.

25. Ibid., 1 Apr. 1963.

26. *News for Leaf Department Men*, 15 June 1959.

27. Correspondence on suggestion plan—in possession of Christopher J. Daye, personnel dept., RJR, as of 1963; Minutes, vol. VIII, p. 378; Christopher J. Daye (21 Feb. 1963) and Gordon M. Black (22 Feb. 1963), interviews with author.

28. Minutes, vol. IX, pp. 56–57, 59–60, 84 (stockholder's question).

29. Based chiefly on Minutes and Exhibits on the Development of the Suggestion Plan—in possession of Christopher J. Daye, personnel dept., RJR, as of 1963; Minutes, vol. IX, pp. 57, 264.

30. Minutes of Suggestion Plan Committee—in possession of Christoper J. Daye, personnel dept., RJR, as of 1963; *MB* 10 (no. 69, 19 Dec. 1958), 11 (no.

53, 5 Aug. 1959—Angel); J. H. Peddicord (12 Apr. 1960) and Christopher J. Daye (21 Feb. 1963), interviews with author.

31. Christopher J. Daye, interview with author, 21 Feb. 1963.

32. John C. Whitaker to Bishop Costen J. Harrell, 11 Aug. 1949—personnel folder of Rev. Clifford H. Peace, personnel dept., RJR. Extensive correspondence with ministers and other tobacco companies began as early as 3 May 1948. See, for example, the letter to Gordon M. Black from Rev. Francis B. Sayre, Jr., East Cleveland, Ohio, 13 May 1948—file: "Religion," personnel dept., RJR. At the time the Reverend Mr. Sayre had served two years as an industrial chaplain under the sponsorship of the Cleveland Church Federation.

33. Clifford H. Peace to Charles B. Wade, Jr., Asheville, N.C., 11 June 1949—personnel folder of Rev. Clifford H. Peace.

34. *TCS*, 6 Dec. 1956.

35. *WSJ*, 27 Sept. 1949; *MIB* 2, no. 22, 26 Sept. 1949.

36. Orientation schedule of the Reverend Mr. Peace, prepared by Fred D. Hauser, 10 Nov. 1949—personnel folder of Rev. Clifford H. Peace; *MIB* 2, no. 42, 2 May 1950. The Reverend Mr. Peace recalled in 1963 that meeting all the supervisors and employees required eight months—*J&S*, 11 Aug. 1963.

37. *MIB* 2, no. 53, 14 Aug. 1950.

38. Minutes of Safety Council, 11 Feb. 1952; *MIB* 4, no. 6, 18 Feb. 1952.

39. Biographical data in personnel folder of Rev. Clifford H. Peace. Note esp. *Tob.*, 17 Apr. 1952 (p. 25), 11 Mar. 1955 (p. 21); *Fortune*, Jan. 1954, p. 40; and numerous clippings in personnel folder of Rev. Clifford H. Peace. When Bishop G. Bromley Oxnam called a conference of Methodist leaders representing church, labor, and management on 16–17 Dec. 1957, the Reverend Mr. Peace participated in the panel on the work of industrial chaplains. His work was mentioned in a leaflet, *The Church at Work in a Working World*, issued by the Methodist church.

40. Leaflet: *Service for Dedication of the Chapel*, 5 June 1951—courtesy of Jane McIver; *J&S*, 19 Aug. 1951; *MB* 4 (no. 34, 31 Oct. 1952), 9 (no. 62, 27 Nov. 1957). Note *MB* 10 (no. 2, 10 Jan. 1958) for the directors' use of the chapel to express their thankfulness for a successful year. Projection of the chapel was most unctuously treated in *Tob.*, 24 May 1951, p. 7, which also mentioned the fact that Norman Vincent Peale had given the chapel national recognition in an article appearing in *Prayer in America*. James A. Gray first made contact with Peale.

41. Letter of James W. Glenn to employees of the R. J. R. Tob. Co., 18 Dec. 1946—office of J. E. Conrad, personnel dept., RJR; Minutes, vols. VII (pp. 410, 465), VIII (pp. 4, 6, 25–34, 41, 45–46, 59); leaflet: *Employee's Retirement Plan of R. J. R. Tob. Co.* Employees often greeted the receipt of retirement checks with the expression: "Old Daddy Reynolds is good to me."

42. Report of Retirement Board of R. J. R. Tob. Co. for 1960, p. 5.

43. Leaflet: *Announcement of Hospital Service Plan of R. J. Reynolds Tobacco Company . . .*, issued 15 June 1939—personnel dept., RJR.

44. Minutes, vol. VII, pp. 192–93; poster (15 Feb. 1940) entitled "Vacation with Pay Plan for Hourly Rated and Piece Work Employees"—courtesy of Effie Fox; *WSJ*, 14 Feb. 1940; Gordon S. Watkins and Paul A. Dodd, *The Manage-*

ment of Labor Relations (New York, 1938), pp. 613–14.

45. Directive from Regional War Labor Board, Atlanta, Ga., 18 Oct. 1944—personnel dept., RJR.

46. Minutes, vol. IX, pp. 195, 198; *MB* 8, no. 52, 14 Dec. 1956; memorandum of Edgar E. Bumgardner to R. N. White, 13 Dec. 1956—payroll dept., RJR. See Minutes, vol. IX, p. 229, for seasonal workers.

47. Leaflet: *Educational Plan for Eligible Employees*, effective 5 Apr. 1957; *MB* 9, no. 17, 4 Apr. 1957; Minutes of Employee Educational Committees, esp. for 11 Apr. 1963—personnel dept., RJR; Minutes, vol. VIII, pp. 186, 239–40.

48. *MB* 14 (no. 47, 17 May 1962), 15 (no. 12, 8 Feb. 1963); leaflet: *Educational Matching Plan of R. J. R. Tob. Co.*

49. *Guideposts*: *MIB* 2, no. 4, 1 Mar. 1949, and no. 14, 8 July 1949; *MB* 7, no. 17, 4 Apr. 1955; orders in purchasing dept., RJR. At first *Guideposts* was mailed to the supervisors' homes; after Mar. 1949 it was delivered to the work place—Roy C. Haberkern, interview with author, 15 Sept. 1963. Service awards: *MIB* 3, no. 24, 20 July 1951; *MB* 7, no. 17, 4 Apr. 1955; leaflet: *In Recognition of Long Service*; Minutes of Personnel Committee, vol. II, p. 657; *Tob.*, 29 May 1941, p. 14. Distinguished service awards: Minutes, vol. IX, pp. 99–101, 119, 195. The following were recommended for the distinguished service award: Charles C. Bodenheimer (manager of structural dept., engineering), James T. Solomon (foreman, engineering), Karl S. Vickers, Jr. (engineering), Charles W. Kirk (asst. superintendent, leaf processing), Charles M. Davis (asst. superintendent, redrying), William W. Rike (dept. foreman, stemming maintenance), Horace P. Harrington (asst. dept. foreman, stemming maintenance), Fred M. Furches (foreman, redrying), Dr. Richard W. Bunn (head of medical dept.), Wilford G. Jones (director, safety dept.), Joseph H. Sherrill (asst. to superintendent of manufacturing), William H. Tucker (superintendent, metal can div.), and James E. (Bill) Thomas (superintendent, cigarette div.). A photograph of the recipients with citations for each appears in *MB* 7, no. 8, 17 Feb. 1955.

50. Minutes, vol. IX, pp. 178–79, 211; *Trust Agreement of Profit-Sharing Plan of R. J. Reynolds Tobacco Company, Effective Jan. 1, 1956*; booklets: *More Profit More Security*, Sept. 1959, 12 Apr. 1961, 1 Jan. 1963; *Amended Trust Agreement on Profit-Sharing Plan of R. J. R. Tob. Co.*, 1 Jan. 1963.

51. Personnel folder of Frederic E. Sturmer—personnel dept., RJR; *WSJ*, 19 Mar. 1946. The name of this publication was changed to *R. J. Reynolds Merchandiser* and a small sketch of the office building added to the masthead with the issue of 10 Sept. 1959. See also *Tob.*, 25 Apr. 1946, p. 7.

52. Erwin W. Cook, interview with author, 28 Feb. 1963; George W. Chandler: personnel folder, personnel dept., RJR; interview with author, 4 Mar. 1963.

53. George W. Chandler, interview with author, 4 Mar. 1963.

54. Wayne L. Tibbets to George W. Chandler, Seattle, Wash.—sales dept., RJR. Note in *MIB* 2 (no. 21, 22 Sept. 1949) an item maintaining that cigarettes were a profitable business.

55. *Tob.*, 5 Mar. (p. 11), 2 Apr. (p. 15), 16 July (p. 4), 5 Nov. (p. 12) 1953; 25 Feb. (p. 5), 10 June (p. 4) 1954; 16 Mar. 1956 (p. 22).

56. George W. Chandler, interview with author, 4 Mar. 1963; *Tob.*, 17 June

1955 (p. 9), 24 Feb. 1956 (p. 9). For an evaluation of this general idea see *MIB* 2, no. 29, 16 Dec. 1949.

57. This account is based generally on the "History and Development of the Leaf Stemming and Blending Process at the R. J. Reynolds Tobacco Company," prepared by Lee R. Salmons—in possession of Mr. Salmons, leaf processing dept., RJR, as of 1963; a file labeled "SPD Reports and Memorandums" in possession of Mebane E. Turner, engineering dept., as of 1963; a graphic description of the Cardwell Machine Company's "Tipping and Threshing" in *Tob.*, 19 June 1952, pp. 16–17; and various interviews with Mebane E. Turner, Lee R. Salmons, John H. Winder, and James E. Chilton. The directors on 13 Mar. 1947 ordered the purchase and installation of necessary equipment and machinery to double the production capacity of the strip preparation dept. at Number 256-2—Minutes, vol. VIII, p. 79.

58. File: Project no. 2292, New Lexington Plant, General Instructions, 8 Nov. 1957—leaf-processing dept., RJR.

59. This question was subject to a congressional hearing. See Statement of John C. Whitaker, Hearing, U.S. Senate Subcommittee on Tobacco, Committee on Agriculture and Forestry and H. H. Subcommittee on Tobacco, 3 May 1958—legal dept., RJR.

60. Contracts: B. F. Sturtevant & Co. of Philadelphia and R. J. R. Tob. Co., 26, 29 June 1916, 11 Sept. 1919, 24 July 1922—files 1360, 1616, 1702, 1703, secretary's dept., RJR.

61. *Tob.*, 19 May 1921, p. 13.

62. Edgar E. Bumgardner, interview with author, 27 Feb. 1962.

63. Samuel O. Jones to John C. Whitaker, Baltimore, Md., 30 Apr. 1935—personnel folder of Samuel O. Jones, personnel dept., RJR.

64. Samuel O. Jones to Edgar E. Bumgardner, Baltimore, Md., 19 Nov. 1934—ibid.

65. Ibid.

66. *MIB* 2, no. 60, 9 Nov. 1950; *WSJ*, 6, 7 Feb. 1953.

67. *WTJ*, Feb. 1963, p. 36.

68. This account of reconstituted leaf is based primarily on the author's interview with Samuel O. Jones, 25 Sept. 1962; in fact, it could not have been written without his assistance.

69. John C. Whitaker, interview with author, 11 Apr. 1962; prospectus, printed estimate, and three letters (Morehead Patterson to John C. Whitaker, New York, 17, 22 May 1951; George S. Hastings to John C. Whitaker, New York, 28 May 1951) in a fancy folder with this printed inscription: "Prepared for the R. J. Reynolds Tobacco Company by American Machine & Foundry Company"—RJR museum.

Chapter 14
Expansion of the Company and Its Enhancement of Life in the Area

1. *Advertising Age* in *Tob.*, 13 Dec. 1957, p. 17.
2. Minutes, vol. IX, p. 272.
3. *Tob.*, 11 Mar. 1954, p. 5. Other filter-tipped cigarettes on the market at this time were Parliament (Benson and Hedges consolidated with Philip Morris on 4 Feb. 1954), Kent (P. Lorillard), and L & M (Liggett and Myers). American introduced its first filter tip, the Herbert Tareyton, in Aug. 1954—American Tobacco Company, *"Sold American!" The First Fifty Years* (New York, 1954), pp. 139–41.
4. "R. J. Reynolds' King-Size Profits," *Fortune*, Dec. 1957, p. 130.
5. Joseph H. Sherrill to Haddon S. Kirk, 13 Aug., 24 Sept. 1952—file: Cigarettes, Filter Tip, box 137C, Records Center, RJR.
6. Haddon S. Kirk, Memorandum for the Record, 9 Dec. 1952—ibid. Early in 1953, the tobacco industry became aware of Reynolds's decision to manufacture and market a filter-tipped cigarette—*Tobacco Leaf,* 21 Feb. 1953, p. 3. Whitaker, Darr, and Gray are credited with having developed the Winston with the timing called by Gray as head of the sales dept.—*Time*, 11 Apr. 1960, p. 110.
7. *Tob.*, 11 (p. 5) and 25 (p. 25) Mar. 1954; *MB* 6, no. 15, 27 Apr. 1954.
8. *MB* 6, no. 10, 25 Mar. 1954.
9. Colin S. Stokes, Memorandum for the Record, 28 Sept. 1953—file: Cigarettes, General, 1953, box 137C, Records Center, RJR; Minutes, vol. IX, p. 97; John V. Hunter, Jr., interview with author, 11 June 1963. As early as Sept. 1953, it was rumored in the tobacco trade that Reynolds planned to introduce a king-size Camel—*Tob.*, 24 Sept. 1953, p. 6.
10. John V. Hunter, Jr. (11 June 1963) and William J. Conrad, Jr. (12 June 1963), interviews with author; letter of confirmation, Percy J. Bartle of Molins Machine Co. to R. J. R. Tob. Co., Richmond, Va., 16 Sept. 1953—file: Cigarettes, General, 1953, box 137C, Records Center, RJR.
11. Labeled sample of first official Winston—RJR museum. This cigarette, made at 10:00 A.M. on 24 Feb. 1954 with Ecusta paper, an estron filter, and a cork tip "of British new type," was undoubtedly preceded by many experimental runs.
12. Joseph H. Sherrill to Haddon S. Kirk, Hamburg, Germany, 13 Feb. 1954 (quotation); circular of Hauni Maschinenfabrik Körber and Co. sent to R. J. R. Tob. Co. on 11 Feb. 1954; Kurt A. Körber to Joseph H. Sherrill, Hamburg, Germany, 22 Apr. 1954—file: Cigarette Machinery, box 139C, Records Center, RJR; purchase agreement: R. J. R. Tob. Co. and Hauni Maschinenfabrik Körber and Co., 6 May 1954—file 2639, secretary's dept., RJR. A copy of this agreement was also in box 139C, Records Center.
13. Haddon S. Kirk to Stuart M. Scott, 22 Nov. 1954—file: Cigarettes, General, 1953, box 137C, Records Center, RJR.
14. *MB* 6, no. 15 (27 Apr. 1954), no. 37 (8 Oct. 1954).
15. "A. M. F.: Patterson Played It Big," *Fortune*, Oct. 1954, pp. 126–31.
16. Percy J. Bartle to R. J. R. Tob. Co., Richmond, Va., 4 Mar. 1955; R. J. R.

Tob. Co. to Molins Machine Co., 10 Mar. 1955—file: Cigarette Machinery, box 139C, Records Center, RJR.

17. Haddon S. Kirk, Memorandum for the Record, 18 Mar., 26 Apr. 1955—file: Cigarette Machinery. Note also another memo dated 4 May 1955 (ibid.) for attempts to find the proper speed for operating the Hauni machine.

18. Memorandum for the Record, 30 June 1955—file: Cigarette Machinery; Charles W. Arelt to R. J. R. Tob. Co., New York, 20 Oct. 1954; Kurt A. Körber to Edward A. Darr, 28 Oct. 1955; American Machine and Foundry Co. to R. J. R. Tob. Co., New York, 29 June 1955—box 139C, Records Center, RJR.

19. Memorandum for the Record, 12 Dec. 1955—file: Cigarette Manufacture, box 137C, Records Center, RJR; Minutes, vol. IX, pp. 192–93; John V. Hunter, Jr., interview with author, 11 June 1963.

20. Minutes, vol. IX, p. 199.

21. Air Way Bills, 8 Feb., 10 June 1956—box 837C, Records Center, RJR.

22. *Printers' Ink*, 25 Dec. 1959, pp. 20–21; *TCS*, 26 Dec. 1959.

23. *Reader's Digest*, Dec. 1952, pp. 738–39.

24. *MB* 6, no. 23, 9 July 1954; Winston Scrapbook: Newspapers, vol. I, passim—advertising dept., RJR.

25. *MB* 6, no. 37, 8 Oct. 1954.

26. Bergen Evans, "Grammar for Today," *Atlantic Monthly*, Mar. 1960, p. 82; Winston Scrapbook: Newspapers, vols. I, II, and Magazines, vols. I, II—advertising dept., RJR.

27. *Business Week*, 20 Feb. 1960, p. 74.

28. *MB* 8, no. 15, 9 May 1956.

29. "R. J. Reynolds' King-Size Profits," *Fortune*, Dec. 1957, p. 131.

30. Minutes, vol. IX, p. 215. See also *Tob.*, 27 Apr. 1956, p. 196.

31. *Tob.*, 27 Apr. 1956, p. 196; Minutes, vol. IX, p. 272.

32. *MB* 8, no. 14, 3 May 1956.

33. John V. Hunter, Jr., interview with author, 11 June 1963.

34. *Printers' Ink*, 22 Dec. 1961, P. 24.

35. *Wall Street Journal*, 6 Apr. 1962.

36. *MB* 14, no. 12, 6 Feb. 1962; *WSJ*, 27 Jan. 1962.

37. *MB* 14, no. 59, 7 June 1962.

38. Ibid., 15, no. 16, 1 Mar. 1963.

39. *Business Week*, 22 Dec. 1962, pp. 78–80.

40. *MB* 8, no. 31 (17 Aug. 1956), no. 43 (19 Oct. 1956); *Tob.*, 15 Mar. (p. 24), 17 May (p. 9), 27 Sept. (p. 25) 1957; Minutes, vol. IX, p. 244; Carter Hall Scrapbook: Newspapers and Magazines, vol. I, passim—advertising dept., RJR.

41. *MB* 8, no. 12, 19 Apr. 1956.

42. *Am. Tob. Co. et al. v. U.S., Record on Appeal*, docket no. 9137–9139 (6th Cir., 1944), transcripts, 5: 3873.

43. Minutes, vol. VIII, p. 104; John V. Hunter, Jr., interview with author, 19 June 1963; R. J. R. Tob. Co. to division managers (DM-16F), 22 May 1940—sales dept., RJR.

44. Haddon S. Kirk to G. H. Transou, 4 Feb. 1955—file for 1955, box 172, Records Center, RJR.

45. *Tob.*, 6 June 1946 (p. 7), 14 Nov. 1958 (p. 29); *MB* 10, no. 54, 3 Oct. 1958; Minutes, vol. X, p. 66; Roy C. Haberkern, interview with author, 2 Nov. 1961.

46. *Tob.*, 13 Mar. 1959, p. 15.

47. *WSJ*, 13 Oct. 1950.

48. *Tob.*, 4 Dec. 1952, p. 12.

49. *Wall Street Journal*, 20 July 1960.

50. *TCS*, 29 Dec. 1959.

51. *MB* 9, special issue, 20 June 1957; *WSJ*, 21 June 1957; *North Carolina: Session Laws and Resolutions*, 1956–1957, pp. 1336–1414.

52. *Tob.*, 28 June 1957, p. 12; *WSJ*, 8 June 1957.

53. *MB* 10, no. 57, 21 Oct. 1958, and 13, no. 39, 28 Apr. 1961; John V. Hunter, Jr., interview with author, 20 June 1963.

54. Minutes, vol. X, pp. 131, 140. For dedication of the plant see *WSJ*, 3 Oct. 1961.

55. Minutes, vol. IX, pp. 36, 195.

56. *J&S*, 4 Mar. 1956. The company's total city and county taxes for 1961 amounted to $2,764,189.

57. Minutes, vol. IX, p. 199.

58. This matter was well aired in the *WSJ*, 6, 7 June 1957. At the same time the company held an option on a tract of land belonging to Stokes County Senator William F. Marshall, who introduced the bill. See also *Tob.*, 14 June 1957, pp. 36–37.

59. Minutes, vols. IX, pp. 306, 308, 321, 334, and X, p. 34; William R. Lybrook, interview with author, 4 Aug. 1960.

60. *MB* 11, no. 83, 16 Dec. 1959; *WSJ*, 14 Dec. 1959.

61. *Tob.*, 31 July 1952 (p. 173), 9 Mar. 1956 (p. 14); *Lexington Leader*, 1 Mar. 1956.

62. Minutes, vols. IX, p. 341, and X, pp. 42, 77, 94, 102; *Tob.*, 22 Aug. 1958, p. 8.

63. Minutes, vol. IX, pp. 226–27, 322–23.

64. File: Project 2292, New Lexington Plant, 1956–1959—leaf-processing dept., RJR.

65. *MB* 14, no. 56, 1 June 1962; various deeds made to R. J. R. Tob. Co. for this property in file 388, secretary's dept., RJR. Comparable to the Brook Cove plant in storage facilities, and the Davie plant was estimated to cost $25 million—*J&S*, 28 Sept. 1962.

66. Property Book of Real Estate, Buildings, Machinery, and Equipment Committee—secretary's dept., RJR; records of engineering dept. in care of Sidney J. Walters.

67. *MB* 11, no. 27, 5 May 1959.

68. *MB* 12, no. 23 (28 Mar.), no. 47 (15 June), no. 58 (22 July), no. 62 (8 Aug.), no. 78 (11 Oct.), no. 80 (14 Oct.) 1960; *WSJ*, 16 Mar. 1960; *TCS*, 31 Mar. 1960; Bowman Gray, Jr., and Alexander H. Galloway to the employees, 22 July 1960; Minutes, vol. X, pp. 185, 218. Other firms outside the United States were considered—Minutes, vol. X, p. 140.

69. *Annual Report* of R. J. R. Tob. Co., 1961; *Wall Street Journal*, 20 July 1960.

70. Minutes, vol. IX, pp. 55–56; *MIB* 2, no. 9, 27 Apr. 1949; *MB* 9, no. 27, 17 May 1957.

71. Based chiefly on Robert M. Newsom, Jr., interview with author, 25 June 1963.

72. *MIB* 2, no. 49, 29 June 1950; Minutes, vol. VIII, p. 382.

73. *MB* 10, no. 36, 20 June 1958. The final move was made on 13 June 1958.

74. Ibid., 10, no. 39, 23 July 1958.

75. Ibid., 11, no. 47, 10 July 1959.

76. Ibid., 13, no. 43 (12 May 1961), and 14 (1962): no. 52 (28 May), no. 82 (28 Aug.), no. 101 (23 Oct.); *J&S*, 14 May 1961.

77. *MIB* 4, no. 11, 4 Apr. 1952; personnel folder of C. E. Stephenson—Records Center, RJR; Leonard L. Browning, interview with author, 26 June 1963.

78. Organization chart of chemical dept., 22 Jan. 1948—research dept., RJR.

79. Roy C. Haberkern, interview with author, 29 Oct. 1961.

80. Minutes, vol. VIII, p. 429; *WSJ*, 24 Oct. 1950; *Tob.*, 2 Nov. 1950 (p. 20), 21 June 1951 (p. 22); *MB* 11, no. 75, 12 Nov. 1959.

81. Minutes, vol. IX, pp. 213–14; *Tob.*, 8 Jan. 1953 (p. 3), 18 May 1956 (p. 7); *WSJ*, 6 Feb. 1953.

82. Luther J. Upton, Jr., interview with author, 11 Oct. 1960; leaflets on research dept., 5 Sept. 1958, Sept. 1962—Records Center, RJR.

83. "R. J. Reynolds' King-Size Profits," *Fortune*, Dec. 1957, p. 132.

84. Minutes, vols. VII, pp. 472–73; IX (p. 62).

85. Ibid., vol. IX, p. 292.

86. Ibid., vol. X, p. 100; *MB* 11, no. 12, 4 Mar. 1959; *TCS*, 5 Dec. 1959.

87. *TCS*, 5 Dec. 1959; Captain J. H. Drew, interview with author, 30 July 1963.

88. *Tob.*, 22 Nov. 1957, p. 25; *TCS*, 5 Dec. 1959.

89. File: Special Jobbers Comments (in mail and file dept., RJR), which also included an updated clipping from *Tobacco Leaf.*

90. William J. Conrad, Jr., to Alexander P. English, 2 June 1959—file: Special Stock Exchange of Reynolds A for B, mail and file dept., RJR. See also *MB* 9, no. 57, 8 Nov. 1957; 10 (1958): no. 7 (13 Feb.), no. 23 (25 Apr.), no. 51 (19 Sept.); and 11 (1959): no. 11 (27 Feb.), no. 28 (6 May).

91. Reports of Visitors, 1918–1962, public relations dept., RJR; *MB* 15, no. 15, 19 Feb. 1963; *UR*, 25 Mar. 1962; Golston H. Dalton, interview with author; Walter P. Webb, *The Texas Rangers: A Century of Frontier Defense* (Austin, 1965), pp. 540–41.

92. Report of Le May H. Blakely for 1952—in Reports, public relations dept., RJR.

93. Copy of voucher dated 28 May 1945—legal dept., RJR. According to this and other vouchers, Williams was reimbursed for these luncheons until 29 Aug. 1945; thereafter the vouchers were made to the Reynolds Grill. According to *Who's Who in America, 1950–1951* (22: 2368, 25: 2697), Williams was a director of AT&T from 1943 to 1948. He held this position at his death—Dr. S. Clay

Williams, Jr., interview with author, 26 July 1963.

94. Dudley Doust, (tape-recorded) interview with Bowman Gray, Jr., 18 Mar. 1960.

95. Minutes, vol. VIII, pp. 180–82, 193–96.

96. Ibid., p. 294.

97. Ibid., pp. 343–44.

98. Ibid., pp. 377–78, 423, 465 (Finance Committee).

99. Ibid., vols. VIII, pp. 471–72; IX, pp. 29, 91–92, 149–50, 221.

100. Ibid., vol. IX, pp. 264–65, 281–85, 290.

101. *Forbes*, 15 July 1963, p. 17.

102. Minutes of Executive Committee, 16 Nov. 1950—secretary's dept., RJR; Minutes, vol. VIII, pp. 400–401.

103. Minutes, vols. VIII, pp. 449, 462; IX, pp. 3, 66, 330.

104. "American Business and the Piety of Profits," *Harvard Business Review* 37 (Nov.–Dec. 1959): 54–55.

105. *A. P. Smith Manufacturing Co. v. Barlow et al., Atlantic Reporter*, 2nd ser., 98: 581–90; H. Henry Ramm, interview with author, 16 July 1963.

106. Minutes of Executive Committee, 23 Feb. 1953—secretary's dept., RJR; Minutes, vol. IX, p. 12.

107. Minutes of Winston-Salem Board of Trade, 1889–1922, 30 Jan. and 9 Feb. 1891—Office of Winston-Salem Chamber of Commerce; *Public Laws and Resolutions of the State of North Carolina . . . 1899*, chap. 561, pp. 752–55.

108. *UR*, 17 Nov. 1898.

109. William A. Blair to Hollis B. Frissell, 25 Nov. 1899—Papers of Southern Education Board, Southern Collection, University of North Carolina, courtesy of Louis R. Harlan. Note also *UR*, 23 Nov. 1899. Other white citizens contributed $1,000, but in Nov. 1900 Professor Atkins left for "the North" to raise the remainder. The Board of Managers, which handled this matter, included Mayor Oscar B. Eaton, William N. Reynolds, Adolphus H. Eller, Walter R. Reynolds, William A. Blair, W. A. Lybrook (given as J. A. Lybrook), and Atkins—*UR*, 22 Nov. 1900.

110. *UR*, 16 May, 20 June 1901.

111. Ibid., 4 May 1893, 2 Sept. 1897; R. J. Reynolds Journal—Daybook, 1894–1898, passim—in possession of Charles H. Babcock as of 1963.

112. *UR*, 14 Mar. 1901, 25 June 1903.

113. Ibid., 24 Nov. 1910.

114. Ibid., 11 Oct. 1906.

115. Ibid., 14 Mar. 1901, 25 June 1903.

116. Minutes, vol. IV, pp. 9–10, 28; *WSJ*, 16 Feb., 28 Mar., 1 Apr., 10 Sept. 1916, 16 Nov. 1919; *UR*, 6 Apr. 1916.

117. *UR*, 19 Oct. 1916. See also above.

118. *TCS*, 15 July 1916, 28 Apr., 25 June, 24 Nov. (quotation) 1917, 8, 10 Nov. 1919; *Tob.*, 19 Oct. 1916, p. 4.

119. Will of Richard Joshua Reynolds, Clerk's Office, Forsyth County Courthouse, Winston-Salem, N.C.; *UR*, 15, 29 Aug. 1918; *WSJ*, 28 Aug. 1918. This move trebled the capacity of the Twin-City Hospital, but Katharine Smith

Reynolds added $50,000 to the total amount for enlarging it—*TCS*, 28 Aug. 1919.

120. *WSJ*, 7 June, 4 July 1919; 1 Dec. 1921; *TCS*, 7 June 1919. Apparently the R. J. Reynolds Lecture Series at Davidson College was another gift. At least Archibald MacLeish lectured there in 1960 under the auspices of the lecture series—*J&S*, 30 Oct. 1960.

121. *WSJ*, 26 Apr. 1962. *The Ledger* (11 May 1962) attributed this extraordinary record to insistence on standards of excellence in such disciplines as mathematics, languages, history, and literature instead of introducing "life adjustment" courses and "social promotions." The R. J. Reynolds High School has long been regarded as one of the best in North Carolina.

122. *UR*, 30 Mar. 1899, 28 Sept. 1905.

123. *WSJ*, 29 July 1916; *UR*, 10 Aug. 1916; Minutes, vols. III, pp. 119–20, and IV, p. 28.

124. Minutes, vols. IV, pp. 241, 327, 387; VI, p. 63.

125. Joseph L. Graham (*J&S*, 23 June 1946); John Neal (*UR*, 16 Sept. 1920, and *WSJ*, 12 Sept. 1920); William N. Reynolds (*WSJ*, 24 Sept. 1921, and *Tob.*, 23 June 1921, p. 3); D. Rich (*WSJ*, 4 Nov. 1922, *Biblical Recorder*, 29 Oct. 1924, and *Creek Pebbles*, 24 Sept. 1926); James Sloan (*UR*, 24 May 1923); Katharine Smith Reynolds (*UR*, 22 Mar. 1923, and Margaret Fulton of Mount Airy, N.C., interview with author); Bowman Gray, Sr., and wife (*UR*, 15 Feb. 1923, clipping dated 10 Feb. 1923 in Scrapbook of Bowman Gray, Sr., and *WSJ*, 2 Mar. 1892); Robert E. Lasater (*WSJ*, 15 Oct. 1927, and Fries, p. 212); Mrs. William N. Reynolds (*J&S*, 14 Apr. 1929).

126. Louisa Wilson Bitting Dormitory (*J&S*, 1 June 1930); Nancy Reynolds Memorial School (*WSJ*, 23 June 1930); Stratford Hall (*WSJ*, 23 Jan. 1930); hospital for whites (*WSJ*, 14 Apr. 1936); Kate Bitting Reynolds Memorial Hospital (*WSJ*, 10 Aug. 1937).

127. William A. Law Scholarship (*WSJ*, 14 Jan. 1937); Bowman Gray Memorial Stadium (*WSJ*, 19 Feb. 1937); Z. Smith Reynolds Foundation (*J&S*, 19 Dec. 1937).

128. Minutes, vol. VII, pp. 424–25, 428–29; *WSJ*, 20 Dec. 1945.

129. File 2631—secretary's dept., RJR; Minutes, vol. VIII, pp. 44–45; William J. Conrad, Jr., interview with author, 4 Sept. 1963.

130. Minutes, vol. VIII, p. 211.

131. *WSJ*, 14 June 1946; *Tob.*, 20 June 1946, p. 17; Minutes, vol. VII, pp. 465–66.

132. Minutes, vol. VIII, pp. 364, 386, 414, 429, 444, 475, 482.

133. Ibid., vols. VIII, pp. 374, 403, 449, 496; IX, p. 37.

134. Ibid., vols. VIII, pp. 298, 357–58, 408, 497; IX, pp. 35–36. For information on the YMCA and YWCA building, see *WSJ*, 13 Apr. 1949.

135. *J&S*, 10 Sept. 1961. See also ibid., 29 Dec. 1946.

136. Minutes, vols. IX, pp. 53, 242, 266; X, pp. 52, 68, 80, 198.

137. Reynolds Park (*J&S*, 26 May 1940); airport (*WSJ*, 27 June 1940); recreation area (*WSJ*, 11 July 1940); coliseum (*J&S*, 4 Dec. 1949); Craige Chair (*J&S*, 14 Sept. 1941, and *Tob.*, 18 Sept. 1941, p. 26); Blackwell Memorial Fund

(*WSJ*, 13 Mar. 1944); Rondthaler Chair (Dr. George G. Higgins, interview with author, 14 June 1960); agricultural research (*WSJ*, 6 May 1948); public library (*WSJ*, 9 Dec. 1948); Memorial Industrial School (*J&S*, 5 June 1949).

138. *WSJ*, 3 Oct. 1946.

139. Ibid., 2 Jan. 1947.

140. *J&S*, 11 Aug. 1946.

141. *WSJ*, 4 Dec. 1959.

142. Ibid., 18 July 1953.

143. Minutes, vols. X, p. 14; XI, pp. 171–72, 292.

144. Ibid., vol. X, pp. 151–52.

145. Community Center at Critz (*J&S*, 16 July 1950); public library (*WSJ*, 25 Jan. 1951); N.C. State College (*J&S*, 21 Jan. 1951); Lasater bequest (*WSJ*, 16 July 1954); Sweet Briar College (*J&S*, 30 Oct. 1960); R. J. Reynolds–Patrick County Memorial Hospital (*J&S*, 20 Nov. 1960).

146. William Neal Reynolds Memorial Scholarships (*WSJ*, 20 Nov. 1961); Katharine Smith Reynolds Scholarships (*WSJ*, 14 Dec. 1962, and *Greensboro Daily News*, 6 June 1963); bequest to Bowman Gray School of Medicine (*WSJ*, 21 Dec. 1961).

147. *J&S*, 28 Feb. 1960, 20 May 1962; *WSJ*, 17 May 1963.

148. Annual Reports of Contributions and Membership Committee, 1960, 1961, 1962—secretary's dept., RJR.

INDEX

entry, 301–3, 523; race relations in, 374; philanthropic contributions of RTC, RTC employees, and Reynolds family to, 523–34

Winston-Salem and Forsyth County Hospital, 528

Winston-Salem Art Center and Council, 532

Winston-Salem Chamber of Commerce, 63, 64, 297

Winston-Salem Foundation, 527, 533

Winston-Salem Journal, 244, 245, 246, 301, 398, 399–400, 403, 407, 487, 502

Winston-Salem Journal and Sentinel, 223, 393, 397, 410, 411

Winston-Salem State University, 524, 531

Winston Tobacco Association, 205

Winston Water Company, 52

Wise, G. D., 52

Witten, Ancil D., 119

Wofford College, 527

Woman's College of the University of North Carolina, 525, 533

Womble, Bunyan S., 299

Women: employment of in RTC factories, 37, 248–49, 267, 268–69; employment of in RTC office, 140, 149; housing for while working at RTC, 270–71; and cigarette smoking, 330, 331, 340–42

Wons, Tony, 336

Wood, W. W., 227

Woodward and Tiernan Printing Company, 160–61

Worker Magazine, 399

Worker's Voice, 388–89

Working conditions. *See* Labor: hours and conditions of at RTC

Work Projects Administration (WPA), 528, 530

World War I, 221, 223, 256, 285, 306, 314–18, 355, 526

World War II, 351, 367, 369, 454, 486, 489

W. P. Pickett and Company, 122

Wright, Richard H., 164–69, 173, 204, 207–8, 209, 237–38, 310, 311, 312

W. T. Gray and Company, 113

W. T. Hancock (company), 263

W. W. Wood and Company, 68

Wyatt, Wortham, 280

Wynder, Ernest L., 496

YMCA, 526, 529, 531

York, Fred, 233

Young, J. W., 75–76

Young, James R., 257

Yuille, Thomas B., 126

YWCA, 273–74, 525, 526, 529

Ziglar, Pauline, 461

Zinzendorf Laundry, 391

Z. Smith Reynolds Foundation, 528, 530, 531, 533